(for more extraordinary praise, from professionals and readers, please turn the page . . .)

DAVID D. BURNS, M.D. graduated magna cum laude from Amherst College, received his M.D. degree from Stanford University School of Medicine, and completed his psychiatry residency at the University of Pennsylvania School of Medicine. He has served as Acting Chief of Psychiatry at the Presbyterian-University of Pennsylvania Medical Center and Visiting Scholar at the Harvard Medical School. He is currently Clinical Associate Professor of Psychiatry and Behavioral Sciences at the Stanford University School of Medicine, where he is actively involved in research and teaching. Dr. Burns has received numerous awards, including the A. E. Bennett Award from the Society for Biological Psychiatry and the Distinguished Contribution to Psychology through the Media Award from the Association of Applied and Preventive Psychology. In 1998 and in 2000 he received the Teacher of the Year award from the graduating psychiatric residents at Stanford.

"Dr. Burns has done it again. He has provided us with clearly described and practical guidelines for dealing with fears, anxieties, panic attacks, procrastination, and communication problems . . . invaluable."
—Marvin Goldfried, Professor of Psychology and Psychiatry, State University of New York at Stony Brook

"The best of what modern psychotherapy has to offer to people suffering from anxiety, depression, and marital problems."
—M. Anthony Bates, Ph.D., Clinical Psychologist, Dublin, Ireland

"If you are looking for sound, workable advice on how to change your life a little or a lot, this is the book for you."
—Robert L. Leahy, Ph.D., Director, Center for Cognitive Therapy, New York

OTHER BOOKS BY DAVID D. BURNS, M.D.

Feeling Good: The New Mood Therapy
(1980; revised, 1999)

Intimate Connections
(1985)

Ten Days to Self-Esteem and
Ten Days to Self-Esteem: The Leader's Manual
(1993)

The
Feeling Good
Handbook

David D. Burns, M.D.

REVISED EDITION

PLUME

PLUME
An imprint of Penguin Random House LLC
penguinrandomhouse.com

First Plume Printing (Revised Edition), May 1999
First Plume Printing, September 1990

REGISTERED TRADEMARK—MARCA REGISTRADA

THE LIBRARY OF CONGRESS HAS CATALOGUED THIS BOOK AS FOLLOWS:
Burns, David D.
    The feeling good handbook / David D. Burns.—Rev. ed.
      p.   cm.
    ISBN 978-0-452-28132-5
      1. Cognitive therapy.   2. Psychotropic drugs—Therapeutic use.
    3. Psychopharmacology.   I. Title.
    RC489.C63B87   1999
    616.89'142—dc21   99-18102
                                              CIP

ISBN: 9780593189788

PRINTED IN THE UNITED STATES OF AMERICA
1 2 3 4 5 6 7 8 9 10

PUBLISHER'S NOTE
The ideas, procedures, and suggestions contained in this book are not intended as a substitute for consulting with a mental health professional.

All names and identities of individuals have been disguised to protect their anonymity.

This book is dedicated to my colleagues
Tony Bates and Sheila Flynn,
who are very dear to me.

Acknowledgments

I owe a debt of gratitude to many people who have contributed to this book in so many ways. First, I want to thank my colleagues, Dr. Tony Bates and Sister Sheila Flynn. Their vision and creativity were crucial to the birth of this book and have been a constant source of joy to me. I would also like to thank several Stanford colleagues who helped me with the revised chapters on antidepressant and anti-anxiety medications for the 1999 revision of the *Handbook.* They included Alan Schatzberg, M.D., our department chairman, Joe Bellenoff, M.D., a psychopharmacology fellow, and Greg Tarasoff, M.D., a senior psychiatric resident. In addition, many of my patients, who wish to remain anonymous, read and critiqued various chapters of the *Handbook* while it was being written and edited. This feedback was essential in showing me what was genuinely helpful and what was not. The result was the development of a much stronger manuscript. Thank you!

I would like to thank Mary Lovell, Wendy Brusick, and Sharon Barksdale for the huge volume of meticulous word processing that was necessary in the creation of this book. I am indebted to many individuals who have provided help with the editing. I want to thank my two editors, Arnold Dolin and Maria Guarnaschelli, for their generous support and technical expertise when the *Handbook* was first published. I am also indebted to Deborah Brody at Plume for her wonderful help with the 1999 revision. In addition, I want to thank my wife, Dr. Melanie Burns, and my daughter, Signe Burns, for many creative suggestions and invaluable editing of this revised edition.

I would like to thank the thousands of readers who have written to me after reading my first book, *Feeling Good: The New Mood Therapy.* Sharing your personal experiences about the help you received from that book has meant more to me than you will ever know. Your ideas and suggestions helped in the development of this *Handbook.* I also want to thank the many psychiatrists, psychologists, clinical social workers, nurses, clergymen, and counselors who have recommended *Feeling Good* to the clients they work with. I know of no higher possible endorsement than yours!

Finally, I want to emphasize that I am not the sole creator of the many ideas and techniques in this book. Cognitive therapy has been a team effort, with hundreds if not thousands of talented clinicians and researchers throughout the world contributing to this important movement, which has revolutionized our understanding and treatment of depression, anxiety, and marital discord. Although I could not begin to acknowledge every contributor, I want to emphasize that much of the early pioneering work was done by Drs. Albert Ellis and Aaron T. Beck. The field of mental health owes much to their vision and leadership.

Contents

Preface to Revised Edition

This book is about a relatively new type of treatment for depression, anxiety, and other disorders called cognitive behavioral therapy (CBT). Although CBT may seem like a complicated name, it has a simple meaning. A "cognition" is just a fancy name for a thought. If you have ever been very depressed or anxious, you are probably aware that you think about things very negatively when you are down in the dumps. Depressed people also have a tendency to behave in self-defeating ways—you may avoid work, pleasurable activities, and other people, for example. CBT can help you change these negative thinking and behavior patterns so you can experience greater happiness, productivity, and intimacy.

I have been very gratified by the overwhelming positive response to the *Feeling Good Handbook.* In 1994 the results of a nationwide survey about the use of self-help books by mental health professionals were published in the *Authoritative Guide to Self-Help Books.* In this study the researchers surveyed 500 American mental health professionals and asked if they "prescribed" books for patients to read between sessions to speed recovery. Seventy percent of the therapists polled indicated that they did use "bibliotherapy" with their patients, and 86 percent reported that the books were helpful to their patients. The therapists were also asked which self-help books, from a list of 1,000, they most frequently recommended for their depressed patients. I was surprised that *The Feeling Good Handbook* was the second most frequently recommended book. *Feeling Good: The New Mood Therapy* was the most frequently recommended book.

I have also been gratified by the immense interest that has been generated in CBT among mental health professionals as well as the general public. Since my first book, *Feeling Good*, was published in 1980, CBT has emerged as one of the most popular and intensively researched forms of psychotherapy ever developed, both in the United States and throughout the world.

There are many reasons for this popularity. First, CBT is based on common sense, and so it makes sense to patients and therapists alike. In addition, the methods really do seem to help, and they often work fairly quickly. The effectiveness of CBT has been confirmed in large numbers of controlled-outcome studies comparing CBT with other established treatments for depression, such as antidepressant medications or other forms of psychotherapy. These studies* indicate that patients treated with CBT improve rapidly and continue to remain undepressed for periods of several years following the initial recovery. CBT compares quite favorably with other forms of psychotherapy as well as with antidepressant drugs, and many therapists now regard it as the treatment of first choice for severe and mild depression as well as all the anxiety disorders. In fact, in his article entitled "Psychotherapy for Depression: No Stronger Medicine," which appeared in the prestigious journal *American Psychologist,* Dr. David Antonuccio from the University of Nevada School of Medicine and the Reno Veterans Affairs Medical Center, stated, "The preponderance of the available

*Santrock, J. W., Minnett, A. M., & Campbell, B. D. 1994. *The Authoritative Guide to Self-Help Books.* New York: Guilford Press.

Jamison, C., and Scogin, F. 1995. Outcome of cognitive bibliotherapy with depressed adults. *Journal of Consulting and Clinical Psychology, 63,* 644-50.

Scogin, F., Hamblin, D., and Beutler, L. 1987. Bibliotherapy for depressed older adults: A self-help alternative. *The Gerontologist, 27,* 383-87.

Scogin, F., Jamison, C., and Davis, N. 1990. A two-year follow-up of the effects of bibliotherapy for depressed older adults. *Journal of Consulting and Clinical Psychology, 58,* 665-67.

Scogin, F., Jamison, C., and Gochneaut, K. 1989. The comparative efficacy of cognitive and behavioral bibliotherapy for mildly and moderately depressed older adults. *Journal of Consulting and Clinical Psychology 57,* 403-407.

Smith, N. M., Floyd, M. R., Jamison, C., and Scogin, F. 1997. Three-year follow-up of bibliotherapy for depression. *Journal of Consulting and Clinical Psychology, 65(2),* 324-27.

Antonuccio, D. June 1995. Psychotherapy for Depression: No Stronger Medicine. *American Psychologist,* 450-52.

scientific evidence shows that psychological interventions, particularly cognitive-behavioral therapies (CBTs), are generally as effective or more effective than medications in the treatment of depression, even if severe."*

CBT is gaining popularity in the treatment of many other disorders as well. For example, at a recent conference, I was intrigued by the presentation by a colleague of mine from Stanford, Dr. Stuart Agras. Dr. Agras is a professor of psychiatry and a world-renowned eating-disorders expert. He presented the results of numerous recent studies on the treatment of eating disorders with medications, such as the new SSRI antidepressants like Prozac, and different types of psychotherapy. These studies indicated that CBT is the most effective treatment for eating disorders—far better than any known drug or any other form of psychotherapy.

The first controlled-outcome study of cognitive behavioral therapy for depression was conducted when I was doing my postdoctoral fellowship in depression research at the University of Pennsylvania in the mid-1970s.[†] In that study depressed patients were randomly assigned to one of two treatment groups. Patients in the first group were treated with imipramine, one of the most widely used antidepressants at the time. These patients received medication alone without any psychotherapy. Patients in the second group received cognitive therapy alone without any antidepressant medications. At the end of the 12-week treatment period, the patients in the cognitive therapy group had improved as much as, if not more than, the patients in the antidepressant drug group. This was the first time that any form of psychotherapy had been shown to be as effective as medications. The study caused considerable controversy and led to a tremendous increase in interest in cognitive therapy and in psychotherapy research.

During the two decades since that study was published, dozens of similar studies comparing CBT with antidepressant medications as well as other forms of short-term psychotherapy have been published in psychology and psychiatry journals throughout the world. Drs. Antonuccio and William Danton, from the University of Nevada, and

*Antonuccio, D. O., Danton, W. G., & DeNelsky, G. Y. 1995. Psychotherapy versus medication for depression: Challenging the conventional wisdom with data. *Professional Psychology, 26,* 574-85.
†Rush, A. J., Beck, A. T., Kovacs, M., & Hollon, S. 1977. Comparative efficacy of cognitive therapy and pharmacotherapy in the treatment of depressed outpatients. *Cognitive Therapy and Research, 1(1):* 17-38.

Garland DeNelsky, from the Cleveland Clinic Foundation, recently reviewed these studies in order to answer several basic questions:

- The conventional wisdom holds that depression is a genetic, biological disorder caused by a chemical imbalance in the brain. In addition, most people believe that drugs are the most effective treatment for depression. Are these beliefs supported by the facts?
- Are drugs or psychotherapy more effective in the treatment of mild or severe depression?
- Which type of treatment—drugs or psychotherapy—is associated with fewer relapses following recovery?
- What guidelines should we have for the treatment of depressed adults as well as depressed children or adolescents?

These investigators published their findings in an article entitled, "Antidepressants vs. Psychotherapy in the Treatment of Depression: Challenging the Conventional Wisdom with Data."* They concluded that for depressed adults, cognitive behavior therapy is at least as good as, and probably better than, antidepressant drugs for severe or mild depressions. For depressed children and adolescents, they concluded that there is little or no convincing evidence that antidepressants are effective and that psychotherapy should be used first.

Based on their analysis of long-term follow-up studies, the authors concluded that patients treated with CBT do better than patients treated with medications or other forms of psychotherapy—they remain undepressed longer and have fewer relapses following recovery. The authors also suggested that for some patients, long-term drug treatment might have negative effects. For example, new data suggest that the effects of the newer antidepressants sometimes seem to "wear off" after a while, so that a medication that once worked no longer does. Although this does not always happen, sometimes it can leave the patient more vulnerable to relapses of depression and treatment resistance. If you would like to learn more about this and have access to the Internet, you might find a recent article from *New York* magazine interesting. You can read it at this web site: http://www.nymag.com/critics/view.asp?id=1740.

Dr. Antonuccio and his colleagues emphasized that these findings have largely been ignored by the media and by the general public. This is because of a strong societal bias that depression is a biological and

*Antonuccio, D. June 1995. Psychotherapy for Depression: No Stronger Medicine. *American Psychologist,* 450-52.

genetic disorder and that antidepressant drugs represent the most powerful form of treatment—beliefs that are not solidly grounded in the facts.

You might question these conclusions and wonder if Dr. Antonuccio and his co-authors interpreted the literature in a fair and unbiased manner. Certainly, their conclusions are controversial. Yet there have been several other scholarly review articles summarizing research studies on antidepressant drugs versus psychotherapy in the treatment of depression,* and their conclusions are consistent with those of Dr. Antonuccio and his colleagues. There is strong evidence from many independent studies that CBT is at least as good as antidepressant medications. For many patients CBT actually seems to work better.

Is there any evidence that a cognitive therapy self-help book such as this one can have antidepressant effects? If you are feeling down in the dumps and you diligently study this book and complete the exercises in it, what is the chance that your mood will improve?

Self-help books are quite controversial. Many people are skeptical about the motives of the individuals who write them. They believe that self-help authors are primarily out to help themselves make money. In addition, self-help authors are often criticized for offering overly simplistic formulas for the complex problems of daily living. I think these impressions are justified. When I look through the self-help sections of popular bookstores, the superficial jargon and quick fixes that are promised in many books turn me off as well.

However, there are two sides to every coin, and academic researchers have begun to take a serious look at self-help books as a new form of therapy. This type of treatment is called *bibliotherapy*, or reading therapy. It can be administered in one of two ways. First, therapists can "prescribe" a self-help book for their patients to read between therapy sessions to increase the speed of learning and recovery. Second, individuals suffering from depression or anxiety can be given a self-help book to read as a self-administered treatment without any other drug therapy or psychotherapy.

The second approach—bibliotherapy without other therapy—has been recently evaluated in five published studies over the past decade

*Dobson, K. S. 1989. A meta-analysis of the efficacy of cognitive therapy for depression. *Journal of Consulting and Clinical Psychology, 57(3),* 414-19.

Hollon, S. D., & Beck, A. T. 1994. Cognitive and cognitive behavioral therapies, in A. E. Bergin & S. L. Garfield (eds.), *Handbook of Psychotherapy and Behavioral Change.* New York: John Wiley.

Robinson, L. A., Berman, J. S., & Neimeyer, R. A. 1990. Psychotherapy for the treatment of depression: A comprehensive review of controlled outcome research. *Psychological Bulletin, 108,* 30-49.

conducted by a team of investigators headed by Dr. Forrest Scogin from the University of Alabama. These researchers evaluated the effectiveness of my first book, *Feeling Good: The New Mood Therapy* as well as Dr. Peter Lewinsohn's *Control Your Depression,* as self-administered treatments for depression. Their first study was published in the medical journal *The Gerontologist,* and the next four were published in the prestigious *Journal of Consulting and Clinical Psychology.* To make a long story short, the investigators concluded that *Feeling Good* was as effective as a full course of individual psychotherapy or as treatment with the best antidepressant drugs. Given the tremendous pressures to cut health care costs, this finding is of considerable interest, since a paperback copy of *Feeling Good* costs less than one day of antidepressant drug treatment—and is presumably free of any troublesome side effects as well!

By the way, I don't want you to get panicky and think you are reading the wrong book. Although all these studies were conducted using *Feeling Good, The Feeling Good Handbook* is ten years newer and should be at least as effective, if not better. *The Feeling Good Handbook* shows you how to apply these new methods to a much broader range of problems. These include depression, all the anxiety disorders, and interpersonal conflicts as well (such as how to repair a troubled marriage or get along with an overly critical boss or colleague).

What did these bibliotherapy studies demonstrate? In the first study Dr. Scogin and his colleagues, David Hambling and Dr. Larry Beutler, randomly assigned 29 adults with mild to moderate depression to one of three treatment conditions for a four-week period. The researchers gave the depressed individuals in the first group a copy of *Feeling Good* and asked them to read it within four weeks. This was the *Feeling Good* bibliotherapy group. The researchers gave the patients in the second group a copy of a book that was not expected to have any antidepressant effects. It was Victor Frankl's classic book about concentration camps entitled *Man's Search for Meaning.* This was the "placebo" bibliotherapy group. The patients in the third group were not given any book to read. This was the no-bibliotherapy group. All the patients in this study were over 60 years of age, because the researchers wanted to determine if bibliotherapy would help older adults who are depressed.

At the beginning of the study, all the patients in the three groups were given two highly regarded depression tests used in research. As you can see in Figure 1, there were no statistically significant differences in the measures in the three groups, indicating that the average depression levels in these groups were similar at the start of the study.

At the end of four weeks, the researchers administered the depression tests again to assess any changes that might have occurred. As shown in Figure 1, the patients in the *Feeling Good* group improved considerably, but the patients in the placebo and no-bibliotherapy groups did not improve. These differences were statistically significant, indicating that the superior improvement in the *Feeling Good* group was not simply due to chance. In addition, the lack of improvement in the patients who read the Victor Frankl book indicated that the antidepressant effects of *Feeling Good* were not just "placebo" effects, but specific antidepressant effects.

It is important to understand this last point. It is possible, at least in theory, that any book depressed patients read would help to improve their moods, by virtue of merely the activity or the distraction. In addition, the expectation that the book might help could raise the patients' hopes, and this could lead to a reduction in depression. This is what is meant by the "placebo" effect. However, the Victor Frankl book did not seem to help the patients who read it. The researchers concluded that while a self-help book could have significant antidepressant effects, this would not necessarily be true of any self-help book. The book must contain sound information about how to overcome depression.

Next, the researchers gave *Feeling Good* to the patients in the no-bibliotherapy group. You can see in Figure 2 that they improved during the next four weeks when they were reading *Feeling Good.* These results replicated the findings from the first four weeks of the study. In addition, the mood scores of the patients who read *Feeling Good* were not significantly different at the follow-up evaluation two months later. This indicated they did not simply relapse back into depression after reading the book but maintained their gains, at least for a two-month period.

This study was quite encouraging but needed replication for several reasons. First, a positive outcome could be due to chance. Scientists believe a result is real only if they can replicate the same finding over and over again in different settings. Second, the study was conducted with older individuals, and it would be useful to know if bibliotherapy is helpful for people of all ages. And third, the follow-up period was too short. Depression tends to become a chronic disorder for many individuals, marked by relapses. Follow-up studies of patients treated with

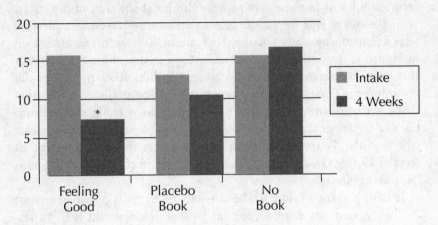

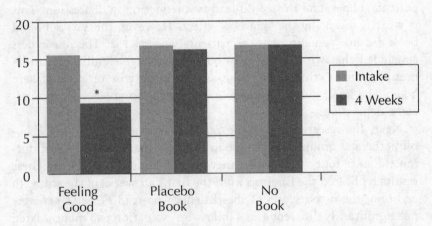

Figure 1. Scores on the Hamilton Depression Test and the Geriatric Depression Scale for all patients at initial evaluation and after four weeks. Higher score indicate more severe depression. As can be seen, the patients who were given a copy of *Feeling Good* improved significantly, but the patients who read the placebo book and the patients on the waiting list (no book) did not. *$p < .05$

drugs and with psychotherapy have often been disappointing, since a substantial percentage of the patients always seem to relapse, often within the first year or even sooner. The crucial question was this: would the results of the new bibliotherapy treatment last? And finally, many of the patients in the bibliotherapy study were only mildly or moderately depressed. How effective would this new bibliotherapy treatment be with patients with more severe depressions?

In a study published in the *Journal of Consulting and Clinical Psychology* in 1995, Drs. Christine Jamison and Forrest Scogin changed the design in order to address these concerns. First, they expanded the number of depressed individuals to 80. Second, they studied patients for three months following the completion of the four weeks of bibliotherapy, and then they initiated a three-year follow-up study. Third, the study was not limited to individuals over 60 years. Fourth, all the patients in the new study had to meet the criteria for a major depressive episode. This is the type of depression normally treated by psychiatrists in outpatient and inpatient settings. This allowed the researchers to determine if the bibliotherapy treatment helped individuals with more serious depressions, as opposed to those with only mild mood swings.

Otherwise, the design of the new study was similar to the first. The investigators randomly assigned the 80 patients to one of two groups. The researchers gave the patients in the first group a copy of *Feeling Good* and encouraged them to read it within four weeks. This group was called the Immediate Bibliotherapy Group. These patients also received a booklet containing blank copies of the self-help forms in the book in case they decided to do some of the suggested exercises.

The patients in the second group were told they would be placed on a four-week waiting list before beginning treatment. This group was called the Delayed Bibliotherapy Group because these patients were not given *Feeling Good* until the second four weeks of the study. These patients served as a control group to make sure that any improvement in the Immediate Bibliotherapy Group was not just due to the passage of time.

At the initial evaluation the researchers administered two depression tests to all the patients. One was the Beck Depression Inventory (BDI), a time-honored self-assessment test that patients fill out on their own, and the second was the Hamilton Rating Scale for Depression (HRSD), which is administered by trained depression researchers.

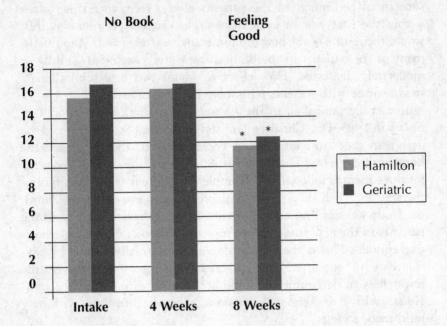

Figure 2. Scores at 4 and 8 weeks on the Hamilton Depression Test and the Geriatric Depression Scale in the Delayed Bibliotherapy Group. Higher scores indicate more severe depression. These patients did not receive *Feeling Good* during the first four weeks of the study and failed to improve. They were then given a copy of *Feeling Good* and improved significantly during the second four weeks. *$p < .05$

As you can see in Figure 3, there was no difference in the depression levels in the two groups at the initial evaluation. The average scores for both groups were around 20 or above. These levels indicate that the patients were more severely depressed than those in the first study, and were similar to patients in most controlled-outcome studies of antidepressants or psychotherapy. For example, this score is nearly identical to the average depression score at intake of approximately 500 patients seeking treatment at my clinic in Philadelphia during the late 1980s.

Every week a research assistant called the patients in both groups and administered the Beck Depression Inventory by telephone. The assistant also answered any questions patients had about the study and encouraged the patients in the Immediate Bibliotherapy Group to complete the book within four weeks. These calls were limited to ten minutes, and no counseling was offered.

At the end of the four weeks the two groups were compared. As shown in Figure 3, the patients in the Immediate Bibliotherapy Group improved considerably. The average scores on both the BDI and HRSD were around 10 or below, scores in the range considered normal. These changes in depression were statistically and clinically very significant. You can also see that these patients maintained their gains at the three-month evaluation and did not relapse. In fact, there was a tendency for continued improvement following the completion of the "treatment." The scores on both depression tests were actually lower at the three-month evaluation.

In contrast, the patients in the Delayed Bibliotherapy Group barely changed, remaining around 20 at the four-week evaluation. This showed that the improvement from *Feeling Good* was not just due to the passage of time. Then Drs. Jamison and Scogin gave the patients in the Delayed Bibliotherapy Group a copy of *Feeling Good* and asked them to read it during the second four weeks of the study. Their improvement in the next four weeks was similar to that in the Immediate Bibliotherapy Group during the first four weeks. You can see in Figure 3 that both groups did not relapse but maintained these gains at the three-month evaluation.

The results of this new study confirmed the results of the first study—*Feeling Good* appeared to have substantial and lasting antidepressant effects. The investigators did several additional analyses to assess the strength of the antidepressant effects of *Feeling Good.* First, they determined the percentage of the patients who actually recovered according to the diagnostic criteria for a major depressive episode, as outlined in the American Psychiatric Association's official *Diagnostic and Statistical Manual (DSM).* At the end of the first four-week period, 70 percent of the patients in the Immediate Bibliotherapy Group no longer met the criteria for a major depressive episode. In contrast, only 3 percent of the patients in the Delayed Bibliotherapy Group recovered during the first four weeks. These results paralleled the results from the Hamilton and Beck depression tests. At the three-month evaluation, when both groups had read *Feeling Good,* 75 percent of the patients in the Immediate and 73 percent of the patients in the Delayed Bibliotherapy Groups no longer qualified for a diagnosis of major depressive episode according to *DSM* criteria.

Second, the researchers compared the magnitude of the improve-

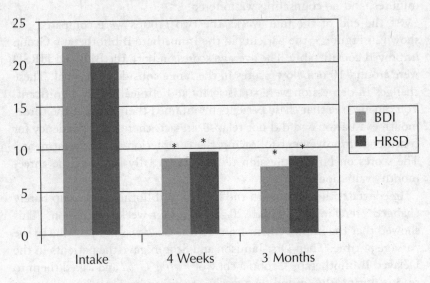

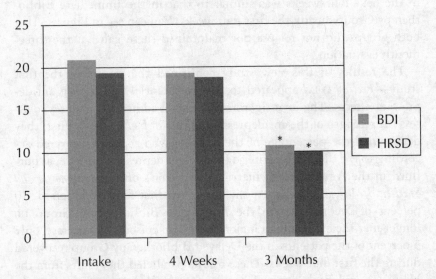

Figure 3. The patients in the Immediate Bibliotherapy Group (top chart) received *Feeling Good* at the intake evaluation. Higher scores indicate more severe depression. The patients in the Delayed Bibliotherapy Group (bottom chart) received *Feeling Good* at the four-week evaluation. BDI = Beck Depression Inventory. HRSD = Hamilton Rating Scale for Depression. * $p < .05$

ment in the bibliotherapy with the amount of improvement in published outcome studies using antidepressant medications or psychotherapy or both. For example, in the large National Institute of Mental Health Collaborative Depression study, there was an average reduction in the Hamilton depression test of 11.6 points in the patients who received cognitive behavioral therapy from highly trained therapists for 12 weeks. This was very similar to the 10.6 point change observed in the patients who read *Feeling Good* after just four weeks. Thus, the amount of improvement in the bibliotherapy treatment appeared to be comparable to other current treatments, but seemed to work significantly faster. My own clinical experience confirms this. Very few patients have recovered during the first four weeks of treatment.

Third, the percentage of patients who dropped out of the bibliotherapy studies was very small, around 10 percent. This is less than most published outcome studies using drugs or psychotherapy, which typically have dropout rates from 15 to over 50 percent. Finally, the patients developed significantly more positive attitudes and thinking patterns after reading *Feeling Good.* This was consistent with the premise of the book—namely, that you can defeat depression by changing the negative thinking patterns that cause it.

The researchers concluded that the bibliotherapy was effective not only for patients suffering from depression, but it might also have a significant role in public education and in depression-prevention programs. They speculated that *Feeling Good* bibliotherapy might help prevent serious episodes of depression among individuals with a tendency toward negative thinking and mild levels of depression.

While the results of this study were encouraging, the three-month follow-up evaluation was still not long enough to determine if the antidepressant effects of *Feeling Good* would last. Motivational speakers can get a crowd of people fired up and feeling optimistic for brief periods of time—but these mood-elevating effects often don't persist. The same problem holds for the treatment of depression with psychotherapy or with drugs. After a period of time many patients relapse. Some develop a pattern of chronic depression that can be difficult to treat. These relapses can be devastating because patients feel so demoralized and hopeless.

In a recent study, published in the summer of 1997, investigators reported the results of a three-year follow-up study of the patients in the study I just described. The authors were Drs. Nancy Smith, Mark Floyd, and Forrest Scogin from the University of Alabama and Dr.

Christine Jamison from the Tuskegee Veterans Affairs Medical Center. The researchers contacted the patients three years after the completion of the bibliotherapy study and administered the depression tests once again. They also asked the patients several other questions about how they had been doing since the study. The researchers learned that the patients had not relapsed but maintained their gains during this three-year period. The scores on the two depression tests at the three-year evaluation were slightly better. Many of the patients (58 percent) said that their moods continued to improve following the completion of the initial study.

The diagnostic findings at the three-year evaluation confirmed this—72 percent of the patients still did not meet the criteria for a major depressive episode, and 70 percent had not sought or received any further treatment with medications or psychotherapy during the follow-up period. Although they experienced the normal ups and downs we all feel from time to time, approximately half indicated that when they were upset, they opened up *Feeling Good* and reread the most helpful sections. The researchers speculated that these self-administered "booster sessions" may have been important in maintaining a positive outlook following recovery. Forty percent of the patients said what they liked about the book was that it helped them change their negative thinking patterns, such as learning to be less perfectionistic and to give up all-or-nothing thinking.

Of course, the study had limitations, like all studies. For one thing, not every patient was "cured" by reading *Feeling Good.* No treatment is a panacea. A 70 percent recovery rate is similar to the improvement rates reported for antidepressant medications as well as for cognitive behavioral therapy and for interpersonal therapy. It is encouraging that so many patients seem to respond to self-help therapy alone, but it is also clear that patients with more severe or chronic depressions need the help of a therapist and possibly an antidepressant medication as well. This is nothing to be ashamed of, because different individuals respond better to different approaches. It is good that we now have three types of effective treatment for depression: antidepressant medications, individual and group psychotherapy, and bibliotherapy.

If you seek professional therapy, remember that you can use cognitive bibliotherapy between therapy sessions to speed your recovery. In fact, when I first wrote *Feeling Good,* this is how I intended the book to be used. I never dreamed that it might someday be used alone as a treatment for depression.

You may be wondering about antidepressant drugs versus CBT or some other form of psychotherapy—which type of treatment is better? Although research studies are often set up to compare the effectiveness of a drug therapy with a psychotherapeutic treatment, therapists who are not researchers often combine the two treatment methods. Many patients receive antidepressants or other needed medicines at the same time they receive counseling. The combination can often be quite effective.

However, a number of recently published studies raise serious questions about the effectiveness of antidepressant medications, especially if they are used alone without psychotherapeutic intervention. These studies suggest that antidepressants, including the new, expensive medications, may not be as effective as we have been led to believe. In fact, a number of investigators have concluded that antidepressants may not be much more effective than placebos, if at all.

You can read one of these articles yourself if you have a computer with a modem, because it was recently published on-line in a new all-electronic scientific journal published on the Internet by the American Psychological Association. The name of this journal is *Prevention and Treatment*. Anyone can go to the web address and read the articles without a subscription (http: //journals.apa.org/prevention).

The first issue of *Prevention and Treatment* features a highly controversial article called "Listening to Prozac but Hearing Placebo" by Irving Kirsch, Ph.D., from the University of Connecticut, and Guy Sapirstein, Ph.D., from the Westwood Lodge Hospital in Massachusetts. These authors carefully reviewed 19 controlled-outcome studies comparing a large variety of antidepressant medications, including the new SSRIs like Prozac, with two kinds of placebos (pills with inert ingredients) in the treatment of depression. "Inactive" placebos are like pills with no active ingredients at all. In contrast, an "active" placebo is a drug that produces side effects, like an antihistamine that produces dry mouth and sleepiness, but it is not an antidepressant. Patients who take active placebos are more likely to believe they are taking a real antidepressant because of the side effects.

These investigators concluded that inactive placebos are usually 75 percent as effective as the best current antidepressants. What does this mean? Well, let's suppose you start out with a score of 25 on a depression test such as my own Depression Checklist number one in Step One of this program. This score would indicate you have a moderately severe depression. Now let's imagine that you participate in a research study comparing an antidepressant, such as Prozac, with a placebo, but you don't know whether you are getting the antidepressant or the placebo.

If you received the antidepressant, the expected reduction in your depression score might be 8 points, judging from data of published studies. This would represent a significant improvement, but with a score of 17 you would still be quite depressed. Keep in mind that a score under 10 is normal, and a score under 5 is even better. So there would be a need for some additional treatment, such as cognitive behavioral therapy, to get the job done.

Now suppose you were in the placebo group, and you got only an inert pill that looked like Prozac. The expected reduction in your depression score would be 6 points, or almost as much as the expected reduction if you had received the antidepressant. Furthermore, the difference between the real drug effect and the placebo effect would be only 2 points—a small amount by anyone's accounting.

What was even more shocking was the discovery that active placebos may be 100 percent as effective as antidepressants. One likely interpretation is that active placebos do a better job of fooling patients and their doctors because of their side effects. Finally, the strength of the antidepressant effects in the studies reviewed by Drs. Kirsch and Sapirstein correlated highly with the strength of the placebo effects. In other words, in some studies the antidepressant medications had somewhat stronger effects, but in these studies the placebo medications also had stronger effects. The actual size of the correlation was so large as to suggest that antidepressants and placebos might be the same.

Clearly these findings are highly controversial. They are not consistent with the impressions about antidepressants conveyed in the media and in popular books and shared by the general public. I do not know what the final word on this will be—new and better studies are needed to sort this out. I think one fact is certain, however, and this has been clear to me since I began treating depression in the mid-1970s. Although some people respond to antidepressants (just as they respond to placebos), the current antidepressants are not sufficiently effective for many people, and other types of psychological treatments are usually needed.

I have never been opposed to antidepressants; I started out my career as a full-time researcher in this area. However, many of the patients I treated with antidepressant medications over the years did not respond in a satisfactory manner. Some patients responded beautifully to antidepressants, and in these instances I was grateful to have the medications available. But many others improved only a little or not at all. Certainly they did not return to joyous, productive living when they took these drugs. This is why I have spent so much of my career researching and developing new psychological treatments, to have more weapons to fight depression than just drugs.

Keep in mind that *Feeling Good* is not a panacea any more than any other approach. If it works for you, that's great. But 30 percent of the individuals who read *Feeling Good* did not recover. If you find that your mood does not improve when you read this book, it should not be a problem, because we now have so many helpful types of interventions. These negative thinking patterns can be immensely deceptive and persuasive, and change is rarely easy. But with patience and persistence, I believe that nearly all individuals suffering from depression can improve and experience a sense of joy and self-esteem once again. Observing this has always given me tremendous satisfaction, and I hope it is something you will experience as you begin to understand and apply the ideas in this book.

—David D. Burns, M.D.
Clinical Associate Professor of Psychiatry and
Behavioral Sciences,
Stanford University School of Medicine

Introduction

In *Feeling Good: The New Mood Therapy* I described a revolutionary, drug-free treatment for depression called cognitive therapy. The word *cognition* simply means thought or perception. Cognitive therapy is based on the simple idea that your thoughts and attitudes—and not external events—create your moods.

When you are upset, you may have noticed that you think about yourself and the world in a pessimistic way. If you feel depressed you may think, "Everything seems so hopeless, I'm such a loser. I'll *never* feel good again." If you feel anxious and panicky, you may think, "What if I lose control and crack up?" During an argument with your spouse, you may tell yourself, "That SOB! What a jerk!" Although these negative thoughts are often distorted and illogical, they can seem deceptively realistic, so you believe things really are as bad as you think they are. Cognitive therapy can help you break out of these mood slumps and develop more positive and realistic attitudes.

Although cognitive therapy was largely unknown at the time that *Feeling Good* was first published, it has exploded into one of the most widely practiced forms of therapy in the world. Extensive research sponsored by the National Institute of Mental Health at universities and medical centers throughout the country has proved that cognitive therapy is as effective and fast-acting as antidepressant medications in the treatment of depression. Even more exciting are recent studies showing that patients treated with cognitive therapy stay free of depression longer than patients treated with drugs alone. This means that the treatment can help you feel better in the here-and-now and deal with future periods of stress and disappointment so you can feel better about yourself and others for the rest of your life.

I wrote *Feeling Good* because I was tremendously excited about how helpful these methods had been to my patients, and I wanted to share these exciting developments with as many people as possible. However, I did not know whether my book would really be helpful to people who were not receiving therapy. I had intended *Feeling Good* to be a supplement to therapy, thinking I would assign chapters to my patients to read between sessions.

Soon after the book was first published, I began to receive heartwarming letters—hundreds at first, then thousands of them—from readers who were kind enough to share their experiences with me. I can recall a man from Oklahoma who described his decades-long unsuccessful struggle with depression. He wrote, "God bless you. Because of your book, I have had my first happy Christmas in over twenty years!"

Many of those who wrote suggested I prepare a sequel that would illustrate how to apply the new mood therapy to the entire range of everyday problems, including low self-esteem, anxiety and panic, and personal-relationship problems. To these many people I owe a debt of gratitude. Your vision inspired the creation of this *Handbook*. I hope it will be equally helpful to you.

People often ask me, "Do you still believe in this approach? Have your methods or theory changed since you wrote *Feeling Good?*" Although there is much that is new and different in this *Handbook,* the vision and techniques described in *Feeling Good* are like pure gold. There's not a day in my office when these ideas do not surprise and enlighten me and my patients, just as if I had discovered them for the first time.

However, there have been many exciting developments since I wrote *Feeling Good.* I have discovered that the new mood therapy can be tremendously helpful for the entire range of mood problems that we all encounter in our daily lives. These include feelings of insecurity and inferiority, procrastination, guilt, stress, frustration, and irritability. Recent door-to-door surveys of thousands of American households sponsored by the National Institute of Mental Health have indicated that nearly 20 million Americans suffer from chronic nervousness, panic attacks, or phobias. You may be afflicted by some type of anxiety such as the fear of heights, public speaking anxiety, nervousness in social situations, agoraphobia, or test anxiety, to name just a few. In this *Handbook* you will discover why you are plagued by these irrational worries. You will also learn how to confront and conquer your worst fears without having to rely on addictive tranquilizers or alcohol.

Another important development has been the application of the new mood therapy to personal-relationship problems. Cognitive therapy has sometimes been criticized as being too self-centered and preoccupied with personal happiness and fulfillment. There is nothing wrong with wanting to grow as an individual, but it is equally important to learn how to get closer to other people so you can resolve conflicts and enjoy greater intimacy.

For the past ten years I have been doing intensive research on the causes and cures for marital and personal relationship problems. I have discovered that certain attitudes cause people to get stuck in endless cycles of blame, hostility, fear, and loneliness. I will show you how to express your feelings more effectively and to listen and really hear how the other person is thinking and feeling during a conflict. The goal is to help you feel closer to the people you care about the most.

As you read the *Handbook,* I will ask you to complete a number of self-assessment tests once a week, just like my patients do. These tests will help you monitor your progress as you read the book. I will also ask you to write down how you might think, feel, and act in a variety of situations that typically make people angry, sad, frustrated, or anxious. Then I will suggest some new and different ways to communicate or think about the situation. If you want to make actual, tangible changes in your life as you read this book, these exercises are vital. Some people may neglect them. They may tell themselves, "I don't need to fill this out. I'll just read what he has to say and that will be enough." I strongly urge you to resist this temptation!

Many of the people who read *Feeling Good* emphasized the importance of these written exercises. They told me that they did not actually begin to experience a profound transformation in their moods and outlook on life until they picked up a pencil and paper and did the exercises that I described. I have taken this feedback seriously and substantially improved and simplified these exercises in the *Handbook*. Although I will ask more of you than most authors or therapists, the potential rewards are great. I want you to enjoy better self-esteem, greater productivity, and enhanced intimacy for the rest of your life as a result of reading this *Handbook*.

Some people have told me, "You seemed to be writing specifically with me in mind. I don't understand how your descriptions of depression and anxiety could be so accurate. It's almost as if you had experienced these mood slumps in your own life." And a few have boldly asked if I have.

Let me share an experience when my son, David Erik, was born. . . .

He was born around 6:00 P.M. on October 13, 1976. While his birth was a normal one it was obvious that he was having difficulties breathing. He was bluer than a healthy baby should be and he was wheezing and gasping for air. The obstetrician reassured us that the problem didn't appear to be serious but explained that they were sending him to an incubator in the premature intensive-care unit as a precautionary measure because he wasn't getting enough oxygen into his blood. I panicked and thought, "God! He needs oxygen for his brain cells. What if he ends up with brain damage or is mentally retarded?"

As I walked through the hospital corridors, frightening thoughts raced through my mind. I developed tunnel vision and I felt as if I were floating across the ceiling. I had fantasies of taking him to clinics for the rest of his life as he struggled with various handicaps. As the night wore on, I was flooded with wave after wave of panic and I felt like a nervous wreck.

Then I asked myself: "Why don't you do what you tell your patients to do? Aren't you always suggesting that distorted thoughts— and not realistic ones—upset people? Why don't you write your negative thoughts down on a piece of paper and see if there's something illogical about them?" Then I told myself, "Oh, that wouldn't work because this problem is real! A silly paper and pencil exercise wouldn't do me any good at all!" Then I countered this with "Why not try it as an experiment and find out?"

The first thought I wrote down was "Other people might think less of me if I have a mentally retarded son." I'm a little ashamed to admit that my own ego was already caught up with the accomplishments and intelligence of my own son. But that was how I was thinking! This is such a common trap. We're programmed to believe that if we're number one in athletics or scholastics or in our careers, then we're no longer "average" or "ordinary" but "special." Our children incorporate this value system as they grow up and their feelings of self-esteem get connected with how talented, successful, or popular they are.

Once I wrote my negative thought down and thought about it, I began to see how distorted and unloving it was and I decided to look at it this way instead: "It's not very likely that people will evaluate me based on how intelligent my son is. They're more likely to evaluate me on what I do. Their feelings about me will depend more on how I treat them and how I feel about them than on my own or my son's success."

The more I thought about it, the clearer it became that my own feelings of happiness and my love for my son didn't have to be connected with his intelligence or career at all. And then a rather sweet realization came to mind. It dawned on me that even if he was only average or below average, it didn't need to diminish the joy we would share by one iota. I thought of how wonderful it would be to be close to him and to do things together as he grew up. I had the fantasy of going into the coin-collecting business with him when I was old and ready to retire from psychiatry. I had always had an interest in coin collecting, and my daughter, who was five years old at the time, was quite bright and independent. She had always developed her own interests and hobbies and never had much interest in coins. The fantasy of going to coin shows with my son and wheeling and dealing Lincoln pennies and buffalo nickels was so exciting that my anxiety vanished entirely.

By this time it was around 3:00 in the morning. I had the sudden urge to go to see him so I drove back to the hospital. Since I was on the hospital staff, the nurses were kind enough to let me visit him. As he lay in the incubator he was still bluish and his nostrils flared with every labored effort to move air in and out. He was crying, frightened, struggling, and exhausted. My heart went out to him. I wanted to touch him. I put on a surgical glove and reached through the hole in the side of the incubator. As I placed my hand on his forehead I felt all the love I had for him. He seemed to settle down and it appeared that his breathing became more relaxed.

When I got home I had the impulse to call the intensive-care unit to see how he was. The nurse said that right after I left he began to breathe normally and his skin turned pink. The order had already been written to discharge him to the regular nursery so he could be with his mother!

Ultimately it turned out that he had no deficiencies or brain damage due to his breathing difficulties. My negative thoughts were quite unrealistic. This crisis helped me learn to love and cherish him as he is, and not because of his intelligence or talents. The joy he radiates every day is my reward.

The story shows that all of us succumb at times to feelings of doubt and despair. These vulnerabilities are universal, and are part of numerous methods that have helped hundreds of thousands of people to break out of their bad moods and experience greater joy, greater self-esteem, and greater intimacy. But *changing* the way you feel is only one of our goals. The other goal is *self-acceptance.* I want you to learn to accept and love yourself as a flawed and imperfect human. I want you to accept your strengths as well as your weaknesses without a sense of shame or embarrassment.

One of the spiritual principles at the root of cognitive therapy is a paradox: Your weaknesses can become your strengths. Your short-comings can become your greatest assets, your windows of opportunity, once you surrender and accept them. The fear and desperation that I experienced when David Erik was born have given me the opportunity to develop unconditional love for him and to reach out to you. Perhaps you and I can also form a more meaningful bond because you can see that I am not a guru who knows all the answers but simply a flesh-and-blood human being like yourself. I often hurt and experience irritability, anxiety, and disappointment, just like you do. I believe that sharing these feelings can make us feel closer. It's our shortcomings and not our successes that give us the opportunity for genuine caring.

That's what I mean when I say that your weakness can be your secret source of strength. I hope that you will come to comprehend this and to discover a profound sense of self-acceptance, compassion, and joy as you read this book.

Understanding Your Moods

1

•

You Can Change *the* *Way You* Feel

Many people believe that their bad moods result from factors beyond their control. They ask, "How can I possibly feel happy? My girlfriend rejected me. Women always put me down." Or they say, "How can I feel good about myself? I'm not particularly successful. I don't have a glamorous career. I'm just an inferior person, and that's reality." Some people attribute their blue moods to their hormones or body chemistry. Others believe that their sour outlook results from some childhood event that has long been forgotten and buried deep in their unconscious. Some people argue that it's realistic to feel bad because they're ill or have recently experienced a personal disappointment. Others attribute their bad moods to the state of the world—the shaky economy, the bad weather, taxes, traffic jams, the threat of nuclear war. Misery, they argue, is inevitable.

Of course there's some truth in all of these ideas. Our feelings undoubtedly are influenced by external events, by our body chemistry, and by conflicts and traumas from the past. However, these theories are based on the notion that our feelings are beyond our control. If you say, "I just can't help the way I feel," you will only make yourself a victim of your misery—and you'll be fooling yourself, because you *can* change the way you feel.

If you want to feel better, you must realize that your thoughts and attitudes—not external events—create your feelings. You can learn to change the way you think, feel, and behave in the here-and-now. That simple but revolutionary principle can help you change your life.

To illustrate the important relationship between your thoughts and your moods, consider the many ways you might react to a compliment. Suppose I told you, "I really like you. I think you're a neat person." How would you feel? Some people would feel pleased and happy. Others might feel sad and guilty. Some people would feel embarrassed, and some would react with anger and annoyance. What explains such different reactions? It's because of the different ways they might *think* about the compliment. If you feel sad, you're probably thinking, "Ah, Dr. Burns is just saying that to make me feel good. He's just trying to be nice to me, but he doesn't really mean it." If you feel annoyed, you might be thinking, "He's flattering me. He must be trying to get something from me. Why isn't he more honest?" If you feel good about the compliment, you're likely to be thinking, "Gee, Dr. Burns likes me. That's great!" In each case the external event—the compliment—is the same. The way you feel results entirely from the way you think about it. That's what I mean when I say that your *thoughts* create your moods.

This is also true when something bad happens. Suppose someone you respect criticizes you. How would you feel? You may feel guilty and inadequate if you tell yourself you're no good and the problem is all your fault. You will feel anxious and worried if you tell yourself that the other person is looking down on you and is going to reject you. You'll feel angry if you tell yourself that it's all their fault and they have no right to say such unfair things. If you have a good sense of self-esteem, you might feel curious and try to understand what the other person is thinking and feeling. In each case, your reaction will depend on the way you think about the criticism. The messages you give yourself have an enormous impact on your emotions. And what's even more important, by learning to change your thoughts, you can change the way you feel.

The powerful methods described in this book have helped thousands of people take greater charge of their emotions, their careers, and their personal relationships—and they can help you. It's not always easy. Considerable effort and persistence are sometimes required to snap out of a bad mood. But it *can* be done! The techniques are practical and straightforward, and you can make them work for you.

This new approach is called "cognitive behavior therapy" because you learn to change the way you *think,* the way you *behave,* and the way you *feel.* A "cognition" is simply a thought. You may have noticed that when you feel depressed or anxious you are thinking about yourself and your life in a pessimistic, self-critical way. You may wake up feeling discouraged and tell yourself, "Ugh! What's the point in getting out of bed?" You may feel anxious and inferior at a social gathering because you tell yourself, "I don't have anything witty or interesting to say." Cognitive therapists believe that these negative thinking patterns actually *cause* you to feel depressed and anxious. When you think about your problems in a more positive and realistic way, you will experience greater self-esteem, intimacy, and productivity.

If you want to break out of a bad mood, you must first understand that every type of negative feeling results from a specific kind of negative thought. *Sadness and depression* result from thoughts of loss. You think you have lost something important to your self-esteem. Perhaps you were rejected by someone you cared a great deal about. You might have retired or lost your job or missed out on an important career opportunity. *Frustration* results from unfulfilled expectations. You tell yourself that things should be different from the way they really are. For example, "That train shouldn't be so late when I'm in such a hurry. Darn it!" *Anxiety and panic* result from thoughts of danger. Before you give a speech in front of a group of people, you feel nervous because you anticipate that your voice will tremble and your mind will go blank. You imagine that you'll make a fool of yourself. *Guilt* results from the thought that you are bad. When a friend makes an unreasonable request, you may feel a twinge of guilt and think, "A really nice person would say yes." Then you may agree to something that isn't really in your best interest. *Feelings of inferiority* result from the thought that you're inadequate in comparison with others. You think, "She's so much better looking than I am" or "He's so much smarter and more successful. What's wrong with me?" *Anger* results from feelings of unfairness. You tell yourself that someone is treating you unjustly or trying to take advantage of you.

The list on pages 6–7 illustrates the connection between your thoughts and your feelings. Study this table carefully. It will help

YOUR THOUGHTS AND YOUR FEELINGS

Emotion	Thoughts that lead to this emotion
Sadness or depression	Thoughts of loss: a romantic rejection, the death of a loved one, the loss of a job, or the failure to achieve an important personal goal.
Guilt or shame	You believe that you've hurt someone or that you've failed to live up to your own moral standards. Guilt results from self-condemnation, whereas shame involves the fear that you'll lose face when others find out about what you did.
Anger, irritation, annoyance, or resentment	You feel that someone is treating you unfairly or trying to take advantage of you.
Frustration	Life falls short of your expectations. You insist that things should be different. It might be your own performance ("I shouldn't have made that mistake"), what someone else does ("He should've been on time!"), or an event ("Why does the traffic always slow down when I'm in a hurry?").
Anxiety, worry, fear, nervousness, or panic	You believe you're in danger because you think something bad is about to happen—"What if the plane crashes?" "What if my mind goes blank when I give my talk in front of all those people?" "What if this chest pain is the start of a heart attack?"
Inferiority or inadequacy	You compare yourself to others and conclude that you're not as good as they are because you're not as talented, attractive, charming, successful, intelligent. "She's really got what it takes. She's so cute. All the men are chasing her. I'm just average. There's nothing very special about me."
Loneliness	You tell yourself that you're bound to feel unhappy because you're alone and you aren't getting enough love and attention from others.

Emotion	Thoughts that lead to this emotion
Hopelessness or discouragement	You feel convinced that your problems will go on forever and that things will never improve. "I'll never get over this depression," or "I just can't lose weight and keep it off," or "I'll never find a good job," or "I'll be alone forever."

you understand why you're in the mood you're in, and this can make it easier to change the way you feel.

What you will learn here is that even though you are convinced they are valid, most of the negative thoughts that make you feel bad are distorted and unrealistic. Example: Following a romantic breakup or divorce you tell yourself, "It's all my fault. I must be unlovable. I'll never be close to anyone." You feel so rotten that it seems absolutely true, and you think your life is over. Months later you begin to date and you start to feel close to people again. It suddenly dawns on you that you are lovable after all, that you *weren't* entirely responsible for the breakup of your relationship. You wonder how in the world you could have believed all the put-downs you were heaping on yourself. But at the time, your negative thoughts seemed completely valid.

That's one of the peculiar things about bad moods—we often fool ourselves and create misery by telling ourselves things *that simply are not true.* And the strange thing is that we usually don't have the vaguest suspicion that we're being conned by our misery and self-doubt.

The ten forms of distorted thinking that lead to negative moods are listed on pages 8–11. Study this list carefully, because you will refer to it frequently as you do the exercises in the book. Many people have told me that this list changed their lives.

One disclaimer is necessary. There are many times when negative feelings are healthy and appropriate. Learning when to accept these feelings and how to cope with a realistically negative situation is just as important as learning how to rid yourself of distorted thoughts and feelings. If a loved one is seriously ill, you will feel concerned. These sad feelings are a sign of caring. If the house you had your heart set on is sold to someone who made a slightly higher offer, it is natural to feel disappointed. If you're having an argument with your spouse, you will probably feel angry and hurt. If you have to give a speech or

THE TEN FORMS OF TWISTED THINKING

1. All-or-nothing thinking

You see things in black-or-white categories. If a situation falls short of perfect, you see it as a total failure. When a young woman on a diet ate a spoonful of ice cream, she told herself, "I've blown my diet completely." This thought upset her so much that she gobbled down an entire quart of ice cream!

2. Overgeneralization

You see a single negative event, such as a romantic rejection or a career reversal, as a never-ending pattern of defeat by using words such as "always" or "never" when you think about it. A depressed salesman became terribly upset when he noticed bird dung on the windshield of his car. He told himself, "Just my luck! Birds are *always* crapping on my car!"

3. Mental filter

You pick out a single negative detail and dwell on it exclusively, so that your vision of all of reality becomes darkened, like the drop of ink that discolors a beaker of water. Example: You receive many positive comments about your presentation to a group of associates at work, but one of them says something mildly critical. You obsess about his reaction for days and ignore all the positive feedback.

4. Discounting the positive

You reject positive experiences by insisting they "don't count." If you do a good job, you may tell yourself that it wasn't good enough or that anyone could have done as well. Discounting the positive takes the joy out of life and makes you feel inadequate and unrewarded.

5. Jumping to conclusions	You interpret things negatively when there are no facts to support your conclusion. **Mind reading:** Without checking it out, you arbitrarily conclude that someone is reacting negatively to you. **Fortune-telling:** You predict that things will turn out badly. Before a test you may tell yourself, "I'm really going to blow it. What if I flunk?" If you're depressed you may tell yourself, "I'll never get better."
6. Magnification	You exaggerate the importance of your problems and shortcomings, or you minimize the importance of your desirable qualities. This is also called the "binocular trick."
7. Emotional reasoning	You assume that your negative emotions necessarily reflect the way things really are: "I feel terrified about going on airplanes. It must be very dangerous to fly." Or "I feel guilty. I must be a rotten person." Or "I feel angry. This proves I'm being treated unfairly." Or "I feel so inferior. This means I'm a second-rate person." Or "I feel hopeless. I must really be hopeless."
8. "Should statements"	You tell yourself that things *should* be the way you hoped or expected them to be. After playing a difficult piece on the piano, a gifted pianist told herself, "I shouldn't have made so many mistakes." This made her feel so disgusted that she quit practicing for several days. "Musts," "oughts" and "have tos" are similar offenders. "Should statements" that are directed against yourself lead to guilt and frustration. Should statements that are directed against other people or the world in

general lead to anger and frustration: "He shouldn't be so stubborn and argumentative."

Many people try to motivate themselves with shoulds and shouldn'ts, as if they were delinquents who had to be punished before they could be expected to do anything. "I shouldn't eat that doughnut." This usually doesn't work because all these shoulds and musts make you feel rebellious and you get the urge to do just the opposite. Dr. Albert Ellis has called this "*must*erbation." I call it the "shouldy" approach to life.

9. Labeling

Labeling is an extreme form of all-or-nothing thinking. Instead of saying "I made a mistake," you attach a negative label to yourself: "I'm a loser." You might also label yourself "a fool" or "a failure" or "a jerk." Labeling is quite irrational because you are not the same as what you do. Human beings exist, but "fools," "losers," and "jerks" do not. These labels are just useless abstractions that lead to anger, anxiety, frustration, and low self-esteem.

You may also label others. When someone does something that rubs you the wrong way, you may tell yourself: "He's an S.O.B." Then you feel that the problem is with that person's "character" or "essence" instead of with their thinking or behavior. You see them as totally bad. This makes you feel hostile and hopeless about improving things and leaves little room for constructive communication.

10. Personalization and blame	Personalization occurs when you hold yourself personally responsible for an event that isn't entirely under your control. When a woman received a note that her child was having difficulties at school, she told herself, "This shows what a bad mother I am," instead of trying to pinpoint the cause of the problem so that she could be helpful to her child. When another woman's husband beat her, she told herself, "If only I were better in bed, he wouldn't beat me." Personalization leads to guilt, shame, and feelings of inadequacy.
	Some people do the opposite. They blame other people or their circumstances for their problems, and they overlook ways that they might be contributing to the problem: "The reason my marriage is so lousy is because my spouse is totally unreasonable." Blame usually doesn't work very well because other people will resent being scapegoated and they will just toss the blame right back in your lap. It's like the game of hot potato— no one wants to get stuck with it.

start a new job or ask your boss for a raise, you will probably feel a little nervous. It's often best to accept these negative feelings.

I don't believe that you should try to be happy all the time, or in *total* control of your feelings. That would just be a perfectionistic trap. You cannot always be completely rational and objective. Certainly I'm not! I have my share of shortcomings, my dark moments of self-doubt, my periods of irritability. I believe these experiences give us the opportunity for growth, for intimacy, and for a deeper comprehension of what it means to be human.

Self-Awareness Exercise

Let's summarize the most important ideas in this chapter. First, you learned that your thoughts, and not external events, create your moods. Second, you learned that specific kinds of negative thoughts cause specific kinds of negative emotions. For example, the belief that you are in danger will make you anxious or frightened. Third, you learned that the negative thoughts that make you depressed, anxious, guilty, angry, or frustrated are frequently distorted and unrealistic, even though they seem absolutely valid. Recognizing the vital connections between your thoughts and your emotions is the first step in breaking out of a bad mood. This exercise will make you more aware of the kinds of distorted thoughts that are most frequently associated with different kinds of negative feelings, including anger (page 12), anxiety (page 17), stress (page 19), and depression (page 23), as well as for bad habits such as alcoholism (page 25).

ANGER

Think of a time when you were angry or irritated. Write down a brief description of the situation that made you angry. What actually happened? Were you upset with yourself or someone else?

_____

_____

_____

_____

_____

Did you fill that out? I have found that some patients—and some readers—do the written self-help exercises that are so crucial to the success of cognitive therapy. Others do not—they seem to be along for the ride. Research has indicated that people who actually do the written exercises improve far more than those who do not. Do you want to feel better and change your life as a result of reading this book? If your answer is yes, then I want you to fill in the description before you continue reading.

Now I want you to tell me about the negative thoughts and feelings you were having in the situation you described. Did you feel hurt? Annoyed? Frustrated? What messages were you giving yourself? Did you tell yourself that the other person was a self-centered bum or that they were being unfair to you? Describe your negative thoughts and feelings here:

_____

_____

_____

_____

_____

A common irritating situation is when someone is late. The later they become, the angrier you get. By the time they finally show up you feel as if you could strangle them. When George was late coming home from work, Marge felt angry and had these thoughts: "He's *never* on time. What a jerk! If he cared about me, he wouldn't be so late. He should be home by now."

Let's examine these thoughts and see if they contain any distortions. Her first thought is "He's never on time." Review the list on pages 8–11 and see if you can find the distortion in this thought. This one is fairly easy. Put your ideas here before you read on:

_____

_____

It's an example of an "overgeneralization," because Marge sees this negative event as a never-ending pattern of defeat. George may *sometimes* be late, or he may be *frequently* late, but he's not *always* late. If you called it the "mental filter," you would also be right. Marge is concentrating on all the times George is late and ignoring or filtering out the times he's on time.

The problem with overgeneralizing is that it will make the situation seem worse than it really is. This may trigger a pointless argument when George comes home. Marge might accuse George of "always being late." He will feel indignant and insist, quite rightly, that he isn't "always late." They'll get into a frustrating argument that misses the point entirely. They'll both feel misunderstood and absolutely convinced that the other one is to blame. Do you recognize this pattern? If you've ever been involved in a marital squabble, I'm sure you know how exasperating this type of interaction can be.

Marge's second thought is "What a jerk!" What distortions are there in this one? Put your ideas here after you review the Ten Forms of Twisted Thinking:

_____

_____

This is an example of "labeling," because Marge is attacking George rather than what George did. You might also view it as an example of "all-or-nothing thinking" since Marge is writing him off entirely. Being late may have been thoughtless or it may have been due to factors beyond George's control, such as a traffic jam on the expressway. Either way, it doesn't make George "a jerk." Contrary to popular opinion, there are actually no "jerks" in the United States at this time. There's certainly plenty of jerky behavior, however!

What is the main distortion in Marge's third thought, "If he cared about me, he wouldn't be so late"? Put your ideas here:

_____

_____

The major distortion in this thought is "mind reading" or "jumping to conclusions." Marge is automatically assuming that a lack of caring explains why George is late. Although he may not care, there could be other explanations for why he's late. Can you think of any possibilities?

List them here:

1. _____

_____

2. _____

_____

3. _____

_____

Here are several possibilities: George might be working late because his boss is pressuring him about a deadline. He may be working overtime so he and Marge can save up enough money for a down payment on a new house. Or he may be annoyed with Marge about something. If so, it may mean that George and Marge don't deal with conflicts openly and directly. This wouldn't mean that George "doesn't care"—his anger would probably mean that he *does* care and he feels hurt. If this were the case, George and Marge could benefit from some communication training so they can learn to share their feelings more openly instead of acting them out through nagging and arguing.

Marge's last thought was "He should be home now." What is the distortion in this thought? Check the list on pages 8–11 and put your ideas here:

_____

This is a classic "should statement." It might be better for Marge to tell herself that she'd *like* George to be on time. This would sound less judgmental and it would create a less antagonistic atmosphere for discussing the problem.

Some readers may feel that I am attacking Marge. You may want to defend her and think, "What if George *is* a jerk? Maybe he's having an affair with someone. Maybe she has the right to be angry!" Certainly there are times when anger is healthy and appropriate. There will be other times when your thinking is way off base and your anger is not particularly valid. And even when someone is treating you unfairly, your feelings will still result from the way you think about what's happening. When you think about a genuinely upsetting situation in a distorted way, your feelings will get blown up out of proportion so much that the real problem becomes harder to resolve. If you're willing to think about the problem more realistically, you'll find it far easier to express your feelings in a constructive way so that the other person will listen and not get so defensive.

Marge just doesn't have enough information yet. She hasn't found out the facts, but she has already convicted and sentenced George. This attitude of blame will guarantee that there will be a fight when George gets home. Her thoughts are so inflammatory that she'll overreact. This will simply make the problem worse. She may pout and cry or accuse him of being a thoughtless jerk. I can't imagine that this will lead to a productive exchange of feelings. Can you?

What *could* Marge say when George comes home? Put your ideas here:

_____

_____

_____

_____

_____

She might say, "George, I was really worried about you, and I'm angry because you're so late and you didn't call. I cooked this great meal for you because I love you, and when you didn't show up on time I felt really hurt. Can you tell me what's going on? Did we have a misunderstanding about when you were going to be home, or what?" This statement is far more powerful than telling him off, because she is sharing how she feels without hurling accusations or putting George down. She invites him to explain what the problem is instead of acting as if she already knew.

Now review the angry thoughts you wrote down at the beginning of this section. See if you can identify any of the distortions that are most frequently associated with anger. Look for:

- **Should statements:** "He shouldn't have said that" or "She's got no right to feel that way."
- **Labeling:** "He's an S.O.B."
- **Mind reading:** "She obviously doesn't have any respect for me."
- **Blaming:** "This is entirely his fault."
- **All-or-nothing thinking:** "I'm right and she's wrong about this."
- **Overgeneralization:** "All she ever thinks about is herself."

ANXIETY AND FEAR

Think of a time when you felt anxious or worried. What was happening at the time? Were you nervous about an important test? An airplane flight? A talk you had to give? Perhaps you were worrying about your health or a bill you forgot to pay. Describe the situation that made you feel nervous:

_____

_____

_____

_____

Next, try to identify your negative thoughts. What were you telling yourself? What were you thinking? Perhaps you were thinking that something bad was going to happen or were worrying about what other people would think of you. Record your negative thoughts here:

_____

_____

_____

_____

Henry felt anxious before an important job interview. I have listed his negative thoughts in the left-hand column. Cover up the right-hand column and see if you can identify the distortions in each of his thoughts. You can refer to the list on pages 8–11.

Negative thoughts	Distortions
1. I'll probably blow it. My mind will go blank and I won't be able to think of anything to say.	1. This thought is an example of "fortune-telling," because Henry is predicting that something bad will happen. Fortune-telling is the commonest distortion that leads to anxiety.

Negative thoughts	Distortions
2. He's probably just giving me the interview out of courtesy because he knows my father.	2. This is an example of "mind reading." Henry is assuming he knows how his prospective boss is thinking.
3. I don't really have anything to offer. He probably has a lot of applicants who are much better than I am.	3. This is an example of "disqualifying the positive," because Henry is overlooking his positive qualities. He's also "jumping to conclusions" since he's assuming that all the other applicants are more qualified than he is. Henry has no information about this.
4. I'll probably make a fool of myself.	4. This is an example of "labeling," since Henry is calling himself "a fool." We all occasionally say or do foolish things, but this makes us human beings, not "fools." This is also an example of "fortune-telling" since he's predicting a bad outcome.
5. That would be terrible.	5. Henry's last negative thought is an example of "magnification." Henry is blowing the importance of this particular interview way out of proportion. The Holocaust of World War II was "terrible." If you have a bad interview and you don't get a particular job, it isn't "terrible," it's simply "unfortunate." Not getting the job could still be a good learning experience. Henry may need to go out on as many as ten interviews before he finds the job that's right for him. His entire future does not hang on any one interview.

Now review the anxious thoughts you wrote down at the beginning of this section. See if you can identify any of the distortions that are most frequently associated with anxiety, panic, or nervousness:

- Fortune-telling: "What if I get so nervous that I pass out or crack up?"
- Mind reading: "People would look down on me if they knew how nervous and insecure I feel."
- Should statements: "I *shouldn't* feel so panicky. This is abnormal. What's wrong with me?"
- Emotional reasoning: "I *feel* frightened. Therefore it must be very dangerous to be on this airplane."
- Magnification: "This is *awful*! What if I lose control?"

Write down the distortions in your negative thoughts here:

1. _____

2. _____

3. _____

4. _____

STRESS

Harry is a successful attorney who feels tense the moment he walks into his office each morning. He can't seem to relax or enjoy his work. The following negative thoughts flood his mind when he sits down at his desk. Cover up the right-hand column and see if you can identify the distortions in them, using the list on pages 8–11 as your guide.

Negative thoughts	Distortions
1. This is awful! Just think of everything I have to do! I just have too much work.	1. This is an example of "all-or-nothing thinking," because Harry's dwelling on everything he has to do rather than the specific things he has to do this morning. You could also call this "magnification."

Negative thoughts	Distortions
2. There's always so much work left at the end of the day!	2. The second negative thought is the "mental filter," since Harry thinks about all the things he hasn't done and overlooks the many things he has done.
3. I'll never catch up.	3. This is an example of "all-or-nothing thinking." Harry is actually on schedule in his preparation for the majority of his cases. A busy and successful attorney is not supposed to be completely caught up. The reason he has so much work is that he has a prosperous practice with a constant flow of new clients. It's actually good that he's never completely caught up!
4. I'll make a mistake or forget to do something important.	4. This is an example of "fortune-telling," because he's telling himself that he's going to foul up. He'd feel better if he told himself that he was doing well and was going to have a productive day.
5. What if I lose this case?	5. This is another example of "fortune-telling." Every lawyer wins some trials and loses others, but Harry's track record has been excellent. Since he has prepared a strong case for this particular client, it would be more realistic to tell himself that the odds are in his favor and that things will probably turn out well.
6. My client will be teed off at me if I lose.	6. This involves "mind reading" and "fortune-telling." Harry's assuming that he will lose and that if he

Negative thoughts	Distortions
	does his client will be dissatis-fied. The majority of Harry's clients have told him they were pleased with his work. Harry told me that when he has lost, his clients have usually been even more apprecia-tive because they recognized that Harry did the best possible job in a difficult situation.
7. Then I won't get any new cases.	7. This thought is an extreme exam-ple of "fortune-telling." In fact, Harry's had so many referrals re-cently that he can hardly keep up.
8. Then I'll lose money and end up destitute.	8. I'm sure it's obvious to you that this is one more example of "fortune-telling." Harry's income has been growing substantially. He will continue to enjoy a comfortable standard of living, and he will not end up in the poorhouse!

See if you can think of a time when you felt stressed. You may have been pressured by your boss about a deadline at work or overwhelmed by all your commitments to your family, your church, or your friends. Describe that stressful situation here:

_____

_____

_____

Now I'd like you to tell me what kinds of negative feelings you had when you felt stressed. Simply check "yes" or "no" for each of the following:

	Yes	No	
1.	_____	_____	Sad or depressed
2.	_____	_____	Nervous, panicky, worried, anxious, or fearful
3.	_____	_____	Annoyed, irritable, resentful, or angry
4.	_____	_____	Frustrated
5.	_____	_____	Pressured, tense, or stressed
6.	_____	_____	Guilty or ashamed
7.	_____	_____	Hopeless or discouraged
8.	_____	_____	Inadequate or inferior
9.	_____	_____	Exhausted, tired, drained, or overwhelmed
10.	_____	_____	Bored, unmotivated, or uninterested
11.	_____	_____	Lonely, unloved, or alone
12.	_____	_____	Other (describe any additional emotions):

Now write down several of your negative thoughts in the left-hand column like the example on pages 8–11.

Negative thoughts	Distortions
1. _____	_____
_____	_____
2. _____	_____
_____	_____
3. _____	_____
_____	_____

Review Table 2 and see if you can identify the distortions in each negative thought. Record the distortions in the right-hand column. Look for:

* **Fortune-telling:** "I'll never get everything done."
* **All-or-nothing thinking:** "I've got to do a perfect job."
* **Should statements:** "I shouldn't make any mistakes."
* **Disqualifying the positive:** "I didn't get anything done today."
* **Mind reading:** "My boss will think this is crummy."
* **Magnification:** "I've got so much work to do."

DEPRESSION

Joanne is a 28-year-old woman who lives in New York and works as an options trader. As you probably know, options traders buy and sell futures on stocks, and they can make or lose vast amounts of money in incredibly short periods of time. The profession can make you or break you, and either way, it's enormously stressful.

Joanne recently formed a partnership with a man who put up $100,000 as capital for her to invest. They agreed to share the profits. Joanne decided to pursue a conservative, low-risk investment strategy. For the past three months, Joanne made $4,000 a month in profits. For several months before that, she had averaged $12,000. She was distraught because of the decrease in profits and felt suicidal.

I was curious why Joanne was so despondent and asked her to write down the negative thoughts that made her feel so bad. They included, among others, the thought that she was a failure and the belief that when her partner found out about her shoddy performance he would be terribly disappointed and fire her. Can you identify the distortions in her thoughts? Check the Ten Forms of Twisted Thinking and put your ideas here:

1. _____

2. _____

3. _____

4. _____

5. _____

One of the distortions is "all-or-nothing thinking": Joanne thinks that if she isn't doing stupendously and making a fortune every single month, then she's a total failure. This may seem ridiculous to you, since $4,000 profit per month is hardly a "failure." However, it feels like a failure to Joanne because of her perfectionist attitude. She reasons, "I feel like a total failure, therefore I must really be one." This illustrates a second distortion, "emotional reasoning," since Joanne assumes that her negative feelings necessarily reflect the way things really are.

A third distortion is "fortune-telling," since Joanne is predicting that the return of the investment will continue to be mediocre. There's no real evidence for this. You could also call this an "overgeneralization," since she imagines that the low-profit months will continue endlessly.

A fourth distortion would be "should statements." Joanne is telling herself she should always make big profits. But if you look at her overall performance, this is clearly an unrealistic expectation. She's had some $12,000 months and she's had some $4,000 months, so her average monthly profit is actually $8,000. That's not bad—it actually amounts to an annual rate of appreciation of nearly 100 percent. She simply hasn't accepted the fact that market conditions are inherently unpredictable, and that her income will fluctuate greatly from month to month. There's no such thing as an investor who *always* scores big. Joanne would do well to stop demanding so much of herself and to make her expectations more realistic.

She's also involved in "mind reading." She assumes with absolutely no evidence that her partner will be as angry and disappointed as she is, and that he will fire her. As part of her psychotherapy homework, I insisted that she talk things over with her partner. Joanne was quite reluctant to do this and procrastinated for weeks.

I twisted her arm and she finally agreed. Joanne was amazed to learn that her partner was quite satisfied with her performance. He told Joanne she could feel free to take even greater risks, and that even if she lost the entire $100,000 she'd still have a job.

You can see that the solution to Joanne's depression involved a combination of self-acceptance and change. Joanne had to *change* her distorted thinking patterns so she could assess her situation more realistically. She wasn't making an absolute killing, but she wasn't a complete failure either. At the same time, she had to *accept* the fact that she wouldn't always be a big winner, and that good months would be followed by bad ones—and vice versa. Sometimes more humble and modest expectations can be tremendously liberating. Although it may stimulate our egos to think we're so brilliant and hardworking that we will always succeed, carrying the burden of having to be so great and so perfect can be overwhelmingly frustrating and lonely.

TEMPTATIONS

Many people have problems controlling their impulses. They can't resist temptations like overeating, smoking, gambling, drinking too much, using drugs, or having sex with the wrong person. Can you think of a time when you succumbed to a temptation? The thoughts that tempted you to give in to these bad habits probably contained positive distortions that are mirror images of negative ones listed on pages 8–11.

Frank had the habit of eating and drinking too much. His family physician advised him that his drinking was a serious problem and that he was in the early stages of cirrhosis of the liver. Frank was overweight and had elevated triglycerides and blood cholesterol levels, along with increased blood pressure. This meant that he was in a high-risk group for a heart attack. He was chronically stressed and irritable, and overeating and drinking were his way of coping with the tension in his life.

Although every morning his "rational self" felt it was a good idea to diet and to quit drinking, Frank's "emotional self" would decide to have a drink—and then another, and another—every night when he came home from work. This urge to drink was caused by positive tempting thoughts. I've indicated the positive distortions in each thought in the right-hand column.

Positive thoughts	Distortions
1. Gee, I'll really feel good if I have a beer now. And it will taste so good.	1. This is an example of positive "fortune-telling," since Frank is predicting something that isn't entirely true. Although Frank usually experiences a brief mood elevation when he starts to drink, he

Positive thoughts	Distortions
	nearly always ends up feeling worse because his drinking gets out of hand. After three or four beers he gets angry and depressed and starts to argue with his wife. He ends up flying off the handle and feels guilty. He wakes up with a hangover and a lack of self-respect the next morning.
2. I really shouldn't have that beer.	2. This is a "should statement." The problem with saying "I shouldn't" is that it sounds moralistic and controlling. This makes Frank feel rebellious and it increases his urge to have a beer.
3. I'll only have one beer. That won't hurt me.	3. This is another example of positive "fortune-telling," because Frank is predicting something very unrealistic. While it's true that an occasional beer is harmless, Frank won't stop after just one. Once he starts drinking, his inhibitions will disappear and he will quietly devour one or two six-packs.
4. Life is so boring. I deserve a little fun.	4. This is "emotional reasoning." Frank may deserve a little fun, but his life won't be much fun if he keeps drinking. His alcoholism makes him chronically depressed and bored with his life and keeps him from getting close to his wife.
5. Gee, that beer tasted good! I think I'll have another one. I'll feel even better!	5. This is more "emotional reasoning" and "fortune-telling." One drink may be relaxing, but five or ten drinks will make Frank irritable and unhappy.

Can you think of any temptations that you succumb to, such as smoking, overeating, drinking excessively, using drugs, or shoplifting? Describe the problem here:

_____

_____

_____

_____

Can you think of the positive thoughts that cross your mind when you feel tempted to do this? Write them down in the left-hand column and number them. Then see if you can identify the positive distortions in these thoughts and record them in the right-hand column.

Positive thoughts	Distortions
_____	_____
_____	_____
_____	_____
_____	_____
_____	_____
_____	_____
_____	_____
_____	_____

OTHER EMOTIONS

Distorted negative thoughts can be associated with any emotion such as loneliness, guilt, jealousy, depression, or frustration. Maybe you're mad at yourself because you snapped at a friend during a moment of irritability and fatigue. Maybe you feel depressed because you didn't do as well on a test as you had hoped. Write down a brief description of any situation that upset you. It could be a recent problem or something that happened many years ago:

_____

_____

_____

_____

How did you feel? Record your negative feelings here:

	Yes	No	
1.	_____	_____	Sad or depressed
2.	_____	_____	Nervous, panicky, worried, anxious, or fearful
3.	_____	_____	Annoyed, irritable, resentful, or angry
4.	_____	_____	Frustrated
5.	_____	_____	Pressured, tense, or stressed
6.	_____	_____	Guilty or ashamed
7.	_____	_____	Hopeless or discouraged
8.	_____	_____	Inadequate or inferior
9.	_____	_____	Exhausted, tired, drained, or overwhelmed
10.	_____	_____	Bored, unmotivated, or uninterested
11.	_____	_____	Lonely, unloved, or alone
12.	_____	_____	Other (describe any additional emotions): _____

Now, write down your negative thoughts and number them. Then look for the distortions in these thoughts, using the list on pages 8–11 as a guide.

Negative thoughts	Distortions
1. _____	_____
_____	_____
2. _____	_____
_____	_____
3. _____	_____
_____	_____
4. _____	_____
_____	_____

I don't expect you to be able to *change* your thoughts and feelings yet. I just want you to practice tuning in with your "third ear" so you can begin to learn more about the vital connection between the way you think and the way you feel. This is the crucial first step.

Answers to Questions Most Commonly Asked About Cognitive Therapy:

Doesn't cognitive therapy just lead to intellectual change without changing how a person really feels on a gut level? No. The purpose of cognitive therapy is to transform your emotions and your perceptions of yourself and your life. Providing rationalizations or intellectual excuses for things is not a part of cognitive therapy. The purpose of the treatment is to develop profound feelings of joy and happiness.

What kinds of problems does cognitive therapy work best for? When does it not work well? Cognitive therapy is an excellent treatment for mood problems such as depression, anxiety, panic attacks, phobias, anger, guilt, and feelings of inferiority. The therapy can be exceptionally helpful for the kinds of problems that we all confront in the course of daily living. These include personal relationship problems, rejection, criticism, procrastination, and the fear of failure. The techniques can be extremely effective and often work rapidly, even without the use of medications.

Cognitive therapy alone is not especially effective for severe psychotic disorders such as schizophrenia or the manic phase of manic-depressive illness. As described in Chapter 3, manic-depressive illness is a cyclic mood disorder characterized by abnormal highs and episodes of deep depression. Manic-depressives frequently need treatment with medication. Effective psychotherapy is also a crucial aspect of the treatment. Cognitive therapy can help manic-depressives develop greater self-esteem so they can cope with personal problems more effectively.

Isn't it normal to feel depressed and angry? Isn't it ridiculous to think that people should be happy all the time? One of the greatest misconceptions about cognitive therapy is that you should try to feel happy all the time. Negative feelings are frequently healthy and appropriate. Sometimes it's best just to accept bad feelings and pamper yourself and ride things out until the clouds pass and you feel better again.

Isn't cognitive therapy just a little bit too simplistic? Just too good to be true? This sounds like the "Power of Positive Thinking"! The principles of cognitive therapy *are* extremely simple. The treatment is based on the idea that your thoughts and attitudes have a huge impact on the way you act and feel. The actual procedures to change your negative thinking patterns, however, are quite sophisticated and require hard work.

Do cognitive therapists promote the idea that you should make yourself happy and ignore other people's feelings? Some pop psychologists have created the impression that you should "do your own thing" and ignore how other people react to you. My own position is quite different. I believe that if you ignore other people's feelings, you will set yourself up for enormous problems in your relationships.

Many people are self-centered. They don't seem to care about people and they use others to achieve their own goals. They often appear to be extremely happy, and they sometimes achieve a considerable level of fame or success. In spite of the external trappings, however, they may feel lonely and insecure because they never learned how to accept themselves or to get close to others. I do not envy them.

By the same token, there is a profound difference between *wanting* other people's love and approval and *needing* their love and approval. If you *need* love and approval, you may be too dependent on other people and feel terribly afraid of conflict or criticism. When someone is angry with you, you may be too threatened to express your own feelings, because you are afraid the other person won't like you if you do, and you cannot truly hear what they say because their anger is so upsetting to you. Like the narcissist who cares only about himself, people who need too much love and approval may be unable to develop mature, open, caring relationships with others. They end up feeling desperate and alone because they have not learned to love themselves.

How does a cognitive therapist deal with subconscious attitudes and feelings? About two thirds of the patients I see in my practice have straightforward problems that can be dealt with in a fairly short time—say, fifteen to twenty-five sessions. These patients find the cognitive methods helpful, and they usually get excellent results. About one third appear to have subconscious fears that cause them to resist therapy. On one level they want to feel better, but on a deeper level they are afraid to change. They ask for help, but soon they resist the therapy. They complain that they aren't getting better, and yet they appear to sabotage the therapeutic process so that progress is extremely slow. For example, some patients refuse to do any of the self-help assignments between sessions, even though these assignments have been helpful to them.

These patients can be a real challenge. When they become more aware of the subconscious fears that are holding them back, they often develop the courage to move forward with their lives. When they finally recover, it's a real cause for celebration. One of my goals has been to learn more about this puzzling phenomenon of resistance and to develop more effective treatment. Part VI illustrates techniques that can help therapists motivate these patients and facilitate greater feelings of trust and rapport.

2

•

How to Measure Your Moods

In this chapter, you will find out if you have been feeling depressed or anxious, and how severe these problems are. In addition, you will learn the answers to the questions people most frequently ask about the causes and treatments of mood problems.

To help you determine if you are suffering from depression or anxiety, I have developed two mood tests, the Burns Anxiety Inventory (BAI) and the Burns Depression Checklist (BDC). Think of them as emotional thermometers that will show whether you have a mood "fever." You can complete and interpret either one of them in under two minutes. I want you to repeat each test weekly to chart your progress while you are reading this book. If you are in therapy, you may want to show your weekly scores to your therapist, just as the patients at my clinic do. When your scores go down, you have proof that you are feeling better. When your score on either mood test is 4 or less, you'll be feeling terrific.

The Burns Anxiety Inventory lists 33 common symptoms of anxiety. Fill out the BAI now. All you have to do is check off how much each symptom has been bothering you in the past week. Each symptom is scored 0 for "not at all," 1 for "somewhat," 2 for "moderately," and 3 for "a lot."

THE BURNS ANXIETY INVENTORY*

Instructions: The following is a list of symptoms that people sometimes have. Put a check (√) in the space to the right that best describes how much that symptom or problem has bothered you during the past week.

Symptom List CATEGORY I: ANXIOUS FEELINGS	0–NOT AT ALL	1–SOMEWHAT	2–MODERATELY	3–A LOT
1. Anxiety, nervousness, worry, or fear				
2. Feeling that things around you are strange, unreal, or foggy				
3. Feeling detached from all or part of your body				
4. Sudden unexpected panic spells				
5. Apprehension or a sense of impending doom				
6. Feeling tense, stressed, "uptight," or on edge				

CATEGORY II: ANXIOUS THOUGHTS

7. Difficulty concentrating				
8. Racing thoughts or having your mind jump from one thing to the next				
9. Frightening fantasies or daydreams				
10. Feeling that you're on the verge of losing control				
11. Fears of cracking up or going crazy				
12. Fears of fainting or passing out				
13. Fears of physical illnesses or heart attacks or dying				
14. Concerns about looking foolish or inadequate in front of others				
15. Fears of being alone, isolated, or abandoned				

	0–NOT AT ALL	1–SOMEWHAT	2–MODERATELY	3–A LOT
16. Fears of criticism or disapproval				
17. Fears that something terrible is about to happen				

CATEGORY III: PHYSICAL SYMPTOMS

	0–NOT AT ALL	1–SOMEWHAT	2–MODERATELY	3–A LOT
18. Skipping or racing or pounding of the heart (sometimes called "palpitations")				
19. Pain, pressure, or tightness in the chest				
20. Tingling or numbness in the toes or fingers				
21. Butterflies or discomfort in the stomach				
22. Constipation or diarrhea				
23. Restlessness or jumpiness				
24. Tight, tense muscles				
25. Sweating not brought on by heat				
26. A lump in the throat				
27. Trembling or shaking				
28. Rubbery or "jelly" legs				
29. Feeling dizzy, lightheaded, or off balance				
30. Choking or smothering sensations or difficulty breathing				
31. Headaches or pains in the neck or back				
32. Hot flashes or cold chills				
33. Feeling tired, weak, or easily exhausted				

Add up your total score for the 33 symptoms and record it here: _____

Date: _____

After you have completed the BAI, add up your total score. It will be somewhere between 0 (if you answered "not at all" on all 33 symptoms) and 99 (if you answered "a lot" on all 33 symptoms). Use this key to interpret your score:

Total score	Degree of anxiety
0–4	Minimal or no anxiety
5–10	Borderline anxiety
11–20	Mild anxiety
21–30	Moderate anxiety
31–50	Severe anxiety
51–99	Extreme anxiety or panic

There is an extra copy of the Burns Anxiety Inventory on pages 43 and 44, along with an answer sheet. You can use the answer sheet to record your answers each week when you take the test. At the bottom, add up your score and put the date in the box provided. You can use the score to monitor the effects of drug therapy, psychotherapy, or the self-help exercises in this book.

If you like, you can take the BAI more frequently than once a week. If you take the test when you're feeling especially nervous and insecure, put a note to indicate this at the bottom of the answer sheet. For example, if your score was 67 during a panic attack, that would indicate an extreme level of anxiety. You could write "when at my worst" next to your score. Similarly, you may want to take the test when you're feeling your best. By comparing your best and worst scores, you will see the range of moods that you have recently experienced.

The Burns Depression Checklist can also be completed and scored in under two minutes.* As you can see, the BDC lists 15 common symptoms of depression. All you have to do is put a check to the right of each symptom to indicate whether it has recently bothered you "not at all" (scored 0), "slightly" (scored 1), "moderately" (scored 2), or "a lot" (scored 3).

---

*Some readers may recall that in Chapter Two of *Feeling Good: The New Mood Therapy,* I presented the Beck Depression Inventory (BDI). The BDI is a slightly different but excellent self-assessment test for depression. I developed the Burns Depression Checklist because the wording of several items on the BDI was not as clear to my patients.

THE BURNS DEPRESSION CHECKLIST*

Instructions: The following is a list of symptoms that people sometimes have. Put a check (√) in the space to the right that best describes how much that symptom or problem has bothered you during the past week.

	0—NOT AT ALL	1—SOMEWHAT	2—MODERATELY	3—A LOT
1. **Sadness:** Have you been feeling sad or down in the dumps?				
2. **Discouragement:** Does the future look hopeless?				
3. **Low self-esteem:** Do you feel worthless or think of yourself as a failure?				
4. **Inferiority:** Do you feel inadequate or inferior to others?				
5. **Guilt:** Do you get self-critical and blame yourself for everything?				
6. **Indecisiveness:** Do you have trouble making up your mind about things?				
7. **Irritability and frustration:** Have you been feeling resentful and angry a good deal of the time?				
8. **Loss of interest in life:** Have you lost interest in your career, your hobbies, your family, or your friends?				
9. **Loss of motivation:** Do you feel overwhelmed and have to push yourself hard to do things?				
10. **Poor self-image:** Do you think you're looking old or unattractive?				

*Copyright © 1984 by David D. Burns, M.D., from *The Feeling Good Handbook*, copyright © 1989

	0–NOT AT ALL	1–SOMEWHAT	2–MODERATELY	3–A LOT
11. Appetite changes: Have you lost your appetite? Or do you overeat or binge compulsively?				
12. Sleep changes: Do you suffer from insomnia and find it hard to get a good night's sleep? Or are you excessively tired and sleeping too much?				
13. Loss of libido: Have you lost your interest in sex?				
14. Hypochondriasis: Do you worry a great deal about your health?				
15. Suicidal impulses†: Do you have thoughts that life is not worth living or think that you might be better off dead?				

Add up your total score for the 15 symptoms and record it here: _____

Date: _____

†Anyone with suicidal urges should seek immediate consultation with a qualified psychiatrist or psychologist.

After you have completed the test, add up your total score. It will be somewhere between 0 (if you answered "not at all" for each of the 15 categories) and 45 (if you answered "a lot" for each one). Use this key to interpret your score.

Total score	Degree of depression
0–4	Minimal or no depression
5–10	Borderline depression
11–20	Mild depression
21–30	Moderate depression
31–45	Severe depression

There is an extra copy of the Burns Depression Checklist on pages 46 and 47, along with an answer sheet. You can use the answer sheet to record your answers each week when you take the BDC. At the bottom, add up your scores and enter the date. Ultimately, I would like your score on the BDC and the BAI to be under 5, but any reduction will be a positive sign of progress.

Many people are unclear about the difference between anxiety and depression, since the two feelings often go hand in hand. If your score is elevated on the anxiety test, it will probably also be elevated on the depression test, and vice versa. *Depression* is the feeling of loss. You feel defeated and discouraged because of something bad that's already happened. Maybe you feel you failed at work or were rejected by someone you loved. *Anxiety* is the feeling of fear. It has more to do with the future—you believe that some disaster is ready to strike at any moment. Anxiety is like hanging from the edge of a cliff by the tips of your fingers. Depression feels more like you've already fallen and you're lying at the bottom of the ravine with your arms and legs broken beyond repair.

Suppose you have an elevated score on one or both of these mood tests. Does this mean you're sick or neurotic? Absolutely not. Feelings of anxiety and depression are nearly universal. Almost everyone feels this way from time to time. While one of my main goals is to show you how to deal with these feelings more effectively, I also want to encourage you to *accept* your negative feelings. You will need to understand this paradox to overcome your anxiety. When you fight your negative feelings and refuse to accept them, they become more and more intense. In contrast, when you *accept* your feelings, they become far easier to deal with. You will learn more about this "acceptance paradox" as you read this book.

Some of these questions about anxiety and depression may have crossed your mind:

How accurate and reliable are the mood tests? Do people try to make themselves look better or worse than they really feel? Not in my experience. Even a small change of a few points from week to week is an indication that a person is feeling better or worse. Most people answer honestly, and the tests continue to be remarkably accurate over time. You can take them as frequently as you want.

You can monitor the effectiveness of your progress as you read this book if you take the depression and anxiety tests in this chapter once a week. If you are in therapy, show the results to your therapist. If the scores go down, you are improving. If the scores go up or stay the same, you haven't started to move forward yet. This is crucial information—I cannot imagine how therapy could be successful without this kind of "quality control." I ask my patients to show me their scores at the start of every session so I know how they're doing.

What is the difference between depression and healthy sadness? When a friend dies or you fail to achieve an important goal, it's normal to feel sad. These feelings are a part of life. Your grief shows that you're human. Depression is different from healthy sadness in many ways:

- Depression involves a loss of self-esteem.
- Depression goes on and on.
- People who are depressed may not function productively.
- Depression is not realistic, and always results from distorted thoughts.
- Depression is an illness.
- Depression feels hopeless, even though the prognosis is excellent.

When should a person seek professional help? You should seek professional help if you have been unsuccessful in your own efforts to overcome a mood problem and you feel stuck. We all get upset when something disappointing happens, but we generally bounce back and feel good again in a few days. For some people this natural recovery can be very delayed, and the feelings of depression and anxiety may persist for weeks, months, years, or even decades. A good psychiatrist or psychologist can often speed up the process of healing.

What can I do to help a loved one who feels depressed? The techniques in this book are intended to help you with your own emotional problems. If you are not a therapist, do not attempt to apply these methods to someone else who is upset. Your efforts will probably backfire.

The best thing you can do to help someone who feels anxious or depressed is to show that you care. Try to understand them. Learn to listen so you can understand their problems and their feelings, using the three listening skills described in Chapter 19.

What can I do if a friend or family member needs psychiatric treatment? If someone is severely disturbed, you can recommend they go for therapy. If they resist, it's not your job to sell them on the idea or to force them to go. If you show concern and understanding, they may change their mind. Ultimately, people have the right to decide whether or not to seek treatment for themselves.

One exception would be if your child is depressed. As a parent, you have the right to bring them to a therapist. However, keep in mind that part of the problem may be a conflict between you and your spouse. Frequently when the parents are treated, the child gets better.

If someone is actively suicidal and threatening to kill themselves, you can bring them to a hospital or to a community mental health facility for evaluation. If that is impossible, you can call the police and ask for guidance.

How can I know if someone is suicidal? The answer to this question is simple: you ask them. Some readers may wonder, "But won't I push them over the brink if I ask?" No. The biggest mistake is *not* to ask. If a friend or loved one appears despondent or discouraged, ask these questions—in the same order—to find out if they are seriously considering suicide:

- **"Have you been feeling sad or unhappy?"** A "yes" will confirm that he or she has been feeling some depression.
- **"Do you ever feel hopeless? Does it seem as if things can never get better?"** Over half the people with depression feel hopeless. Feelings of hopelessness are often associated with suicidal thoughts.
- **"Do you have thoughts of death? Do you ever think you'd be better off dead?"** A "yes" indicates suicidal wishes but not necessarily suicidal plans. Many depressed people say they think they'd be better off dead and wish they'd die in their sleep or get killed in an accident. However, most of them say they have no intention of actually killing themselves.
- **"Do you ever have any actual suicidal impulses? Do you have any urge to kill yourself?"** A "yes" indicates an active desire to die. This is a more serious situation.
- **"Do you feel you can resist these impulses, or do they sometimes tempt you?"** If the person feels tempted, the situation is much more dangerous.
- **"Do you have any actual plans to kill yourself?"** If the answer is "yes," ask about their specific plans. What method have they chosen? Hanging? Jumping? Pills? A gun? Have they actually obtained the rope? What building do they plan to jump from? Although these questions may sound grotesque, they may save a life. The danger is greatest when the plans are clear and specific, when they have made actual preparations, and when the method they have chosen is clearly lethal.

- **"When do you plan to kill yourself?"** If the suicide attempt is a long way off—say, in five years—the danger is clearly not imminent and you have plenty of time to get the person into treatment. If they say they plan to kill themselves soon, the danger is grave and you must take immediate action.
- **"Is there anything that would hold you back, such as your family or your religious convictions?"** If they say that people would be better off without them and if they have no deterrents, suicide is much more likely.
- **"Have you ever made a suicide attempt in the past?"** Previous suicide attempts indicate that future attempts are more likely. Even if a previous attempt did not seem serious, the next attempt may be fatal. All suicide attempts should be taken seriously. If someone takes fifteen aspirin tablets in front of his or her spouse, they clearly don't have a strong desire to die at that moment. If someone scratches their wrists superficially and then calls the local hospital, they have mixed feelings about dying. These unsuccessful suicide attempts that are not immediately dangerous are sometimes viewed as "gestures" or manipulative attempts to get attention. This is often true, since suicidal individuals often feel unloved and angry. They frequently have a subconscious desire to get attention or to get back at lovers, family, and friends for not loving them enough. However, these suicidal "gestures" can be more dangerous than they seem, since many of these people ultimately do kill themselves.
- **"Would you be willing to talk to someone or seek help if you felt desperate? Whom would you talk to?"** If the person who feels suicidal is cooperative and has a clear plan to reach out for help, the danger is less than if they are stubborn, secretive, hostile, and unwilling to ask for help.

The answers to these questions will give you an idea of how severe the problem is. In my experience, people who feel suicidal are usually quite honest. If you discover that a friend or a loved one is actively suicidal, then they will need immediate emergency intervention. You may have to bring them to the emergency room of a local hospital or to a community mental health facility. If they refuse, you can call the police and ask for help. They can direct you to an emergency mental health facility where you can sign a warrant instructing the police to bring the person to a hospital to be evaluated. If the person continues to threaten suicide, he or she may be committed involuntarily for a three-day evaluation in most states.

This action will frequently anger the person who feels suicidal, but you could save a life! Bringing the anger to the surface may be intensely uncomfortable, but it's not nearly so horrible as the anguish and tragedy of a needless death. In addition, there is some evidence that people who express their anger may be less likely to make a sudden suicide attempt than people who keep their feelings bottled up.

My doctor did a blood test and said I had a chemical depression. Does this mean I need to be treated with drugs? Although people who are depressed often have abnormalities in their levels of a number of hormones, this does not necessarily mean that the depression is caused by a chemical imbalance, or that only medications should be used in treatment. (See Chapter 23 to learn more about the medications that can be used to treat anxiety and depression.)

I believe that good psychotherapy enhances the treatment of mood problems, and that people should never be treated with drugs alone. Ultimately the decision of whether or not to use medications is an individual one that needs to be discussed frankly with your therapist or physician.

THE BURNS ANXIETY INVENTORY*

Instructions: The following is a list of symptoms that people sometimes have. Put a check (√) in the space to the right that best describes how much that symptom or problem has bothered you during the past week. If you would like a weekly record of your progress, record your answers on the separate "Answer Sheet" instead of filling in the spaces on the right.

Symptom List	0–NOT AT ALL	1–SOMEWHAT	2–MODERATELY	3–A LOT
CATEGORY I: ANXIOUS FEELINGS				
1. Anxiety, nervousness, worry, or fear				
2. Feeling that things around you are strange, unreal, or foggy				
3. Feeling detached from all or part of your body				
4. Sudden unexpected panic spells				
5. Apprehension or a sense of impending doom				
6. Feeling tense, stressed, "uptight," or on edge				
CATEGORY II: ANXIOUS THOUGHTS				
7. Difficulty concentrating				
8. Racing thoughts or having your mind jump from one thing to the next				
9. Frightening fantasies or daydreams				
10. Feeling that you're on the verge of losing control				
11. Fears of cracking up or going crazy				
12. Fears of fainting or passing out				
13. Fears of physical illnesses or heart attacks or dying				
14. Concerns about looking foolish or inadequate in front of others				
15. Fears of being alone, isolated, or abandoned				

*Copyright © 1984 by David D. Burns, M.D., from *The Feeling Good Handbook*, copyright © 1989

	0—NOT AT ALL	1—SOMEWHAT	2—MODERATELY	3—A LOT
16. Fears of criticism or disapproval				
17. Fears that something terrible is about to happen				

CATEGORY III: PHYSICAL SYMPTOMS

18. Skipping or racing or pounding of the heart (sometimes called "palpitations")				
19. Pain, pressure, or tightness in the chest				
20. Tingling or numbness in the toes or fingers				
21. Butterflies or discomfort in the stomach				
22. Constipation or diarrhea				
23. Restlessness or jumpiness				
24. Tight, tense muscles				
25. Sweating not brought on by heat				
26. A lump in the throat				
27. Trembling or shaking				
28. Rubbery or "jelly" legs				
29. Feeling dizzy, lightheaded, or off balance				
30. Choking or smothering sensations or difficulty breathing				
31. Headaches or pains in the neck or back				
32. Hot flashes or cold chills				
33. Feeling tired, weak, or easily exhausted				

Add up your total score for the 33 symptoms and record it here: _____

Date: _____

THE BURNS ANXIETY INVENTORY*
Answer Sheet

Instructions: Put a 0, 1, 2, or 3 in the space to the right after each of the 33 symptoms from the "Symptom List," depending on how much it has bothered you in the past week: 0 = Not at all; 1 = Somewhat; 2 = Moderately; 3 = A lot. Then add up your total score for all 33 symptoms at the bottom.

1.	1.	1.	1.	1.	1.	1.
2.	2.	2.	2.	2.	2.	2.
3.	3.	3.	3.	3.	3.	3.
4.	4.	4.	4.	4.	4.	4.
5.	5.	5.	5.	5.	5.	5.
6.	6.	6.	6.	6.	6.	6.
7.	7.	7.	7.	7.	7.	7.
8.	8.	8.	8.	8.	8.	8.
9.	9.	9.	9.	9.	9.	9.
10.	10.	10.	10.	10.	10.	10.
11.	11.	11.	11.	11.	11.	11.
12.	12.	12.	12.	12.	12.	12.
13.	13.	13.	13.	13.	13.	13.
14.	14.	14.	14.	14.	14.	14.
15.	15.	15.	15.	15.	15.	15.
16.	16.	16.	16.	16.	16.	16.
17.	17.	17.	17.	17.	17.	17.
18.	18.	18.	18.	18.	18.	18.
19.	19.	19.	19.	19.	19.	19.
20.	20.	20.	20.	20.	20.	20.
21.	21.	21.	21.	21.	21.	21.
22.	22.	22.	22.	22.	22.	22.
23.	23.	23.	23.	23.	23.	23.
24.	24.	24.	24.	24.	24.	24.
25.	25.	25.	25.	25.	25.	25.
26.	26.	26.	26.	26.	26.	26.
27.	27.	27.	27.	27.	27.	27.
28.	28.	28.	28.	28.	28.	28.
29.	29.	29.	29.	29.	29.	29.
30.	30.	30.	30.	30.	30.	30.
31.	31.	31.	31.	31.	31.	31.
32.	32.	32.	32.	32.	32.	32.
33.	33.	33.	33.	33.	33.	33.
TOTAL SCORE						
TODAY'S DATE						

*Copyright © 1989 by David D. Burns, M.D., from *The Feeling Good Handbook*

THE BURNS DEPRESSION CHECKLIST*

Place a check (√) in the box to the right of each of the 15 symptom clusters to indicate how much this type of feeling has been bothering you in the past several days. Make sure you answer all the questions. If you feel unsure about any, put down your best guess. If you would like a weekly record of your progress, record your answers on the separate "Answer Sheet" instead of filling in the spaces on the right.

	0—NOT AT ALL	1—SOMEWHAT	2—MODERATELY	3—A LOT
1. **Sadness:** Have you been feeling sad or down in the dumps?				
2. **Discouragement:** Does the future look hopeless?				
3. **Low self-esteem:** Do you feel worthless or think of yourself as a failure?				
4. **Inferiority:** Do you feel inadequate or inferior to others?				
5. **Guilt:** Do you get self-critical and blame yourself for everything?				
6. **Indecisiveness:** Do you have trouble making up your mind about things?				
7. **Irritability and frustration:** Have you been feeling resentful and angry a good deal of the time?				
8. **Loss of interest in life:** Have you lost interest in your career, your hobbies, your family, or your friends?				
9. **Loss of motivation:** Do you feel overwhelmed and have to push yourself hard to do things?				
10. **Poor self-image:** Do you think you're looking old or unattractive?				

	0–NOT AT ALL	1–SOMEWHAT	2–MODERATELY	3–A LOT
11. **Appetite changes:** Have you lost your appetite? Or do you overeat or binge compulsively?				
12. **Sleep changes:** Do you suffer from insomnia and find it hard to get a good night's sleep? Or are you excessively tired and sleeping too much?				
13. **Loss of libido:** Have you lost your interest in sex?				
14. **Hypochondriasis:** Do you worry a great deal about your health?				
15. **Suicidal impulses†:** Do you have thoughts that life is not worth living or think that you might be better off dead?				

Add up your total score for the 33 symptoms and record it here: _____

Date: _____

†Anyone with suicidal urges should seek immediate consultation with a qualified psychiatrist or psychologist.

THE BURNS DEPRESSION CHECKLIST*
Answer Sheet

Instructions: Put a 0, 1, 2, or 3 in the space to the right of each of the 15 symptoms to indicate how much it has bothered you in the past week: 0 = Not at all; 1 = Somewhat; 2 = Moderately; 3 = A lot. Then add up your score for all 15 symptoms at the bottom.

	1.	1.	1.	1.	1.	1.	1.
	2.	2.	2.	2.	2.	2.	2.
	3.	3.	3.	3.	3.	3.	3.
	4.	4.	4.	4.	4.	4.	4.
	5.	5.	5.	5.	5.	5.	5.
	6.	6.	6.	6.	6.	6.	6.
	7.	7.	7.	7.	7.	7.	7.
	8.	8.	8.	8.	8.	8.	8.
	9.	9.	9.	9.	9.	9.	9.
	10.	10.	10.	10.	10.	10.	10.
	11.	11.	11.	11.	11.	11.	11.
	12.	12.	12.	12.	12.	12.	12.
	13.	13.	13.	13.	13.	13.	13.
	14.	14.	14.	14.	14.	14.	14.
	15.	15.	15.	15.	15.	15.	15.
TOTAL SCORE							
TODAY'S DATE							

3

•

How to Diagnose
*Your Moods**

In the last chapter you learned whether you are feeling depressed or anxious. If you have ever been to a psychiatrist or psychologist, your therapist may have used terms like "manic-depressive illness" or "panic disorder," which could frighten or confuse you. You may also have wondered whether words like "neurosis," "psychosis," "mental illness," or "nervous breakdown" applied to you. This chapter will demystify psychiatric diagnoses. Once you understand how professionals classify emotional problems, you will no longer feel intimidated by these terms.

In 1980 the new *Diagnostic and Statistical Manual of Mental Disorders* was published by the American Psychiatric Association. Based on years of research and clinical experience, this manual has had a remarkable impact on mental health professionals, providing them with a common language for talking about disorders such as depression and anxiety. In 1983 work was begun to revise and improve this manual, culminating in the publication in 1987 of a new manual, the *Revised Diagnostic and Statistical Manual*.

*The descriptions of the disorders in this chapter are based on the *Diagnostic and Statistical Manual of Mental Disorders* (Third Edition, Revised), published by the American Psychiatric Association, Washington, D.C., 1987.

The diagnostic categories you will read about in this chapter, such as "major depressive disorder" or "social phobia," are based on this new diagnostic system. As you will see, these terms do not refer to mysterious entities like "neuroses" but simply describe clusters of familiar symptoms such as sadness or nervousness.

The difference between your score on a mood test, such as the Burns Anxiety Inventory (BAI) or the Burns Depression Checklist (BDC), and the diagnostic categories described in this chapter is similar to the difference between a photograph and a movie. The two mood tests show how bad you are feeling at any given moment. If those same symptoms persist over a period of time or in certain situations, then they are given a diagnostic label. For example, if you get nervous around other people at social gatherings, your score on the anxiety test (BAI) would be very elevated in those situations. The diagnostic name for this would be a "social phobia."

As you read about the symptoms for each diagnostic category, you will probably know whether or not you have experienced those symptoms. Keep in mind that the occasional experience of one or two of the symptoms is quite normal. To qualify for a diagnosis, nearly all the symptoms for that disorder must persist over a period of time. Check "yes" or "no" for that disorder in the table on page 51. When you finish the chapter, you will have an overview of where you fit into the diagnostic system.

As you read this chapter, remember that self-diagnosis with the help of a book like this can never substitute for a professional evaluation by a qualified psychiatrist or psychologist. In my professional practice, all new patients undergo a formal diagnostic procedure much more detailed than this chapter, along with psychological testing. My goal is not to turn you into your own doctor, but to make you more familiar with the diagnostic process.

Anxiety and Panic

Clinicians diagnose several types of anxiety. If your score on the Burns Anxiety Inventory is elevated, see if any of the following fits your symptoms. These categories are not mutually exclusive; there can be considerable overlap between them.

DIAGNOSTIC SUMMARY		
Anxiety and Panic		
Yes	**No**	
____	____	Generalized anxiety disorder
____	____	Social phobia
____	____	Simple phobia
____	____	Panic disorder
____	____	Agoraphobia
____	____	Obsessive-compulsive disorder
____	____	Hypochondriasis

Depression and Mania		
Yes	**No**	
____	____	Major depressive episode
____	____	Dysthymic disorder
____	____	Bipolar disorder (manic-depressive illness)
____	____	Cyclothymic disorder

GENERALIZED ANXIETY DISORDER

People with phobias feel frightened in specific situations. For example, if you have a snake or a spider phobia, you'll feel anxious only when you're around those particular creatures. If you feel anxious and tense all day long, regardless of where you are or what you're doing, and if these symptoms persist more or less continuously for six months or longer, the problem is called generalized anxiety. This problem often first occurs between ages 20 and 40 and is equally common among men and women.

Some people with generalized anxiety harbor the superstitious belief that anxiety and worry will help them. You may think that if you worry enough about a test or paper you're writing, you'll do a better job on it. This attitude is usually not realistic. It may be true that a little anxiety can motivate you to hustle and try your hardest, but a lot of anxiety will simply get in the way and make the job more difficult. In fact, I find that I do my best when I'm not at all anxious.

Chronic worriers frequently believe that anxiety will protect their family and friends from danger. A woman named Anne got agitated whenever her children were five minutes late. She worried that something terrible had happened to them. When her daughter visited a friend in Florida, Anne constantly obsessed about traffic accidents and hurricanes.

Anne was reluctant to give up this habit of worrying because she was afraid that something terrible would happen to her kids if she stopped. There may be another deeper reason why Anne worries constantly about her kids. She may be unhappy about some problem in her life she's afraid to face, such as a marital conflict, or ambivalence about completing college and pursuing a career. She manages to avoid dealing with these frightening issues when she uses up all her energy worrying about her family.

If you have had symptoms of chronic worry and nervousness for at least six months, check "yes" in the Diagnostic Summary table now.

SOCIAL PHOBIA

A social phobia is the fear of other people. Social phobias are tremendously common and afflict both sexes, but they are more widespread among men. People with social phobias feel shy and are afraid of looking foolish in front of others. They don't want to be in any situation where people will notice how anxious they are. You may have a social phobia if you are afraid of public speaking, being with groups of people at meetings or social gatherings, introducing yourself to others, going out on dates, eating in front of others, saying foolish things at parties, or urinating in a public restroom.

A 24-year-old woman with a social phobia was talking to a handsome man at an office party. She grew more and more self-conscious because of her thought, "What if he notices how ill-at-ease I am?" This thought made her unbearably uncomfortable and tense. She got so flustered that she had to excuse herself and go home. Then she felt humiliated and began to berate herself.

SIMPLE PHOBIA

A simple phobia is the fear of something specific like heights, a certain animal, flying in an airplane, choking, thunder, driving, darkness, closed spaces, being buried alive, elevators, blood, dirt or germs, or bridges. Many phobias have Greek names. For example, the fear of heights is called acrophobia; the fear of closed spaces is called claustrophobia; and the fear of being buried alive is called laphephobia.

These terms create the impression that phobias are dreadful and dangerous and that scientists understand a great deal about them. Nothing could be further from the truth. Phobias are uncomfortable, but they are not symptoms of severe mental illness or a weak character. They can usually be treated effectively and quickly, but there is surprisingly little scientific knowledge about what causes them.

Simple phobias are extremely common. Between 10 and 20 percent of the population will develop phobias during their lives. Phobias can occur at any age but often first appear in childhood. They are about twice as common among women as among men.

PANIC DISORDER

A panic attack is a burst of intense, overwhelming anxiety that generally lasts for a brief period—sometimes for as little as a few minutes and rarely for more than several hours. The attacks seem to come out of the blue for no apparent reason. During a panic attack you will notice at least four uncomfortable sensations like dizziness, a pounding of your heart, a lump in your throat, racing thoughts, lightheadedness, trembling or shaking, tightness in your chest, palpitations, diarrhea or upset stomach, rapid breathing, a choking or smothering sensation, shortness of breath, numbness or tingling fingers, hot flashes, chills or sweating. You may feel strange and think that you are unreal or the world may seem unreal.

These symptoms develop suddenly and increase dramatically in intensity within ten minutes. At the height of the panic attack, you may be terrified by one or more of these fears:

What if I lose control?

What if I go crazy?

What if I have a heart attack?

What if I faint?

What if I die?

After a short time the episode wears off. You were hanging on for dear life and you think it's a miracle that you didn't crack up entirely. You don't want anyone to know what happened to you because you feel ashamed, abnormal, and weird. You live in dread of another attack. Your life becomes a constant vigil as you look for some sign that this terrible experience is about to hit again. This leads to the fear of fear itself.

If you've had at least four panic attacks in a four-week period, it's called panic disorder, but this definition is somewhat arbitrary. If you've had only one panic attack but you felt upset about it for a month, you would also qualify for this diagnosis.

Some people who have panic attacks worry that they are "going crazy"—becoming schizophrenic. But the symptoms of schizophrenia are quite different from the symptoms of anxiety. People with schizophrenia may hear nonexistent voices; they may believe that electrical forces or secret radio waves are controlling them; they may think that their thoughts are being broadcast over the television networks and radio stations; or they may feel that God Himself is sending them messages. People with schizophrenia rarely worry about going crazy. They're convinced that they're normal and they believe their delusions are completely real. If you're terribly worried about cracking up, you're not! Anxiety, not insanity, is your problem. Although panic attacks *feel* terrifying, they're quite harmless and very treatable.

AGORAPHOBIA

Agoraphobia is the fear of being in open spaces alone or traveling away from home. A 47-year-old married agoraphobic woman had an overwhelming dread of leaving her house alone. When she drove her car, she would worry that the car might break down and she'd get mugged. This fantasy was so frightening that she refused to drive or leave the house unless her husband came along. She became housebound and insisted on being with him any time she was away from home.

People with agoraphobia are afraid of being in situations where help might not be available in the event they develop frightening or embarrassing symptoms, such as dizziness or fainting, losing bladder or bowel control, having a heart attack, smothering, or cracking up. As a result of these fears, agoraphobics restrict their travel and may need a trusted companion when they travel away from home. Feared situations include being in a crowd, standing in line at the grocery store, being on a bridge, or traveling in a bus, train, or car.

Agoraphobia is one of the most common phobias, affecting an estimated 1 million Americans, and is far more common among women. The problem usually develops during adolescence or early adult life. Because agoraphobics are afraid of leaving home, many of them often have difficulty going to a clinic for therapy. As a result, they often do not receive the treatment they so desperately need to overcome this affliction.

OBSESSIVE-COMPULSIVE DISORDER

Obsessions are persistent, intrusive, nonsensical thoughts that you can't shake out of your head. For example, you may worry that the dirt on your hands will contaminate your children and give them leukemia, even though you know rationally that this is not realistic. A compulsion is a ritualistic act that you feel compelled to repeat over and over in order to ward off the danger. Thus, the obsession is the repetitious, frightening *thought* and the compulsion is the repetitious *action* that results from this thought.

According to the *Diagnostic and Statistical Manual*, the most common kinds of obsessions concern violence, contamination, or doubt. An example of a violence obsession would be a patient of mine who was troubled by the belief that he would suddenly throw his child out of the window or jump out in front of a car in heavy traffic. He had no real intention of doing these things, but was terrified by the irrational fear that he would suddenly lose control and act impulsively. An example of obsessive doubt would be a housewife who worried that the house would burn down because she forgot to turn off the stove at night, so she would get up to check the stove repeatedly. The most common compulsions include hand washing, cleaning things, counting, checking things, or touching things. The compulsive act is logically connected to the obsessive thought. For example, a physician obsessed while driving that he might have inadvertently killed a pedestrian and then forgotten about it. He felt the urge to stop his car and look around for a body to make sure that he hadn't hit anyone. Even though he realized intellectually that it was exceedingly unlikely that he had hit anyone, his fears were so emotionally charged that he couldn't resist the urge to stop and look around for a body.

HYPOCHONDRIASIS

People with this disorder are preoccupied with the idea that they are suffering from a serious illness such as cancer or heart disease. They usually go from doctor to doctor, getting repeated examinations and reassurances that they are in perfect health. Hypochondriasis can occur at any age but often begins when people are in their twenties, and is equally common among men and women. It is one of the most common problems seen by internists and physicians in general practice. Hypochondriacs usually resist the idea that stress or psychological problems may create their symptoms. Because they insist on finding a medical explanation, they can be a great source of frustration to physicians.

Hypochondriasis, like all the other forms of anxiety described in this chapter, is nearly always caused by other problems that the individual is ignoring. I recently treated a businessman who worried constantly about his health. He felt that every little bump, ache, or pain was a sign of some dreadful disease. He constantly ran from doctor to doctor for examinations, which invariably turned out to be normal. His anxiety was not caused by any real illness, and his frequent trips to doctors were simply a way of reacting to the conflicts in his life.

His wife, who was much younger, had recently received her MBA degree and had started her own business. She was working hard at her new career. Although he "rationally" saw that this was a wonderful idea, inside he felt insecure and resentful. They were already financially comfortable, and he wanted to retire and spend more time with her so they could enjoy the fruits of his labor. But she was so busy that he felt lonely and abandoned. He had trouble admitting that he felt this way because he thought he should be "strong." He was ashamed of his negative feelings and tried to ignore them. When he brought in his wife for some couples therapy and they learned to share their feelings more openly, his aches and pains went away as mysteriously as they had come.

Depression and Mania

Clinicians diagnose several types of depression. If your score on the Burns Depression Checklist (page 36) is elevated, see if any of the following fits your symptoms.

MAJOR DEPRESSIVE EPISODE

In a major depressive episode, a person feels sad or experiences a loss of interest in pleasurable activities for at least a two- to four-week period. In addition, there are several of the following symptoms: loss of appetite (or eating too much), trouble sleeping at night (or sleeping too much), feelings of agitation and extreme restlessness (or feeling dull, fatigued, and slowed down), feelings of worthlessness or guilt, difficulties concentrating, and thoughts of death. Many people with these symptoms do not realize they are depressed. They may feel convinced they are inferior and that life is not worth living.

Major depressive episodes occur twice as often in women as in men, but the reason for this is not known. Between 10 and 25 percent of all adult women have had at least one major depressive episode. The estimates for men are between 5 and 12 percent. These figures indicate that at least 15 million Americans have suffered from this affliction. Of course, the number who have experienced milder mood swings is substantially higher. Small wonder that depression is often referred to as the common cold of psychiatric disorders.

DYSTHYMIC DISORDER

This is an extremely common milder form of depression which lasts for two years or more. People with this problem tend to be chronically unhappy for much of their lives, but their depression is not severe enough to qualify as a major depressive episode. Dysthymic disorder usually begins somewhere between childhood and young adult life and is more common among women. It has sometimes been called depressive personality, or depressive neurosis, because chronic unhappiness and pessimism seem to be a part of the individual's personality and view of life.

BIPOLAR DISORDER

Recurrent depressions are sometimes called "unipolar depressions," since they have only one pole—the depressed side. In contrast, "bipolar depressions" have two poles—highs and lows. A person may go down into a deep depression, and then at other times may suddenly develop an abnormal and potentially dangerous mood elevation. The bipolar disorder has also been called manic-depressive illness, because it swings from mania to depression and back again.

There are two kinds of abnormal mood elevations, which differ in severity. Severe mood elevations are called manic episodes or mania. They can be extremely serious and often require hospitalization. Milder mood elevations are called hypomanic episodes, or hypomania.

Manic episodes usually develop rather unexpectedly in individuals who were quite normal before the episode began. The symptoms are just the opposite of the symptoms of depression. Instead of feeling sad, they feel joyous. Instead of suffering from a loss of self-esteem, they enjoy unlimited self-esteem and believe they can achieve anything. They suddenly feel brilliant, alert, creative, and euphoric, a fountain of energy and ideas. They feel *so good* that they cannot accept the idea that there may be something wrong or that they need treatment.

Manic patients often become quite delusional, but they have absolutely no insight about this. They behave in ways that are dangerous and foolish without any awareness of the consequences of their behavior. One of my manic patients, a young woman named Sarah, was walking past a government building in New York where she saw people picketing and television crews filming them. Apparently there was a complex labor disagreement between the municipal government and the employees' union. She stopped to talk to people in the crowd and developed a sudden "insight." She felt convinced she could negotiate a quick solution to the problem and demanded that the television cameramen interview her for the evening news. She also demanded an interview with Mayor Koch and said that she wanted to deliver a major address to the United Nations.

Another characteristic of mania is an extraordinary degree of physical and psychological energy. Manic patients talk constantly and excitedly, jumping from subject to subject. They may pace about or exercise vigorously for prolonged periods of time.

Some manic patients become extremely irritable if crossed or thwarted, and may be arrested or brought to emergency rooms after altercations with the police.

Although the symptoms of mania can be extremely dramatic, this disorder is not as rare as you might think. Many famous politicians and entertainers have suffered from manic-depressive illness. Current estimates indicate that approximately 0.5 to 1 percent of the adult population suffers from manic-depression. That means that between 1 and 2 million Americans have had or will have this affliction. Unlike unipolar depression, which is more common in women, bipolar disorder is equally common among men and women.

There is strong evidence that bipolar illness is inherited and caused by some, as yet unknown, chemical imbalance in the brain. Treatment with appropriate medications, such as lithium, can be extremely helpful to individuals with this affliction. (See Chapter 23 for a description of medications that can be used to treat depression, mania, and anxiety.) Psychotherapy is also crucial in the treatment of this illness. Between the episodes of mania, bipolar patients often suffer from low self-esteem and experience significant difficulties with their careers and personal relationships. A good therapeutic relationship can help to correct these problems and significantly improve the prognosis for this puzzling disorder.

CYCLOTHYMIC DISORDER

You may have known someone whose personality seems to run hot and cold. At times they are turned on by life—perhaps excessively so—and at times they are overly negative, pessimistic, and discouraged. They never seem to find the middle ground. If these oscillations between mild depression and mild elation have persisted for at least two years, the disorder is called cyclothymic disorder. This simply represents a combination of dysthymic disorder and hypomania. It isn't known whether cyclothymic disorder is a separate illness or a milder version of manic-depressive illness.

Suppose you feel that you fit into one or more of these diagnostic categories. What should you do? First, read the appropriate sections in this book. For example, if you have a social phobia, Chapter 14 should be of particular interest to you. If you suffer from public speaking anxiety, Chapter 15 may help.

When is professional therapy indicated? Any time a mood problem is chronic or severe or interferes with your normal functioning, you should seek a consultation with a qualified psychiatrist or psychologist. Many people do not have insight into the causes of their mood problems. If you suffer from anxiety or panic attacks, there's a good chance that you feel angry because of someone or something in your life that is bugging you. However, you may not be aware of this because you are avoiding the problem and pushing it out of your mind. It can sometimes be much easier to unearth and confront these difficulties with the help of a skillful and caring therapist.

If you qualify for one or more of the diagnoses in this chapter, it does not make you a weirdo or a neurotic, but a human being who's hurting. At my clinic we see large numbers of people with these problems. With a little persistence, compassion, and teamwork, these difficulties can be dealt with effectively, and the prognosis to *feel good* again is excellent!

Should *You Change the Way You Feel?*

Cognitive therapy is based on the idea that distorted thoughts, and not realistic ones, lead to unhealthy negative emotions like depression and anxiety. When you learn to think about your problems in a more positive and realistic way, you can change the way you feel. The effects are often dramatic.

This approach is exciting but quite controversial. Are your negative thoughts and feelings *always* unrealistic? Are you justified in changing the way you feel? In an article in the *New York Times* on June 17, 1981, entitled, "In Praise of Depression," David Ives wrote:

> Considering the state of the world, why does science still consider depression an aberration? . . . History, it would seem, is telling us that there is something compelling about the dark side of things. . . . For some of us, optimism is seen for what it is: a form of escapism. . . . Optimism is, in fact, a form of desperation that science would do well to investigate. . . . Depression, let it be said, is nothing more than realism.

There is clearly some truth in this. Life has many frustrations and disappointments. You make a trip to buy an appliance and when you get home and take it out of its box you discover that it doesn't work.

A friend is forty-five minutes late meeting you for lunch after promising to be on time. Your boss criticizes your work in front of other people and then pressures you to meet an impossible deadline. In addition to these day-by-day irritants, we are all confronted by real tragedies—the sudden death of a friend or family member, divorce or rejection by someone we love, or the loss of a job. You may work hard to make your dream come true and then your plans come crashing down. Isn't it appropriate to feel upset? Aren't these feelings inevitable?

I believe that the argument that stress and depression are always realistic is just as absurd as the suggestion that people should try to be happy and successful all the time. Sometimes negative feelings are healthy, and sometimes they are unhealthy. A young man hospitalized for depression told me how he once poured boiling coffee on his leg in an attempt to distract himself from his feelings of worthlessness and emptiness. The despair he felt was not the same as healthy sadness, and his actions were hardly an appropriate response to the problems in his life! By the same token, genuine remorse is not the same as neurotic guilt, realistic fear is not the same as an anxiety attack, and healthy anger is not the same as hostility and aggression.

If you feel that someone you care about is treating you badly, it's natural to feel hurt. You may feel angry and put down. Sharing these feelings openly can often help you understand each other and resolve the problem. When two people respect each other, the ability to be vulnerable and to reveal hurt feelings can create a powerful emotional connection that is the source of real intimacy and friendship.

Anger and irritability can also be unhealthy and destructive. I was recently working in my living room, attempting to write. I didn't feel very creative because it was the end of a long stressful day. My son, who was almost five, walked up to me and innocently asked if I could help him get an apple out of the refrigerator. Before I had even comprehended his question I snapped angrily, "Shut up! Can't you see that I'm busy? Go downstairs and stop bothering me!" He was stunned. Shock and grief swept across his face. In slow motion he turned and walked dutifully downstairs, weeping.

I suddenly realized the impact of what I'd said—crushing, totally without justification. By shouting at my son I had hurt someone I loved without any provocation—clearly a violation of my own moral code. I felt intense remorse. I rushed over to him, picked him up in my arms, and said, "Erik, please forgive me. What I did was wrong.

You didn't do anything wrong. Sometimes we do bad things without thinking when we're in a bad mood. I love you so much and I want you to forgive me." He gave me a wonderful hug and we got his apple and felt like pals again. It was a painful but tender moment that brought us closer together and made our love more vital.

From a practical point of view, how can you know when you should *accept* your feelings, when you should *express* your feelings, and when you should *change* them? The following questions can help you decide:

- How long have I been feeling this way?
- Am I doing something constructive about the problem, or am I simply brooding and avoiding it?
- Are my thoughts and feelings realistic?
- Will it be helpful or hurtful if I express my feelings?
- Am I making myself unhappy about a situation that's beyond my control?
- Am I avoiding a problem and denying that I'm really upset about it?
- Are my expectations for the world realistic?
- Are my expectations for myself realistic?
- Am I feeling hopeless?
- Am I experiencing a loss of self-esteem?

How long have I been feeling this way? Sometimes we hang on to feelings far beyond the time when they could serve any useful purpose. If you are still feeling guilty or angry about something that happened in the past, ask yourself, "Just how much longer do I intend to make myself miserable about this? What is the point of feeling so bad for so long?" A woman named Elaine obsessed constantly about a sexual affair she had nearly two decades earlier. All day long she berated herself. Even a convicted felon is usually set free long before that much time has expired!

Am I doing something constructive about the problem, or am I simply brooding and avoiding it? Sometimes a negative feeling becomes a way of life. You may feel sorry for yourself instead of doing something about the problem that's bothering you. You may be annoyed with someone and go around feeling sour and avoiding them so you won't have to tell them how you honestly feel.

It's natural to feel disappointed when you get rejected or when you fail to achieve a goal and things don't go as well as you hoped. It's important to grieve over the loss of a loved one and to surrender to the tears, to the feelings of loss, and to remember how much you cared about the one who died. You may feel remorse when you think of times you may have let that person down. I believe that these feelings, which seem so painful at the time, can be our greatest opportunities for growth and for experiencing our humanity, especially if we're not afraid to feel some pain and some despair. Most people bounce back and carry on with their lives after a period of time. We can only feel healed and whole if we will allow ourselves to feel broken.

On the other hand, when some people get depressed, they become cynical and hopeless and give up on life. They crawl into bed and avoid pleasurable activities, friends, and work because they're so convinced that life is pointless and that the future holds nothing but deprivation and misery. This is not healthy sadness but depression.

Are my thoughts and feelings realistic? Healthy negative feelings are based on a realistic appraisal of your circumstances. It is often best to express these feelings as constructively as possible, to confront problems squarely and honestly, and to take action to deal with things more effectively. But when your negative feelings are based on distorted and unrealistic thoughts, it is often better to change the way you think about the situation.

The list of cognitive distortions in Chapter 1, page 8, can help you see whether your negative thoughts are illogical. When you write them down, you will frequently discover that you're involved in "all-or-nothing thinking," "fortune-telling," "personalization," and so on. This means that you're viewing a situation in an unrealistic manner. When you modify these thoughts, your feelings will often change.

Will it be helpful or hurtful if I express my feelings? When you feel angry, you might tell yourself, "I have the right to feel this way!" Of course you have the right to feel any way you want, but the real question is whether or not you *want* to feel like that. Will it help you deal with the situation if you express your negative feelings? If the answer is yes, you should probably express them. If the answer is no, it may be better to change your feelings.

Suppose your five-year-old son runs out in the street to chase a ball. You may feel frightened and shout at him in an angry voice. This might make a more powerful and lasting impact than a calm and rational discussion about the dangers of getting killed in traffic.

Your anger would be healthy and it might someday save his life. On the other hand, if a police officer is giving you a ticket, shouting at him in an angry voice might have severe consequences. You might do better to count to ten and admit your error.

Many people are afraid to express their feelings, even when it's clearly indicated. I recently treated a young woman who was reluctant to break up with her boyfriend because she felt guilty about hurting his feelings. For six months she kept stringing him along. She wasn't really being kind to him, she was submitting him to slow torture. For months he'd been depressed and confused because he couldn't figure out where he stood with her. Once they talked things over honestly and she made it clear how she really felt, they broke up. Although he felt disappointed, he got over his disappointment in a couple of weeks and was able to get on with his life.

Am I making myself unhappy about a problem that's beyond my control? Sometimes we refuse to accept situations that are beyond our control, but it doesn't do much good. You may be caught in a traffic jam or stuck on an airplane that's delayed in taking off. If you tell yourself "This shouldn't have happened—how unfair!" or "I can't stand this," you'll have to cope with the stress and aggravation you feel as well as the inconvenience of the delay. You have plenty of other options if you're willing to be creative and to think about the situation more positively. Recently I was stuck on a commuter train for two hours. It was hot and muggy, and I was tired and eager to get home. I began talking with the man next to me and learned a great deal about the Iran-Iraq war from him. Although he didn't consider himself an expert, he knew far more about it than I did. The conversation was more enjoyable than sitting and fuming about the incompetence of the people running the railroad or the "injustice" of the delay!

Am I avoiding a problem and denying that I'm really upset about it? Sometimes one emotion can be a substitute for another. You may be angry with someone, but you don't admit it to yourself. You repress your feelings and get anxious and panicky instead. Your anxiety is simply a way of disguising a problem that you'd prefer to avoid.

I recently treated a 26-year-old interior decorator named Annie who had developed the obsession that she was going crazy. Annie had read my first book, *Feeling Good*, and had memorized the symptoms of schizophrenia described there. All day long she would review them over and over and would feel temporarily reassured that she wasn't crazy, since she didn't have any of them. However, the very act of compulsively reviewing the symptoms made her feel abnormal. This would get her even more upset, so she would review the list again.

If Annie is not really going crazy, what *is* going on? What's she really so anxious about? Six months ago Annie started living with her fiancé, Jim. Both of them have a "conflict phobia": they are afraid of anger and don't know how to talk about their problems, so they avoid anything that's upsetting.

When Annie was growing up, no one in her house ever fought or worked out problems. She grew up with the notion that nice people don't argue or get mad. When she feels annoyed, she doesn't know what to do with her feelings and she sweeps them under the carpet. She denies that she's upset with Jim. Then her feelings eat away at her, and her obsession about going crazy is the result. By worrying, Annie distracts herself from the real problem and doesn't have to admit that she's angry. I suspect that her anxiety and her fears about going crazy will be greatly improved once she and Jim have some couples communication training and learn to talk about their feelings more openly.

Are my expectations for the world realistic? After I finished a lecture to a group of mental health professionals in New York, a psychiatrist in the audience took issue with the idea that distorted thoughts and unrealistic expectations lead to negative emotions. She pointed out that life is filled with annoying experiences and argued that it's realistic to feel frustrated.

At first I thought she was right, but when I thought about it further, it dawned on me that frustration is rarely, if ever, "realistic," but it's eminently human. Frustration always results from a discrepancy between your expectations and reality. If you feel frustrated, it's because you expected something different from what really happened. You expected the subway to be on time, but it was late, so you got frustrated. This means that your expectations were, by definition, unrealistic. After all, the subway, *in reality*, was late. But it can be difficult to change these expectations because you may strongly believe that life *should* or *must* or *ought* to be the way you want it to be.

Frustration can be healthy when we take it as a signal for creativity and change. The irony is that for some people frustration becomes a way of life. Their theme is "Life stinks! Life should be different from the way it is," but they rarely do anything to make it better.

One evening I told my wife that I was frustrated with a particularly difficult patient who seemed determined not to give up her irrational self-criticism. No matter what this patient accomplished, she stubbornly insisted that it wasn't good enough and claimed that she was a totally worthless human being. I tried dozens of ways to help her turn this around, but she always found a way to be negative and defeat me. I told my wife that people *shouldn't* be so unreasonable!

My wife pointed out it wasn't particularly realistic to expect someone with a severe depression to be logical and optimistic. She also pointed out that if there weren't so many self-critical people in the world, I'd be out of business! She was right, so I thanked my lucky stars that there were so many "unreasonable" people who needed help!

I decided to view my work with this patient as a challenge instead of a burden. I became curious about *why* she was resisting me. Maybe she was mad at me but couldn't admit it openly. Or maybe she was afraid to change. As I became more supportive and less demanding, she began to let down her defenses. Soon we were working together productively. She couldn't change until I had accepted her as she was.

I call this the "acceptance paradox." If you try too hard to fight a problem within yourself or someone else, the very act of fighting will often create resistance. Sometimes when you accept the problem and stop trying so hard, things will suddenly begin to change.

Are my expectations for myself realistic? Some people beat on themselves because they think they're not as good or as happy or as successful as they should be. Do you ever have thoughts like these?

"I should always be able to help friends and family members solve their problems."

"I should always be able to please people and live up to everyone's expectations for me."

"I should always succeed at whatever I do and never fall short of any goal."

"I should always be in control of my feelings and never get overly anxious or upset or have any irrational feelings."

"I should always feel close to the people I care about and never fight or bicker."

"I should be able to get everybody's approval and make everybody like me."

"I should try to be perfect and never fail or make mistakes."

You may have difficulty accepting your imperfections and your limitations. You may harangue yourself whenever you fall short of a personal goal and tell yourself, "I *shouldn't* have made that mistake! I'm such a jerk. How could I screw up?" Although all this self-abuse creates guilt and depression, there may be a hidden payoff. Only a very special person could be expected to be so perfect. After all, most of us more average people make lots of mistakes! When we do, we try to learn from them and carry on again. But if you punish yourself and act as if your mistakes are unthinkable and unacceptable, it means you're superior to the rest of us!

Many people find it difficult to accept their feelings. If you have panic attacks, you may think that anxiety is abnormal and dangerous. You may fight your anxiety and insist that you should always be in control of your emotions. When you get any little twitch of nervousness, you may feel that something terrible is happening and think you're about to go crazy. As a result, normal feelings of anxiety mushroom into full-blown panic attacks.

Some people refuse to accept their anger. You may think you should never fight or argue or get mad. You may be afraid to express your negative feelings for fear you'll be rejected or will hurt the person you're mad at. Then your feelings may get bottled up and you may end up constantly bickering and feeling irritable. Because you are afraid of anger, you end up knee-deep in bitterness and conflict. In contrast, if you accept your anger as a normal part of any healthy, loving relationship, you'll discover that you can often resolve problems far more easily and your anger will more quickly disappear.

Am I feeling hopeless? Hopelessness is nearly always a sign of unhealthy emotions. People who are suffering from depression or anxiety frequently feel this way. You reason, "I *feel* so hopeless. Therefore I must really *be* hopeless." You give up, and nothing changes. Then you conclude that things really are hopeless. Many of my patients tell me, "I'm the one who will never get better. My problems are insurmountable. I'll feel this way forever. Why don't you just give up on me, Dr. Burns?" These feelings are nearly always based on a distorted assessment of yourself and your future. I tell my patients that I will *never* buy into their conviction that they are hopeless. Your chances of feeling joy and self-esteem again are extremely high, even if it doesn't seem so.

Am I experiencing a loss of self-esteem? Low self-esteem can lead to unhealthy anger, anxiety, guilt, and depression. If you feel good about yourself and someone has treated you badly, then expressing your feelings can show that you respect yourself. You can share your anger in a constructive way so that the problem can get resolved fairly. If you feel inferior, however, you may be defensive and constantly look for little signs of rejection and unfair treatment. You may lash out at people because you don't feel very worthwhile inside.

I recently had to reschedule a therapy session with a patient because of the death of a friend. Although I called her two days ahead of time and explained the circumstances, she got furious and wrote an angry letter terminating treatment. In the letter she stated that if I really cared about her I wouldn't have canceled the session. Fortunately she threw the letter away before mailing it and was able to work on her low self-esteem and fears of rejection during the next therapy session.

If you've ever been criticized or rejected or have failed to achieve an important goal, you know how natural it is to feel hurt and disappointed. But if you berate yourself as worthless and unlovable, you'll be giving yourself distorted messages and destroying your self-esteem. Being rejected and failing are universal human experiences. They don't make you "a reject" or "a failure"—they make you a human being.

Even if you behave badly, it won't do much good to write yourself off as a "bad person." You will simply waste time and energy ruminating about how lousy and terrible you are. This will only incapacitate you and make the problem worse. In addition, this is very self-centered because you're entirely caught up in yourself! Genuine self-esteem is based on humility and an acceptance of your shortcomings. This makes it possible to assume responsibility for your actions, to feel remorse, to apologize and make amends, and to get on with productive and joyous living.

PART TWO

Feeling Good About Yourself: How to Conquer Depression and Build Self-Esteem

5

•

How to Change the Way You Feel: The Four Steps to Happiness

Let's assume you want to change the way you feel. First you will need a pen or pencil. It's far better to confront your problems by writing them down than by simply thinking them through. I can't emphasize the importance of this enough, if you want positive changes in your life! You can jot down your negative thoughts whenever you feel upset—in your office, at home, on a plane or bus. Once you get in the habit, you will see in black and white just how unrealistic they are.

Many people will tell themselves, "I'll just read this book and try to think things through a little better and that will be enough." This is a real trap. When you're upset, your negative thoughts will chase each other around in your mind in endless circles. Once you get them down on paper, you develop a more objective perspective. As you read the following pages, try the techniques I describe, even if you're convinced they won't work for you. I think you'll be surprised to discover how helpful they can be.

There are four steps to becoming a happier person.

Step 1: Identify the Upsetting Event

The first thing I want you to do is to write a brief description of a specific problem that's bothering you at the top of the blank Daily Mood Log on page 75, where it says "STEP ONE: DESCRIBE THE UPSETTING EVENT." A completed example is illustrated on pages 78–79. As you can see, when Marge was baby-sitting her two grandchildren she inadvertently let her granddaughter use her grandson's toothbrush. Her grandson had a sore throat and Marge started worrying that her granddaughter might catch it from him. When she went to bed that night Marge obsessed about the incident. She was concerned that her daughter, who was often quite critical of Marge, would become angry when she found out. Marge described the situation this way: "I inadvertently let Luci use her brother's toothbrush. Now I feel tormented and I can't sleep."

Perhaps you feel annoyed because a friend made a rude remark. Or you're embarrassed because you wrote a check that bounced, or received an upsetting letter in today's mail. Some people even get upset when something good happens. A graduating law student heard that his roommate had just received a job offer from a prestigious law firm. He felt jealous because he hadn't yet received such an appealing offer.

Sometimes bad moods are triggered by a negative memory or fantasy that comes out of the blue. While editing this paragraph, I suddenly felt as if I'd been kicked in the stomach. I realized I had been thinking about a patient who was angry with me for being charged for a late cancellation of a therapy session—I was imagining being hauled into court for a malpractice suit.

The most important principle to keep in mind when you identify the upsetting event is to be *specific*. Don't write down "Life stinks." If you told me that you wanted help with this problem, I would ask you, "What time of day was it stinking? Where were you when you noticed the smell?" Obviously I wouldn't really know what your complaint meant. If you just had an argument with your spouse or your boss, that would be something specific we could work on.

An attractive but shy young woman named Rita with a mild chronic depression told me that the problem she wanted help with was that she didn't have enough fun in life. I think you can see the difficulty with this: it's a little too vague. I asked Rita *when* she

THE DAILY MOOD LOG*

STEP ONE: DESCRIBE THE UPSETTING EVENT _____

_____

STEP TWO: RECORD YOUR NEGATIVE FEELINGS—and rate each one from 0 (the least) to 100 (the most). Use words like sad, anxious, angry, guilty, lonely, hopeless, frustrated, etc.

Emotion	Rating	Emotion	Rating	Emotion	Rating
1.		3.		5.	
2.		4.		6.	

STEP THREE: THE TRIPLE-COLUMN TECHNIQUE—

Automatic Thoughts	Distortions	Rational Responses
Write your negative thoughts and estimate your belief in each one (0–100).	Identify the distortions in each Automatic Thought.	Substitute more realistic thoughts and estimate your belief in each one (0–100).

(Continue on next page)

THE DAILY MOOD LOG* (continued)

Automatic Thoughts	Distortions	Rational Responses

(Continue on next page)

Automatic Thoughts	Distortions	Rational Responses

STEP FOUR: OUTCOME—Re-rate your belief in each Automatic Thought from 0 to 100 and put a check in the box that describes how you now feel:

□ not at all better □ somewhat better □ quite a bit better □ a lot better

---

CHECKLIST OF COGNITIVE DISTORTIONS*

1. All-or-nothing thinking: You look at things in absolute, black-and-white categories.
2. Overgeneralization: You view a negative event as a never-ending pattern of defeat.
3. Mental filter: You dwell on the negatives and ignore the positives.
4. Discounting the positives: You insist that your accomplishments or positive qualities "don't count."
5. Jumping to conclusions: (A) Mind reading—you assume that people are reacting negatively to you when there's no definite evidence for this; (B) Fortune-telling—you arbitrarily predict that things will turn out badly.
6. Magnification or minimization: You blow things way up out of proportion or you shrink their importance inappropriately.
7. Emotional reasoning: You reason from how you feel: "I *feel* like an idiot, so I really must be one." Or "I don't *feel* like doing this, so I'll put it off."
8. "Should statements": You criticize yourself or other people with "shoulds" or "shouldn'ts." "Musts," "oughts," and "have tos" are similar offenders.
9. Labeling: You identify with your shortcomings. Instead of saying "I made a mistake," you tell yourself, "I'm a jerk," or "a fool," or "a loser."
10. Personalization and blame: You blame yourself for something you weren't entirely responsible for, or you blame other people and overlook ways that your own attitudes and behavior might contribute to a problem.

THE DAILY MOOD LOG*

STEP ONE: DESCRIBE THE UPSETTING EVENT___ I inadvertently let Luci use her brother's toothbrush. Now I feel tormented and can't sleep.

STEP TWO: RECORD YOUR NEGATIVE FEELINGS—and rate each one from 0 (the least) to 100 (the most). Use words like sad, anxious, angry, guilty, lonely, hopeless, frustrated, etc.

Emotion	Rating	Emotion	Rating	Emotion	Rating
1. Anxious	90	3.		5.	
2. Guilty	90	4.		6.	

STEP THREE: THE TRIPLE-COLUMN TECHNIQUE—

Automatic Thoughts	Distortions	Rational Responses
Write your negative thoughts and estimate your belief in each one (0–100).	Identify the distortions in each Automatic Thought.	Substitute more realistic thoughts and estimate your belief in each one (0 and 100).
1. If Luci gets a sore throat it will be my fault. (100%) (20%)	1. personalization fortune-telling	1. I made an honest mistake. Luci probably won't get a sore throat. It won't be the end of the world if she does. I don't deserve to be punished like this. (100%)

(Continue on next page)

Automatic Thoughts	Distortions	Rational Responses
2. If Bess finds out, she will be angry with me. (100%) (20%)	2. fortune-telling personalization	2. I don't know for certain that she'll blame me. If she is critical, I can apologize for making a mistake. If she continues to be angry and upset with me, I can tell her that I made an innocent mistake and that I'm uncomfortable with the way she's treating me. (100%)

STEP FOUR: OUTCOME—Re-rate your belief in each Automatic Thought from 0 to 100 and put a check in the box that describes how you now feel:

☐ not at all better ☐ somewhat better ☐ quite a bit better ☒ a lot better wanted to have more fun. At first she said "all the time." I pointed out that I didn't know *anybody* who had fun *all* the time! With some encouragement, Rita admitted that she wanted to have more fun on the train home to New York after her session. When I asked her to tell me what she had in mind, it turned out that she wanted to talk to other people instead of feeling left out. When I asked whom, she reluctantly admitted that she hoped to talk to a cute guy.

This seemed like an easy assignment, since Rita was as cute as a bug in a rug! I can imagine that practically any young man on the train would jump at the chance to meet her. However, Rita had many negative thoughts in social situations that made her feel inhibited, such as, "It would be embarrassing to get shot down or rejected" and "What if I make a fool of myself in front of the other passengers?" After we dealt with these fears, we talked about how she could be more outgoing so she could start conversations with attractive fellows on the train.

A high school senior told her therapist she wanted help with "an identity crisis." You could talk about that problem for years without getting anywhere. The expression doesn't really mean anything. Her therapist asked her if there were any specific problems in her life she needed help with. She answered that she couldn't decide whether to go to college at Vassar or Bryn Mawr. After two sessions reviewing the relative merits of each option, she decided on Vassar. She said she felt great. Then her therapist asked if she still wanted help with her "identity crisis." She said she didn't think she had one anymore, and she felt ready to terminate her therapy. Defining the specific problem was the key to success.

Remember: only *real* problems can be solved. To be real, a problem must occur at some place and at some time of day. Sometimes you may have a nagging feeling that something isn't quite right but you can't put your finger on it. When this happens to me, I review on an hour-by-hour basis the various things I've done in the past day or two. I often go through my appointment book to see what I've been doing. Usually this helps me figure out what's bothering me. If I still can't figure it out, I may ask my wife or an associate at work who will often know why I'm upset even when I don't!

If worse comes to worst and you can't think of the specific problem, just write a general description of what you were doing when you felt bad. Examples: "At home washing the dishes and feeling lousy" or "Reading this book and feeling discouraged."

Now I want you to write a brief description of a situation that is bothering you at the top of the blank Daily Mood Log on page 78. Once you've done this, you can proceed to the next step.

Step 2: Record Your Negative Feelings

Write down your negative emotions and rate each of them on a scale from 1 to 100. Use words like sad, frustrated, discouraged, angry, hurt, anxious, embarrassed, upset, or guilty. A score of 1 for any emotion would be the least you could feel and a score of 100 would be the most. You can put down several negative feelings, because you will usually have more than one. You can see in her Daily Mood Log that Marge rated her feelings as "anxious—90" and "guilty—90." This indicated she was quite upset about the toothbrush incident.

Some of you won't like to rate your emotions with numbers because it seems artificial or overly compulsive. However, it can be a surprisingly effective device because then you can estimate how much better you feel after you complete the Daily Mood Log. It can also help you break the habit of thinking about your emotions in an all-or-nothing manner. If your anxiety goes down from 100 to 50, you might still be feeling tense, but you're nevertheless feeling quite a bit better. Giving yourself credit for this improvement will boost your morale and keep it high until you've resolved the problem completely. By the same token, there may be times when you still feel upset after completing the Daily Mood Log. This is important information. You can review the Troubleshooting Guide on page 86 to find out why you're stuck. Once you know what the problem is, it will help you to turn your feelings around.

I want you to write down and rate each of your negative emotions about the upsetting event you described in your Daily Mood Log. Once you've done that, you will be ready for the next step.

Step 3: The Triple-Column Technique

Ask yourself, "What are the negative thoughts that are associated with my bad feelings? What am I saying to myself about the upsetting situation?" Tune in to your inner dialogue. Listen with your "third ear." For example, during an argument with your husband you may be telling yourself, "If he really loved me he would listen to what I have to say." If you didn't get the promotion you had your hopes pinned on, you might be telling yourself, "I'll be stuck at this crummy job forever" or "I'm not getting fair treatment" or "I just don't have what it takes." If you're on a diet and you overeat, you might tell yourself that you're a fat pig with no willpower. If you notice an ache or pain or a tightness in your chest, you might feel panicky because you think you're on the verge of a heart attack or are dying of some dreadful disease.

As you become aware of your negative thoughts, write them down and number them in the "Automatic Thoughts" column of your Daily Mood Log. They're called Automatic Thoughts because when you feel upset, they come into your mind automatically, without any effort on your part. Getting in the habit of recording these Automatic Thoughts is one of the most important things you will learn in this book!

Many of my patients resist doing this when they feel upset. They believe that the Daily Mood Log won't help them. Don't succumb to these feelings! These methods are much more likely to help if you will grab a pen and do some writing while you read! Turn to page 75 now, if you have not done so already, and write a brief description of any upsetting event. Then record your negative emotions and write down your Automatic Thoughts. Do it now!

Sometimes you might not be able to pinpoint your Automatic Thoughts. If so, there's a simple solution. Draw an unhappy stick figure with a bubble above its head, like the one on page 83. Make up some negative thoughts that are upsetting the stick figure and write them down in the bubble. Ask yourself, "Why is this stick figure so unhappy?" Just make something up—anything will do. What you write down will usually tip you off to what's bothering you. A woman who insisted she didn't know what she was feeling upset about wrote this in the bubble: "I'll never be able to finish my graduate studies and get my master's degree." This led to a productive discussion of her perfectionism and fears of failure. Psychologists call this a "projective" technique, because the thoughts you put in the cartoon figure's mind are ones that you are projecting from your own mind. So it's not so surprising that they turn out to be the same ones that are actually bugging you!

After you have written down your Automatic Thoughts, estimate how much you believe each of them from 0 (not at all) to 100 percent (completely), and write the figure down in parentheses. The first

"Nothing ever goes right for me. I'm so far behind in my work. . . . This is going to be a lousy day."

When you can't figure out what your gloomy thoughts are, draw an unhappy stick figure. Make up some negative thoughts that are making the stick figure upset and write them down in the bubble over his or her head.

negative thought Marge wrote down was "If Luci gets a sore throat it will be my fault," and the second one was "If Bess finds out she will be very angry with me." She recorded her belief in each thought as 100 percent, because they both seemed absolutely true.

When these negative thoughts first cross your mind, you will nearly always believe that they are the gospel truth. After all, if you don't believe a negative thought, it can't affect the way you feel. For example, you probably don't believe the thought "The world is coming to an end today." Therefore this thought won't make you feel anxious or depressed. If you did believe it, you'd be *quite* agitated! You will eventually discover that the thoughts that upset you are nearly always quite unrealistic, although they seem completely valid when they are running through your mind. Your Automatic Thoughts are deceptive. They create the illusion of truth, even when they're extremely illogical. When you write them down, it will be easier to put the lie to them. The moment you see how unrealistic and pessimistic they are, you will feel better.

After you have written down and numbered each of your Automatic Thoughts, identify the distortion(s) in them in the middle column. You can refer to "The Checklist of Cognitive Distortions" on page 77 when you do this. What are the distortions in Marge's first negative thought, "If Luci gets a sore throat it will be my fault"? Put your ideas here:

1._____

2._____

Answer: One distortion is "personalization," because Marge is blaming herself for a negative event that is beyond her control. A second distortion is "fortune-telling," since she is predicting that Luci will catch her brother's sore throat.

You can see that her second negative thought contains the same two distortions. She's predicting that her daughter will be angry with her, and she's prepared to blame herself for her daughter's reaction. Many people with depression automatically blame themselves and get terribly self-critical whenever anyone is angry with them. Do you ever react this way? I know that I sometimes do, and it can really hurt! You just suddenly feel that you're "no good" inside.

After you identify the distortions in your Automatic Thoughts, substitute Rational Responses in the right-hand column, and indicate how strongly you believe each one from 0 percent to 100 percent. Marge's first Rational Response was: "I made an honest mistake. Luci probably won't get a sore throat. If she does it won't be the end of the world, and I don't deserve to be punished like this." In parentheses, she indicated that she believed this 100 percent. For the second Rational Response, Marge reminded herself that if her daughter did get hostile and critical—as she often did—she could calmly acknowledge that she made a mistake and apologize without getting defensive and without putting herself down. If her daughter continued to harangue her, she could indicate that she was uncomfortable with the way her daughter was treating her.

This illustrates that the solution to a mood problem frequently has both an *individual* and an *interpersonal* dimension. Marge needs to change the way she thinks. She needs to develop better self-esteem and to stop being so self-critical. That's the individual dimension. At the same time, she needs to change the way she relates to other people, including her daughter. That's the interpersonal dimension. This may require some communication training, because Marge is extremely unassertive and she's afraid to express her feelings. She is terribly insecure and afraid of anger or conflict, so she takes too much abuse from other people. She automatically blames herself whenever anyone is annoyed with her. She is like an animal that goes belly up when threatened, hoping the predator will lose interest and go away. In Part IV we will talk about how to solve personal relationship problems and communicate more effectively.

Now I want you to complete your Daily Mood Log. After you write down your Automatic Thoughts, write how much you believe each one on a scale from 0 to 100 percent. In the middle column, identify the distortions in each thought, using the list on page 77 as a guide. Then write down more positive and realistic thoughts in the Rational Response column. Indicate in parentheses how much you believe each of them.

It is not terribly important to do a good job, because this is your first effort. It's much like your first time on roller skates: all you have to do is go through the motions, even if your efforts don't seem terribly graceful or effective. Once you've completed your Rational Responses, you're ready for the next step.

Step 4: Outcome

After you've answered all of your Automatic Thoughts, re-rate your belief in each of them. Cross out the original percent you rate each one, and put a new estimate of how much you now believe it in light of your Rational Response. You can see that Marge crossed out 100% and put in 20%, indicating she no longer believed her two Automatic Thoughts nearly so strongly. You will feel better the moment you see that your Automatic Thoughts are not valid.

Finally, evaluate how much better you feel in the "Outcome"

TROUBLESHOOTING GUIDE*

If you still feel just as upset after you fill out a Daily Mood Log, ask yourself these questions:

1. **Have I correctly identified the upsetting event?** Sometimes you can't put your finger on the problem that's bothering you. You will often discover what it is if you review your activities for the past day or two. Make your description of the negative event specific: What happened? Where were you? What time was it? With whom were you involved?

2. **Do I want to change my negative feelings about this situation?** List the advantages and disadvantages of changing your feelings.

3. **Have I identified my Automatic Thoughts properly?** Remember not to put descriptions of upsetting events or feelings in the Automatic Thoughts column. If you have trouble figuring out what your negative thoughts are, use the stick figure technique.

4. **Are my Rational Responses convincing, valid statements that put the lie to my Automatic Thoughts?** Rationalizations won't make you feel any better. Your Rational Responses must not only be realistic and believable, but they must contradict your Automatic Thoughts. The moment you see that your Automatic Thoughts aren't valid, you'll feel better.

section at the bottom of the sheet. As you can see in her log, Marge indicated she felt considerably relieved. That's because her Rational Responses were more realistic and believable than her Automatic Thoughts.

If you don't feel better after you complete the exercise, review the Troubleshooting Guide on page 86. Ask yourself the following questions:

Have I identified the upsetting event correctly? Remember to make the event specific, not vague. If you feel overwhelmed because you have many problems, then just choose one to work on first. It usually won't make any difference which one it is. Overcoming one problem will give you some inspiration and make it a lot easier to deal with the others.

If you can't put your finger on precisely what's bothering you, then review what's been going on in your life. With whom have you been talking? What have you been doing recently? This is like retracing your steps when you've lost something. Usually it will suddenly dawn on you what the problem is.

Do I really want to feel better? Sometimes you will have mixed feelings about letting go of a negative emotion. In fact your negative feelings may be quite healthy and realistic. If so, it might be better to express them instead of trying to make them go away by using the Daily Mood Log. For example, if someone is mad at you, or you are angry with them, it may be better to talk the problem over with them instead of trying to change your feelings about the situation with cognitive techniques. The chapters in Part IV on communication could be especially helpful in this case.

In deciding whether or not you want to change your feelings, list the advantages and disadvantages of feeling upset. (See page 113 for this "cost-benefit" technique.) Maybe you want to pamper yourself and let the feelings pass, or maybe there's a realistic problem you need to deal with. If you discover that the disadvantages of feeling upset outweigh the advantages, then it will be much easier to modify your feelings using the Daily Mood Log.

Have I identified my Automatic Thoughts properly? When you fill out the Daily Mood Log, remember that the thoughts you write down in the Automatic Thoughts column are the *interpretations* of the upsetting situation, not descriptions of the actual event. If you feel annoyed because your husband is late coming home, it wouldn't be appropriate to put "George was late again" in the Automatic Thoughts column. This is the actual problem, so it goes in the space at the top of the sheet. The premise of cognitive therapy is that only your *thoughts*, and not actual events, upset you. In the Automatic Thoughts column you would put your negative thoughts about this event. You might be thinking, "This shows George doesn't love me" or "He's always late" or "He's probably having an affair with his secretary."

Another common mistake is to put descriptions of your feelings in the Automatic Thoughts column. Don't put "I feel hurt because my boss criticized me," because this is a situation ("My boss criticized me") and a feeling ("hurt"). Describe the situation at the top of the sheet and record your negative feelings. In the Automatic Thoughts column, put the thoughts that are associated with these feelings. Why do you feel hurt? Why was his criticism so upsetting to you? What are you telling yourself? You might be thinking, "He doesn't respect me" or "He's got no right to say that" or "I never do anything right" or "I'm about to get fired."

If you aren't sure what all your negative thoughts are, you can use the stick figure technique described earlier. When Jack was golfing with his friends, he suddenly felt very anxious and nervous. On the Daily Mood Log he recorded this Automatic Thought: "I shouldn't be feeling so nervous, since everything is going well for me." Jack is a stockbroker, and recently the market has been treating him well. He's been making lots of money and his clients are making lots of money. What is the main distortion in his Automatic Thought? Check the list of cognitive distortions on page 77 and put your ideas here:

_____

_____

Answer: Jack is making a "should statement," since he is telling himself he "shouldn't" feel anxious. He was able to come up with this Rational Response: "Human beings are not always perfectly rational. Some people do get nervous, even when things are going well."

This helped somewhat, because Jack was giving himself permission to feel nervous instead of condemning himself for being nervous.

However, Jack still hadn't identified all the thoughts that were making him feel nervous in the first place. Since he drew a blank, I asked him to draw a stick figure of a man very like himself, who was golfing and feeling nervous. I told him to make up some negative thoughts and to write them down in the bubble on top, to show what the stick figure was thinking. As you can see, the stick figure golfer was thinking, "This shot will probably go in the lake. . . .

Jack was upset while he was playing golf, but at first he didn't know why. When he wrote down the negative thoughts in the bubble over the stick figure's head, it became clear what he was worrying about.

I'm doing well at work but I can't keep it up. The stock market will probably go down and everyone will lose money and fire me." I asked Jack if his thoughts were at all similar to those, and he said, "Exactly!" I don't know why the stick figure technique is so effective, but it is! Use it any time you can't figure out what your Automatic Thoughts are.

Are my Rational Responses true and valid statements, or am I just rationalizing? Do they put the lie to my Automatic Thoughts? The purpose of the Daily Mood Log is to help you face reality. It won't be helpful if you deny your problems or try to cheer yourself up with phony rationalizations. After her boyfriend broke up with her, Linda felt guilty and depressed. She told herself she wasn't lovable and that everything was her fault. She felt there was something basically wrong with her personality, and she was terrified she'd never find a husband and end up a lonely old maid.

After talking about the problem with a friend, she decided that the fellow who rejected her was basically a jerk and that the problems in their relationship were actually his fault. This was simply a rationalization. Linda switched from "personalization" ("It's all my fault") to "blame" ("It's all his fault"). I don't think this is the most productive way to deal with the situation. I would prefer to see Linda pinpoint the specific problems in the relationship as fairly and objectively as possible so she can learn from the experience. Why did they break up? What did she do to contribute to the tension? What did he do? How could she deal with a similar problem differently in the future? If she confronts these issues without a loss of self-esteem, she won't get bitter or depressed and she can make her next relationship better.

In order to make you feel better, the statements in the Rational Response column must not only be valid, but they must also put the lie to your Automatic Thoughts. Suppose you meet an old school friend who is more attractive, more intelligent, more successful, and more popular than you. You might have the Automatic Thought, "Gee, I'm not as worthwhile as she is." This thought will make you feel insecure and inferior. You could come up with the Rational Response, "But I'm a better cook." While this might be absolutely true, it's not likely to give your self-esteem much of a boost! For example, your friend might be so successful that she flies to Paris in a Concorde jet and eats in five-star restaurants. Can you think of a Rational Response that would be more effective?

I don't want to create the impression that the solution to your problems will always be easy or magical. The successful application of these techniques can sometimes require persistent work over a period of time. If you want good results, I would recommend using the Daily Mood Log for ten to fifteen minutes per day, five days per week, for at least a month. This regular practice will help you get in shape emotionally, in much the same way that an athlete builds his strength and conditioning through daily workouts. Sometimes it will be easy to change your thoughts and feelings, but at other times it will be difficult because your negative thoughts will seem so powerful and convincing. It's a challenge for me sometimes, and I wrote the book! But if you work at it with determination, you'll get the job done.

Don't go to the other extreme of thinking that this will be too difficult for you. This method is within the reach of the average individual. In a study reported in the *British Journal of Psychiatry*, Dr. Ivy Blackburn and her associates at the University of Edinburgh found that these techniques were very effective for working-class people. This proves that you do not have to be psychologically sophisticated to make cognitive therapy work for you. In a recent study in the journal *Cognitive Therapy and Research*, Dr. Jacqueline Persons and I reported the results of our research, which showed that these methods work equally well for patients with different levels of education and with a wide variety of income levels and cultural backgrounds. We discovered that regardless of whether you're rich or poor, brilliant or of average intelligence, old or young, a change in your thoughts and attitudes will have an enormous impact on the way you feel.

The four steps to happiness are summarized on page 92. Part of the beauty of this approach is that you can apply it to all kinds of problems. You can use it to break out of virtually any kind of bad mood—worry, sadness, anxiety, stress, frustration, guilt, anger. You can use it when you're having problems in your personal relationships, in your career, or in your attempts to modify a bad habit like drinking too much. For your convenience, I've included an additional Daily Mood Log (pages 93 to 96).

Coming up with believable, effective Rational Responses that successfully disprove your Automatic Thoughts takes practice. In the next chapter, I will describe many techniques that will help you develop more positive attitudes and greater self-esteem.

THE FOUR STEPS TO HAPPINESS*

STEP ONE—Identify the upsetting situation. Describe the event or problem that's upsetting you. Who (or what) are you feeling unhappy about?

STEP TWO—Record your negative feelings. How do you feel about the upsetting situation? Use words like sad, angry, anxious, guilty, frustrated, hopeless. Rate each negative feeling on a scale from 1 (for the least) to 100 (for the most).

STEP THREE—Use the triple-column technique. Tune in to the negative thoughts that are associated with these feelings. What are you saying to yourself about the problem? Write these thoughts in the Automatic Thoughts column and record how much you believe each one between 0 (not at all) and 100 (completely). After you identify the distortions in these thoughts, substitute Rational Responses in the right-hand column and record how much you believe each one between 0 (not at all) and 100 (completely). Make sure that your Rational Responses are convincing, valid statements that put the lie to your Automatic Thoughts.

STEP FOUR—Outcome. Indicate how much you now believe each Automatic Thought between 0 and 100. Once your belief in these thoughts are greatly reduced, indicate how much better you feel.

*Copyright © 1989 by David D. Burns, M.D., from *The Feeling Good Handbook*

THE DAILY MOOD LOG*

STEP ONE: DESCRIBE THE UPSETTING EVENT _____

_____

STEP TWO: RECORD YOUR NEGATIVE FEELINGS—and rate each one from 0 (the least) to 100 (the most). Use words like sad, anxious, angry, guilty, lonely, hopeless, frustrated, etc.

Emotion	Rating	Emotion	Rating	Emotion	Rating
1.		3.		5.	
2.		4.		6.	

STEP THREE: THE TRIPLE-COLUMN TECHNIQUE—

Automatic Thoughts	Distortions	Rational Responses
Write your negative thoughts and estimate your belief in each one (0–100).	Identify the distortions in each Automatic Thought.	Substitute more realistic thoughts and estimate your belief in each one (0 and 100).

(Continue on next page)

Automatic Thoughts	Distortions	Rational Responses

(Continue on next page)

Automatic Thoughts	Distortions	Rational Responses

(Continue on next page)

THE DAILY MOOD LOG* (continued)

Automatic Thoughts	Distortions	Rational Responses

STEP FOUR: OUTCOME—Re-rate your belief in each Automatic Thought from 0 to 100 and put a check in the box that describes how you now feel:

□ not at all better □ somewhat better □ quite a bit better □ a lot better

---

CHECKLIST OF COGNITIVE DISTORTIONS*

1. All-or-nothing thinking: You look at things in absolute, black-and-white categories.
2. Overgeneralization: You view a negative event as a never-ending pattern of defeat.
3. Mental filter: You dwell on the negatives and ignore the positives.
4. Discounting the positives: You insist that your accomplishments or positive qualities "don't count."
5. Jumping to conclusions: (A) Mind reading—you assume that people are reacting negatively to you when there's no definite evidence for this; (B) Fortune-telling—you arbitrarily predict that things will turn out badly.
6. Magnification or minimization: You blow things way up out of proportion or you shrink their importance inappropriately.
7. Emotional reasoning: You reason from how you feel: "I *feel* like an idiot, so I really must be one." Or "I don't *feel* like doing this, so I'll put it off."
8. "Should statements": You criticize yourself or other people with "shoulds" or "shouldn'ts." "Musts," "oughts," and "have tos" are similar offenders.
9. Labeling: You identify with your shortcomings. Instead of saying "I made a mistake," you tell yourself, "I'm a jerk," or "a fool," or "a loser."
10. Personalization and blame: You blame yourself for something you weren't entirely responsible for, or you blame other people and overlook ways that your own attitudes and behavior might contribute to a problem.

*Copyright © 1980 by David D. Burns, M.D. Adapted from *Feeling Good: The New Mood Therapy* (New York: William Morrow & Company, 1980; Signet, 1981)

6

•

Ten Ways to Untwist Your Thinking

When you feel bad, you are thinking about things in a negative way. These thoughts, and not what actually happens, are what make you feel upset. Dr. Albert Ellis has called this the "A-B-C" of emotion. "A" stands for the "actual event"—this is what actually happened. Let's assume that you got divorced. "B" stands for your "beliefs" about the event. You may be thinking, "It's all my fault. What will my family and friends think of me?" "C" stands for the "consequences" of your beliefs, including the way you feel and the way you behave. You might be feeling sad and ashamed, and you may crawl into a shell and avoid people because you feel so inadequate and unlovable. As the following diagram illustrates, your thoughts and beliefs make you feel the way you do:

"A" (Actual event = divorce)
↓
"B" (Belief = "I'm no good")
↓
"C" (Consequences = depression)

Your thoughts and beliefs about the event create your feelings. If you had thought, "It's all *his* fault—he's a self-centered jerk," you would feel angry and bitter rather than sad and ashamed.

Cognitive therapists have developed powerful techniques to help you change the way you think and feel. This chapter describes methods that I use every day in my office, and many additional methods will be described in later chapters. These techniques will provide you with a cognitive therapy tool kit that will help you overcome a huge variety of negative thoughts and feelings. Study these methods carefully!

1. Identify the Distortions

As we discussed in the last chapter, the first thing to do when you feel upset is to write down a brief description of the actual situation or problem that's bothering you. Next, identify and rate each of your negative emotions on a scale from 1 to 100. The third step is to write down and number each of your Automatic Thoughts in the left-hand column of the Daily Mood Log. Then identify the distortions in each negative thought, using the list on page 96 as a guide.

To give a simple example, a single man named Nick, who had a fear of intimate relationships, would frequent peep shows and prostitutes whenever he got anxious. Afterward, Nick had an extreme sense of self-loathing and sometimes felt suicidal, thinking, "I'm such a lowlife." What are the distortions in this thought? Review the "Checklist of Cognitive Distortions" on page 96 and put your ideas here:

1. _____

2. _____

Answer: It's an "overgeneralization," because Nick is generalizing from his behavior to his self. You could also call it "labeling," because he's attaching a negative label to himself.

Now you might think that Nick really is a "lowlife" and that he deserves to feel rotten. There are problems with this argument. When Nick thinks of himself as a "lowlife," he convinces himself that he's unworthy of love. Then he is even more likely to continue going to peep shows and prostitutes because that's what a "lowlife" does.

In addition, the shame and low self-esteem Nick feels will make it even harder for him to open up to a relationship with a woman he respects and cares about. He's afraid to risk being rejected, because Nick finds it inconceivable that anyone could ever love him. If he begins to accept himself, he may feel more lovable and find the courage to risk getting close to other people.

When you identify the distortions in any thought, you do not need to be overly precise. There's a lot of overlap between distortions, and the list you come up with may be a little different from mine. The important thing is to try to find at least one or more distortions in each Automatic Thought. That will make it easier to develop an effective Rational Response.

As an exercise, let's suppose someone criticizes you. You get upset and think, "I never do anything right. I'm such a loser." These thoughts make you feel inadequate and guilty. What are the distortions in these thoughts? Review the "Checklist of Cognitive Distortions" on page 96 and put your ideas here:

1. _____

2. _____

3. _____

4. _____

5. _____

6. _____

7. _____

8. _____

Answer: all-or-nothing thinking, overgeneralization, mental filter, discounting the positive, magnification, emotional reasoning, labeling, and personalization.

2. Examine the Evidence

After you write down a negative thought and you identify the distortions in it, ask yourself, "What is the evidence for this thought?" Because we *feel* so bad, we often believe things *are* bad without checking the facts. Once you examine the facts, things will frequently fall into a different perspective.

To continue with the previous example, how could you use the method of examining the evidence to talk back to your thought, "I never do anything right, I'm such a loser"? Put your ideas here:

_____

_____

_____

_____

Answer: You could ask yourself, "Is it true that I *never* do *anything* right? What are some things I do well? What are the things I'm not so good at?" If there's some truth in a criticism, you can try to learn from it in the spirit of self-respect. Focus on the specific problem instead of writing yourself off as a "a loser."

A single man named Eric told me that he could never find a wife because he was "only average-looking." How could Eric Examine the Evidence to find out if this belief was really valid? Put your ideas here:

_____

_____

_____

_____

Answer: I asked Eric to walk around the park on a Saturday and to rate how attractive (on a scale from 1 to 10) the couples were who were walking together. He discovered that some of them were very attractive (with ratings in the 7 to 10 range), some were only average (with ratings in the 4 to 6 range), and some were below average (with ratings in the 1 to 3 range). He also observed that the two partners' ratings were often quite different. Sometimes a very attractive woman was walking happily hand-in-hand with a man who was "only average," and vice versa. This made Eric aware that you don't have to be handsome or beautiful to develop a loving relationship with someone you care about. While it's true that very attractive people find it easier to meet others and to get dates, good looks are no guarantee that you will have a satisfying relationship. Eric's low self-esteem was the real problem. Once he learned to accept himself, he discovered that women were quite interested in him.

3. The Double-Standard Method

When you have a self-critical thought, ask yourself, "Would I say this to a close friend who was very much like me and had a similar problem?" We are frequently much harder on ourselves than on others. If you make a mistake or fail to achieve a goal, you might rip yourself to shreds and think, "I'm such a stupid jerk! I don't know what I'm doing. I'll never succeed at anything!" But if a friend made the same mistake, you'd probably be supportive. Why not be equally encouraging to yourself?

You may reply, "Because I have higher standards for myself." Let's investigate this argument. I would like to know why you have such high standards. You may say, "It's because I want to do my best." So essentially you rip yourself to shreds so you will try hard and do your best, right? I'm sure you'd also like your friend to do his or her best. Why not tell him, "You're such a stupid jerk! You'll never succeed at anything"?

The answer is obvious: because these harsh messages are utterly unrealistic and they won't help your friend do better. They'll just make him or her feel like giving up. These messages won't help you, either!

Why not treat all people, including yourself, with one standard that's both helpful and realistic? Give yourself the same encouraging messages you'd give a friend. This is the essence of the Double-Standard Method. It's an excellent way to answer Automatic Thoughts.

If you suffer from test anxiety, you may tell yourself, "When I take the test I'm going to blow it! I know I'll really screw up." You may give yourself this message hundreds of times while you're trying to study. These thoughts make you extremely nervous and you can hardly concentrate.

Can you imagine leaning over the shoulder of a friend who was trying to study and saying "You're going to blow it! You're really going to screw up"? But that's *precisely* what you do to yourself. That's why you feel so nervous and inadequate.

See if you can use the Double-Standard Method to talk back to those negative thoughts. Put your Rational Responses here:

_____

_____

_____

_____

Answer: Ask yourself what you'd say to a friend who was nervous and trying to study. I suspect you'd tell him or her something helpful and realistic. You might say, "You're doing a good job and all your studying will help you when you take the test." This would give your friend a needed boost of self-confidence. If you say this to yourself, you'll also begin to feel less nervous and more confident.

4. The Experimental Technique

When you have a negative thought, ask yourself if there's a way you could test it to find out if it's really true. Sometimes an experiment will help you get to the truth about things. To take a simple example, let's assume that you sometimes procrastinate. You may need to balance your checkbook, but you tell yourself, "It'll be such a drag," or "I just can't do it," or "It'll be too hard." These thoughts make you feel so upset that you can't stand to do it. The purpose of the Experimental Method is to test these thoughts. You can ask yourself, "Is it really true that it will be a 'drag' and that it will be 'too hard'?" Try to think of an experiment to test these ideas. Put your ideas here:

_____

_____

_____

_____

You could break the task down into small steps. First, locate your checkbook and your bank statement; second, see what checks have come in; third, add up the total amount of money for all the checks that come in; and so on. Then you could complete the first step—locating your checkbook. Ask yourself if it was "too hard" for you or if it was "a drag." You will probably discover that it wasn't nearly as difficult as you predicted. Then you can go on to the next step, and then the next, until the job is done.

The essence of this procedure is to test your negative thoughts by doing experiments. A depressed woman named Phyllis strongly believed that her husband didn't love her and that none of her friends liked her anymore. Consequently she stayed at home. She didn't even answer the phone. After a while people gave up and stopped calling. This convinced Phyllis even more that she was unlovable.

This often happens when you are depressed or annoyed with a friend or family member. Instead of dealing with the conflict, you avoid it. Then it eats away at you and the problem begins to feel far worse than it really is.

How could Phyllis test her belief that nobody liked her? I asked what she thought would happen if she called two or three friends and invited them out to lunch. She predicted they would all make excuses and say they were too busy. I urged her to call them so we could get some real data.

At our next session Phyllis told me that she was surprised: two friends had accepted her invitation, while the third took a rain check until after her vacation. All three seemed happy to hear from her and expressed concern that they hadn't gotten together sooner. This wasn't consistent with Phyllis's claim that nobody liked her anymore.

This doesn't mean that there was no truth whatsoever in Phyllis's negative thoughts. She did harbor resentment toward her husband and sometimes felt jealous of her friends. She may need to deal with these problems with the communication techniques described in Part IV. However, her belief that everybody had rejected her was simply not true.

5. Thinking in Shades of Gray

When you have a negative thought, ask yourself, "Am I looking at things in an either-or, black-or-white fashion? Am I thinking of myself as either a total success or a total failure?" If so, you are probably involved in "all-or-nothing thinking." This is one of the most common distortions. It can lead to anxiety and panic, depression, guilt, feelings of inferiority, hopelessness, perfectionism, and anger. Learning to modify "all-or-nothing thinking" has changed the lives of many of my patients.

One helpful technique is called Thinking in Shades of Gray. The basic principle is very simple: You remind yourself that things are usually somewhere between 0 and 100 percent instead of insisting that they're all one way or the other.

Linda is a spunky, petite 45-year-old woman from Chicago. After her husband died unexpectedly when she was 30, she began to manage his small construction company. Although it was a male-dominated industry, Linda valiantly persisted and eventually developed a booming business throughout Chicago. She constantly had to negotiate with union bosses, contractors, and city officials who could be tough and occasionally ruthless. During the late 1970s, a man who appeared to have mob connections coerced Linda into making several under-the-table payments of thousands of dollars. He threatened that if she refused, she might find that the construction workers would become suddenly uncooperative and unable to complete their jobs. He implied she would be blacklisted and bankrupted if she resisted.

Linda was torn. Out of panic—and greed—she made the payments and completed the project. Linda never again bid for contracts in this part of Chicago. She ran a clean shop and continued to do well and eventually forgot about the incident. Two months ago she received a subpoena from federal investigators. The man who had blackmailed her had been arrested, and a notebook listing payments from construction companies was seized. Linda's name showed up on the list. Linda's attorney was able to obtain immunity from prosecution in exchange for her testimony.

Linda feared for her life because of the possibility that the mob might retaliate if she testified. However, her greatest fear was the possibility of newspaper publicity during the trial. She had the thought, "My family and the people I do business with will find out that I was dishonest. They will think I have no integrity. They'll lose respect for me." She wept out of guilt and shame as she shared these feelings with me.

Can you identify any distortions in her thoughts? Check the list on page 96 and put your ideas here:

1. _____

2. _____

3. _____

Linda is "jumping to conclusions," including both "fortune-telling" and "mind reading." She's predicting not only that she will get negative publicity but also that everybody will look down on her. She really doesn't know this. There may be no publicity. If there is, people may be sympathetic and admire her courage in testifying against organized crime.

An even more profound distortion is the "all-or-nothing thinking." Linda tells herself that she has "no integrity." In the following dialogue, I encouraged Linda to "think in shades of gray."

DR. BURNS: They will see that you have no integrity? How much integrity have you had for the past fifteen years, on a scale from 0 to 100%? Zero? A hundred? How much?

LINDA: I'd have to say 95%. I return checks if people overpay. I try to run my business in a scrupulous way. This was a situation where I did have bad judgment, though.

DR. BURNS: So if you have 95 percent integrity, how do you reconcile this with the claim that you have no integrity? You haven't been perfect, but it sounds like you've done pretty darn well—better than most, I suspect.

LINDA: But what will other people think of me?

DR. BURNS: The most important thing is what *you* think of you. Only *your* thoughts will affect your self-esteem. You're upset because you aren't accepting yourself as an imperfect human being. Let's do some play-acting. I'll be Linda and you can be a business associate. You read about my testimony in the *Chicago Tribune* and you saw me on the network news. I want you to say the worst imaginable things to me. Tell me I have no integrity and that you won't do business with me anymore.

LINDA (*as Critic*): Gee, I read about you in the *Chicago Tribune*. Did you really make those payments to the mob?

DR. BURNS (*as Linda*): Yes, I did. It was bad judgment and I wish I hadn't done it.

LINDA (*as Critic*): So, you did something dishonest. You tried to bribe the unions! You did it out of greed!

DR. BURNS (*as Linda*): That's correct. Greed and fear motivated me. The mob threatened to destroy me if I didn't give in. I was frightened and confused, and what I did was not right.

LINDA (*as Critic*): Well, why should I ever give you any other contracts? You're a real wheeler-dealer!

DR. BURNS (*as Linda*): You might want to give me another contract because of the top-notch work I've been doing for you. I believe my company is one of the best in the city.

LINDA (*as Critic*): But you screwed up! Admit it! I look down on you. I've got no respect for you.

DR. BURNS (*as Linda*): I agree! I *did* screw up and I wish I hadn't. I paid for my mistake and I've learned a lot as a result of it. If you want to look down on me, you can certainly do that. Lots of times I feel exactly the same way. However, I believe I can still do outstanding work for you. If you want the best building at an honest, competitive cost, I'm available and eager to work with you. If you want someone who never screwed up, you may have to look elsewhere. But there are a lot of sharks in the ocean, so be careful!

Obviously people would never really say such insulting things to Linda. The point of the exercise was to show her how to accept herself and to talk back to her own self-critical thoughts. She did screw up, and it was a horrendously difficult situation. She could get defensive and stubbornly insist she was an innocent victim, but that would be defensive and unrealistic. Linda could also condemn herself as a rotten person and give up. Or she could acknowledge her mistake, forgive herself, and move forward with her life.

Linda said that the session caused profound relief because she discovered that she didn't have to be perfect or afraid of admitting her shortcomings. Instead of seeing herself as having either perfect integrity or none at all, she learned to accept reality. Her integrity had been quite high, but not perfect. This insight allowed her to admit her error without a loss of self-esteem, so she could learn from the situation instead of despising herself forever.

6. The Survey Method

One way to evaluate a negative attitude is to ask yourself, "Would other people agree that this thought is valid?" You can often perform a survey to find out.

A man named Richard became very upset whenever he and his wife had an argument, because he told himself, "People who really love each other shouldn't fight." What kind of survey could Richard conduct to find out how realistic this attitude is? Put your ideas here:

_____

_____

_____

Answer: I suggested he ask several happily married friends if they ever fought with their wives. He was surprised that nearly all of them reported that angry feelings and arguments were commonplace.

The head of a prestigious law firm was constantly tense and pressured because he would tell himself, "My associates will think less of me if I lose a case or make a mistake." How could he conduct a survey to find out whether this is true? Put your ideas here:

_____

_____

_____

Answer: The lawyer decided to ask his associates about this. Most of them said they would like him more, not less, if he lost a case because it would make him seem more human. This was a tremendous relief.

A year later he actually did lose a case—the first in over a decade. At a social function of a statewide law organization he told numerous friends and acquaintances that he'd just lost an important case. He was surprised that about half the people were extremely friendly and supportive. The other half were uninterested in the case *he* lost but seemed tremendously eager to talk about cases *they'd* recently lost! It turned out to be the most rewarding meeting he'd ever attended. This helped him discover that it's okay to be human, that sometimes his failures could help him get closer to other people. He also admitted that his many impressive achievements had never really made him feel accepted or close to anyone.

7. Define Terms

When you have a negative thought, ask yourself, "How am I defining terms? What do I mean by this? Am I using vague, pejorative labels that have no real meaning?" This method is especially helpful if you are putting yourself down as "a failure" or "a loser" or "a jerk" or "a fool." Once you try to define what you mean by "loser," "jerk," or "fool," you will usually see that your definition is meaningless or that it doesn't apply to you. Since there really is no such thing as "a loser" or "a jerk" or "a fool," then you cannot possibly be one!

Here's how it works. You feel embarrassed about something and you think, "I'm such a fool." Now, ask yourself: what's the definition of "a fool"? You might define "a fool" as "someone who does something foolish." But according to this definition we're all fools, because we all do something foolish at some time or other in our lives. Unless you concede that all human beings are fools, your definition can't be valid. And if you feel that all human beings are fools, then it can't be so terrible for you to be one, since you're no different from anyone else.

Try again. You might define "a fool" as "someone who does foolish things more often than other people." Now ask yourself what this means. More often than whom? More often than how many other people? You might say that a fool is one who does foolish things more often than half the human race. But now you're in the awkward position of claiming that half the human race—or two billion people—are "fools." In addition, you're now categorizing all people as either "fools" or "non-fools." Can you imagine walking down a crowded downtown sidewalk at the lunch hour and trying to figure out which of the people you see are the "fools" and which are the "non-fools"?

You can go on trying to define "a fool," but your definition will always turn into nonsense. That's because foolish behavior exists, but "fools" do not. Only human beings exist. Is this just semantics, a trick of words? No, it's not. Labels like "fool," "loser," "winner," "jerk," or "inferior person" are useless abstractions. It is far more productive to focus on what you *do*—and what you can do to learn and grow—than on what you *are*. If things don't work out well, ask yourself what you can do differently next time.

8. The Semantic Method

When you feel upset, ask yourself if you're telling yourself, "I *should* do this" or "I *shouldn't* do that." The Semantic Method is an effective way to combat "should statements." Substitute a phrase like "it would be nice" or "it would be preferable" in place of "I should." Instead of saying "I should go on a diet," you could tell yourself that "there would be some advantages in dieting." This change may seem subtle. We're trying to change the emotional coloring so a problem will seem less upsetting and less catastrophic. You stop making rigid, coercive demands on yourself and focus instead on your goals. This sounds less bossy and less judgmental.

You might be interested to know that the word "should" traces its origin to the Anglo-Saxon word "sceolde." The purpose of the Semantic Method is to help you stop scolding yourself. If you motivate yourself with a carrot rather than a stick, you won't feel so guilty and so coerced. When you punish yourself with "should statements," you will frequently just run into resistance because you feel rebellious.

If you feel anxious about public speaking or being at social gatherings, you may tell yourself, "I shouldn't feel this way." Can you see why this is self-defeating? It's self-defeating because it will make you feel worse. You'll feel guilty and anxious about feeling anxious.

What could you tell yourself instead of "I shouldn't feel anxious"? Use the Semantic Method and put your ideas here:

_____

_____

_____

_____

Answer: You could tell yourself that it would be *preferable* not to feel so anxious before a speech. You could also remind yourself that most people do have this problem. You will learn a great deal about how to cope with public speaking anxiety in Chapter 15.

So far we've talked about "self shoulds"—should statements directed against yourself. "Other shoulds" are directed against external events, like trains that arrive late or people who do something you don't like. "Other shoulds" lead to anger and frustration. If your train is late you may think, "It should be on time!" Then you will feel exasperated. Ask yourself if you want to feel this way. There are times when anger is healthy, but is this one of them? Will you do yourself any good if you work yourself into a stew? Will the train arrive any sooner?

How could you use the Semantic Method to talk back to this negative thought? Put your ideas here:

_____

_____

_____

_____

Answer: Instead of demanding perfection from the world, you could say, "It would be great if this train were on time, but it's late. That's inconvenient, but I'll survive. Next time I'll take an earlier train so I won't feel so pressured."

After giving a lecture on my book *Feeling Good*, I spoke with a woman who described her recent vacation to Hawaii with her family. When they arrived she discovered that the airline had lost all their luggage. She had spent so much time carefully buying and packing all the right clothes so they would have a perfect vacation! To make matters worse, their luggage wasn't even located until the last day of their vacation!

How would you have felt? You might have told yourself, "This shouldn't have happened!" Then you would feel miserable. Would you want to feel that way while you were in Hawaii?

She said they made the conscious decision not to get upset. Instead, they viewed the situation as a challenge. They made a game of it to see how much fun they could have without their luggage. She said they had more fun than on any vacation they'd ever had.

9. Re-attribution

One of the commonest cognitive distortions is called "personalization," or self-blame. You put yourself down and blame yourself for a problem you aren't entirely responsible for. One antidote to personalization is "re-attribution": you attribute the cause of a problem to something other than your "badness." Ask yourself, "What other factors may have contributed to this problem?" Then develop a list of possibilities. The aim of the procedure is not to deny any mistakes you might have made, but to assess the causes of a problem more objectively. If you contributed to the situation, accept this and try to learn from the experience instead of wallowing in self-loathing.

A man named Frank became depressed when his wife began to lose interest in sex. They had intercourse less frequently, and sometimes she just seemed to be staring at the ceiling waiting for Frank to finish. Frank's Automatic Thoughts were: "She doesn't love me. She's rejecting me. I must not be worth anything." What are the distortions in these thoughts? Check the list on page 96 and put your ideas here:

1. _____

2. _____

3. _____

Answer: One distortion is "personalization"—Frank is blaming himself entirely for his wife's sexual problem. A second is "mind reading"—he assumes that she doesn't love him. A third is "all-or-nothing thinking"—he tells himself he's "worthless."

To talk back to these thoughts, Frank can use the re-attribution method. He needs to explore other causes of his wife's loss of sexual interest. Are there any other possible reasons? Even if you're not a marriage therapist, I suspect you can come up with a few ideas. List them here:

1. _____

2. _____

3. _____

Answer: There are many possibilities. She might be angry with him about something. If they have trouble dealing openly with negative feelings, as so many couples do, then these feelings could easily get expressed as a lack of sexual interest. This would not mean that she didn't love Frank or that Frank was worthless. It would simply mean they needed to talk about their angry feelings.

There are other possibilities. Frank's wife could have an infection that causes pain during intercourse. She could have religious inhibitions that make it hard for her to enjoy sex. She could feel that Frank's lovemaking is too rushed but may be afraid to talk to him about what she likes and dislikes sexually because she doesn't want to hurt his feelings. She might also be depressed. A loss of interest in sex is a common symptom of depression.

Once Frank finds out what the cause of the problem is, he will be able to deal with it more effectively. Frank asked his wife to join us during his sessions and it turned out that she did have some pent-up anger that was making it hard for her to feel sexually excited. Frank also felt angry and rejected. After they shared those feelings they began to feel much better about each other, and her sexual interest returned.

10. Cost-Benefit Analysis

The Cost-Benefit Analysis is quite different from other cognitive techniques because it deals with your negative thoughts from the perspective of motivation rather than truth. Ask yourself, "How will it help me to believe this negative thought and how will it hurt me?" If it turns out the disadvantages are greater, you will find it easier to talk back to the thought. You can use the blank Cost-Benefit Analysis form on page 114 when you do this.

I recently treated a high school teacher named Chuck, who didn't get very high ratings from his students or from the principal. In addition to his career problems, Chuck had suffered from depression and feelings of inferiority since childhood. One of his recurring negative thoughts was "I'm an inadequate, defective human being." He had this thought many times every day, and whenever it crossed his mind he felt intense self-loathing. However, Chuck was unable to talk back to this negative thought. He believed that he really was an inadequate, defective human being because:

He'd been chronically depressed.

He had no self-esteem.

He was below par in his teaching skills.

He had few friends.

He didn't get along well with his family.

He felt shy and uncomfortable around women.

He'd never accomplished anything special that he could feel proud of.

I tried in vain to persuade Chuck that he was *not* "an inadequate, defective human being." Chuck insisted he was facing the bitter truth about himself and urged me to give up on him.

After months of being stuck on this issue, a light bulb went on in my head one evening when I was thinking about him. I called him the next morning and said that I wanted him to make one list of the advantages and disadvantages of calling himself "an inadequate, defective human being" and a second list of the advantages and disadvantages of thinking of himself as "a human being with defects." He agreed.

When I saw Chuck several days later, his depression had vanished. Chuck said that what I'd been driving at suddenly became clear to

COST-BENEFIT ANALYSIS*

The attitude or belief I want to change:_____

_____

_____

Advantages of Believing This	Disadvantages of Believing This

Revised Attitude:_____

_____

_____

him. The real problem, he explained, was not that he was defective at the core but that he had defects just like everyone else and that he could work on them. He said he could work on becoming a more effective teacher and he could learn to relate to people better. He said that although this difference in his thinking seemed small, the impact on his self-esteem was profound because he viewed himself more positively and realistically.

In the next few weeks, Chuck started dating and making all kinds of changes in his life. He was surprised to discover that the moment he felt better about himself, everyone else started liking him as well. Women were suddenly attracted to him, and his colleagues and students began to treat him with greater respect.

Although this seemed like a miracle, I see similar changes in my office every week. Self-esteem is one of the most powerful forces in the universe. Self-esteem leads to joy, to productivity, to intimacy. That's why I advocate a value system that promotes self-esteem. Self-esteem is like faith: it can move mountains!

The Cost-Benefit Analysis has many useful applications. You can use it to evaluate the advantages and disadvantages of negative emotions, negative thoughts and self-defeating beliefs.

- *Negative feelings:* When you feel angry, anxious or guilty, you can ask yourself, "How will it help me, and how will it hurt me, to feel this way?" When the disadvantages outweigh the advantages, it will be far easier to change your feelings with the Daily Mood Log.
- *Automatic Thoughts:* When you have a thought such as "I'm such a loser" or "I *shouldn't* be so upset," make a list of the advantages and disadvantages of giving yourself this message.
- *Self-Defeating Attitudes:* In the next chapter, you will learn that certain self-defeating attitudes can trigger painful mood swings. An example would be: "I must always try to be perfect" or "I must always try to get everybody's approval." You can ask yourself, "How will it help me, and how will it hurt me, to believe this," as in the example on page 116. When the disadvantages of an attitude are greater than the advantages, try to revise it with a belief that will be more realistic, as on page 116.

You may feel a little overwhelmed and wonder when and how to use each of these techniques. In fact, you can use almost any technichue for any Automatic Thought. By flexible and creative. Try a variety of methods until you find a way to put the lie to each

COST-BENEFIT ANALYSIS*

The attitude or belief I want to change: __I must have everybody's__

__approval to be happy and worthwhile.__

Advantages of Believing This	Disadvantages of Believing This
1. It will feel good when people approve of me. 2. I'll work hard to make people like me. 3. I'll be very sensitive to other people's feelings.	1. I'll feel lousy when people don't like me or approve of me. 2. Other people will control my self-esteem. 3. People may not respect me in the long run if I don't stand up for what I believe in. 4. I may be less sensitive to other people because I'll be so worried about criticism or conflict.

(35)———————————(65)

Revised Attitude: __It can be great to have people like me and approve__

__of what I do. When people are critical of me, I can try to understand__

__their point of view.__

*Copyright © 1984 by David D. Burns, M.D., from *The Feeling Good Handbook*, copyright © 1989

negative thought. Sometimes this will be easy, and sometimes it will require persistence. The summary on page 118 will help you identify the methods that are most likely to help.

You may be wondering when you should use each of the various techniques. I believe that you should always "identify the distortion" first. You will discover that certain techniques work especially well for particular kinds of distortions. For example, if the distortion in your negative thought is "all-or-nothing thinking," the method called "Thinking in Shades of Gray" is likely to help. If your negative thought is a "should statement," the "Semantic Method" will nearly always work well. If you're involved in "emotional reasoning," you may find it helpful to Examine the Evidence, or you could use the Experimental Technique.

Remember that any cognitive technique can usually be used with any negative thought, so don't be rigid in trying to match specific techniques to specific distortions. Also keep in mind that a method that works wonders for one negative thought may not be at all helpful for another. Determination and patience are crucial. If you keep at it, you will succeed!

I once treated a woman who had the thought "I deserve to suffer for the rest of my life because of my abortion." She had had an abortion two years earlier, and she felt enormously guilty. She told herself she was despicable and berated herself mercilessly all day long. I tried numerous methods to help her talk back to this thought, but none of them worked. She said she deserved to suffer and insisted that her problems were hopeless. We worked on her need to condemn herself for many months, with no success. Eventually, I asked her husband to join us for couples therapy sessions. Once they started to feel closer, she was able to forgive herself. After she let go of the guilt and the self-hatred, her depression disappeared. I still hear from her occasionally. She's had two more children and feels an immense joy in living.

I tell you this story because it illustrates the importance of patience and persistence. You may have to be creative and try many ways of challenging the negative thoughts that make you miserable. One of the great strengths of cognitive therapy is its enormous flexibility. Eventually you will learn to talk back to your self-criticisms. When you do, you will experience a profound transformation in your spirit and in your outlook on life.

TEN WAYS TO UNTWIST
YOUR THINKING*

1. **Identify the Distortion.** Write down your negative thoughts so you can see which of the ten cognitive distortions you're involved in. This will make it easier to think about the problem in a more positive and realistic way.

2. **Examine the Evidence.** Instead of assuming that your negative thought is true, examine the actual evidence for it. For example, if you feel that you never do anything right, you could list several things you have done successfully.

3. **The Double-Standard Method:** Instead of putting yourself down in a harsh, condemning way, talk to yourself in the same compassionate way you would talk to a friend with a similar problem.

4. **The Experimental Technique:** Do an experiment to test the validity of your negative thought. For example, if, during an episode of panic, you become terrified that you're about to die of a heart attack, you could jog or run up and down several flights of stairs. This will prove that your heart is healthy and strong.

5. **Thinking in Shades of Gray.** Although this method might sound drab, the effects can be illuminating. Instead of thinking about your problems in all-or-nothing extremes, evaluate things on a range from 0 to 100. When things don't work out as well as you hoped, think about the experience as a partial success rather than a complete failure. See what you can learn from the situation.

6. **The Survey Method.** Ask people questions to find out if your thoughts and attitudes are realistic. For example, if you believe that public speaking anxiety is abnormal and shameful, ask several friends if they ever felt nervous before they gave a talk.

7. **Define Terms.** When you label yourself "inferior" or "a fool" or "a loser," ask, "What is the definition of 'a fool'?" You will feel better when you see that there is no such thing as "a fool" or "a loser."

8. **The Semantic Method.** Simply substitute language that is less colorful and emotionally loaded. This method is helpful for "should statements." Instead of telling yourself "I *shouldn't* have made that mistake," you can say, "It would be better if I hadn't made that mistake."

9. **Re-attribution.** Instead of automatically assuming that you are "bad" and blaming yourself entirely for a problem, think about the many factors that may have contributed to it. Focus on solving the problem instead of using up all your energy blaming yourself and feeling guilty.

10. **Cost-Benefit Analysis.** List the advantages and disadvantages of a feeling (like getting angry when your plane is late), a negative thought (like "No matter how hard I try, I always screw up"), or a behavior pattern (like overeating and lying around in bed when you're depressed). You can also use the Cost-Benefit Analysis to modify a self-defeating belief such as, "I must always try to be perfect."

7

◆

How to Develop a Healthy Personal Value System

While the purpose of cognitive therapy is to help you solve specific problems in the here-and-now, it can also help you develop greater emotional strength and wisdom for the future. As you review your negative thoughts, you may discover certain recurring self-defeating attitudes. You may find that you're overly guilt-prone because you automatically blame yourself for everyone else's problems. You may discover that your anxiety and depression are usually triggered by criticism or arguments with people you care about. You may learn that you're a perfectionist, worrying excessively about failing at work or school or letting others down. You may discover that you are extremely vulnerable to stress because you think about things in an "all-or-nothing" manner and your performance never seems quite good enough.

Common attitudes that often lead to depression and anxiety are listed on page 121. As you review the list you may recognize the ones that are causing problems for you. These are sometimes called "silent assumptions." They make you vulnerable to painful mood swings. Once you identify them, you can work on them from a variety of angles and develop a healthier personal value system.

COMMON SELF-DEFEATING
ATTITUDES AND FEARS

1. "It would be terrible to be rejected, abandoned, or alone. I must have love and approval before I can feel good about myself."

2. "If someone criticizes me, it means there's something wrong with me."

3. "I must always please people and live up to everyone's expectations."

4. "I am basically defective and inferior to other people."

5. "Other people are to blame for my problems."

6. "The world should always be the way I want it to be."

7. "Other people should always meet my expectations."

8. "If I worry or feel bad about a situation, it will somehow make things better. It's not really safe to feel happy and optimistic."

9. "I'm hopeless and bound to feel depressed forever because the problems in my life are impossible to solve."

10. "I must always try to be perfect." There are several kinds of perfectionism that can make you unhappy.

    - Moralistic perfectionism: "I must not forgive myself if I have fallen short of any goal or personal standard."
    - Performance perfectionism: "To be a worthwhile person, I must be a great success at everything I do."
    - Identity perfectionism: "People will never accept me as a flawed and vulnerable human being."
    - Emotional perfectionism "I must always try to be happy. I must control my negative emotions and never feel anxious or depressed."
    - Romantic perfectionism: "I must find a perfect mate and always feel infatuated with him or her."
    - Relationship perfectionism: "People who love each other should never fight or feel angry with each other."
    - Sexual perfectionism: Men may believe "I should always have full and sustained erections. It's shameful and unmanly if I have an episode of impotence or come too quickly." Women may believe "I should always achieve orgasm or multiple orgasms."
    - Appearance perfectionism: "I look ugly because I'm slightly overweight [or have heavy thighs or a facial blemish]."

The Vertical Arrow Technique

The "Vertical Arrow Technique" can help you pinpoint your silent assumptions. The methods described in Chapter 6 involve putting the lie to your negative thoughts. You show that your negative thoughts aren't true by using logic, by examining the evidence, by doing experiments, and so on. The Vertical Arrow Technique involves precisely the opposite strategy. You *buy into* your negative thoughts and see where they lead you. This can help you understand the self-defeating beliefs that are creating unnecessary barriers to self-esteem, intimacy, and productivity.

Here's how you do it. First, identify a negative thought about a situation that's upsetting you. Suppose you're studying for an exam and you think, "If I don't study harder, I may blow it." This thought makes you tense and you have a hard time concentrating. Write this thought down and draw a small downward arrow underneath it, as illustrated on page 124. The arrow means "If this thought were true, why would it be upsetting to me? What would it mean to me?" You might think, "If I blow the test, I may fail the course." Then write this down as your second negative thought and put another arrow underneath it. Remember that the downward arrow always means "If that thought were true, why would it be upsetting to me? What would it mean to me?" These questions will lead to another negative thought, and then another, as illustrated.

After you've generated as many negative thoughts as you can, review what you've written. Ask yourself, "What do these negative thoughts tell me about my value system? What are my basic assumptions about the basis of happiness and self-esteem?" Now study the four Automatic Thoughts that are illustrated on page 124. Ask yourself what the silent assumptions are. Write your ideas here before you read on.

1. _____

2. _____

3. _____

Answer: The Automatic Thoughts contain several silent assumptions: (1) I must always be a success in life to be worthwhile and to be loved and respected by others. (2) I must get everybody's approval to be a worthwhile person. (3) If I fail to achieve any goal, it will be a catastrophe. Review the sample again and see if you agree.

One of the remarkable things about the Vertical Arrow Technique is that you can identify these self-defeating attitudes very rapidly. I often use the procedure in the first or second therapy session with a new patient. This allows me to pinpoint his or her underlying fears within five to ten minutes—considerably quicker than the years it might take to learn about yourself with psychoanalysis! The man whose thoughts are illustrated here in Figure 10 suffered from low self-esteem. He had a terrific fear of failure and abandonment and a desperate need for approval. These attitudes crippled him.

Once you have identified a silent assumption, you should ask yourself these three questions about it: (1) Is it to my advantage to believe this? What are the consequences, positive and negative, of this attitude? (2) Is it realistic to think this way? Is my silent assumption really valid? (3) What would happen if I confronted my worst fear? Would the world really come to an end if I changed this attitude?

The following three-step program will show you how you can develop healthier attitudes that will lead to better self-esteem and improved relationships with others.

STEP ONE: COST-BENEFIT ANALYSIS

You can evaluate the consequences of my silent assumption with the Cost-Benefit Analysis described in Chapter 6: you list the advantages and disadvantages of believing it. This helps you decide if a particular attitude is helping you or hurting you.

Let's work this out together, using the belief "I must always be a success in life to be worthwhile." Can you think of any advantages of thinking this way? Keep in mind that I'm not asking you about the advantages of being successful—I'm asking about the advantages of basing your self-esteem on your success. How will it help you to think you must earn your self-esteem through your achievements?

List the advantages of this attitude here:

1. _____

_____

THE VERTICAL ARROW TECHNIQUE*

Automatic thoughts

1. **If I don't study harder, I may blow the exam.**

   If this were true, what would it mean to me? Why would it be upsetting to me?

2. **If I blow the exam, I may fail the course.**

   And if I failed, why would that be uspetting to me?

3. **That would mean I was a failure and people would think less of me.**

   And if I was "a failure" and if people thought less of me, what then? Why would this be upsetting?

4. **Then I'd feel terrible, because I need people's approval to feel happy and to be worthwhile.**

2. _____

_____

3. _____

_____

4._____

_____

I can think of several: (1) You will work very hard to be successful.
(2) Your value system will be similar to a lot of other people's. After
all, many people believe that more successful people are inherently
more worthwhile. This Calvinist work ethic has actually been around
for over 200 years. (3) Life will seem simple and clear to you. You'll
know exactly what you have to do to be worthwhile. (4) When you
succeed at something, you'll feel good because you'll think, "I'm
worthwhile now because I got an 'A' [or a promotion]."

Now, can you think of any disadvantages to this attitude? List
them here:

1. _____

_____

2. _____

_____

3. _____

_____

4. _____

_____

Here are several that come to my mind: (1) You'll always be on a
treadmill, having to *earn* your self-esteem. You'll never feel truly

worthwhile inside, because you'll never know for sure whether you will continue to be successful. Even highly paid professional athletes can go into slumps. Sooner or later they age and lose their incredible athletic skills. Are they less worthwhile then? (2) You may feel lots of anxiety and avoid doing anything creative because of your fear of failure. (3) When you fail, you may get depressed because you will feel that you're not very worthwhile or lovable. (4) Even when you succeed, you may feel inferior to other people who are even more intelligent and successful—and there will always be someone who's doing better. (5) You may not pursue what *you* want in life because you're too busy figuring out how to be successful so you can get everyone's approval. As a result, you may end up being less happy and successful than if you believed in yourself and pursued the goals that made sense to you.

Once you've listed the advantages and disadvantages of a particular attitude, ask yourself which are greater. Does it help you or hurt you more to believe "I must be a success in life to be worthwhile"? If the disadvantages are greater, you will want to revise this attitude. What new attitude could you adopt instead? Put your suggestions here:

_____

_____

_____

_____

Answer: I like to think about it this way: "It's important to me to be productive and to do my best. Sometimes I'll do well and sometimes things won't turn out the way I hoped. I can enjoy my successes, but they won't make me any better than anyone else. My failures will be disappointing, but I can learn from them and they won't make me any less lovable or worthwhile."

For some readers, this new attitude will be obvious. For others it may be hard to grasp, hard to accept. There are strong influences in our culture that make us think that "winners" are more special and more lovable. I would suggest that the truth is the opposite: You can never be loved for your successes—only for your vulnerabilities. People may be attracted to you and may admire you if you are a great success. They may also resent and envy you. But they can never *love* you for your successes.

The attitude "My worth as a human being depends on my success" is neither true nor false. You are simply defining worthwhile human beings as those who achieve the most. This attitude could never be proven or disproven. Like any value system, it will have certain positive and negative consequences. The Cost-Benefit Analysis allows you to sort them out.

If you decide that you don't like this value system, you can decide to think of your self-esteem as unconditional, as something that doesn't have to be earned. This new attitude will also have certain consequences. One will be that you will always feel worthwhile, even when you fail. Another consequence is that you will never feel inferior to, or better than, any other human being. You will still take great pleasure in being productive, but your degree of success will not dominate your sense of self-esteem. You will never look down on people who are less successful and talented, and you will never feel less worthy than anyone else, no matter how successful or intelligent they are. So it really boils down to the consequences you choose for your life.

As an exercise, choose one of the silent assumptions from the list on page 121, and do a Cost-Benefit Analysis, using the blank form on page 128.

STEP TWO: TEST YOUR BELIEF

Let's assume that you have completed your Cost-Benefit Analysis and decided that an attitude of yours has more disadvantages than advantages. As the next step, you can ask yourself if that attitude is realistic. Sometimes you can do an experiment to test the validity of your silent assumption. I once treated a depressed perfectionistic physician who had complained of feeling frustrated and unrewarded for many years, despite substantial academic accomplishments. He desperately wanted to change because he could see that he was burning up way too much time on projects he couldn't complete because they were never quite good enough. He couldn't seem to let go of his compulsive perfectionism because he had the belief that he couldn't really enjoy anything in life unless he did it in an outstanding manner. He told me: "Dr. Burns, I struggle and struggle to

COST-BENEFIT ANALYSIS*

The attitude or belief I want to change:_____

_____

_____

Advantages of Believing This	Disadvantages of Believing This

*Revised Attitude:*_____

_____

_____

climb to the top of the mountain. But when I get there, I just see an even higher peak in the distance, and I feel tremendously let down. My parents always told me I should try to be number one. But where's the reward? Where's the payoff?"

Like many perfectionists, he believed he couldn't experience satisfaction from any activity unless he performed it perfectly. He found out differently—and thus won a degree of freedom from his perfectionism—after he tested this belief. First, he scheduled a series of activities with a potential for personal growth, satisfaction, or pleasure and predicted how satisfying each of them would be, using a scale between 0 and 100. After each activity was completed, he recorded how satisfying it actually was and estimated how well he performed.

The form he completed is illustrated on page 132. He was surprised to learn that he could experience greater personal satisfaction in doing a below-average job of fixing a broken pipe that had flooded his kitchen than in giving an outstanding lecture to a group of medical students. The discovery helped him realize that an excellent performance was neither necessary nor sufficient for satisfaction. In fact, he was shocked to observe that many activities he did in an "average" or "below-average" way were among the most rewarding. As a result, he began to think about activities in terms of their potential for making him feel rewarded. He reported that this helped him to feel more relaxed and gave him the courage to initiate a number of exciting professional projects about which he had procrastinated for years because he had feared an imperfect outcome.

Many people experience depression after a divorce or a romantic rejection. One reason is their belief that if they are alone, it means they are unlovable and bound to feel unhappy. What experiment could you do to test this belief? Put your ideas here:

_____

_____

_____

_____

Answer: You could use the Pleasure-Predicting Sheet on page 131. First, schedule a series of activities with the potential for pleasure (such as reading a good book) or personal growth (such as jogging) in the Activities column. In the Companion column, record whom you will do each activity with. Make sure you do some activities by yourself (put "self" in the Companion column) and some activities with friends or family (put their names in the Companion column). Before you do each activity, estimate how satisfying it will be on a scale from 0 percent to 100 percent in the Predicted Satisfaction column. After you have completed each activity, record how satisfying it turned out to be between 0 percent and 100 percent in the Actual Satisfaction column.

A woman who was separated from her husband did this experiment. She was surprised to discover that many of her most satisfying activities were the ones she did by herself, even though she anticipated feeling lonely and miserable. This was not consistent with her belief that if she was alone, she was bound to feel miserable. This gave her confidence a boost. Her mood brightened and his interest in her suddenly increased because she was no longer so needy and dependent on him.

STEP THREE: THE FEARED FANTASY TECHNIQUE

The Feared Fantasy Technique is another powerful cognitive method that can help you modify a self-defeating attitude. Essentially, you confront your worst fears in a dramatic way—and you discover that the monster you've been so afraid of is not real but just a hot air balloon.

The method should be of great interest to psychologists and psychiatrists because it represents a synthesis of cognitive therapy and behavior therapy. Behavior therapy is based on the notion that you must confront your fears before you can conquer them. If you have an elevator phobia, you must get on the elevator and stay there, no matter how frightened you feel, until your anxiety has vanished. This method usually does work. With the Feared Fantasy Technique, exactly the same thing happens except that the fear you confront results from a thought or an attitude, such as "I must be a success in life to be worthwhile."

I demonstrated the Feared Fantasy Technique at a recent meeting of the American Psychiatric Association. One of the participants, a psychologist named Manuel, agreed to play the role of a patient so I could show the audience how cognitive therapy actually works. As it turned out, the demonstration became quite real. Manuel had tears in

PLEASURE-PREDICTING SHEET*

Activity	Companion	Satisfaction	
		Predicted	Actual
Schedule activities with a potential for pleasure or personal growth	(If alone, specify "self")	(0–100%) Record this before each activity	(0–100%) Record this after each activity

THE PLEASURE-PERFECTION BALANCE SHEET			
Activity	Predict how satisfying the activity will be	Record how satisfying it actually was	Record how effectively you performed
Fix broken pipe in kitchen	20%	99% (I actually did it.)	20% (I took a long time and made a lot of mistakes.)
Give a lecture to medical school class	70%	50% (I didn't feel particularly gratified about my performance.)	98% (As usual, I got a standing ovation.)
Play squash with Joe	75%	90% (Even though I didn't play especially well, we had a hell of a good time.)	40% (I played subpar. So what?)
Jog to store and get ice cream cone	60%	90% (It was fun!)	50% (I did not improve my time for jogging this distance.)

his eyes once he began to talk about his belief that he had to be perfect to earn people's love. He said he felt ashamed because he cried and showed weakness in front of his professional peers. He was convinced they would look down on him.

I suggested we use the Feared Fantasy method to deal with this concern. I told him he could pretend to be a mean colleague named Jack and I would be Manuel. Jack would put me down and say the cruelest things he could possibly think of.

MANUEL (*as Jack*): Hi, Manuel! Didn't I see you doing that demonstration with Dr. Burns last week at our annual meeting?

DR. BURNS (*as Manuel*): Yes, that was me up in front. What did you think of the demonstration?

MANUEL (*as Jack*): Honestly, Manuel, I was embarrassed. You seemed to be on the verge of crying.

DR. BURNS (*as Manuel*): Actually, tears did come to my eyes during the demonstration. I found it very moving. Why was this embarrassing for you?

MANUEL (*as Jack*): Well, for a grown man, a psychologist no less, to be crying in front of a group of his associates is kind of inappropriate, don't you think?

DR. BURNS (*as Manuel*): You mean it's inappropriate to show my feelings? Or it's inappropriate to have strong feelings? Or what? I don't exactly get your drift.

MANUEL (*as Jack*): Well honestly, Manuel, crying in public like that isn't the most professional or put-together thing in the world.

DR. BURNS (*as Manuel*): I see. You think that a "put-together" person would not be moved to tears. Do you think less of me because I was moved to tears?

MANUEL (*as Jack*): As a matter of fact, I do. I don't intend to be cruel, but I feel you deserve to know the truth. I think you're a jerk.

DR. BURNS (*as Manuel*): Well, I could understand you might not approve of crying during a psychotherapy demonstration. I *do* think it's okay, and we could have a gentlemen's disagreement about that. The experience turned out to be extremely valuable for me because I learned to believe in myself and to stop being so afraid of criticism. You might not approve of being moved to tears or crying. You might think that it's more professional or manly to control your emotions in certain situations. For my part, I think we'd be better off if we were more natural and felt free to show our feelings. But I still can't grasp why you think I'm "a jerk." Am I "a jerk" because I cried? Or because I disagree with you? Or what?

MANUEL (*as Jack*): Touché. I give up!

We then reversed roles, and I became the ruthless critic. I tried to put Manuel down for crying, and he talked back to me. He did beautifully. He said the exercise gave him tremendous self-confidence. After the workshop was over, one of the participants said that the demonstration was one of the most moving experiences he'd had in many years. He said he was grateful that Manuel had dared to share his feelings with the group. It shows just how off-base we can sometimes be with our fears and self-doubt. Sometimes the vulnerabilities we try so hard to hide can be our greatest assets in terms of getting close to others!

You can do the Feared Fantasy exercise with a therapist or with a friend, or you can do it as a written exercise on your own. The following is an example that a patient of mine, Linda, completed as a homework assignment between sessions. Linda is attractive and personable and has a great career as a stockbroker, but she is afraid to flirt with men and to develop an intimate relationship because of her intense fears of becoming vulnerable and risking rejection. The Vertical Arrow Technique (see page 124) indicated that Linda's problems stemmed from "emotional perfectionism." She believed that she should never have or reveal negative feelings like anger, anxiety, or sadness. She thought that to be loved, she had to be a "perfectly mature" woman who was always completely poised and in control of her emotions. She felt that as soon as any man discovered her real self, she'd be rejected. Rather than risking this, she settled for loneliness.

I asked her to write out a dialogue with an imaginary man who was rejecting her after several dates because she was "too emotional." I told her to make him much worse than any real man would ever be, and to say the cruelest, most upsetting things she could think of. The purpose of the exercise was to get her to confront her worst fears so she wouldn't have to spend the rest of her life feeling afraid of intimacy. The following is a brief excerpt from the dialogue she wrote.

REJECTING MAN: Well, Linda, I've decided that I need a little "space," so I won't be seeing you for a while.

LINDA: I find that upsetting. Can you tell me what the problem is?

REJECTING MAN: Yes, I'll be happy to. You're emotionally retarded. You worry and you get upset about things. You're not strong. Now that I know you well, I'm disgusted, so I'm going to leave you.

LINDA: It sounds like your main complaint is that I get upset at times and I'm not strong and tough enough emotionally.

REJECTING MAN: Yes, that's just the problem. You always overreact. You're such a neurotic. When I met you, I thought you had it all together, but now I see you're an emotional invalid.

LINDA: Well, it's true that I do get upset about lots of things. I worry when the market goes down and my clients lose money. I also feel quite annoyed right now. These are just two things I have strong feelings about—there are many more. Do you think these strong feelings make me an "emotional invalid"? Are you looking for a woman with no feelings? Or am I misreading you? What exactly *is* your point?

The dialogue illustrates how Linda confronted her belief that a man could love her only if she met some ideal of how a perfectly mature woman feels and behaves. Writing out the dialogue helped Linda see that this ideal really represented an emotional strait-jacket, and that if someone did reject her because she had feelings, it might be a blessing in disguise. Who would really want to be married to a man who didn't want his wife to have feelings? As obvious as it might seem, this insight helped her accept herself as a spontaneous and emotional woman. This gave her the courage to break out of her self-imposed isolation and to reach out to others.

Cognitive therapy has two goals: to help you feel better in the here-and-now, and to help you develop a more realistic personal value system so that you will not be so vulnerable to painful mood swings and conflicts with others in the future. The Vertical Arrow Technique can make you more aware of the beliefs and attitudes that may be causing problems for you. These silent assumptions are always operating in your mind, and they influence the way you react to the good and bad things that happen to you.

Once you identify one of your silent assumptions, you can evaluate it with a Cost-Benefit Analysis. This will help you sort out the advantages and disadvantages of believing it. You will see that these attitudes are always two-edged swords, with a healthy side and a hurtful, destructive side. When the disadvantages of an attitude outweigh the advantages, it can motivate you to think about things in a more self-enhancing way.

After you perform the Cost-Benefit Analysis, you should ask yourself if your silent assumption is realistic. Sometimes you can do an experiment to test the validity of your belief. When you see that an attitude is both self-defeating and unrealistic, you will be far more motivated to develop a new attitude that is more positive and helpful.

The Feared Fantasy Technique can help you transform your new attitude into an emotional conviction. This technique can be valuable because even when you have made an intellectual decision to change your attitude, you may still wilt in the face of adversity. But when you confront your own worst fears you will begin to realize that they're not nearly as terrifying as you thought. This experience can be liberating!

8

•

Cognitive Therapy in Action: How to Break Out of a Bad Mood

In the last two chapters you learned about a variety of methods that can help you develop more positive attitudes and greater self-esteem. These techniques are the basic tools you will need in order to talk back to the Automatic Thoughts that upset you. In this chapter, I'll show you how you can integrate these methods in a creative and effective way so you can deal with a variety of common mood problems, such as feelings of inferiority and insecurity, irritability and low self-esteem, frustration, guilt, stress, and depression.

Mood Problem #1: Feelings of Inferiority and Insecurity in Social Situations

I recently treated a single man from Miami named Chuck. Chuck was concerned because he had a mild congenital chest abnormality in which the breastbone is curved inward, giving the chest a sunken appearance. Aside from this, Chuck is tall and good-looking. Whenever he thinks about going to the beach he feels so self-conscious that he decides to stay home instead. Chuck says he could never take his shirt off in front of other people because he tells himself: "I'm inferior to all these other men who have such better physiques. If I take off my shirt, everyone will stare at me and think I am abnormal."

For the moment, put yourself in Chuck's shoes. There may have been a time when you felt inferior to other people because you felt your figure wasn't good enough—you weren't tall enough, or thin enough, or smart enough. What are the distortions in Chuck's first negative thought: "I'm inferior to all these other men who have such better physiques"? Review the list on page 96 and list the distortions here:

1. _____

2. _____

3. _____

4. _____

Answer: It's clearly an "overgeneralization." Chuck is generalizing from his chest to his self. It may be that his *chest* is inferior, but does that make *him* an inferior person? You could also call this the "mental filter" plus "discounting the positive," since Chuck is thinking only about his one weak point, his chest, and he's ignoring his many good features. (He's tall, broad-shouldered, athletic, attractive, bright, warm and friendly, and he earns a good living.) Finally, he's involved in "emotional reasoning." He says, "I *feel* inferior and abnormal, therefore I must *be* inferior and abnormal."

As an exercise, see if you can identify the distortions in his second Automatic Thought: "If I take off my shirt, everyone will stare at me and think I am abnormal." Review the list on page 96 and list the distortions here:

1. _____

2. _____

3. _____

4. _____

5. _____

Answer: Chuck is involved in an "overgeneralization." Some people might stare at him, but not *everyone* will. He's also "jumping to conclusions," including "mind reading" and "fortune-telling." He doesn't know what other people will be thinking. Most people probably have better things to think about and won't dwell on the idea that he's abnormal. He's also "labeling" himself in a negative way: "abnormal" is a heavily loaded word. "Emotional reasoning" is a fourth distortion. He *feels* that he'll be the center of attention, so he concludes that he really will be. Finally, he's "magnifying" the importance of his chest to the people on the beach. He would probably be surprised to discover that most people just don't care very much about what he looks like.

How could Chuck talk back to these two negative thoughts, using the methods described in the last two chapters? One method would be to "examine the evidence." Chuck could go to the beach and see if it's true that all the men there have better physiques. He'd probably see a few muscle builders who did have magnificent bodies, but he'd also see lots of other men—and women—who weren't so fabulous looking. There would be fat people and skinny people and old people with wrinkles. You see *all kinds* of people at a public beach! This would not be consistent with Chuck's belief that everyone there has a better physique.

I recently stumbled across a nude beach while on vacation with my family at Lake Tahoe in California. I was floating along the water on my air mattress and suddenly, behind some rocks, I saw all these naked people! I noticed a man who looked like he might have been a Vietnam veteran because his left leg was missing below the knee. He seemed to be having just as much fun as anyone else. If I had been Chuck, I could have asked myself, "Is it true that everyone is staring at this man and thinking he's inferior or abnormal?" I noticed his missing leg, but I wasn't staring at him or looking down on him. Nobody else was either. In fact, he looked tough and was drinking beer and partying with a group of his buddies as well as with some attractive ladies. I don't think that anyone would have dared to cross any of them! I was happy that the one-legged man was there because he was accepting himself and having fun. This made me feel better about my own body, which is *far* from perfect.

Chuck could also use the Experimental Technique to test the validity of his negative thoughts. He could go to a beach and take his shirt off—something he'd never actually done!—and check out his prediction. He can find out if it's *true* that everyone will be staring at him. How many people are staring? How long will they stare? This method would have two advantages. First, Chuck would probably discover that his thoughts were exaggerated. Second, Chuck would have to confront his fears. When you confront your fears, you usually get over them; when you harbor them and hang on to them, they gain power over you. I'm sure Chuck would feel very self-conscious for the first few minutes after he took his shirt off. I also suspect that quite soon his anxiety would begin to fade away. Eventually he'd be swimming or playing volleyball and forget all about his chest.

Let's stop and do a little cognitive therapy quiz. Why does Chuck feel anxious and self-conscious at the beach?

a. Because of his chest.
b. Because of the way people would react to his chest.
c. Both a and b.
d. Neither a nor b.

If you answered a, b, or c, you haven't quite gotten the central idea of cognitive therapy yet—namely, that only your thoughts can upset you. Chuck feels uncomfortable because he tells himself that he's grotesque and inferior and that it would be awful to have everybody look down on him. Once he stops believing these thoughts, his feelings will change.

What are some additional strategies Chuck could use to talk back to his negative thoughts? We could list dozens of approaches, but here are just a few:

• *The Cost-Benefit Analysis.* Chuck could list the advantages and disadvantages of thinking of himself as an inferior person because of his chest. He could also list the advantages and disadvantages of being so hung up on his chest that he can't go and have fun at the beach. Maybe he feels just as happy never going to the beach. If so, he doesn't really have a problem. On the other hand, if he wants to feel free to go swimming, and wants to rid himself of his fears and inhibitions, then it would be worth it to confront his fears.
• *The Double-Standard Technique.* What would he say to a friend with the same problem? He certainly wouldn't say, "Gee, your chest looks like a satellite dish! People will be staring at you and squirming with discomfort all day."
• *Define Terms.* What is the definition of an "inferior" person?

- *Thinking in Shades of Gray.* How worthwhile does Chuck think he would be, in a range between 0 and 100, if he had a big muscular chest? How worthwhile does he think he is now, with the chest he has?
- *The Survey Technique.* He could ask people if they would like a friend any less if he or she had a physical imperfection, like fat thighs or a flat chest. He could ask people how frequently they think about other people's physical imperfections when they are at the beach.
- *The Vertical Arrow Technique.* Chuck could ask himself why it would be upsetting if someone thought he was inferior. He might say that people wouldn't like him or respect him. Then he could ask himself why that would be upsetting. He might discover that he has a fear of disapproval and learn that he's basing too much of his self-esteem on what other people think of him. If so, he can do another Cost-Benefit Analysis and list the advantages and disadvantages of believing that he always has to get everybody's approval. How will it help him, and how will it hurt him, to think this way?
- *The Feared Fantasy Technique.* Chuck could write out a dialogue with an imaginary group of strangers, the "hostile crowd," who were insulting him and saying cruel things about his chest. They should say far worse things than any real group of people would ever say to him. The dialogue might go like this:

HOSTILE CROWD: Gee, you really have a weird-looking chest. You should be in a freak show.

CHUCK: Yes, my chest is sort of hollow. I notice you all have massive, hairy chests.

HOSTILE CROWD: Yes, we lift weights and take hormones. Our chests are like the Rocky Mountains. Yours looks like a soup bowl.

CHUCK: I've always admired men with large chests. Mine does look like a soup bowl in comparison. You have some of the biggest chests on the beach!

HOSTILE CROWD: Yes, people all admire us because we're such handsome studs. But nobody admires you. In fact, everyone's staring at you and thinking that you're gross, deformed, and disgusting. Nobody wants to be seen with you.

CHUCK: It sounds like even being near me is making you real uncomfortable. Why is that? Perhaps you should go and see a psychiatrist I know, named Dr. Burns. They call him the Mood Doctor and he may be able to help you with your nervousness. Or if you feel so uncomfortable, perhaps you can hide your eyes while I walk past.

I find it helpful to think of a negative thought or a self-defeating attitude as a trap represented by the box in the illustration below. Each intervention, which is represented by an arrow, is a way of breaking out of the trap. The diagram shows that there are *numerous* ways to turn any negative thought around. If one technique doesn't work, try another, and then another. When you finally put the lie to a negative thought, you will experience a profound change in the way you feel at a gut level. If you feel stuck, just keep knocking until the door swings wide open and you feel good again!

You may be wondering when you should use each of the various techniques. I believe that you should always "identify the distortion" first. You will discover that certain techniques work especially well for particular kinds of distortions. For example, if the distortion in your negative thought is "all-or-nothing thinking," the method

THERE ARE NUMEROUS WAYS TO CHALLENGE
ANY AUTOMATIC THOUGHT

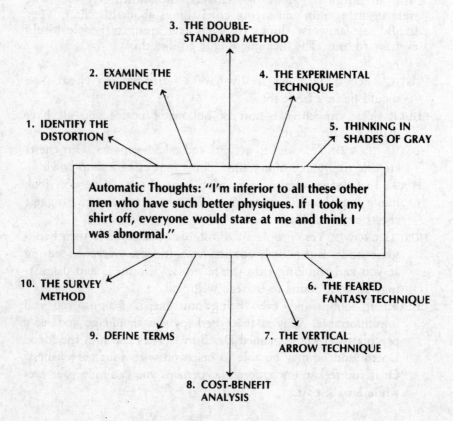

3. THE DOUBLE-
STANDARD METHOD

2. EXAMINE THE
EVIDENCE

4. THE EXPERIMENTAL
TECHNIQUE

1. IDENTIFY THE
DISTORTION

5. THINKING IN
SHADES OF GRAY

Automatic Thoughts: "I'm inferior to all these other men who have such better physiques. If I took my shirt off, everyone would stare at me and think I was abnormal."

10. THE SURVEY
METHOD

6. THE FEARED
FANTASY TECHNIQUE

9. DEFINE TERMS

7. THE VERTICAL
ARROW TECHNIQUE

8. COST-BENEFIT
ANALYSIS

called "Thinking in Shades of Gray" is likely to help. If your negative thought is a "should statement," the "Semantic Method" will nearly always work well. If you're involved in "emotional reasoning," you may find it helpful to Examine the Evidence, or you could use the Experimental Technique.

Remember that any cognitive technique can usually be used with any negative thought, so don't be rigid in trying to match specific techniques to specific distortions. Also keep in mind that a method that works wonders for one negative thought may not be at all helpful for another. Determination and patience are crucial. If you keep at it, you will succeed!

Mood Problem #2: Irritability and Low Self-Esteem

Mary told me that she'd been feeling irritable toward her husband, Bob, and overreacting to things: "If Bob says something I don't like, I feel shocked. It's like I was stabbed by a knife and I get unglued. If we're at a church meeting and something happens that I don't like, I get suddenly angry and I feel like leaving. If we're even watching a movie on TV, I get annoyed with the program and I insist we should change to another one."

When you are feeling irritable, there's often something bothering you that you're not dealing with. When you find yourself flying off the handle, ask what's going on in your life. Think about the things that have happened recently. Usually you will come up with the problem that's bugging you.

Mary said that Bob, who is 61, had been advised by his accountant to sell his business within eighteen months to take advantage of favorable IRS regulations. (If he waited beyond that time, his taxes on the sale would be substantially higher.) When Bob told Mary about the accountant's recommendations, she said, "It just wiped me out. I felt devastated. I feel hot and upset just talking about it now."

It seemed we'd located the source of Mary's irritability, so I asked her to write this as the "Upsetting Event" at the top of a Daily Mood Log. She recorded her emotions as "Panic—99; Sad—99." It's interesting that she didn't feel angry. Apparently the sale of her husband's business was very threatening to Mary, since she felt panicky, and she also anticipated a loss, as indicated by her strong feelings of sadness. I was curious why Bob's retirement and the sale of the business were so upsetting to her. One of the great strengths of cognitive therapy is that the therapist doesn't have to rely on intuition to figure out what's going on. Any therapist's interpretations are frequently incorrect, and they sometimes say more about the therapist's feelings and beliefs than about what's actually going on in the patient's psyche! In contrast, a cognitive therapist will ask, "Why is this so upsetting to you? What are your negative thoughts?" These questions will usually reveal the essence of what's really bothering you.

Why don't you write down *your* theories about why Mary felt panicky and upset about the sale of Bob's business? Then you can compare your hunches with what was really going on in Mary's mind. Put your ideas here:

1. _____

_____

2. _____

_____

3. _____

_____

I asked Mary to write down her negative thoughts about the sale of the business. They were:

1. "How will it turn out?"

2. "What will happen to us?"

3. "We'll be 'has-beens.' "

4. "After Bob has worked so hard for thirty-five years to build his business, I hate to see him step down. He's finally doing well. He should have the chance to enjoy the fruits of his labor."

5. "It stinks."

I wanted to learn a bit more about this, so I used the Vertical Arrow Technique, described on page 122. I asked Mary to choose one of these thoughts that was particularly upsetting. She chose number 2, "What will happen to us?" I told her to draw a small downward arrow under it. This arrow means "Suppose this is true. Why is it upsetting to me? What am I really afraid of?" Using this technique, Mary generated several additional Automatic Thoughts:

6. "We won't be able to enjoy the same standard of living we've had in the past year."

   And why would that be upsetting to me?

7. "We'll have to go back to the more frugal life-style we had in the past."

   And why would that be upsetting?

8. "I won't be able to spend money for the things I love, such as jewelry, clothes, crystal, and so forth. We won't be able to get a larger boat."

   And why would that be a problem to me?

9. "I'm addicted to shopping and I'll have to break the addiction."

   And why would that be upsetting?

10. "Shopping is my escape from loneliness. If I can't go out and shop, I'll have to sit home and be depressed."

    And why would I be depressed if I couldn't go out shopping?

11. "I need to spend money to feel happy. Otherwise my life will be a bore."

Once we generated this list of negative thoughts, it became clear why Mary felt so threatened by Bob's imminent retirement. Mary was a shop-a-holic and thought she needed to spend money and buy attractive things to make life interesting. I asked Mary to review her negative thoughts to see if she could come up with any self-defeating beliefs that were causing this attitude. She said that her "silent assumption" appeared to be: "I'm lazy and I need to spend money to feel good." Although you might feel judgmental and think Mary is being selfish and childish, I admired her honesty in facing this. It's an attitude that many of us share. It *does* feel good to have extra money to buy things. We're a consumer society and we are constantly bombarded with advertising that implies that wealth confers status and happiness.

Mary said that this addiction to spending began after all her children had finished college and gotten married. Since her whole purpose in life had been to raise them, she suddenly felt lonely and her life seemed to have no focus. She felt frightened and bewildered. Bob was actively involved with his career and Mary felt resentful, lonely, and unfulfilled. Bob's business was finally beginning to pay off so they had plenty of extra money to enjoy the finer things in life. Mary naturally slipped into a pattern of spending money as a way of coping with the emptiness she felt inside. She said that she could see herself getting increasingly unhappy and more demanding, much like a drug addict who has to take more and more "stuff" to get high.

Mary sadly acknowledged that she also had a second self-defeating belief: "If I don't always get what I want, I'm bound to feel miserable." This attitude made her very irritable in her dealings with Bob. Any time they differed on where to go for dinner or what movie to see, she pouted. Since Bob felt terribly guilty whenever Mary was upset, she usually got her way.

In the last chapter you learned that one powerful way to deal with these "silent assumptions" is to do a Cost-Benefit Analysis. I asked Mary to make a list of the advantages and disadvantages of believing "I'm lazy and I need to spend money to feel good." The advantages included: "(1) There will be no effort required. I can just go and spend money if I'm in a bad mood. (2) I don't have to expose myself to the risk of failure." The disadvantages of her belief included: "(1) I won't grow and change. (2) Nothing in my life will get better. (3) I won't confront the problems in my life. I'll just get a quick fix at the shopping center instead. (4) We may run out of money if I spend it excessively. Then I'll feel, 'Ugh! I let Bob down.' (5) I don't believe in myself. (6) I'm a slave to another master. The money I possess will actually possess me. (7) Life has no real goals and no sense of accomplishment."

After weighing the two advantages against the many disadvantages, Mary clearly saw that her silent assumption was hurting her far more than it was helping her. I asked if she could think of another, more realistic belief she could substitute in its place. She suggested this one: "I can feel good as a result of doing things and getting creatively involved in life."

The advantages of this attitude were: "(1) I will make Bob happy.

(2) Our marriage will be less stormy. (3) My self-esteem won't be controlled by the amount of money we have." The disadvantages were: "(1) I will have to take more initiative. (2) I will have to face my fears." The advantages of this new belief outweighed the disadvantages.

The Cost-Benefit Analysis can help you with the *motivation* to change your thinking. Once you can see that your negative attitudes are hurting you more than they are helping you, you will be more likely to give them up. But you may still believe that these attitudes are *true*. Even though Mary can see that her preoccupation with spending money is unhealthy, she may still believe at the gut level that people with a lot of money to spend are inevitably happier than people on limited incomes. She may feel convinced that life will be more rewarding and exciting if she can go on these buying sprees. You may believe this at a gut level, too!

I suggested we take things one step further. I asked Mary to do an experiment to test her belief that spending money was the key to feeling happy and exhilarated (the Experimental Technique is described on page 102). I told Mary to write the following statement at the top of a Pleasure-Predicting Sheet: "Hypothesis: I need to buy things and spend lots of money to experience true pleasure and satisfaction in life." Then, in the Activity column, I asked Mary to write down a number of activities with a potential for pleasure, learning, or personal growth that might give her a feeling of satisfaction or a sense of accomplishment. Mary said that there were many things she might enjoy that she'd been putting off. These included sewing, doing psychotherapy self-help assignments between sessions, learning to use a computer, and getting more involved in church work. After listing each activity, she recorded whom she would do it with and estimated how much it would cost. This would allow her to compare the enjoyment she got doing things alone with the enjoyment she got from being with Bob and with friends. It would also allow her to see if spending money was always more satisfying than free or inexpensive activities.

In the Predicted Satisfaction column, Mary estimated *ahead of time* how rewarding each activity should be, between 0 (the least satisfying) and 100 percent (the most satisfying). The predictions she made reflect her belief that spending lots of money would make her happy, and that anything else would be a bore. She predicted the highest

PLEASURE-PREDICTING SHEET

Hypothesis: I need to buy things and spend lots of money to experience true pleasure and satisfaction in life.

Activity	Companion	Satisfaction	
		Predicted	Actual
Schedule activities with a potential for pleasure or personal growth	(If alone, specify "self")	(0–100%) (Record this before each activity)	(0–100%) (Record this after each activity)
Eat a dish of Häagen-Dazs Macadamia Nut ice cream at the train station	Self ($2.50 for the large dish)	75	75
Go window-shopping	Self ($0)	25	75
Shop for jewelry and buy something expensive	Self ($300)	90	10
Spend time sewing	Self ($0)	50	80
Rent a movie with Bob and watch it on the VCR	Bob ($2)	60	90
Fill out the Daily Mood Log between sessions	Self ($0)	20	90
Register for a class at the community college	Self ($200)	50	75
Play volleyball with the church group	Friends ($0)	60	85
Balance the checking account	Self ($0)	25	75

satisfaction for buying jewelry, and the lowest satisfaction for window-shopping.

In the Actual Satisfaction column, she was to record the outcome—how satisfying each activity actually turned out to be. As you can see, she felt so guilty after she purchased an attractive gold bracelet that her satisfaction turned out to be only 5 percent. In contrast, many of the activities that were free and that had frightened her, such as doing her psychotherapy homework between sessions, turned out to be very enjoyable. These experiences put the lie to Mary's hypothesis that spending lots of money was inherently more rewarding than less costly activities. This made it abundantly clear that her moods were not, in reality, connected to her pocketbook. She realized that some of life's greatest sources of satisfaction are absolutely free.

This is not exactly a revolutionary or new idea. Sometimes the rediscovery of an old truth can make a profound difference in your outlook and your self-esteem.

Mood Problem #3: Frustration, Guilt, and Stress at Work

Susan is a 32-year-old pediatric nurse at Children's Hospital in Philadelphia. She does direct patient care and also has some administrative and supervisory duties since she is the assistant head nurse on her ward. Susan came for treatment because she had felt mildly depressed, irritable, and burned-out at work for several years.

Sunday she was scheduled to work until 4:00 p.m. At 3:00 she was all caught up and was looking forward to going home on time when the lab called to say that a white blood cell transfusion was ready for one of her patients. This frustrated Susan because these transfusions require two hours of close supervision by one nurse and it meant she couldn't leave on time. White blood cells are supposed to be delivered at the beginning of the shift in the morning to prevent this problem. The cells had been sitting around in the blood bank and were about to expire, so Susan couldn't pass the job on to the next shift. To make matters worse, the attending physician, a woman doctor, arrived on the ward and started "swinging her weight around" when she learned the transfusion was behind schedule. She complained that the nurses were incompetent and that the patients were getting lousy care.

Susan described this in the Upsetting Event space at the top of a Daily Mood Log. She recorded her negative feelings as: "Angry—80; Frustrated—90; Guilty—95." The first thought she recorded in the Automatic Thoughts column was: "Here's a kid who's dying. I should be glad to give him his white blood cells."

This thought made her feel guilty. Can you identify the main distortions in it? Check the list of cognitive distortions on page 96 and put your ideas here:

1. _____

2. _____

Answer: It's a "should statement." Susan is telling herself she *shouldn't* get annoyed. Can you see why this is self-defeating? In addition to having to cope with a frustrating situation, she's turning her anger against herself and getting extremely self-critical. She's also involved in "personalization," because she's blaming herself for a problem she didn't cause.

What Rational Response would you suggest? Put your ideas here about how Susan could talk back to her negative thought:

_____

_____

_____

_____

Answer: In Chapter 6 we talked about two techniques that can help you deal with "should statements." One is the Semantic Method— you simply substitute an expression like "It would be nice if" or "It would be preferable if" in place of the "should." Another approach would be the Cost-Benefit Analysis. Susan could list the advantages and disadvantages of believing that she should be like Florence Nightingale and always feel happy when she encounters an annoying situation.

Susan's Rational Response was "It's natural to get annoyed when people foul up and you have to stay late." By giving herself permission to feel upset, she won't have to feel so guilty and self-blaming. This involves a substantial shift in Susan's attitudes. She is very perfectionistic and believes that she should *never* get angry and that she should *always* be pleasant and in control of her emotions.

Susan's second Automatic Thought was: "Why should I have to do this?" Susan recognized immediately that this was another "should statement." Just as she was expecting emotional perfection from herself, she was expecting perfection from the world.

What Rational Response would you suggest?_____

_____

_____

_____

_____

Answer: Susan couldn't come up with one. I suggested that one approach would be to use the Semantic Method. Instead of thinking "I shouldn't have to do this," she could tell herself, "It would be a lot better if I could go home on time and I didn't have to supervise this transfusion. I can let the blood bank know that I was uncomfortable because the late delivery caused problems for me. I can ask them to be sure to make their white cell deliveries in the morning."

When I proposed this Rational Response, Susan became extremely defensive. She insisted that calling the lab "wouldn't do any good." I was a little surprised by her reaction. I pointed out that I'd worked in the clinical laboratory at a hospital when I was a medical student and that we always tried to respond to the needs of the nurses and doctors who were involved in patient care. I wondered if she might be underestimating the extent of her influence as an assistant head nurse. I also pointed out that sometimes it helps to express your feelings—in a tactful but clear way—even if it doesn't bring about any real changes. I asked Susan if she wanted to work on learning how to express her feelings more effectively.

Susan got even more annoyed and insisted that I "didn't understand." She said she didn't want to pursue the matter any further. After the session, I felt somewhat put down. I felt I had missed the boat. However, it also seemed possible that I had hit the target and that Susan was very reluctant—for reasons that weren't yet clear—to change.

The next week Susan said she'd listened to the tape of our session twice and had reread the chapters on dealing with criticism and anger in *Feeling Good*. She had written some notes, which I have excerpted with her permission:

I have come to the conclusion that I may be repressing anger . . . because I'm afraid of what may happen if I express hostile feelings. I have never learned to express angry feelings constructively. In the past, whenever I was angry or frustrated, I have reacted in one of three ways.

The first way is to throw a fit. This usually involves ranting, raving, yelling, cursing, or crying. After these outbursts, I feel embarrassed, ashamed, guilty. I feel physically upset and may end up with a headache.

The second way I react is to sulk. Instead of expressing my feelings, I mope and complain. I generally feel guilty because I know I've acted like a jerk.

The third way is the martyr method. I have this one down pat. While other people are yelling at me or complaining, I maintain a calm exterior while they give me the business. Afterwards I feel bitter and disgusted. I accept all the blame for whatever it is that has upset that individual. I usually apologize and assure them that I will attend to the problem. This is my usual method of dealing with angry co-workers or parents of patients. Afterwards, I end up with jaw pain because I've been gritting my teeth.

Lately, I have felt that I may lose control if I allow myself to feel anger. I'm afraid I may do physical harm to someone if I don't keep a tight rein on my emotions. I frequently feel like beating the hell out of someone. These impulses frighten me and I feel ashamed of them. I feel like I deserve to be punished.

I agree with you that I allow things to happen to me and I make no effort to change things. I have an almost fatalistic outlook. When I am treated badly by someone, it reinforces my belief that I deserve no better.

I was thrilled with this analysis. It seemed accurate and it showed me that Susan had the capacity for some pretty honest introspection. Anyone who can look at herself with that degree of openness and honesty has a great opportunity for growth. Some people are so fearful of change and so committed to maintaining the *status quo*—in spite of how miserable they feel—that they resist therapy. They sometimes deny their problems, or they may insist that everyone else is to blame. Others, like Susan, say, "This is where I'm at. I admit it and I'm hurting." Then some exciting personal changes become a very real possibility.

As we discussed her analysis, it seemed clear that Susan had a "conflict phobia." She has an intense fear of disagreements or angry interactions and tries very hard to avoid them. This is like trying to run away from a monster in a nightmare. It seems as if you're running through molasses and you just can't get away. Although Susan tells herself repeatedly that she should always try to be happy and loving, she just can't avoid feeling irritated. Then she doesn't know what to do. Blowing up, sulking, and acting like a martyr all make her feel even more miserable. Blaming herself is equally unsatisfactory.

Susan agreed that learning to deal with people in a more direct way would be an important goal of her therapy, one that would have important ramifications in her professional life and in her personal life as well. After this discussion, we decided to complete the analysis of her negative thoughts about the blood bank.

Susan's third Automatic Thought was: "I probably was incompetent and should have called the blood bank earlier."

What are the distortions in this thought?

1. _____

2. _____

3. _____

Answer: You can see that this is another "should statement." It is also an example of "fortune-telling," because Susan expects herself to foresee other people's errors. The third distortion is "personalization," because she is automatically blaming herself for the blood bank's error. It seems that Susan either directs the "shoulds" inwardly and blames herself, or else she directs "shoulds" outwardly and blames the world. When she blames herself, she hates herself and feels guilty and inadequate. When she blames the world, she feels frustrated and furious. Either way, life becomes extremely unrewarding and exhausting. Since her work as a nurse is filled with numerous unexpected irritations and disappointments, it's little wonder that she feels so burned out! What Rational Response would you suggest?

_____

_____

_____

_____

Answer: The Rational Response Susan came up with was quite simple: "I had no way of anticipating this problem."

Susan's fourth Automatic Thought was: "Dr. Jones thinks I'm incompetent and no good. She acts as if the kid wouldn't get his cells if she didn't take over and 'save the day.' "

This thought angered Susan. She felt *furious* with Dr. Jones. What are the distortions in Susan's Fourth Automatic Thought?

1. _____

2. _____

3. _____

The most obvious distortion is "mind reading," since Susan's jumping to conclusions about what Dr. Jones is thinking. It may also be a hidden "should statement," since she thinks Dr. Jones shouldn't act bossy and insensitive. The third distortion is "blame"—Susan thinks Dr. Jones is making her feel guilty and inadequate. What Rational Response would you suggest?

_____

_____

_____

_____

Answer: Susan's Rational Response wasn't very good. It was: "I don't know what Dr. Jones is thinking, but she has the right to think whatever she wants." The difficulty is that this sounds defensive and hostile. Furthermore, Susan hasn't challenged her Automatic Thought—she's simply buying into it. She still seems convinced that Dr. Jones doesn't respect her.

I used the methods of Re-attribution (see page 111) and Examine the Evidence (see page 100) to help Susan come up with a better Rational Response. I asked, "Is there any evidence that Dr. Jones thinks you are 'incompetent' and 'no good'?" Susan told me that she and Dr. Jones were actually good friends. She said that Dr. Jones had frequently expressed admiration for her professionalism and compassion for her patients. This was clearly inconsistent with Susan's Automatic Thought. I asked if there might be any other explanation for why Dr. Jones was acting irritable and throwing her weight around. Susan mentioned that she was recently widowed; her husband had unexpectedly died of a heart attack several months earlier. This, along with the daily stresses of caring for seriously ill children, was an equally plausible explanation for why Dr. Jones might be feeling on edge. Susan was able to come up with a better Rational Response: "Dr. Jones probably feels tense and frustrated with the situation, as I do, and she's just letting off a little steam. Maybe we need to talk it over and try to clear the air."

Changing her Automatic Thoughts by using the Daily Mood Log reduced a good deal of the guilt and frustration Susan was feeling. We then worked on how she might communicate more effectively in situations like this. Certainly some annoyance is natural. It's not realistic to expect that cognitive therapy—or *any* form of therapy—can eliminate all your negative feelings. Sometimes it's appropriate to tell people how you feel. The five principles of effective communication will be described in detail in Chapter 19, but we can discuss the issue briefly here. What could Susan say to the people at the blood bank and to Dr. Jones? Put your ideas here:

_____

_____

_____

_____

Answer: She could tell the people at the blood bank something like this: "I was uncomfortable that we were notified about the white blood cells at 3:00 on Sunday. This means that someone on the day shift has to stay late to administer them. This is demoralizing because the staff is always eager to leave on time. Would it be possible to alert us in the morning whenever a white cell transfusion has been ordered?" This statement has the following characteristics: (1) She expresses her negative feelings in a direct, honest way. However, she does this tactfully when she says, "I was uncomfortable. . . ." (2) She tells the people at the blood bank specifically what she wants them to do differently so she won't come off a complainer. Although there are no guarantees that she will get a friendly, cooperative response, at least she will feel she's standing up for herself in a dignified, professional way instead of acting like a wounded and resentful victim.

What could Susan say when Dr. Jones complains and "throws her weight around"? Put your ideas here:

_____

_____

_____

_____

Answer: There are, of course, many ways Susan might respond. Here's just one idea. She could say, "I'm also frustrated that we were notified so late about the white blood cells, and I share your concern that this patient should get the best possible care. I'm a little uncomfortable because you may think I'm not doing a good job for your patients. Is this true? I respect you a lot and I want to hear about any problems you've noticed on the ward. Do you have any ideas on how I could deal with the blood bank more effectively? I'm planning to call them to remind them that we need these white cells delivered in the morning." Notice that she shows some appreciation of how Dr. Jones is feeling, and she also expresses her own feelings in a tactful way. Instead of getting defensive or ignoring Dr. Jones's irritation, she asks Dr. Jones to say exactly what's on her mind. She compliments Dr. Jones, so Dr. Jones will not view this as some kind of battle or put-down. Dr. Jones will probably calm down and stop acting so frazzled and will communicate in a friendlier way.

However, it's possible that Dr. Jones might continue to gripe and complain. If she's in a really bad mood, Dr. Jones could say, "I *can't believe* you haven't already taken care of this transfusion! Don't you know that timing is essential? If the patient doesn't get these cells right away, they won't be fresh anymore. Then we'll have to order a new batch." What could Susan say next?

_____

_____

_____

_____

Answer: Susan could say, "You're absolutely right about that, and I feel every bit as annoyed as you do. I'm going to have to stay late to supervise the transfusion. I'm feeling blamed for this problem and I'd like your help in finding a solution. You may have more clout with the blood bank. Could you back me up and stress the importance of delivering these white cells in the morning? Then we wouldn't be under so much pressure at the end of the shift." Notice that Susan finds truth in Dr. Jones's criticism, but at the same time she expresses her feelings so she doesn't appear to be a doormat. She asks for Dr. Jones's help in solving the problem instead of allowing feelings of antagonism to develop.

This brief excerpt from Susan's treatment illustrates an important aspect of cognitive therapy. Part of the treatment is individualistic—we will work hard on changing Susan's distorted negative thoughts and self-defeating attitudes. At the same time, we will work on developing the skill necessary to communicate more effectively with others, so Susan can build more rewarding relationships at work and in her personal life. The goal of the therapy is to reduce the rage, the guilt, and the loneliness Susan feels so that she can develop greater self-esteem and feel closer to others.

Mood Problem #4: Irritability, Frustration, and Marital Conflict

Let's look at another example of how cognitive therapy can help deal with feelings of irritability and frustration. Frank is a 34-year-old dentist who recently married a 36-year-old woman named Fran, after enjoying many years of happy bachelorhood. Several weeks after the wedding Frank told me, "I feel irritable all the time. I feel like Fran's intruding on my territory. I feel trapped. When I come home from work I feel exhausted. I want to have a beer and unwind for a while. But I feel I have to talk to Fran, make love to Fran, and be interested in her day. I try to watch TV and Fran climbs all over me. She does this erotic dance and tries to turn me on. She thinks I should be constantly making love to her. All I want is to be alone."

Frank explained that his feelings of annoyance weren't just limited to coming home from work: "I get irritated when I see her things in the medicine cabinet. We've moved into a small apartment and we've got no space at all. This morning I couldn't find the toothpaste and I said, 'Where the hell did she put it!' Then I saw it right in front of me on the sink.

"When we're out with friends I have a lot of escape fantasies about having sex with other women. I feel trapped. I feel like my independence has been taken away from me. It's been five years since I was living with someone. I feel like I want to make love with another woman just to prove I can be free."

Frank said that when he comes home from work, he has these feelings: "Angry—75; Trapped—75; Anxious—80; Frustrated—80." I asked Frank to write down the Automatic Thoughts that were associated with these feelings. They were:

1. "Fran shouldn't intrude on me."

2. "I should want her sexually right now. If I don't want her sexually *all the time*, then there must be something wrong with this marriage and I should find someone I'm more attracted to."

3. "She doesn't respect my feelings or my need to be by myself and unwind."

4. "I should never allow anyone to control me. I should get angry."

5. "Things will get worse. I made a mistake getting married."

One of the things I like the most about cognitive therapy is that it shows so clearly and accurately where a person is coming from. It's as if all your secret inner thoughts and negative attitudes come spilling right out of your head, so they can be understood and dealt with.

Frank's negative thoughts tell us a great deal about why he feels so upset, and they also point the way to the cure. You can see that it's not Fran who makes Frank feel trapped and dissatisfied—it's Frank. He has very perfectionistic expectations about what marriage should be like. He thinks he and Fran should *always* want to be together and that he should *always* feel romantic and sexual and excited by her.

He also expects Fran to read his mind. He wants her to respect his need to be alone, but he stubbornly refuses to tell her that he feels this way! Of course, he cannot tell her that he needs a little time by himself when he comes home at night because that would be an admission of defeat and failure. He would have to admit his marriage is more "ordinary" and less "special." It's amazing to me how our desires for perfection so often condemn us to misery and loneliness!

Frank found it relatively easy to talk back to his negative thoughts. Let's work on his first one. When Fran approaches him, he tells himself, "She shouldn't intrude on me." What are the distortions in this thought?

1. _____

2. _____

3. _____

4. _____

Answer: First, it's an obvious "should statement," since he's telling himself she should automatically be just the way he wants her to be. Second, it's an example of "mind reading," since Frank thinks about her motives in a negative way. She probably doesn't feel like an "intruder," but like a wife who misses her husband. Finally, it's an example of "discounting the positive," since he turns something positive—Fran's love—into something negative when he labels her enthusiasm as an "intrusion."

What Rational Response would you suggest? Put your ideas here:

_____

_____

_____

_____

Frank came up with this one: "Fran doesn't intend to be intrusive but to be affectionate because she misses me. She loves me and her motivations are positive. She may feel insecure and want some affection. That's a normal reaction."

What's the distortion in Frank's second thought: "I should want her sexually right now . . . and *all the time*"? Put your ideas here:

1. _____

2. _____

Answer: This is another obvious "should statement." Frank's first "should statement" was directed toward Fran, and this one is directed toward himself. He seems to be very demanding and has exceedingly high expectations for himself and for other people. In addition, like most perfectionists, he's trapped by "all-or-nothing thinking." He thinks that if he isn't always wildly turned on by Fran, it means his marriage is a failure. If you were Frank, what Rational Response could you come up with?

_____

_____

_____

_____

Answer: Frank's was quite simple: "It's not realistic to assume I should be sexually excited and active all the time." This thought made him considerably less tense.

In the last chapter you learned about the Vertical Arrow Technique. This method can help you discover certain self-defeating attitudes, called "silent assumptions," that are lurking underneath your negative thoughts. Once you identify these assumptions, you can modify them and grow as a person. When you refute your negative thoughts you will feel better at the moment, but when you modify a silent assumption, you will be developing a healthier value system that can pave the way for greater joy and intimacy and personal meaning throughout your life.

In order to unearth Frank's silent assumptions, I asked him this question: "Suppose you're not sexually turned on by Fran all the time. Why would that be upsetting to you? What would that mean to you?"

FRANK: That would mean I was getting old and my life was becoming boring. I feel like I should always seek out excitement.

DR. BURNS: And suppose your life was becoming boring and you weren't always seeking out excitement. Why would that be upsetting to you?

FRANK: Then I would be just like everyone else.

DR. BURNS: And then what?

FRANK: Then my life would be empty.

DR. BURNS: And suppose your life was empty. What then? Would that be a problem for you?

FRANK: Then I couldn't be happy. I feel I should strive to be happy *all the time*. I think I shouldn't have negative emotions.

This brief dialogue revealed the "emotional perfectionism" lurking underneath Frank's annoyance. He has a rule in his mind which states that he should try to be a very "special" kind of person who's constantly filled with passion and zest for life and who never feels bored or unhappy. You could also say that Frank suffers from "emotophobia," which literally means "phobia about negative emotions." Frank appears to be afraid of feelings such as boredom, sadness, or anger.

One of the elusive things about these silent assumptions that get us into so much trouble is that they're not completely irrational— they're often a subtle mixture of good and bad. Certainly there's nothing wrong with Frank's desire to make his life meaningful and exciting and fulfilling. His enthusiasm and zest for living are among his strengths. But these very strengths can also become weaknesses when he lets them dominate his life. As Frank put it, "This fear of negative emotions has made me leave *every* job and *every* woman I've ever had. This belief that I'm entitled to be happy all the time has caused endless frustration and anger, because I can't tolerate any negative feelings. I'm demanding and impatient, and I panic when I get any unpleasant emotion. This makes me terribly lonely because I can't share my feelings with Fran."

One of the advantages of giving up the expectation that he should always be happy and have a constantly thrilling marriage is that he will be free to communicate more openly with Fran. He can tell her how he feels when he comes home at night, and they can talk about how much time they want to spend doing things together. Too much togetherness can ruin any marriage. Frank's trapped feelings are simply his way of reminding himself that he needs some time to be alone and that he and Fran need to talk things over. Fran may think that it's perfectly okay for Frank to unwind alone for a while when he gets home after a hard day at the office. She may agree that they don't have to spend every single minute of their lives together. They may decide to spend a night or two each week doing things separately. They may want to spend an occasional weekend apart. It's a matter of negotiating a balance that will make sense to both of them. Frank will have to compromise with some of his grandiose expectations for his marriage. He will have to swallow some of his pride and give up the idea that his relationship with Fran will be perfect and thrilling at every moment. As he gives up his goal of an ideal relationship, he may discover the rewards of a real one.

Frank and Fran may benefit from some communication training along the lines described in Part IV. He needs to learn to share his negative feelings more openly with Fran. The capacity to reveal hurt and vulnerable feelings is hardly a sign of marital failure; it is the very meaning of true intimacy. Comprehending this may require a transformation in Frank's basic values, because he will no longer view his negative emotions as a bad thing. He will begin to see them as a pathway to a more profound appreciation of his uniqueness as well as what he shares with the rest of humanity.

Mood Problem #5: Depression

George, who is 36 years old, recently experienced his second serious depression. The first episode, which lasted six months, occurred around the time he got married, ten years ago. Up to the time of his most recent depression, George felt happy. He opened a successful restaurant, and he and his wife started a family. Their two lovable boys are now 5 and 7 years old.

Prior to seeking treatment at my clinic, George had been treated unsuccessfully with medications and psychotherapy by a psychiatrist near his home. Because this wasn't helpful, George was hospitalized for three weeks. A nurse on the ward gave him a copy of *Feeling Good*. George experienced a strong mood lift when he read it and worked on some of the exercises in the book. He called my office after he was discharged, because he was still depressed.

Testing at my clinic indicated that George had a severe "biological depression," since his serum cortisol level was markedly abnormal. His treatment was particularly interesting since it indicates that irrational negative thoughts do occur in these so-called "chemical depressions." Helping George talk back to these negative thoughts relieved his feelings of hopelessness and despair. This can be crucial early in the treatment when you are trying to find an effective antidepressant medication.

During a recent session, George showed me twenty upsetting thoughts that he had written down for homework between sessions. The list included:

1. "I'm a failure. I never succeed at anything."

2. "I'm a rotten father because I don't love my children. My boys are afraid of me."

3. "I'm hopeless and I will never get well. My state of mind will go on forever."

4. "This depression means I don't love my wife. If I really loved her, I wouldn't feel this way."

5. "Everyone, including Dr. Burns, is getting disgusted with me."

6. "I'm letting everyone down."

7. "I shouldn't be feeling this way."

These thoughts made George feel hopeless, ashamed, and worthless.

I asked George to identify the distortions in the first thought: "I'm a failure. I never succeed at anything." Review the list on page 96 and see what distortions you can identify in this thought:

1. _____

2. _____

3. _____

4. _____

Answer: It's certainly an example of "emotional reasoning." George is thinking, "I *feel* worthless. I *feel* like a failure. Therefore I must really *be* a failure." It's also an example of "discounting the positive," since he is overlooking the many things he's succeeded at. (He's hardworking, he's managed to build a successful business, he's gone to work every day in spite of intense feelings of depression, and he has a loving family.) It's also an example of "all-or-nothing thinking," since he thinks of himself as a total failure just because he's depressed. Finally, it's an example of "personalization," since George is blaming himself for his depression. He really did nothing to deserve it or to bring it on.

It was relatively easy to help George turn this thought around. I used the method called Examine the Evidence. I simply asked George to list a number of the many things he'd accomplished, and then asked how he reconciled this with the claim that he was "a failure." I also used the Double-Standard Method, and asked if he would say "You're a failure" to a friend with a similar level of depression who was struggling so hard to overcome it. This helped George see that he was being unreasonably hard on himself.

I used a similar strategy on his second Automatic Thought: "I'm a rotten father because I don't love my children. My sons are afraid of me." He had come to this conclusion for two reasons. First, there were times when he felt anxious and irritable around his children. In the past week he'd snapped at his son for misbehaving, and he concluded he must be a cruel ogre. In addition, because of his depression George didn't have strong feelings of love for his children or for his wife—or for anyone. George concluded that he must not love them anymore. Interestingly, George wept constantly when he told me about this.

What are the distortions in George's second Automatic Thought?

1. _____

2. _____

3. _____

Answer: First, he's "discounting the positive," since there was abundant evidence he *did* love his children and there was no evidence that they were afraid of him. For example, after the previous session, when he joined his wife and sons in the waiting room, his two boys ran up to him. One hugged his leg and the other jumped into his arms and started talking to him excitedly. Then he picked up the son who was hugging his leg and stood with one child in each arm with tears in his eyes. It was clear that his boys were absolutely delighted to be with him. This hardly supported his belief that they were afraid of him or that he hated them! In addition, why would a man who didn't love his children be sobbing about them? George's tears were evidence that he did care a great deal—probably more than 99 percent of the fathers in Philadelphia that day!

Another distortion in his thoughts was "emotional reasoning." George was saying, "If I don't *feel* love at every minute, then I must not love them." But it's extremely difficult to feel *any* positive emotion, such as love or happiness, when you are severely depressed. Fortunately those positive feelings return when the depression disappears.

Finally, George was involved in a "should statement." He's telling himself that he should always want to be with his children and should never feel irritable or annoyed with them. Although an ideal imaginary father might be like that, real fathers are not.

The same two methods—Examine the Evidence and the Double-Standard Technique—helped George turn his second negative thought around. He was able to see that he was a loving and committed father even though he didn't always *feel* that way when he was depressed. Although this insight may seem obvious to you, it was a tremendous relief for George.

As an exercise, see if you can identify the distortions in one of George's five other Automatic Thoughts. Then see if you can substitute an effective Rational Response, using one or more of the methods described in the list on page 118. George's responses can be found in his Daily Mood Log on page 167. You can see that he initially believed all his Automatic Thoughts 100%. After we came up with convincing Rational Responses, his belief in each Automatic Thought went down considerably, and he felt much better. That's the essence of cognitive therapy.

THE DAILY MOOD LOG

Automatic Thoughts	Distortions	Rational responses
1. I'm hopeless and I will never get well. My state of mind will go on forever. ~~(100%)~~ (30%)	Fortune-telling; emotional reasoning; all-or-nothing thinking; discounting the positive	1. I may *feel* hopeless but that doesn't mean I *am* hopeless. My first depression ten years ago eventually disappeared, so this depression probably will too. The therapy has already been helpful to me, so I can't be completely "hopeless." (100%)
2. The depression means I don't love my wife. If I really loved her, I wouldn't feel this way. ~~(100%)~~ 30%	Emotional reasoning	2. Men who love their wives can get depressed. I don't *feel* a lot of love, but that's probably just a symptom of my depression. If we have some problems, we can talk them out. I don't have any desire for any other women. (75%)
3. Everyone, including Dr. Burns, is getting disgusted with me. ~~(100%)~~ 25%	Overgeneralization; mind-reading; magnification	3. I may think that everyone is disgusted with me because I'm disgusted with myself. Is there any evidence that Dr. Burns is disgusted? I can ask him about this and see. If he is feeling frustrated with me, I can find out why. (100%)
(Continue on next page)		

THE DAILY MOOD LOG (continued)

Automatic Thoughts	Distortions	Rational responses
4. I'm letting everyone down. ~~(100%)~~ 0%	Overgeneralization; mind reading	4. I can't be letting *everyone* down because I don't know everyone. Furthermore, there's no evidence that I'm letting anyone down. I'm putting tremendous pressure on myself to get well, but no one else is pressuring me. Dr. Burns says I may be trying too hard and that it's okay to be patient and to give myself a little time to recover. (100%)
5. I shouldn't be feeling this way. ~~(100%)~~ 25%	Should statement	5. I should feel this way because I'm depressed. It will eventually pass. (75%)

9

•

Why People Procrastinate

In the previous chapters, we've talked about changing your thoughts and attitudes when you feel upset. You can also do a great deal to brighten your moods by becoming more productive and involved with life. However, many people procrastinate and become immobilized when they feel anxious or depressed. In this chapter you will discover why you procrastinate. In the next chapter, I provide a unique program that has helped many people put an end to their procrastination and unleash their full potential for productivity and creativity.

To start, take the Procrastination Test on page 171. Each statement on the test describes a mind-set that I often see in patients who have difficulties being productive. You'll notice that some of the causes of procrastination are internal—they have to do with your own thoughts and attitudes. Other causes have to do with your relationships with others. There's considerable overlap between the various categories, so don't be surprised if you recognize yourself in several of them!

1. **Putting the cart before the horse.** In your opinion, which comes first—motivation or productive action? If you said "motivation,"

don't feel bad. You made a good guess. That's the way a lot of procrastinators think. But it's not the correct answer.

Procrastinators tell themselves, "I don't feel like it. I'll wait until I'm in the mood." The problem is that if you wait until you're "in the mood," you may be waiting forever. Did you really think you were going to feel like mowing the lawn, cleaning the garage, or balancing your checkbook? You're never going to "feel like it"! These are boring, unpleasant tasks!

People who are extremely successful know that motivation doesn't come first—productive action does. You have to prime the pump by getting started whether you feel like it or not. Once you begin to accomplish something, it will often spur you on to do even more.

When I give lectures or workshops, I find that as the time of the presentation approaches, I begin to dread it. I wish I didn't have to go through with it. The night before, I feel petrified, and I want to get sick so I can bow out gracefully. I tell myself that I don't have anything interesting to say. The idea of standing up in front of hundreds of psychologists and psychiatrists and talking for several hours seems terrifying.

Shortly after I begin speaking, my feelings begin to change. I notice warm smiles and receptive faces. Many of the people seem intrigued by what I'm saying. As they begin to ask questions, my enthusiasm builds. By the end of the presentation I feel exhausted, but I can't wait to have the chance to do it again.

The same principle can apply to any job you're putting off. Once you get started, it usually turns out to be far less horrible than you had imagined, and you feel more like doing it.

The diagram below illustrates how action can lead to motivation and then to further action:

$$\text{ACTION}$$
$$\downarrow$$
$$\text{MOTIVATION}$$
$$\downarrow$$
$$\text{MORE ACTION}$$

The message is simple: the more you do, the more you'll feel like doing; but *doing something* comes first!

2. **The mastery model.** People who procrastinate often have an unrealistic view of how a productive person really functions. You may

THE PROCRASTINATION TEST*

This test describes attitudes that some people have when they procrastinate. Put a check (√) in the box that best describes your feelings:

	0–NOT AT ALL	1–SOMEWHAT	2–MODERATELY	3–A LOT
1. I often put things off because I don't feel like doing them or because I'm not in the mood.				
2. I sometimes give up on tasks because they turn out to be more frustrating and difficult than I anticipated.				
3. I sometimes procrastinate because I'm afraid of failure.				
4. I don't like to start something if I feel I won't be able to do it perfectly.				
5. I often feel that I haven't accomplished anything worthwhile because I'm so critical of my work.				
6. When I procrastinate, I feel guilty and I tell myself I really *should* get started.				
7. I sometimes put things off when I feel annoyed or upset with people.				
8. I often agree to do things I don't really want to do because it's so hard for me to say no.				
9. I sometimes put things off because I feel that people are acting bossy and making unreasonable demands on me.				
10. I often feel like I have lots of things to do that I'm not very committed to or enthusiastic about.				

assume that successful people always feel confident and easily achieve their goals without having to endure frustration, self-doubt, and failure. This "mastery model" of success is quite unrealistic. Achieving personal goals is stressful. You will usually have to overcome numerous obstacles and setbacks along the way. If you think that life should be easy and that other people don't have to struggle, you will conclude that something is "wrong" and give up when things get tough. You'll have such a low tolerance for frustration that any disappointment will be unbearable.

Highly productive people are more likely to have a "coping model" of success. They assume that life will be frustrating and that there will be numerous rejections and failures on the road to success. When they encounter these obstacles, they simply assume that things are as they should be, and they persist. They rise to the occasion with renewed determination and commitment.

My daughter was not studying her chemistry book very ambitiously during her sophomore year of high school, and she was barely getting C's on the tests. Although she read each chapter once, she wasn't persisting and putting in the long hours necessary to master the material. Every time she studied she got frustrated, because a lot of what she was reading didn't make sense to her. As a result, she put off studying until the night before her exam.

The "mastery model" was the problem. She had never challenged the notion that the material should be easy. I explained that I often had difficulty learning things and that I simply put in lots of extra time and effort. At first she did not accept this. She thought I was just saying it to be nice. Then I showed her a chapter of a statistics book I'd been studying for over a year but still didn't understand very well. She could see for herself how worn and underlined the pages were. I told her that my slow progress didn't frustrate me because I understood a little more each time I read the chapter, and I was proud of what I had been able to learn on my own. Once she accepted this, she began to think about chemistry as a challenge instead of an enemy. Her moods and her study habits improved enormously.

3. **The fear of failure.** Although we often think of people who procrastinate as "lazy" and "irresponsible," the real problem is sometimes just the opposite—success may be overly important to you. Rather than risk failure, you may do nothing at all.

People with the fear of failure often base their self-esteem on their accomplishments. If you fail at your work, you may feel that you are a failure as a human being. This makes it too dangerous to try. The stakes are simply too high.

Ted had purchased a small established chocolate manufacturing company near Chicago that had been run as a family business. Although the company was only breaking even, it seemed that with effort it could grow and prosper. However, Ted was neglecting the business. Instead of going to the office in the morning, he would dawdle at home or run errands that weren't really important.

Ted told me that he was terribly afraid of failure. This was the first time in his life he'd ever owned his own company—previously he'd always worked for large corporations. I explored Ted's fear of failure during a session.

DAVID: And suppose you did try and failed? What would that mean to you?

TED: The last corporation I worked for had a serious financial setback, but it never upset me because I was working for someone else. I always felt I could be helpful to the company. But if my own company failed, I'd feel like it was a personal failure.

DAVID: And why would that be upsetting to you?

TED: It would mean I was a failure.

DAVID: And suppose you were a failure. What would that mean to you?

TED: Well, people would find out I was a failure.

DAVID: And then what?

TED: Then they wouldn't love me anymore.

DAVID: Who wouldn't love you?

TED: My wife and kids . . . my son. My son is working with me. Maybe he'd lose respect for me.

This brief conversation made us both aware that Ted felt he had to *earn* the love of the people he cared about. I suggested that he could confront this attitude head on, if he was willing, using the Feared Fantasy Technique (see page 130). I told him that we would do some role-playing and pretend that his business had failed. I would play the role of his son, but I would be more hostile than any real son would ever be. I instructed Ted to play himself. Here's how the dialogue evolved:

SON: Gee, Dad, how's the business doing?

DAD: Not well, son. I'm afraid we'll have to file for bankruptcy. There just isn't any way we can pay all the bills.

SON: Bankruptcy! You mean the business is going under? Will we lose our house? How could you do this to us?

DAD: The business is going under and there's a chance we may have to move.

SON: Wow, you really blew it! Here I am ready to start college, and when I need your financial help the most, you let me down.

DAD: Well, you'll have to work and help out, too. We can make it, but we'll have to pull together as a family.

SON: Come on, Dad! This is terrible!

DAD: I can appreciate how you feel. But why is this so terrible?

SON: No one else's father has these problems. Everyone else is doing well. Why can't you? What are people going to think of us?

DAD: I'd be more interested in what *you* think of me. You sound pretty angry.

SON: Well I am! What do you expect when your father's a loser?

DAD: It sounds like I have to be successful and make a lot of money for you to love and respect me. Do I read you right?

Now Ted was confronted—in fantasy—with his worst fear. He'd dreaded failure and rejection since he was a little boy, but he'd never really faced it head on. Instead of feeling shocked or overwhelmed, he started giggling—and so did I—because his worst fear seemed so ludicrous! It dawned on him that his worries were based on several distortions. First, he was "magnifying" (or "catastrophizing") the financial consequences of a business reversal. He actually had other assets, so even if the company failed, his family wouldn't end up penniless. Second, he was involved in "mind reading." His wife and son wouldn't really be so crass and rejecting if he failed, and the family would probably feel closer in the face of adversity. Finally, and most important, he saw that he was "personalizing" his son's rejection. If someone did reject him because of a failure, it would be a reflection on that person and not on Ted. This insight was illuminating to Ted.

He felt immediate relief. One week later he reported that his depression had vanished and he was working happily in his new business.

4. **Perfectionism.** Finding a publisher for my first book, *Feeling Good,* was a tremendous chore. I was an unknown author, and a self-help book on depression seemed unappealing to most publishers. In addition, the first draft of the book was rather dull and long-winded. Ultimately I found a publishing house and an editor, Maria

Guarnaschelli, whom I really liked. When I went to New York to meet with her and sign the contract, we discussed how I should revise the book. Maria showed me how to rewrite it so it would sound more lively and appealing. She said she loved the book and told me it was sure to be a best-seller.

I went home with a check for the advance in my pocket. It was more money than I'd ever seen at one time, and Maria's accolades were ringing in my ears. I should have felt on top of the world, but for some reason I was discouraged.

After I got home, I sat at my desk, staring into space, for ten days. I just couldn't get started on the revision. In fact, I couldn't come up with one good sentence! I also felt physically exhausted and couldn't run more than half a mile without getting winded, in spite of the fact that I was in perfect health. I knew I was upset, but I couldn't figure out what was bothering me.

Finally I reached for a sheet of paper and wrote down my negative thoughts. The first one was: "This book has to be a best-seller. But I'm a psychiatrist, not an author, and I don't know how to write a best-seller. Maria will be disappointed in me."

The moment I got the thought on paper, I felt a flood of relief, because I decided to think about it like this instead: "It's not my job to write a 'best-seller.' However, I can write a helpful book if I write it in exactly the same personal style that I use with my patients. That will be easy for me, and that's all I'm really responsible for. How well the book sells is the publisher's responsibility." My energy suddenly returned and I went out and ran over seven miles without getting tired. I felt like an antelope! I came back and revised *Feeling Good* over the next several months without any stress at all.

Many of us were raised with the belief that we should always try to do things perfectly and that there would be some special reward for being "the best." Unfortunately, we perfectionists sometimes reach for the stars and end up clutching air. When I try too hard and put too much pressure on myself, I may feel so stressed that I procrastinate and do nothing at all. In contrast, when I lower my standards just a tad, I sometimes feel more relaxed and become far more productive and creative.

I don't want to give you the impression that it's wrong to have high standards. Without a concern for quality and excellence, great achievements in science and in the arts would be a rarity. However,

PERFECTIONISM VS. THE HEALTHY PURSUIT OF EXCELLENCE*

Perfectionism	The healthy pursuit of excellence
1. You are motivated by the fear of failure or by a sense of duty.	1. You are motivated by enthusiasm and you find the creative process exhilarating.
2. You feel driven to be number one, but your accomplishments, however great, never seem to satisfy you.	2. Your efforts give you feelings of satisfaction and a sense of accomplishment, even if you aren't always "the greatest."
3. You feel you must earn your self-esteem. You think you must be very "special" or intelligent or successful to be loved and accepted by others.	3. You enjoy a sense of unconditional self-esteem. You do not feel you have to earn love and friendship by impressing people with your intelligence or your success.
4. You are terrified by failure. If you do not achieve an important goal, you feel like a failure as a human being.	4. You are not afraid to fail because you realize that no one can be successful all the time. Although failure is disappointing, you see it as an opportunity for growth and learning.
5. You think you must always be strong and in control of your emotions. You are reluctant to share vulnerable feelings like sadness, insecurity, or anger with others. You believe they would think less of you.	5. You're not afraid of being vulnerable or sharing your feelings with people you care about. This makes you feel closer to them.

*Copyright © 1989 by David D. Burns, M.D., from *The Feeling Good Handbook*

compulsive perfectionism is not the same as the healthy pursuit of excellence, as you can see in the comparisons on page 176.

5. **Lack of rewards.** The greatest motivating force in the world is a feeling of excitement and satisfaction in what you do. If you feel rewarded for your efforts, it will motivate you to work harder. But if nothing you do is ever good enough, life will become an exhausting, joyless treadmill.

People who are highly successful and productive usually give themselves credit for what they do. Because they think about their work in a positive way, they feel excited and involved.

Procrastinators sometimes do just the opposite. They constantly put themselves down. If you clean the house, you may tell yourself that what you did "wasn't good enough" or "didn't count" or "wasn't very special." Then at the end of the day you feel drained and you don't think you've accomplished anything worthwhile.

In fact, some procrastinators display a brilliant ability to discount the value of anything they do. A woman who worked for a computer company told me that for over two years she had been hiding in her office, doing virtually nothing aside from clipping her nails, making personal phone calls, and reading magazines. She was afraid her boss might discover how little she was doing and fire her. She wanted me to help her become more productive.

I wanted to find out what her idea of "becoming more productive" would be. Notice how unwilling she is to give herself credit for anything positive:

DAVID: Let me see if I can understand what you have in mind when you say you want me to help you become more productive. Suppose you made a plan for yourself and you were able to work four hours a day for the next week. Would you consider that a step in the right direction?

SUSAN: That wouldn't count because I'm supposed to put in seven hours a day. [Notice how she discounts the positive.]

DAVID: Okay. Let's suppose you then continued to improve and during the second week you put in seven hours a day. What would you think about that?

SUSAN: I'd say it wouldn't count at all. You see, I was supposed to start working on this project last February. Even if I put in seven hours a day, I'd still be way behind. [Notice that she discounts the positive again.]

DAVID: And suppose you started putting in ten hours a day, seven days a week, and eventually you got all caught up. Would you give yourself credit? Would you feel you were becoming a little more productive?

SUSAN: Well, if I did . . . then I'd think that I was still behind everybody else and worry about all the time I've wasted in the past two years.

DAVID: Okay. Suppose you continued working ambitiously and your efficiency went up to some incredibly high level and they started raving about you as one of their most productive, efficient employees. Let's say they even promoted you. What would you think then?

SUSAN: That would be spooky. I'd say I must have made a pact with the devil and it had nothing to do with me.

DAVID: I see. So I take it then that regardless of whatever you do at work, whatever effort you put in and whatever degree of success you achieve, you'll continue to believe that you're incapable of being productive and undeserving of any praise or credit?

SUSAN: Yeah.

I've included this dialogue to illustrate Susan's enormously persistent tendency to put herself down. Do you ever do this yourself? Do you tell yourself that your efforts and accomplishments aren't any good? If so, you'll feel beaten down no matter how hard you try, and you'll feel unappreciated and unmotivated.

We usually think of rewards as coming from the outside. A compliment for a job well done feels good. Getting a high grade on a test or making a sale to a difficult customer can be highly motivating. But ultimately all rewards must come from within. Only your thoughts can make you feel good or bad. If you never give yourself credit, you will feel that you can never do anything well enough to satisfy yourself, so it will become pointless to try. Why keep banging your head against a wall?

6. **"Should statements."** Procrastinators often tell themselves: "I really *should* write those letters. I *ought to* get started." These "should statements" usually aren't very effective, because they make you feel guilty and resentful, so you avoid the task. The moment you tell yourself "I really *should* do it," you will probably have the thought ". . . but I don't really have to right now. I'll wait until later."

Sometimes, the more you tell yourself that you *should* do something, the harder it is to do it!

You may have difficulty with this idea. You may insist that there's nothing wrong with using the word "should." You may think that it's your duty to clean your desk or to study hard. You may feel it's something you really *should* do!

There are actually three valid uses of the word "should" in the English language. One is the "moral should." You "should" not intentionally take advantage of someone, because this violates your moral code. The second is the "legal should." You "should" not drive at 90 mph because it's dangerous and you'll probably get a ticket. The third is the "laws of the universe should." Things "should" happen because the forces of nature make them happen. For example, if you drop your pen, it "should" fall because of the force of gravity.

When you say "I should straighten up my desk," is this a "moral should"? Obviously not, unless one of the Ten Commandments says "Thou shalt not have a messy desk." Is it a "legal should"? Obviously not, unless there are laws that prohibit messy desks. Is it a "law of the universe should"? Obviously not, since there's no law of nature that says that people with messy desks will always straighten them up right away.

Since it's not a "moral should," a "legal should," or a "law of the universe should," the word "should" really isn't appropriate here. When you say "I should straighten up my desk," I suspect what you really mean is "It would be to my advantage to straighten up my desk." But then why not simply think about it like that instead? Keep the word "should" out of the picture. Every time you tell yourself "I really *should* do X or Y," change it to "It would be desirable for me to do X or Y." Since this doesn't sound so moralistic, it won't make you feel rebellious and guilty.

Of course, this is based on the assumption that you've thought the matter through and have decided that it really is important to you to clear up your desk. You may discover that there is no compelling reason to have an organized desk. One of my friends at college prided himself on having one of the messiest rooms of anyone on campus. Papers and clothes were strewn several inches deep all over the room in what looked like total chaos. He said that people were always telling him to straighten it up, but that it *was* organized and he liked it just the way it was. He said he knew where everything was, even though it looked messy to other people. In fact he was a superb student, and he was the most organized person I ever knew. His messy room was not a real problem for him.

Maybe procrastination isn't a problem for you, either. The fact is, you've probably been getting along okay for a long time with your desk the way it is. Cleaning it up will be time-consuming and anxiety provoking and you probably have better things to do. And if you do straighten up your desk, it will just get messy again. Remember that there's a certain amount of status in having a messy desk. And if you do clean it up, people may begin to expect more of you. This will put you under tremendous pressure. With a messy desk they'll be reminded that you're a rather disorganized person and you may be able to get away with a lot more.

In addition, there may be someone you're annoyed with who gets upset every time they see your desk. By leaving it messy, you can let them know indirectly that you're upset without being too obvious about it. This way, you won't have to confront them directly with how you feel. You can avoid an argument or a fight, which could be very upsetting for both of you.

Do you still want to clean up your desk, in light of all those reasons not to? If so, you will need some compelling reasons to do it. What are they? Keep these reasons in mind so you will know why you're cleaning it up. Then you will be doing it because you want to and not because you think you "should."

7. **Passive aggressiveness.** People who procrastinate are often afraid to express negative feelings openly and directly. You may avoid conflicts and deny that you're upset because you think it's not "nice" to be angry. Your true feelings may come oozing out indirectly. You may fail to return an RSVP for a party you don't really want to go to, or you may "forget" to repay a debt because you're annoyed with the person who lent you the money. You may chronically show up late for appointments because you're annoyed with your boss. You may "forget" to take out the trash because you feel upset with your spouse for nagging you about it.

You may not be completely aware that your procrastination is provocative or frustrating to others. You may push your negative feelings out of your mind and say "I just forgot." That way you can deny how you really feel.

You can develop some insight about this if you ask yourself if a family member, a teacher, or someone you work with feels frustrated or annoyed because of your procrastination. If so, ask yourself if you feel upset or annoyed with them. This could be the cause of your procrastination.

8. **Unassertiveness.** Many people procrastinate because they are unassertive and agree to do things they don't really want to do. You may give in to unreasonable demands from others because you think you should be nice. You may think you should meet everybody else's expectations and base too much of your self-esteem on what other people think of you. You may be terrified of disapproval or criticism. You may be afraid to say no and run the risk that someone would get annoyed with you. Then you may put something off and get anxious every time you think about doing it. You could think of your procrastination as a way of being on strike.

Of course, there are times when we all do things we don't want to do to help others, but this niceness can go too far if you feel that you always have to say yes and please everybody. You may get overcommitted and procrastinate instead of being honest and direct with people about how you feel.

9. **Coercion sensitivity.** You may procrastinate because you feel that people are acting bossy and making unreasonable demands on you. You may be stubborn and refuse to do what they ask as a way of rebelling. Other people may find this behavior annoying and act even pushier. This leads to a power struggle, because no one wants to give in.

Your procrastination may be an indirect way of expressing your annoyance with the person who's nagging you. Even if it is to your advantage to go along with them, you may feel the need to resist so you can show that you won't let them control you. One morning a woman named Sarah made a decision to start her diet. She did well all day. That evening her husband, who was unaware of her decision, reminded her that she shouldn't eat so many sweets. She felt hurt and told him, "I can eat anything I darn well please!" She ate a giant hot fudge sundae in front of him to prove her point!

10. **The lack of desire.** This last cause of procrastination may sound ridiculously obvious, but it's the commonest cause of all. When you procrastinate, it's often because you simply don't want to do whatever it is that you're putting off. Most procrastinators aren't in touch with this. All you know is that there's some task you vaguely feel you should do, but you get really uncomfortable when it's time to do it,

so you do something else. Instead of telling yourself that you didn't want to do it and admitting that you made a conscious choice not to, you act as if the whole process is mysterious. You think, "Gee, I really am a procrastinator. I must really be lazy. That must be why I didn't balance my checkbook [or study or clean my desk or mow the lawn]." But this is just a lot of fancy talk. The real reason you didn't do it was because you didn't want to!

Now you might say, "So what? Everyone knows that!" However, admitting that you don't want to do something can be a useful insight. Once you become aware of why you're procrastinating, it may put the problem into a different perspective. If you're procrastinating, ask yourself why. You may have good reasons.

You may put something off because it's not a high priority. You may feel that it wouldn't be wise for you to do it, and in your heart of hearts you may not really want to do it or need to do it. Perhaps your family, friends, or boss has encouraged you to pursue a goal that you don't really feel committed to or ready for. Maybe it isn't quite right for you, but you haven't admitted this to yourself. Instead of owning up to the fact that the task may not be right for you, you may postpone it while you tell yourself that you "should" do it or that you "need" to do it. Then you may berate yourself and get anxious. Your procrastination may really be a healthy response that you need to listen to.

Soon after *Feeling Good* was published, I obtained a contract for *The Feeling Good Handbook*. However, I didn't feel ready to write the book. I forced out a number of chapters, but my writing was wooden and the material seemed boring. I wasn't convinced that I had anything new or important to say because it seemed I had already said nearly everything in *Feeling Good*. Furthermore, I couldn't think of a format for the *Handbook* that excited me. This state of affairs dragged on for years. Every now and then my editor would call or write to tell me how well *Feeling Good* was doing and would ask about the new *Handbook*.

One evening it suddenly occurred to me that I was ready to write the *Handbook*—for years I had been teaching and treating patients and doing research, and I had learned a great deal that I wanted to share. It also dawned on me that there were probably a lot of people who would appreciate learning more about how to break out of bad moods. I felt full of new ideas and rapidly produced a draft of the *Handbook*. The experience of writing it was exhilarating, and I was glad that I had put the project off until I felt ready.

10

•

A Prescription for Procrastinators

The following five-step program can help you become more productive and successful. What is one thing you've been putting off? It might be calling the doctor or dentist for a checkup, paying your bills, writing an overdue letter, calling on a customer, balancing your checkbook, organizing your desk, outlining a proposal, asking someone for a date—it can be anything. Choose one thing. Make sure it's specific and not vague. Think about this for a moment and see if you can come up with one thing you're putting off before you read on.

Some people might tell me, "Dr. Burns, I'm procrastinating about everything." This problem is too abstract. It's overwhelming. The best way to get your life together is to get started on one specific task. This will often give you the momentum to do other things you've been putting off. Select something concrete and real that you'd like to do, like cleaning the garage. Describe the task you've chosen:

_____

_____

Have you thought about something and written it down? If not, I really want you to do this before you read on. I want you to interact with me and to do the written exercises as you read this. Are you willing to? If so, that's great! You will be rewarded for your efforts!

Step 1: Cost-Benefit Analysis

First, ask yourself *why* you should stop procrastinating. Make a list of the advantages of putting this task off:

1. _____

_____

2. _____

_____

3. _____

_____

4. _____

_____

5. _____

_____

When you make your list, remember that procrastination has many advantages: it's easy; you can do something else that would be more relaxing; you can put the problem out of your mind so you won't feel so upset; you can avoid hard work; you don't have to face the possibility of failure; you can frustrate the people who are unfairly nagging you to get it done; and you can prevent people from pressuring you and making so many demands on you. If you put the task off long enough, they may begin to accept the fact that you're not going to do it and they'll expect less of you.

Procrastination may also give you some status. After all, it's only very lucky or very wealthy people who don't have to work hard at things. If you procrastinate and take it easy, you may be saying, "I'm a special kind of person—I'm one cut above the rest. I shouldn't have to work hard and hustle. I deserve to play and have fun."

It's crucial to be aware of these advantages of procrastination because they may be too good to give up. You'll need some pretty powerful reasons to change. Developing some insight into the rewards of procrastinating will make you more aware of why you put things off. You wake up and tell yourself "I'm really going to get started on X today." "X" could be dieting or cleaning your desk or any chore you've been putting off. At the end of the day, you realize that you haven't followed through on your plan. Instead of dieting, you binged. Your desk is even more littered. You still haven't studied or gone out on a job interview. You get frustrated and mad at yourself, and you wonder why you're being so irrational. Maybe you're *not* being so irrational. You undoubtedly have a lot of powerful reasons why you procrastinate.

You may decide that you don't want to change. Remember the discussion in the last chapter—that procrastination is sometimes healthy? You may be doing something, like going to college or selling life insurance, because you think it's what you *should* be doing. Everyone pressures you to do it, but in your heart of hearts it's not what you really want to be doing. Maybe you cut classes and avoid studying because you don't want to be in school right now. Maybe you want to take a year off and bum around and think about what you really want to do with your life. I took a year off from medical school on two different occasions because I wasn't sure I wanted to be a doctor. I was not a pre-med student in college, and I only went to medical school so I could become a psychiatrist. I didn't enjoy medical school, and on many occasions it just didn't seem worth all the hassle. Those years off helped me get in touch with what I really wanted to do with my life, and I discovered a far greater degree of commitment than was there when I left.

Can you think of any disadvantages in procrastinating about the task you chose? You may feel guilty; you may get tired of people nagging you; you won't enjoy the satisfaction of completing the job. List the disadvantages of procrastinating here:

1. _____

_____

2. _____

_____

3. _____

_____

4. _____

_____

5. _____

_____

Now weigh the advantages of procrastinating against the disadvantages. Ask yourself whether the costs or the benefits of putting it off are greater. The man whose Cost-Benefit Analysis is illustrated on the next page was procrastinating about cleaning his desk. He decided that the disadvantages of procrastinating outweighed the advantages by a 60–40 margin.

Now make a similar list of the advantages and disadvantages of getting started on the task *today*. Notice that I did not say "sometime." Also notice that I've asked you to list the advantages and disadvantages of *getting started*, and not of completing the task. This is important, because the task may seem overwhelming. While I've been writing this book, lots of papers have piled up in my office. I haven't taken the time to keep up with all the filing that needs to be done. I would estimate that I have at least five hours of organizing and straightening up to do. When I decide to get started, I'll only do a little bit at first. Then I'll chip away at it over a period of a couple of weeks. That way it won't seem overwhelming. If I told myself I had to do it all at once, I might never get started.

PROCRASTINATION
COST-BENEFIT ANALYSIS

What are you procrastinating about? Describe the task here:

Straightening my desk

List the advantages and disadvantages of procrastinating:

Advantages	Disadvantages
1. I can do something else I want to do.	1. I feel guilty every time I look at it.
2. It seems like a hideous chore.	2. I feel disorganized and I lose respect for myself.
3. If I put it out of my mind, I won't have to think about it.	3. I can't find the things I need.
	4. It looks like a mess and my wife is annoyed about it.
	5. I don't enjoy the satisfaction of getting it done.

(40)—(60)

Outcome: Weigh the advantages of procrastinating against the disadvantages on a 100-point scale, and put the score in the circles.

List the advantages and disadvantages of getting started today:

Advantages	Disadvantages
1. I'll probably feel better about myself if I at least get started.	1. It will make me uncomfortable to face the mess.
2. I'll be more organized and able to find the things I need.	2. There are other things I'd rather be doing.
3. The room will look better.	3. It may take a long time.
4. My wife will be pleasantly surprised.	

(55)——(45)

OUTCOME: Weigh the advantages of getting started today against the disadvantages, and put that score in the circles.

Think about the advantages of getting started today on the task you've been putting off: you may feel greater self-esteem; other people may get off your back and respect you more; you may experience a mood lift; you might feel more motivated once you get started. List the advantages of getting started today:

1. _____

_____

2. _____

_____

3. _____

_____

4. _____

_____

5. _____

_____

The disadvantages of getting started could include: the task may be difficult; you may feel frustrated and nervous; you may feel obligated to do even more once you get started; you may fail; people may get ticked off at you if you don't do a good job; you won't be able to use the time to do something that's more enjoyable. List the disadvantages of getting started here:

1. _____

_____

2. _____

_____

3. _____

_____

4. _____

_____

5. _____

_____

After you've completed these lists, weigh the advantages of getting started today against the disadvantages. Which seem greater to you? You can see that the man who completed the form on page 188 decided that the advantages slightly outweighed the disadvantages, by a 55–45 margin.

Once you've compared the costs and benefits of getting started today with the costs and benefits of procrastinating, you can decide which option is the best. I've included a blank Cost-Benefit Analysis for your use at the end of this chapter.

Your analysis may indicate that even though you don't want to do a particular task and you don't "feel like it," it may still be in your best interest to get started. This insight can help you break the habit of thinking you always have to feel motivated or "in the mood" before you do something.

The Cost-Benefit Analysis can be especially helpful if someone is putting pressure on you to do something and you feel the urge to resist them. Maybe your spouse or a parent or a teacher is nagging you to lose weight, to jog, to study, to apply for a job, or to clean up your room. You may feel stubborn and dig in your heels. You need to decide what *you* want to do. Sometimes it turns out to be better to do something in spite of the fact that someone's being obnoxious and nagging you about it!

By the same token, after you review your Cost-Benefit Analysis, you might discover that you really don't want to get started at this time. You may discover that you may *never* want to do the thing you've been putting off. That's perfectly okay, because you've made a free choice. Once you make this decision, you're no longer procrastinating. Procrastination, by definition, is avoiding a task that you've chosen to do. If you decide not to do it, your problem has been solved. There's really no reason to read any further! On the other hand, if your Cost-Benefit Analysis indicates that you do want to get started, then you're ready for the next step.

Step 2: Make a Plan

Have you decided that the advantages of getting started today outweigh the disadvantages? If so, I want to know exactly what time you will start. Write the time down here:

Have you written the time down? If the answer is no, I'm puzzled. This indicates that you do not plan to get started on the task today. Either you're reading this chapter out of curiosity, or else you have decided not to get started on the task. This is okay, but we should be perfectly clear with each other that you do not have any intention of overcoming your procrastination at this time.

On the other hand, if you *have* written the time down, congratulations! You are beginning to change your life one step at a time. You've already taken the biggest step. If you keep filling out the blanks as you read, I believe that you'll be able to lick this problem. Keep it up! If you haven't written the time down, you can still do it. Grab your pen and fill in the blank now!

Many patients complain that they want help with their procrastinating. They express a vague commitment to doing something to solve the problem. They may say they'll go home and start jogging or they'll apply for a job or do whatever it was they've been putting off. In the early days of my practice, I would get my hopes up, only to discover when they came back the next week that they hadn't followed through. The typical story was "I forgot" or "Gee, I didn't get around to it."

After feeling puzzled and frustrated by this for several years, I finally found a good way to combat it. If you were my patient and you told me you planned to do something you had been putting off, I would ask, "At what specific time today do you plan to do it?" After squirming, you might name a time. Then I would say, "Can you think of any distractions or problems that would conceivably prevent you from following through?" We would list these together. Then I would say, "Now, I want you to tell me how you will combat each of these obstacles so you can guarantee that nothing can prevent you from following through." Once I felt convinced that you meant business, I would ask you to call my office at an agreed-upon time and report either that you had completed the job or that you "stubbornly refused."

This may seem insulting and heavy-handed, but I have found that once you make a commitment to getting started at a specific time, the likelihood of success is enhanced.

Since you may not have put down a specific time when I asked you to several paragraphs back, let me give you the chance again here:

Have you done this? If so, the chances are high that you're about to change your life in a very fundamental and important way.

Now make a list of any problems or obstacles that could prevent you from following through. Fred, a perfectionistic professor, kept procrastinating about writing the outline for his book because he was afraid that it wouldn't be good enough. After completing the Cost-Benefit Analysis in my office one morning, he agreed to work on it from 3:00 to 4:00 that afternoon. I asked him to list any problems that could conceivably prevent him from carrying out this plan. These were:

1. "I won't feel like it when 3:00 rolls around."

2. "I'll get distracted by other things. I'll decide that I should straighten up my office first."

3. "A student might want an appointment."

4. "Once I try to write the outline, I'll feel inadequate. I'll tell myself that I don't have anything important to say."

I asked Fred how he would solve each of these problems. This was his "solution" list:

1. "I can tell myself I've made a decision to work on the book between 3:00 and 4:00 whether I feel like it or not."

2. "I can work on it at the library instead of my office. Then I won't feel so tempted by the distractions in my office."

3. "If a student wants an appointment, I can say that I have a commitment from 3:00 until 4:00 p.m."

4. "I can decide to jot down some ideas for one hour, whether or not it seems like I have anything worthwhile to say. Then I will give myself credit for that."

Fred called my office at 4:15 and left the message that he'd written steadily during the entire hour and felt great about it.

This simple method can be effective for you too. Think about the task you've decided to get started on today. In the left-hand column below, list any problems or obstacles that could sabotage your good intentions. Then put solutions to these problems in the right-hand column.

Problems	Solutions
1. _____	1. _____
_____	_____
2. _____	2. _____
_____	_____
3. _____	3. _____
_____	_____

Once you've decided when you will get started and have thought of ways to deal with any problems that might sabotage your good intentions, you're ready for the next step.

Step 3: Make the Job Easy

You can make a difficult job easy if you have modest, realistic goals instead of grandiose, perfectionistic ones. You might think that if the first sentence of your report isn't a masterpiece of modern prose, it won't be any good at all. This expectation will put enormous pressure on you and you may end up doing nothing. Why not try to write an "adequate" first sentence instead? That would be far easier, and at least you could get started. Once you have one "adequate" sentence on the paper you can add another and another, until you complete an "adequate" paragraph or a page. Then you can do some "adequate" editing the next day and make this material even better. Often things turn out the best for me when I'm not trying so hard. The same may be true for you.

Another way to make a tough job easy is to do a little bit at a time. You may feel overwhelmed because you tell yourself you have to do things all at once. Instead, break the job down into its smallest component parts and concentrate on one part at a time.

The secret involves getting into the here-and-now instead of worrying about everything you have to do in the future. Life exists one minute at a time, so all you'll ever have to do at any time is one minute's worth of work. That's not so hard, is it?

There are two ways to break a big job down into small parts. One is to tackle the job in a step-by-step fashion. If you have to paint your porch, the first step might be to select a color. The second step would be to go to the hardware store to buy the paint. The third step would be to carry the ladder out to the porch. And so forth. Make sure each step of the task is reasonably easy.

The second way to break a task down is to work in short spurts. Would you be willing to work at a big job you've been putting off for only fifteen to thirty minutes today? You may resist this suggestion. Nearly every procrastinator tells me, "That would be useless. I'm not going to study [or work at my taxes] for only fifteen to thirty minutes! That would be only a drop in the bucket compared to all I have to do!"

Remember that no one could possibly do any more than fifteen to thirty minutes of productive work in any fifteen- to thirty-minute period. So telling yourself you have to do more than that is pointless! Of course, once you've put in fifteen or thirty minutes, there's nothing to prevent you from deciding to put in another fifteen to thirty minutes. Once I get rolling on a difficult job I often feel so good about it that before I know it several hours have passed. But I rarely tell myself to do more than fifteen minutes worth of work at any one time. I tell myself that everything beyond fifteen minutes is gravy. This is, admittedly, a way of fooling myself, but I'm quite gullible and the method is enormously effective. Give it a try!

Here are the advantages of working in short spurts:

- You'll break big jobs down into small parts that can be completed in short periods of time. This will make your task seem less overwhelming.
- You can accomplish your goal of doing fifteen minutes worth of work soon after you begin. The sense of accomplishment will often reduce the feelings of tension and motivate you to do more. You'll begin to feel more relaxed and productive.
- You won't be so tempted to procrastinate and put things off, because you'll never be obligated to do more than fifteen minutes worth of work at any one time. It's really not so hard to sit down and work at an unpleasant task if you feel you have to stick with it for only a little while.

- Trying to cram everything in at once is usually not the best way to master a difficult assignment. You can often work more creatively and efficiently by doing things in short bursts. If you're studying or writing a report, your mind will digest ideas between these short work periods. You will produce a higher-quality product than you thought you were capable of, with far less effort and stress.

Once you've made a plan to make the task easier and less of a hassle, you can move on to the next step.

Step 4: Think Positively

When you think about a task you've been avoiding, you may feel upset and want to do something else instead. This is because you give yourself negative messages that make you feel guilty and overwhelmed. Suppose you're procrastinating about writing thank-you letters. You may tell yourself: "Oh, I have all those letters to write. I can put them off until later when I'm more in the mood. I really should write them now, but I don't feel like it. It'll be so unpleasant. I think I'll watch television for a while instead."

You can learn how to deal with these negative thoughts so they won't undermine your efforts. Ask yourself, "When I procrastinate, what am I telling myself? What negative thoughts are running through my mind?" Write these thoughts down. This is crucial—you cannot change the way you think and feel if you refuse to write your thoughts down. Write down any negative thoughts you may have about the task you're putting off:

1. _____

_____

2. _____

_____

3. _____

_____

Once you write them down, you may see that you engage in a subtle process of self-deception when you procrastinate. It's not the actual task, but the unrealistic way you think about it that makes you want to put it off. Let me repeat that: You procrastinate because you think about the job in an unrealistic, illogical way. When you avoid a task, you are always fooling yourself about something!

Dr. Aaron Beck has called these distorted negative thoughts "TICs," for "Task-Interfering Cognitions," because they interfere with your ability to get started. You can replace them with "TOCs," for "Task-Oriented Cognitions," with the help of the "TIC-TOC Technique." TOCs are positive and realistic thoughts that will make you feel more productive and motivated.

For example, the first negative thought, or TIC, illustrated on the next page is "I have all those letters to write." The distortion in this thought, which you would write down in the middle column, is "all-or-nothing thinking." You're telling yourself you have to write all those letters today. This will make you feel overwhelmed, and you'll give up before you even begin. You could substitute this TOC in the right-hand column: "I don't have to do them all tonight, but I'd probably feel a whole lot better if I finished at least one of them." You could even decide that all you have to do tonight is locate some stationery and address one or two envelopes. That would be a good first step.

The second TIC is "I can put them off until later when I'm more in the mood." Can you identify the distortion in this thought? Review the list on page 206 and put your ideas here:

_____

_____

The distortion is "emotional reasoning," because you're waiting until you feel like writing the letters. This is putting the cart before the horse. Usually action comes first and motivation comes second.

What could you tell yourself instead? Put your TOC here:

_____

_____

_____

THE TIC-TOC TECHNIQUE

What are you procrastinating about? Describe it here:
Writing thank-you letters

What negative feelings do you have when you think about doing it? Use words like "anxious," "guilty," "frustrated," or "overwhelmed" and indicate how strong each one is between 0 and 100.

	Emotion	Rating		Emotion	Rating
1.	Guilty	80	3.	Unmotivated	90
2.	Bored	90			

TICs (Task-Interfering Cognitions)	Distortions (See list on page 206)	TOCs (Task-Oriented Cognitions)
1. I have all those letters to write.	1. All-or-nothing thinking	1. I don't have to do them all tonight, but I'd probably feel a whole lot better if I did at least one of them.
2. I can put them off until later when I'm more in the mood.	2. Emotional reasoning	2. I don't have to be "in the mood" to get started. Once I get started I'll probably feel more like doing it.
3. I really should write them now, but I don't feel like it.	3. "Should statement"; emotional reasoning	3. It would be to my advantage to start them now.

TICs	Distortions	TOCs
4. It'll be such a drag. I think I'll watch TV for a while instead.	4. Fortune-telling	4. How do I know it will be a drag? Maybe it won't! I can write one letter and find out. Watching TV may not be so great, because I'll feel guilty about not doing the letters.

You could think about it this way instead: "I don't have to be 'in the mood.' Once I get started, I'll probably feel more like doing it."

As an exercise, cover up the middle and right-hand columns in the following examples. The TICs in the left-hand colum are upsetting thoughts that patients of mine have had about tasks they were putting off. Try to identify the distortions in these TICs and see if you can substitute TOCs. Then compare your answers to the ones I've suggested. Don't be concerned if your responses are different from mine. Part of the beauty of this technique is that there's a lot of room for your own unique approach.

You may have the thought: "This TIC-TOC technique is just a silly gimmick that wouldn't work for me. How dumb!" This is another TIC that will make you procrastinate. Can you see what distortions it contains? Check the list on page 206 and put your ideas here:

1. _____

2. _____

3. _____

The thought is an example of "fortune-telling," because you're predicting that this technique won't help you. We don't have any real evidence for that. It's also an example of "emotional reasoning," because you feel that these methods won't help, so you conclude they really won't. Finally, you're "labeling" the technique a "gimmick." This is pejorative. If you think of it as a "method," you will be more open-minded and willing to give it a try.

TICs	Distortions	TOCs
1. I'll never get the garage cleaned. The junk's been piling up for years.	1. Fortune-telling; all-or-nothing thinking	1. I can do a little bit. I don't have to do it all today.
2. I don't want to study for the exam!	2. Emotional reasoning	2. I don't have to *want* to study, but it would be advisable to do it anyway.
3. I have so much to study. It's overwhelming!	3. All-or-nothing thinking	3. The sooner I get started, the sooner I'll get done. I can think of what I need to do in the next hour instead of worrying about all I have to do.
4. I have no confidence. I don't know how to work some of the problems in the book.	4. Emotional reasoning; "should statement"	4. I'm not supposed to feel confident yet. That's why I need to study.

TICs	Distortions	TOCs
1. I should ask my boss for a raise—but I really don't feel like it.	1. "Should statement"; emotional reasoning	1. It would be to my advantage to ask my boss for a raise because I've been working hard and it's time for a salary review. Asking him for a raise is scary, but I can do it even if I don't feel like it.

Can you think of a way to talk back to this negative thought? Put your ideas here:

_____

_____

_____

_____

You could substitute this TOC: "It seems as if writing down my negative thoughts wouldn't help, but I can't know this until I try. Maybe the method will work, and it will only take a few minutes to find out!"

Now write down your negative thoughts about the job you've been avoiding in the left-hand column of the blank form at the end of this chapter. Identify the distortions in these thoughts, and substitute more positive and realistic thoughts in the right-hand column. You will be surprised by how helpful this can be!

Step 5: Give Yourself Credit

Once you've begun a job you've been avoiding, it's important to give yourself credit instead of discounting your efforts. A mental reward will boost your motivation. A housewife told me that she worked like a hornet all day long. At the end of the day she'd obsess about all the things she hadn't had time to squeeze into her crowded schedule. This made her feel as if she hadn't accomplished anything at all! She felt burned out and unrewarded. I suggested that she could make a list of everything she accomplished each day. Simply reviewing this list at the end of the day made her feel better, because she could see that she had done a great deal.

Let's assume that she still continued to feel inadequate and miserable in spite of the fact that she was doing a great deal every day. What would you think the real problem is? You be the psychiatrist, and put your diagnosis here. Why does she feel burned out each day?

_____

_____

_____

_____

I would speculate that doing housework and errands all day long may not be what she really wants to do. Her negative feelings may be her way of telling herself that she would like to go back to school or pursue a career. She may be pushing herself to do what she thinks she *should* do, rather than doing what she *wants* to do.

There can be some advantages to this. It may protect her from taking a chance of doing something new and risking failure. Being an unhappy but dutiful, perfectionistic housewife may be less threatening. But by the same token, life becomes a joyless treadmill, and the chronic resentment and unhappiness she feels may poison her marriage.

You may wonder how you can tell if your goals are appropriate for you. I would say that if you feel a sense of commitment and excitement about what you're doing, you're in good shape. This doesn't mean that you constantly have to feel high and exhilarated.

Pursuing any goal involves lots of hard work and frustration along the way. But if you have a sense of meaning and purpose, all the hard work falls into a different perspective. This is what is meant by the expression "a labor of love." Your discomfort becomes like the pain of labor, because you're giving birth to your own destiny.

Let's summarize the five steps to greater productivity. First, pinpoint one specific task that you've been putting off and do a Cost-Benefit Analysis. This will help you decide if you really do want to get started on the task. Many people have a knee-jerk reaction and tell themselves "I should do this" and "I ought to do that" when they don't really feel committed. You may discover that your procrastination is not a bad habit but simply your way of telling yourself—and the world—that a particular activity is not right for you. You may want to rethink your priorities instead of feeling guilty.

The second step is to decide on a specific time to get started today and to anticipate ways you might sabotage yourself. Make a plan to handle these distractions. The third step is to make the job easy, either by breaking it down into parts or by working at it for short periods of time. Then it won't seem so overwhelming. Next, use the TIC-TOC technique to change the negative thoughts that create emotional barriers, such as guilt, frustration, and anxiety.

Finally, give yourself credit for the things you accomplish instead of insisting that your efforts are never good enough. When things don't turn out as well as you had hoped, you can learn from the experience and move forward instead of giving up and deciding that you're "a failure."

PROCRASTINATION
COST-BENEFIT ANALYSIS*

What are you procrastinating about? Describe it here:

_____

List the advantages and disadvantages of putting it off:

Advantages	Disadvantages

OUTCOME: Weigh the advantages of procrastinating against the disadvantages on a 100-point scale, and record the score in the circles.

(Continue on next page)

List the advantages and disadvantages of getting started today:

Advantages	Disadvantages

Outcome: Now weigh the advantages of getting started today against the disadvantages on a 100-point scale, and record the score in the circles.

THE TIC-TOC TECHNIQUE*

What are you procrastinating about? Describe it here:

_____

What negative feelings do you have when you think about doing it? Use words like "anxious," "guilty," "frustrated," or "over-whelmed" and indicate in parentheses how strong each one is between 0 percent and 100 percent.

Emotion	Rating	Emotion	Rating
1. _____		3. _____	
2. _____		4. _____	

TICs (Task-Interfering Cognitions)	Distortions (See list on page 206)	TOCs (Task-Oriented Cognitions)

(Continue on next page)

TICs	Distortions	TOCs

CHECKLIST OF COGNITIVE DISTORTIONS*

1. All-or-nothing thinking: You look at things in absolute, black-and-white categories.
2. Overgeneralization: You view a negative event as a never-ending pattern of defeat.
3. Mental filter: You dwell on the negatives and ignore the positives.
4. Discounting the positives: You insist that your accomplishments or positive qualities "don't count."
5. Jumping to conclusions: (A) Mind reading—you assume that people are reacting negatively to you when there's no definite evidence for this; (B) Fortune-telling—you arbitrarily predict that things will turn out badly.
6. Magnification or minimization: You blow things way up out of proportion or you shrink their importance inappropriately.
7. Emotional reasoning: You reason from how you feel: "I *feel* like an idiot, so I really must be one." Or "I don't *feel* like doing this, so I'll put it off."
8. "Should statements": You criticize yourself or other people with "shoulds" or "shouldn'ts." "Musts," "oughts," and "have tos" are similar offenders.
9. Labeling: You identify with your shortcomings. Instead of saying "I made a mistake," you tell yourself, "I'm a jerk," or "a fool," or "a loser."
10. Personalization and blame: You blame yourself for something you weren't entirely responsible for, or you blame other people and overlook ways that your own attitudes and behavior might contribute to a problem.

PART THREE

Feeling Confident: How to Conquer Anxiety, Fears, and Phobias

11

•

Understanding Anxiety

There are three competing theories about the causes of anxiety. A cognitive therapist would claim that negative thoughts and irrational attitudes cause anxiety. For example, if you believe that you must always get everyone's approval, you might feel very nervous if your boss was criticizing you or if you had to give a speech before a large audience.

A psychoanalyst would argue that repressed conflicts make you anxious. When you were growing up, you may have gotten the idea that children should be seen but not heard. You might have been afraid of sharing any negative feelings with your parents. As an adult, you may still be afraid of expressing anger or telling people how you really feel. When you have a conflict with your boss, you may clam up because you feel he will put you down, just as your parents did. The effort to avoid the conflict makes you repress your feelings, and you get terribly nervous and panicky.

Some psychiatrists think that an imbalance in your body chemistry causes feelings of fear and panic. These therapists might tell you that all you need is the right drug to correct the problem. Many patients are equally convinced that their nervous problems are medical. Some think their anxieties are caused by food allergies or low blood sugar.

Others fear they have a brain tumor or a heart condition. They go from doctor to doctor looking for a diagnosis and cure that never seem to materialize.

Which of these three ideas is correct? In this chapter, we will examine the merits of each.

How Your Thoughts Can Frighten You

Cognitive therapy is based on the premise that your thoughts, not external events, make you upset. This is just as true for anxiety and panic as for any other negative emotion. You have to interpret a situation and give it a meaning before you can feel worried or nervous about it. This idea has tremendous practical importance, because when you change the way you think, you can change the way you feel. You can overcome fear, worry, anxiety, nervousness, and panic.

Many people find this idea exciting. Others react with irritation. They insist that it can't be so. They tell me that if you're about to be hit by a train, it's the event, and not your thoughts, that makes you frightened. What do you think about this?

One evening recently I was going home from the airport in a taxi. As we crossed the railroad track about a mile from my house, I noticed a train coming in the distance. I was alarmed to see that a man was slowly driving his car down the railroad tracks—not crossing them, but actually driving down the tracks! I had no idea why anyone would be doing that, but I could see that he was on the same set of tracks as the oncoming train. If he didn't immediately back up, turn, and get off, it was clear that his car would be crushed.

I told the driver to stop and jumped out of the taxi. I shouted, "Get off the tracks!" The man simply pulled to a stop and waited. I rushed up to the window and urged him to back up, to get his car off the tracks immediately. He smiled at me in a leisurely, friendly way and asked if I knew the way to City Line Avenue. I couldn't comprehend why he would ask such a dumb question! The train was approaching at high speed and City Line Avenue is about ten miles away. He had less than thirty seconds to back up his car and get to safety. I exclaimed, "Back up! Back up!" He slowly backed up his car and then turned and positioned it so the hood was directly in the path of the oncoming train.

I ran and stood directly in front of his car, waving my arms wildly.

I screamed, "Back up! Back up!" He only had to back up five or ten feet to save himself.

Instead, he did the opposite! He slowly crept forward, inch by inch. By now the train was just a hundred yards away, coming fast with the horn blowing. I shouted "Faster! Faster!" Instead of speeding up, he smiled again and pulled to a stop. A crash seemed inevitable. The moment before the impact, I ran to avoid the collision. The train hit his car at high speed and crushed it.

The train was over a mile long and it was nearly a minute before it came to a full stop. I rushed up to the demolished car. The point of impact was directly behind the driver's head. The back half of the car was smashed to bits, but the front half was relatively intact, except for lots of broken glass. My heart was pounding as I peered through the mangled window. I saw that the driver was a frail, skinny, elderly gentleman. Miraculously, he appeared uninjured. He slowly turned to me, still smiling. Then he asked me in a lazy, relaxed voice if I could direct him to City Line Avenue. He explained that he'd been looking for City Line Avenue for some time—he thought he might be lost and asked if I'd kindly point him in the right direction. He said that all he needed was a few directions. I was flabbergasted.

"Direct you to City Line?" I asked incredulously. "That's over ten miles from here and your car is smashed!"

"Smashed?" he asked. He sounded surprised and skeptical.

"Look at it," I replied. "You've just been hit by a train! I'm astonished that you weren't killed."

"What train?" he asked in a disbelieving voice.

"*That* one!" I said, pointing at the train. He slowly turned and looked at the smashed rear half of his auto and at the train a few feet behind him.

He finally became animated. He seemed filled with enthusiasm and exclaimed: "Oh! Hit by a train? Can I sue?" I told him, "You'll be lucky if they don't sue *you*! You've been driving down the railroad tracks."

It suddenly dawned on me what had happened. This elderly man was apparently getting senile and he was confused by the dark. This experience underscored a simple concept at the heart of cognitive therapy. You cannot have *any* emotional reaction to an event until you have a *thought* about it and have given it meaning. He had no anxiety whatsoever because he did not perceive that he was in danger.

He did not have the thought "I'm about to be hit by a train," so he had no emotional response to the event.

The railroad engineers soon appeared on the scene. When the police and the ambulance arrived, I gave them my story and went home. The next day when I was jogging I noticed a man inspecting the scene of the accident. I learned that he was the elderly man's son. When I described what had happened, he explained that his father was getting old and confused and had lots of difficulties driving at night.

The story also illustrates a second principle of cognitive therapy: There is a difference between healthy fear and neurotic anxiety. The thoughts that lead to healthy fear are realistic; they alert us to a danger that we need to deal with. My fear probably saved the old man's life. In contrast, neurotic anxiety results from distorted thoughts that have little or no basis in reality. If you are having a panic attack, you may believe that something terrible will happen if you let your anxiety get out of hand. You might think you'll pass out from a stroke or have a heart attack or go crazy. Although these fears seem legitimate, they're quite unrealistic because: (1) Anxiety *never* causes strokes or heart attacks. (2) Most people who are afraid of passing out during a panic attack have never once passed out when in a state of panic. In fact, you *cannot* pass out during a panic attack because your heart is beating rapidly and pumping extra blood to the brain. (3) Panic attacks never lead to insanity or a loss of control. You are worrying about something that's blatantly unrealistic.

And why do you believe these distorted thoughts? Because of the way you *feel*. You feel as if you're in danger, so you think you really must *be* in danger. You say, "I feel so frightened and out of control that I must be on the verge of losing control." Or "I'm dizzy and confused. I feel like I'm about to pass out, so I must be on the verge of fainting."

Although you may easily see that other people who feel depressed or anxious are being irrational and illogical, it is not so easy to accept the fact that your own negative thoughts are equally unrealistic. You may feel convinced that your fears and insecurities are absolutely valid. Changing them may require hard, persistent effort. Many powerful techniques to help you get rid of these frightening thoughts will be illustrated in the following chapters.

How Repressed Feelings Can Make You Anxious

Freud said that repressed anger causes depression. He thought that people get depressed because they're afraid to express their angry feelings, for fear of being rejected or abandoned by the people they care about. Then they turn these feelings inward and direct their anger against themselves. Depression, Freud thought, is a form of self-hatred which results from this bottled-up anger.

I have seen few, if any, patients whose depression resulted from repressed anger. I do not believe Freud's theory has a great deal of merit, although large numbers of people still believe it. However, my clinical experience has led me to the overwhelming conviction that anxiety and panic—and not depression—do result from repressed anger. People who suffer from anxiety and panic attacks nearly always have unexpressed negative feelings about some problem in their lives. You may not be completely aware of these feelings because you push them out of your mind. When you deny your feelings and avoid the conflicts that are bothering you, you will start to feel nervous and panicky. When you confront these problems, your anxiety will frequently diminish or disappear.

There are two kinds of feelings that people with anxiety are likely to deny: anger and unexpressed wishes or desires. Let me give you an obvious example. Ted is a businessman from San Francisco who was very unhappy when he was growing up. He had a variety of allergies that caused him to miss a lot of school. He often had to go to the doctor. He was sickly and had few friends. He was often teased because he couldn't participate in sports. The allergies caused severe skin problems, and Ted felt ugly and unpopular. He told himself, "If I'm really successful when I grow up, everything will be okay. People will like me."

So that's exactly what Ted did. He got an MBA, and although he wasn't a top student, he was determined to succeed. Following graduation, Ted took over his uncle's business which was on the verge of bankruptcy. He took out a second mortgage on his house and invested every penny in the company. It was a highly speculative gamble, and Ted worked his tail off from early morning till late at night seven days a week to make it work. In a few years the business recovered and started to prosper. Then the business boomed. Profits began pouring in. The company went public and was listed on the

New York Stock Exchange. The stock soared in value, and soon Ted's company was worth millions of dollars. He started new business ventures that turned into bonanzas. Soon he was featured in national magazines such as *Time* and *People*. Ted had become the "golden boy," married to a beautiful woman and considered handsome and debonair himself.

But there was one problem. Ted was still unhappy. He was constantly anxious. He worried all day long about his health, his business, and his popularity. He was a bundle of fears and phobias. He looked me up one day after reading *Feeling Good*, and told me sadly that in spite of all his money, the only happy days he could recall were when he'd been nearly penniless, working as a lifeguard during the summers when he was in college at U.C.L.A. He felt free then, working in the day and having fun with friends at night.

The cognitive techniques were helpful to Ted. He was able to see how irrational his fears were. He began to have days and then weeks when he felt relaxed and free of anxiety. Life began to seem like fun again. But every now and then, Ted's fears would return. Sometimes his airplane phobia would come back. This was especially inconvenient because his business required him to travel extensively. On other occasions, Ted would worry that he was about to have a heart attack. Then he'd worry that he was about to go broke. In spite of his rational awareness that these fears were unfounded, they would come back over and over to plague him.

One day it occurred to me that every time Ted got anxious, there was some problem that he was avoiding. During a session when we were dealing with his airplane phobia and his fears of bankruptcy, I asked him in passing how things had been going at work and at home. He told me they were going great except for his irrational worries. I asked again if anything was bothering him or upsetting him. He insisted there was not. He explained that he and his wife had been staying at their spacious new home overlooking the Pacific Ocean and that there were several relatives staying with them. He said that everyone was having a great time.

When I asked how long these relatives had been there, Ted said "Several weeks." My eyebrows went up. I asked if he was feeling at all uncomfortable with relatives camping out at his house and whether he knew when they planned to leave. At first Ted insisted that this wasn't a problem. He reasoned that since it was such a large house, it was only fair that he should share it with everybody! He said it would be selfish to live there with just the servants and his family. He said he was worried that the relatives might get mad at him if he tactfully asked how long they planned to stay.

Well, I suspect you get the drift. The theme in Ted's life was "I need everybody's approval. I must make sure that everybody likes me, even if I have to ignore my own needs and feelings." After we talked about this, Ted admitted that he felt very uncomfortable with all those people living in his house. In spite of his generous desire to share his wealth and good fortune, he felt trapped and missed his privacy. He talked this over with his wife, and the relatives moved out. His anxieties about going broke or dying in an airline crash suddenly vanished.

This pattern is common. You may deny your feelings and ignore certain problems in your life because you don't want to upset anyone or hurt their feelings. Suddenly you're worrying and having panic attacks and you have no idea why! It becomes so important to be nice that you get distracted from what's really bothering you. It's as if you think you don't have permission to feel the way you do. When you ignore these feelings of resentment and frustration, they may get converted into anxiety. You may dwell on your anxiety and your feelings of panic instead of dealing with the problems that are bothering you. When you confront them, you will often feel relief.

Will Ted's dramatic improvement last forever? Of course not. He will probably get upset and deny his feelings again on many occasions, just as you and I do. When he does, he'll have to have a little chat with himself and ask, "What am I *really* upset about?" Then he'll have to do something about the situation that's bothering him.

All of this may seem obvious to you. I hope it does. But I have been to professional symposia on the treatment of anxiety and panic by some of the world's leading experts, where the idea that patients may have family or career problems that need to be addressed is usually not even mentioned as a possible cause of anxiety. Instead, patients may be told that they have a "chemical imbalance" needing treatment—possibly indefinitely—with drugs. Although medications can be helpful for some patients, this is rarely, if ever, the whole story.

Medical Causes of Anxiety and Panic

So far we've talked about the two common psychological causes for anxiety: negative thoughts and repressed negative feelings. Many patients and many doctors think that the origin of anxiety and panic is not psychological but medical. In one study, over 90 percent of the patients with panic attacks had consulted at least one physician because they believed that they had some disease or chemical imbalance. Over 70 percent of these patients had seen ten or more physicians in the search for some medical illness that would account for their symptoms of anxiety!

This is not so surprising. Most patients with anxiety or panic attacks are convinced that something is physically or mentally wrong with them. In fact, the distorted belief that something is wrong with you is one of the most common symptoms of anxiety and panic. When you feel depressed you may reason, "I feel hopeless, therefore I must really be hopeless." When you feel anxious you may reason, "I feel like there's something terribly wrong with me, therefore there must really be something wrong."

Another reason for the preoccupation with medical illness is that many of the symptoms of anxiety are physical, as described in Chapters 2 and 3. When you feel nervous you may get lightheaded and develop a headache and worry that you have a brain tumor. Your chest may feel tight and you may think you have a heart condition. You may feel short of breath or feel a lump in your throat and think that your windpipe is closing down.

A third reason that people with anxiety go to physicians is because they would feel so much better if they had a real illness rather than an emotional or psychological problem. I first became aware of this when I was a medical student working in the outpatient medical clinic at Stanford University Medical Center. Patients came to this clinic from all over the western United States, with thick medical charts and long histories of aches and pains no one could diagnose. The majority of them had nothing medically wrong with them.

I can vividly recall the day when an ambulance pulled up and a woman was rushed in on a gurney for "emergency surgery." This was slightly unusual because emergencies were generally sent to the emergency room, but for one reason or another she ended up in the clinic. She was screaming and complained of excruciating abdominal pain. I wondered if she had a ruptured appendix, but I became a little suspicious when I examined her stomach. It was soft, not hard and rigid as it should have been with a ruptured internal organ. As I reviewed her medical chart, which was two inches thick, I discovered that she'd had seven previous operations on her abdomen for unexplained stomach pain! The biopsy reports of tissue samples obtained during these operations were always perfectly normal.

I asked her husband to wait in the waiting room while I spoke to her. She told me that he had shot her in the stomach during an argument seven years earlier. Since that time, she'd been working in his factory, packing sardines into cans fourteen hours a day. She admitted that she hated the job and was very unhappy with her marriage. As we talked, her pain disappeared. Then she told me that the mysterious stomach pain always got worse when her husband was around and usually disappeared completely when she wasn't with him.

Well, I guess you can make the proper diagnosis. She didn't need X-rays or surgery, but she did need marital counseling. The couple made the decision that day to separate for several weeks, to reduce the pressure they both felt so they could decide either to deal with the anger that was eating her alive or to get divorced.

You may think, "That's so obvious. How could any doctor miss it?" Physicians are trained to think about medical problems rather than human ones. Once your doctor has done a physical exam and ordered the proper tests, he or she feels the job is done. Talking to you about personal problems is time-consuming and costly. And many patients often strenuously resist a psychological interpretation. They pressure their physicians to do medical tests and to prescribe drugs. When physicians inquire about personal problems or suggest a referral to a psychiatrist or psychologist, many people feel deeply offended.

You may think that the woman with abdominal pain was very different from you. You may think her situation is dramatic and unusual and believe there really is something wrong with you. Certainly if you have headaches or pains or if you feel dizzy, it's reasonable to have a consultation with your doctor. He or she will listen to your symptoms and perform a physical examination, possibly ordering a blood test or an electrocardiogram. In the vast majority of cases, there will be no abnormalities to account for your symptoms. If so, you should suspect that a problem in your life, not in your body, is at the root of your difficulties.

However, there are several medical problems that can occasionally cause the symptoms of anxiety. Stimulants such as amphetamines or even coffee, as well as sedatives such as alcohol or marijuana, can make some people feel panicky and out of control. Many people with panic attacks report that the first episode occurred when they were high on a drug. Afterward the panic attacks can occur spontaneously.

In addition, if you abruptly stop taking any sedative drug—including alcohol, sleeping pills, tranquilizers, and most antidepressants—you may have feelings of anxiety and panic as well as other withdrawal symptoms. Research indicates that treating anxiety with large doses of tranquilizers or sleeping pills for more than a few weeks can be hazardous (see Chapter 23). The potential for addiction is great. I saw a woman recently who told me that after she stopped taking an average dose of Dalmane—a commonly prescribed sleeping pill—which she'd used nightly for several years, she was completely unable to sleep for two months!

Patients with panic, anxiety, or depression may rarely have abnormalities of the thyroid gland. "Hyperthyroidism" means an abnormal increase in thyroid output. This stimulates the body's metabolism. In addition to anxiety, people with this disorder may feel speeded up, experience increased appetite, weight loss, and an inability to tolerate heat, and have bulging eyes. The disease is uncommon and can easily be diagnosed with appropriate blood test. The opposite disorder, hypothyroidism, is caused by insufficient thyroid output. This leads to a slowing of the metabolism along with mood changes, including psychosis and depression. This disorder, too, is rare.

It has been known for decades that extraordinarily low levels of blood sugar can cause symptoms of anxiety, including sweating, trembling, racing heart, lightheadedness, and hunger. However, this syndrome, called hypoglycemia, is rare in the general population and it is almost never the cause of panic disorder. Although 25 percent of the normal adult population appear to have low blood sugar levels during testing, this usually does not cause the feelings of panic or anxiety that afflict so many people. One obvious exception would be a diabetic who made a mistake and injected too much insulin. This would cause a temporary severe fall in blood sugar with the symptoms of hypoglycemia. However, the cause of the symptoms is obvious, and this problem is not ordinarily confused with panic disorder. The only time that hypoglycemia would be suspected as a cause of panic attacks would be if your symptoms only occur one to two hours after eating and are always quickly eliminated by eating something sweet like candy or drinking orange juice or soda. (This is because the sugar goes into your blood and corrects the problem.)

Another extremely rare medical problem, a tumor of the adrenal gland called a pheochromocytoma, can cause a sudden dramatic increase in blood pressure along with headache, palpitations, flushing, sweating, and nausea. These tumors are exceedingly rare, and most people who have them do not experience typical panic or anxiety attacks.

In recent years, there has been a great deal of publicity about the relationship between panic attacks and a cardiac disorder called mitral valve prolapse. The mitral valve closes when the heart contracts to pump blood into the aorta. In some people, the leaflets of the mitral valve may bulge excessively during the heartbeat. Your doctor might pick this up when he hears an extra "click" while he listens to your heart with his stethoscope. The finding can be confirmed with an echocardiogram.

A number of studies have suggested that mitral valve prolapse is somewhat more common in patients with panic attacks than in the general population. However, estimates of how many panic attack patients have mitral valve prolapse are controversial, because of wide differences in the precise criteria that physicians use to diagnose mitral valve prolapse. The meaning of the association between mitral valve prolapse and panic attacks is unclear. There is no evidence that mitral valve prolapse causes panic, and there is no evidence that panic attacks cause mitral valve prolapse. In addition, mitral valve prolapse tends to be benign and does not need to be treated, whether or not you also have panic attacks. The treatment of the panic attacks will be the same regardless of whether or not you have this condition.

In summary, medical problems only rarely cause symptoms of anxiety and panic. The pursuit of a nonexistent disease is costly and time-consuming and often distracts people from dealing with the problems in their lives.

Psychiatrists are just as likely as internists to reinforce this notion that the causes of your anxiety are chemical or physical. Even in the absence of any medical problem, patients are frequently told that a "chemical imbalance" is responsible for their anxiety, and that their symptoms must be treated with drugs that will correct this "imbalance." Let me make one thing abundantly clear: We do not know of any physical or chemical imbalance that causes anxiety or panic.

Psychiatrists who tell you that you have a "chemical imbalance" are confusing theory with fact. Although psychiatrists strongly believe that there may be some physical tendency that makes some people more likely to develop anxiety or panic attacks, there is as yet no proof of this theory. And although much interesting research is being done, we still do not have the answer.

I do not mean to imply that your anxiety is "all in your head." Anxiety is a total body reaction. Your heart may speed up, your fingers may tingle, and you may perspire. However, most of these bodily changes are not causes but simply the effects of anxiety. And when you feel better as a result of treatment, these physical sensations will diminish or disappear entirely.

I do not mean to argue that medications should never be used in the treatment of anxiety and panic. Although the majority of patients with milder forms of anxiety and panic can be treated without drugs, many with more severe problems can be helped with medications. However, these drugs should never be used as a substitute for counselling or psychotherapy. With a little courage and some compassion, you can conquer your fears and resolve the problems that gave birth to the feelings of fear and panic in the first place.

12

•

How to Fight Your Fears and Win

A 32-year-old man was lying on his bathroom floor, writhing in agony from a sharp stomach pain. He felt as if he was about to explode. He pleaded with his wife to call an ambulance. Terrifying images of emergency rooms and intravenous tubes raced through his mind. By the time the ambulance arrived, twenty-five minutes later, the "attack" had mysteriously vanished. A careful medical examination by his doctor the following week revealed no organic cause for the pain.

Four weeks later the man was walking with his wife through a department store when he suddenly felt overwhelmed and confused. He developed tunnel vision and felt as if he was floating across the ceiling. He was consumed by an irresistible urge to flee from the building, so he told his wife that it was time to go and rushed her outside. As he stood in terror waiting for a taxi, sweat rolled down his forehead. He was ashamed of his feelings and fought desperately to appear calm. By the time the cab arrived his symptoms had disappeared.

Do you get the idea that this man is an oddball? In fact he is a relaxed, articulate young professional with a lovely wife and family and an impeccable reputation. The dreaded disease he suffers from is simply a common panic attack.

A panic attack is usually triggered by a negative thought or a frightening daydream. Once a panic attack develops, your thoughts, feelings, and physical symptoms feed each other in a vicious cycle, as illustrated on pages 223–224. You can see in these diagrams that your panic is triggered by your negative thoughts. Your heart pounds and your thoughts race as adrenaline pours into your blood. These sensations alarm you and you think, "Gee, something must really be wrong." This thought creates even more fear and frightening physical symptoms.

At the same time, your negative thoughts and feelings feed each other. You feel so anxious and tense that it seems that something dreadful must be wrong. After all, why would you feel so frightened if you weren't in real danger? This is called "emotional reasoning," because you take your emotions as evidence for the way things really are.

Finally, your actions also make things worse. If you think you're dying or cracking up, you may crawl into bed with the lights off and try to hang on for dear life. This is like a sensory deprivation experiment, and it lets your fantasies run wild! You feel abnormal and impaired. This convinces you that there must be something terribly wrong.

These fears can feel absolutely terrifying and absolutely realistic, but there is usually no real danger. That's because distorted thoughts, not realistic ones, cause anxiety. If there's one message I want you to understand as you read this book, that's it!

The problem, of course, is that you won't know how unrealistic your fears are during a panic attack. Between attacks you may realize that it's absurd to think you're on the verge of a heart attack or going crazy, but when you feel anxious you will need some concrete evidence to show you how irrational these fears are.

Margaret is a 32-year-old mother of two children who took up jogging in an effort to lose weight. While jogging, Margaret would become obsessed with the idea that she might be putting too much strain on her heart. When she was done, she'd sit down in a particular living room chair and wait to see if she was okay. Her heart would pound, since she'd just been exercising strenuously, and she would notice a certain tightness in her chest. This made her suspect she might be in the beginning stages of a heart attack. She would develop fantasies of being in a coronary care unit with intravenous needles in her arms and tubes in her chest. The images would send waves of panic through her body. Her fears would build to such

THE PANIC CYCLE: THE FEAR OF A HEART ATTACK

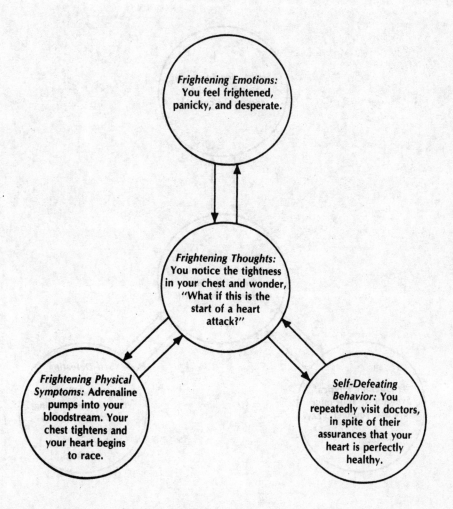

THE PANIC CYCLE: THE FEAR OF GOING CRAZY

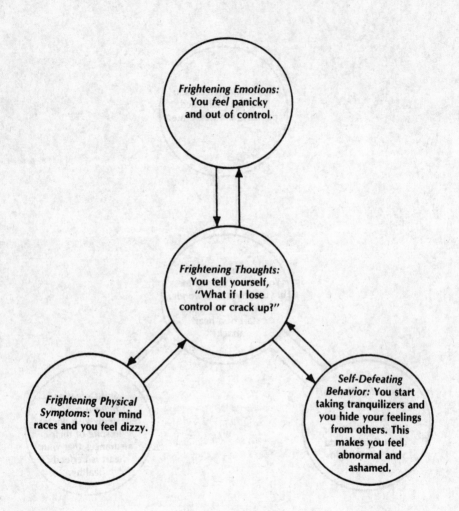

a crescendo that she couldn't stand the suspense, so she would walk outside and stand in front of the medical building next door. Her rationale was that if she did suddenly have a heart attack, the doctors and nurses in the building would see her collapse on the grass and would rush out and save her. After standing there for ten to fifteen minutes, Margaret's symptoms would subside and she'd go home, feeling relieved but humiliated.

Margaret had gone to several cardiologists for elaborate studies of her heart including electrocardiograms, treadmill tests, and so on. In spite of repeated assurances that she was in excellent health, her neurotic behavior persisted. Each time she went jogging she would ask herself, "Maybe it really is a heart attack this time. How can I know for sure?"

During a session, I asked Margaret to hyperventilate (breathe rapidly and deeply) and to picture herself in a coronary care unit. Within thirty seconds she became pale and clutched at her chest. She got lightheaded and said she was afraid this might bring on an actual heart attack. I asked her to estimate how nervous she felt on a scale from 0 to 99. She blurted out "Ninety-nine— the worst—I can't stand it!" Her intense reaction proves what a powerful impact your negative thoughts and fantasies can have on your feelings.

Now before we go on, I'd like to ask a very simple question: What was the cause of Margaret's intense, overwhelming fear? Why was she having this panic attack in my office? I'm asking because I want to see if you understand the basic principle of cognitive therapy. Write your answer here:

_____

_____

_____

_____

When I pose this question to audiences during lectures or workshops, I get a variety of answers. Some people say it's a hormonal reaction. Others say her anxiety must be due to subconscious conflicts. My experience leads to a very different answer: She feels anxious because of her thoughts. She believes she's about to have a heart attack. This irrational thought is the cause of her panic.

Now let me ask a second simple question. What would have to happen to make Margaret's fear disappear? What would make her feel immediately calm and happy as a lark? Put your ideas here:

_____

_____

_____

_____

When I ask professionals or lay people these questions, again I get a variety of answers. Some people say she needs years of psychoanalysis. In fact, Margaret had eight years of unsuccessful psychoanalytic treatment. Some people say she needs large doses of tranquilizers to suppress her panic attacks. This would probably only cover up her symptoms, and she could become addicted. She may still be vulnerable to these panic attacks when she tries to go off the medication. Others say she should go to a cardiologist for testing and reassurance, but she's already been to many.

I believe that Margaret can eliminate her anxiety if she eliminates the cause. Doesn't that make good sense? Her negative thoughts make her anxious. She believes something that isn't true—namely, that she's on the verge of a heart attack. If she became convinced that this thought wasn't true, her symptoms would vanish. How could Margaret put the lie to the thought that she's about to have a heart attack? Think about this for a moment before you read the next section.

THE EXPERIMENTAL METHOD

In Chapter 6, you saw that there are many ways to untwist distorted thoughts. I have developed a number of techniques that are especially effective for anxiety and panic attacks. One of these is called the Experimental Method. It can help you prove beyond the shadow of a doubt that your fears are just a figment of your imagination. The calming effects can be dramatic and immediate.

I asked Margaret if she could think of a way to test her belief that she was on the verge of a heart attack. Could she think of an experiment that would prove with absolute certainty whether or not she was having a heart attack? She suggested "I could get an electrocardiogram." I replied, "But I don't have one in my office and you don't have one at home. Can you think of any other test?" She replied, "I could take my pulse and see if it's racing." I replied, "But it could be racing because of your anxiety, so that won't prove anything one way or the other. If you were having a heart attack right now, what would be something you could not do?" She thought about this for several moments and replied, "I'd be weak and in terrible pain. My heart would be failing, so I could barely move." I replied, "Exactly. So what experiment could you do to find out right now whether or not you're having a heart attack?" Her face lit up and she said, "I could see if I could stand up. Then I could see if I could walk. Then I could see if I could jog. If I could do those things, it would show I wasn't having a heart attack!"

I suggested that she do just that. She stood up—no problem. She walked across the office—no problem. Then I suggested we jog together down the hall outside my office. She did this with no problem. Then I suggested we jog up and down several flights of stairs together. In the process, her symptoms vanished. Margaret tried the method at home the next time she developed the fear of a heart attack, with equally dramatic results. She terminated treatment after several sessions and wrote to me the next Christmas to report that she was still doing well.

The results of the Experimental Technique aren't always so dramatic, but this method is frequently extremely helpful. The instant that you see with absolute certainty that your fears are groundless, you'll have no reason to feel upset.

You may have the thought: "I will never get well that fast. I'm hopeless." In fact, most people *don't* get well that fast. Successful treatment with a difficult mood problem can often require trust and persistent hard work over a period of time. Remember, too, that Margaret had struggled unsuccessfully for eight years before she came to me and we quickly found the intervention that "clicked." This often happens with my own patients—we work and work and work, seemingly making no progress. The patient feels hopeless and wants to give up, but I urge them on, saying, "Keep trying! We'll eventually get it." Then one day, long after they've given up believing there's any chance, the clouds suddenly lift and they experience the joy and relief that Margaret did. This can happen for you as well.

Some people are afraid to put their fears to the test. A businessman named Jack had symptoms similar to Margaret's. Whenever he felt upset, he'd obsess about some ache or pain, notice a tightness in his chest, and become convinced he was dying of heart failure. In the six months prior to our first session, Jack had spent over $10,000 getting physical examinations, X-rays, electrocardiograms, and laboratory tests from numerous physicians. The results of these tests always proved to be entirely normal. I demonstrated the Experimental Technique in my office and asked Jack to jog down the hall. Like Margaret, he experienced instantaneous relief and agreed to try this at home instead of running to a doctor the next time he felt he was having a heart attack.

Several days later, Jack got anxious and felt some chest pain, but he was so petrified that he refused to get out of his chair for two hours. He was afraid that the slightest movement might trigger a heart attack! Jack's resistance to testing his fears illustrates how enormously convincing your negative thoughts can seem, even when they're absolutely unrealistic.

As a way of getting around Jack's resistance, I suggested that he begin with very minimal exercise the next time he felt he was having a heart attack, and then he could try exercise that was increasingly demanding. He devised the following plan:

1. I will see if I can take five deep breaths. That will show I can still breathe properly.

2. I will raise my right arm five times.

3. If that works, I will raise both arms five times.

4. Then I will stand up and sit down.

5. If this goes okay, I will walk back and forth across the room.

6. Then I will touch my knees, toes, and floor.

7. Then I will try five sit-ups.

8. Then I will try five push-ups.

9. Then I will see if I can walk around the block slowly.

10. Then I will run around the block rapidly.

He concluded that if he could do all ten things, it would prove that he was not really having a heart attack.

The next time I saw Jack he was pleased but embarrassed. Between sessions he had gotten anxious and felt convinced he was having a heart attack. By the time he'd completed five of the ten tests, it became crystal clear that he wasn't having a heart attack. His chest pain and his anxiety vanished.

The Experimental Technique can be an effective way to put the lie to your irrational fears. Here's how you do it: First, identify the negative thoughts that upset you during a panic attack. The commonest ones are: "I may be cracking up," "I may be having a heart attack," "I may be losing control," "I may be about to faint," and "Maybe I'm about to die." Second, devise an experiment to test this fear. Ask yourself, "If I *were* losing control and cracking up, how would I know this for sure? Do I have any symptoms of schizophrenia now?" List the symptoms on a piece of paper and see if you have any of them. When you prove that your fears aren't valid, you will feel better.

If you would like to learn how to use the Experimental Technique to deal with your feelings of panic, turn to the four examples at the end of this chapter (page 254). When you have worked through these practice exercises, you will have a much better feeling for how to use this powerful technique.

PARADOXICAL TECHNIQUES

There's another method that can show you that your fears of insanity are irrational. It works like this: If a patient becomes anxious during a therapy session and tells me he's afraid he's about to crack up, I may reply, "I know you've been afraid of cracking up for many years. This would be as good a time as any to go ahead and get it over with. After all, you are with a psychiatrist. Why don't you go ahead and do it? Please try your hardest to lose control and crack up."

The patient usually looks shocked and protests that he doesn't understand what I am asking him to do. I tell him that he could stand up and flail his arms and legs about or babble gibberish and try his best to go crazy. In order to help inhibited clients, I sometimes demonstrate this myself. One time I did a somersault on the floor of the office, another time I stood on my desk and sang the "Battle Hymn of the Republic."

After I have demonstrated this bizarre behavior, I invite the patient to try to go insane. They usually laugh and feel relieved once it dawns on them that they can't crack up, even if they try with all their might.

If you would like to try this, when you're in a good mood, act crazy or eccentric for several minutes in the privacy of your home. You can talk in tongues, flail your arms about, dance, make baby sounds, or do whatever you like. After you've practiced this and you're comfortable with it, you can try it again during an anxiety attack when you feel convinced you're cracking up. It can be reassuring to discover that you cannot go crazy, no matter how hard you try.

This type of intervention has been called "paradoxical treatment" by psychologists and psychiatrists, because you do the opposite of what you are inclined to do. Instead of desperately clinging to your sanity, you try your hardest to go insane. However, because this technique could conceivably backfire and upset you, it might be best to try it under the supervision of a professional therapist if you have any doubt about it.

SHAME-ATTACKING EXERCISES

People with panic attacks often suffer from the fear of losing control and looking foolish in front of others. In a recent session a woman told me about her fear of being in situations she can't easily escape from—like being at the hairdresser's or in the dentist's chair or attending a church service. She said she feels trapped and gets a panic attack. She imagines becoming hysterical and running out of the room and making a fool of herself in front of other people.

Like many anxiety-ridden people, she believes she should be in complete control of her emotions at all times, and she thinks that people would look down on her for feeling nervous or insecure. These attitudes make her so tense that she loses all her spontaneity in social situations.

One antidote to this fear involves purposely doing something foolish in public. I believe that this "Shame-Attacking" method was originally developed by Dr. Albert Ellis, a noted psychologist. The idea is to do what you're most afraid of so you can learn that the world doesn't come to an end after all.

Because I don't like to recommend any self-help method that I haven't tried myself, I performed a "Shame-Attacking" Exercise one summer, while on vacation with my family at a casino resort on Lake Tahoe. I put on a cowboy hat and dark glasses and got on a crowded hotel elevator with my two children. Then, at every floor, from the twelfth floor down, I called out the numbers. I had to force myself to blurt out, "This is floor number eleven," because I told myself, "My gosh! What will all these people think of me?" It was much like the feeling just before you jump off a high dive for the first time. People began to chuckle more and more at each floor as I continued to announce, "Tenth floor . . . ninth floor. . . ." By the time we reached the main floor, everybody was laughing and giggling. As we walked off the elevator and the passengers merged with the crowd, I realized that nothing terrible had happened. It turned out to be a lot of fun to make "a fool" of myself. This helped me feel more relaxed and willing to be spontaneous around other people.

Other Shame-Attacking Exercises could include:

* Go into a crowded store and announce the time of day. You can say, "It is now 3:42 p.m." Wait for a moment until people have turned to stare at you. Then repeat the time loudly and clearly.
* Announce the street stops on a crowded bus.
* During a serious conversation with a friend, stick your pencil in your nose and let it hang there (insert the eraser end!)

CONFRONT YOUR FEARS

The reason the Experimental Method, the Paradoxical Technique, and the Shame-Attacking Exercises can be so effective is that you confront your fears instead of running away from them. People with fears and phobias usually do just the opposite—they avoid situations they're afraid of. When you avoid frightening situations, you simply make your problems worse. This is a guarantee! It's like running away from a bully—he will just continue to chase you and frighten you. And the opposite is just as true: Facing your fears will help you conquer them. You learn that the catastrophe you fear will not really happen.

The best way to confront your fears is to stop avoiding the situation you're most afraid of. Instead of trying to control your anxiety, surrender to your symptoms. Let them run their course. Do not fight them. Let the worst occur, if there is a worst. If you stick it out, you will discover that there are no terrible consequences after all.

Flora had agoraphobia—the fear of being away from home alone. Whenever she left her house, her mind was flooded with images of being arrested by the police for a crime she didn't commit. If she was walking down the street she would reason, "Just suppose I accidentally dropped my wedding ring here, and then coincidentally a murder was committed on this very spot. The police might find the ring and link me to the crime. Then I'd have no way to prove I didn't commit it. I'd be arrested and thrown in jail. Then I'd be separated from my son and daughter and they'd have to be raised by someone else."

In my office she realized that this chain of events was extremely unlikely, but she nevertheless believed it was at least remotely possible. Whenever she was out and feeling frightened, these ruminations seemed perfectly realistic and were so frightening that she would rush home. As a result, Flora would never leave her house unless she was accompanied by a friend. Her rationale was that a friend could testify to her innocence in the event she was brought to trial for murder.

Flora is not insane. She's attractive, bright, and friendly. She's from a prominent New York family, and she's considered a pillar of the community. You would never suspect that she had such irrational fears. Yet anxieties like hers are very common.

After Flora and I talked about how important it was to confront her fears, she agreed to walk alone to a nearby park on a Saturday around noon. She promised to sit down on a park bench and to stubbornly refuse to give in to the compulsion to go home, no matter how frightened she got.

When Flora left her home, her anxiety began to increase. She sat on the bench and every two minutes recorded how anxious she felt, on a scale from 0 to 99. Terrifying thoughts and feelings began to flood her mind. She didn't budge. She was determined to sit there no matter how nervous she got. Her anxiety shot up to 99—sheer panic. A policeman walked by and she felt certain he was about to arrest her. Her heart pounded and a voice inside screamed, "Go home!" But she bravely stayed glued to the bench in sheer terror for ten or fifteen minutes. The policeman didn't arrest her but smiled and said hello. Her anxiety started to melt away. After twenty minutes, the anxiety disappeared entirely. Freedom! She had called the bluff on her fears and won! This gave her the courage to get up and do some shopping. As she entered the grocery store she began to feel ecstatic—it dawned on her that she had surrendered to the anxiety and nothing terrible had happened!

During the experiment, Flora found it helpful to repeat the following statements to herself: "This attack can't go on forever. No matter how bad it gets, it will eventually go away, and I can take it. It will not destroy me. I am not on the edge of a nervous breakdown, even though it feels that way. I will sit here and confront my worst fears. I will defeat them and become stronger." She also found it helpful to talk to her symptoms in this way: "Go ahead and do your worst. This is your big chance. I am not going to run away from you any longer. I have not committed any crime, and I have the right to sit here as long as I want."

The technique of surrendering to your symptoms has been called "flooding" or "exposure" by psychiatrists and psychologists. Essentially, you "expose" yourself to your fears and you allow yourself to become "flooded" with uncomfortable symptoms. After a time, they reach their crest and fade away. As they disappear you will often experience exhilaration instead of the shame and humiliation you felt when you let your fears get the better of you.

Example: If you're afraid of elevators, you could get on an elevator and ride it up and down as long as necessary until your anxiety goes away. No matter how terrified you get, stay on the elevator! Do not get off until your fears have vanished.

Some readers may think, "But what if my phobias really *are* dangerous? What if I'm afraid of snakes or insects or dogs? These animals actually *can* kill you!" Again, I want to remind you that phobias, by definition, are irrational fears that get in the way of productive living. The fear of a rattlesnake about to strike is no phobia. But people with snake, insect, or dog phobias are afraid of *all* snakes, insects, and dogs, even the ones that are not dangerous. For example, tarantula spiders are not poisonous to humans, and they can be quite friendly. In my high school biology class in Arizona, all the students were required to let tarantulas crawl across their hands so we could overcome our fear of spiders. You could do this at home by letting a daddy longlegs crawl across your hands. If you have a dog phobia, you could force yourself to pet and play with a neighbor's friendly dog.

When you expose yourself to something you fear, you can keep an ongoing record of your feelings. Divide a sheet of paper into three columns. In the left-hand column, record the time every two minutes. In the middle column, record how anxious you are, between 0 and 99. In the right-hand column, jot down any frightening thoughts or daydreams you may be having. This written log will make you more aware that your anxiety will not go on forever. After a while, your fears will begin to fade away.

I recently treated a 26-year-old systems analyst named Steve, who had been troubled by severe anxiety, panic attacks, and depression since he graduated from college several years earlier. These feelings were the worst when he was at work or when he was on airplanes or away from home. The constant anxiety, stress, and tension had worn him to a frazzle. Steve was feeling pretty beaten down and hopeless when he first sought treatment.

Steve's problems stemmed from an intense fear of being alone. Although we could have spent years trying to analyze the childhood origins of this fear, I doubt this would have helped him. And to be quite honest, I don't believe that psychiatrists or psychologists really know where these deeper fears come from. They may come from traumatic experiences when we were small, from our genes, or from cultural influences like school, television, and advertising. Regardless of the cause, Steve was afraid of being alone and in need of a cure.

The intervention that was the most helpful to Steve was spending a week alone in Washington, D.C., staying in the apartment of a friend who was away on vacation. This was terrifying to him at first. He was afraid he'd crack up or have a nervous breakdown and be unable to take care of himself. But he did survive, and as the hours passed, his self-confidence began to grow. This put the lie to his belief that he was inadequate and unable to survive on his own. His fears continued to fade until they were gone. This experience gave him a tremendous boost. He experienced a sense of triumph and completed his therapy shortly after this. I have heard from him on many occasions since then, and he has continued to do well.

Some people don't like to face their fears so dramatically. They prefer to expose themselves to anxiety-provoking situations more gradually, so they can back off whenever their anxiety becomes too intense. This approach can also be helpful. The most important thing is to confront your fears persistently and courageously until they disappear. Confronting the fear can be terrifying, but the beneficial effects are often dramatic.

Dr. Stanley Rachman of the University of British Columbia has capitalized on this idea to devise a slightly different approach to treating agoraphobia. His technique is to move through your fears toward the person you feel safe with. Suppose you feel safe with your spouse but are afraid of going on a bus alone or waiting alone at a bus stop. You could walk to a bus stop together. Your spouse boards the bus and gets off at the next stop. Then you can wait alone for the next bus, take the bus, and get off at the first stop, where your spouse will be waiting for you.

Next, ask your spouse to go to the second or third stop and wait for you. Each time you can go a little farther on the bus alone. The advantage of this technique is that you're going *toward* safety instead of thinking you have to bite the bullet and confront your fears all at once, without any moral support. Another advantage is that you and your spouse will be able to work together as a team. Many friends and family members of agoraphobics want to help, but they feel frustrated because they don't know what to do. I like to think of Dr. Rachman's technique as the "partnership method" because someone who wants to help can be a partner in your treatment.

Let's see if you can think of an application of this method. Suppose you are afraid of walking away from home alone. How could you work with your spouse to overcome this fear? One approach would be for him to go outdoors with you and walk ahead one block and wait for you to meet him. Then he could walk two blocks ahead and wait while you walk toward him. You could gradually build up your distance until you walk a mile or even more alone.

THE DAILY MOOD LOG

The Daily Mood Log, described in Chapter 5, is another useful method for fighting anxiety and panic attacks. When you feel anxious, write down the negative thoughts that make you feel so frightened. Then identify the distortions in these thoughts, using the list on page 260. When you substitute more positive and realistic thoughts, it will often turn your fears around.

A 45-year-old woman named Victoria avoided going on trains because she would get anxious and have fantasies of fainting in the aisle. The first Automatic Thought Victoria wrote down was: "What if I get so uptight that I pass out?" She identified the distortion in this thought as "fortune-telling," since she was making an unrealistic prediction. She substituted this Rational Response: "It is unlikely that I will pass out on the train since I haven't actually passed out once in my entire life."

Then she wrote down a second Automatic Thought: "But what if I did pass out? That would be terrible! And who can say I won't?" See if you can identify the distortion(s) in this thought.

1._____

2._____

Victoria noted that she was again involved in "fortune-telling," because she was predicting a disaster. She was also "magnifying" how terrible it would be if she did faint. She countered it with a new Rational Response: "Why would it be so terrible if I did pass out? I would simply fall on the floor and wake up a moment or two later. I would then probably notice a circle of people around me who would offer to help. I could stand up and thank them for their concern and tell them I was okay. I would sit down in my seat and get off at my destination."

Then a third Automatic Thought crossed her mind: "But they'll look down on me. They'll think I'm a fool because I caused a commotion." What are the distortions in this thought?

1._____

2._____

3._____

Victoria noted that this involved "mind reading" and "fortune-telling," because she was assuming that people would look down on her if she did faint. She was also "labeling" herself as "a fool." What Rational Response would you suggest?

_____

_____

_____

_____

Victoria's Rational Response was: "There's no evidence they'll be looking down on me. Would I look down on someone or call them a fool simply because they fainted? That would be absurd!"

Her final Automatic Thought was: "But what if someone did look down on me? I couldn't stand it! That would be terrible!" She noted that this was "fortune-telling" and "magnification" again. Her Rational Response was: "Why would that be so terrible? What can they do to me? Shout at me? Frown? Call up my friends and tattle? Put a headline in the paper? If someone looked down on me for fainting, it would mean that they had an immature attitude and it wouldn't reflect on me."

The next time I saw Victoria she announced with a sense of triumph that she had taken a commuter train to the therapy session. It hadn't been easy, but she'd done it! This was a major victory.

I've included an extra Daily Mood Log for you at the end of this chapter on page 258. When you use it, you will see that your Automatic Thoughts are nearly always predictions that something bad is about to happen. To illustrate this, write down the kinds of negative thoughts you might have in each of the following anxiety provoking situations:

You have an airplane phobia. As you're boarding the plane at the beginning of your vacation you're drenched with sweat and your heart is pounding. What are you thinking?

_____

_____

_____

_____

You have a big test coming up in school. You're really nervous about it. What are you thinking?

_____

_____

_____

_____

In each situation you're undoubtedly making dire predictions about all the terrible things that are going to happen. As you board the airplane you may be thinking, "What if it crashes?" Then you picture the plane going down in flames. These thoughts scare the living daylights out of you. Before an examination you may tell yourself, "It's going to be so tough." Then you imagine getting an "F" on the test. These thoughts make you so nervous that you can't concentrate on what you have to study.

In all of these situations, you're involved in the cognitive distortion called "fortune-telling." *All* anxiety results from this distortion. Do you know why these negative predictions are distortions? It's because the catastrophes you predict are *not* realistic. The fact is, the plane you are boarding *won't* crash. And if you prepare diligently for the test, it's very unlikely that you'll fail.

One way to deal with fortune-telling is to make positive, realistic predictions instead of unlikely, negative ones. If you feel nervous about an airplane flight, you can tell yourself that it's going to be a pleasant flight. Imagine landing safely at your destination and having a good time on vacation. When studying for a test, tell yourself that you *are* learning the material and that the more you study, the higher your score will be.

Many people seem taken aback by this advice. They tell me: "That's silly! It sounds like The Power of Positive Thinking. I don't want to be Pollyanna and look on the bright side all the time. It's not realistic. It is possible that I might do lousy on the test. What if I get petrified and my mind goes blank? So why tell myself I can study effectively and do well? That's just plain stupid!"

If this is how you think, you may be caught up in a self-fulfilling prophecy. You may use up all your energy worrying and telling yourself how awful you'll do instead of preparing systematically to do the best you can. When I feel confident and I anticipate doing well, I usually perform much better than when I worry and catastrophize about failure.

Some people defend their worrying with this argument: "It's safer to worry. I may protect myself against danger if I'm nervous. Maybe I can keep the airplane up if I worry about a crash. Maybe I'll study harder if I worry about flunking the test. If I relax and think about things positively, something bad may happen." Can you see any loopholes in these arguments? A

small amount of anxiety may boost your performance by helping you "psych up," but too much anxiety will only make you
miserable.

THE COST-BENEFIT ANALYSIS

If you have a fear or a phobia, you will need to decide whether or not
you really *want* to get over it. One part of you may want to stop
worrying and start feeling better, while another part may resist changing
because you believe your fears are helping you or protecting you.

One way to deal with this problem is with the Cost-Benefit Analysis.
Ask yourself, "How will it help me to worry and predict catastrophes,
and how will it hurt me?" List the advantages and disadvantages
and weigh them against each other. Then make a second list of the
advantages and disadvantages of thinking positively and imagining
that things will turn out well. Again, balance the costs against the
benefits of being optimistic. This may make it easier for you to let
go of your worrying and to start believing in yourself.

An elderly woman who sought treatment for agoraphobia stubbornly resisted her therapist's suggestions to go out of the house
alone. She explained that she was afraid that she might get mugged
or murdered. She pointed out that there were newspaper reports of
mugging almost every day.

There are two issues here. First, does she want to be so preoccupied with this fear that she loses the freedom to leave her
house? The Cost-Benefit Analysis can help her sort this out.
What are the advantages and disadvantages of being housebound?
The big advantage of staying in is feeling safe. The disadvantage
is a loss of freedom. She needs to think this through and make
a choice. Otherwise she will be at odds with herself and with her
therapist.

If she decides to confront her fears and leave her house, she may
need to perform a second Cost-Benefit Analysis. What are the advantages and disadvantages of worrying constantly when she's away from
home? She has to ask herself if panic and worry will prevent something terrible from happening. Certainly there are commonsense
precautions that every citizen should consider: you should always
walk with a friend if your neighborhood isn't safe; you shouldn't go
out alone at night; you shouldn't carry large amounts of cash with
you; you should keep a list of your credit card numbers at home in

the event they're lost or stolen; and you should not attempt to fight or argue with a robber.

Once you've taken these precautions, further worrying won't help much. I suppose she could argue that if she's in a constant state of panic she'll be especially careful and suspicious of every stranger, but the cost of such excessive vigilance is emotional misery. There's a point at which you have to say: "Okay, I've taken every rational precaution to protect myself. Beyond this, absolute safety is impossible, so I might as well assume that I'll be safe and relax and enjoy myself."

If you have a phobia, you should pay careful attention to this issue. You may have a vague desire to feel better, but you may resist my suggestion to confront your fears. Sometimes there are hidden advantages in your fears that you're unaware of. Some agoraphobics get a lot of attention from others and this can be hard to give up. We all like attention—it's just a fact of human nature. At the same time, change involves pain and hard work. And that may not sound like much fun! You will need a pretty strong reason to change if that's what you want to do.

The Cost-Benefit Analysis can help you develop the motivation you need to change. You might be anxious about going on planes or elevators, being in crowds, or leaving home alone. In the left-hand column list the advantages of worrying: it makes you cautious, so you don't take reckless chances; you don't risk making a fool of yourself; you may get extra attention from other people; and so on. In the right-hand column, list the disadvantages of worrying: it's uncomfortable; it restricts your freedom; other people get frustrated with you; and so on.

Once you've completed these lists, balance the advantages against the disadvantages. Ask yourself: "Do my fears help me more? Or do they hurt me more?" If you decide that the disadvantages of your fears outweigh the advantages, you'll be more motivated to change. The Cost-Benefit Analysis may not cure you, but your determination and commitment will be the key to getting better.

POSITIVE IMAGING

People with panic attacks or phobias are often preoccupied with frightening fantasies and daydreams. A 22-year-old musician would imagine losing control and screaming whenever she was in a crowd.

This fantasy was so upsetting that she avoided groups or social situations. Hypochondriacal individuals worry constantly about getting diseases; they picture themselves in hospitals whenever they notice a slight ache or pain.

These images are not hallucinations but simply daydreams. Most of us have daydreams throughout the day, but we usually don't pay much attention to them. To understand this better, try to picture something vivid and harmless, like a red apple in a brown basket. Can you see it? These are the kinds of pictures that pass through your mind when you daydream. If you daydream about something pleasurable, like sex or hitting a good shot while playing tennis, you'll feel good. When you daydream about the things you fear, you will frighten yourself.

You may not be aware of these frightening daydreams and fantasies unless you look for them when you feel nervous. Once you notice them, you can trace the obvious connection to your fears. It's important to realize that since you create these frightening fantasies, you can learn to control them. If you modify them in a creative way, you will feel less anxious.

You might want to choose to substitute a peaceful image of a place you love, like being on vacation at the shore or in a cabin in the mountains. Breathe slowly and deeply when you picture it. One anxious patient found it helpful to imagine herself walking along the beach in the evening, since she loved the ocean. She would visualize the moon and waves. Her imagination was such that she could even feel the cool ocean breeze across her skin and faintly smell the salty ocean air. She said she could almost feel the sand under her feet.

I suggested that she repeat this message to herself while she visualized the scene: "I have no cares in the world. Everything is taken care of. My husband and children are well. The bills are all paid. I have many people to be close to and many happy activities to look forward to. It is so peaceful here." As she imagined this scene, she was flooded with a wave of inner peace, and her anxiety disappeared within moments.

Another patient with strong religious feelings found it helpful to recite the words of the Twenty-third Psalm during the visualization exercise: "He makes me lie down in green pastures. He leads me beside still waters. He restores my soul."

Why can this simple exercise reduce your anxiety? It's because you change the pictures in your mind, just as a movie director prepares for a totally different scene. And the effect of the peaceful scene can be quite profound.

Try the technique to see how it works for you. Sit down in a comfortable chair. Begin by putting a frightening image or day-dream in your mind. Choose the one that ordinarily upsets you. You could imagine dying, cracking up, or saying something foolish at a social gathering. You can intensify the effect by breathing rapidly and telling yourself things like "This is terrible. I can't stand it." You may notice how your tension builds up.

Now erase those images and project some peaceful ones in your mind. Breathe slowly and deeply and select a scene that appeals to you: fishing in a quiet lake, receiving your diploma the day you graduated from high school or college. The scene can be a happy memory or a pleasant fantasy. Give yourself positive reassuring mes-sages. You will notice how your mood improves.

DISTRACTION

Some people find it helpful to distract themselves from the frighten-ing thoughts and images that become so intense during a panic attack. If you concentrate on something else, it will frequently take the edge off the uncomfortable symptoms.

Several types of distractions can be helpful. The first is mental distraction. You could purchase an inexpensive puzzle that requires concentration and manipulation. It should be small enough to fit in your wallet or handbag. One woman used one of those little square puzzles where you have to rearrange the numbers or letters to con-form to a certain pattern. Another woman found a small plastic dome in which you flip tiny plastic doughnuts onto a hoop. The puzzle should be one that requires several minutes of concentrated activity to solve. A Rubik's Cube would be ideal.

During an anxiety attack, take the toy out and concentrate on it, focusing all of your mental energy on every detail of the game. This can interrupt the flow of frightening images in your mind. Other people have distracted themselves by performing calculations in their heads, balancing their checkbooks, or engaging in some other men-tally demanding task.

The second form of distraction is physical. When you feel anxious or stressed, strenuous exercise like swimming, jogging, aerobics, or speed walking might be helpful. You might prefer a competitive sport like squash or tennis. Long, slow runs have been reported to be especially helpful for people who feel down and depressed. Shorter, more intense exercise seems to be helpful for anxiety and panic. It isn't known for sure whether the exercise creates an actual chemical change in your brain or simply serves to break the flow of negative thoughts. Exercise does give you a sense of accomplishment and self-control when you feel helpless and terrified. As a result, you calm down and feel more relaxed.

A third type of distraction is to get involved in productive work or a hobby. You might read your favorite novel, work on your coin collection, or work in the garden. You might find it helpful to do something you've been putting off, like straightening up the house or writing thank-you letters.

When you feel anxious, you may resist doing this. You may give yourself endless excuses: "I just can't concentrate now" or "I don't feel like it." Don't give in to this urge—that will only make the anxiety worse, because you will flood your mind with frightening thoughts and fantasies. Instead, do something productive. You'll be surprised to find that you *can* get involved. As you do, you'll begin to feel better.

THE ACCEPTANCE PARADOX

Many of the techniques in this chapter will help you reduce your anxiety. However, that's only half the battle. Although one purpose of the therapy is to help you *change* your negative feelings, a second and somewhat contradictory goal is to help you *accept* your negative feelings. I call this the "Acceptance Paradox," and grasping it is a crucial part of the cure. The essential message is that you cannot overcome your negative feelings until you have first learned to accept them.

But that's just the rub. You may have a great deal of difficulty accepting your negative feelings because of attitudes like these:

1) Emotional Perfectionism: You may feel that you should always be happy and in control of all your feelings. You may think that "normal" people don't get anxious and label yourself as "weirdo" or a "neurotic" whenever you feel nervous, frightened, insecure, or panicky. Do you ever think this way?

————yes   ————no

2) Castastrophizing: You may think that anxious feelings are very dangerous and will lead to insanity if you let them get out of control. This makes you fight your anxiety and it mushrooms into sheer panic. Do you ever think this way?

_____yes   _____no

3) Fear of Disapproval: You may be convinced that others would look down on you if they found out how nervous, shy, lonely, or insecure you feel in certain situations. You may think you have to impress people as a "winner" who is always poised and confident. Do you ever feel this way?

_____yes   _____no

4) Conflict Phobia: You may feel that "nice" people with good relationships don't ever feel upset or annoyed with each other. This makes it hard to express your anger as well as other vulnerable feelings such as loneliness, insecurity, or jealousy. This attitude makes it difficult to resolve conflicts or to achieve genuine intimacy. Do you ever feel this way?

_____yes   _____no

5) Emotophobia: Emotophobia is the fear of negative emotions. You may believe that you should not have to endure any negative feelings like anxiety, panic, frustration, anger or sadness. When you feel upset, you may overreact and harangue yourself, thinking that something is terribly wrong. This mind-set doubles your troubles, because you not only get upset, but you get upset about being upset. Do you ever feel this way?

_____yes   _____no

If you think you *must not* feel anxious or upset and you believe you should be happy and in control all the time, you may be creating extra grief for yourself because no one really can feel happy, loving, and confident all the time. When you feel nervous or annoyed with someone, you will get self-critical and feel like a failure. This robs you of self-esteem and makes it far more difficult to get close to others. We are lovable because of our flaws and imperfections; it is our vulnerability that makes us human.

You may see this intellectually, without really believing it at the gut level. Like so many of my patients, you may embark on a crusade of self-abuse whenever you feel anxious, or angry, scolding yourself and insisting you *shouldn't* feel that way.

Helen is a 32-year-old woman I treated for panic attacks with the methods described in this chapter. She improved rapidly, but feared that the panic attacks might return. I pointed out that this was quite likely and asked what her negative thoughts would be the next time she did feel panicky. They included, among others:

1. "I'm a hopeless case."

2. "These anxiety attacks are a sign of weakness."

3. "I'm inferior. There must be something wrong with me."

4. "This is shameful. People will look down on me."

The fear of exposure and disapproval is extremely common among people who suffer from anxiety. Helen feels as if her panic is a dreadful, shameful secret. I suggested that we could deal with this with the "Feared Fantasy Technique" which is described on page 130. I told Helen to pretend to be a really mean person who was looking down on her, and I would be Helen. I told her to be as ruthless as she could possibly be and to say cruel things that she imagines people would be thinking about her if they knew she had panic attacks.

As you will recall, in this exercise Helen is not playing the role of a real person, but simply a frightening fantasy that represents the projection of her own worst fears. I am asking her to verbalize all her own self-criticisms, so that I can show her how to deal with them more effectively and develop greater self-acceptance.

HELEN (*as the Feared Fantasy*): Helen, I understand that you suffer from depression and panic attacks. Is this true?

DAVID (*as Helen*): Oh, I do! I have *tremendous* panic attacks!

HELEN (*as the Feared Fantasy*): Well, it doesn't make any sense. What could possibly be going on in your life to upset you or make you anxious? You have a beautiful family and you have loads of money. What's wrong with you?

DAVID (*as Helen*): Probably a lot more than what meets the eye. You're right that my anxiety and depression don't make a lot of sense. That's one of the funny things about these feelings. They don't always make a lot of sense. It's one of the most interesting aspects of it.

HELEN (*as the Feared Fantasy*): Well, this is all very irrational and disturbing. I don't think I like you, now that I know all this about you.

DAVID (*as Helen*): Oh? Why's that?

HELEN (*as the Feared Fantasy*): Because I just can't understand how someone in your position can be so weak and give in to these irrational feelings. You're just making a mountain out of a molehill. I mean, come on! Get off it!

DAVID (*as Helen*): I'm probably even weaker than you think I am. I have all kinds of weaknesses that you don't even know about, yet. So if you like real strong people, I may not be your cup of tea.

HELEN (*as the Feared Fantasy*): What's wrong with you? I've never had panic attacks. I've never been depressed like you. I am rational and sane and in control of my feelings.

DAVID (*as Helen*): You're a pillar of strength. I think of you as the Rock of Gibraltar.

HELEN (*as the Feared Fantasy*): I love your sarcasm. It's great. But I find people like you so pathetic.

DAVID (*as Helen*): You sound annoyed with me. Are you?

HELEN (*as the Feared Fantasy*): Yes, I *am* annoyed with you. I really despise you because I'm so strong and I know that everyone can be this way. If I can do it, everyone can do it. I really look down on pathetic people like you. I'm going to tell people that you are such a basket case. They'll know how emotionally unstable you are.

DAVID (*as Helen*): I can let you borrow the phone if you'd like to call them all now. Or, if you prefer, you could just drive up and down the streets shouting out my name out on a megaphone and telling people how sick I am.

HELEN (*as the Feared Fantasy*): Touché.

DAVID (*as self*): What's the point of this? What are we driving at here?

HELEN (*as self*): Actually, I'm not sure, but it's funny. I can see some humor in it, so at least that's something.

DAVID (*as self*): I'm glad humor is helpful. But aside from the humor, there's a point to this.

HELEN (*as self*): I'm not sure what the point is. Am I blowing out of proportion what other people would think?

DAVID (*as self*): Well, I guess that's probably true, but I'm driving at something deeper. The point is this: If someone wants to look down on you for being an imperfect human being, it's more of a reflection on them. You suffer from depression and anxiety so we could say that you're emotionally imperfect. Some people get divorced and they may be imperfect in their ability to resolve conflicts and to get close to others. Some people have very limited incomes and they could be imperfect in their ability to earn money. You may not be a genius, so we could say that your intelligence is imperfect or you may be overweight and out of shape so your figure is imperfect. If people want to throw rocks at you for *any* imperfection you might have, they can. But the question is, who is being irrational? Is this anything you really need to be concerned about? If you accept yourself as a human being with flaws, then you don't need to be afraid of anybody's put-downs. That's the point I'm trying to illustrate in a dramatic way.

Throughout the session, Helen and I continued to work on her belief that her anxiety made her a "weak" person. She was convinced that other people would never accept her the way she was, but the real problem was her inability to accept herself. This "emotional perfectionism" and fear of disapproval are extremely common among people who suffer from anxiety and depression. Sometimes you cannot deal with your feelings effectively until you surrender and accept them. This accomplishes two things: First, you learn that you *can* handle negative emotions, and the world doesn't come to an end simply because you're feeling angry or anxious or discouraged. Second, once you accept your emotions, they will frequently diminish and become a positive force in your life. But if you try to avoid or deny your feelings, insisting that you *shouldn't* feel that way, they will often intensify and mushroom way out of proportion.

If you still believe that you *shouldn't* get so upset, do a Cost-Benefit Analysis, as described on pages 113 and 123. List the advantages and disadvantages of always trying to be happy and in control of your emotions. Ask yourself, "How will this attitude help me, and how will it hurt me?"

It can also be helpful to ask yourself if this attitude is realistic.

I find life very stressful at times, and I frequently get annoyed or anxious or sad. This seems pretty normal, and I don't know many people who are dramatically different from me in this regard. I often tell my patients that if they could aim for five happy days per week, on the average, and two miserable days, that would be a pretty good deal. How would you feel about a goal like that? One advantage would be that when you felt upset, you could use your energy to deal with the problem that's bothering you instead of catastrophizing about feeling bad.

The secret of successful treatment is not to become a perfect, shining star or to learn to be in complete control of your feelings. These strategies are doomed to failure. In contrast, when you accept yourself as an imperfect but eminently lovable human being, and you stop fighting your emotions so strenuously, your fear will often lose its grip over you.

Helen improved rapidly. One key to her rapid recovery was her willingness to listen to the tapes of therapy sessions and to do the homework exercises between sessions. However, I don't want to create the impression that therapy is always easy and magical. If you have long-standing or severe difficulties, it may require more time and patience before you get better. I believe that you will be successful if you persist, and I have always felt that the sweetest victories are the battles that were the hardest fought!

GETTING IN TOUCH

In the last chapter you learned that if you are anxious, you may be avoiding certain problems and conflicts in your life that you feel angry or upset about. Getting in touch with what's really upsetting you can often be very liberating.

When you were growing up, you may have learned that you weren't supposed to express your feelings. When you tried, you got punished. Your family may have operated on the philosophy that people should try to be happy and loving all the time, and that if you've got something bad to say you shouldn't say it. As a result, you may have no models for how people can deal with problems successfully and share vulnerable feelings openly.

One consequence of this mind-set may be that you get anxious and obsess about something completely unrelated to the real problem when you feel upset, and you may not even be aware that you're doing this. Like many of my patients, you may become hypochondriacal and go from doctor to doctor in search of a disease when in reality you're upset with your spouse. You may fear you have cancer or heart disease because you feel so convinced that something is wrong. You are right—something *is* wrong! But it has to do with your life—the people you care about or perhaps your career. You're pushing the problem out of your mind because you don't know how to deal with it or because you think you've got no right to feel angry or upset in the first place.

Anxiety is like living a dream. The real problems in your life are disguised symbolically so that you don't recognize them. The solution, of course, is to confront the problem you've been avoiding. This usually involves expressing your feelings more openly.

A medical student named Mickey became upset when his fiancée, Gail, decided to go home for the weekend to attend her high school class reunion. Mickey and Gail had talked things over and the plan made good sense to Mickey. He had to spend the entire weekend studying for his final exams, so there was no reason for Gail to hang around.

However, soon after Gail left, Mickey began to feel tense and uncomfortable. He sensed that something was wrong. He noticed a bruise on his arm and developed a mild cough. For no apparent reason, he started to worry that he might be coming down with AIDS. This wasn't especially likely, since he'd had sex with only one other woman in his life. Nevertheless, Mickey began to obsess about dying from AIDS. He asked himself, "How can I be absolutely sure? People are dying of AIDS right and left." He became so overwhelmed with anxiety that he went to the emergency room of the hospital where he worked and got a blood test. The results several days later confirmed the obvious: he was in perfect health.

This pattern of obsessing about medical illnesses is extremely common with people who are anxious. There's generally no logical reason to suspect they have a disease. I have seen many people with an AIDS phobia, and none of them were at risk. They were not intravenous drug users and they had not had many sexual partners. Their fears were completely irrational and developed whenever they were upset about something.

What was really going on? Inside, Mickey felt bad about spending the weekend alone, even though he'd made the rational decision that it was a good idea for Gail to attend the reunion. Mickey felt lonely and jealous and insecure, but he felt he shouldn't express these feelings. He told himself that his feelings weren't reasonable, and that it made perfect sense for her to go. He was afraid that if he told her he felt hurt about spending the weekend alone, she might think he was weak and unmanly. He thought a man was supposed to be strong and rational and not have feelings like these. Finally, Mickey was concerned that he might appear manipulative or controlling. He told himself he had no right to tell Gail what to do.

People nearly always have lots of good reasons not to express their feelings! I have a hunch that there may be times when you don't tell people how you feel, either. Am I right?

What could Mickey have said to her? He could have told her, "I'll be feeling lonely and a little jealous when you're gone, because I really love you. I know it's a good idea for you to go, but part of me wishes you could stay." This would show Gail how he felt without demanding that she stay. Sharing his inner feelings—even if they didn't seem completely rational—probably would have made Gail feel a lot closer to him. The tenderness would have reassured him and prevented his anxiety attack.

I suggested that Mickey and Gail come in together for a few sessions. When they sat down, he was still agitated. He told me he was still worrying that he'd contracted AIDS, in spite of the fact that his blood test was normal. He said he'd read dozens of articles about the symptoms and was worried that they'd confused his lab test with someone else's. He wondered if he should perhaps have a second test just to be sure.

I told Mickey that checking out his symptoms in that way was unacceptable, and urged him to share his feelings with Gail. At first they both admitted that they were afraid of being open with each other. They were worried about hurting each other's feelings. But once they got started, they did beautifully. At the end of the session, Mickey said that his depression and worry about AIDS had suddenly and mysteriously vanished and he felt much closer to Gail.

Does this mean that Mickey was miraculously "cured" because of this experience? Obviously not. The tendency to repress your feelings can be deeply entrenched. In the future when Mickey is upset, he may begin to obsess again about AIDS or some other dreadful catastrophe. When this happens, he can ask himself "Am I upset with someone?" Instead of using his energy worrying about his obsessions, he can try to pinpoint what's really bothering him. His obsessions are really a reminder that something's bugging him that he's trying to ignore. Dealing with his feelings more openly and directly will require ongoing effort to reinforce the communication skills he is beginning to learn.

Sharing angry and vulnerable feelings in an atmosphere of trust can often have profound mood-elevating effects. If you cannot tell someone how you feel, true intimacy is impossible. Although anger can drive people apart, it can also draw people closer together when there's no threat to anyone's self-esteem, when the feelings are expressed honestly and listened to nondefensively, when there's no threat of rejection or retaliation, and when the underlying attitude is one of caring, trust, and respect.

The anti-anxiety techniques described in this chapter are summarized on page 252. It isn't necessary to master all of them, but it should be encouraging for you to know that there are numerous ways to overcome fears and phobias. You may find that you can apply these techniques on your own and get gratifying results. Or if you feel overwhelmed, you may want the help of a professional therapist. Once you call the bluff on your fears, you will win. Sometimes this takes time and effort. If you're determined, I believe you will eventually discover the inner peace and confidence you so richly deserve!

HOW TO OVERCOME
FEARS, PHOBIAS, AND PANIC ATTACKS*

1. **The Experimental Method:** Do an experiment to test your belief that you're "cracking up" or "having a heart attack" or "losing control."

2. **Paradoxical Techniques:** Exaggerate your fears instead of running away from them. If you have the fear of cracking up or having a stroke, you try your hardest to crack up or have a stroke.

3. **Shame-Attacking Exercises:** Purposely do something silly in public, in order to overcome your fear of appearing foolish.

4. **Confront Your Fears:** Expose yourself to whatever you're afraid of instead of running away and letting your fears cripple you. There are three ways of doing this:

   • **Sudden exposure or "flooding."** You allow yourself to experience all your symptoms, no matter how bad they get. You endure your fears until they run their course and wear out.
   • **Gradual exposure.** You gradually expose yourself to whatever you're afraid of (like being away from home alone, going into grocery stores, or taking buses or elevators). You back off when your anxiety becomes too great.
   • **The partnership method.** If you're afraid of being alone, you can ask someone you feel safe with to walk a certain distance ahead of you and wait for you. Then you walk and meet them there. The next time you ask them to go a little farther, so you can gradually increase the distance you can walk alone.

5. **Daily Mood Log:** Write down the negative thoughts that make you feel anxious or frightened. Identify the distortions in these thoughts and replace them with more realistic, positive thoughts. Instead of worrying yourself sick by constantly predicting failure and catastrophes, tell yourself that things will turn out reasonably well.

6. **The Cost-Benefit Analysis:** Make a list of the advantages and disadvantages of worrying and avoiding whatever you fear. Weigh the advantages against the disadvantages. Make a second list of the advantages and disadvantages of confronting your fears. Weigh the advantages against the disadvantages.

7. **Positive Imaging:** Substitute reassuring and peaceful images for the frightening daydreams and fantasies that make you feel so anxious.

8. **Distraction:** Distract yourself with intense mental activity (like working on a Rubik's Cube), strenuous exercise, or by getting involved in your work or a hobby.

9. **The Acceptance Paradox:** When you feel anxious or panicky, you may make matters worse by insisting that you *shouldn't* feel this way. This is like throwing gasoline on a fire, and your anxiety gets worse. One way to develop greater self-acceptance is to write out a dialogue with an imaginary hostile stranger who puts you down for feeling anxious. The hostile stranger is simply a projection of your own self-criticisms. When you talk back to them, you will develop greater self-acceptance, and your anxiety will usually diminish or disappear.

10. **Getting in Touch:** When you feel anxious or panicky, you are probably ignoring certain problems that need to be dealt with. Review your life and try to get in touch with the situation that's making you feel so upset. When you find the courage to deal with the problem more openly and directly, it can be very liberating!

Practice Exercises for the Experimental Technique

Each of the following patients used the Experimental Technique successfully. See if you can figure out how they tested their fears. Don't look at the solutions until you've thought about each problem first.

PROBLEM #1. THE FEAR OF LOSING CONTROL WHILE DRIVING

Emily had a freeway phobia. When driving on a busy highway she would become nervous and tell herself, "What if I lose control of the car?" Then she would panic and pull off to the side of the road to avoid a wreck. She would wait there until a policeman would come along to help her. These experiences were so frightening and humiliating that she stopped driving on freeways entirely. How could Emily test her belief that she's "losing control" when she's driving? Put your suggestions here:

_____

_____

_____

Solution: While she is driving, Emily can test her belief that she is "losing control" by (1) turning the radio on and off, (2) looking in the rearview mirror, (3) using the turn signal and changing lanes, (4) speeding up and slowing down, (5) keeping the speed at 50 mph.

These maneuvers convinced Emily that she was in control. Her anxiety went away almost immediately and she was able to continue driving without having to pull off to the side of the road. Her self-confidence increased and she began to use freeways more and more frequently.

PROBLEM #2. THE FEAR OF LOSING CONTROL AT WORK

Jane is a secretary who sometimes feels as if she's "losing control" at work. Her heart suddenly begins to pound and her mind races wildly. Then she goes to the women's lounge and lies down on the couch in a cold sweat, trying to hang on to her sanity. This is about as helpful as throwing gasoline on a fire. How can Jane test her belief that she's "losing control" when she suddenly feels anxious and panicky at work? Put your ideas here:

_____

_____

_____

Solution: Jane developed these tests to see if she was really losing control: "(1) I can see if I can stand up and walk around the room. This will prove I can control my arms and legs. Then I can try to walk to the drinking fountain. (2) I can try to read a sentence from the newspaper and see if I can summarize what it says. This will prove that I can control my thinking. (3) I can try to perform calculations by adding up numbers in my head. This will prove that I can concentrate. (4) I can call up Information and ask for the telephone number of a friend. This will prove that I can communicate properly. Then I can call up the friend and talk for a few minutes. This will prove I can carry on a normal conversation."

Jane performed these tests the next time she was anxious, and she was able to complete each of them successfully. This convinced her that she was in control in spite of her anxiety, and she felt better.

PROBLEM #3. THE FEAR OF BEING UNABLE TO BREATHE

People with panic attacks often develop a mistrust of their bodies. When they get nervous they may breathe too rapidly, and this makes them feel dizzy. This is a perfectly normal physiological reaction, because your body takes in too much oxygen and blows off too much carbon dioxide. If you breathe extremely rapidly for several minutes right now, you'll see what I mean.

Whenever she's alone, Cindy breathes too rapidly and gets very frightened. She thinks she might suffocate and lose control of her breathing and imagines that her windpipe will suddenly "close up." Because of this intense fear, Cindy spends nearly twenty-four hours a day with her husband. They work together, they play together, they sleep together. I asked Cindy how it would help to be with her husband if her windpipe "closed." She hadn't thought this through very clearly, but felt he might in some way be able to "open it up" for her or at least to call for emergency medical help. This excessive togetherness has put a strain on their marriage because they both feel trapped and resentful at times.

How can Cindy test her belief that she's about to lose control of her breathing and suffocate whenever she's alone and feeling anxious? Put your ideas here:

_____

_____

_____

Solution: Whenever Cindy felt she was losing control of her breathing she performed this test: "(1) Can I inhale slowly? (2) Can I hold my breath? (3) Can I exhale smoothly and slowly?" She agreed that if she could do all three things, it was proof that she could breathe properly.

This put the lie to her belief that she was suffocating or that her windpipe was closing off, and she was able to tolerate being alone for longer and longer periods. She also began a jogging and exercise program. The intense breathing and exertion helped her gain greater self-confidence because she learned that rapidly breathing is not dangerous.

PROBLEM #4. THE FEAR OF CRACKING UP

While he's studying, Jerry gets anxious and his thoughts race. This makes it difficult to concentrate. He tells himself, "I must be cracking up." Then he gets fantasies of being a catatonic schizophrenic in a mental hospital. This terrifies him and he paces about for hours, trying to hang on to his sanity. Fears of "cracking up" or having a nervous breakdown are extremely widespread among anxiety-prone individuals. While anxiety attacks can be intensely uncomfortable, they do not represent the onset of insanity.

How can Jerry test his belief that he's "cracking up"? Put your ideas here:

_____

_____

_____

Solution: Jerry agreed that the following are the symptoms of schizo-phrenia: visual hallucinations; hearing imaginary voices; feeling that you are like God; the belief that some important group like the FBI or the KGB is plotting against you; the conviction that your thoughts are being broadcast on radio and television programs. He developed this "insanity test":

Yes	No	
_____	_____	1. Am I hallucinating? Do I see things that aren't there?
_____	_____	2. Do I hear voices coming from outside my head?
_____	_____	3. Do I feel that I am a god or a great genius?
_____	_____	4. Do I feel the FBI is conspiring against me?
_____	_____	5. Do I feel that people are reading my mind or that my thoughts are being broadcast on loudspeakers?

The next time Jerry felt he was "losing his mind," he took his "insanity test." Since the answer to all these questions was no, he realized there was not one shred of evidence that he was going insane. This was not consistent with his belief he was "cracking up," and it took the edge off his fear.

THE DAILY MOOD LOG*

STEP ONE: DESCRIBE THE UPSETTING EVENT _____

_____

STEP TWO: RECORD YOUR NEGATIVE FEELINGS—and rate each one from 0 (the least) to 100 (the most). Use words like sad, anxious, angry, guilty, lonely, hopeless, frustrated, etc.

Emotion	Rating	Emotion	Rating	Emotion	Rating
1.		3.		5.	
2.		4.		6.	

STEP THREE: THE TRIPLE-COLUMN TECHNIQUE—

Automatic Thoughts	Distortions	Rational Responses
Write your negative thoughts and estimate your belief in each one (0–100).	Identify the distortions in each Automatic Thought.	Substitute more realistic thoughts and estimate your belief in each one (0 and 100).

(Continue on next page)

Automatic Thoughts	Distortions	Rational Responses

(Continue on next page)

Automatic Thoughts	Distortions	Rational Responses

STEP FOUR: OUTCOME–Re-rate your belief in each Automatic Thought from 0 to 100 and put a check in the box that describes how you now feel:

☐ not at all better; ☐ somewhat better; ☐ quite a bit better; ☐ a lot better.

CHECKLIST OF COGNITIVE DISTORTIONS*

1. All-or-nothing thinking: You look at things in absolute, black-and-white categories.
2. Overgeneralization: You view a negative event as a never-ending pattern of defeat.
3. Mental filter: You dwell on the negatives and ignore the positives.
4. Discounting the positives: You insist that your accomplishments or positive qualities "don't count."
5. Jumping to conclusions: (A) Mind reading—you assume that people are reacting negatively to you when there's no definite evidence for this; (B) Fortune-telling—you arbitrarily predict that things will turn out badly.
6. Magnification or minimization: You blow things way up out of proportion or you shrink their importance inappropriately.
7. Emotional reasoning: You reason from how you feel: "I *feel* like an idiot, so I really must be one." Or "I don't *feel* like doing this, so I'll put it off."
8. "Should statements": You criticize yourself or other people with "shoulds" or "shouldn'ts." "Musts," "oughts," and "have tos" are similar offenders.
9. Labeling: You identify with your shortcomings. Instead of saying "I made a mistake," you tell yourself, "I'm a jerk," or "a fool," or "a loser."
10. Personalization and blame: You blame yourself for something you weren't entirely responsible for, or you blame other people and overlook ways that your own attitudes and behavior might contribute to a problem.

13

◆

Dealing with the Fear of Death

Since death represents the ultimate confrontation with the unknown, it's not surprising that people who suffer from anxiety and panic are often afraid of death. Many people think that the fear of death is inevitable, but nothing could be further from the truth. The fear of death is one of the easiest fears to overcome if you apply some simple techniques.

One disclaimer is necessary here: The methods described in this chapter were not developed for people with serious illnesses, although they may also find these concepts helpful. Those who will benefit the most are people who are in good health but who become terrified by fears of death during panic attacks.

The first step is to examine specifically what you're afraid of. It can be helpful to conceptualize death in terms of three stages. Stage One is the dying process, up to the point when you pass into unconsciousness. Stage Two is the instant that you slip into unconsciousness, the actual moment of death. Stage Three is the period of time after you have died. Let's look at each of these stages and find out what you're afraid of.

If you are concerned about Stage One, the process of dying, then what you're really afraid of is life, not death. While you are in the process of dying you are still alive. What is it that you're afraid of? Is it the pain? The discomfort? Ask yourself, "Have I ever been sick or uncomfortable before? Was I able to cope with it then?" If you were able to cope with an illness at other times in your life, then there's no reason to think you won't be able to cope with the process of dying. Have you ever had a fever of 102°? Were you able to cope with that? Have you ever had a broken arm? Were you able to cope with that? What did you do for the discomfort? Did you take medication? Painkillers are generally available to individuals suffering from terminal illnesses, and the pain can usually be managed in a humane manner.

Perhaps you have experienced great pain in the past and you dread the thought of having to endure such suffering again. It's important to realize once again that it's not death, but life, that you fear. If someone with a terminal illness is in great agony, they are usually not at all afraid of death. Death, to them, is frequently a blessing and a welcome escape.

Your concerns might be different. You might have negative thoughts like "If I'm dying I will know I didn't fulfill all my dreams for my life. There are so many things I wanted to do, and I'll realize I only had a chance to do some of them." Once you've identified a negative thought like this, write it down. Then try to identify the distortions in it. Can you? Review the list on page 260 and see if you can find it.

One distortion is "all-or-nothing thinking," since you're telling yourself you didn't fulfill *all* your dreams and you didn't do *everything* you wanted during your life. It's also an example of the "mental filter," since you are thinking about all the things you *didn't* do rather than the many things you *did* do during your life.

Can you think of a more realistic way to look at it? One patient came up with this response:

No one can fulfill all of their dreams, but there are many things that I have been able to do. I always wanted to be a schoolteacher, and I have spent many years as a schoolteacher. I wanted to raise a family, and I have raised a family. I haven't done everything I wanted, but very few people could make that claim. When I die I will have to make a compromise between the dreams I had as a child and the reality of what I accomplished as an adult. I can think about all the things that I have done and feel a sense of satisfaction, or I can think about the many things I haven't done and make myself unhappy. The latter would be arbitrary and cruel.

Once she thought about it this way, she began to feel better because she no longer felt that death represented the ultimate defeat. Her perfectionism, and not the fear of death, was the real culprit.

The second stage of death involves the actual moment of dying, the instant when you slip into unconsciousness. Many patients tell me this would be terribly frightening because it represents the ultimate loss of control. But is this such a terrifying or unknown experience? Not really. You've actually had this experience every day of your life. The experience of slipping into unconsciousness is just like the experience of going to sleep. If you're not afraid of falling asleep, why be afraid of the moment of dying? You have also had this sensation if you were anesthetized. One moment you're conscious, and at the next instant you're asleep. There's literally nothing to it.

The third stage of death is the period after you have died. Again, ask yourself, "What is it that I am afraid of?" Try to pinpoint the negative thoughts that cross your mind when you think of being dead. One patient had the thought, "What if I wake up and I'm buried alive?" If this is your concern, then once again it's life, not death, that you're afraid of, because you'd be alive. But instead of getting upset about the situation, you could thank your lucky stars you are still alive! That's about the best thing that could happen to someone who thought they were dead! Concentrate on digging your way out so you can plan a big celebration! You could also put a provision in your will that you have to be buried with a small garden spade just in case this unlikely but wonderful event should happen.

Most people aren't so afraid of being buried alive, but they worry about being in an unconscious state and unaware of what's going on. In fact, there's no unpleasantness involved in this. Why do surgeons anesthetize people before they operate on them? It's to make sure that they will not experience any discomfort.

One patient was terrified by the thought "After I die there will be nothingness. I couldn't stand that!" After he wrote it down on his Daily Mood Log, he was able to substitute this Rational Response: "Then there will be 'nothing' to be upset about!" This helped him feel better, because he'd never really tried to think about it logically before.

The Daily Mood Log below lists several negative thoughts another patient had about being dead. You may recognize some of the fears that you have had at times. Notice how he refuted each of his negative thoughts.

THE DAILY MOOD LOG*

STEP ONE: DESCRIBE THE UPSETTING EVENT
<u>Thoughts of being dead.</u>

STEP TWO: RECORD YOUR NEGATIVE FEELINGS—and rate each one from 0 (the least) to 100 (the most). Use words like sad, anxious, angry, guilty, lonely, hopeless, frustrated, etc.

Emotion	Rating	Emotion	Rating	Emotion	Rating
1. Fear	99	3.		5.	
2.		4.		6.	

STEP THREE: THE TRIPLE-COLUMN TECHNIQUE—

Automatic Thoughts	Distortions	Rational Responses
Write your negative thoughts and estimate your belief in each one (0–100).	Identify the distortions in each Automatic Thought.	Substitute more realistic thoughts and estimate your belief in each one (0 and 100).
1. After I die, there will be many things that I won't be able to enjoy anymore. I won't be able to play tennis. I won't be able to go to work. I'll have to give up all these activities. ~~(100%)~~ 20%	Mental filter	1. There are many times when I'm not playing tennis now, and that isn't so terrible. I'm not playing tennis at this moment, for example. If it's not necessary for me to be playing tennis now, it certainly won't be necessary for me to play tennis after I die. Furthermore, I'll be unconscious and unaware of the fact that I am not playing tennis, so I won't feel disappointed! (80%)
2. There will be no one to care for my wife and children. They may face hardships without me, and my children may not grow up successfully	Fortune-telling	2. There are many times when I have been away from my family on weekends and on other occasions, and nothing terrible has happened. Other in-

(Continue on next page)

*Copyright © 1984 by David D. Burns, M.D., from *The Feeling Good Handbook*, copyright © 1989

Automatic Thoughts	Distortions	Rational Responses
without my guidance. ~~(75%)~~ (10%)		dividuals cope with the loss of a loved one. There's no reason to feel that my family wouldn't be able to cope. They would undoubtedly feel a sense of loss if I died, and that's natural. It would show they loved me. Eventually they will find happiness again, just as other people do. (100%)
3. But I'm afraid of the unknown, and I have no idea what death would be like. ~~(100%)~~ (25%)	Fortune-telling	3. Death will either be "something" or "nothing." If it's "something" it won't be "un-known," and if it's "nothing," there will be "nothing" to worry about! Since I don't know what will happen one minute from now, that also represents the unknown. Tomorrow is the unknown, and the day after that is unknown. I have been living with the unknown since the time I went down the birth canal. I have been coping with it so far, so there's no reason to think I won't be able to cope with it in the future. (100%)

STEP FOUR: OUTCOME—Re-rate your belief in each Automatic Thought from 0 to 100 and put a check in the box that describes how you now feel:

☐ not at all better; ☐ somewhat better; ☐ quite a bit better; ☒ a lot better.

I'd like you to identify the stage of death you're concerned about. Is it the period just before you die (Stage One), the actual moment of death (Stage Two), or the time after you're dead (Stage Three)? Write it down here:

_____.

Now record your negative thoughts about it on a Daily Mood Log (a blank form is included on pages 269–271). Identify the distortions in your thoughts, and substitute Rational Responses in the right-hand column. Once you record your negative thoughts, you may discover that your fears about death aren't particularly realistic. This can help you feel a lot better about life.

You may feel the way many of my patients do when I first describe these techniques. They tell me, "Dr. Burns, I can see that these methods are extremely logical, but they won't really help me get over my feelings. You see, I know my fear is irrational, but it's very real and I've felt this way all my life." I tell them to go ahead and write down their negative thoughts about death on the Daily Mood Log anyway, even though they feel convinced that this "logical" approach won't help. The next session they nearly always report that their fear of death "spontaneously" disappeared, and I usually never hear about the problem again. I hope the method proves to be as helpful to you!

You might even want to go one step further and think about death in a positive way. Although that might seem ludicrous at first, it really isn't.

The other day I discovered the mutilated corpse of a rabbit in our garden. Apparently our cat had captured and killed it. This rabbit used to come to feed in a certain section of our lawn, so I had a hunch it would only be a matter of time until our cat captured it.

Its moment of death must have been unbearably painful and terrifying. Death was a blessing, an escape. Just think how horrible it would have been if the rabbit had been unable to die!

If you have trouble identifying with a rabbit, then think about yourself or someone you love. Suppose your body was riddled with cancer and you couldn't die. Imagine that you were smashed to bits in a plane crash and you couldn't die. Now are you so sure that death is such a bad thing?

Can you imagine what it would be like to grow old if there were no such thing as death? Consider how feeble and sickly people in their eighties and nineties can become. Now try to imagine how decrepit you'd be if you lived to be 180! Or 580!

If you think that life without death would be a good thing, think the scenario through to its ultimate conclusion. I think you'll discover that the consequences are more grotesque and terrifying than anything you have ever imagined.

Suppose, for example, that everybody stopped growing old at the age of 21 and we all lived forever. You might add that there would be no illness and no violence in the world. To make the fantasy even more appealing, let's assume that everyone is attractive, healthy, and intelligent. You might think this would be wonderful. But would it be?

What would happen is that we'd have a population explosion of unparalleled proportions. People would reproduce like bacteria—after all, there would be an endless abundance of young, attractive, healthy people to mate with. Soon there would be not billions, but trillions and trillions of people competing for space on the planet. Eventually there wouldn't even be one square inch of soil left and people would be stacked five feet deep over the entire surface of the earth. There'd be absolutely no way of getting rid of anyone since people couldn't die. Just imagine how uncomfortable it would be if you had claustrophobia, with all those attractive people lying on top of you and no way to get out!

The existentialist philosophers like Sartre, Camus, and others claim that when you face the ultimate inevitability of death, life becomes meaningless. I believe the truth is exactly the opposite. Accepting death can make life more meaningful, more rewarding.

When I was a child, time crawled at a snail's pace. I can remember long summer days that seemed like an eternity. The week I drafted this chapter, I turned forty-two. It could be a few years or it could be thirty years before I die, but either way, it won't seem all that long. These days, the days fly by like minutes and weeks can seem like hours. Today I saw a patient whom I hadn't seen in over six months, and yet it seemed as if I'd just seen him yesterday.

Noticing how short life is may seem morbid. But the knowledge that time is running out can help us understand how precious life is and make us more aware of the importance of sorting out our priorities. My eight-year-old son won't be a little boy much longer. Soon he'll be a grown man. But he's still a little boy today, and if I want to love him and spend time with him, I can do that. So this evening we played some badminton and hit the birdie over the net fourteen times without missing. That's our new record. While we were playing I told him that I was writing a chapter about the fear of death. I reminded him that someday, I would die, and so would he. I was curious how he felt about it. He told me he loved me and said that people wouldn't worry so much about death if they were having fun. Then he asked me to serve.

THE DAILY MOOD LOG*

STEP ONE: DESCRIBE THE UPSETTING EVENT _____

_____

STEP TWO: RECORD YOUR NEGATIVE FEELINGS—and rate each one from 0 (the least) to 100 (the most). Use words like sad, anxious, angry, guilty, lonely, hopeless, frustrated, etc.

Emotion	Rating	Emotion	Rating	Emotion	Rating
1.		3.		5.	
2.		4.		6.	

STEP THREE: THE TRIPLE-COLUMN TECHNIQUE—

Automatic Thoughts	Distortions	Rational Responses
Write your negative thoughts and estimate your belief in each one (0–100).	Identify the distortions in each Automatic Thought.	Substitute more realistic thoughts and estimate your belief in each one (0 and 100).

(Continue on next page)

Automatic Thoughts	Distortions	Rational Responses

(Continue on next page)

Automatic Thoughts	Distortions	Rational Responses

STEP FOUR: OUTCOME–Re-rate your belief in each Automatic Thought from 0 to 100 and put a check in the box that describes how you now feel:

☐ not at all better; ☐ somewhat better; ☐ quite a bit better; ☐ a lot better.

CHECKLIST OF COGNITIVE DISTORTIONS*

1. All-or-nothing thinking: You look at things in absolute, black-and-white categories.
2. Overgeneralization: You view a negative event as a never-ending pattern of defeat.
3. Mental filter: You dwell on the negatives and ignore the positives.
4. Discounting the positives: You insist that your accomplishments or positive qualities "don't count."
5. Jumping to conclusions: (A) Mind reading—you assume that people are reacting negatively to you when there's no definite evidence for this; (B) Fortune-telling—you arbitrarily predict that things will turn out badly.
6. Magnification or minimization: You blow things way up out of proportion or you shrink their importance inappropriately.
7. Emotional reasoning: You reason from how you feel: "I *feel* like an idiot, so I really must be one." Or "I don't *feel* like doing this, so I'll put it off."
8. "Should statements": You criticize yourself or other people with "shoulds" or "shouldn'ts." "Musts," "oughts," and "have tos" are similar offenders.
9. Labeling: You identify with your shortcomings. Instead of saying "I made a mistake," you tell yourself, "I'm a jerk," or "a fool," or "a loser."
10. Personalization and blame: You blame yourself for something you weren't entirely responsible for, or you blame other people and overlook ways that your own attitudes and behavior might contribute to a problem.

14

•

Social Anxiety:
The Fear of People

The *Diagnostic and Statistical Manual* of the American Psychiatric Association defines a social phobia as "a persistent fear of . . . [social] situations in which the person is exposed to possible scrutiny by others and fears that he or she may do something . . . that will be humiliating or embarrassing." These situations might be dating, attending social functions and parties, or being introduced to strangers. Common fears include saying foolish things or being unable to answer questions when making conversation in a group, choking on food while eating in front of others, being unable to urinate in a public bathroom, having your hand tremble when signing your name in public, or having your mind go blank when giving a talk in public.

Dr. Aaron Beck has pointed out an interesting contrast between social phobias and agoraphobia. The agoraphobic fears that something terrible will happen if he or she is lost or alone. In contrast people with social anxiety fear the opposite—being around others and being the center of attention. Agoraphobics have been compared to children who are afraid of being lost and abandoned by their parents in a strange place, whereas people with social phobias feel more like children who are afraid of being under the critical scrutiny of a group of adults. Unlike agoraphobia, which is far more common in women, social phobias are more common in men. Perhaps this is because men experience greater pressures to perform, to assume leadership, to be emotionally "strong," and to initiate social contacts with the opposite sex.

Here are some common attitudes of individuals with social anxiety. Do you recognize these feelings?

- You feel that you're in the limelight, being judged by others. You believe that people are cold and would readily hurt or humiliate you.
- You believe you have to impress people to get them to like and respect you. However, you don't think you have anything interesting or worthwhile to say that will impress them. You are more preoccupied with pleasing people and acting the way they expect you to act than in being yourself.
- You don't believe that people will like the "real" you. You fear that if people found out about the "real" you, they would brand you as a fraud or look down on you. You feel inferior and defective in comparison with others.
- You believe that people have X-ray eyes and can always see how you are feeling inside, and that feelings of shyness or anxiety will be noticed and judged as foolish and unacceptable. This makes you avoid social situations. You would rather die than let anyone know how nervous you feel.
- You think that people are very judgmental and expect you to be polished, poised, and perfect. You have stereotyped ideas of appropriate social behavior. You have rigid standards of how you should feel, how you are supposed to act, and so on.
- You are terrified that you will make a fool of yourself in front of others. You feel convinced that if you do, the word will spread like wildfire and soon everyone will look down on you.
- You have extreme difficulty expressing negative feelings like anger. You are very unassertive and you avoid conflicts or disagreements with others.

Although we often think of people with social phobias as timid and shy wallflowers, they are sometimes highly successful and prominent individuals whom you would never suspect of having this problem. Gregory is the executive vice-president of a prestigious New York corporation. He confided to me that in the past thirty years he has rarely, if ever, said anything during staff meetings. He lives in constant terror that someone might ask for his opinion or ideas. I asked Gregory why this was so frightening. He confessed, "I

probably wouldn't have anything very intelligent or creative to say."
I was curious about why this was so threatening to him:

DAVID: And suppose you didn't have anything intelligent or creative to say. What then?

GREG: I'm a professional man and I'm expected to have something significant to say.

DAVID: And what if you didn't?

GREG: People would think I'm not a very capable person.

DAVID: And then what?

GREG: It would hurt my professional career.

DAVID: What would that mean to you?

GREG: Then I'd be a failure.

DAVID: And then?

GREG: I'd have no money. I couldn't pay the bills or the children's college tuition.

DAVID: What would that mean to you?

GREG: That would be a catastrophe because my style of living would collapse. I wouldn't be able to have the things I want. I'd be miserable.

This dialogue revealed the self-defeating attitudes at the root of Gregory's fears: he feels he must always appear competent, and he thinks he should never make mistakes. He believes that his colleagues are extremely judgmental and won't accept him unless he's perfect.

It's easy to see that these attitudes would make Gregory awfully uneasy, but there are also hidden benefits. As long as Gregory thinks he should be perfect, he'll put a tremendous effort into his work. He won't have to take risks and he'll always play it safe. Furthermore, he can secretly think of himself as a very "special" person. After all, only someone very "special" would be expected to be so perfect.

At the same time, Gregory pays a price for thinking this way. He feels constantly stressed; he rarely dares to express his own creative ideas; he's terrified of mistakes and criticism; and he often feels lonely, because he can't open up and share his feelings.

SELF-DISCLOSURE

Gregory feels insecure only in groups where he is expected to speak up. In one-to-one interactions, he feels fine. Some people with social phobias are a little different. They experience great anxiety even when talking to a friend when no one else is present. A college freshman at the University of Arizona named Jed told me that he felt especially anxious around a friend named Terry. He admired Terry because Terry seemed like a "cool dude." Terry was polished and good-looking and self-confident, and all the girls liked him. At the same time, Terry seemed a little too slick and glib, and Jed felt intimidated.

Jed's difficulties began one night when he and a bunch of friends, including Terry, were out drinking. Jed became intoxicated and started clowning around. He became the "life of the party," and all his friends seemed to be impressed by him. Jed said he felt he was being "cool."

The next day, Jed ran into Terry. Terry tried to strike up a conversation and said he had a lot of fun the night before. Without the benefit of a couple of drinks, Jed no longer felt loose and flippant. Instead, he felt nervous and self-conscious. He stared at the ground, hoping Terry wouldn't notice how anxious he felt, and mumbled brief replies.

After that, whenever he ran into Terry, Jed's heart started racing and he panicked. He tried to avoid Terry and acted uninterested whenever they spoke. Terry made overtures of friendship on several occasions and suggested they should get together, but Jed never followed up. Eventually they drifted further and further apart. Terry joined one of the "snobby" fraternities and they saw each other less frequently.

Jed said that this was not an isolated example but was typical of his relationships with friends. He said he put Terry on a pedestal and saw him as better than he was. Then he felt terribly pressured to compete and to impress Terry to prove he was Terry's equal. This made Jed extremely anxious and insecure.

Jed exemplifies many of the self-defeating attitudes described earlier that lead to social anxiety. He feels he must impress people and put on a show to be likable; he has stereotyped ideas of proper, acceptable behavior; he feels that his anxiety is shameful and unacceptable; and he is convinced that his "true self" would not be acceptable to his buddies. Jed constantly wears a mask, a manufactured "social self," that he presents to the world in hopes of being liked. This creates constant tension. Jed always has the terrible fear that someone will find him out and see his real, unacceptable self hiding behind the mask.

I suggested that Jed might want to tell Terry how he felt as a way of breaking the ice and making Terry more aware of why he had been acting aloof. I explained that he could let Terry know that he liked him but that he also felt a little nervous around him. I suggested he could point out that while he admired Terry, he felt that Terry was so smooth and polished that he sometimes felt uncomfortable when he was with him.

Jed replied, "No way, José!" He explained emphatically that students don't say stupid things like that and that if he did, which he never would, Terry would think he was a "real wimp." Jed's greatest fear was letting Terry know he felt nervous and anxious.

Jed's reaction is typical of nearly every socially anxious individual I've ever treated. He has rigid ideas of "right" and "wrong" social behavior. He is dogmatically convinced that sharing his feelings openly would not be socially acceptable. This was *not* the kind of help Jed had in mind! What he hoped was that I could teach him to *eliminate* his anxious feelings so he'd feel bold and relaxed and confident, as he did when he was intoxicated.

Notice the contradiction in what Jed is asking for. On the one hand he says, "Help me develop better self-esteem." But at the same time he says, "P.S. Make me into a very different person. Help me become the mask I wear. Don't ask me to accept myself the way I am! The real me is no darn good. A real stud doesn't feel nervous!"

Jed wants to believe that his real self is that joking, charming, totally self-confident guy who was impressing everyone when he was drunk. He feels that the nervous, insecure guy who usually inhabits his body isn't his real self, but an alien. He thinks that the shy, insecure Jed is a shameful, sick aberration, a mentally defective twin, who must be hidden behind locked doors.

Jed might outgrow some of his social anxiety through greater personal disclosure. Instead of feeling anxious and nervous and holding all his feelings inside, he could tell people how he feels. This can be remarkably helpful. If you suffer from social anxiety you may dig in your heels and hesitate to use this technique, just as Jed did, because of your "emotional perfectionism." You may think it's shameful to feel nervous and insecure. This attitude intensifies your anxiety, because you carry a double burden: you feel anxious and you feel that you have to hide your anxiety.

Jed and I became increasingly frustrated with each other because we seemed to have different agendas. It seemed that he was determined to become Mr. Cool. All he wanted was for me to teach him how to impress guys and score with women. In contrast, I wanted him to accept himself as a real human being, so he could admit his feelings of insecurity and nervousness without shame or a loss of self-esteem. I encouraged him to tell his friends that he sometimes felt nervous, but he wouldn't budge. He said he'd rather die than do that. I didn't disagree with his goal of feeling more comfortable and self-confident, but I felt certain he was using the wrong approach.

One day in a staff meeting my assistant, Retta Jo Bender, told me that whenever Jed was waiting for his appointment he came on "real strong" and talked a lot. She said Jed seemed like a nice person but he always seemed to be trying to impress her. She said this made her uncomfortable.

I realized that this was probably what he did with classmates at school, which would explain why he didn't have anyone he felt close to. The next time I saw Jed I told him what Retta Jo had shared with me. I said, "You know, Jed, I think she's fond of you but she's real turned off by you. You're trying to be so great, so special. The fact is that most of us don't feel so high and mighty. You seem determined to be better than everybody else. I want you to know that I resent it and I'm sick of it and it just won't wash. I bet that most of the people you know are real turned off by you, just the way I am!"

After I said this there was a long silence, and I felt very awkward. I was concerned that I'd overstepped my bounds and that I'd been unprofessional and too aggressive. But Jed's whole attitude suddenly seemed to change. He appeared humbled and said he understood what I'd been trying to tell him. He said that I was honestly expressing my feelings to him, and he could see why it was so important for him to express his feelings. He said it was the best session we'd ever had, and asked why I had waited so long to tell him how I felt!

After the session he began to feel much more relaxed and open with people. He even told his girlfriend that he'd been bothered by anxiety in social situations for several years. He was surprised that she said she felt the closest to him that she'd ever felt.

We often make the mistake of thinking that people will accept and admire only our strengths and will reject us if they know of our vulnerabilities and weaknesses. Because of this belief, we are afraid to tell people that we feel uncomfortable or that we have negative feelings about them. This is the mistake that I had been making with

Jed. I noticed how annoying and inappropriate his behavior was, and yet I was afraid of hurting his feelings or portraying myself as anything other than kind and helpful. As a result, I had been just as dishonest with him as he was being with the rest of the world. Once I opened up, our relationship became much more genuine, and he was able to experience real trust and closeness.

Personal disclosure is a powerful antidote to social anxiety, if you are willing to muster the courage. Tell people that you feel anxious in certain situations. Ask them if they ever feel nervous or worried. If you're afraid they might think less of you, ask them.

Like Jed, you may be thinking, "I couldn't tell people I feel anxious! It's a ridiculous idea. I'd make a fool of myself." Let's look at each of these objections carefully. When you say, "I *couldn't* do that," what you really mean is, "I don't *want* to tell anyone how anxious I feel." That's your prerogative, but you could if you chose to. If you insist on hiding your feelings, you'll continue to believe that you're somehow "different" or "defective." If you share your feelings, you might learn that other people are also quite human and willing to accept you.

Shortly after I opened my psychiatric practice, my wife and I bought a home in a nice neighborhood. Our daughter began playing with a girl who lived in a nearby house that looked like a mansion. One night, dressed in Levi's and an old T-shirt, I stopped by to pick up my daughter. Janice, the mother of the girl, met me at the door. She was dressed to the hilt and looked like a model in *Vogue* magazine. Janice invited me in and I found myself in a large hallway filled with expensive antiques. The walls were covered with oil paintings that looked several hundred years old—it was like a museum.

I felt quite awkward. Janice noticed how nervous I seemed and asked if I was feeling uncomfortable. I had the urge to deny how I felt in a defensive tone of voice, but instead I confessed that I did feel tense because I wasn't used to being in such a fancy house. She said she was quite surprised that a "shrink" would ever feel insecure! I felt even more embarrassed and teasingly reassured her that this was the only time since 1955 that I had felt any small tinge of nervousness! Janice laughed and we became good friends.

I believe that being open about my insecurities disarmed her, and we both felt more comfortable. Denying how I felt would have added to the tension and made me appear phony. Although some people do appear very glamorous and successful, most of us feel pretty human underneath. Sharing your vulnerabilities can be one of the best ways to overcome social anxiety and to develop close relationships with others.

THE FEARED FANTASY TECHNIQUE

Let's look at the worst possibility. Suppose you told someone you felt anxious and they *did* conclude you were a basket case. Would this be so terrible? How would you handle it?

A young woman named Joan, who works as an administrative assistant for a sportswear manufacturer, always felt very anxious around good-looking men. One of Joan's duties was to take sales representatives on tours of the plant facilities. Because many of these salesmen were attractive young men, she'd often get tense and the muscles of her neck would tighten up. Then her head would start to shake. She'd become preoccupied with the fear that one of the men would notice her head bobbing and look down on her. This thought made her anxiety unbearable, and the more she tried to hide her feelings the worse she felt. When I suggested that she might relieve some of the pressure by simply telling the group she felt a little nervous, she seemed as shocked as if I'd asked her to take her clothes off and run naked through the plant!

I proposed we examine her concerns with the Feared Fantasy Technique (see page 130). I suggested that she pretend to be a handsome man and insult me because I was nervous and my head was shaking. I told her to try to make me feel as foolish and humiliated as she could, by saying the things that a person would never really say but might be thinking. The purpose of the role-playing was to show her that even if the worst happened, it wouldn't be nearly as terrible as she imagined.

JOAN (*as the hostile handsome young man*): I noticed that your head is shaking. Why is that?

DAVID (*as Joan*): My head is shaking because I feel nervous.

JOAN (*as the hostile man*): Gee, that looks funny to have your head shaking like that.

DAVID (*as Joan*): It probably does look funny. It does that when I'm nervous.

JOAN (*as the hostile man*): Only a nut would let their head shake in public!

DAVID *(as Joan, smiling)*: I've suspected that I was a little bit nutty for some time now. As a matter of fact, I think that might even become one of my better qualities.

JOAN *(as the hostile man)*: Well, I don't think it's such a great quality. You've got to be some kind of a weirdo to have your head shaking like that in public. You must be ready for the loony bin!

DAVID *(as Joan)*: Oh, absolutely! In fact, I'm probably much loonier than you think. I'm actually on my best behavior now. Tell me, do you find crazy ladies interesting?

JOAN *(as the hostile man)*: This is ridiculous. I don't know what's wrong with you, except that you seem awfully nervous. I think you're a mental case and I don't want to have anything to do with you!

DAVID *(as Joan)*: Well, I have learned something new. I always thought that being nervous made people human. Now I've discovered that it makes them "mental cases." I think you're quite wise in not getting involved with any "mental cases" like me. That could be quite dangerous! You would have no idea what crazy thing I might do next!

Joan was able to see that I was unperturbed by her attempt to humiliate me. She saw that the foolish behavior belonged to the hostile man. Although a real person would never be so critical, the imaginary stranger represented Joan's own self-critical thoughts. We then did a role reversal so she could learn to talk back to the imaginary put-downs.

You might want to try the Feared Fantasy Technique by role-playing with your therapist or with a friend or by writing out a script. When you talk back to the worst criticisms you can think up, you will begin to see how unrealistic they are. This can liberate you from your deepest fears and help you accept yourself as an imperfect but lovable human being.

THE SHAME-ATTACKING EXERCISE

Another way to squelch this fear is with a powerful technique called the Shame-Attacking Exercise (see page 230). The essence of the exercise is to confront your fears head-on, in a shameless, bold manner.

A handsome New York television anchorman named Steve was recently helped a great deal by a Shame-Attacking Exercise when he participated in the "intensive" program at my institute. Steve seems to have it all together, and you'd never suspect that he suffered from shyness and severe social anxiety. Steve has a mild, inherited tremor, so that his hands shake whenever he tries to hold a cup of coffee or write his name. He'd been to numerous neurologists in the hope of finding a cure, but they all said it was essentially untreatable and he'd just have to learn to live with it.

One of Steve's most terrifying fears was that someone would notice his tremor and look down on him. The tremor became noticeably worse whenever he was around people, and he constantly worried that they would discover his secret. He had developed all kinds of mannerisms to try to hide the tremor—for example, he never drank any fluid in front of other people. He was afraid that his producers would notice the tremor and decide he was defective and abnormal. He felt this would end his television career.

Steve had never actually challenged any of these beliefs. He had no real evidence that anyone would look down on him because of his tremor. He was so good at hiding it that no one had ever found out about it. I suggested that his problem was not his tremor, but his negative thoughts and feelings about it. These were his negative thoughts: "(1) It would be awful if anyone saw my hand shaking. (2) They would think there was something wrong with me. (3) This would be humiliating."

I wanted Steve to test these thoughts and confront his fears. I instructed him to go to a fashionable boutique where there were attractively dressed men and women shopping for expensive clothes. I suggested he could buy something inexpensive, like a tie or a handkerchief, and charge it on his credit card. Then, when the sales clerk asked him to sign his name—which terrified him—he could say in a loud, clear voice that everyone could hear, "Oh, there goes my shaky, trembling hand. My, oh my! Look at that tremor!" While he spoke, he could let his hand shake as much as possible so everyone could see it.

I told Steve that once he'd done this, he should tear up the charge slip and ask for a new one, explaining that his signature was too shaky. When he signed the second charge slip, he could call attention to his tremor again. Finally, before he left the boutique, he could ask for a drink of water. When he received the cup, he could hold it so that everyone could see the cup shaking and the water splashing about. Then he could say, "There goes my shaky hand again!"

Steve was not at all enthusiastic about this assignment! In fact, he stubbornly refused to do it for several days. Finally he gave in. I assigned a psychology graduate student to go along and observe him so we could be sure that he did the exercise completely.

With great misgivings, Steve entered a boutique in a fashionable area and purchased a tie. While he was signing his name as planned, he experienced sheer panic. However, nobody seemed terribly preoccupied with his shaky hands. One of the saleswomen started flirting with him when he was filling out the charge slip. By the time he left, his anxiety had diminished substantially. He felt encouraged and went into several additional stores and repeated the exercise. Each time, people seemed interested in him and no one seemed put off by his shaky hands. These experiences put the lie to his belief that it would be unbearable to let someone see his hands shaking.

Although he was partially relieved, Steve still thought that people were just acting polite. He believed that most people would secretly think he was abnormal, that something was terribly wrong with him, because of his tremor. To test this, he began telling people he met at my clinic—as well as strangers he met on the street—that he was in Philadelphia to get treatment for his "shaky hands." He was surprised that people were warm and friendly and didn't seem at all turned off by him.

The Shame-Attacking Method is similar to a method many therapists call "flooding" or "exposure." Essentially, you expose yourself to your fears and you allow yourself to be flooded with anxiety. It's like confronting a bully and saying, "Take your best shot." Usually your fears will peak, and then plateau, and then subside. Often they will disappear entirely! The effects can be profound. I strongly recommend this method for people with social anxiety.

Let's see if you understand how to use the Shame-Attacking Exercise. Imagine that you're a good-looking 26-year-old carpenter man who feels intensely shy and nervous in any social situation. When you go to singles' bars, you tell yourself, "These people are all so much more poised and self-confident than I am. If they knew how nervous I felt, they'd all think there was really something wrong with me." These thoughts make you so tense you can barely stand being in social situations for more than a few minutes. How could you attack these fears with the Shame-Attacking Exercise? Put your ideas here:

_____

_____

_____

_____

Answer: You could go to a singles' bar and strike up a conversation with someone. While you're getting to know them, you could tell them that you get very nervous in crowds and ask them if they ever feel that way. A man named Frank who received intensive treatment for a social phobia actually did this, with good results. He reported that the candid disclosure of how nervous he felt actually put other people at ease and made it easier for him to get to know them. This was not consistent with his belief that people would think his anxiety was shameful, and he felt much more relaxed.

THE EXPERIMENTAL TECHNIQUE

We often assume that our negative thoughts and beliefs are true without really questioning them. A young man from England named Martin worked in New York as a chemist. Martin had severe social anxiety and felt extremely awkward around groups of people. Standing in grocery store lines was a nightmare. He thought that all the people in the line were chitchatting with each other in a friendly, charming way. He imagined that they expected him to be equally witty and charming. He would stare anxiously at the floor, hoping no one would notice how inappropriate and klutzy he felt. He berated himself and told himself he wasn't supposed to stare at the floor. He told himself he should move his head and eyes around in a relaxed, spontaneous fashion. Needless to say, all the pressure he put on himself made him feel exceedingly awkward.

The moment it was time to pay for the groceries was terrifying. Martin felt that everyone was watching him and expecting him to say something clever and lighthearted to the cashier. Since he could never think of anything at all to say, the experience was sheer hell. He would leave the store feeling ashamed, embarrassed, and humiliated.

A student therapist at my unit suggested that he could test his belief that all the people in grocery lines were chitchatting amicably. She told Martin to forcibly lift his eyes from the floor and look at the other people in line. Since Martin was a scientist, she told him to calculate what percent of the people were actually socializing with one another. She also asked him to study and analyze what the other people in line did with their eyes. Did they always gaze into each other's faces in an animated manner, or did they sometimes stare off into space, just as he did?

Martin was extremely reluctant to perform this experiment. He felt that all the people would notice him staring at them. He was convinced that they would scowl at him in a judgmental way. It seemed much safer just to keep staring at the floor. Nevertheless, she twisted Martin's arm and he finally agreed to do it.

The next session, Martin reported with relief and surprise that most of the people in line were not chatting with each other. Many of them were daydreaming or looking at the candy or the magazines next to the check-out line. When they paid the cashier, they didn't act particularly charming, but simply paid their bills and left with their groceries. This discovery was an enormous relief.

In another session Martin told me that when he was walking down the street or standing in line at fast-food restaurants, he often felt that people were glaring at him in a disapproving way because they didn't like his looks. This made Martin feel intensely anxious and angry. He had thoughts like "He's got no right to look down on me! I'd like to punch him in the mouth." Then he would glance at people in a defiant way. Although Martin is a pleasant-looking fellow, he did tend to dress plainly due to his low self-esteem, and he sometimes needed a haircut. However, it did not seem at all likely to me that people were put off by his looks. Nevertheless, the defensive hostility he projected put people on edge, and when he saw the discomfort in their faces he thought, "I was right. They really *don't* like my looks!"

Can you think of an experiment Martin could do to test his belief that people glared at him because they didn't like his looks? Put your ideas here:

_____

_____

_____

_____

Answer: I suggested that he might smile and say hello to twenty strangers when he was walking down the street or standing in line at fast-food restaurants. Then he could keep track of the number of people who smiled back in a friendly way and the number who ignored him or said something rude.

Martin found this assignment difficult at first. In fact, he refused to do it for two months. He said he was so angry and anxious that he didn't feel like smiling. I told him he could just force out a smile and a hello, regardless of how uncomfortable he felt. Finally he agreed to practice smiling in front of a mirror for a few days before he began the experiment.

At the next session, Martin was euphoric. Although a few people did seem sour and ignored him, the majority smiled back and were exceedingly friendly. He got into conversations with several people, and ended up talking for over three hours to a fellow he knew from work. This was very unusual because he'd barely spoken to a fellow employee in over two years. He said he suddenly started to feel confident and charming and he loved meeting people. Not bad for someone who had felt tense, hostile, and lonely for much of his life!

THE SEMANTIC METHOD

Like Martin, most people with social anxiety feel intensely uncomfortable and fearful of saying or doing something foolish in front of others. This is a particularly painful and humiliating form of suffering. In spite of your intense desire to feel close to others, your fears of making a social blunder and making yourself the object of ridicule may prevent you from taking the necessary steps to initiate relationships.

Some of this anguish results from the cognitive distortion called "magnification." When you feel nervous in social situations, you may be using overly colorful language and blowing things out of proportion in your mind. For example:

- You spill a drink on yourself at a party and you tell yourself, "My gosh! This is terrible!"
- You're afraid to say hello or flirt with an attractive person you'd love to have a date with. You think, "If she [or he] gives me a hard time I'll look like an idiot. I couldn't stand that! It would be awful!"

The Semantic Method can be an extremely helpful antidote to this "magnification." You simply use more modest and less colorful language when you think about the problem. For example, when you spill a drink on yourself, you could tell yourself that it's a little embarrassing or inconvenient rather than dramatizing it as "terrible."

Some people may resist this. There may be several hidden payoffs when you catastrophize your shortcomings and magnify your mistakes. First, you may enjoy attracting attention to yourself by carrying on about your problems in a dramatic fashion. Second, when you act helpless and overwhelmed, the hidden message you project is, "I'm really such a remarkably superior person, it's practically inconceivable that I would do something as clumsy as spilling a drink on myself at a cocktail party. I will act terribly upset so you will know this is highly unusual!" Third, you may have the belief that if you blow your problems out of proportion and berate yourself sufficiently, you will improve. Perfectionists often think this way. They beat on themselves endlessly, thinking that somehow they will achieve salvation.

If you stop magnifying your mistakes and overreacting to them, you'll have to give up this kind of self-importance. This means you will have to accept your mistakes in a low-key way instead of viewing them as a federal offense. See if you can do this. Let's suppose that you flirt with someone and they give you the brush-off. What could you tell yourself instead of, "Gee! I really looked like a total idiot"? Put your Rational Response here:

_____

_____

_____

_____

Answer: Some people might tell themselves: "If he doesn't like me, it's his problem! He's probably a snob anyway." I don't like this approach because now you're putting the other person down. This has a hostile, insecure sound to it. I would suggest that you maintain a friendly, lighthearted attitude. Tell yourself that you looked like a human being, and not a "total idiot," and you get credit for trying. Remind yourself that you can flirt with other people and that eventually you will find someone who's fun to talk to.

THE "WHAT-IF?" TECHNIQUE

When you are blowing things out of proportion and predicting social catastrophes, try the "What-If?" Technique. This variation of the Vertical Arrow Technique can be especially helpful for the thoughts that lead to anxiety (see page 122). When you insist that some social foible would be "terrible," ask yourself, "What are the worst possible consequences of this? What if they really did happen?" When you face them squarely, you will frequently discover that your worst fears aren't nearly as terrible as you imagined.

To continue with the previous example, suppose you smile and say hello to an attractive woman who's picking out apples in the grocery store. She tells you to get lost. Several people are watching. You may think, "This is awful!" Ask yourself, "Why is this so awful?" You might say, "All those people will think I'm a jerk." Now ask yourself again: "And what if they do? Suppose they all think I'm a jerk. Why is that so awful?" You might say, "They'll look down on me and tell other people what a klutz I was." Now ask yourself: "And what if this happened? Why would that be so awful? How many people would they tell? What's the worst possible thing that could happen?"

Let's imagine that they'd each told several other people how lame you were. Now ask yourself: "Is that the very worst that could happen? Could I live with that? Why would that be so awful?"

You might not give up so easily. Let's imagine that each of those people told several more people, and so on, until eventually there were several hundred people who knew that you had made a fool of yourself. And they might all agree that you were a loser and decide that they didn't like you.

Once you've pushed your fears to their worst imaginable extreme, ask yourself these two questions: "How likely is this? Could I live with this if it did happen?" You could remind yourself that there are

200 million people in the United States. If several hundred people thought you were a jerk, so what? Could you still survive and find happiness? Do you want to let these people—assuming that this incredibly unlikely chain of events actually happened—have so much power over your life? What could they do to you anyway? Could they arrest you? Would they get together in groups and snicker about you?

If you decide you *could* live with these unlikely consequences, then you're free. You're free to flirt with anybody you want, and you can stop letting your insecurities spoil your life. Certainly not everybody will find you attractive or interesting. Some people *will* think you're a jerk. I can assure you there are hundreds of people who think I'm a jerk! I would be inclined to agree with them, too! I've often felt that being a jerk was actually one of my better qualities.

When you believe in yourself, your supporters will far outnumber your critics. Many people will respond to you positively, and this can lead to rewarding relationships and opportunities. Are you willing to take the risk?

THE DAILY MOOD LOG

So far we've talked about a number of causes and cures for social anxiety. The "Daily Mood Log" should be added to the tools you use because it will show you precisely why you are afraid of people and how you can deal with these feelings more effectively. You may recall the specific steps, which are described in detail in Chapter 5:

Step One: Write a brief description of a social situation that made you feel anxious.

Step Two: Record your negative feelings and rate how intense each one was between 0 (not at all) and 100 (the worst).

Step Three: The Triple-Column Technique: Write down the Automatic Thoughts that made you feel nervous and insecure in the Automatic Thoughts column. Indicate how strongly you believed each one between 0 and 100. Then identify the cognitive distortions in each negative thought, using the list on page 296, and substitute more positive and realistic thoughts in the Rational Response Column. Indicate how much you believe each of them between 0 and 100.

Step Four: Outcome: Re-rate your belief in each Automatic Thought
                on the scale of 0 to 100. Once your belief in each
                negative thought is reduced, indicate how much better
                you now feel.

Let's assume that you usually feel insecure and self-conscious around
groups of people. This is so painful to you that you go to great
lengths to avoid social situations. Imagine that your boyfriend recently asked you to go shopping with some friends who were visiting
from California. You felt panicky and wanted to back out. You
recorded your negative emotions as: "Nervous—100; Frustrated—100;
Hopeless—100."

Next, you wrote down the following "Automatic Thoughts" on
the Daily Mood Log:

1. I will not know what to talk about.

2. I will feel so stupid.

3. His friends will think I'm not very interesting.

4. When I speak they will stare at me and think that what I have
   to say doesn't count.

5. I will feel so tense that I won't be able to walk and talk freely.

6. I *shouldn't* feel this way! What's wrong with me?

7. I'll never change.

I'm sure you can see the connection between your negative thoughts
and your anxious feelings. Let's see how you might deal with some
of them. Your first thought was "I will not know what to talk
about." What are the distortions in this thought? Review this list
of cognitive distortions on page 296 and put your ideas here:

1. _____

2. _____

3. _____

4. _____

5. _____

Answer: first, this is a prime example of "fortune-telling." These negative predictions often function as self-fulfilling prophecies. If you keep telling yourself that you have nothing to say, you may get so nervous that you will have difficulties thinking of things to talk about.

You are also making a "should statement." You are pressuring yourself that you must come up with things that are witty and entertaining in order to be liked by others.

A third distortion would be "discounting the positive." If you went shopping with these people, you probably would have things to talk about, and you could ask questions to get to know the other people a little better. But you may censor all your ideas and feelings because they seem too ordinary to impress people.

A fourth distortion is "emotional reasoning"—you *feel* like you'll have nothing to say, so you assume that you really won't. But you have no evidence for this. A fifth distortion would be "all-or-nothing thinking." You may not be a geyser of conversation and wit, but you'll certainly have *some* things to say.

The Ten Ways to Untwist Your Thinking on page 118 lists many ways of talking back to negative thoughts. What could you tell yourself instead of, "I will not know what to talk about"? Put your ideas here.

_____

_____

_____

_____

Answer: One approach would be to use the "Double Standard Method." If you had a friend who felt nervous before shopping with friends, would you tell her, "Hey, you won't have *anything* to talk about?" You wouldn't say this because it would be mean. Instead, you'd be supportive and you'd encourage her. Would you be willing to talk to yourself in the same supportive way you would talk to a friend? If so, you could tell yourself something like this: "I will have something to say, and I can ask these women about themselves. I can be a good listener, and they might appreciate the fact that I'm interested in them."

A second approach would be the "Cost-Benefit Analysis." You could list the advantages and disadvantages of telling yourself, "I won't be able to think of anything to say." One obvious advantage would be that you'll feel so discouraged that you'll stay home, so you won't have to confront your fears. The main disadvantage would be that you'll spend the day in anguish, hating yourself. Weighing the advantages against the disadvantages can sometimes motivate you to say, "Hey, I'm tired of this. I think I'll take a chance and do things differently for once."

A third approach would be the "What-If?" technique. Suppose you *did* go shopping and couldn't think of much to say. What's the worst that could happen? Conceivably, one or more of these people might decide they didn't like you because you were so shy and quiet. If so, what's the worst thing that could possibly happen? Would they start telling other people about what a nervous and undesirable person you were? How many people would they tell? Would they put an article about you in the newspaper and polarize the entire city against you so you'd never again have the chance of making any friends?

Once you push your fears to their most exaggerated conclusions with the "What-If" technique, ask yourself, "how likely is this? And even more important, could I still accept myself if this unlikely chain of events did occur?" In evaluating this, you might need to do another "Cost-Benefit Analysis." You could list the advantages and disadvantages of believing, "I must have everyone's approval to be a worthwhile human being."

It's important to realize there are numerous ways to change your negative thinking patterns. When one method's not helpful, you can try another, and then another, until you finally find a Rational Response that makes good sense to you.

Now I want you to see if you can talk back to your second negative thought, "I will feel so stupid." Identify the distortions in this thought, using the list on page 296:

1. _____

2. _____

3. _____

4. _____

5. _____

6. _____

Now, substitute your Rational Response here:

_____

_____

_____

_____

A blank Daily Mood Log is located at the end of this chapter on page 294 for your convenience. Remember that to make you feel better at the gut level, any Rational Response must have these two characteristics:

1. It must be absolutely true and realistic. Phony rationalizations will never help you. Ask yourself how much you believe your Rational Response between 0% and 100%. Your belief in it should be close to 100% if it's going to do you any good.

2. The Rational Response must put the lie to your negative thought. The moment you stop believing your Automatic Thoughts, you will feel better.

How much better? The aim is not to reduce your anxiety from 100% (the worst) to 0% (no anxiety at all). That would be unrealistic. If you can reduce your anxiety by about half before a social function, you will be more likely to mix with other people and open up. This *will* be anxiety-provoking at first. But once you do, you'll see that the world doesn't really come to an end, and your self-confidence will increase.

Social anxiety is caused by double-barreled mistrust. First, you don't believe that you can be accepted as a vulnerable and imperfect human being. You imagine that people are extremely vindictive, hostile, and judgmental and will not accept you as you really are. In addition, you do not accept yourself. You may despise yourself for your vulnerabilities and think you must be better than you really are to be lovable and worthwhile. The solution to this dilemma cannot exist in your head but can only be worked out in your relationships with others. Much like someone with an elevator phobia, you've got to get on the elevator and discover firsthand that you won't get trapped or fall after all. This means mixing with other people in social situations and being more open about your feelings. This will be anxiety-provoking at first. If you stubbornly persist and expose yourself to social situations over and over, you will slowly begin to gain greater and greater self-confidence. As you stop running away and begin to connect with other people, you will gain freedom from the fears that have plagued you.

THE DAILY MOOD LOG*

STEP ONE: DESCRIBE THE UPSETTING EVENT _____

_____

STEP TWO: RECORD YOUR NEGATIVE FEELINGS—and rate each one from 0 (the least) to 100 (the most). Use words like sad, anxious, angry, guilty, lonely, hopeless, frustrated, etc.

Emotion	Rating	Emotion	Rating	Emotion	Rating
1.		3.		5.	
2.		4.		6.	

STEP THREE: THE TRIPLE-COLUMN TECHNIQUE—

Automatic Thoughts	Distortions	Rational Responses
Write your negative thoughts and estimate your belief in each one (0–100).	Identify the distortions in each Automatic Thought.	Substitute more realistic thoughts and estimate your belief in each one (0 and 100).

(Continue on next page)

*Copyright © 1984 by David D. Burns, M.D., from *The Feeling Good Handbook*, copyright © 1989

THE DAILY MOOD LOG (continued)

Automatic Thoughts	Distortions	Rational Responses

(Continue on next page)

THE DAILY MOOD LOG (continued)

Automatic Thoughts	Distortions	Rational Responses

STEP FOUR: OUTCOME—Re-rate your belief in each Automatic Thought from 0 to 100 and put a check in the box that describes how you now feel:

☐ not at all better; ☐ somewhat better; ☐ quite a bit better; ☐ a lot better.

CHECKLIST OF COGNITIVE DISTORTIONS*

1. All-or-nothing thinking: You look at things in absolute, black-and-white categories.
2. Overgeneralization: You view a negative event as a never-ending pattern of defeat.
3. Mental filter: You dwell on the negatives and ignore the positives.
4. Discounting the positives: You insist that your accomplishments or positive qualities "don't count."
5. Jumping to conclusions: (A) Mind reading—you assume that people are reacting negatively to you when there's no definite evidence for this; (B) Fortune-telling—you arbitrarily predict that things will turn out badly.
6. Magnification or minimization: You blow things way up out of proportion or you shrink their importance inappropriately.
7. Emotional reasoning: You reason from how you feel: "I *feel* like an idiot, so I really must be one." Or "I don't *feel* like doing this, so I'll put it off."
8. "Should statements": You criticize yourself or other people with "shoulds" or "shouldn'ts." "Musts," "oughts," and "have tos" are similar offenders.
9. Labeling: You identify with your shortcomings. Instead of saying "I made a mistake," you tell yourself, "I'm a jerk," or "a fool," or "a loser."
10. Personalization and blame: You blame yourself for something you weren't entirely responsible for, or you blame other people and overlook ways that your own attitudes and behavior might contribute to a problem.

*Copyright © 1980 by David D. Burns, M.D. Adapted from *Feeling Good: The New Mood Therapy* (New York: William Morrow & Company, 1980; Signet, 1981).

·

15

Public Speaking Anxiety

Imagine that in five minutes you will have to speak or give a talk in front of a group of people. It might be a church group, a class or an important business meeting. How worried or nervous would you be feeling?

_____ Not at all
_____ A little bit
_____ A moderate amount
_____ An extreme amount

If you indicated that you would feel at least a little anxious, I want you to tell me how you would be thinking. Write down any negative thoughts you might have just before you give your talk:

_____

_____

_____

_____

Although everyone is different, you might be telling yourself something like this: "What if they think I'm a bore? What if my mind goes blank? I'll probably look nervous and my voice will tremble and shake. Everyone will see what a dodo I am." You may imagine yourself fumbling awkwardly as you begin to speak. You may anticipate that people in the audience will quietly chuckle or yawn in boredom and slip out the back door before you're done. Or you may be afraid that people will interrupt you and ask embarrassing questions that will make you look foolish.

These fears are extremely common. However, many people with public speaking anxiety think their problems are very unusual.

If you're willing to work at it, you can conquer your fears of public speaking. You'll feel better about yourself and others will respect you more. The ability to speak in front of groups can mean getting better grades in school, getting a promotion at work, or possibly finding a new and more rewarding career.

The crucial first step is to recognize the connection between your negative thoughts and the way you feel. You feel worried and uptight because you give yourself negative messages. When you write these negative thoughts down, it becomes easier to see how distorted and self-defeating they are. Since you put these frightening thoughts and fantasies in your mind, it's within your power to get rid of them.

A businessman named Frank wanted to expand his business by offering a series of seminars to potential clients in his community. He had procrastinated about arranging these seminars for years because he was afraid he would appear nervous and do a bad job. He thought this would damage his professional reputation.

Frank's intense anxiety about speaking in front of a group resulted from these negative thoughts: "If I'm nervous I won't be able to present my ideas very clearly. I shouldn't feel so anxious! People will notice my voice trembling and they'll think, 'Gee! That guy sure is nervous.' Then they'll think I'm not a very worthwhile person and they won't want to do business with me."

Once you write down your negative thoughts, you can identify the distortions in each of them using the list on page 308. Frank's first negative thought was: "If I'm nervous I won't be able to present my ideas very clearly." Can you identify the distortions in this thought? Put your ideas here before you read on:

1. _____

2. _____

It involves "all-or-nothing thinking" because he's telling himself that he will either feel completely relaxed and present his thoughts articulately, or that he will feel extremely nervous and make a totally garbled presentation. In reality, he will probably be able to present his ideas reasonably well even if he does feel nervous. And if he gives a series of seminars, he'll get better and better at it each time.

Frank is also involved in "fortune-telling" (also known as "jumping to conclusions") because he's predicting a bad outcome. You may argue that this prediction is realistic, since he *will* be nervous and he may have some trouble with the presentation. That may be partially true, but it's quite destructive for Frank to give himself this message. If he had a friend who planned to give a seminar, would Frank tell him, "you're going to be nervous and confused" over and over in the days before the presentation? Of course he wouldn't! And yet that's exactly the kind of negative message Frank gives himself!

Once you identify the distortions in a negative thought, you can substitute a Rational Response. What Rational Response would you suggest? What could Frank tell himself in place of, "If I'm nervous I won't be able to present my ideas very clearly"? Write your ideas here:

_____

_____

_____

_____

_____

Frank and I came up with this Rational Response: "I may feel nervous at first, but that's natural. I'll probably feel more relaxed once I get started. I will be able to get my ideas across even if I'm not the world's greatest orator."

Now let's repeat the process with his second negative thought, "I *shouldn't* feel so anxious!" Check the list of cognitive distortions on page 308 and see which ones this thought contains. Write your ideas here:

1. _____

2. _____

This is a classic "should statement," since Frank's insisting he *shouldn't* be nervous. Why shouldn't he be nervous? He may have an imaginary ideal of himself as an invulnerable superman who has total mastery of every situation. This emotional perfectionism is very common among anxious individuals. You *condemn* yourself for having normal feelings of anxiety. Frank's thought also involves "personalization," since Frank is blaming himself for feeling nervous.

What Rational Response would you suggest?

_____

_____

_____

_____

Frank probably wouldn't impose such rigid demands on a friend. If a friend felt nervous before giving a speech, Frank would be more encouraging. He'd say, "It's okay to feel nervous. We *all* feel that way." He can extend the same compassion toward himself by giving himself that same message. This could be Frank's Rational Response.

You may object to this approach. You may argue, "But I have higher standards for myself than for other people. I don't want to tell myself that it's okay to be nervous. That's like giving up!" These high standards may be unrealistic and self-defeating. You apparently do feel nervous about public speaking, like most human beings, or else you wouldn't be reading this! You might feel more relaxed if you would lower your standards just a tad and *accept* the fact that you feel anxious.

Some readers might continue to object: "A normal person may feel a *little* anxious, but I feel *petrified* and that's not normal!" You may feel petrified because you label these nervous feelings as "abnormal." If instead, you tell yourself that nervousness is normal, you won't feel so intimidated by these reactions. This is the "Acceptance Paradox." If you resist your anxiety, and you insist that you shouldn't feel anxious, your anxiety will get worse. If, in contrast, you accept your anxiety, it loses its power over you.

Now look at Frank's third negative thought: "People will notice my voice trembling and they'll think, 'Gee! That guy sure is nervous!'" What distortions can you identify in this thought?

1. _____

2. _____

This is an example of fortune-telling and mind reading, since Frank is predicting that everyone will notice how nervous he is and look down on him. It might also be the "mental filter" since he imagines people will only think about his nervousness and overlook everything else he has to say. What Rational Response would you suggest?

_____

_____

_____

_____

Frank's fourth negative thought was: "Then they'll think I'm not a very worthwhile person and they won't want to do business with me." What distortions does this thought contain?

1. _____

2. _____

3. _____

Once again, it involves fortune-telling and mind reading. These distortions are *extremely* common in nearly all forms of anxiety. Frank's thought is also an overgeneralization, since Frank assumes that if *some* people don't like him, then nobody will. He thinks that everyone will react in exactly the same manner, like sheep. Is this likely, given how different and how unpredictable people are?

Frank is also generalizing from his *performance* to his *self*. If he fails to give an outstanding presentation, he will feel like a failure *as a person*. This means that his ego and self-esteem are always on the line. Even if it turns out that Frank is not a charismatic lecturer, does it follow that he's not a worthwhile *person*? Or a savvy businessman? I have personally given many talks in my life. Some have gone well, but I can remember a few that were real bombs! On those occasions, was I a less worthwhile *person*? Or simply a less effective lecturer? This may seem like a subtle distinction, but the impact on the way you feel about yourself is about as subtle as the Grand Canyon!

Instead of telling himself that people will despise him and not want to do business with him if he appears anxious, how could Frank think about it? Put your Rational Response here:

_____

_____

_____

_____

_____

Here's the Rational Response that Frank came up with after we discussed it: "Getting nervous makes me very human, not less worthwhile. Most of the people who attend the seminar will be more interested in what they can learn about making money than in judging how 'worthwhile' I am as a person."

This exercise gave Frank the courage to take a risk and give one seminar. He did feel nervous at first, but it went well and he got a good response from the participants. Following the seminar he began to feel the best he'd felt in years. As you confront and conquer a fear it often turns into its opposite—exhilaration. This payoff makes it all the more important not to run away from the things you fear.

Before we go on, let's summarize what you've learned about public speaking anxiety so far. What is the cause of your public speaking anxiety? Put your answer here:

_____

_____

_____

_____

_____

Answer: Anxiety results from your negative thoughts. Although they may seem realistic, they are often quite distorted and illogical. Some of the commonest distortions that are associated with public speaking anxiety include:

- Fortune-telling: "I'm going to blow it!"
- Mind reading: "Everyone will notice how nervous I am and look down on me."
- All-or-nothing thinking: "My presentation will be a complete fiasco."
- Overgeneralization: "This will show what a lousy, inferior human being I am."
- Should statements: "I *shouldn't* feel so nervous. I *should* be in total control of my emotions at all times."

When you substitute more positive and realistic thoughts for the ones that are negative and distorted, you will often feel better. John is a television announcer in Boston who lost his job after eight years of broadcasting when the station was sold. This job was a blow to his self-esteem, and he felt angry and depressed. At times John felt old and over the hill.

After several months he landed a job with another television

THE DAILY MOOD LOG*

STEP ONE: DESCRIBE THE UPSETTING EVENT _____
Feeling nervous before television broadcasts.

STEP TWO: RECORD YOUR NEGATIVE FEELINGS—and rate each one from 0 (the least) to 100 (the most). Use words like sad, anxious, angry, guilty, lonely, hopeless, frustrated, etc.

Emotion	Rating	Emotion	Rating	Emotion	Rating
1. Anxiety	80	3.		5.	
2. Shame	80	4.		6.	

STEP THREE: THE TRIPLE-COLUMN TECHNIQUE—

Automatic Thoughts	Distortions	Rational Responses
Write your negative thoughts and estimate your belief in each one (0–100).	Identify the distortions in each Automatic Thought.	Substitute more realistic thoughts and estimate your belief in each one (0 and 100).
1. I'll probably blow it when I get on the air. ~~(100%)~~ 0%	1. Fortune-telling, discounting the positive	1. I usually do quite well once I get started. (100%)
2. I still feel anxious after twenty years in broadcasting. A "true professional" wouldn't feel so nervous. I should feel poised and confident. ~~(100%)~~ 10%	2. "Should statement," labeling	2. There are many times when I do feel poised and confident. Who says I have to feel that way all the time? There's no such thing as a "true professional." I'm a human being, and regardless of my skill or experience, there will be times when I feel nervous. (90%)

STEP FOUR: OUTCOME—Re-rate your belief in each Automatic Thought from 0 to 100 and put a check in the box that describes how you now feel:

☐ not at all better; ☐ somewhat better; ☒ quite a bit better; ☐ a lot better.

*Copyright © 1984 by David D. Burns, M.D., from *The Feeling Good Handbook*, copyright © 1989

station but felt insecure and nervous before broadcasts. His self-confidence was shot because he told himself, "I'll probably blow it when I get on the air. How can I still feel anxious after eight years in broadcasting? A 'true professional' wouldn't be so nervous. I should feel poised and confident."

You can see on page 304 how he identified the distortions in each automatic thought and substituted Rational Responses in the right-hand column. Your Rational Responses might have been different, but this is not a problem. There's tremendous room for your own unique approach.

Now I'd like you to work on some of your own negative thoughts using the blank Daily Mood Log on page 306. In the "Upsetting Event" space at the top describe the type of public speaking situation that you might be confronted with. Next, record your negative feelings—like anxious, ashamed, or nervous—in the appropriate spaces and rate how strong each feeling is between 0 (for the least) and 100 (for the worst). Then record your Automatic Thoughts and number each of them in the left-hand column. See if you can identify the distortions in each thought, using the list on page 308. Finally, substitute Rational Responses in the right-hand column. When you've completed the exercise, indicate how much it helped by checking one of the four "Outcome" boxes at the bottom. You'll be surprised how effective this simple procedure can be. *Don't try to do it in your head!* Doing the exercise on paper is far more effective.

When you write down your negative thoughts and you substitute Rational Responses, you will put things in a more positive and realistic perspective. This will help reduce some of the anxiety. Remember, though, that a certain amount of anxiety is perfectly natural. The goal is not to achieve complete tranquility or total control of your emotions. If you remind yourself that you are not the same as what you do, you can maintain a sense of self-esteem regardless of how well you do when you give your talk.

Your anxiety can make you uncomfortable, but it won't stop you from doing a good job if you don't let it. One way to prove this to yourself is to make a list of all the ways you think your nervousness could louse you up if you were giving a talk. Once you pinpoint the specific problems, it's usually fairly easy to solve them.

Suppose you're afraid that you'll get so nervous that your mind

THE DAILY MOOD LOG*

STEP ONE: DESCRIBE THE UPSETTING EVENT _____

_____

STEP TWO: RECORD YOUR NEGATIVE FEELINGS—and rate each one from 0 (the least) to 100 (the most). Use words like sad, anxious, angry, guilty, lonely, hopeless, frustrated, etc.

Emotion	Rating	Emotion	Rating	Emotion	Rating
1.		3.		5.	
2.		4.		6.	

STEP THREE: THE TRIPLE-COLUMN TECHNIQUE—

Automatic Thoughts	Distortions	Rational Responses
Write your negative thoughts and estimate your belief in each one (0–100).	Identify the distortions in each Automatic Thought.	Substitute more realistic thoughts and estimate your belief in each one (0 and 100).

(Continue on next page)

THE DAILY MOOD LOG (continued)

Automatic Thoughts	Distortions	Rational Responses

(Continue on next page)

THE DAILY MOOD LOG (continued)

Automatic Thoughts	Distortions	Rational Responses

STEP FOUR: OUTCOME—Re-rate your belief in each Automatic Thought from 0 to 100 and put a check in the box that describes how you now feel:

☐ not at all better; ☐ somewhat better; ☐ quite a bit better; ☐ a lot better.

CHECKLIST OF COGNITIVE DISTORTIONS*

1. All-or-nothing thinking: You look at things in absolute, black-and-white categories.
2. Overgeneralization: You view a negative event as a never-ending pattern of defeat.
3. Mental filter: You dwell on the negatives and ignore the positives.
4. Discounting the positives: You insist that your accomplishments or positive qualities "don't count."
5. Jumping to conclusions: (A) Mind reading—you assume that people are reacting negatively to you when there's no definite evidence for this; (B) Fortune-telling—you arbitrarily predict that things will turn out badly.
6. Magnification or minimization: You blow things way up out of proportion or you shrink their importance inappropriately.
7. Emotional reasoning: You reason from how you feel: "I *feel* like an idiot, so I really must be one." Or "I don't *feel* like doing this, so I'll put it off."
8. "Should statements": You criticize yourself or other people with "shoulds" or "shouldn'ts." "Musts," "oughts," and "have tos" are similar offenders.
9. Labeling: You identify with your shortcomings. Instead of saying "I made a mistake," you tell yourself, "I'm a jerk," or "a fool," or "a loser."
10. Personalization and blame: You blame yourself for something you weren't entirely responsible for, or you blame other people and overlook ways that your own attitudes and behavior might contribute to a problem.

---

*Copyright © 1980 by David D. Burns, M.D. Adapted from *Feeling Good: The New Mood Therapy* (New York: William Morrow & Company, 1980; Signet, 1981).

will go blank. Can you think of any solutions to this? Write your solution to this problem here:

_____

_____

_____

_____

One good solution would be to put a brief outline of your talk on a 3" × 5" card and hold it in your hand or place it on the podium so you can refer to it if you get lost. This is far more effective than reading your speech. Reading your speech will make you sound unbearably boring and will guarantee a poor result. Just glance at the outline on the 3" × 5" card from time to time and talk to people just as if you were sharing your ideas with a friend. This will make you come across in a more personable and spontaneous way.

Even if you don't have an outline you can easily solve the problem of having your mind going blank. I was giving my "Feeling Good" lecture to a women's group in Virginia, and there were some temporary problems with the sound system. As I was speaking, I noticed that people in the audience began to snicker, but I couldn't figure out what they were laughing about. Then I noticed that a spare microphone on a stand behind me was slowly and magically "walking" across the stage all by itself! Apparently a stagehand was pulling it by its cord to try to get it off the stage. It looked ridiculous and I started laughing, too.

After the problem got straightened out I discovered I had completely forgotten what I'd been talking about. I looked out at a sea of 600 ladies staring at me. They were patiently waiting for me to say something wonderful. I drew a total blank! After a long, dramatic silence I asked them, "Have any of you ever had the fear that you'd be in front of a large audience and your mind would suddenly go blank? If so, raise your hands." A few hands went up gingerly and then huge numbers of hands went up. Then I said: "Well, that just happened to me! I don't have the vaguest notion what I was talking about! Where was I?" This evoked further laughter and won the audience over to my side. Many hands went up and the women told me where I'd left off. They saw that I was vulnerable and became very relaxed and friendly. As a result, the presentation went unusually well.

Here are some other public speaking problems and suggestions about how you could solve each of them.

Problems	Solutions
1. Someone in the audience might ask a question I can't answer.	1. I could tell them it's an excellent question and I don't know the answer.
2. My heart will pound and I'll feel terribly tense before I have to speak.	2. I could walk or jog or do some calisthenics to work off the excess energy.
3. I might say something stupid.	3. I could acknowledge my error and correct it.
4. I might do a lousy job. People would be bored.	4. I could ask several friends to critique me afterward. I could take a night-school course in public speaking so I could learn how to make my presentations more interesting and useful.

Now I'd like you to try this. Write down problems that you might have if you were to give a presentation in the left-hand column. In the right-hand column, write down solutions to these problems. If you have difficulty, ask a friend who has more experience in public speaking.

Problems	Solutions
1. _____	1. _____
_____	_____
_____	_____
_____	_____
2. _____	2. _____
_____	_____
_____	_____
_____	_____
3. _____	3. _____
_____	_____
_____	_____

Probably the most important key to public speaking success is to make contact with your audience in a friendly way. You may be afraid that someone in the audience will ask a hostile question or make a critical remark during the question and answer session at the end of your talk. This is one of the easiest problems in the world to solve—*if* you follow several simple suggestions. What you must *not* do is argue with them or defend yourself. That *never* works. Instead, find a way to compliment them (called "stroking") and to agree with them (called "disarming"). This nearly always works like a charm.

1. *Stroke them:* Give them a genuine compliment. Say something positive about their ideas. Remember that people who come on

in an aggressive, critical way are frequently insecure and looking for recognition. They want to feel important and they may be jealous because you're in the limelight. If somebody asks an intimidating, hostile question you could simply say, "That's a very important question. Thank you for asking it." If you say this in a genuine way it will immediately make them feel flattered and you will appear cooperative and friendly. You won't end up in an awkward debate that will make everyone tense. There's another big benefit. When you compliment people who ask questions, the others in the audience will feel like it's safe for them to share their ideas and ask questions, too. Pretty soon lots of hands will go up and you'll reap the benefits of a lively audience response instead of a long, dull silence at the end of your talk.

2. *Disarm them:* In addition to stroking them, find some grain of truth in what they have to say. This is the exact opposite of your normal impulse to defend yourself and argue. It's amazingly effective because you'll appear flexible and open-minded and not rigidly stuck to one narrow point of view.

During a radio show last week I was talking about how negative thoughts can lead to depression and anxiety. The host of the show said, "Dr. Burns, can't we go too far with this philosophy of optimism and positive thinking? Isn't negative thinking more realistic?" I replied: "Absolutely (disarming). Some of the latest research shows that too much optimism can be just as destructive as low self-esteem (disarming). For example, Hitler was extremely optimistic. Compulsive gamblers can be overly optimistic. This is an exciting area for new research (disarming)." This response won the host over to my side because he saw me as an ally and not as a competitor. We had a fabulous interview.

You can learn the stroking and disarming techniques if you write down imaginary questions or criticisms that people in the audience might raise during your talk. Then write down how you might respond, as in this example:

AUDIENCE MEMBER: Your ideas about the economy are a lot of bunk. We need higher taxes and a lower defense budget.
YOU: Those are important issues, for sure (stroking). If we can lower the federal deficit, it will mean a stronger economy and less inflation (disarming). This is important, and it deserves serious consideration (disarming).

Now try some script writing yourself. Write down the difficult questions or critical comments that might come up during the question-and-answer period at the end of your talk. Then write down how you might respond, using the stroking and disarming techniques.

Audience member (write out a critical remark that someone might make here):

_____

_____

_____

You (write out how you could respond here):_____

_____

_____

_____

_____

Use additional paper to write responses to other questions or criticisms from audience members. With practice, you'll get the knack of it. If you have difficulty coming up with good answers, ask a friend for help. After you've come up with some good answers on paper, try role-playing with a friend. Let them pretend to ask threatening questions and you can disarm and stroke them. If your response sounds phony or defensive, do a role reversal and let them give it a try. After a while you'll discover that there's really *nothing* that people could ever say or ask that you couldn't turn to your advantage if you use these techniques. This will reduce your fears and your friendly style of fielding questions will make your presentations more effective.

I used this method once to prepare for a Mike Wallace interview on national television. During the early 1980s the staff of "60 Minutes" developed a daytime show called "Up to the Minute." They were interested in new treatments for depression and made an eight-minute documentary film which illustrated excerpts from actual cognitive-therapy sessions with patients in my office. After the film was shown, Mike Wallace was to interview me for twenty minutes on live television.

One of my patients warned me that Mike Wallace could be a tough, hard-hitting interviewer and asked if I knew what I was getting into. This put me into a panic because when I agreed to do the show I wasn't really clear who Mike Wallace was. I had imagined that he was a kindly gentleman who was interested in depression. Then I watched him on "60 Minutes" and got terrified! I began to imagine all kinds of embarrassing and intimidating questions he might ask in order to discredit me. I wrote them down and thought of how I might answer them. I practiced by talking to myself. First I would imagine I was Mike Wallace, and I would say something terribly insinuating: "Dr. Burns, is it true that you make a living on other people's suffering?" The question seemed silly, but there was something terribly guilt-provoking about it.

I decided I could answer Mike Wallace like this: "As a matter of fact, you've raised an important question [stroking]. I do make money by treating illnesses, as does any physician [disarming]. Sometimes it really doesn't really seem right to me—it seems crass [disarming]. I feel bad about it, and I wish we had a better way to deliver medical care [disarming]."

Of course the actual show wasn't at all the way I had imagined it. Mike Wallace turned out to be a very friendly person. He came to my dressing room before the show and said he'd seen the film of the therapy and was impressed with the method. Then he asked if I would teach him how to talk back to *his* Automatic Thoughts!

The show went well and the experience gave me tremendous confidence. You may never be under intense pressure from someone who's trying to discredit you, but it's nice to know there's such a simple and effective way to handle hostile questions and accusations.

Let's suppose you follow all these suggestions and you give a talk. How will you feel if it doesn't go as well as you had hoped? If you flub, you can thank your lucky stars, because this will give you the golden opportunity to discover that the world doesn't come to an end after all. Life goes on even if you're not successful all the time.

You can prepare for this now by writing down all the negative thoughts you'd have if you gave a speech that turned out to be a complete flop. You might be telling yourself, "Those people must really think I'm a jerk. What a loser I am! I made such a fool of myself. I can't stand it!" Study the list on page 308 and try to identify the distortions in these thoughts. One distortion would be "magnification," since you're telling yourself that you "can't stand it." It may be uncomfortable, but you can stand it. It's not nearly as bad as being boiled in oil, for example. Another distortion would be "labeling," since you are calling yourself "a jerk," "a loser," and "a fool." We all behave foolishly at times, but this makes us human beings, not "fools" or "jerks." A third distortion would be "mind reading." You're assuming that everyone in the audience will be as unforgiving and critical as you are.

If you have trouble talking back to your negative thoughts, ask yourself what you would say to a dear friend who didn't do a very good job giving a talk. Would you say, "Gee, you're such a jerk"? Of course you wouldn't! You'd probably be more supportive and helpful and say, "There's a lot you can do to improve your presentation, but you deserve credit for trying." Then you'd help him pinpoint the specific problems so he could do a better job the next time.

Now let me ask you this question: If you would treat a friend in a helpful way, why are you so hard on yourself? Would you be willing to treat yourself the same way you would treat a friend?

What do you do when you fail? Do you mope and tell yourself what a loser you are? Would you treat someone you loved that way? When you fail, why not take yourself out to dinner at a fancy restaurant instead? Anybody can celebrate when they succeed. Why not treat yourself in a special way when you fail? That's when you need the support the most!

Some people not only fear failure, they also fear being average. Several years ago an associate and I gave a workshop in Chicago. The presentation was adequate but not one of our best. He'd been up half the night with the flu and I was in a bad mood as well. I got defensive during the question-and-answer period, and while our workshop was informative, it didn't sparkle. Several days later I told my associate how disappointed I felt. He asked why. I said I thought our presentation was below average. He said, "Remember, Dave, we can only be above average half the time. The other half the time we'll be below average. It's impossible to beat these odds, because 'average' is, by definition, the halfway point. We can look forward to being above average next time!" I felt immediate relief. How great not to have to shine all the time!

The methods described in this chapter can help you cope with your anxiety more effectively. Try not to get too perfectionistic about it. Your goal is not to achieve complete control of your feelings—this would be impossible. A certain amount of nervousness before any performance is inevitable, even for professional entertainers. When you stop fighting your anxiety and accept the idea that it is natural, you can sometimes use it as a positive force that will make your presentation more effective and exciting. This idea has been quite helpful to me.

I used to get very nervous about appearing on television. If I felt tense, I found it difficult to come across in a personable, animated way. A patient once told me how different I was in the office, where I was lively and full of spark, than on a television show she'd seen— I had seemed stiff and awkward. The problem was that I'd freeze up and feel intimidated and lose all my spontaneity. Then I'd tell myself I should relax, and that made things even worse! The harder I tried to relax, the more nervous I got!

People gave me all kinds of advice about ways to beat this problem, but their suggestions weren't terribly helpful. The worst advice was "Just be yourself." That didn't work because I *was* being myself! The "real me" simply felt tense and self-conscious the moment the cameras started rolling.

Eventually I stumbled across a solution. I decided it was okay to feel nervous, but I decided to view the nervousness differently, not as a bad thing but as a form of energy that I could use to come on strong and "sock it to 'em." After all, I have a number of controversial and powerful convictions about the causes and cures for emotional problems. Why worry about coming across in a warm, charming way on television? Why not be strong and exciting instead?

Recently I tried this on the *A.M. Philadelphia* show. They'd arranged a debate between another psychiatrist and me on the relative merits of drugs and psychotherapy in the treatment of mood problems. On the opening segment I felt he hit below the belt by implying that I was "just an author" and not a researcher. I felt angry, because I do a fair amount of research that I'm quite proud of. I decided to fight back and to present my ideas with the conviction they deserved during the next segment. Instead of being polite and courteous and meek, I felt energized and presented myself in the best possible light. I made a conscious effort to win the viewers over to my side and to cast him in a negative light. I shouldn't admit this, but that's the truth! And what's even worse—I loved every minute of the show! I got lots of positive feedback about it.

Giving up on the idea that I should relax paradoxically helped me feel more confident and relaxed. I was able to use my anxiety as a source of energy, because I wasn't fighting it. The key was the decision to believe in myself and to be forceful rather than trying to please everyone and worrying about how other people would judge me.

Therapists call this concept "reframing." You view a problem in a different light so that you think about it as something positive and good. Many people think that public speaking anxiety is "bad." They tell themselves that their nervousness makes them "abnormal" and "inferior." You can reframe your thinking about public speaking anxiety if you think of the anxiety as something good that can lead to a superior performance. View it as a source of energy, and use the anxiety to put extra zest into your performance. Believe in yourself and concentrate on what you have to say, rather than criticizing yourself for feeling nervous. Instead of fighting the anxiety, come on strong and deliver your message with conviction and charisma.

Let's review the methods described in this chapter:

1. *Daily Mood Log:* Write down the negative thoughts that made you anxious, such as: "I'm really going to blow it." Then identify the distortions in these thoughts, such as "fortune-telling" and "all-or-nothing thinking," and substitute more positive, realistic thoughts.

2. *Problem solving:* If you think your anxiety will cause problems for you (like making your mind go blank), list these problems and think of specific solutions to them (such as having a brief outline of your talk available on the podium).

3. *Script writing:* Write out difficult or critical questions that people in the audience might ask. Instead of getting frazzled or defensive, "stroke" them by saying something positive about their ideas and "disarm" them by finding some truth in what they have to say. This will make them feel good, and you'll win them over to your side.

4. *Unconditional self-esteem:* If you base your self-esteem on being a success, you'll be plagued by constant anxiety and stress, because you'll always be afraid of failure. If you have uncondi-

tional self-esteem, you can learn from your failures with a spirit of compassion and self-respect.

5. *Positive reframing:* Instead of worrying about your anxiety or thinking of it as "bad," think of it as a source of energy. Use the anxiety to put extra zest into your performance. Instead of fighting the anxiety, use the energy to come on strong and deliver your message with conviction and charisma.

16

•

How to Give a Dynamic Interview When You're Scared Stiff

It's natural to get nervous before an interview for a new job or for a school admission. It seems like you're in a spotlight and every shortcoming will be examined. You feel as if all the people you're competing with are enormously more talented and poised. You may think you'll look klutzy when they ask you embarrassing questions about your qualifications and experience.

I'd like to show you how to deal with these feelings so you can give a dynamic interview and present yourself in a positive and appealing way. In addition, I want you to have enough self-confidence to really listen during interviews, so you can ask yourself, "How impressed do I feel with the person who's interviewing me? Is this the job [or school] that will really be the best for me?"

In order to learn more about how people react to job interviews, I recently asked sixty individuals how they would be feeling and thinking if they were in the following situation: "You are interviewing for a job. You are presenting yourself in your best light. You can't tell how the prospective employer is reacting to you." Some people said they would feel annoyed with the interviewer. Typical responses were:

"It is not fair to leave you in limbo."

"This person is being very impersonal."

"Why doesn't he act more open and straightforward?"

"I don't like game-playing or power trips."

Other people imagined that the interviewer didn't like them. Typical responses were:

"He is bored."

"Did he notice my short fingernails?"

"I am making a fool of myself. I will probably never get the job."

"I'm thinking he doesn't like me and I'm wasting his time."

"He's probably interviewed other people for the job and I don't compare with them."

"I must try to hide and control the nervousness."

A third group reported more positive thoughts and feelings. These responses were characteristic:

"I'd feel calm. I'm being honest with my presentation."

"I hope this guy likes me. If he does, maybe he'll give me the job."

"I will just keep being myself. I'm happy with the way I present myself, and if it's not what the company is looking for, then the job isn't for me."

I also asked people how they would be thinking and feeling if, during a job interview, the prospective employer said: "Based on the interview and a review of your application, you're by far the most promising candidate I've seen so far."

There was still a wide variation in the way people reacted. One woman wrote that she would feel ecstatic: "Fantastic. I love it. Who should I go out and celebrate with? Maybe I'll make president of the company, maybe even the U.S.A." Most were more cautious in their enthusiasm, and some people even sounded annoyed and self-doubting, because they interpreted the interviewer's compliment as a put-down. One woman wrote: "I'll probably blow it anyway. He's just handing me a line."

The study showed that there can be a tremendous variation in the way people react to interviews and that these reactions depend on how they think about the situation. What kinds of thoughts would you have if you were being interviewed? Would you tell yourself you're doing a lousy job? Would you get defensive? Would you feel panicky and tongue-tied? When you identify the distortions in the thoughts that upset you, you can substitute more positive and realistic ones, and you will often feel better.

Although I obviously can't know precisely how you might be thinking during a stressful interview, many people tell themselves, "I shouldn't be so nervous." Do you recognize the distortion in this thought? Stop for a moment and see if you can find it in the list on page 308. Write down your ideas here:

_____

It's a "should statement." You're telling yourself you shouldn't be so nervous. This is unrealistic, because you're telling yourself you ought to be different from the way you really are. It sounds judgmental and it will make you feel worse.

Instead, you could think about it this way: "It would be nice to feel more confident, but most people do feel nervous about job interviews. It's understandable that I would feel this way." Notice that you accept the fact that you feel nervous instead of demanding complete poise and self-confidence. This involves a shift from self-condemnation to self-acceptance. This is an important key to self-esteem.

A second negative thought you might have would be, "All the other candidates are probably so much better than I am." Can you identify the distortions in this one? Put your ideas here:

1._____

2._____

3._____

It's an example of "jumping to conclusions," since you have no real evidence that all the other candidates are more qualified than you are. In addition, you are using the "mental filter" and are "discounting the positives," because you're thinking about all your shortcomings and overlooking your strengths. Can you imagine saying something like that to a friend: "Hey, Joan, when you apply for that job, just remember that all the other candidates are so much better than you"? Since you wouldn't put someone else down, why be so hard on yourself?

A third negative thought about an interview might be, "I'll stammer and my mind will go blank. I'll look like a jerk." There are several distortions in this one. Can you identify them? One is "fortune-telling"—you're predicting negative results ahead of time. This is like self-hypnosis. If you give yourself negative messages over and over, you'll begin to believe them and they may become self-fulfilling prophecies. Can you imagine saying "You're going to blow it, you're going to blow it!" over and over to your friend before an interview? What could you tell yourself instead? Can you think of a more positive thought? Put your ideas here:

_____

_____

_____

_____

You could tell yourself that you're going to go out on many interviews and that each one will be a learning experience. You could also tell yourself that you'll get better and better at it and that eventually you will find the job you're looking for.

Now see if you can do it. First, indicate how strongly you would feel each of the following kinds of emotions during a job interview. Put a check (√) in one of the boxes to the right of each of the eight kinds of emotions.

TYPE OF NEGATIVE EMOTION	How strongly would you feel this way during an interview?			
	0–NOT AT ALL	1–SOMEWHAT	2–MODERATELY	3–A LOT
1. Nervous, worried, uptight, anxious, tense, panicky, scared, frightened				
2. Inferior, inadequate, second-rate				
3. Angry, annoyed, irritated, ticked off				
4. Frustrated				
5. Guilty, ashamed				
6. Embarrassed, foolish				
7. Sad, unhappy				
8. Hopeless, discouraged				

In the left-hand column on page 324, write down some of the Automatic Thoughts you might have during a job interview. Remember not to just record your emotions, because you've already indicated how you might feel. "I feel nervous" is not an Automatic Thought; it's a description of how you feel. Instead, put the thought that makes you feel nervous. It might be "I'll make a fool of myself." Once you've recorded your Automatic Thoughts, see if you can find the distortions in them, using the list on page 308. Record the distortions in the middle column. Finally, substitute more positive and realistic thoughts in the right-hand column.

If you have trouble with this step, ask someone you respect how they would think about the situation. It can also be helpful to ask yourself what you'd say to a close friend who was about to be interviewed. Would you put them down and tell them they were going to look like a fool? Or would you be upbeat and encouraging? Then why not talk to yourself in the same supportive way?

Automatic Thoughts	Distortions	Rational Responses

What can you expect when you change your thoughts? After you begin to think more positively, you still will feel some anxiety. That's natural—you don't have to gain perfect control over your emotions. Just try to put things into a more positive and realistic perspective so your self-doubts don't get out of hand. Your mind is like a powerful beacon. If you constantly focus that light on dangers and catastrophes, you'll feel frightened. But if you focus on a positive outcome, you'll be more likely to feel good and end up with the job you want.

The Five Principles of Dynamic Interviewing

So far, we've talked about changing your attitudes and feelings. Now let's discuss what you're going to say during the interview.

PRINCIPLE #1: BE PERSONAL AND FRIENDLY

During an interview, you'll probably feel that you're in the spotlight. You may put pressure on yourself to impress the person who is interviewing you. But since you feel so tense and awkward, this seems impossible.

Instead of trying to impress the interviewer, try to get to know him or her. There's no rule that says you have to sit back and answer questions the entire time. You can also ask questions. Express an interest in what he or she has to say. Remember—you're there to learn about the company. How long has the interviewer worked there? What type of work does he or she do? How did he or she get involved in this type of work? What does he or she like and dislike about the firm?

These questions will often lead to informal, friendly conversations that will set you more at ease. Remember that the people who interview you may also feel somewhat nervous. Most people are eager for attention, and if you express a genuine interest in them, they will feel better about you and you'll be more likely to get a job offer.

One of the greatest headaches that administrators have is the sour apple on the staff who demoralizes others with a bad attitude. If you come across in an enthusiastic and friendly way, you'll be a much more attractive candidate. In addition, when you express an interest in the person who interviews you, you'll feel less self-conscious yourself. It's far easier to get excited about someone else's accomplishments than to try to impress them with your own. When you don't try so hard, you often end up making the best possible impression.

I used to do consulting for the University of Pennsylvania Law School. Law students typically get nervous during their first and last semesters. During the first semester, they worry because of doubts about performing adequately under the intense competition from so many bright classmates. During the last semester, they feel anxious because of fears that they won't get any good job offers. Many of the senior students I treated told me they had had as many as ten or fifteen job interviews without a single offer. They felt panicky and depressed.

When I asked them to describe a typical job interview, it was always the same. They would sit down with some intimidating attorney in a pin-striped suit who would let them know there was a huge number of extraordinarily talented applicants for one opening at the firm. Then the attorney would ask the law student to describe his or her qualifications. They would lamely describe themselves as bright, loyal, hardworking, and so on, just as every other applicant did. The interviews were incredibly boring. Needless to say, job offers never materialized.

I discovered a method that dramatically changed this. I told the students that people are almost never hired on merit alone, no matter how talented they are, but also on the basis of a personal relationship. People offer jobs to people they like and whom they consider friends. I said, "Don't bother talking about your qualifications. It just sounds immature and self-centered, and it won't do you a bit of good. They already know you're bright, or you couldn't have made it through law school. They want someone they'll enjoy having in their firm, someone the other attorneys and the clients will like. If the clients like you, they will refer other clients and the firm's reputation will grow. This is as important as a doctor's bedside manner."

I told them to try to get to know the attorneys who interviewed them by asking questions such as these: what do they like and dislike about the practice of law? How did they get the assignment of interviewing new candidates? What type of law do they practice? Why? How do they reconcile the long hours of a law practice with family life?

The students seemed dubious but agreed to try. Their success shot up tremendously. One student who hadn't received a single nibble got seven job offers out of his next ten interviews! He said that what was bizarre about it was that these thirty-minute interviews often went on for an hour or more, and he almost never said anything whatsoever about himself. He just expressed a genuine, friendly interest in the men and women who were interviewing him. He said he sometimes asked if they found the interviews interesting or boring. You can imagine that it might get tiresome having to interview ten or twenty nervous law students in a day! He said they seemed overjoyed to have the chance to talk about themselves. They would talk and talk, and eventually they would say, "My goodness! We went an hour over the time limit and there are all these other students waiting. And I forgot to ask you about yourself. Oh well, we'll have plenty of time to get to that later—when you join our firm!"

PRINCIPLE #2: MAKE THEM SELL THEMSELVES TO YOU!

Don't try too hard to sell yourself during interviews. Instead, make them sell themselves to you. This can work like a charm. Suppose the person interviewing you says, "We have many outstanding candidates for this position. Why should we consider you?"

Instead of getting defensive and trying to recite a list of your best qualities—a strategy that is doomed to failure—use a little reverse psychology. You can say, "You obviously have a top firm [or university] and you deserve someone outstanding for this position. Could you tell me a little bit about the kind of person you really want? Then I'll tell you about myself so we can see whether or not I might fill the bill."

Once you learn about the kind of person the firm is looking for—someone who's honest, hardworking, creative, or whatever—it will be infinitely easier for you to portray yourself in a way that will specifically appeal to the interviewer. Then you can say, "I'd like to hear more about your company [or university]. I've heard some great things but I'd like your point of view. What are some of the potential benefits of working for this firm? What do you like about the company? What are some of the negative aspects of working here?"

Now you've challenged them to sell themselves to you! Instead of acting desperate and reciting a long and boring list of your good points, you're making it clear that you're there to evaluate them in just the same way they are learning about you. It's a two-way street, because the interviewer will have to persuade you to join his or her company. You can afford to pick and choose. When you ask about the positive *and negative* aspects of the company, you make it clear that you have self-esteem, and that you deserve a job that will be good for you. They will try harder to win you over.

Ask specific questions about the job you're interested in. Whom will you be working with? Has the morale of the group been high? What hours will you be expected to work? What are the possibilities for promotion? Why did the last person leave the position?

These questions will give you useful information and make you appear self-confident. Instead of trying to sell yourself, you become the shopper. This has an enormous impact on the balance of power. If you're even vaguely suitable for the job, your value will instantly escalate!

In life there are the pursued and the pursuers. You must choose one role or the other. This is true whether you're looking for a mate or for a job. The pursued usually get what they want, and the pursuers usually get rejected. If you give in to the urge to answer every question and try too hard to sell yourself, you will become the pursuer and you probably won't get the job. Instead, invite the interviewer in a friendly way to sell himself or herself to you, and you will be much more likely to get the job you want.

I don't mean to imply that a job interview is just a game or that you should try to get the better of the other person. However, power is an important issue that you do need to take into account. If you simply answer questions without asking any of your own, it will make you look desperate. It will appear that you don't care what kind of outfit you work for. It may also look as if you're not really interested in the person who interviews you. In contrast, when you ask questions and express an interest in the company, you will project intelligence and self-respect. You'll be far more likely to get the job.

PRINCIPLE #3: BE HONEST—BUT PRESENT YOURSELF IN A POSITIVE LIGHT

Let's assume there's something that makes you a less desirable candidate. Maybe you're inexperienced, you've never worked before, or you didn't get along with your last boss. When you're applying for a new job, you may be asked about these problems. Perhaps you took a year off from school because you were depressed and flunking three subjects. The interviewer may say, "I see you have a year that's not accounted for on your resume. Can you explain this to me?" How can you, without sounding like a liability?

It's simple. Just say that you took a year off to think about your goals in life. Emphasize that it was a valuable experience that made you more aware of your priorities. This is an honest and positive statement. Most interviewers would respect you more for it.

Let's suppose that you're a 34-year-old woman and you're looking for a job for the first time in your life. The man who interviews you says, "I notice that you don't have any previous work experiences listed on your resume." How can you respond without seeming totally inept?

Put your ideas here:_____

_____

_____

_____

_____

You could say, "As a matter of fact, this is the first job I've applied for. I've raised three happy kids and I've completed college in my spare time. I can't offer you a lot of professional experience, but I can offer a lot of human experience along with plenty of persistence and enthusiasm. Can you tell me more about what the job involves so I can see if I could make a contribution to your firm?"

This response is honest and upbeat. I would be impressed if I were interviewing you. Notice that you're asking the interviewer to do some of the talking. This will give you a better idea of what he or she is looking for. If you do have the skills for the job, then point this out. If you don't, just be frank and ask them to keep you in mind for a more suitable opening later on.

PRINCIPLE #4: DON'T GET DEFENSIVE ABOUT YOUR SHORTCOMINGS

Many people are afraid of being asked about something really embarrassing. To take an extreme example, suppose the interviewer says: "I notice that you were asked to leave your position with the XYZ

Corporation because of insubordination. Is it true that you were fired because of a personality conflict with your supervisor?" Let's assume this did happen. It's probably about the worst thing you could hear! How would you respond? Put your ideas here:

_____

_____

_____

_____

Many people would get tense and defensive, but this will make you look bad. You could blame your old boss or deny the accusation, but then your chances of being hired are nil. The interviewer won't believe you. Do you have any winning options? Yes! Disarm the interviewer. Agree, don't argue.

You could say: "As a matter of fact, I think that's pretty accurate. I was inexperienced and I was too dogmatic and inflexible. My supervisor was difficult for many staff members to get along with, but I made the mistake of being too argumentative and I foolishly locked horns with him instead of trying to understand his point of view. I could have handled the situation much better than I did. I learned a lot from the experience. I learned that I can't always expect people to be tactful, reasonable, and pleasant. I think I've gotten a little more tolerant and flexible because of that experience."

The advantage of this response is that you display yourself as a reasonable and open-minded person. There's no way you can erase what happened. If you insist that it was unfair and argue that it was all your supervisor's fault, you'll simply confirm that you're still hard to get along with. You'll be arguing with the person who's interviewing you, just as you argued with your former boss! I guarantee that someone else will get the job. But if you assume responsibility for the problem and genuinely agree that you screwed up, the interviewer might just admire your courage and decide that you're the kind of person they want on their team! (See page 376 for more about "disarming.")

PRINCIPLE #5: WHEN YOU DON'T KNOW WHAT TO SAY, PARAPHRASE THE QUESTION OR PUNT

Some people get rattled during interviews. Their minds go blank and they can't think of anything to say. There's a simple solution to this: Paraphrase the question before you attempt to answer it. Let's say the interviewer asks you, "What are your strengths and weaknesses?" Before you try to answer the question, repeat it like this: "Let's see. You'd like me to tell you about my strong points and weak points? Is that right?"

"Yes."

"I'd be glad to do that."

When you paraphrase a question, you get a few moments to gather your thoughts, and it becomes easier to respond in a meaningful way.

You can also use the "punting" technique, described on page 434, when people try to put you on the spot to gain an advantage in a negotiation. A patient of mine was visiting a law firm in New York to see if he might be interested in working for them. Jerry already had a good position with a firm in Philadelphia, and he hadn't clearly decided that he wanted to move to New York. He was just exploring the possibilities and wanted to learn more about the firm.

The man who interviewed Jerry seemed impressed and invited an associate to join the interview. He told Jerry that he would work with this woman if he joined the firm. She began to ask Jerry pointed questions. She asked how much salary he was asking for and why he thought his skills were good enough to merit a position in their firm. She pointed out that their work was of a highly technical nature and said she was skeptical that Jerry had enough experience and expertise.

Jerry was on the spot. He felt defensive and was squirming with anxiety. In reality, he really didn't have all the technical expertise she required and he hadn't even thought about his salary requirements. He mumbled something about not wanting to take any less than he was getting at his current job in Philadelphia and tried to present his skills in the best possible light. This came across rather lamely. He felt annoyed with the woman and sensed, quite rightly, that the man who had interviewed him was quickly losing interest. Needless to say, Jerry was never asked back for a second interview.

What should Jerry have said instead? How could he have handled the situation differently? This woman wanted to know his salary requirements and precisely how he would fit into their firm, but Jerry hadn't even thought about these issues. If you were Jerry, what would you have said?

———————————————————————————————

———————————————————————————————

———————————————————————————————

———————————————————————————————

———————————————————————————————

He could say, "I haven't really thought about my salary requirements yet. I think that discussion might be premature, because I don't even know how I might fit into your firm. Today I'd like to learn more about what you're doing and to tell you a little about my work. Then if it seems useful, we can meet again to explore the specifics of working together. I wouldn't dream of talking about my salary requirements unless I was convinced I had a real contribution to make. I hope I will, but I don't think either of us knows that yet."

The key technique is "punting." He simply drops back and punts. Jerry isn't obligated to answer all her questions. She has the perfect right to ask him anything she wants, but there's no rule that says he has to answer. The fact is, he doesn't know how much money he wants, and he doesn't even know if he should work for this firm. He can simply say this in a polite way. He will avoid letting her run the show and he won't end up in a fourth-down position.

There's a second benefit to punting: Jerry will reveal himself to be a skillful negotiator. If he doesn't pursue them, then they will have to pursue him. They will have to convince him that he should join their firm. Their interest in him will instantly and dramatically increase.

Script Writing

So far I've given you some insights about successful job interview strategies. You can probably see that some of these ideas have merit and might help you. However, you will need to be able to do it when you're actually having a job or school interview. This is where the "script-writing" method can be helpful. Think of several questions you might be asked during an interview. Imagine one or two routine questions ("What are your qualifications?") along with one or two of the most anxiety-provoking questions you can imagine ("Is it true that you were arrested for assault at your last job?"). Write down several interview questions here:

1._____

_____

2._____

_____

3._____

_____

Have you written the questions down yet? It's very important for you to do this instead of just reading this chapter. If you want to sharpen up your interview skills, these written exercises will be invaluable. We'll come back to the questions shortly.

I recently treated an executive named Tim, who had moved to the United States from Australia to head up a candy company that a friend of his had purchased. After several months it began to dawn on Tim that their product simply wasn't going to be competitive in the American market. The candy was good, but the product didn't have eye appeal. It was packaged in a rather ordinary wrapper that didn't grab the eye. In addition, they were underfinanced and didn't have the millions of dollars they would need to advertise the candy nationally and get it placed on the shelves of grocery stores and drugstores.

After a year and a half of frustrating attempts to boost distribution, the company lost $500,000 and Tim was stuck with a warehouse filled with stale candy. It was clear that he had to start looking for a new job, but he felt depressed and thought of himself as a "loser." He was convinced that his career was over and felt he could never get another decent job. He was in a panic about job interviews because he was afraid he'd be asked about his depression and grilled about why the candy venture had failed.

I asked Tim to list the most intimidating and personally embarrassing questions he could imagine being asked during an interview. Here's the first one he wrote down: "I notice that the candy company lost half a million dollars soon after you took over as president. Is this true? And if so, why should we want you to assume the leadership of our company?" How would you handle this question? Put your response here:

_____

_____

_____

_____

Here's what Tim and I came up with: "It's true that we did lose half a million dollars due to several crucial marketing errors. We were vastly undercapitalized and didn't have a sufficient advertising budget. We also overestimated the American demand for a product that was quite popular in Australia." Notice that this honestly acknowledges the mistakes that were made, but without a sense of shame or humiliation. Business errors of this type are not unusual.

I asked Tim to write the script of a tough interview and helped him edit his responses to the questions. Keep in mind that these are imaginary questions, not ones that would be asked during an actual interview. They represent Tim's worst fears. Learning how to handle these gave Tim a great boost in self-confidence, because he realized that any real interview would be far easier by comparison. It went like this:

INTERVIEWER: Why should we want you? How can we know you won't make the same mistakes with us?

TIM: It depends on how valuable you think a degree in the school of hard knocks is. If you look at my work record during the past twenty years, you'll see many successes along with this failure. I've learned a lot from my successes and a lot from my mistakes. I think I have more to offer because of it.

INTERVIEWER: But I understand that you went into a severe depression and you even had to go to a psychiatrist. Is this true?

TIM: Yes. At first I blamed myself entirely for the failure of the company, and life looked pretty bleak. Now I can see that I made a valiant effort in a tremendously difficult situation, and I feel proud of that, even though the results were disappointing.

INTERVIEWER: How could we be sure you wouldn't get depressed again if you were working for us? Isn't depression a sign of a weak character? We want a strong leader as the head of our group.

TIM: I think almost anyone would feel discouraged by a business reversal, especially when they had worked as hard as I had. I don't think that means I have a "weak character," but simply that I'm human and that I care a great deal about the work I do. Can you tell me a little more about your company and your needs so I can see if I can be of help to you?

We practiced role-playing so Tim could learn to field these insulting questions. He enjoyed the exercise and listened to the tape of the session several times. He said it was a relief to discover that he could even turn hostile questions to his advantage. Then he went out on several job interviews, which went smoothly. He was offered the presidency of two of the three companies that interviewed him, and he was the second choice at the third company. Not bad for a "loser"!

Now it's your turn. You have written down several difficult or embarrassing questions that you might be asked during an interview. Select one of those questions and think about how you might answer it. Keep in mind the six principles of effective interviewing:

- Be personal and friendly.
- Express an interest in the person who interviews you.
- Don't try too hard to impress the interviewer; make the interviewer sell him- or herself to you.
- Be honest, but present yourself in a positive light.
- Don't get defensive about your shortcomings.
- If the question is confusing and you don't know how to answer it, repeat the question and ask for a clarification, or punt.

Write your response to the question here:_____

_____

_____

_____

_____

If you have trouble coming up with a good response, think about it for a day or two, or ask a friend for suggestions. Sometimes you will need several days before an effective answer will suddenly pop into your mind. Practice is the key. After you've worked at this for a while, you'll get the knack of it. It's well worth the time and effort. Once you see that you can handle any question that's thrown your way, you feel more self-confident in an actual interview.

Turning Failure Into Success

When you go out on interviews, some people will like you and some people won't. Sometimes you'll do well, and sometimes you won't. You can turn your failures into successes if you keep several ideas in mind.

Don't put all your eggs in one basket. You may need to go out on many interviews before you find the right job. Pinning all your hopes on one job is foolish. You'll pressure yourself too much, and it will feel like a catastrophe if you don't get the job.

Your "batting average" in a competitive job market may be only one offer in every ten interviews. That means you'll have to endure an average of nine rejections for every offer you get. But every rejection will take you one step closer to your goal. The more rejections you get, the quicker you'll find a job. In fact, you need all the rejections you can possibly get!

Don't base your self-esteem on how well you do. Job interviewing, like golf or cooking, is a skill you can develop—you can get better and better at it over a period of time. Your success at it has nothing to do with what kind of a person you are. People who do well on interviews are often poised and skillful, but they're not more worthwhile human beings.

Don't blame yourself for a rejection. You may be tempted to tell yourself that you're no good, and you may feel as if you'll never get a job. Instead of putting yourself down like this, try to learn from the situation. What are the specific reasons you didn't get the job? Sometimes the person who interviewed you will give you some feedback if you ask in a friendly way. Maybe you were inexperienced; maybe you had good qualifications but they had to pick from many qualified people; maybe you didn't interview well; maybe your skills didn't match their needs; maybe it was politics and the daughter of the company president got the job. If you can find out why you didn't get the job, it usually takes the sting out of it because you won't feel so worthless and defeated. If there's a specific reason, make a plan for what to do next instead of giving up.

Don't blame someone else for a rejection. Instead of blaming themselves, many people go to the opposite extreme. They insist that life is unfair and blame the world. Cynthia lost a public relations job at a New York hospital because she was inexperienced and somewhat disorganized. After she interviewed unsuccessfully for a new position with another hospital, she discovered she had been the second choice among the candidates. Cynthia was furious because she had her heart set on this job. She told me they hadn't given her a fair shake and insisted they didn't understand her full potential. When she later learned that the man they hired had ten years of successful experience in public relations, she understood that being the second choice was a compliment and a basis for optimism. She persisted in her job search and ultimately landed an equally desirable position.

Think about rejections as opportunities. When someone turns you down, don't get defensive or annoyed. Instead, thank them for their time and ask them to keep you in mind if something more suitable comes up in the future. Most successful people have learned that rejections will often turn into successes later on. It's not wise to burn bridges or to view rejections as "the end." Often a rejection is just the first awkward step in what later turns into a productive, successful relationship.

Remember that an offer you don't really want is worth its weight in gold. This is the "Burns Rule": People only want what they can't get, and they never want what they can get. What it boils down to is this:

trying to get the first offer can be tough. Since you're what people can get, you're not in demand. But once you get an offer, even if it's not the one you want, you can easily get many more offers. Since you're what people can't get, you're in demand. Everyone will want you.

Let me give an example of how this works. A divorced woman with two children applied for admission to graduate school in psychology. Her options were limited to programs in Chicago, where she lived, because she didn't want her kids to have to change schools. She had her heart set on a highly competitive program at the University of Chicago, but knew her chances for admission were only marginal because of the large number of applicants. After her interview, she was informed that she had not been selected for the program, but she would be placed on a waiting list of alternate candidates.

Six weeks later another school, in a less desirable area and with only an average reputation, called to tell her that she'd been admitted but without financial assistance. She was told that she had to decide within two hours.

Her heart sank, because she still had the dream of attending the University of Chicago. She called me in a panic. She was distraught and wanted to know what to do.

I explained that this was her golden opportunity, and suggested that all she had to do was to call the University of Chicago and tell them that she was under pressure to accept an offer that very day from another school, so that if they were interested in her they'd have to move quickly.

She was skeptical that this would do any good, but she called the admissions office and explained the situation to the secretary of one of the professors on the admissions committee. Within ten minutes the professor called back to inform her that they were extremely interested in her and if she would consider attending the University of Chicago, they would offer her free tuition plus a stipend of $8,000 per year for living expenses. She immediately accepted and ultimately received her doctorate there.

Why was she suddenly accepted when she'd been ignored? Because she was in demand. They probably thought that if someone else was pressuring her to accept an offer, she was an incredibly desirable candidate. This made them want her as well. It's basic human nature to want something that's a little beyond our grasp, and this is true in school or job interviews.

If you want to take advantage of the Burns Rule, you should court every suitor when you're applying for a position. Once you get an offer, even if it's an unappealing one, you're over the biggest hurdle because you're in demand. Leak this information to the people you're interested in. Let other interviewers know that you've had an offer, but that you like them very much and would be proud to consider their offer as well. If you do this in a friendly manner, I think you'll be pleasantly surprised to discover that you will suddenly get many offers.

You may object to this strategy, thinking it amounts to manipulation. In a way, you're right. I felt a little guilty when writing this section. I was concerned that I might come off as exploitative or insensitive. If I offended you, I apologize. However, I felt that this information was necessary, because the people who conduct interviews wield great power. They've got what you want, and they are intentionally playing you off against many other candidates so they can get the best possible person to work for them or to attend their university. You need a little power too, to balance the situation. I want you to get the best possible offer so you'll feel happy and excited about the opportunity just ahead of you. Then you'll do the best job you're capable of, and everyone will win.

17

·

Test and Performance Anxiety

Our culture places a heavy emphasis on competition and success. While it's healthy to want to do good work, many people believe that success is the only key to happiness and self-esteem. They believe that to be loved and respected by others, they must be outstanding in every respect. This attitude can create a crippling pressure to achieve called "performance anxiety."

You may get performance anxiety when you are studying or taking a test. This is called "test anxiety." You may get performance anxiety when you have to write a paper or a report—this is called "writer's block." You may get performance anxiety when you have to give a talk, take an oral examination, act in a play, or even just introduce yourself to a group of people.

Performance anxiety has two causes. One of them is obvious, and the other is hidden. Fear of failure is the obvious cause. And why is this failure not okay? Because you feel you will be humiliated and ostracized if you don't succeed. Your sense of self-esteem gets tied up with your achievements, and you feel convinced that others would love and respect you less if you fell short of their expectations of you.

The second, more hidden cause of performance anxiety may be that the goals you have chosen are not really the ones you want. Your anxiety may be your body's way of letting you know that you're trying to push a round peg into a square hole. You may be forcing yourself in a direction in your career or in your studies that really isn't right for you.

A troubled first-year law student recently sought treatment because of anxiety attacks in classes. Fred said he was terrified about being called on to answer questions in front of the other students. He confessed, "When the professor calls on me, I'll probably goof up." This fear is especially common among first-year law students because the professors ask intimidating questions to lead the students into contradictions and to make them unsure of themselves. This is intended to toughen the students and prepare them for the competitive rigors of a legal career, but many of them feel traumatized by the experience. I explored what Fred was really afraid of:

DAVID: Suppose you did goof up in class. Why would that be upsetting? What would that mean to you?

FRED: Well, then I'd make a fool of myself.

DAVID: Suppose you did make a fool of yourself? Why would that be upsetting to you?

FRED: Because then everyone would look down on me.

DAVID: Suppose people did look down on you, what then?

FRED: I'd feel miserable.

DAVID: Why is that? Why would you feel miserable if people were looking down on you?

FRED: Well, that would mean I wasn't a worthwhile person. It might ruin my career. I'd get bad grades, I'd flunk out, and I might never become an attorney.

DAVID: And what then? What would that mean to you?

FRED: That would mean I had failed at something I've wanted all my life.

DAVID: And then?

FRED: Life would be empty. It would mean I was a failure. It would mean I was worthless.

This brief dialogue reveals the perfectionism and fear of disapproval at the root of Fred's difficulties. He believes it would be terrible to make a mistake or to fail at achieving a personal goal. He has convinced himself that if one person looks down on him, then everybody will. It is as if the word "Reject" will be stamped on his forehead for everyone to see.

Fred's feelings of self-esteem seem to be contingent upon approval or success. He believes that his achievements have to be outstanding or else they will be no good at all. If his cravings for perfection, approval, and success are not satisfied, Fred senses that he will be an unloved nothing, because he has no true support from within. Because he feels he must be totally competent and confident, he cannot accept his own humanity or cope with the insecurities he feels as a struggling law student.

There may be another reason that Fred feels blocked and tense about his performance in law school. He may not be sure that he really wants to be there in the first place. He may be slaving away dutifully so he can make his parents proud and impress his friends. But inside he may never have asked himself, "Is a high-powered legal career what I really want? Is this *my* vision for my life, or someone else's?"

The following techniques are designed to help you confront and conquer the fears that cripple you so that you can pursue your own goals in life with greater passion and self-confidence.

CONFRONT YOUR FEARS

Some people deal with performance anxiety through avoidance. You may habitually procrastinate and put your work off to the last minute. This allows you to protect yourself from the anxiety for as long as possible. In addition, you may reason that if you don't really hustle and do your best, you won't feel like a complete failure if you do a bad job. You can tell yourself, "I didn't really try, but if I had tried, I'd be the greatest."

People with performance anxiety may procrastinate for another reason. They have the misconception that they can't concentrate or perform effectively when they feel nervous. If you believe you can't function, you will probably give up and stop functioning. Then you'll conclude that you were right: you'll think you really couldn't function. But this is just a self-fulfilling prophecy.

A college student named Henry didn't take his chemistry final because he was convinced that he'd panic and get a bad grade on the test. He was a conscientious student and had never skipped an exam before. He reasoned that only a very disturbed person would be "unable" to complete a course. Consequently he dropped out of school. Letting his anxiety get the better of him in this way was entirely unnecessary. Henry had no real evidence that he wouldn't do a good job on the chemistry final—he simply gave up because he assumed he couldn't perform well.

If you refuse to give up in spite of your doubts and fears, you will usually discover that you can perform far better than you thought. Anxiety is uncomfortable, but it need not prevent you from doing practically anything you choose to do. No matter how nervous you feel, you can write papers, study, take exams, or compete athletically. Your anxiety will try to fool you by making you believe you can't function properly. But when you call the bluff on your fears, you will discover that your "inability" to function is just an illusion, a bogey monster full of hot air.

Penny was referred to me three days before her first final exam of the first semester in law school. She said she was so panicky that she simply couldn't study. She explained that her mind raced uncontrollably and she couldn't understand a single sentence in any of her books. She was convinced she was going to flunk out and wanted me to write a letter to the dean so she could drop out of school with a medical leave of absence.

I told Penny I'd write any letter she wanted, but that I didn't believe she really did need to drop out of school. I explained that the biggest mistake she could make was to stop studying, and that if she just kept studying in spite of how she felt, she would probably do reasonably well on her exams. I told her that anxiety creates the myth that you cannot function properly, but if you refuse to give in, you'll discover that you can function even though it seems you can't.

Penny protested: "But I can't understand what I'm reading when I try to study." I told her just to move her eyes across the page, whether or not it seemed as if she was understanding anything. I said it was crucial to go through the motions and study all day long, even though she felt she wasn't getting anywhere. I emphasized that the only error she could make would be to stop studying.

Penny told me that she would get so nervous when she took the test that she might not even be able to understand the questions. I told her it wasn't at all important to feel that she understood the questions. What was important was for her to agree to keep moving her pencil across the page during the entire two hours of the exam, no matter what she wrote down. I told her she was not allowed to give up or to waste any time thinking or questioning herself.

She protested: "But what if I can't think of anything meaningful to put down?"

"Then put down *anything*. It doesn't have to seem meaningful."

"But what if I can't think of even one sentence?"

"Then just string some unconnected words together and put a period at the end. You may not think it makes sense, but you must keep moving the pencil!"

"But what if I can't think of even a single word to put down?"

"Then just write gibberish. You must agree not to give up or to stop."

Penny reluctantly agreed. She said she was annoyed and insisted that I didn't understand how confused and anxious she felt. She said she was certain she'd flunk and then I'd have to write a letter to the dean for her. I agreed.

When I saw Penny a week later, she was furious. She explained that she'd followed my advice and it hadn't worked. She studied night and day for three days before the test but only got more and more confused, just as she had told me she would. She said that when she got the test she was unable to comprehend even one question on it. She just wrote gibberish in the answer book, the way I told her to. She said she flunked the test and felt enraged and humiliated. She insisted that I call the dean to arrange a leave of absence.

I asked Penny what grade she got. Her face turned red and she said that she hadn't gotten the examination back yet, but she knew she had flunked! I suggested we wait another week and assured her I would write a letter to the dean if she still wanted me to, once she got her grade on the exam.

At our next session Penny was still annoyed with me. I was curious about how she'd done on the test. Peevishly she admitted that she'd received an A. Apparently there was a note on the front of her answer book that said that her essay was the best in the class.

I asked Penny how she reconciled this with her belief that she couldn't study or perform adequately on tests when she was anxious. She replied, "It's obvious that I flunked the exam. They simply must have confused my examination booklet with someone else's!" I asked Penny if I could help straighten this out, and even offered to call the professor to explain that there may have been a mixup and that they had gotten her booklet confused with some other, brighter student's.

She changed the subject and didn't take me up on the offer. I sure would hate to face her in court someday! She doesn't back down very easily!

Penny's story reveals how your anxiety can fool you and make you feel convinced that you can't function when you really can. It illustrates how vitally important it is not to give up when you feel anxious. Suppose that, like Penny, you're trying to study for an important exam and the pressures are intense. Every time you open the book you panic. Your mind races and it seems as if you can't concentrate on what you're reading. You may tell yourself, "I can't think straight! What's wrong with me? I can't understand a single sentence!"

One way to deal with this is to test the validity of what you're telling yourself. Is it really true that you can't think straight? Read one sentence and then see if you can write a brief summary of what it says. You'll discover that you actually did understand it, even though you thought you didn't.

You may argue, "Well, maybe I could read that one sentence, but I could never understand an entire paragraph." If so, repeat the experiment. Read a paragraph twice and then summarize what it said. Once again, you'll discover that you did understand it reasonably well.

If you're struggling to write a report, you may feel that you're too nervous to write one decent sentence. If so, find out if this is true. Force out a sentence, no matter how inept it seems. Once you get it down on paper, you'll discover that it wasn't as bad as you thought. With a little editing you can make it even better. Then you can add several more sentences, and pretty soon you'll have a decent paragraph.

THE COMPARTMENTATION TECHNIQUE

We can learn a great deal about how to cope with performance anxiety by investigating the strategies used by successful athletes. In a study of weight lifters, Drs. Michael J. Mahoney and Marshall Avener, of Penn State University, investigated the impact of anxiety on performance during the final trials for the U.S. Olympic team.* Who

*M. J. Mahoney and M. Avener, "Psychology of the Elite Athlete: An Exploratory Study," *Cognitive Therapy and Research* 1, no. 2 (1977): 135–141.

do you think experienced more anxiety before the competition—the athletes who went on to win, or the athletes who ended up losing?

Drs. Mahoney and Avener discovered that both groups of athletes experienced similar amounts of anxiety. What distinguished the winners from the losers was how they coped with it. The less successful athletes tended to pay a great deal of attention to their fears. They aroused themselves into near-panic states with exaggerated self-doubts and fantasies of impending tragedy. In contrast, the athletes who won were more likely to ignore their anxiety. They reported that they just proceeded as if it weren't there. They were aware of their nervousness, but they concentrated on what they had to do. They gave themselves helpful mental instructions, like "Now I will take a deep breath. Now I will reach up and grip the bar," and so on. Because they assumed their anxiety was nothing more than a nuisance, it didn't get in the way. They were aware of the anxiety but they didn't dwell on it.

I call this technique "compartmentation," because you put your anxiety in a mental compartment—a box—and you ignore it. Instead, you focus on what you have to do. This is a powerful way to deal with performance anxiety. To learn this technique, establish a goal you would like to accomplish. You might have to prepare for an important exam, write a paper, or act in a play. Next, break the task down into a series of small steps and proceed with the task, one step at a time. If at any point your anxiety causes a problem for you, simply develop a strategy to solve the problem. If you persist and refuse to give in to your anxiety, you'll discover that you can always perform effectively, no matter how anxious you feel. There's a double payoff: you'll perform more effectively, and your anxiety will lose its grip.

Ann is a freshman in college. She told me she got so anxious that she could never take written exams. I asked her to imagine she had just been handed a test and to describe how she felt. She said she would feel so panicky that her vision would get blurred and she couldn't even read the questions properly. I asked her how she could cope with this problem. It occurred to her that she could focus her eyes on the first word of the first question. When her eyes were clearly in focus she could read this question, one word at a time. This made it clear that her anxiety could not prevent her from reading.

Then she asked, "But suppose I don't understand the question? When I'm anxious my mind starts racing and I get totally confused. I won't even know what the point of the question is." I asked Ann to think about how she might solve this problem. She decided that she could paraphrase the question in her own words immediately after reading it. For example, if the question read "Who was the first president of the United States?" she would say this to herself: "Let's see, this question is about the first president of the United States. That must be George Washington." She could see that this process of paraphrasing each question would help her understand it. This gave her a little more relief.

The next problem Ann anticipated was that she might feel insecure if she didn't know the answer to the first question on the test. Then she'd panic. I asked her how she could cope with this problem. She thought about it and decided that she could find an easy question to answer first. Then she'd be off to a good start.

Let's review the basics of this compartmentation technique: You put your anxiety in a mental box and ignore it. If you're afraid that your anxiety will prevent you from performing adequately, ask yourself specifically how your anxiety could hurt your performance. Then you develop a method for coping with this problem. Concentrate on the task at hand. This will show you that your anxiety might make you uncomfortable or slow you down a bit, but it will not prevent you from achieving your goal.

Imagine that you have to write a report for your boss. You've been procrastinating for two weeks because you feel so anxious, and the deadline is approaching. In the left-hand column of the chart on page 348 I've listed the specific problems that are holding you back. In the right-hand column, write down how you would solve each problem. Then you can compare your solutions to the ones at the end of the chapter.

When you list the problems that make it hard for you to function, you'll see that there are ways to work around them. Once you get started, your anxiety will usually diminish. This technique is based on the philosophy that you can conquer your fears if you confront them instead of avoiding them. Suppose you have to study for a difficult test. You'll want to put it off because you feel so nervous. If you give in, you'll feel better temporarily because you'll tell yourself, "Whew! What a relief! I can put that out of my mind for a while." You'll feel a momentary mood lift, but in the long run you'll feel

Problems	Solutions
1. I'll get so nervous, I'll feel that I can't even sit down at my desk and write a single word.	1. _____ _____ _____
2. I'll feel so worried and confused that I won't know how to get started on the report.	2. _____ _____ _____
3. I'll tell myself I have to write a really fantastic first sentence. Then I won't be able to think of anything especially brilliant to say.	3. _____ _____ _____
4. I'll feel overwhelmed, thinking about what an enormous task it is.	4. _____ _____ _____
5. I'll tell myself that I'm not in the mood to get started. Then I'll get up and wander around.	5. _____ _____ _____

even more insecure and anxious. If you confront your fears instead, you'll usually discover that the task wasn't nearly as impossible as you thought it was going to be. You'll be on the road to greater self-confidence and productivity.

WORRY BREAKS

You may find that you get distracted by daydreams when you're anxious and trying to study. You may stare into space, fantasizing about being on a Caribbean island, or you may imagine going to pick up your examination after it's been graded and seeing a large red F on it. The harder you try to study, the more powerful and distracting these fantasies become. Pretty soon all the time is gone and you haven't gotten anything done.

Sometimes it helps to schedule "worry breaks" every few minutes. During these breaks, take one full minute to daydream or to fret and catastrophize about how terrible things are. Time it on your watch. Give full vent to your insecurities without trying to fight them. At the end of the minute go back to work again, and concentrate for two or three minutes until your next "worry break." After a while, the distracting thoughts and fantasies will begin to lose their power over you. Then you can sustain your concentration for longer and longer periods of time.

It's probably not good to try to study more than ten or fifteen minutes at a time without at least one "worry break." Your mind is like a finely tuned automobile engine. It just isn't built to run at full speed endlessly. If you try to do too much at once, you'll burn out.

During these "worry breaks," you might find it helpful to dictate your thoughts about how terrible everything is into a tape recorder for one minute. You can say: "I'm such a slow learner. I'm so far behind. Just think of everything else I have to do. I'm not getting anywhere. It's hopeless. Everyone else is so much smarter," and so on. Then play it back and listen to yourself. Although these thoughts might be upsetting at first, after a while they'll lose their power because they'll begin to sound ridiculous and boring.

THE DAILY MOOD LOG

The Daily Mood Log, described in Chapter 5, can help you combat performance anxiety. First, describe the "Upsetting Event," the situation that's making you feel nervous, as illustrated on page 352. Next, write down your negative emotions and rate each one on a scale from 0 to 100. You may feel frightened, anxious, irritable, worried, nervous, pressured, or tense.

In the "Automatic Thoughts" column, write down the negative thoughts that make you feel upset. Try to tune in to the messages you're giving yourself. What are you telling yourself? You may feel petrified because you're thinking: "I'm probably not studying hard enough. There's so much I don't know! Think of everything else I should be doing. I don't understand this very well. I just can't concentrate. What if I flunk?" These thoughts make you feel overwhelmed and disorganized. You may get up and wander about the house or eat compulsively.

After you write down these negative thoughts, identify the distortions in each of them, using the list on page 308. Finally, substitute more realistic thoughts that "call the bluff" on your anxiety in the "Rational Response" column.

Joan is a psychologist who was having a great deal of trouble studying for her certification examination. As you study the "Automatic Thoughts" in her log on page 352, you will see that she was giving herself a number of negative messages that were extremely self-defeating. Each time she opened a book, Joan would berate herself for not having started sooner. Instead of focusing on what she was learning at a particular moment, she would obsess about all the other material she hadn't studied yet. Instead of assuming that her hard work and preparation would pay off, she would tell herself that the material she was studying probably wouldn't even be on the test.

It's little wonder that Joan felt frustrated and overwhelmed! Once she wrote down her negative thoughts, she could see how hard she was being on herself. However, she was convinced that her negative thoughts were absolutely valid. For example, the second negative thought is "I may not pass the exam." She agreed that this was an example of "fortune-telling," since she was predicting a catastrophe, but she couldn't see that there was anything illogical or unrealistic about it. She believed she really might flunk the exam and told me she didn't want to be involved in any ridiculous "power of positive thinking" program.

I suggested we examine the evidence for her claim that she would probably flunk the exam. Joan admitted that out of the hundreds of exams she'd taken in her life, she'd flunked only one test—a health quiz in high school that she hadn't studied for. Based on her track record, it seemed more realistic to assume that if she studied consistently she could probably do well on the exam.

COST-BENEFIT ANALYSIS

Sometimes a logical demonstration that your fears are groundless will not be convincing. Joan was still hesitant to give up her pessimistic predictions. She explained that if she became too confident and stopped worrying, she might get too complacent to study. Then she really *would* blow the exam! She assumed that her constant worrying and fretting was the price she had to pay for success.

This belief that your worry will somehow help you and protect you from danger is extremely common. It's as if God expects us to suffer and we'll be punished if we become too happy or confident! You may also feel that optimism is foolish and think that it's safer and wiser to assume the worst. If so, do a Cost-Benefit Analysis: make a list of the advantages and disadvantages of feeling anxious and worrying about failure. Ask yourself how all the worrying will help you and how it will hurt you. Then make a second list of the advantages and disadvantages of feeling confident and thinking about your work in an optimistic way. Ask yourself how a positive attitude will help you and how it will hurt you. Finally, weigh the advantages against the disadvantages of each option. This may make it clear just how self-defeating your anxiety and worry can be.

Joan listed these three advantages of worrying: "(1) I'll be thinking about my examination constantly, so I won't get overly complacent. (2) People will see how important it is for me to do well, so they'll be more forgiving if I fail. (3) If I worry about failure, I may try harder and do a better job."

Joan listed only one disadvantage: "I'm crippling myself with all this worry and self-doubt." However, this one disadvantage of worrying far outweighed the three advantages in her mind. This insight made Joan more motivated to talk back to her negative thoughts, and the Rational Responses helped her feel more relaxed. She agreed to write down and answer her negative thoughts every night when she was studying at home during the next week. This helped her feel more confident, and she was able to study much more effectively. Ultimately she did quite well on the exam.

I'm not claiming that things will always turn out well simply because you believe they will. That would be just as superstitious as telling yourself that obsessive worrying will protect you from danger.

THE DAILY MOOD LOG*

STEP ONE: DESCRIBE THE UPSETTING EVENT _____
Sitting down trying to study.

STEP TWO: RECORD YOUR NEGATIVE FEELINGS—and rate each one from 0 (the least) to 100 (the most). Use words like sad, anxious, angry, guilty, lonely, hopeless, frustrated, etc.

Emotion	Rating	Emotion	Rating	Emotion	Rating
1. Anxious	99	3. Angry	75	5. Hopeless	65
2. Frustrated	90	4. Disgusted with myself	80	6.	

STEP THREE: THE TRIPLE-COLUMN TECHNIQUE—

Automatic Thoughts	Distortions	Rational Responses
Write your negative thoughts and estimate your belief in each one (0–100).	Identify the distortions in each Automatic Thought.	Substitute more realistic thoughts and estimate your belief in each one (0 and 100).
1. Just think of all the time I've been wasting! (100%) 25%	Mental filter; discounting the positive	1. I did a little studying yesterday, and I'm going to learn something right now. (100%)
2. I may not pass the exam. (100%) 25%	Fortune-telling	2. The exam has four sections. It's unlikely I'll flunk them all. If I look at the situation realistically, the worst that could happen would be that I'd flunk one section and have to

(Continue on next page)

Automatic Thoughts	Distortions	Rational Responses
		make it up. Since I've passed nearly all the exams I've ever taken, there's a good chance that I'll pass this one. (90%)
3. But I can't re-member anything. three days after I study it. (100%) 0%	All-or-nothing thinking	3. I can remember some things. I can also take notes and review them later. (100%)
4. There's too much material to cover. (100%) 0%	All-or-nothing thinking; "should statement"	4. There *is* a lot of material and nobody can re-member all of it. I can focus on the most import-tant ideas and learn as much as possible in the time I have. (100%)
5. I'm going to study the wrong things—they won't appear on the test. (100%) 0%	Fortune-telling	5. Some of the things I'm studying prob-ably will be on the test. Some things won't be on the test, but this hap-pens to everybody.
6. They're just going to ask a lot of trivial questions. What right do they	Fortune-telling; "should statement"	6. I have no evidence that all the ques-tions will be irrelevant or trivial. It would be

(Continue on next page)

Automatic Thoughts	Distortions	Rational Responses
have? They're supposed to be educators! (100%) 0%		unfortunate if the test wasn't a good one, but it wouldn't be a catastrophe, because everyone has to take the same test. (100%)
7. I never do enough. I should be doing more! (100%) 25%	"Should statement"	7. I probably ask too much of myself as it is. If I aim to do a little less, I'll probably feel less pressured and end up doing more. (100%)

STEP FOUR: OUTCOME—Re-rate your belief in each Automatic Thought from 0 to 100 and put a check in the box that describes how you now feel:

☐ not at all better ☐ somewhat better ☒ quite a bit better ☐ a lot better

I'm not saying that you should be a "cockeyed optimist" and ignore the possibility of failure. But things usually will turn out far better if you anticipate success and adopt a positive attitude.

DEFINE YOUR GOALS

It can help to ask yourself, "Why would failure be so upsetting to me?" You might think that people would lose respect for you, that your career would come to an end, or that you'd be a terrible disappointment to your parents or friends. While these concerns may contain a grain of truth, they are frequently exaggerated. The real problem may be that you aren't clear about your own goals in life. For example, after the law students I described earlier began to feel a little less anxious, nearly all of them confessed that they didn't really know if they even wanted to be in law school in the first place. They said they didn't have a burning desire to be lawyers and were in law school because that's what their parents wanted or because they couldn't think of anything better to do. They felt resentful about having to meet their parents' expectations because they had not asked themselves, "Is this what I want for my life?"

When I asked this question, the answer was always "No." Most of them did *not* want to be Wall Street lawyers, but it had never dawned on them they had the right to pursue their own dreams for their lives. Instead of clarifying what they *did* want to do, they were rebelling against what they *didn't* want. Their anxiety was a perfect way out of a trap. Subconsciously they were telling themselves, "I'm so anxious I may have to drop out of school. This will give me a perfect excuse to quit. My parents won't really be angry or disappointed in me. I tried my best, but I just had to quit because of my nerves."

Their anxiety was the result of this conflict. They were divided against themselves, like two teams were pulling against each other in a tug of war. The side that felt they should be in school was competing with the side that didn't want to be there but couldn't admit it. Once they became aware of that struggle, they were free to do one of two things: they could leave law school and put their energies into some other career, or they could stay because they wanted to, and not just to please their parents.

When you feel anxious about your performance, you may not be aware that you have mixed feelings because you're busy telling yourself, "This is what I should want to do. I should just push harder and get through it." But if it isn't what you really want to do, then every psychological technique in the world will fail to make your anxiety go away. Your lack of commitment to a goal will sabotage any possible treatment effect. You can take a tranquilizer to quiet the two teams doing battle, but they will continue to struggle. You can give one of these teams a pep talk and try to energize it to win, but the other team will just fight back a little harder, and you won't gain much ground. You've got to call time out and tell these two opposing teams, "Hey, guys, we're stuck because we're at odds. We've got to pull together toward a common goal. What should that goal be?"

Surprisingly, none of these anxious students ever did drop out of law school. Instead, they decided to stay and pursue very different kinds of career goals that appealed to them. A black student with an interest in international law became excited about the possibility of working with emerging African nations. A woman who loved the theater decided she would like to work in the legal aspects of the entertainment business. A young man from Minnesota decided he wanted a rural law practice in a small midwestern community where his wife, who was studying agricultural engineering, could more easily pursue her career. Once they gave up the need to do what they thought they *should* do and felt free to define personally meaningful goals, their anxiety usually vanished.

FEARED FANTASY TECHNIQUE

You may be concerned that if you pursue your own goals and stop trying so hard to meet everyone else's expectations, other people will be disappointed in you. For example, you might want to take a year off from school or to change your major. How would your family react? When the law students confronted their parents with their new career plans, their parents were usually pleased and relieved that the emotional storms were over. However, there may be times when people will feel let down because you didn't live up to their expectations. You can confront these fears with the Feared Fantasy Technique. Let's pretend that I'm your son. You can pretend to be a critical, angry parent. You're disappointed in me because I've decided I'd like to practice law in the Midwest instead of going to Wall Street. Our dialogue might go like this:

ANGRY FATHER: I'm extremely upset. You say you're not going to Wall Street? You're going to practice in the Midwest? You don't want to do that! You're missing the boat. That's no career.

STUDENT: Yes, I plan to practice in the Midwest, in a rural area.

ANGRY FATHER: But you'll never make any money like that. And with your brains you could do something worthwhile with your life!

STUDENT: It sounds as if you think my choice of a career isn't very worthwhile. That makes me feel like I must fit into your mold. I feel hurt. I want you to love and respect me for the career that I've chosen.

ANGRY FATHER: I don't want you to fit into a mold, I just want you to do what's best for you. I know you'll never be happy in the Midwest.

STUDENT: I feel very committed to a general law practice in the Midwest. Can you tell me why this is upsetting you?

ANGRY FATHER: I've already told you why I'm upset! The top people go to Wall Street and they make a name for themselves. The losers go to Nebraska and grow corn. Your mother and I want to be proud of you.

STUDENT: It sounds as if you won't be proud of me if I go to Nebraska. Am I reading you right? Would you feel that I was a loser? Would you love me less?

Now the father has two choices. He can continue to be judgmental and rejecting because his son isn't doing precisely what he wants him to, or he can accept his son and love him as he is. Most fathers would not be so hostile and rejecting, but at least the son could live with himself. He would have a sense of integrity and self-respect because he pursued a vision for his life that made sense to him. Over the course of time, I suspect that his father would soften.

Let's review the methods for coping with test and performance anxiety:

1. **Confront Your Fears:** You do an experiment to test your belief that you can't function properly when you feel anxious. If you feel so nervous that you think you can't concentrate or understand what you're studying, read one sentence out loud and summarize what it said. You will usually discover that you did understand it, even though it seemed as if you couldn't.

2. **The Compartmentation Technique:** You put your anxiety in a mental box and ignore it. You concentrate on doing the task one step at a time.

3. **Worry Breaks:** You schedule one-minute worry breaks every five or ten minutes. During the worry breaks you give full vent to all your self-doubts and fantasies of failure.

4. **The Daily Mood Log:** You write down your negative thoughts, identify the distortions in them, and substitute more positive and realistic thoughts.

5. **The Cost-Benefit Analysis:** You make a list of the advantages and disadvantages of worrying and predicting failure. Then make a second list of the advantages and disadvantages of feeling confident and giving yourself positive, optimistic messages.

6. **Define Your Goals:** Ask yourself, "Do I really want to be doing this? Am I feeling coerced and trying too hard to meet other people's expectations?"

7. **The Feared Fantasy Technique:** You write out an imaginary dialogue with someone who feels let down and acts excessively critical because you didn't live up to his or her expectations.

SOLUTIONS TO THE EXERCISE ON PAGE 348

1. My anxiety really can't prevent me from sitting down at my desk. I can certainly pick up the pen. Then I can at least write one word on a piece of paper.

2. I can review my notes. Then I can outline the report. Then I can draft the introductory paragraph.

3. I can try to write an average first sentence instead of trying to write a brilliant one. Then I can do some average editing later on, and revise it and make it even better.

4. I can work on one small part of the report at a time. Then it won't seem so overwhelming.

5. I can remind myself that I don't need to "feel like it" in order to get started. Tough jobs are bound to be uncomfortable at first. Once I start to make some progress I'll probably feel more motivated.

PART FOUR

Feeling Good Together: How to Strengthen Relationships Through Better Communication

18

·

Good and
Bad Communication

Communication seems easy, and we all think we're experts. After all, you've been talking since you were a child, and it comes naturally most of the time. You just open your mouth and the words come spilling out. When you feel happy and close to someone, it is easy to communicate well. You feel good and they feel good and everything seems rosy. It's when you have a strong disagreement or a conflict with someone that you find out whether you can really communicate well. How well do you do when you're angry, or when someone is angry with you? How do you deal with criticism? What do you say when the other person is being unreasonable and refuses to listen to your point of view? How well do you communicate when you feel vulnerable and hurt?

People who can communicate effectively in these situations are exceedingly rare. But these are the situations where good communication is vital. The key to intimacy, friendship, and success in business is the ability to handle conflict successfully. People have enormous difficulty with this. Husbands and wives don't communicate well. Friends don't communicate well. Family members often handle conflicts and disagreements very poorly.

Even psychotherapists, who are presumably experts, have difficulties communicating with patients. When I teach psychiatrists and psychologists at workshops, I often ask a volunteer to role-play so we can see how effectively they can communicate with a difficult, hostile patient. Pretending to be the patient, I say something like "Dr. Smith, you don't seem to care about me. I want help with my problems, but all you ever say is 'Hmmm.' " Almost invariably the therapist responds in a defensive or evasive way. He or she might say "Hmmm" or "Tell me more" or "I do care about you." Therapists seem to have little comprehension of how annoying and inappropriate these responses might sound to an angry patient!

Would you like to become a better communicator? First, let's see if we can define good communication and bad communication. Good communication has two properties: you express your feelings openly and directly, and you encourage the other person to express his or her feelings. You say how you are thinking and feeling, and you try to listen and understand what the other person is thinking and feeling. According to this definition, the ideas and feelings of both people are important.

Just as good communication involves self-expression and listening, bad communication involves a refusal to share your feelings openly or to listen to what the other person has to say.

Becoming argumentative and defensive is one sign of bad communication. You may contradict the other person without trying to understand his or her feelings. You may project subtle messages that say "I'm not really interested in what you have to say. I'm only interested in broadcasting my own feelings and insisting that you agree with me."

Another sign of bad communication is denying your own feelings and acting them out indirectly. You may act pouty or get sarcastic. This is called "passive aggression." Active aggression is also bad communication—when you tell the other person off or threaten or issue ultimatums. The list of "Characteristics of Bad Communication" on the next page will make you more aware of what not to do when you are trying to resolve a conflict with someone. Study this list carefully!

You may recognize several bad habits that get you into trouble. Changing these tendencies can make a tremendous difference in the way you relate to people and save you endless grief!

THE CHARACTERISTICS OF BAD COMMUNICATION*

1. **Truth**—You insist that you are "right" and the other person is "wrong."

2. **Blame**—You say that the problem is the other person's fault.

3. **Martyrdom**—You claim that you're an innocent victim.

4. **Put-down**—You imply that the other person is a loser because he or she "always" or "never" does certain things.

5. **Hopelessness**—You give up and insist there's no point in trying.

6. **Demandingness**—You say you're entitled to better treatment but you refuse to ask for what you want in a direct, straightforward way.

7. **Denial**—You insist that you don't feel angry, hurt, or sad when you really do.

8. **Passive Aggression**—You pout or withdraw or say nothing. You may storm out of the room or slam doors.

9. **Self-blame**—Instead of dealing with the problem, you act as if you're an awful, terrible person.

10. **Helping**—Instead of hearing how depressed, hurt, or angry the other person feels, you try to "solve the problem" or "help" him or her.

11. **Sarcasm**—Your words or tone of voice convey tension or hostility which you aren't openly acknowledging.

12. **Scapegoating**—You suggest that the other person has "a problem" and that you're sane, happy, and uninvolved in the conflict.

13. **Defensiveness**—You refuse to admit any wrong-doing or imperfection.

14. **Counterattack**—Instead of acknowledging how the other person feels, you respond to their criticism by criticizing them.

15. **Diversion**—Instead of dealing with how you both feel in the here-and-now, you list grievances about past injustices.

Let's examine the way several of my patients communicate. They are ordinary men and women who are probably similar to you. In each case, I want you to decide if what my patient said was an example of good or bad communication.

Joanne is 26 years old and is completing her law degree. Her husband, Ted, is a surgeon. Ted and Joanne separated several months ago but have been attempting a reconciliation. They are struggling with the issue of whether they should separate permanently or try to resolve their difficulties and get back together again. Joanne complains that Ted has difficulty expressing his feelings. She says that when he's annoyed he gets pouty and gives her the icy treatment instead of telling her how he feels. Ted complains that Joanne is too close to her family. He says she's bossy and self-centered. He tells her that she puts her family and her career ahead of him. This makes him feel like a second-class citizen.

Recently Ted planned a trip to Bermuda, and they argued about whether or not Joanne would go with him. At first he wanted to go alone and Joanne felt hurt. Later he asked her to go with him, but in the meantime she had decided that she needed some time alone. When she told him she wasn't planning to go, he got annoyed and said, "You should get on with your life and not hold any hopes for this relationship!" Joanne replied, "No problem! I have already started to do that." First, let's look at Ted's comment. Would you say it was an example of good communication or bad communication?

_____ good communication

_____ bad communication

I'd say it's bad communication, because he didn't express his feelings or acknowledge hers. If you examine the list on page 365, you will see that he's involved with "Denial." He probably felt rejected and angry but he tried to hide his feelings. He could say, "I'm disappointed and hurt. I care for you and I really wish you'd go with me." Instead, he simply rejects her and puts her down. This is consistent with her image of him as someone who acts pouty and cold when he's upset.

Ted also failed to acknowledge her feelings. Why did she decide not to go? How is she feeling? When he doesn't ask these questions, Ted projects a lack of love and interest in her.

Now let's look at her comment. Would you call this an example of good communication or bad communication? Think about it a little bit and review the list on page 365 before you answer this and read any further.

_____ good communication

_____ bad communication

Her comment is another example of bad communication, because she hasn't acknowledged his feelings or expressed her own. She's involved in "Sarcasm" and "Denial." It seems pretty clear that he feels hurt, angry, and rejected, but she appears to be ignoring his feelings. This will make her seem self-centered and uninterested in him. Joanne is not expressing her own feelings either. She felt stung and wounded by his comment. Instead of expressing this, she simply responded in a cold, rejecting manner.

This denial of the way you really feel is extremely common. Many people have a terrible fear that something awful will happen if they simply state, in an open and direct way, how they feel. I have a strong hunch that you may have this problem too!

Joanne could express her own feelings and acknowledge Ted's by saying something like this: "I feel very bad right now because you told me that I should get on with my life. I feel hurt and angry. I still care for you and I don't want our relationship to be over. You're telling me not to hold out any hopes in this relationship. Your voice has a sharp edge to it. I wonder if you're feeling annoyed because I decided not to go to Bermuda? Can you tell me how you feel about this?" This would make him aware of how she's feeling and would encourage him to talk about his own feelings. That's good communication. It isn't a put-down, it isn't a denial, and she wouldn't be playing the role of a martyr or victim. The response would make Joanne vulnerable, because she would disclose her feelings in a non-defensive way and would invite him to express his anger directly. But at the same time, her response would be powerful because she urges him to open up and come out of his shell, and she has set aside the impulse to get back at him.

Let's look at another example of a separated couple with problems communicating. Henry is a management consultant in New York City. He separated from his wife, Denise, several months ago because of conflicting goals about marriage. Henry very much wants children, but Denise does not want a family and would prefer to pursue her own career instead. Henry has been very disappointed by Denise's lack of interest in sex. Denise complains that Henry is married to his career. She says she wants a husband with a nine-to-five job who would come home in time for dinner so they could spend their evenings together. This is far more important to her than having him put in long hours so he can make lots of money. Henry feels rejected and unappreciated. He takes great pride in all his hard work and has developed an outstanding career and a good salary. Henry's father, an immigrant from Russia, worked long hours as a tailor. When Henry was growing up, the importance of ambition, hard work, and success were stressed. Henry wishes Denise would respect his accomplishments so they could enjoy the good life together.

Henry and Denise have always had a great deal of difficulty discussing conflicts or dealing with angry feelings. Henry sometimes plays the role of a martyr. He feels resentful that Denise doesn't love and appreciate all the sacrifices he's made to raise their standard of living, and he's afraid to tell her how badly he wants to have children. He also is afraid to tell her how unhappy he feels about her lack of interest in sex, because he doesn't want to hurt her feelings. As a result his resentment built up, until he finally moved out and began to date other women.

Like the previous couple, Henry and Denise have not decided whether they should get a divorce or try to work their problems out. Recently they went out on a date, and afterward they were talking about a couple they know who were about to get married. Denise mentioned that the woman in that relationship was "making all the sacrifices." She explained that "to maintain a relationship, people must sacrifice." Henry found this statement annoying because he felt that Denise's definition of "sacrifice" was to submerge all your desires and needs entirely to another person. Since this is exactly what Henry felt he had been doing, and since it had worked out poorly for him, he felt infuriated. He said, "No. Sacrifice causes resentment." Is Henry's statement an example of good communication or bad communication? Review the list on page 365 before you answer this question.

_____ good communication

_____ bad communication

I would say this is an example of bad communication. Henry is not expressing his own feelings openly, and he is not encouraging Denise to express hers. Henry's communication error is "Truth." His statement will only provoke an argument. Can you think of a better response? What could Henry say? Put your ideas here:

_____

_____

_____

_____

My suggestion would be along these lines: "Denise, I feel resentful right now. I think you're talking about our relationship. Maybe you think you've done all the sacrificing. I know this is how I feel. I feel I've done all the sacrificing and it really bothers me. Tell me how you feel about this." If Henry said this, he would be sharing his feelings in a straightforward way, and he would be encouraging Denise to tell him how she feels about their relationship, rather than talking about some other couple.

You might be interested in Henry's response when I suggested this. He said he thought it would be an excellent approach, but he was terribly afraid to be so open with Denise. He said, "It would make me vulnerable. If I expressed my feelings and opened myself up to her left hook, I don't know what would happen!" This fear of making yourself vulnerable is one of many attitudes that can cause poor communication. You end up living in a box and having to communicate by tapping on the wall in Morse Code.

Husbands and wives are not the only ones who have difficulties expressing their feelings. Mildred's 25-year-old son, Jerry, is attending medical school in San Francisco. He is very close to Mildred and they talk frequently on the telephone. He does well in his classes and seems to have lots of friends. However, he tells Mildred that he's going nowhere and that his life seems empty and has no meaning. He sometimes says that if it weren't for the fact that she's still alive, he would commit suicide.

When Jerry says these things, Mildred feels panic and anguish. She tells him that he has a great deal to live for. She emphasizes that he's intelligent and has many friends. She reminds him that he's good-looking and that women like him. Is Mildred's response an example of good communication or bad communication? Review the list on page 365 before you answer.

_____ good communication

_____ bad communication

I would say this is an example of bad communication. Her communication errors include "Truth" and "Helping." Mildred is not encouraging Jerry to express his feelings, and she is not expressing her own. How does Mildred feel when he says these things? She feels shocked, frightened, concerned, frustrated. But she does not say this to Jerry. Instead, she tries to cheer him up by contradicting him. Essentially, he says "My life stinks" and she says "No, your life is good." This will frustrate Jerry. He will feel that she doesn't understand how bad he feels, so he will continue to complain even more persistently. He'll point out five things in his life that stink. She'll try to cheer him up by pointing out five good things. They will both end up feeling anxious and exasperated.

Bad communication nearly always involves some type of argumentative response. We don't listen to what the other person says because it upsets us to hear how they feel. Mildred feels so frightened that she isn't aware she's being contradictory. She loves Jerry and desperately wants to make him feel better. That's understandable, but there are far more effective ways to do this.

The tendency to argue and contradict the other person when you feel upset is practically universal. You may not be aware that you are doing this. It seems to be a deeply ingrained part of human nature. If you believe that intimacy involves emotional closeness and a sharing of feelings, then this habit of contradicting others will defeat you. It always creates distance and prevents intimacy.

Jerry is looking for some understanding. He wants his mom to understand how bad he feels. He must want to communicate with Mildred because he calls her so frequently. If you were Mildred, what would you say to Jerry? Think about it for a moment before you read on, and then put your ideas here:

_____

_____

_____

_____

Mildred could respond like this: "Jerry, I want you to know how bad I feel right now. I get alarmed when you say that your life is empty and that there's no point in being alive. I love you and it breaks my heart to hear so much sadness and despair in your voice. I want to understand you better. Can you tell me why you feel the way you do? Maybe there's something missing from your life that's very important to you. Maybe there is a problem that you've been afraid to share with me. Can you tell me more about how you feel?" This response would be more honest, because she's admitting how frightened and concerned she feels instead of denying her feelings and acting "helpful." She would also be encouraging him to open up. Most people want to be understood and accepted more than anything else in the world. If she tries to understand and gives up the urge to help, she will be helping him. It's a paradox.

Let's look at a mother/daughter interaction. Marilyn is about the same age as Mildred. Her daughter, Susan, is about Jerry's age. Susan lives with Marilyn and they manage a chain of clothing stores that Marilyn founded after her husband died. They do well and have a beautiful home. However, Marilyn's daughter is often bossy and domineering. She puts Marilyn down, and Marilyn simply takes it because she sees herself as a "nice, sweet person."

Recently Marilyn was having her kitchen redone. One evening when she was washing the countertop after work, Susan made the following statement in a very irritable tone of voice: "Mother! I can't believe you're doing this! The workers told me specifically that we're not to run the dishwasher or get any water on the floor until they finish putting in the tiles!" Marilyn's face stiffened, and angry tears welled up in her eyes. She stormed out of the room muttering, "I can't believe she said that!" Would you call this an example of good communication or bad communication? Examine the list on page 365 before you answer.

_____ good communication

_____ bad communication

This is an example of bad communication, because Marilyn is not expressing her feelings and she is not acknowledging what Susan is saying. Holding your hurt feelings inside is called "Passive Aggressiveness." Marilyn is expressing her anger passively and indirectly by walking out and saying nothing. What could she have said to her daughter instead? Remember that good communication has two components: you express your feelings openly, and you acknowledge how the other person is feeling. Put your ideas here:

_____

_____

_____

_____

_____

Look at the response you wrote down. Was it sarcastic or aggressive? Did you tell Susan off or put her down? Active aggression is not the antidote to passive aggression. Marilyn's aim is to communicate with her daughter and to improve their relationship, not just to hit back.

Marilyn needs to point out that her daughter sounds condescending and nasty. Marilyn can tell Susan that she feels put down and annoyed. She doesn't need to say this in an antagonistic or sarcastic way, because then she would be accepting her daughter's invitation to be childish and to have a fight. She would be giving Susan the power to set the tone of the interaction.

Marilyn could say, "I didn't know we weren't supposed to use the kitchen tonight, and I will be careful not to get the floor wet. I'm quite upset right now because I feel talked down to. Your tone of voice sounds condescending, and that makes me angry. I want you to treat me with respect. It sounds like you might be annoyed with me. If you are, I want you to tell me. Are you angry or upset about something?" This response will call attention to Susan's insulting tone of voice and will encourage her to communicate in a more direct way.

Susan probably is annoyed with Marilyn. Instead of bringing the problem up and talking it out, she acts hostile and insulting. When Marilyn runs out of the room, this makes Susan feel very powerful. Marilyn's "sweetness" and her habit of avoiding conflicts hurts both of them. But if Marilyn sticks up for herself, they will both benefit.

Brothers and sisters frequently have trouble communicating. Janice recently discovered that her brother Tom was involved in a homosexual relationship. Janice learned that Tom's lover wanted to be included as co-owner of a house Tom was buying, without helping to pay for it. Janice was disturbed on several accounts. First, she felt that she had never really been close to Tom. She was concerned that she and Tom had never really gotten to know each other very well. Second, she was upset that Tom was gay and she worried about AIDS. Finally, she was concerned that Tom's lover would get half ownership of his house without helping to pay for it.

Janice told Tom that she was afraid that the man he was living with might be taking advantage of him. Tom responded: "He's not!" He said this in a very defensive, irritable tone of voice. If you were Janice, what would you say next? Put your ideas here:

_____

_____

_____

_____

_____

Janice said, "I was concerned because he asked for half ownership of the new house without offering to pay for it." Would you say this is an example of good communication or bad communication?

_____ good communication

_____ bad communication

I would say it's an example of bad communication, because she's ignoring his defensive tone and she is not revealing her feelings about the matter. She's being argumentative. Her communication errors include "Truth" and "Denial." She is pushing the idea that Tom's lover may not be completely fair and honest. Although she may be right, she'll get nowhere. Tom will simply get defensive and they'll end up arguing. Are you familiar with this pattern? Does this ever happen to you?

Janice could respond this way instead: "I hope you're right. I'm worried because I care for you and I don't want anyone to take advantage of you. I noticed a sharp edge in your voice just now. I wonder if you feel that I don't understand the situation. Maybe you think I'm talking down to you. Maybe I'm sticking my nose in where it doesn't belong. If so, I apologize. I really do want to feel closer to you. Can you tell me more about what's going on? I would appreciate it." This response gives Tom the chance to talk about his feelings and encourages him to tell her if he's annoyed instead of arguing defensively.

You may not always like the responses I have suggested. A different style and tone may suit you better. We all have different personalities, and what works for one person isn't always the same as what works for someone else. What I do hope is that you are beginning to comprehend what bad communication is and how enormously common it is. Bad communication is almost as automatic and natural as breathing! Bad communication has two characteristics. What are they?

1. _____

_____

_____

2. _____

_____

_____

They are not expressing your feelings openly, and not acknowledging how the other person is thinking and feeling. Instead you argue and get defensive.

Good communication also has two characteristics. What are they?

1. _____

_____

_____

2. _____

_____

_____

They are expressing your feelings openly and directly, and acknowledging the other person's feelings.

In the next chapter I will describe three powerful listening skills and two self-expression skills that will help you communicate more effectively and more intimately.

19

•

Five Secrets of Intimate Communication

The five communication techniques described in this chapter can change your life. Three are listening skills and two are self-expression skills. You will learn to listen with your "third ear" so you can understand precisely what the other person is thinking and feeling. They will also help you express your feelings more clearly and effectively. Once you have learned each of the five techniques, I will show you how to put them all together so you can communicate more effectively.

Listening Skill #1: The Disarming Technique

This is the most difficult—and the most powerful—listening skill. You find *some* truth in what the other person is saying and agree with them, even if you think that what they're saying is wrong. This is a particularly effective tool when you feel criticized and attacked. It takes the wind out of the other person's sails and has a profound and sudden calming effect. Regardless of how unreasonable their criticism might seem, find some grain of truth in it. When you resist the urge to argue or defend yourself and you instead agree with the other

THE FIVE SECRETS OF EFFECTIVE COMMUNICATION*

LISTENING SKILLS

1. **The Disarming Technique.** You find some truth in what the other person is saying, even if you feel convinced that what they're saying is totally wrong, unreasonable, irrational, or unfair.

2. **Empathy.** You put yourself in the other person's shoes and try to see the world through his or her eyes.

   - **Thought empathy:** You paraphrase the other person's words.
   - **Feeling empathy:** You acknowledge how they're probably feeling, given what they are saying to you.

3. **Inquiry:** You ask gentle, probing questions to learn more about what the other person is thinking and feeling.

SELF-EXPRESSION SKILLS

1. **"I feel" statements.** You express your feelings with "I feel" statements (such as "I feel upset") rather than with "you" statements (such as "You're wrong!" or "You're making me furious!").

2. **Stroking:** You find something genuinely positive to say to the other person, even in the heat of battle. This indicates that you respect the other person, even though you may be angry with each other.

*Copyright © 1984 by David D. Burns, M.D., from *The Feeling Good Handbook*, copyright © 1989

person, you will paradoxically end up a winner. He or she will usually feel like a winner too, and will be much more open to your point of view.

Here's an example. Suppose you told me: "I'm suspicious about these communication techniques. I don't think they will work for me." What could I say to you? How could I respond, using the disarming technique? Put your ideas here:

_____

_____

_____

_____

Answer: I could say, "You're right to be suspicious. I'm not convinced these methods will be helpful to you either. People sometimes find it extremely difficult to change. I'd like to hear more about why the methods don't seem useful to you."

Can you see the value in this response? There is nearly *always* some truth in what another person is saying. When I agree with you, it will be hard for you to keep up the argument.

You may not want to use this disarming technique because when you are criticized you will feel angry, and a voice inside you will be screaming, "I'm right and I have the right to defend myself!" If you give in to this voice—and the temptation will be almost overwhelming—you'll be off to the races in a pointless, frustrating battle. Arguing with a critic almost never works. Agreeing with a critic almost always builds rapport. The effects can be quite magical!

Now let's try it again. Let's assume your spouse says, "You're always late and I'm sick of waiting for you." How would you disarm him or her?

_____

_____

_____

You could say: "It's true. I *am* late and you have the right to be angry." Can you see the value in this response? When you admit that you're late, your spouse will feel listened to and respected and won't feel nearly so mad. But if you get defensive and make excuses for yourself, it will enrage him or her even more.

Let's try another example. Your boss says: "This proposal stinks. Were you daydreaming when you wrote it?" Let's assume you put a great deal of effort into the proposal and you felt proud of it. You know it's not *that* bad, and you'd like to kill your boss. In spite of this, how could you disarm your boss? Put your ideas here:

_____

_____

_____

_____

Answer: You could respond: "It sounds like I really missed the boat on the proposal, even though I worked hard on it. Could you tell me what you liked and disliked about it?" This will calm your boss down, and he or she will probably communicate in a more tactful manner.

When you use the disarming technique, you must be genuine in what you say or it will backfire. You can always find some valid way to agree, no matter how illogical the person's accusations might seem to you. If you agree with them in a sincere way, they will generally soften and will be far more willing to listen to you.

Suppose I say to you, "That green shirt looks awful on you." Let's assume that you're wearing a bright turquoise shirt and everyone's been telling you how great it looks. How could you disarm me?

_____

_____

_____

_____

You could say, "Green may not be my best color. What color would you like to see me wearing?" Notice that this response avoids an argument and puts the ball back in my court. I've invited you to get into a stupid argument about what color your shirt is, and you've tactfully declined by finding some little morsel of truth in what I said. What's the point in arguing with me about the color of your shirt?

Of course, some people seem to love pointless debates. That's perfectly okay—you can argue with people endlessly if that's what turns you on! But if you're tired of arguing and find that people never listen to you, and if you'd like to feel closer to people, then the disarming technique could change your life!

Some readers may resist and think, "I shouldn't have to agree with someone who's being unreasonable." The answer to this is that you don't have to. However, you'll probably be far better off if you do. When you disarm someone who's being unreasonable, you'll often win them over to your point of view. Instead of arguing, look for a common framework so you can begin to understand each other and work together as a team. When you listen more deeply and try to grasp where the other person really is coming from, the relationship will be transformed. No longer are you enemies fighting each other to "win." The other person will frequently do a sudden turnabout and agree with you. This is because you have made a basic decision to build a relationship based on trust instead of doing battle in an effort to tear the other person down.

There are several reasons why this can be so remarkably effective. When two people argue, they always polarize each other and take extreme positions because they both feel they're not being listened to. Inside, the other person knows there's another side to the issue, but they feel you don't appreciate their point of view—you're both being dogmatic and defensive. Once you disarm them, they will recognize that you respect them, and they won't feel so dogmatic and have such an urge to insist that they're right and you're wrong. They will usually soften and acknowledge your feelings and ideas.

Let's try some more disarming. It's a terribly important technique, and you will need to practice it over and over before you catch on. Keep in mind as you practice that I'm only asking you to use this one technique. In an actual conversation, you would combine the disarming technique with the other methods described in this chapter, so that you will come across in a natural and effective way.

But right now, you need to concentrate all your efforts on this one technique.

Let's assume you're a little overweight and your spouse says, "You're a fat slob! You've got no self-control." How could you disarm him or her? Put your ideas here:

_____

_____

_____

_____

Answer: You could say, "You're absolutely right. I *do* need to lose weight and I need better self-control." Keep in mind that you are only using the disarming technique just now. In an actual conversation, you would also want to express your feelings and acknowledge how your spouse is feeling. In this instance, you would probably be feeling hurt and put down. Your spouse, too, sounds angry and frustrated. You would want to encourage him to express his feelings more directly and openly so he doesn't have to resort to hostile jabs. The other methods in this chapter, when combined with the disarming technique, will allow you to do this.

Your husband says, "You're too emotional about things. You get too upset. You're so irrational. You overreact. Why don't you use a little logic? The world won't come to an end!" How could you disarm him?

_____

_____

_____

_____

Answer: You could say, "I agree with you. I often overreact and get illogical, and it turns out later on that I wasn't being realistic."

Your wife says, "You're too logical and rational about everything!" How could you disarm her?

_____

_____

_____

_____

Answer: You could say, "You're right. I tend to be too logical instead of sharing my feelings."

Your husband says, "You get pouty and irritable when you get upset." How could you disarm him?

_____

_____

_____

_____

Answer: You could say, "I think I do act like that when I get mad."

Many readers may be thinking, "These techniques stink! I wouldn't agree with any creep who talked to me like that! Who does he think he is?" You are quite right in thinking this. When someone beats up on you, it's important to express your feelings.

Remember, though, that there is always a grain of truth in what the other person is saying, even if it sounds obnoxious and insulting. Even if their criticism seems very off base, there's still something valid about the way they feel. If you acknowledge this, they'll be more willing to listen and less likely to argue and put you down. They need to be listened to just as much as you do. In fact, the reason most people get so dogmatic and unreasonable is because they feel frustrated. And why do they feel frustrated? Because they think— quite rightly—that nobody's really listening or caring about what they're trying to say.

We will get to your side of things shortly. I do want you to be a winner. But sometimes you have to lose in order to win. You have to give in order to get. If you want respect, you have to give respect first. If you want to be listened to, then listen to the other person first. When you surrender, you will suddenly achieve victory. This is a paradox, but it's a practical, powerful reality.

Epictetus stated this idea nearly 2,000 years ago when he wrote, "If someone criticizes you, agree with them at once. Tell them that if only they knew you well, they would not bother to criticize only that!"

Most people are so preoccupied with standing up for their own ideas that they have trouble grasping the disarming technique. I am treating a businessman from Dallas named Al who is so brilliant that he memorizes every therapy session and then sends a perfectly typed memo the next day, summarizing everything that was said. In addition, he enters this information into a computer so he can cross-reference everything he learns. If he calls and talks to my secretary to change an appointment, I receive a memo the next day that contains a verbatim transcript of the conversation.

Al does a lot of legal work and loves to fight in court. He's extremely competitive and takes great pride in his ability to poke holes in the testimony of his opponents. He's a kind of white-collar cowboy and prides himself on being the fastest gun in town. So why is he in therapy? Al feels lonely and at odds with his wife, and he's concerned that he can't get close to people. His great logical mind is a two-edged sword: he is a success in business, but he is so aggressive that he sometimes drives people away.

His wife, Claire, is often quite timid. She feels angry and intimidated by Al, and she's terribly afraid to express herself. Recently they had their second therapy session as a couple. I told Claire to express her feelings and instructed Al to disarm her:

CLAIRE: You're a totally controlling person. You try to control who I meet, where I go, and what I do.

AL: That just isn't right at all. I don't try to control you in any way! There was a time when I did, but I don't do that anymore and I haven't in a while.

CLAIRE: Yes you do!

At this point I interrupted them because they were off to the races. Instead of disarming Claire by finding truth in her comment, Al couldn't resist the urge to argue that she was "wrong." Of course, by insisting Claire was wrong, he proved that she was right, because his argumentative response was very controlling. Al is putting a wall up and saying, "I don't want to pursue this topic."

If you were Al, how would you have disarmed Claire?

_____

_____

_____

_____

Answer: He could have said, "You're right. I *am* very controlling and I can see that this has really hurt you and angered you." This response would make Claire feel less angry because she would feel listened to. In addition, by agreeing that he was overly controlling, Al would show that he wasn't as controlling as she thought. Do you see this?

There's one caveat. When you disarm someone and you agree with their criticism, it will be effective only if you maintain a sense of self-esteem. For example, suppose you tell me, "You're a jerk." If I feel threatened by the criticism, I might answer you in a defensive or sarcastic way by saying, "Oh, sure. I'm a jerk! Look who's talking!" This hostile response will instantly make things deteriorate. Alternatively, if I feel depressed and believe that I am a worthless loser, I may sigh and sadly say, "Yes, I really am a worthless jerk." This comment probably won't gain many friends either! But if, with a twinkle in my eye, I say, "Yes, I've suspected that about myself for some time now," you will probably feel less irate. My sense of humor and lack of defensiveness may win you over and transform a potential battle into a friendly and productive discussion of the real problem. I have projected the message "I'm not afraid of criticism and I'm willing to listen to what you have to say." This attitude is likely to melt the hostility and win the day.

Let's practice the disarming technique again. Suppose I say, "You'll never understand these methods. You're such a stupid reader—I can't believe it!" How could you respond, using only the disarming technique?

_____

_____

_____

_____

_____

You could say, "As a matter of fact, I don't understand these methods as well as I'd like. I'm sure there are many readers who are much smarter than I am." Of course, you would also want to express your feelings and learn more about mine. You could add, "I feel really put down and I don't like being talked to like that. It sounds like you're frustrated with me. Are you?" This statement illustrates the next skill.

Listening Skill #2: Empathy

Empathy means that you try to put yourself in the other person's shoes and understand what they are thinking (called "thought empathy") and feeling (called "feeling empathy"). Thought and feeling empathy are crucial to practically any conversation.

Thought empathy. Repeat out loud what the other person is saying so they will know you got the point. You can ask a question to see if you got it right. Let's assume your lover has been acting distant and he says, "I feel our relationship has no real future. There's too much of an age difference." Reflect it back to him in a quiet manner. "No real future? Apparently you feel the age gap is too great. Can you tell me more about how you feel about this?" Don't say this sarcastically or defensively. Try to convey a spirit of genuine curiosity. Your goal is to understand where he's coming from and not to argue or state your own point of view. Instead, you mirror what he is saying in a nonjudgmental way so as to grasp the essence of what he is feeling.

This strategy will enable you to develop a much sharper understanding of his mind-set. Try to grasp the meaning behind the words.

Feeling empathy. Once you have paraphrased what the other person said, acknowledge the feelings he or she might have and ask a question to see if you are reading his or her emotions correctly. Suppose your husband suddenly jumps on you by saying: "Why don't you ever listen? Trying to talk to you is like beating my head against a brick wall!" Using feeling empathy, you could respond: "It sounds like I've been closed-minded and stubborn. I can imagine that you might be feeling fed up and frustrated with me. Do you feel that way?" As he begins to ventilate about how he feels, accept his feelings instead of reacting in a critical or hostile way (the aggressive response) or withdrawing and playing the role of wounded victim (the passive response). If he says, "Damn right I'm upset!" you can then say, "I'm glad you told me that, even though this is upsetting to me. I get pretty frustrated when people don't listen to me, so I can understand how you're feeling." This response involves resisting your all-too-human urge to lash out and fight back. You'll probably be feeling just as hurt and angry as he is, and you'll understandably want to prove that he's wrong. Don't.

Let's practice thought and feeling empathy. Remember that you don't have to agree or disagree with the other person. Instead, you repeat what they said and acknowledge how they might be feeling. It may help if you begin with one of these expressions in a gentle tone of voice:

- "What you seem to be saying is . . ."
- "It sounds like . . ."
- "I take it that you think . . ."
- "Let me see if I'm getting this right."
- "I just want to make sure that I understand what you're saying."

Then you can paraphrase what they said and ask a question to see if you grasped their meaning.

I urged Claire to tell Al just how angry she was. I told her to let him have it. She hesitated, but after some cajoling on my part, she said, "Okay. Al, here's my fantasy about you. I often imagine that I'm in a room with ten strong men and you're tied to a chair. I remind you of one of the times you've hurt me, and one of the men comes and smashes you in the face. You mutter, 'I'm sorry, I'm sorry, I'm sorry!' Then I tell you about another time when you humiliated me, as the second man comes up and lets you have it, and you apologize again. We do this again and again." If you were Al, how could you respond using thought empathy and feeling empathy? Put your response here:

_____

_____

_____

_____

Answer: Al could say, "It sounds like there have been many times that I've hurt you and you want to even the score and get back at me [thought empathy]. You must be awfully furious with me [feeling empathy]. It also sounds like you're afraid to tell me how you feel unless I'm tied down and you have ten strong men to protect you when you tell me how upset you feel [feeling empathy]. Perhaps you want me to feel remorse and to apologize for how badly I've treated you."

During a recent session with a separated couple, the woman mentioned some bills that her husband hadn't paid. He became enraged and said, "You're trying to provoke me and get sympathy from Dr. Burns. You're trying to make it look like it's my fault! I won't stand for this bull!" How could she respond, using thought empathy and feeling empathy? Put your ideas here:

_____

_____

_____

_____

Answer: She could say, "It sounds like you're really upset with me for bringing that up [feeling empathy]. You say I'm trying to provoke you and blame you and get Dr. Burns to side with me [thought empathy]. That would make me angry, too [feeling empathy]. It's no fun to be blamed or ganged up on [feeling empathy]."

Let's try it again. Suppose I tell you, "I'm ticked off. You're reading my *Handbook* but you're not filling in the blanks and doing the exercises. Are you looking for magic? How do you expect me to help you? You can't change without doing the written exercises. It just won't work!" How could you respond, using thought empathy and feeling empathy? Put your ideas here:

_____

_____

_____

_____

Answer: You could say, "Dr. Burns, you say that it's important to do the written exercises [thought empathy]. It sounds like you're frustrated because I haven't been doing them [feeling empathy]. You believe that if I really want to change, I'll have to do them [thought empathy]."

At first you may find that you cannot grasp these communication methods very well. Like many of my patients, you may argue when you think you're disarming, and you may preach and attack when you think you're empathizing with the other person. If you really want to change, you'll have to work at it persistently for many weeks. If you do, things will begin to fall into place. And then, Eureka! You'll have the ability to use some incredibly powerful tools that can transform the way you relate to others.

Now suppose you're thinking, "That's a lot of hype. And besides, this is much too complicated and manipulative. I could never keep all this stuff straight and I don't think I'd even want to." How could I respond, using thought empathy and feeling empathy?

_____

_____

_____

_____

Answer: I could say, "You're absolutely right [disarming]. I'm probably bragging too much about how wonderful these methods are, and they don't sound realistic or genuine to you [thought empathy]. You seem a little put off [feeling empathy]. You feel there's too much to learn and it's all a little overwhelming [feeling empathy]. In addition it sounds like you think I'm sounding phony and manipulative, and that turns you off [thought and feeling empathy]."

Many people do feel a little intimidated by these methods at first. They may seem artificial and confusing, and they will go against the grain. During a marital spat, you will tell yourself, "I don't want to agree with the S.O.B.! After all, he's wrong and I'm right!" These and many similar thoughts will get in the way. But if you persist and practice every day, it will start to come together.

Good communication can be extremely powerful. Like any source of power, these methods can be used for good or evil purposes. If your goal is to manipulate others and to "win," then these techniques will not enhance genuine intimacy. However, if your goal is to feel closer to others, then you don't need to fear any awkwardness you may feel when you first try these techniques, because your positive intentions will be obvious.

Remember that we're focusing on single methods which are likely to sound artificial if you say nothing else. If your spouse calls you a jerk, you might respond, "You say that I'm a jerk." This is a technically correct example of thought empathy, but you sound more like a parrot than a real human being. Your spouse will probably feel infuriated because you're not being genuine or real. You can avoid this problem if you express your feelings with "I feel" statements. An "I feel" statement is a simple statement of how you feel. We'll talk more about this later, but I'll give you an example now. You could tell your spouse, "You say I'm a jerk, and you're probably pretty annoyed with me [thought empathy, feeling empathy]. This bothers me. I feel put down ['I feel' statement]. Maybe I have been acting like a jerk [disarming technique]. Can you tell me what I did that turned you off?" This last response also illustrates the next skill.

Listening Skill #3: Inquiry

Inquiry is the use of gentle, probing questions to learn more about what the other person is thinking and feeling. You can ask them to tell you more about their negative feelings, since that's what most people are afraid to talk about. You can also encourage them to tell you more about what you've done or said that turned them off or hurt their feelings.

It's very hard for most people to express angry feelings. They don't want to admit that they feel hurt. That's why the inquiry technique is so important. You give the other person a direct, explicit invitation to criticize you and to tell you how annoyed they feel.

If you use the inquiry technique and get the other person to lay the cards on the table, you can deal with the problem and you'll know where you stand. To give a simple example, if I sense that a patient is uncomfortable with me or with their progress in therapy and I don't encourage them to talk it over, there's a good chance they'll express their dissatisfaction indirectly. They may be argumentative and "forget" to do their self-help assignments between sessions. They may not show up for their next session and drop out of therapy prematurely. They may not pay a bill. I end up feeling frustrated and shot down. On the other hand, if I use the inquiry technique and ask them if they feel turned off, it nearly always leads to an honest exchange of feelings that makes the therapy far more satisfying and useful. The same principle holds for any relationship, whether it's with your spouse, your child, your boss, your customer, or your best friend.

Most of my patients are afraid to use the inquiry technique. They don't want to open Pandora's box and let all the nasty monsters out. They like to avoid anger and conflict. They are often afraid of being criticized. They may argue that "nice" people don't fight or get mad at each other. Do you ever feel like that? Are you afraid of hearing angry criticism from someone you care about?

I know I used to be like that. So was a patient of mine named Sarah. Sarah is separated from her husband, David. David has a great deal of pent-up anger toward her, so I urged Sarah to ask him to tell her about his angry feelings whenever he was acting nasty. But Sarah didn't want to hear about how furious David was. She told me that what he was saying wasn't right; she told me that David was to blame; she told me that it wasn't fair for David to be so mean and angry with her; she told me that it was too upsetting to hear all those awful things.

Sometimes she got defensive and argued with David when he seemed annoyed. That shut him up. Sometimes she would apologize and promise to be a better wife in the future if only he would come back to her. She would tell David what a wonderful relationship they could have if he would just forget about the past. That shut him up. She also learned to change the subject when David appeared angry. That also shut him up.

David got more and more icy and distant. He called less and less frequently. He began to speak more often about divorce. Sarah complained that the therapy wasn't helping.

One Sunday, out of desperation, Sarah decided to ask David about all his negative feelings. She agreed to listen to what he had to say. She used the disarming technique to find some truth in his criticisms. She used the inquiry technique and asked him to tell her about his dissatifactions with their marriage. She used thought and feeling empathy to try to see the world through his eyes and understand how he was feeling. At last David opened up. It wasn't pleasant. He began to rip into her. She disarmed him and asked for more criticisms. He ventilated more. This went on and on. It was rather traumatic. He raged at Sarah and finally stormed out of her apartment. Sarah went to bed discouraged and tearful and alone. She was convinced of what she'd been telling me all along—the stupid communication techniques had only made things worse.

When I saw Sarah two days later, she was elated. On Monday David had called her. He was affectionate and said that she seemed changed. After he left the apartment he began to realize that a lot of what he'd said wasn't entirely fair. He said he had also contributed to their problems and he thought he was beginning to fall in love with her again!

Although the effects of the three listening skills are not always so magical, they often are. A similar thing happens to me frequently in psychotherapy sessions. At the beginning and the end of every session I say, "Please tell me what you liked and disliked about our last session [or the session we had today]. Let's start with the negative things. Was there anything I said that hurt your feelings or turned you off?" Then, regardless of what the patients tell me, I look for the truth in their criticisms.

Let's assume the patient says, "You laughed and made fun of me." Now I might feel that I had been laughing at myself, but that's irrelevant because the patient felt laughed at and is hurt. If I defend myself, it will only alienate the patient. I might say, "I'm glad you said that. I feel bad that it hurt your feelings when I made a joke [feeling empathy]. I would feel angry if I felt someone was laughing at me [feeling empathy]. Do you feel that way [inquiry]? It's not my intention to make fun of you. You deserve my support and my respect [disarming]."

The purpose of a response like this is to make it safe for patients to express their feelings. If they're afraid to tell me when they're angry, my efforts will be sabotaged. If they tell me when they feel turned off and I respond with respect, feelings of trust and rapport will nearly always develop.

You're probably not a therapist and you may be wondering, "What does all this have to do with me?" Answer: Everything! I don't care if you're talking to your spouse, your son, your boss, or your customer. Everyone gets hurt and angry from time to time. Most people won't tell you—they feel too inhibited. If you make it your responsibility to encourage people to open up, you can deal with these negative feelings and they won't rob you of joy, intimacy, and success.

When you use inquiry, your tone of voice will be crucial. If you ask a question sarcastically or defensively, the method won't work. To state an extreme example, if someone accuses you of being selfish, you could get sarcastic and say, "Oh, I'm being selfish, am I?" This sounds like a question, but it's not. It's a rhetorical question. It's a thinly disguised put-down. What you're really saying is, "How dare you say such an insulting, unkind thing to a wonderful and innocent person like me!" Don't be surprised if the other person doesn't respond in the kindly, agreeable way you were hoping! A more valid use of inquiry would be: "Can you tell me what I've done or said that seemed selfish?" If you say this in a spirit of genuine curiosity, it will prompt the other person to open up in a more direct way.

Inquiry is not only used to learn more about how the other person is thinking and feeling, it can help transform vague negative reactions into concrete problems that you can deal with in a more productive manner. Suppose you are trying to get a promotion and your supervisor tells you he has some doubts because of your lack of experience. Don't succumb and feel defeated for the next six months.

Instead, use the inquiry technique: "Just what kind of experience do you feel I lack?" When your boss describes the qualities or experience you lack, respond with empathy and use the disarming technique: agree with your boss and show you understand his or her point of view. Make a plan to get that experience. Learning precisely what your boss is looking for will help you improve your marketability and will demonstrate your ability to listen and learn. Your boss will respect you more and will be more likely to help you. He or she might eventually give you the promotion you want or suggest another interesting option you hadn't considered.

Let's practice the inquiry technique. The man you've been dating says, "I need more space. I need my freedom." How could you respond?

_____

_____

_____

Answer: You need to focus on his feelings. What's he really saying? What's the message behind the words? You could say: "You say you need more space, more freedom [thought empathy]. It sounds like you feel trapped and dissatisfied with our relationship [feeling empathy]. Maybe you want to date other people [feeling empathy]. Can you tell me what some of the problems in our relationship are [inquiry]? I'd like to know what you like and don't like about it [inquiry]."

Your spouse says, "You're always leaving your socks around the house." How can you respond?

_____

_____

_____

Answer: "It's true. I have [disarming]. Are there other things I've been doing that you feel annoyed about [inquiry]?" Notice that you're not defending yourself or apologizing and promising to do better. Maybe you *should* try to be more consistent about throwing your dirty socks in the clothes bin. However, it would be unwise to focus prematurely on the solution to the problem because then the exchange of feelings will be cut short. Your spouse needs to talk about how he or she feels. Your spouse probably has *ten* complaints, but underneath all of them there's only one: "I feel hurt and angry because I feel unloved." It isn't terribly important if you think that some of these complaints are unreasonable. What is important is that you give your spouse a chance to tell you how he or she feels. Show that you're willing to listen and want to understand. Encourage your spouse to talk about the angry feelings. Respond with openness and show that you care. Then you've hit the jackpot. This is infinitely more important than picking up a pair of socks. This is the real secret of intimacy.

The three listening skills—disarming, empathy, and inquiry— capture the essence of effective listening. These skills are frequently overlooked, even by professionals whose very work demands expert communication. In a recent study at Presbyterian Medical Center in Denver, more than 300 clinical interviews by physicians were observed and evaluated. The investigators commented: "To our surprise all did not seem as it should be. Physicians at all levels [of training] who had previously been thought quite competent appeared defective in their interaction with patients. Our initial reaction was to distrust our observations, but repeated observations have shown great consistency." One of the problems: Doctors did not listen carefully to patients.

Sensitive listening skills are rare. Responding with empathy is especially difficult when you feel frustrated and upset, and when you feel you are being criticized or not listened to. But this is when you need listening skills the most, because your attempts to defend yourself and get your point across will just infuriate the other person. They have their heels dug in, and the more intently you try to contradict them, the more stubbornly they will insist that you are "wrong."

If you don't want to be involved in an exasperating no-win war of wills, find truth in what the other person is saying. You can often put the lie to their criticism without ever putting up a single argument in your own defense. It sounds like a paradox, and I call it the "Persuasive Law of Opposites": Agree with your critic, and you will disprove what he or she is saying about you. Try to disagree with your critic, and you will increase his or her conviction that the accusations are absolutely valid.

This startling phenomenon is illustrated on page 396. As you can see, when you respond to a harsh attack with a combination of empathy, disarming, and inquiry (the "persuasive answer"), the critic will soften and will revise his or her entrenched ideas about you. In contrast, if you become defensive or insist on contradicting the critic (the "defensive answer"), this will be about as helpful as throwing gasoline on a fire. He or she will feel certain that every accusation is true.

Persuasion through effective listening captures a form of verbal power that might be viewed as Eastern. I like to think of the method as "zeroing in," because you allow yourself temporarily to become a zero. Instead of being preoccupied with promoting your own ideas and forcing the other person to listen to your feelings, you *zero* in on the other person's thoughts and feelings. The moment you give up your urge to control or to convince the other person you are right, you will paradoxically gain enormous influence.

Let's assume you have listened and are ready to express your own point of view. How do you proceed? You can use two self-expression skills, "I feel" statements and stroking.

Self-Expression Skills #1: "I feel" Statements

Instead of arguing or getting defensive, you can express your feelings with "I feel" statements. The method is incredibly simple. All you do is say "I feel" and add a word that describes how you feel. You can use a word like annoyed, hurt, worried, frustrated, concerned, or sad. For example you can say, "I feel nervous" or "I feel angry."

There are several types of feelings that you can express with "I feel" statements:

1. **Negative feelings.** Examples include "I feel angry," "I feel criticized," "I feel put down," "I feel frustrated," "I feel coerced," "I feel misunderstood."

2. **Vulnerable feelings.** "I feel sad," "I feel rejected," "I feel hurt," "I feel unloved," "I feel disappointed," "I feel ignored," "I feel intimidated," "I feel attacked," or "I feel inadequate."

THE PERSUASIVE LAW OF OPPOSITES

If you agree with an angry critic by finding a grain of truth in what is said, you will paradoxically put the lie to the criticism. This is illustrated as the "Persuasive Answer." In contrast, if you defend yourself or disagree with the criticism, you will frequently make the critic more upset and convinced about his or her accusations. This is illustrated as the "Defensive Answer."

EXAMPLE #1

Your partner attacks you by saying:	"You obviously don't care about anyone but yourself."
Persuasive answer:	"What you're saying upsets me ['I feel' statement]. I guess I've given you the impression I don't care about you {thought empathy]. You certainly don't deserve to be treated like that [disarming]. I don't like to be ignored either, and I can understand that you might feel pretty irritated with me [feeling empathy]. Do you [inquiry]?"
Why you disprove the criticism:	You have demonstrated a genuine concern for the other person and expressed a regard for his or her feelings. You have avoided defending yourself in a self-centered manner. This demonstrates that you *do* care about him or her. Hence, the accusation is invalidated. By agreeing with the criticism, you have disproved it!
Defensive answer:	"That's a lie. I *do* care about you and when I don't give in, you whine and accuse me of not loving you. You're the one who's selfish!"
Why you confirm the criticism:	You sound angry and blaming. Your message doesn't convey the love and warmth you claim to feel, so the response sounds phony. Your partner will see you as cold, critical, and defensive and will feel justifiably convinced that you don't care about anybody but

	yourself. Your attempt to contradict the accusations will backfire. By contradicting the criticism, you have proven that it's valid!
EXAMPLE #2	
Your partner attacks you by saying:	"It's all your fault. I'm right and you're wrong. Why don't you just admit it, and stop being so stubborn?"
Persuasive answer:	"I probably have been acting stubborn [disarming]. You say things are my fault, and I'm willing to accept my share of the blame [thought empathy, disarming]. There is truth in what you're saying, and I want to understand your point of view a little better [disarming, inquiry]. I'm frustrated too, because I'm not getting my ideas across ['I feel' statement]. I want you to try to understand how I feel ['I feel' statement, feeling empathy]."
Why you disprove the criticism:	Because you are assuming some responsibility for the problem, you are rising above your partner's childish blame-casting. By showing your flexibility and willingness to listen, you have proven that you're not as "stubborn" or as "wrong" as your partner claims.
Defensive answer:	"You can blame me until kingdom comes, but you'll just be proving how childish you are. It's sheer stupidity to insist you're entirely right and I'm entirely wrong. The fact is, you're just as much to blame. Why don't you just admit it!"
Why you confirm the criticism:	Because you are contradicting your partner in an argumentative way, he or she will feel even more convinced that you are stubborn and inflexible. Your partner will feel attacked and will counterattack. The war of words will continue.

3. **Wishes and desires.** "I would like to spend more time with you," "I want us to work out this problem and feel close to each other," "I really want you to be on time," or "I would like you to try to understand my point of view."

"I feel" statements are in sharp contrast to "you" statements, like "*You're* making me mad" or "*You've* got no right to say that" or "*You're* wrong about that." These "you" statements sound critical, blaming and judgmental. They will always trigger a fight or an argument.

The three listening skills will help you deal with someone else's negative feelings. The self-expression skills will help you express your own. People have the greatest trouble expressing anger. We learn to attack when we're angry or we act our feelings out instead of stating them openly. We fear sharing our angry feelings because this makes us vulnerable. It's far easier to say, "Screw you!" and to reject someone rather than to tell them, "I feel annoyed about this. Let's talk it out."

"I feel" statements are crucial when you find yourself getting defensive or argumentative. I've observed hundreds and hundreds of times that when people are angry they start arguing instead of saying how they feel. They defend what they believe to be the "truth." You will tell yourself, "I'm right about this." You will argue and try to convince the other person that they are "wrong." But they are just as certain that they are right, so you will get locked into an argument. And no one will ever win!

The solution to this is simple. What you call the "truth" is, in reality, a disguised form of anger! Let me repeat that: TRUTH is just a form of hostility! And if you don't mind being shocked, then I'll tell you this: Your TRUTH is your ENEMY! Don't ever defend the "truth" again! Instead, simply say, "I feel angry" or "I feel frustrated right now." These statements will be a whole lot more honest and a whole lot more effective than arguing about the TRUTH!

Now, let's see if you can get the hang of it. Let's assume a family member says, "You're wrong about this. You're such a stupid jerk!" How would you respond, using "I feel" statements? Put your ideas here:

Answer: You could say, "I'm feeling attacked and put down. I feel defensive and hurt." This is infinitely better than, "Oh no I'm not! *You're* the one who's wrong about this! You're a jerk if I *ever* saw one!" This will just lead to an argument. Can you see this?

Suppose a friend says, "I'm ticked off at you." You feel annoyed because you feel they're blaming you for something that was primarily their fault. How would you respond, using "I feel" statements?

_____

_____

_____

_____

Answer: You can say, "I feel angry, too." This is infinitely preferable to getting defensive and criticizing them. The idea is to *share* your feelings rather than to *attack* with your feelings. The "I feel" statements simply provide information about how you feel. You tell them how you feel instead of arguing about who's right and who's wrong.

You're an attractive college student talking to your professor about your paper. He's an inspiring teacher, but he has a lecherous reputation. He says, "I think there's a special chemistry between us." You feel confused, embarrassed, upset. What can you say, using "I feel" statements?

_____

_____

_____

_____

Answer: You could say, "I'm feeling really pressured and uncomfortable right now. I came to get some help with the paper."

Although these ideas may sound quite straightforward, most people have an intense fear of expressing their feelings directly and openly. When they feel upset or annoyed, they deny their feelings and act them out instead. A patient became annoyed with me during a conference with several staff therapists who were all involved in her treatment. She felt I was discussing problems that were quite personal and she didn't feel ready to talk about them in the group setting. Her concerns were valid, but instead of saying "I'm not comfortable with this and would prefer to work on other problems," she suddenly stood up, complained of a headache, and stormed out of the room.

Although she felt and acted helpless, this was in reality a powerful maneuver that stunned everyone in the room. She projected the message "Don't mess with me or I'll make you pay!" Later on she denied that she was angry and claimed to be unaware that her actions might have been upsetting to others! This "passive-aggressive" behavior seems obvious when you see it in others, but it's all too easy to get sucked into it when you feel hurt, because you don't want to admit how you feel. You may pout, slam doors, play the role of the martyr, or gossip about people behind their backs instead of telling them how you feel face to face. You may express your feelings in a disguised form—being critical, or getting sarcastic and defensive and argumentative. You may express your feelings with judgmental body language like frowning, crossing your arms in front of you, or shaking your head to signal "no" while the other person is trying to talk.

The problem with this behavior is that although you let people know that *something* is going on that you don't like, you're not really clear about what it is. If you openly and honestly share how you're feeling, you and the other person will have the opportunity to deal with what's bothering you.

Self-Expression Skill #2: Stroking

More than anything else, people want to be cared about and appreciated. What we fear the most is being rejected or put down or judged. Therefore I always try to express a positive regard for the other person, even in the heat of battle. I try to let them know that I respect them and that they're important to me. This can relieve unspoken fears that someone is going to get rejected.

Many people have the hidden assumption that anger and caring are opposites. You may jump to the conclusion that if two people are mad at each other, it means they don't respect each other or care for each other. This makes you overreact, and any difference of opinion becomes a federal case. You may feel the need to reject the other person before you get rejected, so you can save face. You can often prevent this if you let them know that although you're at odds, you still think highly of them. This will make it easier for them to open up and to listen, because they will feel less threatened.

If a patient is angry with me and I also feel annoyed, I might say, "It seems that we're both frustrated with each other. I believe we can talk this out, even though it's uncomfortable to feel angry and to be criticized. I'm convinced that in the long run, this will make our work together more rewarding." The purpose of this message is to acknowledge honestly that we both feel angry and to let them know that I think it's okay to feel this way. I want it to be crystal clear that my agenda is to make things better and not to reject them.

You can express this same message in slightly different language to your spouse or to a friend or to someone you're doing business with. You might tell your spouse, "I'm mad as hell, but I do care about you." If you're having an argument with a close associate at work, you could say, "We have a strong difference of opinion about this, and I'm not at all comfortable with your point of view. However, I know we'll work this problem out, and I want you to know that I respect you and like working with you." The purpose of this is to keep the machine well oiled so it doesn't overheat and blow up. Most of us can tolerate considerable frustration if we feel cared about. It's easy to get that message across if you're willing to.

The philosophy behind stroking is that you can still respect someone even when you feel furious with something they did or said. This is similar to the philosophy of unconditional self-esteem that's behind so much of cognitive therapy. You can dislike what a person is *doing,* you can disagree with what they're *thinking,* and you can be uncomfortable with what they're *feeling.* But you won't gain anything if you judge or condemn them *as a person.* Remember that they are a collection of strengths and weaknesses, just as you are. If you maintain an attitude of respect or liking, the other person will sense this and will be far easier to deal with.

You may be thinking, "But what if that person really *is* a bum and I don't like them and I don't even want to have anything to do with them?" There will be many times when you will choose not to have anything to do with someone. They may be too exploitative, too self-centered, or too insensitive to be worth the effort. The costs of maintaining the relationship will simply outweigh the benefits. The only question is how to part ways with them. When you express your negative feelings, it may be a good idea to say something positive about them as well. If you allow them to salvage some self-esteem, they'll be less likely to get defensive and more likely to hear at least some of what you have to say. Your message will be more realistic and have a more powerful impact.

Communication Exercise #1

Now let's see if you can integrate good listening skills with good self-expression skills. A man named Harry runs a dry cleaning establishment. He has a tendency to feel irritable and harassed by customers. Last Saturday, several people complained about spots on their slacks. By the time the third customer complained, Harry felt he'd had it. A lot of four-letter words were flying through his mind as he explained in an icy tone of voice that *some* spots *cannot* be removed and that they simply become more obvious when the garment is *properly* dry cleaned. Would you call that an example of good communication or bad communication?

———— good communication

———— bad communication

Why?_____

_____

_____

_____

_____

I would say it's bad communication, because Harry's defending himself and alienating the customers. They will feel put down and take their business elsewhere. Then Harry will get even more irate as his business dwindles. He'll complain about how unreasonable and ungrateful people are. He sees himself as a victim, and this mind-set operates as a self-fulfilling prophecy.

Although your life is probably very different from Harry's, there may be times when people complain when you feel you've done a good job. If you were Harry, how could you respond to the complaining customer, using the techniques you've been learning?

_____

_____

_____

_____

_____

Answer: You could say, "I'm disappointed that the slacks aren't satisfactory to you ['I feel' statement]. I know how frustrating it can be to have a bad spot like that on a nice pair of trousers [feeling empathy]. Your business is important to me and I want you to be pleased [stroking]. Sometimes a spot like that will show up more when a garment is cleaned, and it may not be possible to remove it without ruining the slacks ['I feel' statement]. What would you like me to do [inquiry]? I don't want you to leave here feeling annoyed or thinking you're not getting the very best service [thought and feeling empathy]." The purpose of this statement is to create an attitude of friendliness and cooperation. Harry might offer to clean another pair of slacks free as a gesture of goodwill, even though he's not at fault. Over the years, he'll make the money back a hundredfold if he has a happy customer. If he empathizes and shows some genuine concern for the customer's frustration, the customer will probably accept Harry's explanation and not demand any compensation at all.

Some readers may raise the question: "But what if the customer is totally unreasonable and insists that Harry ruined the slacks? What if the customer demands $100 for a new pair?" I'm curious about your answer to this question. If you were Harry, what would you say, using the listening skills and self-expression skills?

_____

_____

_____

_____

Answer: Harry could say, "I know how annoying it is not to be able to wear a fine pair of slacks because of a stain [feeling empathy]. It sounds like you're pretty angry, and I would be, too [feeling empathy]. I'm not comfortable paying for the slacks, because they were cleaned properly ['I feel' statement]. If we ruin a garment because of negligence, we do pay for it, because that's only fair [disarming]. I value you and don't want to lose you as a customer [stroking]. Is there any other way I could compensate you as a token of my goodwill [inquiry]? I'd be happy not to charge for this bill, since the slacks are no good to you, and I'd also be willing to give you a credit for another cleaning."

Communication Exercise #2

A teenage girl named Linda was shopping with her boyfriend, Ray, in a record store. Linda told him she was going next door to use the ladies' room at a fast-food restaurant. As she left she said, "I'll meet you at the car in five minutes." Ray misunderstood and thought Linda said "I'll meet you here."

On the way out of the restaurant, Linda bought Ray a milkshake. She waited for him at the car in the hot sun. After five minutes she got furious, dumped the melting milkshake on the ground, and stormed into the store. Linda glared at Ray. He said, "What's wrong?" She refused to talk and pouted. Ray became upset and pleaded for her to tell him what was wrong. She still refused to talk. They left the store and went for a drive. Linda ignored him and he begged her to talk to him.

You can see that her passive-aggressive reaction has many payoffs.

Linda's pride was hurt and she can make Ray pay! In addition, she gets loads of attention from him! She gets to take out her frustration on him by glaring while he says all the right things, such as "I love you! I want to talk to you!" This makes Linda feel enormously powerful and important.

Why shouldn't she behave like this if it's so rewarding? One danger is that she may get into this pattern with friends who may not be so willing to put up with her. As her relationship with Ray progresses, he too may begin to get sick of her, once he realizes he's being manipulated and is jumping through a hoop like a trained dog. Finally, Linda's selfish, self-righteous behavior is not consistent with her value system, with her personal happiness, or with real sharing and intimacy.

How could she have expressed her feelings, using "I feel" statements, when she went into the store?

_____

_____

_____

_____

Answer: She could have said: "I'm feeling ignored and annoyed. I said I was going to wait at the car and I thought you'd be right out. I bought you a milkshake. I've been waiting out there in the sun and the milkshake has almost melted."

How could Ray have expressed his feelings, using "I feel" statements, when she was pouting at him and glaring and refusing to talk?

_____

_____

_____

_____

Answer: He could say, "You seem real upset with me, and I don't know what you're upset about [feeling empathy, inquiry]. It bothers me when you glare at me and refuse to talk ['I feel' statement]. I feel punished ['I feel' statement]. I don't like it ['I feel' statement]. If I did something to make you mad, I want you to tell me what it was so we can clear it up [inquiry]."

Sometimes when people pout, they don't want to talk. They want to be left alone for a few minutes. How could Linda express this, using "I feel" statements?

Answer: She could say, "I'm upset and I don't want to talk right now. I need to be left alone for a few minutes. Then it will be easier for me to talk about it."

Summary of Communication Skills

LISTENING SKILL #1: THE DISARMING TECHNIQUE

1. Find some truth in what the other person says. They have to be right to some extent, since no one is ever 100 percent wrong. Usually, when you agree with the other person they will then stop arguing and agree with you! This remarkable phenomenon is called the "Law of Opposites."

2. If you feel angry or attacked, express your feelings with nonchallenging "I feel" statements, such as "I feel upset that . . ." Avoid the temptation to argue or strike back. Don't get defensive.

3. Answer in such a way that your dignity and self-esteem are maintained, even if you agree with the other person's criticism.

4. Give up your desire to lash out or blame the other person. Try to maintain an attitude of mutual respect so that nobody has to lose face or feel put down.

5. Avoid getting into who is "right" or "wrong." This serves no purpose!

LISTENING SKILL #2: EMPATHY

1. Put yourself in the other person's shoes. Listen carefully and try to understand accurately what they are thinking as they are talking. State what you think the other person is thinking by saying something like "It sounds like . . ." and then paraphrase respectfully what you understood them to say.

2. Also try to understand what the other person is feeling. Listen with your "third ear." Notice their body language. Do they appear tense? Angry? Hurt? Acknowledge what the person is feeling, based on what they said and the manner in which they said it.

3. Ask a question to confirm how they are feeling, such as "I can imagine you must be feeling frustrated with me. Is this true?" Ask them if you have accurately understood what they are thinking and feeling.

4. Use an "I feel" statement to let them know how you would feel if you were in their shoes. You might say, "I would be feeling the same way if this had happened to me."

5. Accept the other person's feelings. Do not be hostile, critical, or defensive. Let them know that you are willing to hear what they have to say.

LISTENING SKILL #3: INQUIRY

1. Most people have an intense fear of expressing their feelings openly. They are always afraid of conflict and will avoid telling you they're angry with you. They deny their feelings, and then act them out. You can prevent this if you ask the other person to tell you more about their negative feelings.

2. You can also ask the other person to tell you more about the specific problem that makes them feel upset. What are the

details? How often does it happen? How do they feel about it? What did you do that turned them off?

3. Ask the person to tell you directly what you did or said that hurt their feelings. When they tell you, don't get defensive. Instead, use empathy and the disarming technique. Find some truth in what they have to say. If you feel upset or irritated or put down, express your feelings with an "I feel" statement.

4. Use a tone of voice that is respectful, not challenging, when asking what made them unhappy or angry. Do not use any form of sarcasm.

5. Don't be afraid of anger and conflict. They are healthy. Don't let the other person's unhappy feelings go unexpressed. That makes the feelings much more intense.

SELF-EXPRESSION SKILL #1: "I FEEL" STATEMENTS

1. When expressing your feelings, use "I feel" statements, such as "I feel upset." Avoid "you" statements, such as "You're making me upset." These "you" statements sound critical and judgmental and always trigger fights and arguments! Here are some examples:

"You always" or "You never . . ."
"You are wrong."
"You shouldn't . . ."
"You've got no right."
"It's your fault."
"You're making me angry."

2. Don't act out your feelings! State them! Use "I feel" statements. Acting out emotions can take the form of:

Pouting	Being sarcastic
Stony silence	Being critical
Gossiping	Being argumentative
Door slamming	Frowning
Martyr playing	Being rude
Drinking too much	Negative body language

3. Negative feelings can be expressed by saying, "I feel . . ." with words like:

concerned	pressured
frustrated	misunderstood
angry	uncomfortable
coerced	

4. Vulnerable feelings can be expressed by saying, "I feel . . ." with words like:

sad	nervous
rejected	ignored
hurt	inadequate
unloved	intimidated
disappointed	

5. Wishes and desires can be expressed by saying something like:

"I would like to spend more time with you."
"I really want us to work out this problem and to be closer."
"I really want to feel close to you."
"I want you to try to understand my point of view."

SELF-EXPRESSION SKILL #2: STROKING

1. Generally speaking, most people want to feel cared about and appreciated. The greatest fear that people have is being put down, rejected, or judged.

2. Reassure the other person by clearly letting them know that you respect them and that they are important to you, even if you are angry or disagreeing with them at the moment.

3. Let the other person know that you want to work out the problem in a mutually satisfactory way.

4. Don't criticize or condemn them as a person. Nothing is ever gained by doing this. Attacking them personally is very different from commenting negatively on something they are doing or thinking.

5. The listening and self-expression skills are only techniques. Real communication results from the spirit of genuine respect for yourself and for the other person. If your goal is to prove

yourself right, to blame the other person, or to get back at them, any communication technique will fail. But if your goal is to resolve the problem and to understand how the other person is thinking and feeling, these powerful methods will help you resolve conflicts and enjoy greater intimacy.

·

20

How to Change the Way
You Communicate

So far you've learned what good and bad communication are and how to listen and express your own feelings more effectively. I have devised a three-step written exercise that can help you make these ideas a natural part of the way you communicate. This exercise can make the difference between intellectual understanding and actual changing. If you read a book on dieting or jogging, you would learn a great deal about losing weight and getting in shape, but your body wouldn't actually change a great deal unless you began to eat less and exercise regularly. By the same token, if you do the written exercise in this chapter over a period of weeks, the insights you've gained will be transformed into a new and more effective way of communicating with others.

I decided to change the way I communicated in the late 1970s. I found that I sometimes got into conflicts with uncooperative patients, and I wasn't always satisfied with the outcome. If an angry patient expressed feelings of hopelessness and said that I didn't really understand his or her problems, I often got defensive. I would say that I thought I could understand their problems reasonably well and that I felt convinced they weren't hopeless. I would urge them to start doing more of the self-help assignments between sessions. The patient might reply, "That won't work! I've already tried it." Then I might point out that the one time he or she tried it, the symptoms of depression actually improved. Then the patient would say it was a fluke and it didn't count. On and on the argument went!

Going home on the train at night, I would write out a little script of what the patient and I had said to each other. Although my statements always appeared valid and logical, I could see that they weren't especially effective. The conflict usually hadn't been resolved, and the patient and I felt frustrated with each other.

I got tired of these logjams and asked myself, "What could I have said instead? How might I have handled it differently?" I started rewriting those scripts. If I felt stuck, I showed the scripts to colleagues and asked what they would say. After revising my statements several times, I usually found a new approach that I was more comfortable with. Then I tried this out the next time I saw the patient—with a much better result. The patient felt understood, there was a meeting of the minds, and we began to work together effectively.

The disarming technique and the "I feel" statements were especially helpful, but I sometimes resisted the disarming technique because I felt that I was "right" and the patient was "wrong." I also sensed that a kind of battle was going on, and I didn't want to back down or lose face. I found that it helped enormously if I told myself, "Win by losing, remember to surrender," during these confrontations.

I worked at these written scripts every day for several months, and the method was extremely helpful. I really did change the way I communicated with patients. The change was dramatic, not subtle, and it became second nature after a while. Now when a patient becomes annoyed or uncooperative, I switch into the listening skills and the self-expression skills almost as if I'm going on automatic pilot. The plane usually navigates through the storm and lands safely.

You can master these same skills. First, think of a conflict you had with someone that didn't work out well. In the left-hand column of the Revise Your Communication Style form, write down what they said that was upsetting to you, as shown in the sample on page 413. David, one of my patients, had an argument with Terri, his wife. Terri said, "You criticize every single thing I do." As you can see David wrote this down verbatim.

REVISE YOUR COMMUNICATION STYLE		
S/he says	**I ordinarily say**	**Revised version**
In this column record something your partner typically says that you find upsetting.	In this column record what you usually say. Point out why your statement is self-defeating.	Substitute a more effective statement.
Terri: "You criticize every single thing I do."	David: "Terri, I don't! That's a stupid thing to say!" (This sounds critical and disrespectful. I dismissed what she said and contradicted her. It's a put-down. She'll feel hurt and frustrated.)	David: "I've got to agree with you [disarming]. I do feel angry and left out of your life ['I feel' statement]. I often feel hurt ['I feel' statement] and I criticize you to get back at you [disarming]. And it only makes things worse [disarming]."

In the middle column, write down what you said to the other person. (If you pouted and said nothing, just put "I said nothing.") David responded by saying, "Terri, I don't! That's a stupid thing to say!" Once you write it down, think about why this response didn't work very well. You will notice that your responses are often an example of bad communication because you're not expressing your own feelings with "I feel" statements and you're not acknowledging how the other person is thinking and feeling. You will find that your comments are nearly always argumentative and that you are preoccupied with your version of the "Truth." When you analyze your middle-column responses, review the list of "Characteristics of Bad Communication" on page 365. This list will help you figure out why your statement precipitated an argument instead of a good exchange of feelings.

You can see how David analyzed his comment. By insisting that Terri was wrong, he proved that she was right! His statement was critical, and this provoked an argument. Arguing or avoiding each other is just about all David and Terri have done for several years.

Finally, in the right-hand column, labeled "Revised Version," write down what you might have said. Try to use the three listening skills and the two self-expression skills. Remember to express your feelings and to paraphrase what the other person is saying. Try to find some truth in it.

You can see that David has been doing his homework. He was able to apply those methods skillfully. You will probably agree that his revised response would have a markedly different impact.

There are two blank Revise Your Communication Style forms at the end of this chapter. Practice with one of them, and save the other one to copy. If you have trouble coming up with good "revised versions," or if you can't see why your middle column answers aren't satisfactory, think it over for a couple of days. Reread the previous chapter. Then come back to the form and read over what you wrote. Usually the light bulb will suddenly come on, and you will think of a better response! I often find it useful to ask a friend or colleague. They frequently have the objectivity I may lack when I'm overly involved in a situation.

Let's look at another example. Joanne is the woman described in Chapter 18, who was separated from her husband, Ted. When she finally encouraged Ted to express his anger, his interest in the relationship was rekindled. They were having a good time on a date when Ted suddenly said in an irritated tone of voice: "Why are you being so sweet? Why are you being so fake? This is how you were when we were first dating! Everything was 'fine.' " Joanne replied: "That's how I feel. I have missed you. I'm not being fake." This led to an argument. Later Joanne wrote his comment in the left-hand column of the form and put her response in the middle column, as illustrated on page 415.

Can you see why her comment triggered a bad response? She forgot to express her feelings or to acknowledge his. That's the definition of bad communication. She responded defensively and contradicted him. This tendency is nearly universal, and it never works well. This is the most important thing for you to understand about communication! It may seem obvious when you see these argumentative reactions in other people, but when *you* do it, you won't notice. You'll think you're being reasonable.

REVISE YOUR COMMUNICATION STYLE		
S/he says	**I ordinarily say**	**Revised version**
In this column record something your partner typically says that you find upsetting.	In this column record what you usually say. Point out why your statement is self-defeating.	Substitute a more effective statement.
Ted: "Why are you being so sweet? Why are you being so fake? This is how you were when we were first dating. Everything was 'fine.' "	Joanne: "That's how I feel. I have missed you. I'm not being fake." (I'm being defensive. I'm contradicting Ted. This triggered an argument.)	Joanne: "I feel upset right now ['I feel' statement]. I feel put down ['I feel' statement]. You seem annoyed with me [feeling empathy]. Have I been acting fake [inquiry]? Were you uncomfortable with me when we were first dating [inquiry]?"

There's something else about Joanne's middle column remark that I find amazing. Do you remember the "Persuasive Law of Opposites" from the previous chapter? If you agree with a criticism you will put the lie to it, but if you argue with the critic, you will always prove that he or she is right. You can see that Joanne argued with Ted. She insisted she wasn't being "fake." She insisted she did feel "sweet." Can you see that these argumentative responses proved that Ted was right? In reality, she felt hurt and put down at that moment. By insisting that she felt loving and that she had missed him, she came across in a way that was quite "fake." She wasn't being honest with herself or with Ted.

In the right-hand column Joanne put a revised version of how she might have responded. You can see that she expresses the annoyance she feels when Ted attacks her. She doesn't do this in a blaming or defensive way—she's simply sharing her feelings by using "I feel" statements. She also asks about his feelings and urges him to tell her what he's thinking. This will be more likely to lead to an honest exchange of feelings that will bring them closer together.

REVISE YOUR COMMUNICATION STYLE*

S/he says	I ordinarily say	Revised version
In this column record something your partner typically says that you find upsetting.	In this column record what you usually say. Point out why your statement is self-defeating.	Substitute a more effective statement.

REVISE YOUR COMMUNICATION STYLE*

S/he says	I ordinarily say	Revised version
In this column record something your partner typically says that you find upsetting.	In this column record what you usually say. Point out why your statement is self-defeating.	Substitute a more effective statement.

THE FIVE SECRETS OF EFFECTIVE COMMUNICATION*

LISTENING SKILLS

1. **The Disarming Technique.** You find some truth in what the other person is saying, even if you feel convinced that what they're saying is totally wrong, unreasonable, irrational, or unfair.

2. **Empathy.** You put yourself in the other person's shoes and try to see the world through his or her eyes.

   • **Thought empathy:** You paraphrase the other person's words.
   • **Feeling empathy:** You acknowledge how they're probably feeling, given what they are saying to you.

3. **Inquiry:** You ask gentle, probing questions to learn more about what the other person is thinking and feeling.

SELF-EXPRESSION SKILLS

1. **"I feel" statements.** You express your feelings with "I feel" statements (such as "I feel upset") rather than with "you statements" (such as "You're wrong!" or "You're making me furious!").

2. **Stroking:** You find something genuinely positive to say to the other person, even in the heat of battle. This indicates that you respect the other person, even though you may be angry with each other.

21

◆

How to Deal with Difficult People

In this chapter we will talk about dealing with difficult people, including:

- People who are "passive-aggressive." Instead of telling you they're upset, they pout and refuse to talk to you.
- People who are actively aggressive. They put you down and sound hostile, sarcastic, or condescending.
- People who are stubborn and argumentative.
- People who are critical and judgmental.
- Pushy people who put you on the spot and make excessive demands on you.
- Chronic complainers.
- People who need help.
- People who are boring and superficial.

How to Communicate with Someone Who Refuses to Talk to You

Many people ask me, "Dr. Burns, the listening skills you describe are all well and good, but what do you do when someone refuses to talk to you?"

Here are some examples:

- Steve's 14-year-old son misbehaved. When Steve tried to discuss this with him, he threw a tantrum and slammed the door to his room.
- Mary has had an argument with her friend Susan. They both flew off the handle and made a lot of inflammatory statements. A few days later Mary suggested it might help to talk things out. Susan replied: "There's *nothing* to talk about. You're not the kind of person I care to have anything to do with!"
- Harold's wife seemed sullen. Harold didn't know what the trouble was, so he asked her if she was upset with him. She bristled: "Of course I'm not upset. Why don't you get off my back and leave me alone!?"

Steve, Mary, and Harold have been thwarted. Thwarters rely on passive-aggressive tactics. They stone you with silence and insist they're not upset. They relish their power to frustrate and upset you. If you try to persuade them to talk to you, they'll just continue to thwart you.

So what's the solution? It's easy. You can neutralize their "thwarting" with the potent "anti-thwarting maneuver."

Step 1: Empathize. Instead of insisting they talk, ask in a friendly way why they don't want to. This often opens up the communication immediately. Eventually Steve's son will have to come out of his room. Steve could say, "It must be hard to talk things over when you feel criticized. Is that how you feel?" Mary could use a similar technique to respond to Susan's thwart: "I'm not the kind of person you care to have as a friend? Maybe you'd be willing to tell me some of the ways I've let you down. Would you?" Harold could say this to his wife: "I see that you don't much feel like sharing your feelings with me. Maybe you think I'm not an easy person to talk to. Is this the case?"

If you empathize in an accurate and nonjudgmental way, the chances are good the other person will soften up and talk. Use the inquiry technique to probe gently for more information about how he or she thinks and feels. If the other person says something critical—which probably will happen, because he or she feels angry with you—make sure you use the disarming technique to find some truth in the criticisms. This will set the other person more at ease.

Good listening skills are especially important in dealing with thwarters, because their thwarting habits show that they lack good assertive skills. They're annoyed and they don't know how to express their feelings in an effective manner. When you disarm them, empathize, and use the inquiry technique, it will be much easier for them to say what's on their mind.

Step 2: The Anti-Thwart. Let's assume the worst. Even when you empathize, they still refuse to talk. This frequently happens, especially if they're boiling. What can you do? It's quite simple. You zap them with the Anti-Thwart.

Here's how it works. Briefly agree that this isn't a good time for them to talk. Emphasize that you feel some communication is needed and suggest that you can talk things over later, when they're more in the mood. That's all you have to do.

Suppose Steve's son refuses to open up and says, "I've already told you, I'm not going to talk about this. Leave me alone!" Steve can say: "I can see you're not in the mood to talk now, and you shouldn't have to. I respect that. Every man needs to be alone at times. Nevertheless, we *do* have something we need to talk over. We can do this sometime in the next day or two, when you're more in the mood."

Typically, the other person will respond to our Anti-Thwart with another desperate attempt to thwart you. Steve's son might say, "Don't hold your breath" or "I won't talk to you now *or* later! Leave me alone, dammit!" In this case, just stick to your strategy and repeat your position gently—like this:

STEVE: You've got the right to be alone now, and you need to be alone. That's why I'm not going to talk to you any more right now. Nevertheless, we do have some things we need to talk over later. Even though you don't want to just now, eventually we will find a time. Tomorrow or the next day, I'll ask you if you're in the mood. In the meantime, if the spirit hits you and you want to talk, let me know.

SON: I'll *never* be in the mood. Not *now*, not *ever*!

STEVE: I know exactly how you feel. But never is a long time. I'll check with you in a day or two. When you feel ready, we'll work this problem out. We do have some things that we need to look at.

Essentially, this anti-thwarting strategy allows Steve to avoid getting caught up in a power struggle, and it leaves the ball in his son's court. His son is acting childish—and probably knows it—and Steve reminds him that sooner or later he'll have to deal with the problem. Steve wins because he doesn't try to control his son—he gives him his freedom. At the same time, Steve doesn't have to compromise on the principle that ultimately the problem must and will be talked out.

The anti-thwarting maneuver accomplishes a lot for you. It allows both parties to withdraw temporarily without losing face. You have responded to the other person's adolescent tactics in an adult way—they'll have to come up to your level if you don't descend to theirs. You have refused to accept the invitation to feel frustrated, to act pushy, or to get involved in a nonproductive battle of wills. You relinquish the urge to control. You avoid blaming, making demands, or polarizing the other person.

The thwarter may *want* you to get uptight and combative. This gets them off the hook so they can focus on your irrational behavior. Why give in to this? By reminding them that you do need to talk, but only when they're ready, you've left the ball in their court. The onus is on them, not you, and they know it!

THE ANTI-THWARTING DO'S AND DON'TS

- *Don't* insist they talk to you right now. They have a right to be alone. Respect that right. You'll only lose by trying to control them.
- *Don't* thwart them by saying, "Okay, then I won't talk to you, either." In this case, you're buying into the rejection.
- *Don't* blame yourself or judge what you're doing by the other person's haughty and childish reactions. They're refusing to talk. It's a reflection on them, not on you.
- *Don't* get judgmental. Although they are behaving in a hostile and immature way, keep your eye on your two goals—empathy and a postponement of the discussion.
- *Don't* allow yourself to get frustrated by insisting they talk right now, because you will give them the gratification they crave. They want you to feel upset so they can switch the spotlight onto your irritation. Keep your cool. Don't get sucked into their trap.
- *Do* empathize with their reasons for being unwilling to talk things over. They may think you're overly critical or judgmental; they may think you're not a sympathetic listener; they may be feeling ashamed or embarrassed about something they did; or they may be clamming up because they feel it's inappropriate to express angry feelings. Ask them about these possibilities in a gentle, nonjudgmental way. This will frequently open them right up.

• *Do* postpone the discussion if they still refuse to talk. Emphasize the importance of discussing things later, and give them permission to back off temporarily. This prevents a polarization. If they continue to thwart you later on, simply empathize and postpone again.

How to Deal with Someone Who Is Hostile

Sometimes, instead of refusing to communicate, the other person may be aggressive and give you a verbal blast. He or she may talk down to you or use a condescending or sarcastic tone of voice. Your first reaction will usually be to get defensive and blast right back, or to feel hurt and to blame yourself. In both cases, you're letting the other person call the shots. You're putting him or her in charge. Either response will just make the unpleasantness escalate.

So what can you do? Good listening and self-expression skills are nearly always the key to the resolution of any conflict. You need to listen and hear the truth in what the other person is saying, and to acknowledge how he or she is feeling. At the same time, you need to express your feelings about the way you are being treated. I call this method "changing the focus," because you draw attention to the hostile way the feelings are being expressed.

Changing the focus is a listening skill: you acknowledge the other person's anger and you describe the hostile way they are expressing it. Changing the focus is also a self-expression skill: you let them know that you feel upset about the way you're being treated. This technique can soften a hostile exchange and bring about greater feelings of trust. For example, if someone puts you down you can say, "I'm feeling put down right now ['I feel' statement]. Your tone of voice has a sharp edge [changing the focus]."

When you draw attention to the way you are being treated, don't get hostile. Think in terms of sharing the way you feel instead of attacking the other person. You don't want to say "You're putting me down." It makes you sound like a self-pitying victim, because you're blaming the other person. It will infuriate the other person. He or she can say, "What a pity! Little baby feels put down!"

You will also want to use the three listening skills to learn more about what the other person is feeling. If a family member calls you an idiot, you could say, "It sounds like you're pretty annoyed with me [feeling empathy]. I want you to tell me what I did that turned you off [inquiry]. I suspect you've got a good reason to feel ticked off [disarming]."

The other person undoubtedly has a valid point. The only problem is that the two of you are battling. Use the inquiry technique to prompt the other person to become more direct with you. Try to maintain a spirit of respect when you do it. Use the disarming technique and try to put yourself in the other person's shoes to see if you can grasp why he or she is acting in such an aggressive way.

Debbie was enraged when she discovered that her husband, Tom, a Wall Street investment banker, had been having an affair with a colleague for many years. After several months of turbulence, they got divorced. Tom subsequently married this woman, and Debbie maintained custody of their 12-year-old son, Bob.

Debbie felt devastated and intensely jealous. She had difficulties letting go, and the hope that Tom would leave his new wife and return to her kept her from getting genuinely interested in any of the men she dated. To make matters worse, Tom and his new wife purchased the very house that Tom and Debbie had once dreamed of owning. When Tom's new wife got pregnant, he seemed to gloat and Debbie felt crushed. She felt that Tom had everything—a successful career, good looks and charm, and an attractive wife—and that she had nothing but bitterness and loneliness.

One night when Tom was on the phone telling his son Bob about his new wife's pregnancy, an argument ensued. Bob blurted out that Tom seemed more interested in his new baby than in him or Debbie. Then Bob hung up on his dad. Tom called back and Debbie answered. Tom was enraged and demanded to talk to Bob. Debbie explained that Bob was in his bedroom sobbing, too upset to come to the phone. Tom became abusive, hurling four-letter words at Debbie. He even accused her of being an unfit mother and said he was going to sue for custody of their son.

If you were Debbie, how would you have handled this? Would you defend yourself? Would you fight back? Debbie's best bet may be to change the focus. Remember that the essence of the technique is to change the focus of the conversation from the content of the discussion to the style of the interaction.

First, Debbie must empathize with Tom's angry feelings. She needs to draw him out, using the three listening skills, so she can try to see the world through his eyes.

Debbie could say, "I know you love Bob a lot and it hurts you that he won't come to the phone [feeling empathy]. You two do need to talk this over, and I'm willing to support you in this [disarming]. I'm sure Bob feels just as hurt and threatened by the new baby as I do ['I feel' statement]. After he's settled down a bit, I'll encourage him to call you back so the two of you can talk things over." This response would mean that Debbie is giving up the urge to get revenge. Her goal becomes to work with Tom toward a solution rather than allowing their son to become a pawn in the struggle. She validates his concerns instead of opposing him and doing battle.

Next, Debbie needs to share her feelings about the way she is being treated. She could say, "I feel put down, and it bothers me greatly that we're fighting like this over Bob. ['I feel' statement]. You've got a valid need to talk to him [disarming], but when you swear at me and threaten me, it makes it hard to work together."

This concept is not new to you, since I've repeatedly emphasized the vital importance of good listening skills throughout the last several chapters. These skills are *exceptionally* important in hostile interactions. Tom does not feel respected or understood. That, in fact, is the very reason that he feels so hostile and acts so aggressive.

Aggressive individuals like Tom are generally just as afraid of intimacy and sharing as are the passive-aggressive people described in the last section. It just doesn't seem that way because they blast their negative feelings at you with full intensity. Tom lashes out instead of sharing his negative feelings because he feels afraid. He fears being vulnerable and saying, "Debbie, I feel hurt and frightened. It seems like I'm losing my son's respect. I need your support." Instead, he intimidates Debbie and provokes a fight. This keeps Debbie on the defensive and he doesn't have to risk feeling vulnerable or appearing weak and inadequate.

Notice that when you change the focus, you point out how you feel about the hostile style of relating instead of arguing about the issue at hand. One reason this is so difficult is that you'll get distracted by the content of what the other person is saying and you'll overlook the hostile style and tone in which they say it. Tom sounds self-righteous and intimidating, and it's easy for Debbie to get confused and to fight back.

When should you apply this technique? When you feel threatened, put down, or exasperated, you can use these emotions to your advantage if you take them as signals that you need to change the focus. Changing the focus calls attention to Tom's hostility and shifts the tone if Debbie is willing to hear what he has to say. He obviously feels frustrated and probably thinks she doesn't respect him. That is why he's acting so hostile in the first place. She needs to acknowledge his concerns in a sympathetic way, and to let him know that she also wants to be treated with greater respect. This conveys an attitude of self-esteem as well as a basic respect for Tom. Neither of them will have to lose face or be reduced to the status of an object.

Does this mean she's supposed to like Tom after he betrayed her and left her in so much anguish? No. She has every right to feel angry and hurt. But she has a basic decision to make, the same decision we all have to make during an angry encounter. There's a fork in the road, and we have to go down one road or the other. One is the road of hostility and defensiveness. You are intent on winning because you are so afraid of being the loser. You feel beaten down and have the overwhelming desire to even the score.

The other road is based on self-esteem and respect for the other person. Although you may feel angry, your goal is to share your angry feelings in a way that will enhance your chances of being heard, and to listen to the truth and the hurt feelings behind the other person's angry blasts. You are working from the assumption of "us," as opposed to "me versus you." Your goal is not to wage war but to work together to resolve the problem.

How to Communicate with Someone Who Is Stubborn and Argumentative

One of the commonest complaints I hear is "My spouse always has to be 'right.' He [or she] is never willing to listen to my point of view." The biggest mistake you can make in this situation is to promote your own ideas and try to persuade the other person that they should listen to you. This never works. You need to give in order to get. If you want to get some understanding, you may have to give some understanding first.

First, ask yourself why the other person is being so argumentative and stubborn. Maybe part of the problem is that you're not listening to them! Why would they keep harping away at you if they felt you had gotten the point? They wouldn't! Every stubborn, argumentative person has an equally stubborn partner who is defensive and argumentative and who refuses to listen to them.

This problem will disappear if you use the three listening skills: the disarming technique, empathy, and inquiry. Of the three, disarming is probably the most powerful and important. The moment you find the truth in the other person's point of view, they will soften and suddenly become more open to your point of view. In order to do this, you must give up the notion that you are the only one who's right and that what they have to say is pure and utter nonsense. There's always something important and valid about what the other person is saying that's being ignored and resisted. That's precisely why they get dogmatic and furious.

Linda and Fred participated for several weeks in our intensive program for depression at my clinic in Philadelphia. Part of the treatment included therapy sessions with them together because they both admitted their marriage had been cold and unfulfilling for decades. Linda had caught Fred in an affair thirty years earlier, and she had never forgiven him. She felt he was an untrustworthy, narcissistic liar, and she wasn't about to open up and become vulnerable and let herself get hurt again. They'd practically never had sex ever since. Linda's feelings of chronic depression, bitterness, and unfulfillment were the price she gladly paid to get back at Fred and to protect herself from the risk of trusting him.

During their sessions, Linda would frequently say, "I can't trust you. You don't tell the truth. You betrayed me and showed your true colors when you had the affair." Then Fred would defend himself and insist this wasn't the truth and that it wasn't fair. He would explain that he'd learned his lesson and he'd never had any more affairs. He insisted that had been faithful to her ever since. Then Linda would repeat that he was basically dishonest and untrustworthy. On and on the argument raged. They both admitted that they'd been trying unsuccessfully to resolve this for decades.

Now, put yourself in Fred's shoes. Assume that you have been faithful and trustworthy ever since. How would you get Linda to see your point of view? How would you get her to agree with you? What can you say when she accuses you of being unfaithful? Put your ideas here:

_____

_____

_____

You must acknowledge the truth in her point of view before she will soften and open up to you. You could say, "You know, you're right [disarming]. I did have an affair and I betrayed you [disarming]. I hurt you terribly [feeling empathy]." Notice that instead of trying to defend his innocence—which will annoy her and make him seem even more dishonest—he admits his guilt. Paradoxically, Linda may suddenly sense the possibility of forgiving him. As they talk, he may also want to express his feelings—he feels punished and rejected—instead of arguing that he's "right." This will have a far more powerful impact than insisting that he's been faithful. That's because sharing his feelings *is* intimacy. In contrast, when he argues about what a good guy he has been, he simply sounds phony and dishonest. Furthermore, he *is* dishonest when he defends himself, because he's hiding how annoyed and put down he feels!

With considerable encouragement, Fred did begin to communicate more openly with Linda. When he acknowledged her feelings and shared his own feelings of anger and rejection, she wept and admitted how lonely she felt and how much she wanted to feel close to him again. She said she knew that she'd been punishing him because of her fears of being let down. She asked him to be patient with her because the process of forgiveness and building trust would take some time.

How to Deal with People Who Are Critical and Judgmental

Recently I was having a therapy session with a businessman named Frank who tends to be rather overbearing when he is upset. Frank told me that I was too preoccupied with money and that he shouldn't have to pay at each session. He said he wanted to be billed monthly. I felt annoyed because I told myself "He always has to have things his own way." I also felt guilty because I told myself, "He's probably right. Maybe I *am* too preoccupied with money." I got defensive and explained in a terse, polite voice that I had tried a monthly billing system, but it hadn't worked out very well because some patients had run up substantial bills without paying. He didn't appreciate this comment and argued that he had impeccable credit and knew much more about credit and billing than I did. Then we launched into a frustrating debate about billing systems.

Notice how my negative thoughts and feelings functioned as a self-fulfilling prophecy. I felt attacked and had the urge to defend myself. This caused me to be attacked! Suddenly I told myself, "Whoa! I don't need to be so defensive about this." Then I decided to try a different approach. I turned to him and said, "You know, I think you're right. I've been too concerned about getting paid and I'm being defensive. You have every right to feel annoyed and I owe you an apology. We should focus on the problems in your life and not worry so much about money." He immediately softened and told me how much he appreciated working with me. He began to share his feelings of insecurity and started to talk about what was really bothering him. The next time we met, he handed me a check for twenty sessions in advance!

Many people have a great deal of trouble dealing with criticism. It's natural to feel hurt and to get defensive. Since most of us are programmed to base our self-esteem on how much other people like and approve of us, criticism feels like a blow to our egos. Part of the solution involves learning to communicate more effectively when you are criticized, and part has to do with a basic change in your attitudes and values.

The most important principles to keep in mind when you are being criticized are these:

1. Disarm the person who is criticizing you. Find some truth in the criticism instead of getting defensive. There is always truth in a criticism. When you acknowledge it, the person who is criticizing you will usually back off and calm down. This is the single most important technique in dealing with criticism.

2. Use the empathy and inquiry techniques. Encourage the other person to express all their criticisms and negative feelings.

3. Express your feelings with "I feel" statements instead of arguing.

You may be thinking, "But how can I disarm someone if their criticism is unfair and wrong?" If so, it's even more important to find some truth in it. Do you remember the "Persuasive Law of Opposites," described in Chapter 16? When you agree with a criticism, you will immediately put the lie to it. On the other hand, when you argue and contradict the criticism, you will prove that it is valid. To understand this concept a little better, review pages 396 to 397.

People who are judgmental and critical often have a lot of unexpressed anger or dissatisfaction. They may act that way because they never have the chance to get their feelings off their chest. You will contribute to this problem if you are argumentative and defensive. Instead, encourage the other person to say everything bad they can think of about you. If they open up and tear you to shreds, don't defend yourself. Instead, find truth in what they say. Acknowledge how they feel. Urge them to tell you more. This can work wonders.

When you are criticized, you will probably feel upset. You may feel defensive, inadequate, annoyed. You may not want to admit these feelings openly. Instead, you get defensive. This is a huge mistake. It makes you appear phony and culpable. Instead, tell the person how you feel. If you feel put down, say "I'm feeling put down." If you feel defensive, say "I'm feeling defensive." If you feel inadequate, say "I'm feeling inadequate." If you feel angry, say "I feel angry." But when you do, add "But I know there's a lot of truth in what you're saying, and I want you to tell me more."

Your ego can get in the way of this. You may tell yourself you're not supposed to feel the way you do. I see this problem frequently in the therapists I train. Some patients have an uncanny ability to sense their therapists' greatest vulnerabilities and they "go for the jugular" when they're angry. The therapist generally feels tense and becomes more formal and more "professional." This alienates the patient, because the therapist doesn't appear genuine. Instead, he or she sounds condescending.

To take a simple example, suppose an angry patient says this to a student therapist: "Aren't you a little on the young side? Do you have your license yet, or are you just a novice?" The therapist may feel annoyed and threatened by the question. He or she *does* feel insecure—that's quite natural. Instead of owning up to this, the therapist may get defensive and begin to look like a *real* jerk.

What could the student therapist say that would be effective? Put your ideas here:

_____

_____

_____

_____

The therapist could say, "As a matter of fact I *am* a novice, and I do feel like a beginner at times [disarming, 'I feel' statement]. I know that I will feel more comfortable once I get to know you better and once we're working together productively ['I feel' statement]. You may feel awkward about this and wonder if I will be able to help you or understand your problem [thought and feeling empathy]. Do you [inquiry]?"

Many readers will resist the approach I'm describing. You may feel you have a right to defend yourself when you are criticized. You may feel that something terrible will happen if you use the disarming technique, the inquiry technique, and "I feel" statements. Agreeing with a critic goes against the grain of human nature. We feel we're supposed to be competitive and to stand up for what we believe. Try to resist this urge. You will discover that these techniques are tremendously powerful—far more so than you might imagine.

A patient of mine named Hal has a short fuse, and he frequently gets angry while driving. Last week he inadvertently cut in front of another car in traffic. When Hal pulled up to a stoplight, the other driver pulled up next to him and started screaming obscenities, telling him in four-letter words what a lousy driver he was. If you were Hal and you were subjected to all this humiliation and abuse, what would you do? Put your response here:

_____

_____

_____

_____

Hal decided to use the disarming technique. He simply turned to the other driver and said in a friendly voice: "You're right [disarming]. It *was* my mistake [disarming]. I shouldn't have cut in front of you [disarming]." The driver was dumbfounded and turned bright red. Hal smiled inwardly, and as the light turned green he drove off in triumph!

This example illustrates that the disarming technique alone is usually enough to deal with criticism, especially when the other person is irate and trying to put you down in an extremist, childish way. Suppose someone says, "You're ugly!" How would you disarm this criticism?

_____

_____

_____

_____

You could simply say, "I'm not the best-looking person in the world, that's the truth!"
Suppose someone says, "You're a jerk!" How would you disarm this criticism?

_____

_____

_____

_____

You could say, "Yes, I am a bit of a jerk. In fact, I've probably done quite a few jerky things you don't even know about yet!"
The critic says, "You're to blame for this. It's your fault!" How could you disarm him or her?

_____

_____

_____

_____

"I think I *have* contributed to the problem. I feel bad and I'm concerned that I've let you down."
As an exercise, make a list of several sincere or insulting criticisms

that have been leveled at you at one time or another. Then see if you can write down a brief disarming response. I have done this exercise on many occasions, and it has made a huge difference in the way I relate to people who are critical of me.

How to Deal with People Who Put You on the Spot and Make Unreasonable Demands

It's easy to get overcommitted and become overwhelmed by all you have to do. You may be constantly driving your children from place to place and trying to keep up with the cooking and the housework and dozens of other chores that never seem to end. Your boss may tell you to do this and do that and it seems it would take an army to keep up with all the demands. You go home each night feeling drained and exhausted and guilty. You feel even further behind than when you went to work that morning.

One of the reasons we get overcommitted is because of guilt and the feeling that we should always say yes to people. The real problem isn't that people make demands on us, but that we don't know how to deal with these demands in a tactful way. A method that I've found extremely helpful is called "punting." You tell the person you need to think about their request and that you'll get back to them. In the meantime, you can figure out what you want to do. If you feel overwhelmed and their request does not seem reasonable, you can practice how to say no.

I'm often asked to give lectures or workshops. There are times when I enjoy lecturing, but at other times when I am committed to my writing, patient care, and research, lecturing seems like too much of a burden. Let's suppose a colleague calls and pressures me to give a lecture at his university. I've learned to say, "I'm really flattered that you thought of me. Let me check my schedule and see if it will be possible. I'll call you back in a day or two." This gives me time to think about the proposal and deal with any feelings of guilt. If in my heart of hearts I know it's better to say no, I think about what I will say when I call back. Usually it turns out to be easy. I just say, "I really appreciate being asked but I find that my schedule is overcommitted right now. Please think of me again in the future."

Now you might think, "That's so simple! But why not just say no right away instead of 'punting'? You'd save yourself two days of worry." I have a tendency to believe I must always say yes and please everybody. Saying no when someone puts you on the spot can sometimes be difficult. If you're like me, you'll find it far easier to "punt" when you feel pressured. This gives me the time I need to regroup and to rehearse a friendly, assertive response.

How to Cope with a Complainer

Do you know anyone who always bitches and complains? Whatever you do to try to cheer them up, they just complain louder. When you try to give them some helpful advice they just say, "that won't work," and they continue to complain. Then you get frustrated because you don't know what to do.

You need to recognize that complainers usually don't want any advice, they simply want to be listened to. All you have to do is to use the disarming technique and *agree* with them instead of trying to "help" them. They nearly always feel better and they quiet down. It works like a charm! This is because you've given them what they really want—a little T.L.C. and some understanding.

I want you to try it. Suppose an elderly parent tells you, "No one spends any time with me anymore." You feel a sudden pang of guilt and annoyance. How could you respond?

_____

_____

_____

_____

Answer: You could say, "I think what you're saying is true {disarming}. People don't spend much time with you, and it sounds like you've been feeling pretty neglected {feeling empathy}. Have you {inquiry}?"

Notice that you find some way to *agree* with a complainer. Do *not* argue or give advice or try to help in any way! The disarming technique alone is frequently the most effective approach.

Suppose a complainer says, "Oh, my hemorrhoids are aching and the doctors never do me any good." How could you disarm him or her?

_____

_____

_____

_____

Answer: "It sounds like your hemorrhoids are real sore and the doctors aren't giving you *any* help [thought empathy]. Doctors really can be a waste [disarming]!"

Suppose an associate moans that, "Nobody respects me! I work my fingers to the bone and nobody ever cares or notices." You suddenly feel resentful. How can you respond?

_____

_____

_____

_____

Answer: "You're right [disarming]. You work awfully hard and you don't get the credit you deserve [disarming]. Everyone takes you for granted [disarming]. It's not fair [disarming]!"

Now, you might resist this approach. You might say, "I don't want to be phony. I shouldn't have to agree with someone who's complaining." The answer to this is that you don't "have to." It's just an option. But it works wonders. The complainer will nearly always calm down and stop complaining. Every other approach I'm aware of will fail, and you'll both end up feeling frustrated.

When should you use this approach? The tip off is that you're starting to feel frustrated because you're hearing the same complaints over and over and you notice that the complainer simply isn't listening to you. You feel irritated, and you can't wait to get away from the complainer. Concentrate on the listening skills and stop trying to be helpful. The complainer just wants his or her feelings validated. He or she only wants you to agree with him or her. I used to hate complainers because I never knew what to do. I felt guilty, inadequate, and frustrated. Now I love complainers because the disarming technique works like magic. Give it a try. I think you'll be amazed.

How to Help a Troubled Loved One

If you are having difficulties helping someone who is upset, ask yourself the following questions:

1. Is this person really asking for my help?

2. Is it appropriate to help him or her?

3. Is this person asking me to help solve problems, or is he or she simply asking me to be a good listener and to provide emotional support?

The first question may make you aware that you are trying to help someone who hasn't really asked for help. This may be due to an irrational attitude I call the "help addiction." You may feel it is always your duty to help friends and loved ones find solutions to their problems. You try to help even when help hasn't been asked for. As a result, you may appear intrusive and controlling.

Mildred was upset because her son, Jack, a 28-year-old stockbroker, had left his wife and two daughters to live with an 18-year-old girl whom Mildred described as "low class." Mildred lamented: "I just don't understand it. He met her at a bar and she smokes marijuana. He was always such a lighthearted, model boy when he was growing up. He was so poised, and everybody loved him. What's happened to him now? I thought I raised him right."

Mildred refused to let Jack's girlfriend set foot in her home, and she repeatedly urged him to straighten out. She warned him that he was ruining his career, breaking his poor mother's heart, and damaging his daughters. She complained that Jack didn't spend enough time with her. She was bewildered by how selfish and insensitive he'd become.

Mildred felt it was her duty to make sure he changed his ways. She felt accountable for his actions and afraid that her friends would look down on her because of Jack's affair. She blamed Jack for her misery and was determined not to feel any better until Jack repented.

What are the consequences of Mildred's attitude? She will drive Jack away because he feels judged and guilty whenever he is around her. Then she will complain that she feels lonely and abandoned!

Jack may be going through a "crazy period," a delayed adolescent rebellion, but Mildred's blaming attitude will only feed the fire. She will lose his respect. Although she insists she loves him and only wants to help him, the message Jack hears is "I will punish you until you do exactly what I want you to. I am determined to control you. I will not accept you until you fall in line."

What could Mildred do? Her feelings are important, and she would have a far greater chance of being heard if she expressed them with "I feel" statements instead of trying to "help" Jack. She could say, "I feel upset that you have left your wife to live with this young woman. I feel terribly disappointed and ashamed and hurt." These "I feel" statements convey direct information about her feelings without implying that Jack is entirely responsible for them. At the same time, she could express a genuine concern for Jack if she asked him about his feelings in a nonjudgmental manner. Why did he leave his wife? What were the problems they were having? How does he feel about the separation? Communication, rather than helping, would be the goal because Jack has not asked for help.

One reason we may jump in and "help" is because our egos are on the line. We may link our self-esteem with the happiness of others. We may get upset if a loved one is having difficulties because we think this is a reflection on us. We feel we have failed.

The second question to ask yourself is whether it's appropriate to help someone. There are times when people would benefit more from working things out for themselves.

Ned dropped out of college impulsively. He persuaded Harry, his father, to lend him $7,000 to start a business. Harry felt uneasy about this but gave in because he told himself "A loving father should be willing to help his son." Ned had poor judgment and soon squandered the money. Harry felt manipulated and angry, but he was reluctant to discuss this with Ned for fear of hurting Ned's feelings.

A short while later, Ned persuaded his dad to give him a credit card. Ned explained that he couldn't get his own because he had no previous credit record. He said that if his dad would help him, he could establish a line of credit, which would be useful for a new business venture. Several months later, Harry started getting calls from a collection agency: the card was overextended and no payments had been made.

You can probably see how Harry's efforts to help backfired in his dealings with his son. He felt that a caring father should be ready and willing to be supportive when his children need something. He behaved as though the message "I will help you" means "I care about you." But this message is a two-edged sword because it also implies "You need me and you can't do it on your own." If someone really *can* do it on their own, the impact of your help can be destructive. If you reward people with love and attention every time they get upset or act sick, they may learn to manipulate you. This can rob them of the motivation to become more self-reliant.

If you decide that you do want to help someone, the third question to ask yourself is *how* you are going to help them. There are two very different ways to offer help. You can help simply by listening, or you can help by doing favors or giving practical advice. You can think of these approaches as the "listening mode" and the "problem-solving mode." If you and the other person are on the same wavelength, there's no problem. However, you will have difficulties if you are in the problem-solving mode while the other person only wants you to be a good listener. Your message is: "Why don't you pull yourself up by your bootstraps? Think more positively. Try doing X." The other person may resent all this "logical" advice. He or she just wants you to say, "I hear how lousy you feel. I know how awful it can be." Unfortunately, you may not know that some emotional support is all that's needed, so you offer advice that sounds intrusive and insensitive to the other person.

You may wonder when you should be a good listener and when you should be more active in helping someone solve a problem. Sometimes you simply have to ask them. Many of my patients genuinely want help, and they will work actively to solve their problems along the lines I suggest. But others simply want to be listened to. They don't want help or advice. If I try to help them, they get annoyed and start complaining. That's when it's time to listen and to avoid trying to be helpful by solving problems.

I'm just like everyone else, and when I feel upset, I want someone to listen to me as well. There are times when I come home from the office and I feel like complaining about how unreasonable the world is. I don't want my wife to give me advice—if I want advice I generally ask for it. I just want her to say, "There, there, you're right. People shouldn't be so irrational." Then I feel relieved because somebody understands. I cheer up right away and I stop complaining!

How to Instantly Transform a Boring Conversation into an Exciting One

This week a young man asked me what he was supposed to do when he was on a date with someone who was uninteresting or when he was stuck at a party, talking to someone who seemed boring. This problem can also come up in your relationships with friends or professional colleagues. You may know someone who talks too much about nothing very interesting. He or she drones on and on and all you can think is, "How can I get away from this person?"

There's only one cause of boring interactions, and there's always one instantaneous solution. Before I reveal the secret, you will first have to decide if you *want* to have a more exciting interaction with the person who seems boring. You always have the right to excuse yourself and look for someone you naturally feel more attracted to. There's no rule that says that you're obligated to be interested in everyone. If the chemistry's not there, you can pass.

However, you have another option. You can transform the most boring interactions into incredibly exciting ones within less than thirty seconds with a 100% success rate if you use this simple but bold technique: Comment, in a tactful and friendly way, on the fact that you feel bored. Ask the other person if they feel the same way. That's all you have to do!

If you're chatting about trivia with someone at a party and you're crawling out of your skin, you could say: "Have you ever noticed how easy it is to get involved in really boring small talk at parties like this?" They'll probably say yes. Then you could say, "Well, that's how I feel right now ['I feel' statement]. Do you feel the same way [inquiry]? We're just talking about nothing at all. I don't know why, because I'll bet you're an interesting person and I'd like to get to know you a little better [stroking]." The moment you admit that you feel bored there will be a certain electricity in the air. It's a fairly daring statement, and your boredom will be history! The compliment "I'll bet you're an interesting person" is included to reassure the other person that you don't want to put them down and that you simply want to get to know them better.

You may be *afraid* to use this technique. Lots of people go through life playing games, censoring their own feelings and being petrified about being open and honest with others. Your boredom is just your way of reminding yourself that you're not being honest with yourself or with the other person. You're pretending. You're lying. If you're willing to be honest and to step out from behind your mask, your boredom will vanish.

Dave, a divorced man in his thirties, told me about a woman he'd dated several times. He said she was attractive but he didn't like her very much because she seemed superficial and "not very deep." He wondered whether he should stop taking her out. What could Dave say to her? Put your ideas here:

_____

_____

_____

_____

Dave could say, "Sarah, you're a really attractive woman [stroking], but when we go out I have trouble because I feel I'm not getting to know you very well ['I feel' statement]. We seem to stick to superficial topics ['I feel' statement]. Have you noticed this [inquiry]? It makes me uncomfortable ['I feel' statement]. I don't know why that is, and I'd like to get to know you better as a person [stroking]."

Dave tried this approach after we rehearsed it during a session. The next week he was euphoric. To his amazement, Sarah opened up immediately. They began to talk about past disappointments in romantic relationships. He told me that Sarah was a "very exciting" and "very deep" person with all kinds of feelings and ideas. He couldn't imagine how he'd ever thought she was superficial or boring.

There's actually no such thing as a boring person. Boring interactions exist, but boring people do not. There's only one cause of boring interactions, and there's one cure. Inassertiveness is the cause, and assertiveness is the cure. This method always works. It never fails. Do you have the guts to try it?

22

·

Why People Can't Communicate with Each Other

In the last several chapters we've talked about the difference between good and bad communication, and you've learned how to listen and express your feelings more effectively. It will take some work to master these skills, but with effort it can be done. Patients of mine find that it takes a good five or six sessions, with a reasonable amount of homework and practice between sessions. Those who work at it consistently get good results, and many report that the techniques are astonishingly effective.

However, many people find that they resist these methods. They can see that they do not communicate well, and yet they stubbornly dig in their heels when it's time to try something new. I predict that you will have to battle with some powerful feelings that could sabotage your efforts to communicate more effectively. See if you can recognize yourself in any of the attitudes described on pages 443 and 445.

How Your "Truth" Keeps You Stuck

"Truth" is probably the greatest barrier to good communication. During an argument with a friend or your spouse, you may have such a powerful conviction that you are right that you don't try to see the

TEN ATTITUDES THAT KEEP YOU
FROM EXPRESSING YOUR FEELINGS*

1. **Conflict phobia.** You are afraid of angry feelings or conflicts with people. You may believe that people with good relationships shouldn't fight or argue. You may also believe that the people you care about would be hurt and couldn't take it if you told them how you felt or what was really on your mind. I call this the "ostrich phenomenon," because you bury your head in the sand instead of dealing with the problems in your relationship.

2. **Emotional perfectionism.** You believe that you shouldn't have irrational feelings like anger, jealousy, depression, or anxiety. You think you should always be rational and in control of your emotions. You are afraid of being exposed as weak and vulnerable. You believe that people will look down on you if they find out how you really feel.

3. **Fear of disapproval and rejection.** You are so terrified by rejection and ending up alone that you'd rather swallow your feelings and put up with some abuse than take the chance of making anyone mad at you. You feel an excessive need to please people and to meet everybody's expectations. You are afraid that people would not like you if you expressed your own ideas and feelings.

4. **Passive-aggressiveness.** You pout and hold your hurt and angry feelings inside instead of sharing them openly and honestly. You give others the silent treatment and try to make them feel guilty instead of sharing your feelings.

5. **Hopelessness.** You feel convinced that your relationship cannot improve no matter what you do, so you give up. You may feel that you've already tried everything and nothing works. You may believe that your spouse is just too stubborn and insensitive to be able to change. This acts as a self-fulfilling prophecy. Once you give up, things get stuck and you conclude that things really are hopeless.

*Copyright © 1989 by David D. Burns, M.D., from *The Feeling Good Handbook*

6. **Low self-esteem.** You believe that you aren't entitled to express your feelings or to ask others for what you want. You think you should always please other people and meet their expectations.

7. **Spontaneity.** You believe that you have the right to say precisely what you think and feel when you are upset. You may feel that any change in the way you communicate will sound phony and ridiculous.

8. **Mind reading.** You believe that people should know how you feel and what you want without your having to express yourself directly. This gives you a perfect excuse to hold your feelings inside and to feel resentful because people don't seem to care about your needs.

9. **Martyrdom.** You are afraid to admit that you're angry, because you don't want to give anyone the satisfaction of knowing they've upset you. You take enormous pride in controlling your emotions and suffering silently.

10. **Need to solve problems.** When you have a conflict with someone, you go around and around in circles trying to solve the problem instead of sharing your feelings openly and hearing how the other person feels.

TEN ATTITUDES THAT PREVENT YOU FROM LISTENING*

1. **Truth.** You believe that you are right and the other person is wrong. You are preoccupied with proving your point instead of expressing your angry feelings more directly or trying to grasp how the other person is thinking and feeling.

2. **Blame.** You believe that the problem is the other person's fault. You feel overwhelmingly convinced that you're completely innocent and tell yourself that you have every right to blame him or her.

3. **Need to be a victim.** You feel sorry for yourself and think that other people are treating you unfairly because of their insensitivity and selfishness. Your stubborn unwillingness to do anything assertive to make the situation better gives people the impression that you like the role of a martyr.

4. **Self-deception.** You cannot imagine that you contribute to a problem because you cannot see the impact of your behavior on others. For example, you may complain that your wife nags you, but you don't think about the fact that you repeatedly "forget" to follow through on your promise to repair the fence. You may complain that your husband is dogmatic and stubborn and unwilling to listen to your ideas, but you don't notice that you constantly contradict everything he tries to say.

5. **Defensiveness.** You are so fearful of criticism that you can't stand to hear anything negative or disagreeable. Instead of listening and trying to find some truth in the other person's point of view, you have the urge to argue and defend yourself.

6. **Coercion sensitivity.** You are afraid of giving in or being bossed around. Other people seem controlling and domineering, and you feel that you must dig in your heels and resist them.

7. **Demandingness.** You feel entitled to better treatment from others, and you get frustrated when they do not treat you as you expected. Instead of trying to understand what really motivates them, you insist that they are being unreasonable and have no right to feel and act the way they do.

8. **Selfishness.** You want what you want when you want it, and you throw a tantrum if you don't get it. You are not especially interested in what others may be thinking and feeling.

9. **Mistrust.** You put up a wall because you believe you will be taken advantage of if you listen and try to grasp what the other person is thinking and feeling.

10. **Help addiction.** You feel the need to help people when all they want is to be listened to. When friends or family members complain about how bad they feel, you make "helpful" suggestions and tell them what to do. Instead of being appreciative, they get annoyed and continue to complain. You both end up feeling frustrated.

other person's point of view. Instead, you argue and try to force them to agree with you. This never works. You've probably noticed that the more you try to persuade the other person to agree with you, the more argumentative he or she becomes. This is because you're not really listening to their viewpoint. They believe their feelings are being ignored, and they'll argue louder and longer to try to get you to listen. You both end up feeling angry and frustrated.

You may be completely unaware you're doing this. A woman's husband recently said, "Sarah, you always do exactly what you want without considering my needs. You put your career and your needs first." Sarah replied, "No, I don't. You are my priority, Harold, but sometimes my studies have to take precedence if I have a big exam coming up." Although Sarah might think she's being honest and reasonable, she has made the mistake of suggesting that she's right and he's wrong about this. The moment she contradicts him, she proves that he's right. In point of fact, she's not trying to understand his point of view, she's only tuned in to her needs and her own view of the situation. That's exactly what he's complaining about!

So what's the alternative? She could express her feelings with "I feel" statements. How does she feel? She feels ticked off! So why not just say this instead of being argumentative? She could also try to understand what he's thinking and feeling. How does he feel? He feels shut out and ignored. She could say, "I feel put down and angry ['I feel' statement], but I know there's some truth in what you say [disarming]. Apparently you think I've put my career first and you feel rejected [thought empathy]. Is this the way you feel [inquiry]? If so, I could understand why you feel hurt and angry [feeling empathy]."

I've worked with hundreds of people with troubled relationships, and practically every one of them has made the same mistake of arguing about the "truth." This strategy never helped anyone resolve a problem. When you feel upset, you will have a tremendous urge to explain why your ideas and feelings are valid. *Don't do it!* You will have a tremendous urge to defend yourself and argue. *Don't do it!* What usually happens when you try to point out the truth to someone? When you argued and got defensive, did your spouse ever stop arguing and say, "Thank you, thank you for opening my eyes. I see now where I was so wrong"? Of course not!

The key to resolving an argument is often to back off and try a different approach. The bottom line is that you must never defend the "truth"! Your "truth" is your enemy! When you give up the idea that you have a monopoly on the truth and you try to understand the other person's point of view, you will find that people will be much more willing to listen to you and to understand your own point of view.

Now you may be thinking, as so many of my patients do, "But what if I *am* right and my partner *is* wrong? Doesn't the truth count? I don't want to be a liar. I *won't* be a liar." There are two difficulties with this position: It won't work, and it's not valid. The reason it won't work should be clear to you by now. Whenever you're having a dispute with someone, you will both feel upset. Any attempt on your part to insist that you are right and the other person is wrong will only fan the flames.

The second difficulty is that the other person's feelings are just as valid to him or her as your feelings are to you. Defending your "truth" is foolish because there really isn't any one truth in a situation. People have feelings that need to be accepted and understood. These feelings are neither true nor false.

In a session recently, Erika told her husband that he was always talking down to her and treating her as though she was inferior. Erika had been battling a long-standing drinking problem and had purchased a book on Alcoholics Anonymous. Before she had a chance to read it, John had read it and presented her with a computer printout highlighting all the ideas in the book. She said she was furious because she felt that he was trying to control her and was implying that she was unable to understand the book on her own. John replied that this wasn't true and insisted he was just trying to help her.

Now, who is "right"? Is Erika "right" that he's talking down to her and trying to keep her under his thumb? Or is John "right" that he's trying to help her so they can feel closer? There are worlds of truth in what each of them has to say. She's right that he's overly aggressive and intellectual. She felt inferior in school and resentful of her domineering father when she was growing up. She feels intimidated by John's active mind. Erika would feel more comfortable with him if he were a little warmer and more low-key.

John is also right. She does have a drinking problem and she needs to do something about it. He feels lonely and he desperately wants to feel closer to her. If either one of them tries to develop a sympathetic and accurate understanding of how the other one feels, the conflict will probably disappear, because they will both feel respected and cared about.

What could John say to break the stalemate? Instead of defending himself he could say, "I understand how you feel [feeling empathy]. I must have seemed kind of thoughtless and controlling to have gone through the whole book like that [disarming]. I know that probably made you angry [feeling empathy]. At the same time I'm feeling kind of frightened about your drinking, and lonely, and I really want to be close to you ['I feel' statement]. Maybe we need to talk about what's going on between us. Are you feeling upset with me now [inquiry]?"

What could Erika say to break the stalemate? She could say, "I felt resentful when you outlined the book ['I feel' statement]. I feel like you're the brilliant, impatient teacher and I'm the dumb student ['I feel' statement]. But I know you feel lonely and rejected by me, and you're trying to be helpful [feeling empathy]. Is that how you feel [inquiry]?" This response would shift the focus away from who's right and who's wrong. John will learn what she's feeling, and he will see that she's trying to understand his point of view.

When you argue and defend the "truth," it becomes nearly impossible to feel close to your partner or to resolve any conflict. You'll simply fight on and on. If, instead, you reveal your feelings and encourage your partner to share his or hers, you will be on the path to greater intimacy.

How Self-Deception Keeps You Stuck

Another great barrier to communication is the tendency to blame others and to deny that we are contributing to the problem. Part of the difficulty is that during an argument we can literally see what the other person is doing to us—we see them being hostile, self-centered, defensive, and narrow-minded—but we cannot see what we are doing that may be contributing to the problem. That's because there are usually no mirrors or television cameras around when we're having a fight with someone, so we literally cannot see ourselves in action. This blindness to the impact of our own actions on others can be quite profound.

A depressed woman named Molly complained bitterly that her

husband, Frank, never expressed his feelings. Molly told me she had had the bad luck to marry a cold fish. She said Frank was like a lot of men—he didn't care about intimacy or about talking about feelings. She was feeling discouraged and hopeless about their relationship and spoke about her marital problems at nearly every session.

To find out what was really happening, I encouraged Molly to invite Frank to come with her so I could observe firsthand what was going on. I proposed that we work on improving the way they communicated. Possibly I could help Frank get over his inhibitions about expressing how he felt. Molly was quite enthusiastic about this plan, and Frank was very willing to participate in the therapy.

During a session with the two of them together, I summarized Molly's feelings of loneliness and asked Frank if he'd be willing to take a stab at opening up and sharing some of his feelings with her. Frank said he spent most of his time working and avoiding Molly. He said he would have no inhibitions about sharing his feelings, but he felt pretty sure that Molly didn't really want him to communicate more openly.

Molly seemed annoyed and insisted that what Frank was saying wasn't true! I was puzzled and asked Molly if she wanted Frank to open up. She reassured me that indeed she did. I told Frank to go ahead.

Frank told Molly that he, too, felt lonely and hurt. He said he felt she was quite critical of him and put him down a great deal. He told her that he often tried to express his feelings and ideas, but that she jumped all over him whenever he did. He said it just didn't seem worth it. He said he felt just as angry and rejected as she did.

As he was speaking, Molly got more and more agitated and finally interrupted him. She was furious and said he had "no right" to say things like that. She said what he was saying was "unfair" and "untrue." She began sobbing and stormed out of the office, slamming the door behind her.

I was quite taken aback. Molly was so fragile and threatened by Frank's negative feelings that she couldn't stand to hear what he had to say. When he did try to open up, her punishment of him was instantaneous and severe. She hit him with her most powerful weapons—anger, depression, and rejection. But Molly was totally unaware of the way Frank might feel about her behavior. She couldn't see that she was partially responsible for their poor communication and was convinced the difficulties were entirely due to his shortcomings. On pages 451–452 you can see several additional examples of how people unknowingly create the very problems they complain so loudly about.

How Blame and Mistrust
Keep You Stuck

A woman from Cleveland named Laura told me what an insensitive lover her husband, Dave, was. She complained that she'd never once experienced an orgasm in over thirty years of marriage. I asked Laura to tell me specifically about the problems she and Dave were having in the bedroom. One of Laura's main complaints was that Dave, a strong and athletic man, pinched her nipples tightly and constantly during intercourse. She told me that her nipples were quite sensitive and she didn't want them touched, at least not like *that*!

I asked Laura whether she had ever talked this over with Dave and told him what she liked and disliked sexually. She seemed shocked and protested, "I shouldn't have to! Don't you think he'd get the idea after thirty years?" Like Molly, Laura saw herself as the victim of someone else's insensitivity. She had never stopped to ask, "What am I doing to contribute to this problem?"

You might be thinking, "Okay, that's interesting, but it's not really so serious. All you have to do is encourage Laura to be more open with Dave. Encourage them to have some sessions together so they can talk about their sexual problems. Once she tells Dave where and how she likes to be touched, he'll probably respond differently. They both have a lot to gain and nothing to lose."

If that's what you are thinking, you took a page out of my book! I encouraged Laura to bring Dave to the sessions for that precise reason. She agreed, with some reluctance, but warned me that she thought the situation was "hopeless."

After several sessions with them together, I got to know Dave. He agreed that something important was missing from their marriage. For years he had been troubled by Laura's dissatisfaction with him. He felt he wasn't sufficiently manly to excite her sexually, and told me with embarrassment how he'd taken up long-distance running to try to build up his stamina. He was jogging over 60 miles a week and had competed in numerous marathons. He thought that if he

ARE YOU CONTRIBUTING TO THE PROBLEM?

Problem	How you may explain the problem	How you may be contributing to the problem
1. Your partner is uncommunicative and won't talk to you about how he or she feels.	You tell yourself that your partner is a cold fish who doesn't care or know how to express his or her feelings.	When your partner does try to express feelings, especially negative ones, you may feel put down and act hurt. You may get defensive and criticize him or her. Your partner feels attacked and reluctant to talk about his or her feelings.
2. Your partner seems rigid, dogmatic, and argumentative and won't listen to your point of view.	You tell yourself that your partner is stubborn, closed-minded, and controlling. You think that he or she has to be "right" all the time. You tell yourself that he or she doesn't care about your feelings and ideas.	You may be equally argumentative. You may insist on getting your ideas across without truly listening or trying to find truth in what your partner is trying to say.

Problem	How you may explain the problem	How you may be contributing to the problem
3. Your spouse and family seem selfish. They constantly make demands on you and rarely take your needs into account. You feel more like a hired maid than a wife and mother.	You tell yourself that your husband and children are insensitive to your needs and care only about themselves.	You may be unassertive and afraid to say no or to tell others what you want. You may think people should be sufficiently sensitive to be able to read your mind and know how you feel without your having to express yourself. You may have low self-esteem and feel you don't deserve to be happy or treated well by others. You may fear disapproval and think you have to be "nice" all the time to keep from being rejected.

became more athletic, that might please her and turn her on. With tears in his eyes, he admitted that no matter how hard he worked at it, he simply couldn't excite her. He felt like a real "loser" at sex.

I felt we were on the verge of a real breakthrough, so I asked Laura if she'd be willing to tell Dave about some of her sexual needs and feelings. I suggested she might tell him specifically what she liked and disliked about his lovemaking.

There was a long, tense moment of silence. Then Laura turned to me and said, "Dr. Burns, you're just like Dave. You really don't understand! I won't stand for this ridiculous conversation any longer!" She got up and bolted from the room.

Why did Laura walk out instead of talking about the problem that we had agreed to discuss? One reason has to do with Laura's feelings of fear and mistrust. She may have never felt loved or lovable. She may have never learned that it was possible to be open with the people she cared about. She may have never discovered that although these problems can be painful at first, there can be a reward after you confront your fears and resolve the problem. She may not have believed that she and Dave could feel close as a result of working things through. Laura is much like someone with a severe phobia. She is terribly afraid of talking about a conflict openly, in much the same way that some people are terrified of elevators. She believes that if she opens up, something awful will happen.

Reality often reinforces these fears. When people try to work through a problem, it usually *is* stressful at first. For one thing, Laura may have always felt ashamed of her sexual impulses. Talking about her feelings may make her feel embarrassed, vulnerable, and unfeminine. In addition, she may not express herself well at first, and Dave might feel hurt or he could get defensive. This might make her all the more convinced that expressing her feelings just won't work. She might conclude it isn't worth all the grief and pain it causes.

Since Laura is extremely angry at Dave for not loving her as she wants to be loved, there may be another motivation for storming out of the room instead of staying to work on the problem. Laura may feel so angry with him that she prefers to punish him and sabotage the therapy.

I am always amazed when I see people choosing the road to revenge over the path to intimacy. It seems that there is something seductive and appealing about our hostility, and it can be very difficult to let go of it. It can be hard to admit that we're choosing to hang on to our anger instead of resolving the problem. There's something strangely comforting about blaming another person and imagining that they are the sole cause of our unhappiness. Let's face it, revenge fantasies are enormously appealing. And if we have to choose between what seems like the outside chance of being loved and the virtual certainty of perpetuating the war, it can be awfully hard to resist the temptation of inflicting further pain.

How Your Conflict Phobia Keeps
You Stuck

The desire to get back at others can prevent you from opening up and getting closer to them. Many people have the opposite problem—they are afraid of anger and conflict. They think they should be nice all the time and never have any negative feelings. I call this a "conflict phobia." People with this attitude will go to great lengths to avoid talking openly about disagreements or hurt feelings.

Many of us were raised with the belief that negative emotions like anger are bad. This attitude can make it hard for you to express your feelings. You may be afraid to say "I feel angry right now" or "I feel lonely," because you think you shouldn't feel this way. This attitude may also make it hard for you to listen. If someone you respect is angry with you, you don't want to hear it because you feel you have failed or that your relationship is less than what it should be.

The following is an excerpt from a therapy session with Andy, a businessman who has suffered from chronic anxiety, depression, and loneliness for much of his life. Andy doesn't feel nearly as close to his wife, Mary, or to his daughters as he would like. Every time he tries to raise this issue at home, he gets nowhere.

As the session unfolds, Andy is telling me how bad he feels because Mary and his youngest daughter, Betsy, ignore him at the dinner table. The problem is especially poignant for Andy because his other daughters are away at college in California and this is Betsy's last year at home.

ANDY: I got into a hassle with Mary about our youngest daughter, Betsy. Betsy and Mary usually ignore me at the dinner table. I feel like Betsy excludes me from the conversation. What really hurts is—I feel alone. I tried to talk to Betsy but it didn't work out too well. She cried and said she was unhappy and felt guilty. She said she felt she was trying her best and that nothing more could be done.

DAVID: If Betsy is ignoring you, maybe she's angry with you. You need to find out how she feels and to share your feelings with her. Otherwise you're not connecting with her.

ANDY: I didn't realize it was important to do that. I've never done it, and I'm not sure I can handle a lot of negative emotions. I can try to draw her out but I'm afraid if I do I'll feel like I've screwed things up by causing all this conflict.

DAVID: How does it follow that you've screwed things up?

ANDY: I feel those negative emotions wouldn't have been there if I hadn't stirred them up.

NOTE: Andy's tendency to blame himself makes him fear conflict. If Betsy gets upset, he feels like he's done something wrong. Do you ever feel this way?

DAVID: Let me see if I understand. Prior to the conversation, Betsy had nothing but sweet emotions for you?

ANDY (*Laughs*): Right! Yes! That's correct. And then when I got angry it stirred up all these negative feelings that weren't there. That's what I was thinking. I guess I tend to blame myself when Betsy gets upset. I feel I caused her to feel that way. When I was growing up my mother used to say, "If you want to talk about something bad, I don't want to hear it." Maybe my whole family has the belief that people shouldn't talk about negative feelings. If someone expresses negative feelings, then I feel I've failed. It seems there's something wrong if someone is angry. I dislike conflict, and so I must project that attitude to the kids.

DAVID: Yeah, they're obviously avoiding conflict just like Dad and Mom do.

ANDY: How can I change this? How can I get Betsy to open up? When I told Betsy I wanted to talk, she said, "Yeah," in a cool way, as if to say, "Dad's here. Ugh!"

DAVID: What was your response?

ANDY: I said, "I'd like to talk to you about what happened yesterday when the three of us were talking at dinner."

DAVID: Okay. Now, what's wrong with that? Let me remind you about the two principles of good communication: you express your own feelings and acknowledge how the other person is feeling. Can you see that you failed to tell her how you were feeling or to acknowledge where she was coming from?

ANDY (*Laughs*): Oh, *I* see! Yeah, sure. Whenever I walk into the room, it's always the same. She acts cold, as if she doesn't want to talk to me. I don't comment on that. I ignore it.

DAVID: Yeah—and how does it make you feel when she treats you like that?

ANDY: Not good. She's real cool. I feel defensive.

DAVID: Exactly! Now instead of intellectualizing about what happened yesterday, could you tell her how you feel? What would you say?

ANDY: I could tell her that I feel defensive and uncomfortable and shut out, and that I really *do* want to talk.

DAVID: That would be a good statement of how you feel. That's quite good. You might also want to ask her about her feelings, like this: "Betsy, when you said 'Yeah' you seemed so cool. You seem annoyed, and that tone of voice hurts me. I feel real put down. This happens between us an awful lot. This is what I wanted to talk to you about. If you feel upset with me, I want you to tell me how you feel more directly. Do you feel annoyed?"

ANDY: Yeah . . . that's good.

DAVID: I don't think you need to go any further than this. Ask her how she's feeling, and tell her how you're feeling. That's the solution, to focus on how you both feel.

ANDY: I try to talk about my feelings, but I get intellectual and confused and I don't know what's going on.

DAVID: The reason you get confused is because you're not really paying attention to your emotions. Your feelings need to be shared, and her feelings need to be expressed as well. But instead, you kept trying to solve the problem of being excluded at the dinner table. You failed to get together emotionally.

ANDY: I guess she was unhappy with me and I was unhappy with her.

DAVID: Exactly! And instead of dealing with that, you probably kept focusing on your so-called agenda.

ANDY: Right! But how do you deal with being unhappy with each other?

DAVID: All you have to do is say, "It sounds like you're feeling a little unhappy with me. I'm not comfortable either. Tell me a little more about how you feel right now." The purpose of a close relationship is simply to share your feelings with someone you trust. But that's the one thing that many people have great difficulty doing.

ANDY: Okay, but *then* what do you do? She may say she's unhappy with me. What then?

DAVID: Be a good listener. Find some truth in what she's saying. Empathize with how she feels. Be curious and ask her questions so you can learn more about her feelings. Be open and friendly and let her know how you feel.

ANDY: So she's unhappy with me, and I'm unhappy with her because I feel alone.

DAVID: There you go. That's it! That's what needs to be said—and heard.

ANDY: I *told* her I felt ignored. She came out with all these reasons she was acting that way. I can't deal with that crap.

DAVID: Of course not. But you do need to listen. You can tell her that you feel lonely and hurt and that you want to feel close because you care about her. And you need to hear that she's unhappy too. You don't need to look for a solution, because the moment you share your feelings in a spirit of trust and caring, you will feel closer to each other. That's the real meaning of intimacy.

The next week Andy told me that the session made a strong positive impact on him. He saw that he had to take a risk and open up emotionally in order to feel close to his wife and daughter. He also saw that his lifelong struggle to intellectualize and to avoid conflict had become more uncomfortable than simply dealing with the negative feelings that are inherent in any close relationship. Although revealing these feelings may be painful and frightening in the short run, it can provide an opportunity for real sharing and growth.

How Martyrdom Can Keep You Stuck

Marge is a 52-year-old woman who decided to start dating after being divorced for many years. She's a sweet, petite, spunky woman who's done well in business, but she sometimes strikes people as being a little too formal and too "nice." For several months we talked about how to flirt and how to dress in a more casual and appealing way. Marge was an enthusiastic student and her phone was ringing frequently. Lots of men wanted to date her.

One fellow, Nate, was attracted to Marge, but he seemed a little bit unstable and irresponsible. One thing he did that was annoying was to call her late at night after he'd been drinking, to brag about his real or imaginary sexual exploits with various women. Marge was turned off by this obnoxious behavior, but she was nevertheless attracted to him because she felt inhibited and he seemed wild and exciting.

One Friday, Nate called at midnight to invite Marge to have

dinner with him and a business associate on Nate's yacht the next evening. He told Marge to meet them at the dock at 6:00. Although it was a last-minute invitation, Marge accepted. She showed up at 6:15 because of a traffic jam, and Nate's yacht was nowhere in sight. She was perplexed and waited several minutes. No Nate. Then she asked a man who worked on the dock if he'd seen Nate's boat. Marge learned that Nate and another man had taken the boat out two hours earlier. Marge felt furious and embarrassed for being stood up.

She left and didn't contact Nate. Several days later he called at 3:00 a.m. Marge was away and her daughter took the call. Nate was intoxicated and demanded to know why Marge had stood *him* up. Marge's daughter explained that her mother wouldn't do something like that, and said that Marge was gone for the weekend.

During the next session, a student co-therapist asked Marge what she wanted to do about the situation. Marge said she really wanted to call Nate and tell him he was acting like a jerk. I asked Marge if she would be willing to do that. Marge pulled back and turned red and said she wouldn't *dream* of doing something like that! Her reasons? She had many excuses, including:

"I'm supposed to be a nice person."

"It's my fault for choosing the wrong kinds of guys."

"When I was raised, I was told that you shouldn't make yourself vulnerable by letting someone know that you're angry or that they hurt you."

Marge told us that when she was growing up, her mother, a bitter and unhappy woman, always told her she should *never* show her feelings. A girl Marge knew constantly picked on Marge and Marge wanted to tell her off. Marge's mother told her to "rise above it." She said she should never let this girl know she was getting to Marge.

While there's some value in turning the other cheek and not letting someone get your goat, playing the role of a martyr can be destructive. Marge learned to blame herself and to hide all her feelings. This is unfair to her *and* to other people. In the first place, she comes off as too sweet and doesn't seem genuine. In addition, how can people know how she feels if she doesn't tell them?

This type of interaction occurred repeatedly while I was seeing Marge. Acting sweet and ignoring people's hostile behavior was as natural to her as breathing. The most recent incident involved an exciting and successful lawyer who proposed to her after they'd been dating for several months. Marge was thrilled with his proposal. The only problem was that she never heard from him again. Marge finally began to realize that her "niceness" simply wasn't working, and that she was just a doormat and was getting used. It took considerable courage and persistence for her to express herself. She finally took the risk of being more open and assertive, and she's feeling a lot happier with herself and more satisfied in her relationships.

Men are just as frequently afraid of expressing angry feelings. I have just started treating a 30-year-old architect named Ben who developed a severe depression after he and his wife separated. Ben separated from his wife because he had an affair with a lady client whom he found terribly exciting. Ben told me that he had lost interest in his wife and the excitement and the romance just weren't there any longer. However, the real problem in Ben's marriage wasn't the absence of romance, but the inability to deal with anger. Ben believed that it was "wrong" to feel upset, and he took great pride in the fact that he never displayed any angry feelings. Since he never let his negative feelings out, they simply built up and sabotaged the sexual and tender ones. He had recently lost his job for a similar reason: his boss, an aggressive man, told him, "You have no blood in your veins. You're too cold and calculating. I never know what you feel."

During his third therapy session, Ben discussed yet another problem—a conflict with his parents. He felt annoyed with them but told himself, "I have no right to be angry with them, because they're trying to help me. I shouldn't feel angry with them." This thought made him feel inadequate and guilty. He said he felt like a failure in his marriage, in his work, and as a son.

Ben insisted that he was being realistic. He said he felt strongly that he should never get angry. Although he acknowledged that most people feel angry at times, he said he took great pride in the fact that he always hid his anger and suffered silently. He could see that this was rather self-defeating, but said he didn't want to give in and lower his standards and end up like any other "average" man who lost his cool and got mad. This reveals the tremendous sense of pride that often lurks beneath our pain.

To help Ben deal with his problem, I asked him to list the advantages and disadvantages of believing he should never get angry. You can see in his Cost-Benefit Analysis (page 461) that there are many benefits, as well as a number of disadvantages, to this mind-set.

Probably the greatest benefit is a sense of self-righteous perfectionism. By refusing to express his anger, Ben can stay in control and keep people at a distance, in a one-down position. "I'm just a tad better" is the message he projects, "so I won't let you get to me." In spite of all the misery he feels, he can tell himself, "I'm one cut above the rest." The disadvantages include constant stress, loneliness, and depression, because Ben can never feel close to himself or to other people. Is it worth paying such a heavy price?

How Your Need to Solve Problems Keeps You Stuck

One attitude that gets in the way of good communication is the need to solve problems. I often tell troubled couples that they must refuse to solve the problems in their relationship if they hope to experience greater love and closeness. This may sound like a paradox, but it's really not. If two people are upset with each other and are arguing about some "problem," they will usually go round and round in circles when they are trying to solve it. This bickering will continue as long as they feel angry with each other. Their feelings need to be expressed in a nondefensive way—and listened to. But if their anger isn't shared openly—and it almost never is—all their attempts to solve the problem will fail. As long as they feel angry and at odds, they will need to get back at each other. This makes it impossible to solve the problem. In contrast, if they share their feelings and listen in a spirit of trust, and feel cared about and respected once again, they will find it far easier to solve the problems that bother them.

To take a simple example, let's say that Marilyn wants to go out Thursday nights to attend a class at the local college. Ron, her husband, is uncomfortable about having to make dinner that night and eat alone with their daughter. They have been arguing about this problem and they just can't seem to find a solution that would be fair to both of them.

Marilyn argues that it's her right to go out one night a week. She

COST-BENEFIT ANALYSIS

The attitude or belief I want to change:

I should never get angry

Advantages of Believing This	Disadvantages of Believing This
1. I'll avoid confrontations and conflicts with people.	1. The anger will come out in some other way that may be destructive.
2. When I'm aware that I'm getting angry, I'll be able to criticize and scold myself.	2. I will deny myself a part of being human.
3. That way I'll never be out of control.	3. I'll set a bad example for my daughter.
4. The world, other people, and outside stimuli won't be able to exert any influence over me.	4. I'll set an impossible standard for myself. This will lead to further frustration and pain as I reprimand myself for not being perfect.
5. I'll be able to deceive myself into thinking I have risen above mere average people and I'll think that I'm somehow better.	5. I won't feel comfortable with myself.
6. I'll feel like Mr. Cool.	6. I may not come across as genuine to other people.
7. It makes life simple because I'll always know what to do.	7. I may deprive myself of a source of self-esteem and intimacy.
8. I can keep people at a distance.	8. My anger could help me deal with many situations more effectively.
	9. Life loses its complexity and richness.

(40)——————————————(60)

Revised Attitude: Anger may be uncomfortable but there are times

when it's better for me and for the relationship to tell the other person

how I feel.

says that Ron needs to spend more time with their daughter, so it shouldn't be a problem. Ron half-heartedly agrees with this but says he feels uncomfortable with the arrangement because he and Marilyn don't ever have much time together anymore.

Can you see why their attempts to solve this problem might fail? Marilyn feels controlled and housebound. Ron has had a successful career and she's dutifully raised their children. Now she would like to make her life a little more interesting and complete her undergraduate degree. If Ron recognizes this and listens to her feelings, Marilyn will feel respected and cared about. But if he criticizes her plans and only complains about being alone every Thursday, he'll appear selfish and insecure. This will make her angry and she'll get more and more demanding, because she doesn't want to feel controlled.

By the same token, Ron has slaved away at his career and developed a good income, and he would like to feel closer to Marilyn and to his daughter. He wants to spend more time with them. He feels lonely and needs greater intimacy. If she listens and shows concern for how he feels, then Ron will feel respected and cared about. But if she just proclaims her right to do her thing, she will appear selfish, and this will make him feel even more hurt and lonely. Ron doesn't want to feel rejected and cast aside.

If they attempt to solve the problem of what to do on Thursday night, failure is almost guaranteed. No external arrangement can ever meet their needs to feel loved and respected by each other. But if they refuse to solve this problem and try instead to listen to each other in a spirit of trust and caring first, their problem will no longer exist. The problem of what to do on Thursdays doesn't really need a solution. What they are craving is intimacy and self-esteem.

You may protest. You say, "All that touchy-feely stuff is missing the point. The bottom line is that they have to figure out what they're going to do on Thursdays. Will she go to her class or won't she? They've got to compromise and find a solution." I don't believe that a compromise is indicated, and I think that looking for a solution would be a mistake. Ron and Marilyn need to express their feelings and be heard. If Ron feels loved and respected, I doubt that he'll mind cooking and spending a couple of hours on Thursdays with their daughter. He might see cooking as an expression of his love for Marilyn and for his daughter and not as an imposition. By the same token, if Marilyn feels loved and cared about, she will take Ron's needs into account as she plans more time outside the home to complete her studies and to develop her own career. She will view her relationship with Ron as a haven and as a complement to her independence rather than as a restriction of her freedom. It will be important to spend time with him and to make sure he feels loved and happy.

I have written this chapter to warn you that even though you may be hurting a great deal and desperately want to make your personal relationships better, you may find it exceedingly difficult to change. When you're annoyed with someone, it's natural to focus on what the other person is doing wrong and to hide the many things you are doing that may contribute to the difficulties. This is a trap from which very few can escape. Over and over, patients are extremely enthusiastic when they first learn about the two principles of good communication—sharing your own feelings and drawing out your partner. But when it's time to put these principles into practice, they suddenly have a change of heart. They find that they can't resist a good argument about the "truth," in much the same way that an alcoholic can't resist the urge to take a drink.

People always have lots of reasons why they shouldn't have to express their feelings with "I feel" statements or to draw out how the other person feels. They may insist that their situation is hopeless and tell me that these techniques wouldn't do any good. They may explain that their spouse "really *is* wrong" and emphasize that it's terribly important to point this out to him or her. The list of reasons not to share your feelings openly or to listen goes on and on. Arguing and blaming your partner may feel good in the short run, and it's awfully tempting to pout and to lash out. Making yourself vulnerable by listening and by sharing your feelings in a spirit of trust frequently gets forgotten in all the sound and fury. When it comes to a choice between love and hatred, between sharing and attacking, between working together or doing battle, it's hard to resist the more hostile approach.

Learning to listen and to share your feelings more openly will not come easily, but I believe that with persistent determination, you can experience greater intimacy.

Mood-Altering Medications

•

23

Answers to Your Questions About Commonly Prescribed Medications for Depression and Anxiety

In this book I have emphasized drug-free treatments for depression and anxiety. You may be wondering whether or not you would also benefit from an antidepressant medication or from an anti-anxiety medication. In this chapter I will answer a number of basic questions about these medications. You will learn whether depression and anxiety result from a chemical inbalance in the brain. You will also learn how effective these drugs are, if some are better than others, and how you can tell if they are really helping you.

In the next two chapters I will tell you about the medications that are currently used to treat depression, bipolar manic-depressive illness, and the anxiety disorders, such as chronic worry, panic attacks, phobias, shyness, obsessive-compulsive disorder, post-traumatic stress disorder, and others. You will learn about costs, dose ranges, side effects, drug interactions, and dangers of all the currently prescribed antidepressant drugs, mood stabilizers, and anti-anxiety medications. You will also learn about a number of common errors in prescribing that you should be aware of.

You may be thinking, "Why should I have to deal with all these complicated issues? Isn't it my doctor's responsibility to know which drugs I need and to inform me about them?" In an ideal world that would be true, but in the real world we live in, it may not always be a safe assumption. It pays to be well informed about any medications you are taking, and it doesn't hurt to be assertive with the physician who prescribes them for you.

I don't mean to stir up conflict between you and your physician. Quite the contrary. The dialogue you have with your doctor about drugs and side effects is a crucial part of therapy. Your knowledge can enhance the feeling of teamwork and increase the chances for a positive result.

If I am depressed or anxious, does it mean I have a chemical imbalance of some type in my brain? No, this is not a safe conclusion. There have been theories, dating back nearly two thousand years to Hippocrates, the father of modern medicine, that depression may result from some type of abnormal chemical or hormone. Theories have been proposed linking depression with abnormalities in a wide variety of transmitter chemicals that nerves use to send messages to each other. Chemical transmitters that have been studied include serotonin, norepinephrine, dopamine, GABA (gamma-aminobutyric acid), glutamate, and many others. To date, no conclusive proof of a cause-and-effect relationship linking any of these chemicals to depression has been forthcoming. In addition, there is no laboratory test that can be performed which would tell us if any specific patient, or any group of patients, has any kind of chemical imbalance that causes depression or anxiety.

Some psychiatrists appear to confuse theory with fact. They tell depressed patients that they have chemical depressions that must be treated with antidepressants. I would prefer that psychiatrists not do this, because it creates an impression of certainty in the patient's mind that is not justified by current scientific evidence. In addition, it may make at least some patients feel helpless—they may wrongly conclude that their depression results from chemical factors beyond their control that can only be treated with medications. This belief can act as a self-fulfilling prophecy. If you do not try to cope with the stressful events that may have triggered your depression, it is not likely that you will identify and resolve these problems.

There has also been a great deal of research suggesting that negative thinking patterns may cause depression. From a clinical perspective, it is easy to see that these negative thinking patterns are present in practically every individual suffering from depression, anxiety, and low self-esteem. These negative thinking patterns could be inherited—pessimism may be something we are born with—or learned when we are growing up.

As a clinician, the most important question is this: how can I best help the individuals I am treating who are suffering from depression and anxiety? I find that the new forms of psychotherapy are invaluable, and I use them with every patient I treat. I find that the medications can also be quite helpful for some patients, although they are clearly not helpful for everyone.

Although the causes of depression are not yet known, the evidence is much stronger that schizophrenia and bipolar manic-depressive illness are biological disorders that have extremely strong genetic components. Medications are usually needed to treat these conditions, although psychotherapy can also play an important role.

How can I decide whether I should be treated with drugs only, psychotherapy only, or a combination of both? At my clinic in Philadelphia, about 60 percent of the patients receive psychotherapy alone and 40 percent receive psychotherapy plus medication. I have not had good success treating depression and anxiety with medications alone. I usually do not offer this type of treatment, even though it is currently in vogue.

I always ask my patients during the initial evaluations whether or not they would prefer to take antidepressants. Some patients strongly feel that they would prefer to be treated without an antidepressant. I usually treat them with cognitive therapy alone, and this is often successful. However, if the patient has been working hard in therapy for six to ten weeks without any improvement, I sometimes suggest we try to add an antidepressant to put some "high octane" in the tank, so to speak. In some cases this makes the psychotherapy more effective.

Some patients strongly feel that they would like to receive antidepressants. I treat them with a combination of an antidepressant medication and psychotherapy. However, I almost never treat patients with antidepressant medications alone. I began my career using this approach, but found that too many patients had unsatisfactory outcomes. The combination of medications with psychotherapy seems to produce better results in both the short term and the long term than drugs alone.

It may sound unscientific to base the medication decision on the patient's preferences, and certainly in some cases I have to make a recommendation that differs from my patient's wishes. But the majority of the time I have found that patients do well when treated with the approach they are the most comfortable with.

Who would be most likely to benefit from a medication? The following guidelines are not rigid. They are intended to provide a general framework.

- People who are out of touch with reality and who have delusions or bizarre hallucinations. These individuals nearly always need antipsychotic medications to control their symptoms, at least during the time when the symptoms are quite severe. Psychotherapy can often also be beneficial, but is usually not nearly powerful enough for the psychotic symptoms. Psychotic symptoms are not generally seen with depression or anxiety disorders. They are more characteristic of schizophrenia, severe mania, drug intoxication or withdrawal, or other brain disorders.
- If you are so severely depressed or anxious that you cannot function or do anything to help yourself, you may need the help of an antidepressant medication.
- If your depression is characterized by many physical symptoms such as insomnia, severe changes in appetite, agitation, or retardation; a loss of interest in sex; a worsening of symptoms in the morning; and an inability to feel cheered up by positive events.
- If you feel suicidal, you should probably be treated with the best of everything available, including a good antidepressant medication and intensive psychotherapy.
- If you have been working hard in your psychotherapy for a couple of months and you feel stuck, you may benefit from a medication. Often the right antidepressant will get things moving forward more rapidly.
- If you have positive feelings about being treated with medications for your mood problems, or if you have had a positive response to an antidepressant in the past.
- If you have never been treated with an antidepressant.
- If you do not abuse alcohol or other drugs.
- If your depression has had a reasonably clear-cut beginning and your symptoms are quite different from the way you normally feel.
- If your depression is of fairly short duration and has not gone on and on for many years or even for a decade or more.
- If you have a strong desire to get better.
- If you are not receiving financial compensation for your depression (such as disability payments) and you are not involved in a lawsuit and hope to receive money because of your psychiatric symptoms.

Most of these guidelines are based on clinical wisdom and anecdotal evidence and not on systematic research, so you should take them with a grain of salt. There are lots of exceptions to the rules. Many people who looked like they would be poor drug responders have positive responses to antidepressants, and others with all the characteristics of drug responders have not been helped by antidepressant medications. As noted above, I always combine medications with psychotherapy, and so there are lots of other ways to help an individual if the medication does not work.

How can I tell which antidepressant drug will be the best one for me? All of the currently prescribed antidepressant drugs tend to work about equally well, and equally rapidly, for most patients. Therefore, it may not make a great deal of difference which one you take.

So far no new type of antidepressant medication has been shown to be more effective or faster-acting than the older drugs that have been available for several decades. However, there are dramatic differences in the costs and side effects of the different types of antidepressants. The newer medications are far more expensive than the older ones because they still are patented. They are also more popular because they usually have fewer side effects than the older, cheaper drugs. In addition, if you have certain kinds of medical conditions, some antidepressants will be relatively safer for you than others. I will discuss these issues in greater detail in the next chapter.

Many doctors select an antidepressant for a particular patient based on the kinds of side effects the drug has. For example, some antidepressants tend to make you sleepy, and others tend to be stimulating. If you are nervous and agitated and having trouble sleeping, your doctor will probably prescribe a medication that has sedative side effects. In contrast, if you are fatigued and unmotivated and sleeping all the time, your doctor may prescribe a drug that is more on the stimulating side. Similarly, some drugs that stimulate the appetite will be helpful if you are depressed and losing weight. Other drugs without this effect may be better for you if you are overweight and eating too much because of your depression.

Sometimes a patient will respond particularly well to one antidepressant but not to others. Unfortunately, we cannot usually predict this ahead of time, and so most physicians use a trial-and-error approach. There are a few generalizations about the kinds of antidepressants that work best for certain kinds of problems. For example, drugs that have stronger side effects on the serotonin systems in the brain are generally considered to be more effective for patients who suffer from obsessive-compulsive disorder (called OCD for short). Patients with

OCD have recurrent illogical thoughts (like the fear their stove will catch fire and burn the house down), and they perform compulsive rituals over and over (such as checking repeatedly to make sure that they turned the stove off). Drugs that may be especially helpful for OCD include several of the tricyclic antidepressants such as clomipramine (Anafranil), the SSRIs such as fluoxetine (Prozac) or fluvoxamine (Luvox), or the MAOIs such as tranylcypromine (Parnate).

If you have symptoms of anxiety, such as panic attacks or social anxiety, your physician might choose one of the SSRI or MAOI antidepressants, since these often seem to be quite effective. Your physician might also choose one of the more sedative antidepressants, such as trazodone (Desyrel) or doxepin (Sinequan), since the relaxation might help reduce your anxiety.

Over the years I have treated many patients with a particularly difficult type of chronic and severe depression known as Borderline Personality Disorder (called BPD for short). Patients with this disorder have intense and constantly fluctuating negative moods such as depression, anxiety, and anger. Patients with BPD also experience lots of turbulence in their personal relationships. In my experience, some BPD patients respond dramatically to the MAOI antidepressants, and so I might be more inclined to choose an MAOI for patients with these features. Of course, some patients with BPD have poor impulse control, and they may do better with one of the newer and safer antidepressants. This is because the MAOIs can be quite dangerous if patients mix these drugs with certain forbidden foods and medications that I will describe in detail in the next chapter.

The bottom line is this: any depressed patient has a reasonably good chance of responding positively to almost any antidepressant medication if it is prescribed at the correct dose for a reasonable period of time. Most physicians prescribe the antidepressants they are the most familiar with. This is good practice. Few doctors can master the myriad details about all the currently prescribed antidepressants, and most doctors try to become very familiar with a few medications and they use them frequently. As a result, your doctor will usually be very familiar with the medication they are recommending for you.

What are the most common kinds of side effects? All of the medications prescribed for depression, anxiety, and other psychiatric problems cause side effects. For example, many of the older antidepressants (such as amitriptyline, trade name Elavil) cause fairly noticeable side effects such as dry mouth, sleepiness, dizziness, and weight gain, among others. Many of the newer antidepressants (such as fluoxetine, trade name Prozac) can cause nervousness, sweating, upset stomach, or a loss of interest in sex as well as difficulties having an orgasm.

I will describe the specific side effects of every antidepressant and anti-anxiety drug in the next two chapters. You will see that some medications produce lots of side effects, whereas others produce very few.

The Side Effects Checklist beginning on page 475 can provide you and your physician with accurate information about any side effects that you experience while you are taking a medication. If you take this test a couple times per week, this will show how the side effects change over time.

Remember that many of these so-called "side effects" can occur even if you are not taking any medication, since many are also symptoms of depression or anxiety. Feeling tired, having trouble sleeping at night, or a loss of interest in sex are good examples. It can be very useful to complete the Side Effects Checklist at least once or twice before you start any medication. That way you can see if a side effect began before or after you started the drug. Obviously, if you had the same side effect before you started taking a drug, then the drug is probably not to blame for it.

Also, remember that patients who take only placebo medications (sugar pills) during research studies tend to report side effects as well. This is because they think they are taking a real drug. So there is no proof that a particular side effect is necessarily caused by the drug you are taking. When in doubt, talk this over with your physician.

How will I know if the medication is working? I am pretty demanding in terms of what I expect from an antidepressant—I believe that any antidepressant medication should have a profound and dramatic effect in order to justify its continued use. I believe that every patient taking antidepressants should take mood tests like the ones in Chapter 2 at least once a week. Your scores on these tests will be a highly reliable measure of how well the medication is working.

I do not encourage patients to continue taking drugs that have only modest or questionable beneficial effects on mood. When the score on the test goes down only a little bit (for example, a 30 or 40 percent improvement), I am inclined to call this a placebo effect and not a real drug effect. This amount of improvement could be due to the passage of time, the psychotherapy, or the belief that the drug will work. If the improvement in mood is minimal, and if the patient has had a sufficient dose of the medication for a sufficient period of time, I would probably take the patient off the drug and try another medication, a combination of medication and psychotherapy, or psychotherapy alone.

Now, you may think, "But a 40 percent improvement in my mood sounds pretty good. I'm almost halfway better." Certainly any improvement is desirable, but research studies indicate that inactive placebos can also have significant antidepressant effects. A 40 percent improvement is typical of a placebo response.

The only justification for taking any antidepressant drug is this: Is the drug doing its job? To my way of thinking, the goal of treatment is to recover from depression. Most patients want complete recovery, not just a slight or moderate improvement in their mood. If an antidepressant is not accomplishing this goal after a reasonable trial, I would recommend switching to another drug or treatment approach.

How well do most of the antidepressant drugs work? Most studies indicate that approximately 50 to 70 percent of depressed patients respond to an antidepressant medication. Since approximately 30 to 50 percent of depressed patients also respond to a sugar pill (a placebo), most of these studies indicate that an antidepressant increases your chances for recovery at least somewhat.

However, remember that the word *respond* is different from the word *recover,* and the improvement from an antidepressant is often only partial. In other words, your score on a mood test like the one in Chapter 2 may improve without going into the range considered truly happy (less than 5). This is why I nearly always combine antidepressant medication treatment with cognitive and behavioral techniques like those described in this book. Most people are not interested in just partial improvement. They want the real McCoy. They want to get up in the morning and say, "Hey, it's great to be alive!"

As I have emphasized, most of the depressed and anxious people I have treated have problems in their lives such as a marital conflict or a career difficulty, and nearly all of them beat up on themselves with negative thinking patterns. In my experience, medication therapy is usually more effective—and more satisfying—when good it is combined with good psychotherapy.

How long does it take for an antidepressant or anti-anxiety medication to work? On average, antidepressants require two to four weeks to work, although there are exceptions. As a general rule, I don't keep a patient on any drug unless it is having a fairly dramatic beneficial effect. If there's no obvious reduction in your scores on mood tests

SIDE EFFECTS CHECKLIST*

Instructions: Put a check (✓) after each item to indicate how much you have been bothered by each type of side effect during the past several days. Please answer all the items.

	0–NOT AT ALL	1–SOMEWHAT	2–MODERATELY	3–A LOT	4–EXTREMELY
MOUTH AND STOMACH					
1. Dry mouth					
2. Frequently thirsty					
3. Loss of appetite					
4. Nausea or vomiting					
5. Stomach cramps or upset stomach					
6. Increase in appetite or eating too much					
7. Weight gain or loss	/				
8. Constipation					
9. Diarrhea					
EYES AND EARS					
10. Blurred vision					
11. Overly sensitive to light					
12. Changes in vision, such as halos around objects					
13. Ringing in your ears					
SKIN					
14. Sweating too much					
15. Rash					
16. Excessive sunburn when exposed to sun					
17. Change in skin color					
18. Bleeding or bruising easily					

SIDE EFFECTS CHECKLIST (cont.)	0–NOT AT ALL	1–SOMEWHAT	2–MODERATELY	3–A LOT	4–EXTREMELY
SEX					
19. Loss of interest in sex					
20. Difficulties getting sexually excited					
21. Difficulties getting an erection (men)					
22. Difficulties having an orgasm					
23. Difficulties with your period (women)					
STIMULATION AND NERVOUSNESS					
24. Stimulated					
25. Agitated					
26. Anxious, worried, or nervous					
27. Feeling strange or "spaced out"					
28. Excess energy					
SLEEP PROBLEMS					
28. Feeling tired or exhausted					
30. Loss of energy					
31. Sleeping too much					
32. Trouble falling asleep					
33. Sleep that is restless or disturbed					
34. Waking up too early in the morning					
35. Nightmares or strange dreams					
MUSCLES AND COORDINATION					
36. Muscle jerks or twitches					
37. Slurred speech					
38. Tremor					
39. Difficulty walking or loss of balance					
40. Feeling slowed down					

SIDE EFFECTS CHECKLIST *(cont.)*	0–NOT AT ALL	1–SOMEWHAT	2–MODERATELY	3–A LOT	4–EXTREMELY
41. Stiffness of the arms, legs, or tongue					
42. Feeling restless, like you have to keep moving your arms or legs					
43. Hand-wringing					
44. Constant, regular, rhythmic leg jiggling					
45. Abnormal movements of your face, lips, tongue					
46. Abnormal movements of other parts of your body, such as your fingers or shoulders					
47. Muscle spasms of your tongue, jaw, or neck					
OTHER					
48. Difficulty remembering things					
49. Feeling dizzy, light-headed, or faint					
50. Feeling your heart race or pound					
51. Swelling in your arms or legs					
52. Trouble starting urination					
53. Headache					
54. Breast swelling or enlargement					
55. Milk secretion from the nipples					

Please describe any other side effects: _____

_____

_____

_____

like the Burns Depression Checklist or the Burns Anxiety Inventory (see Chapter 2) after several weeks, I would switch to another, more promising antidepressant. Often you can find one that will be helpful.

One common error is to stay on an antidepressant for many months or years, even though you are still quite depressed and your scores on the mood tests confirm that you have not improved much if at all. This has never made sense to me, and yet many patients referred to me over the years were in just this position. They had been taking some medication like amitriptyline (Elavil) or fluoxetine (Prozac) for many years, and yet they were depressed or anxious the entire time! When I asked why they were taking the drug, they have often said, "Oh, my doctor told me I needed this for a chemical imbalance in my brain, just like a diabetic needs to take insulin every day."

The reason diabetics take insulin is because *insulin works.* But if an antidepressant does not work—which is often—I do not see any reason to keep taking it. It would be better to change the therapy in some way. Your doctor can add an "augmenting drug" which can sometimes make the antidepressant more potent, or your doctor can switch to a different type of antidepressant. In addition, good psychotherapy often works when drugs do not. Sometimes the combination of antidepressants plus cognitive therapy can be quite effective.

The purpose of the medication is to speed your recovery. This means feeling happy and free from depression, anxiety, and worry. *When a medication is not working, there is simply no reason to keep taking it.* As noted above, the idea that depression and anxiety result from a chemical imbalance in the brain is just a theory, not a fact, and we still have no laboratory test that could diagnose this chemical imbalance if it did exist. Further, even if a chemical imbalance caused your depression, there would be no reason to take any drug unless that drug had a fairly dramatic beneficial effect.

In contrast to the antidepressants, many anti-anxiety drugs, such as the benzodiazepines like diazepam (Valium) or alprazolam (Xanax) and others, work rapidly, usually within an hour or less. Unfortunately, these drugs can also rapidly produce sleepiness and confusion. In addition, the anxiety comes back when the drug wears off, and so you have to keep taking it. Once you have taken the benzodiazepines for more than several weeks, the probability of physical dependence (addiction) increases significantly. Therefore, I do not encourage most patients to use these drugs for prolonged periods of time.

Fortunately, there are safer and more effective treatments for anxiety.

Many psychiatrists now use the antidepressants to treat anxiety as well as depression. Although the antidepressants take longer to work, they can be quite effective for anxiety as well as depression and they are not habit-forming. The cognitive behavioral treatments for anxiety described in this book have also been shown to be very effective for anxiety disorders, even when patients receive no medications at all.

If the medication does help, how long should I stay on it? As noted above, anti-anxiety drugs (minor tranquilizers) can be extremely addictive if you take them on a daily basis for more than several weeks. If you take large doses of benzodiazepines, the likelihood and severity of the physical dependency increases. I rarely use these drugs and encourage my patients to taper off them after a few days or a few weeks at most.

Since most antidepressants are not addictive, your doctor may suggest a treatment period of six to twelve months before you taper off. Some patients have asked me to taper off their antidepressant after they have been feeling really good for just a few months. This has usually been successful. Most psychiatrists prefer a longer depression-free period, since relapse is less likely.

Some psychiatrists tell their patients that they need to stay on their antidepressants for the rest of their lives to prevent relapses in the future. There are a number of long-term studies of patients for several years following treatment of the initial depression. Some studies suggest that patients who continue taking antidepressants have fewer relapses than patients who do not. However, other long-term studies indicate that patients treated with cognitive behavioral therapy (with or without drugs) also do well. Several studies suggest patients treated with cognitive therapy (and no medications) have fewer relapses than patients treated with medications (and no cognitive therapy).

Other kinds of psychiatric disorders may require ongoing treatment, or episodic treatment, over a prolonged period of time. Schizophrenia is an example. The cause of this disorder seems very likely to be biological, and the hallucinations and other psychotic symptoms, such as paranoia, may require treatment with one of the neuroleptic medications throughout the patient's life. Patients with bipolar manic-depressive illness may also require indefinite treatment with lithium or another of the mood stabilizers described in the next chapter. The medication smoothes the abnormal highs and lows and helps prevent future mood swings. Efforts to discontinue lithium may result in severe mania or depression. The situation is somewhat analogous to diabetes, where daily insulin may be needed to stabilize the metabolism of blood sugar. In addition, there is evidence that in some individuals lithium becomes less effective if it is stopped and then restarted at a later time.

What should I do if the depression comes back when I go off the antidepressant? The great majority of the patients I have treated have been able to discontinue their antidepressants following full recovery without any significant return of the depression. If the mood tests indicate the depression is increasing when you are tapering off the antidepressant, you can simply raise the dose slightly for a week or so until you are feeling undepressed again. Then you can slowly continue to taper off the medication again. Usually this works.

If a patient experiences a return of the depression at a later date, I encourage them to return for a "tune-up." We use the same cognitive therapy techniques that helped them recover initially. I might also use an antidepressant if the depression is severe. Generally I use the same medication that helped them previously. Although every individual is different, the great majority of my patients have responded to these relapses quite rapidly—often within a session or two.

Many doctors believe that depressed patients should stay on antidepressants indefinitely. I have rarely found long-term medication treatment necessary for depression, and I have asked myself why my experience is so different from that of my colleagues. I believe it is because all my patients receive intensive self-help treatment as described in this book. The main emphasis of our work is always on understanding and changing the negative thinking patterns and personal relationship or work problems that triggered the depression in the first place. When my patients complete therapy, they have a sense of mastery. They know the causes of their own depression or anxiety, and have a clear-cut understanding of what they need to do to overcome it. Specifically, they know the cognitive therapy method that proved most helpful to them. Using the same technique in the future usually works for that specific patient. It is like the combination to the lock on his or her emotional "safe."

In addition, prior to treatment I specifically train each patient to prepare for relapse ahead of time. During these relapses every patient tends to have the same thoughts. They are usually these:

1. This relapse proves I am hopeless.
2. I didn't really recover.
3. The therapy was just a fluke.

4. I never really improved—I was just fooling myself.
5. I am worthless after all.
6. Even if I do improve, it will just be temporary, and pretty soon I will fall back into this horrible depression again.

I encourage the patient to write these thoughts down on the Daily Mood Log. Then we identify the distortions in each negative thought. These include all-or-nothing thinking, fortune telling, discounting the positive, emotional reasoning, hidden "should" statements, and so forth. Then I encourage the patient to talk back to these thoughts, and we practice this in a role play. I play the role of these negative thoughts, and the patient plays the role of the positive thoughts. I verbalize the negative thoughts out loud, and the patient argues with my statements. We also do role reversals and continue until the patient can absolutely demolish the negative thoughts.

I also tape-record the session and give the tape to the patient so that she or he can play it if a relapse occurs. I attempt to complete this systematic relapse prevention (or relapse minimization) training for every patient prior to discharge. I believe this helps greatly, because only a handful of patients over the years have called for the treatment of relapses, and when they did, the treatment of the relapse rarely required more than a couple sessions.

How can I prevent potentially dangerous interaction between antidepressants and other drugs I may be taking, including non-prescription (over-the-counter) drugs? In recent years doctors have become increasingly aware that certain types of drugs may interact with each other in ways that are dangerous. Thus, two drugs may be quite safe and have few or no side effects if you take either one separately, but if you take the two drugs at the same time, there could be serious consequences because of how the two drugs interact with each other.

This problem of drug interactions has become increasingly important in recent years for two reasons. First, there is an increasing trend among psychiatrists to prescribe more than one psychiatric drug at a time. Second, more and more patients are being put on antidepressant drugs (as well as other types of psychiatric drugs) for prolonged periods of time, sometimes indefinitely. If you do take a psychiatric drug for a long time, eventually you will probably receive one or more prescriptions from other doctors for other medical problems. For example, your doctor might prescribe a medication for an allergy or high blood pressure or pain or an infection. In addition, you might take an over-the-counter medication for a cold, a cough, a headache, or an upset stomach. Now the very real possibility of drug interactions has to be considered, because these drugs may interact with the psychiatric drug you have been taking.

Of course, it goes without saying that psychiatric drugs can also interact with tobacco and alcohol as well as street drugs such as cocaine or amphetamines. In some cases these interactions can also be quite dangerous and even fatal. Some antidepressants interact in extremely dangerous ways with commonly used drugs, including over-the-counter medications. I am not trying to be overly alarmist here. With a little education and good teamwork with your physician, you can take an antidepressant safely.

In the next two chapters I will describe a number of important drug interactions for each drug or category of drug you might be taking. Remember that knowledge about these drug interactions is rapidly changing and evolving. New information comes out on almost a daily basis. Make certain each doctor you see has a complete and accurate list of every drug you are taking, including any over-the-counter drugs you take. Ask your doctor if there are any drug interactions that could be important. Ask your pharmacist the same thing. If they are not sure, ask them to check for you. It is virtually impossible to keep all potential drug interactions in your mind, because so much new information is constantly emerging. References and computer programs that list dangerous drug interactions are readily available to help with this task. If you are appropriately assertive and have a little education about the topic, you will be in a better position to have an intelligent discussion with your doctor about interactions among the drugs you are taking.

You will see in the next two chapters that I have prepared detailed charts or lists of important interactions for antidepressants, mood stabilizers, or anti-anxiety drugs. So, for example, if you are taking fluoxetine (Prozac), you can review the table that lists its drug interactions.

You may think that you shouldn't have to study these charts because your doctor should know all about any dangerous drug interactions and ensure that nothing bad happens to you. There are several problems with this line of reasoning. First, though your doctor may be extremely knowledgeable, he or she is also human and cannot keep up with all the new information that is emerging. Second, even if your doctor told you about every conceivable drug interaction, there is no way you could remember all of them! And third, in this era of managed care, doctors have to manage more and more patients, and you may get only a few minutes with your prescribing physician at infrequent intervals to review your symptoms and the dose of the medication. There may simply not be enough time to discuss all the possible drug interactions you need to know about.

This discussion represents my own philosophy about antidepressants and anti-anxiety medications. Keep in mind that psychiatry is still less standardized than internal medicine, and there is a lot more room for disagreement. Psychiatric treatment is still a blend of art and science, and your doctor's approach may differ from mine. If you have questions about the doses, side effects, drug interactions, or the effectiveness of any drug you are taking, review your concerns with your physician. My goal is to make you a more enlightened consumer and to improve your relationship with the physician who treats you. I believe that a sense of teamwork, trust, and support are crucial to recovery, in psychotherapy and in medication treatment as well.

24

◆

*The Complete Consumer's Guide to Antidepressant Medications**

This chapter gives you practical information you need about the costs, doses, side effects, and drug interactions for all the currently available antidepressant and mood-stabilizing drugs. I would recommend you use it as a reference source rather than trying to read it all at once—there is just too much detailed information to digest at one sitting. If you want to learn about a specific drug that you or a family member may be taking, the Table of Antidepressants on page 485 will help you locate the information you need. Let's assume, for example, that you are taking fluoxetine (Prozac). You can read the section on the SSRI antidepressants starting on page 505. In addition, the section on drug costs starting on page 487, should be of general interest to all readers.

*I would like to thank Joe Bellenoff, M.D., a psychopharmacology fellow at Stanford University Medical School, and Greg Tarasoff, M.D., a senior psychiatric resident at Stanford, for helpful suggestions during the revision of this chapter. In addition, much useful information was obtained from the excellent *Manual of Clinical Psychopharmacology,* Third Edition, by Alan F. Schatzberg, M.D., Jonathan Cole, M.D., and Charles DeBattista, D.M.H., M.D. (Washington: American Psychiatric Press, 1997). This scholarly but highly readable book is an invaluable reference. I highly recommend it for individuals who would like more information on the medications currently used in the treatment of emotional problems.

TABLE OF ANTIDEPRESSANTS

Antidepressant Drug Class	Chemical Name (and Trade Name)*	Page #
Tricyclic Antidepressants		492
	amitriptyline (Elavil, Endep)	
	clomipramine (Anafranil)	
	desipramine (Norpramin, Pertofrane)	
	doxepin (Adapin, Sinequan)	
	imipramine (Tofranil)	
	nortriptyline (Aventyl)	
	protriptyline (Vivactil)	
	trimipramine (Surmontil)	
Tetracyclic Antidepressants		492
	amoxapine (Asendin)	
	maprotiline (Ludiomil)	
SSRI Antidepressants		505
	citalopram (Celexa)	
	fluoxetine (Prozac)	
	fluvoxamine (Luvox)	
	paroxetine (Paxil)	
	sertraline (Zoloft)	
MAO Inhibitors		524
	isocarboxazid (Marplan)	
	phenelzine (Nardil)	
	selegiline (Eldepryl)	
	tranylcypromine (Parnate)	
Serotonin Antagonists		552
	nefazodone (Serzone)	
	trazodone (Desyrel)	
Other Antidepressants		557
	bupropion (Wellbutrin)	557
	mirtazapine (Remeron)	565
	venlafaxine (Effexor)	562

*Many of the antidepressants are now available as generic brands (see Table 24.1). Only the trade names of the original brands are listed in this table.

Antidepressant Drug Class	Chemical Name (and Trade Name)*	Page #
Mood Stabilizers		567
	carbamazepine (Tegretol)	584
	gabapentin (Neurontin)	594
	lamotrigine (Lamictal)	597
	lithium (Eskalith)	567
	valproic acid (Depakene) and divalproex sodium (Depakote)	580

Costs of Antidepressant Medications

We often think that more expensive means better, but this is not always the case with antidepressants. There are some very dramatic differences in the costs of the antidepressants that do not reflect differences in effectiveness. In other words, sometimes a drug is just as effective, or even more effective, than another drug that costs 40 times more. If the cost of the medication is a concern for you, a little education may save you a great deal of money.

The costs and doses of the most commonly prescribed antidepressants and mood stabilizing agents are listed in Table 24.1 on page 487. Note that the table quotes *the cheapest wholesale price* for each antidepressant drug. The retail price for the same medication at the drugstore will probably be higher. If you choose a different brand of the same medication, it may be higher yet. Please keep this in mind in all of the following discussions of drug costs.

Comparing the costs of the different types of drugs and the different doses provides some interesting information. For example, many of the older drugs are now available generically. When a drug is first manufactured, the drug company gets a 17-year patent so they can market the drug exclusively. The relatively high cost of the newer drugs still protected by patents helps to cover the costs of the research, development, and testing. After the patent expires, other companies can compete and manufacture the drug, and so the price goes down dramatically.

TABLE 24.1
NAMES, DOSES AND COSTS OF ANTIDEPRESSANT MEDICATIONS

Chemical Name*	Trade (Brand) Name†	Available sizes (mg) & cheapest wholesale cost per 100 pills‡		Daily Dose Range§	Are Generics Available?**
		Tricyclic Antidepressants			
amitriptyline	Elavil	10 mg	$1.73	75–300 mg	Yes
		25 mg	$1.85		
		50 mg	$2.78		
		75 mg	$3.53		
		100 mg	$4.28		
		150 mg	$2.09		
clomipramine	Anafranil	25 mg	$78.29	150–250 mg	No
		50 mg	$105.57		
		75 mg	$138.97		
desipramine	Norpramin	10 mg	$15.75	150–300 mg	Yes
		25 mg	$7.14		
		50 mg	$10.91		
		75 mg	$12.42		
		100 mg	$40.89		
		150 mg	$109.95		
doxepin	Sinequan	10 mg	$3.98	150–300 mg	Yes
		25 mg	$4.43		
		50 mg	$6.60		
		75 mg	$8.93		
		100 mg	$11.25		
		150 mg	$14.96		

*If your doctor prescribes the chemical or "generic" name on the prescription, your pharmacist can often substitute an inexpensive brand that can be much less costly than the trade-name drugs.

†Only the brand name of the original drug is listed. Generic versions of these drugs have their own brand names.

‡Cost source: *Mosby's GenRx, 1998 (8th Edition): The Complete Reference Guide for Generic and Brand Drugs.* St. Louis: Mosby. The average wholesale price for 100 pills of the least expensive brand currently available is listed. This is the price your local retail pharmacist would have to pay for the product without any special discounts. Your cost will be more and will depend on the markup by your pharmacist.

§The doses would be used for the treatment of an episode of depression. Some patients may benefit from doses higher or lower than the normal range. If prolonged treatment is necessary following recovery, a smaller dose may be sufficient. Always consult with your doctor before changing the dose.

**These are drugs with generic brands available in 1998. More of the current antidepressant drugs will become available as generic brands when their original drug patents expire.

Chemical Name	Trade (Brand) Name	Available sizes (mg) & cost per 100 pills		Daily Dose Range	Are Generics Available?
Tricyclic Antidepressants					
imipramine hydrochloride	Tofranil	10 mg 25 mg 50 mg	$1.88 $2.33 $3.08	150–300 mg	Yes
imipramine pamoate	Tofranil-PM (sustained release)	75 mg 100 mg 125 mg 150 mg	$103.67 $136.29 $169.95 $193.73	150–300 mg	No
nortriptyline	Aventyl	10 mg 25 mg 50 mg 75 mg	$11.55 $15.90 $19.43 $24.83	50–150 mg	Yes
protriptyline	Vivactil	5 mg 10 mg	$46.46 $67.36	15–60 mg	No
trimipramine	Surmontil	25 mg 50 mg 100 mg	$64.08 $108.14 $157.20	150–300 mg	No
Tetracyclic Antidepressants					
amoxapine	Asendin	25 mg 50 mg 100 mg 150 mg	$32.87 $53.44 $89.16 $43.87	150–450 mg	Yes
maprotiline	Ludiomil	25 mg 50 mg 75 mg	$19.43 $29.10 $40.88	150–225 mg*	Yes

*Maprotiline should not exceed 175 mg per day if a patient is kept on the drug for an extended period. The manufacturer suggests that the dose should not exceed a maximum of 225 mg for periods of up to six weeks.

Chemical Name	Trade (Brand) Name	Available sizes (mg) & cost per 100 pills		Daily Dose Range	Are Generics Available?
SSRI Antidepressants					
citalopram	Celexa	20 mg	$161.00	20–60 mg	No
		40 mg	$168.00		
fluoxetine	Prozac	10 mg	$218.67	10–80 mg	No
		20 mg	$224.54		
fluvoxamine	Luvox	50 mg	$198.67	50–300 mg	No
		100 mg	$204.37		
paroxetine	Paxil	10 mg	$189.33	10–50 mg	No
		20 mg	$189.20		
		30 mg	$214.80		
sertraline	Zoloft	50 mg	$176.23	25–200 mg	No
		100 mg	$181.33		
MAO Inhibitors					
phenelzine	Nardil	15 mg	$40.24	15–90 mg	No
selegiline	Eldepryl	5 mg	$215.90	20–50 mg	No
tranylcypromine	Parnate	10 mg	$45.80	10–50 mg	No
isocarboxazid	Marplan	10 mg	NA	10–50 mg	NA
Serotonin Antagonists					
nefazodone	Serzone	100 mg	$83.14	300–500 mg	No
		150 mg	$83.14		
		200 mg	$83.14		
		250 mg	$83.14		
trazodone	Desyrel	50 mg	$5.03	150–300 mg	Yes
		100 mg	$11.70		
		150 mg	$58.43		
Other Antidepressants					
bupropion	Wellbutrin	75 mg	$62.17	200–450 mg	No
		100 mg	$82.96		
venlafaxine	Effexor	25 mg	$105.53	75–375 mg	No
		37.5 mg	$108.68		
		50 mg	$111.93		
		75 mg	$118.66		
		100 mg	$125.78		
	Effexor XR (extended-release capsules)	37.5 mg	$193.88	75–375 mg	No
		75 mg	$217.14		
		150 mg	$236.53		
mirtazapine	Remeron	15 mg	$198.00	15–45 mg	No

Chemical Name	Trade (Brand) Name	Available sizes (mg) & cost per 100 pills	Daily Dose Range	Are Generics Available?
Mood Stabilizers				
lithium*	Eskalith	150 mg $7.63 300 mg $5.25 600 mg $13.23	900–1,500 mg†	Yes
	Lithobid, Eskalith CR (sustained-release)	300 mg $15.53 450 mg $35.80		
carbamazepine*	Tegretol	100 mg $14.67 200 mg $10.08	800–1,200 mg	Yes
valproic acid*	Depakene	250 mg $12.98	750–3,000 mg	Yes
divalproex sodium*	Depakote‡	125 mg $30.95 250 mg $60.76 500 mg $112.08	750–3,000 mg	No
lamotrigine	Lamictal	25 mg§ — 100 mg $175.54 150 mg $184.43 200 mg $193.33	50–150 mg**	No
gabapentin	Neurontin	100 mg $37.80 300 mg $94.50 400 mg $113.40	900–2,000 mg	No

*The doses of this mood stabilizer must be monitored by blood tests and will therefore be highly individualized for each patient, depending on your age, gender, weight, diagnosis, and individual metabolism, as well as other medications you may be taking.

†Higher doses may be required during acute mania because the body appears to metabolize lithium more rapidly during manic episodes.

‡This is also available as Depakote Sprinkle (125 mg) and can be sprinkled onto food.

§The price of the 25mg Lamictal was not listed in *Mosby's GenRx* (1998 edition).

**This is the recommended dose range for epilepsy when given in conjunction with valproic acid. When given alone, the recommended dose range for epilepsy is 300 mg to 500 mg per day.

As shown in Table 24.1, these so-called "generic" medications are much cheaper than the newer drugs that are still under patent. Let's assume that your doctor prescribes a dose of 150 mg per day of imipramine. The cost of three 50mg pills is less than 10 cents per day, or roughly $3 per month. This is because imipramine is now available generically. In contrast, if your doctor prescribes two 20mg Prozac pills per day, the cost is nearly $4.50 per day or $135 per month—over 40 times more than the imipramine. And if she or he prescribes four Prozac pills—the maximum dose—the cost is $270 per month—

nearly 100 times the cost of a month's supply of imipramine. This is a steep price for many people. Don't forget these are *wholesale* prices—you may pay even more.

Is Prozac 40 to 100 times more effective than imipramine? Definitely not. Most antidepressants tend to be equally effective. Research studies have not confirmed that Prozac is any more effective than imipramine—in fact, it may be slightly less effective for severe depressions. However, the big advantage of Prozac is that it has fewer side effects (such as dry mouth or sleepiness). This may be important to some people and make the price difference worthwhile. On the other hand, Prozac has some side effects of its own, such as problems with sexual functioning (a loss of interest in sex and difficulties achieving orgasm) in as many as 30 to 40 percent of patients, and possibly more. Prozac can also cause upset stomach, nervousness, and difficulties sleeping. People who don't like these side effects might actually prefer one of the cheaper medications like imipramine.

Table 24.1 also shows that pills which contain a larger quantity of a particular drug are not necessarily more expensive than pills which contain a smaller quantity. This is especially true if you are taking one of the newer drugs that are still under patent, so you may be able to save money by buying pills containing a larger dose. For example, the cost of 100 nefazodone (Serzone) tablets is $83.14 for the 100mg size. The price for 100 of the larger tablets (150 mg to 250 mg) is exactly the same. So if you are taking a large dose, say 500 mg per day, you could either take five 100mg pills (cost of $4.16 per day) or two 250mg pills (cost of $1.66 per day).

In addition, you can often save money by buying a larger size of a medication and breaking a pill in half. To continue with the same example, if you are taking two 250mg pills of nefazodone per day, it will only cost you approximately half as much if your doctor prescribes 500mg pills and you break them in half.

This does not hold true for generic drugs. On average, the costs are low overall and depend on the dose, and the savings at higher doses are not as drastic. In addition, because so many different companies manufacture these drugs, the prices for the different doses are not always entirely consistent—sometimes a smaller dose actually costs more than a larger dose. For example, look at the pricing structure for the tricyclic antidepressant desipramine (trade name Norpramin). 100 of the 10mg pills cost $15.75, while 100 of the 25mg pills costs only $7.14. In this case the larger pill is cheaper. This is because different companies manufacture the two sizes.

To make comparison even more confusing, in other cases a larger dose of the same drug costs substantially more and you can save money by taking a smaller size. For example, take another look at the costs of desipramine. 100 75mg pills cost $12.42, and 100 150mg desipramine pills cost $109.95. So you can save lots of money by taking two 75mg pills instead of one 150mg pill. Again, this is because different companies manufacture the 75mg and 150mg sizes. This may strike you as odd, but the pricing structure in some instances is completely out of whack.

If you or a family member is taking an antidepressant, make sure you study Table 24.1 and discuss the cost issues with your druggist. A little research on your part may result in large savings.

Another important point, not illustrated in the table, is that the cost of the same generic drug and dose can vary greatly because the generics often have so many different manufacturers. Table 24.1 always lists the least costly generic brand of each pill; other, more costly versions of the same pill are not listed. For example, 100 50mg imipramine pills manufactured by the drug company HCFA FFP cost only $3.08. In contrast, 100 of the same size imipramine manufactured by Novartis, another drug company, cost $74.12—more than 20 times more. Keep in mind that if your doctor prescribes the antidepressant by its chemical name (as listed in Table 24.1), your druggist has the freedom to provide you with the least costly generic brand if one is available.

My goal is not to promote any one drug or class of drug. All antidepressants have merit, and they all have drawbacks. The key point is this: more expensive does not always mean better. If you review the costs of these drugs, you can work with your doctor and pharmacist to choose the medication and brand that makes the most sense for you.

Specific Kinds of Antidepressants

TRICYCLIC AND TETRACYCLIC ANTIDEPRESSANTS

The first drugs listed in the Table of Antidepressants on page 485 are called *tricyclic* and *tetracyclic* antidepressants. These two differ slightly in their chemical structures. *Tri-* means three and *tetra-* means four; *cyclic* refers to a circle or ring. Thus, the tricyclic compounds consist of three linked molecular rings while the tetracyclics consist of four.

Eight tricyclic and two tetracyclic antidepressants are listed in the table. The eight tricyclic drugs include amitriptyline (Elavil), clomipramine (Anafranil), desipramine (Norpramin), doxepin (Sinequan), imipramine (Tofranil), nortriptyline (Aventyl), protriptyline (Vivactil), and trimipramine (Surmontil). These used to be the most widely prescribed antidepressants, and they are still among the most effective of all the antidepressants. Many of them are also the least expensive because generic brands have become available. However, the tricyclics do tend to have more side effects than the newer drugs, and so they are less popular than they used to be. On the other hand, they have been prescribed for several decades and have a long track record of reasonably good effectiveness and safety.

The two tetracyclic antidepressants listed in the table are called amoxapine (Asendin) and maprotiline (Ludiomil). These tetracyclics were synthesized and released after the tricyclics had been in use for some time. It was hoped that they would represent significant improvements in treatment, either because of increased effectiveness for certain types of depression or because of fewer side effects. Unfortunately, these expected improvements did not really materialize. For the most part, the effectiveness, mechanism of action, and side effects of the eight tricyclic and the two tetracyclic antidepressants are very similar.

Doses for the Tricyclic and Tetracyclic Antidepressants

Table 24.1 on page 487 lists the costs and dose ranges of the eight tricyclic and the two tetracyclic antidepressant medications. As noted above, many of them are inexpensive because generic brands are available. Don't be fooled into thinking that cheaper antidepressants are less effective, however. A number of studies suggest they may be slightly more effective than many of the newer antidepressants such as Prozac, especially for patients with severe depression.

The most common error your doctor is likely to make is to prescribe a tricyclic antidepressant dose that is too low. This statement may run against the grain if you feel you should take the lowest dose possible. Yet in the case of tricyclics, if the prescribed dose is too low, the medication will not be effective. On the other hand, dosages above those recommended in Table 24.1 can be toxic and may make your depression worse.

Having said that, let me also say that there are cases in which some people (especially the elderly) do respond to doses that are smaller than those listed, and there are also times when people need larger doses. One reason for this is the considerable differences in how rapidly people metabolize antidepressant drugs. These differences are partially genetic, due to levels of certain enzymes in your liver that metabolize these drugs. Some people have livers that remove certain drugs from their bodies very rapidly. They may need larger doses to maintain an effective blood level. Other people have livers that remove drugs from their bodies far more slowly. They may need smaller doses. In addition, you will learn below about other drugs that can make tricyclic blood levels fall and lose their effectiveness, or increase and become more toxic.

If you suspect you are taking an inappropriately large or small dose, review the dose ranges in Table 24.1 and discuss your concerns with your physician. Blood-level testing for most of the tricyclic antidepressants is readily available, so your doctor may order a blood test to make sure that your dose is neither too high nor too low.

The best way to begin taking a tricyclic medicine is to start out with a small dose and to increase the amount each day until a dose within the normal therapeutic range is achieved. This buildup is usually completed within one or two weeks. For example, a typical daily dose schedule for imipramine, a common tricyclic antidepressant, might be the following:

> Day one—50 mg at bedtime
> Day two—75 mg at bedtime
> Day three—100 mg at bedtime
> Day four—125 mg at bedtime
> Day five—150 mg at bedtime

You and your doctor may prefer to build up the dose more gradually. Doses of up to 150 mg per day can be conveniently taken once a day at night. The antidepressant effect will last all day long, and the most bothersome side effects will occur when you are asleep, when they will be least noticed. If doses larger than 150 mg per day are required, the additional medicine should be given in divided doses during the daytime.

For the more sedating tricyclic antidepressants, up to half the maximum indicated dose may be taken on a once-per-day basis before bedtime. This dosage promotes sleep. Several of the tricyclic antidepressants, including desipramine, nortriptyline, and protriptyline, can be stimulating. They can be taken in divided doses in the morning and at noon. If taken too late in the day, they may interfere with sleep.

If you reduce the dose of a tricyclic antidepressant or if you decide to stop taking the medicine, it is best to reduce the dose gradually. Sudden discontinuation of any antidepressant may result in side effects. These include upset stomach, sweating, headache, anxiety, or insomnia. Usually, you can go off a tricyclic antidepressant safely and comfortably by tapering the dose gradually over a one- or two-week period.

Side Effects of the Tricyclic Antidepressants

The most frequent side effects of the tricyclic antidepressants are listed in Table 24.2 on page 496. The table shows that all the tricyclic antidepressants have quite a number of side effects, and this is their greatest drawback. The most common side effects include sleepiness, dry mouth, a mild hand tremor, temporary light-headedness when you suddenly stand up, weight gain, and constipation. They can also cause excessive sweating, difficulties with sex, twitches or jerking when you fall asleep at night, and a number of other effects listed in Table 24.2. Most of these side effects are not dangerous, but they can be annoying.

The side effects of antidepressant drugs can be predicted if you know how strongly they block histamine receptors, alpha-adrenergic receptors, and muscarinic receptors (also called cholinergic receptors) in the brain. Each antidepressant in Table 24.2 has a different profile of side effects depending on its action on these three receptor systems in the brain.

What are these receptors with such big names? They are actually not very complicated. If a nerve is stimulated, it sends an electrical impulse along its long, thin *axon* in much the same way that an electrical impulse travels down a wire. However, the ends of the nerve do not touch the other nerves they want to stimulate. This is because all the nerves in the brain are separated from each other by a very thin layer of fluid. This fluid layer is called the *synaptic region,* or simply *synapse.* The electrical impulses of the nerves are too weak to jump across the fluid-filled synaptic region, so what can they do?

To solve this problem, nerves in the brain communicate with each other by sending chemical messengers across the synapses. Here's how it works. When the electrical impulse comes to the end of the axon, the nerve releases a chemical transmitter substance. Each nerve uses a specific kind of transmitter. These include serotonin, norepinephrine, dopamine, acetylcholine, and many others. Once released, these chemical transmitter molecules swim across the narrow fluid-filled synapse and become attached to the nerve on the other side of the synapse. Once they attach to the second nerve, they trigger an electrical reaction. The

TABLE 24.2
SIDE EFFECTS OF TRICYCLIC ANTIDEPRESSANTS*

Note: This list is not comprehensive. In general, side effects that occur in 5 or 10 percent or more of patients are listed, as well as rare but dangerous side effects.

Side Effect[†]	Sedation and Weight Gain[‡]	Light-Headedness and Dizziness	Blurred Vision, Constipation, Dry Mouth, Speeded Heart, Urinary Retention	Common or Significant Side Effects
Brain Receptor	histamine (H₁) receptors	alpha-adrenergic (α₁) receptors	muscarinic (M₁) receptors	
amitriptyline (Elavil, Endep)	+++	+++	+++	dizziness; speeded heart; abnormal ECG; dry mouth; constipation; weight gain; trouble urinating; blurred vision; ringing in ears; sweating; weakness; headache; tremor; tiredness; insomnia; confusion
clomipramine (Anafranil)	++ to +++	+++	++ to +++	dizziness; speeded heart; abnormal ECG; dry mouth; upset stomach; loss of appetite; constipation; weight gain; trouble urinating; menstrual changes; disturbed sexual functioning; blurred vision; sweating; weakness; muscle cramps; tremor; tiredness; insomnia; anxiety; headache; rash; seizures

*The + to +++ ratings in this table refer to the likelihood that a particular side effect will develop. The actual intensity of the side effect will vary among individuals and will also depend on how large the dose is. Reducing the dose can often reduce side effects without reducing effectiveness.

[†]Many side effects, if troublesome, can be minimized by a reduction in dosage. Side effects are usually greatest in the first few days and tend to disappear later.

[‡]The drugs that are the most sedative may also have greater anti-anxiety effects. In other words, they may calm you and make you less nervous. When given at night, the sedative agents help reduce insomnia.

Side Effect Brain Receptor	Sedation and Weight Gain histamine (H_1) receptors	Light-Headedness and Dizziness alpha-adrenergic (α_1) receptors	Blurred Vision, Constipation, Dry Mouth, Speeded Heart, Urinary Retention muscarinic (M_1) receptors	Common or Significant Side Effects
desipramine (Norpramin, Pertofrane)	+	+	+ to ++	dry mouth; rashes; agitation; anxiety; headache; insomnia; stimulation
doxepin (Adapin, Sinequan)	+++	+++	++ to +++	dizziness; speeded heart; dry mouth; constipation; weight gain; blurred vision; sweating; sleepiness
imipramine (Tofranil)	++	++ to +++	++ to +++	dizziness; speeded heart; abnormal ECG; dry mouth; constipation; weight gain; trouble urinating; blurred vision; sweating; weakness; headache; tiredness; insomnia; anxiety; stimulation; rash; seizures; sensitivity to light
nortriptyline (Aventyl)	+ to ++	+	++	dry mouth; constipation; tremor; weakness; confusion; anxiety or stimulation

Side Effect	Sedation and Weight Gain	Light-Headedness and Dizziness	Blurred Vision, Constipation, Dry Mouth, Speeded Heart, Urinary Retention	Common or Significant Side Effects
Brain Receptor	histamine (H₁) receptors	alpha-adrenergic (α₁) receptors	muscarinic (M₁) receptors	
protriptyline (Vivactil)	0 to +	+ to ++	+++	dizziness; decreased or increased blood pressure; abnormal ECG; nausea; constipation; blurred vision; sweating; weakness; insomnia; stimulation; headache
trimipramine (Surmontil)	+++	++ to +++	++ to +++	dizziness; decreased or increased blood pressure; abnormal ECG; dry mouth; constipation; weight gain; blurred vision; sweating; weakness; headache; tremor; sleepiness; confusion; intolerance to heat or cold

process is a bit more complicated than this, of course, but that's basically how it works.

Nerves that use acetylcholine have different kinds of cholinergic receptors on their surfaces. One type of cholinergic receptor is the muscarinic receptor. The cholinergic nerves control many physiologic systems in the body, including the lubrication of the mouth. If you stimulate the muscarinic receptors on the cholinergic nerves, your mouth will become wet. Conversely, if you block these muscarinic receptors, your mouth will become dry. Because many of the tricyclic antidepressants tend to block these muscarinic receptors, they cause dry mouth.

Blockade of the brain's histamine receptors makes you hungry and sleepy. Table 24.2 indicates that four of the tricyclic antidepressants (amitriptyline, clomipramine, doxepin, and trimipramine) have rather strong effects on the histamine receptors. Consequently, these four antidepressants are more likely to make you feel sleepy and hungry. If you are having trouble sleeping, this side effect could be a benefit, but if you are already feeling sluggish and unmotivated, these drugs may make things worse for you. If you have been losing weight due to depression, the appetite boost could be beneficial. However, if you are overweight, you might have to pay added attention to your diet and exercise more in order to avoid weight gain, which can be demoralizing. Since many antidepressants that do not cause weight gain or sleepiness are now available, it might be better to switch to one of them. You can see in Table 24.2 that three of the tricyclics (desipramine, nortriptyline, and protriptyline) have only weak effects on the histamine receptors. These antidepressants will be less likely to cause sleepiness and weight gain. There are many antidepressants in other categories as well that do not cause sleepiness and weight gain.

Blockade of the brain's alpha-adrenergic receptors causes a drop in blood pressure. This can result in temporary light-headedness or dizziness when you suddenly stand up because your leg veins become more relaxed, and blood pools in your legs. As a result, your heart temporarily does not have enough blood to pump up to your brain, and so your vision may go black or you may feel dizzy or woozy for a few seconds. Antidepressants with relatively strong effects on the brain's alpha-adrenergic receptors are more likely to cause dizziness when you suddenly stand up. Many tricyclics have strong effects on alpha-adrenergic receptors, but two of them (desipramine and nortriptyline) have only weak effects on these receptors. Consequently, these two drugs are less likely to cause dizziness or a drop in blood pressure.

Finally, blockade of the brain's muscarinic receptors causes side effects such as dry mouth, described above, along with constipation, blurred vision, difficulties in getting your urine flow started, and a speeding up of the heart, even when you are resting. Because of the effects on the heart, the tricyclic medications in Table 24.2 with the strong effects on muscarinic receptors may not be advisable for patients with cardiac problems. Drugs with anticholinergic effects can also create problems with memory. Many patients have told me that they cannot remember a word they want to use, or they forget someone's name when they take these drugs. The memory effects are dose-related and should disappear when you stop taking the drug.

Two of the tricyclic drugs in Table 24.2 (desipramine and nortriptyline) have relatively weak anticholinergic effects. These two drugs are the least likely to cause side effects like dry mouth and forgetfulness. They also tend to have weaker effects on the histaminic and alpha-adrenergic receptors. Because they have fewer side effects, they are among the most popular tricyclic antidepressants.

The effects of antidepressant drugs on these three brain receptor systems do not completely explain all their side effects. In the right-hand column, I have listed many of the more common or significant side effects for each drug. For example, you will see that all of them can cause skin rashes. Some tricyclics, most notably clomipramine (Anafranil), can cause seizures. This drug would not be a good choice for individuals with epilepsy.

If you and your doctor are choosing one of the antidepressants listed in Table 24.2, you might want to consider the side-effect profile when making your choice. All these medications are comparably effective, so their side effects may be the most important criteria for you. If you are having trouble sleeping at night, one of the more sedative antidepressants may be useful. The sedative agents are also somewhat calming and might be helpful if you are experiencing anxiety.

Many side effects of tricyclic antidepressants occur only in the first few days. With the exception of dry mouth and weight gain, the side effects frequently diminish as you become accustomed to the drug. If the effects are strong enough to make you uncomfortable, your doctor may decide to reduce the dose, which usually helps.

Some side effects suggest that you are taking an excessive dose. These include difficulty in urination, blurred vision, confusion, severe tremor, substantial dizziness, or increased sweating. A dose reduction for such symptoms is definitely indicated. A stool softener or laxative can help if constipation develops. As noted above, lightheadedness is most likely to occur when you stand up suddenly because the blood flow to your brain is temporarily diminished. The dizzy feeling usually persists for only a few seconds. If you get up more carefully and slowly, or if you exercise your legs before standing (by tightening and then relaxing your leg muscles, as when you run in place), this should not be a problem. The movement of your legs causes your leg muscles to "pump" the blood back up to your brain. Support stockings can also help.

Some patients describe feeling "strange" or "spaced out" for several days when they first start taking a tricyclic antidepressant. In my experience, doxepin (Sinequan) is more likely to cause this "spaced-out" effect. When patients report feeling strange on the first day or two of taking an antidepressant, I usually advise them to stick with it. In nearly all cases the sensation disappears completely within a few days.

If patients are given sugar pills (placebos) that they think are antidepressants, they report side effects that are similar to those reported by patients taking antidepressants. For example, in one study 25 percent of the patients taking clomipramine reported difficulties sleeping, so you might conclude that this drug causes insomnia in a quarter of those who take it. However, 15 percent of the patients in the same study who received only a placebo also reported insomnia. So the likelihood of insomnia caused by clomipramine is really only 10 percent. Clearly, this side effect is "real," but it is somewhat less common than what you might at first expect.

Such studies indicate that many "side effects" may not be caused by the medication you are taking. Some side effects may result from fears about the medication, or from the depression itself, or from other stressful events in your life such as a conflict with your spouse rather than from the drug itself.

Side Effects of the Tetracyclic Antidepressants
You can see in Table 24.3 on page 503 that the side effects of the tetracyclic antidepressants are similar to those of the tricyclic antidepressants. However, they have some side effects of their own that you should be aware of if you are thinking about taking one of these drugs. Maprotiline (Ludiomil) appears to be more likely than the eight tricyclic antidepressant drugs to cause seizures, a particularly troublesome

side effect. Although the likelihood of seizures is low, patients with a history of seizures or head trauma should probably avoid this drug. Recent studies suggest that the likelihood of seizures with maprotiline is significantly greater when the dose is increased too rapidly, or when patients are kept on higher than recommended doses (225 to 400 mg per day) for more than six weeks.* Therefore the manufacturer has suggested that maprotiline be started and increased very slowly, and that the dose be maintained at no more than 175 mg per day if patients take this drug for more than six weeks.

Amoxapine (Asendin) has a troublesome type of side effect not shared with most other antidepressants. This is because one of its metabolites blocks dopamine receptors in the brain, much like antipsychotic drugs such as chlorpromazine (Thorazine) and many others which are used in the treatment of schizophrenia. Thus, patients who take amoxapine can in rare instances develop some of the same types of side effects. For example, women may experience galactorrhea (the production of breast milk). Any of several so-called "extrapyramidal" reactions can also develop. One of them, called akathisia, is a motor restlessness syndrome. This is an unusual kind of muscular "itchiness"—your arms or legs feel intensely restless and so you cannot sit still. You feel the compulsion to keep moving or pacing about. Akathisia is uncomfortable but not dangerous.

In rare instances amoxapine can also cause symptoms that mimic Parkinson's disease. Symptoms include passive inactivity, a "pill-rolling" tremor of the thumb and fingers while at rest, decreased swinging of the arms when walking, stiffness, stooped posture, and others. If these symptoms develop, notify your doctor right away. She or he will probably want you to stop the drug and try an alternative medication. Although alarming, these symptoms are not dangerous and should disappear when you stop taking amoxapine.

However, a more serious side effect of amoxapine (as well as many other antipsychotic drugs) is called *tardive dyskinesia.* Patients with tardive dyskinesia develop involuntary, repetitious movements of the face, especially the lips and tongue. The abnormal movements can also involve the arms and legs. Once it begins, tardive dyskinesia sometimes becomes irreversible or difficult to treat. The risk appears to be the highest among elderly women, but it can occur with any patient. The risk of tardive dyskinesia increases the longer you have been on

---

*Dessain, E. C., Schatzberg, A. F., & Woods, B. T. (1986). *Archives of General Psychiatry, 43:* 86-90.

TABLE 24.3
SIDE EFFECTS OF TETRACYCLIC ANTIDEPRESSANTS*

Note: This list is not comprehensive. In general, side effects that occur in 5 or 10 percent or more of patients are listed, as well as rare but dangerous side effects.

Side Effect — Brain Receptor	Sedation and Weight Gain — histamine (H₁) receptors	Light-Headedness and Dizziness — alpha-adrenergic (α₁) receptors	Blurred Vision, Constipation, Dry Mouth, Speeded Heart, Urinary Retention — muscarinic (M₁) receptors	Common or Significant Side Effects
amoxapine (Asendin)	++	++	+ to ++	dizziness; speeded heart; dry mouth; stomach upset; constipation; trouble urinating; blurred vision; rashes; tremor; tiredness; insomnia; EPS†; lactation; restlessness; excessive stimulation; tardive dyskinesia; galactorrhea; NMS‡
maprotiline (Ludiomil)	++	+	+	dry mouth; constipation; weight gain; blurred vision; rashes; sleepiness; seizures; stimulation; sensitivity to light; edema (swelling of ankles)

*The + to +++ ratings in this table refer to the likelihood that a particular side effect will develop. The actual intensity of the side effect will vary among individuals and will also depend on how large the dose is. Reducing the dose can often reduce side effects without reducing effectiveness.

†EPS = extrapyramidal symptoms (described in text) including akathisia and dystonic reactions and tardive dyskinesia.

‡This is a potentially fatal reaction that also occurs in reaction to antipsychotic drugs (also known as neuroleptics). The symptoms include increased fever, rigid muscles, altered mental status, irregular pulse or blood pressure, rapid heart, profuse sweating, and abnormal heart rhythms.

the drug, but it can develop after only a brief period of treatment at a low dose.

Finally, as if that weren't enough to frighten you, amoxapine can, in rare cases, cause a frightening complication known as neuroleptic malignant syndrome, or NMS. NMS consists of high fever, delirium, and muscle rigidity, along with changes in blood pressure, heart rate and rhythm, and sometimes death. All these risks obviously should be carefully balanced against any potential benefits of amoxapine; it may be difficult to justify using this medication when so many equally effective and safer drugs are readily available.

Tricyclic and Tetracyclic Antidepressant (TCA) Drug Interactions

When you are taking more than one drug, the drugs may interact in ways that will be detrimental to you. One drug may cause the level of a second drug to increase or to decrease in your blood. As a result, the second drug may cause excessive side effects (if its blood level gets too high) or it may become ineffective (if its blood level falls). In addition, sometimes two drugs can interact to create toxic reactions that are quite dangerous.

A number of drug interactions for the tricyclic and tetracyclic antidepressants are listed in Table 24.4 on page 506. This list is not comprehensive, but it does include many of the more common and important interactions. If you are taking any other medications along with these antidepressants, you should review this table. Note that both prescription and nonprescription drugs are listed, and that psychiatric and nonpsychiatric drugs are included. In addition, be sure to ask your physician and pharmacist if there are any drug interactions among the drugs you are taking.

You can see in Table 24.4 that smoking cigarettes and drinking alcohol can both cause the blood level of these antidepressants to fall, thus reducing the likelihood that the drug will be effective. Your doctor may need to do a blood test to find out if your blood level is adequate. In addition, alcohol can enhance the sedative effects of the tricyclic antidepressants, a combination that can be hazardous if you are driving or operating dangerous machinery.

Certain antidepressants can be particularly hazardous for individuals with specific medical conditions. In particular, the tricyclics can be dangerous to individuals with cardiovascular disease, including those with a previous heart attack, abnormalities in heart rhythm, or high blood pressure. Special precautions should also be taken for individuals with thyroid disease. Make sure you mention any medical problems you have to the doctor who is prescribing your antidepressant so that she or he can take the proper precautions.

As noted above, several tricyclic and tetracyclic antidepressants can cause seizures in rare instances. An incidence of seizures as high as 1 to 3 percent has been reported with clomipramine, imipramine, and maprotiline.* These estimates may be overly high. At any rate, the risk can be reduced by making sure the dose is not excessive and by raising the dose gradually. Nevertheless, these drugs should be used with caution, if at all, by individuals with a history of seizure disorders, head trauma, or other neurologic disorders associated with seizures. In addition, caution should be used if these drugs are combined with other drugs that can lower the seizure threshold, such as the major tranquilizers (neuroleptics). Rapid withdrawal from sedative agents, such as alcohol, minor tranquilizers, and barbiturates can also trigger seizures. Clomipramine, imipramine, and maprotiline should be used with great caution in combination with these agents.

SELECTIVE SEROTONIN REUPTAKE INHIBITORS (SSRIs)

Currently, the most popular antidepressant drugs are the selective serotonin reuptake inhibitors, or SSRIs. At this time five SSRIs are prescribed in the United States. These include citalopram (Celexa), the newest SSRI, which was released in this country in 1998, and fluoxetine (Prozac), the first SSRI, which was released in 1988. The other three are fluvoxamine (Luvox), paroxetine (Paxil), and sertraline (Zoloft). Unlike the older tricyclic and tetracyclic drugs discussed above, which interact with many different systems in the brain, the SSRIs have selective effects on nerves that use serotonin as a transmitter substance.

When Prozac first appeared on the market, there was a great deal of excitement because it was chemically quite different from the older antidepressants. Unlike the tricyclic and tetracyclic drugs, it had specific effects on the serotonergic nerves in the brain. Since a serotonin deficiency was hypothesized to be the cause of depression, it was hoped that Prozac would be dramatically more effective than the diffuse effects of the tricyclic and tetracyclic drugs. It was also expected that Prozac (and the other SSRIs) would have fewer side effects than the older drugs.

*Maxmen, J. S., & Ward, N. G. (1995). *Psychotropic Drugs Fast Facts,* Second Edition. New York: W. W. Norton & Company.

TABLE 24.4
DRUG INTERACTION GUIDE FOR TRICYCLIC AND TETRACYCLIC ANTIDEPRESSANTS (TCAs)

Note: The drugs in the left-hand column can interact with TCAs. The comments describe the types of interactions. This list is not exhaustive; new information about drug interactions comes out frequently. If you are taking a TCA and any other medication, ask your doctor and pharmacist if there are any drug interactions.

Antidepressants

Drug	Comment
tricyclic and tetracyclic antidepressants (TCAs can interact with other TCAs)	desipramine causes an ↑ in other TCAs — abnormal heart rhythms can result
SSRIs	TCA levels can ↑ (as much as 2- to 10-fold); abnormal heart rhythms can result; SSRI levels can also ↑
MAOIs	serotonin syndrome* [especially clomipramine (Anafranil)]; low blood pressure; hypertensive reactions
serotonin antagonists, including trazodone (Desyrel) and nefazodone (Serzone)	nefazodone may cause low blood pressure
bupropion (Wellbutrin)	↑ in risk of seizures; extreme caution required
venlafaxine (Effexor)	probably okay; in theory TCA could cause ↑ in venlafaxine blood levels
mirtazapine (Remeron)	information not yet available

Antibiotics

Drug	Comment
chloramphenicol (Chloromycetin)	TCA levels and toxicity may ↑
doxycyline (Vibramycin)	TCA levels and effectiveness may ↓
isoniazid (INH, Nydrazid)	TCA levels and toxicity may ↑

Antifungal Agents

Drug	Comment
imidazoles such as fluconazole (Diflucan), itraconazole (Sporanox), ketoconazole (Nizoral) and miconazole (Monistat Vaginal Suppositories or Cream)	TCA levels may ↑, especially nortriptyline
griseofulvin (Fulvicin)	TCA levels may ↓

Diabetes Medications

Drug	Comment
insulin	greater than expected drop in blood sugar
oral hypoglycemic drugs	greater than expected drop in blood sugar

*This is a dangerous and potentially fatal syndrome which includes rapid changes in vital signs (fever, oscillations in blood pressure), sweating, nausea, vomiting, rigid muscles, myoclonus, agitation, delirium, seizures, and coma. Information in this table was obtained from several sources including the *Manual of Clinical Psychopharmacology* (Schatzberg et al. [1997]) and *Psychotropic Drugs Fast Facts* (Maxmen et al. [1995]). These excellent references are highly recommended.

Medical Conditions	
Condition	**Comment**
glaucoma	highly anticholinergic TCA can trigger attacks of narrow-angle glaucoma; symptoms include eye pain, blurred vision, and halos around lights
heart disease	use TCA with extreme caution; may trigger abnormal heart rhythms
liver disease	use TCA with caution; the metabolism by the liver may be impaired, with excessively high blood levels and increased side/toxic effects
seizure disorder	use TCA with caution; TCA may cause ↑ in seizures (TCA lowers the seizure "threshold")
thyroid disease	use TCA with caution in patients with thyroid disease, or those taking thyroid medication; may trigger abnormal heart rhythms
Medications for Abnormal Heart Rhythms	
Drug	**Comment**
disopyramide (Norpace)	abnormal heart rhythms
epinephrine	TCA may enhance the effects, leading to rapid heart, abnormal heart rhythms, and ↑ in blood pressure
quinidine	blood levels of quinidine and TCA may ↑ ; abnormal heart rhythms and weakened heart muscle can lead to congestive heart failure
Medications for High Blood Pressure	
Drug	**Comment**
beta-blockers such as propranolol (Inderal)	beta-blockers may cause increased depression; TCA may cause greater than expected drop in blood pressure
clonidine (Catapres)	TCA [e.g., desipramine (Norpramin)] may reduce effectiveness of clonidine because blood levels ↓
calcium channel blockers	blood-pressure drop may be greater than expected
guanethidine (Ismelin)	may lose antihypertensive effect when combined with TCA [e.g., desipramine (Norpramin)]

Medications for High Blood Pressure

Drug	Comment
methyldopa (Aldomet)	blood-pressure drop may be greater than expected, especially with amitriptyline (Elavil); some TCAs [e.g., desipramine (Norpramin)] may reduce antihypertensive effect
prazosin (Minipress)	blood pressure may ↑ because levels of prazosin may ↓
reserpine (Serpasil)	may cause greater than expected drop in blood pressure; may also cause excessive stimulation
thiazide diuretics such as hydrochlorothiazide (Dyazide)	blood-pressure drop may be greater than expected; effects of TCA may increase

Medications for Low Blood Pressure (Used for Patients Who Are in Shock)

Drug	Comment
epinephrine	TCA may enhance the effects, leading to rapid heart, abnormal heart rhythms, and ↑ in blood pressure

Mood Stabilizers and Anticonvulsants

Drug	Comment
carbamazepine (Tegretol)	blood levels of TCA and carbamazepine may ↓; TCA can make seizures more likely
lithium (Eskalith)	may enhance antidepressant effects
phenytoin (Dilantin)	blood levels of TCA may ↓ or ↑; TCA can make seizures more likely
valproic acid (Depakene)	↑ in blood levels of amitriptyline (Elavil) and valproic acid

Pain Medications and Anesthetics

Drug	Comment
acetaminophen (Tylenol)	TCA levels may ↑; acetaminophen levels may ↓
aspirin	TCA levels may ↑
halothane (Fluothane)	TCA levels may ↑; TCA with strong anticholinergic effects may cause abnormal heart rhythms
cyclobenzaprine (Flexeril) (a muscle relaxant used to treat muscle spasm)	may cause abnormal heart rhythms

Pain Medications and Anesthetics

Drug	Comment
methadone (Dolophine)	may have greater than expected narcotic effect; for example, desipramine (Norpramin) may double the blood level of methadone
meperidine (Demerol)	greater than expected narcotic effect; lower doses of meperidine or another painkiller may be needed
morphine (MS Contin)	greater than expected narcotic effect and sedation; TCA levels may ↓
pancuronium (Pavulon)	abnormal heart rhythms, especially TCA with strong anticholinergic effects

Sedatives and Tranquilizers

Drug	Comment
alcohol	may have enhanced sedative effects; this could be hazardous when driving or operating dangerous machinery. May cause TCA levels to ↓
barbiturates (such as phenobarbital)	enhanced sedative effects; may cause TCA levels to ↓
buspirone (BuSpar)	enhanced sedative effects as described above
chloral hydrate (Noctec)	TCA levels may ↓
ethchlorvynol (Placidyl)	temporary mental confusion has been reported when combined with amitriptyline (Elavil), but could conceivably occur with other TCAs as well
major tranquilizers (neuroleptics)	levels of TCA and phenothiazine neuroleptics [such as chlorpromazine (Thorazine)] may ↑, leading to more side effects and greater potency; abnormal heart rhythms have been observed with thioridazine (Mellaril), clozapine (Clozaril), and pimozide (Orap)
minor tranquilizers (neuroleptics)	enhanced sedative effects

Stimulants (Pep Pills) and Street Drugs	
Drug	**Comment**
amphetamines ("speed" or "crank") cocaine benzedrine benzphetamine (Didrex) dextroamphetamine (Dexedrine) methamphetamine (Desoxyn) methylphenidate (Ritalin)	these drugs may boost the blood levels and effects of some TCA [(e.g., imipramine (Tofranil), clomipramine (Anafranil), desipramine (Norpramin)] and vice versa; abnormal heart rhythms and increased blood pressure have been observed with cocaine, but seem possible when any stimulants are combined with TCA
Weight Loss and Appetite-Suppression Medications	
Drug	**Comment**
fenfluramine (Pondimin)	possible serotonin syndrome when combined with clomipramine; increased TCA levels
Other Medications	
Drug	**Comment**
antihistamines	increased drowsiness; it is safer to use antihistamines that are not sedative
acetazolamide (Diamox)	TCA blood levels may ↑; blood pressure may ↓
birth-control pills and other medications containing estrogen	TCA blood levels may ↑, with greater side effects; higher doses of estrogen may reduce the effects of TCA
caffeine (in coffee, tea, soda, chocolate)	TCA blood levels may ↑
charcoal tablets	TCA blood levels may ↓ due to poor absorption from the stomach and intestinal tract
cholestyramine (Questran)	TCA blood levels may ↓

Other Medications	
Drug	**Comment**
cimetidine (Tagamet)	TCA blood levels may ↑ (greater side effects)
disulfiram (Antabuse)	TCA blood levels may ↑ (greater side effects); in two reported cases, disulfiram plus amitriptyline (Elavil) caused a severe brain reaction (organic brain syndrome) with mental confusion and disorientation
ephedrine (can be found in Bronkaid, Marax, Primatene, Quadrinal, Vicks Vatronol nose drops, and several other asthma and cold medications)	TCA may block the ↑ in blood pressure ordinarily caused by ephedrine; ephedrine levels and effects may ↓
high fiber diet	TCA blood levels may ↓ due to poor absorption from the stomach and intestinal tract
liothyronine (T3, Cytomel)	can enhance the effects of TCA; abnormal heart rhythms can result; TCA blood levels may ↑
prochlorperazine (Compazine)	TCA blood levels may ↑ with increased side effects and toxic effects
psyllium (Metamucil)	TCA blood levels may ↓ due to poor absorption from the stomach and intestinal tract
scopolamine (Transderm)	may cause ↑ in TCA blood levels
l-dopa (Sinemet)	absorption of TCA from the stomach and intestinal tract into the blood may ↓; effects of both TCA and L-dopa may ↓
theophylline (Bronkaid)	TCA blood levels may ↑
tobacco (smoking)	TCA blood levels may ↓

This is because Prozac does not have such strong effects on the histaminic, alpha-adrenergic, and muscarinic receptors.

Only one of these two hopes was fulfilled. Prozac and the other four SSRIs do cause significantly fewer side effects than the tricyclic and tetracyclic antidepressants. For example, they are less likely to cause sleepiness, weight gain, dry mouth, dizziness, and so on. They are also much safer since they are less likely to have adverse effects on the heart, and they are much less likely to result in death if a patient intentionally or unintentionally takes an overdose. The biochemists who created these new drugs deserve credit in this regard.

Unfortunately, the SSRIs are not more effective than the older drugs. As many as 60 to 70 percent of depressed patients improve when treated with SSRIs, and these percentages are not better than those of the older drugs. Among chronically depressed patients, the probability of responding appears to be lower. The SSRIs also appear to be slightly less effective than the older tricyclic antidepressants for more severely depressed patients. In addition, the amount of improvement is often only partial—the patient may become less depressed, but may not return to full self-esteem and joyous daily living. This is a problem for all the antidepressants, and not just the SSRIs. Although they are no more effective, the SSRIs are dramatically more expensive than the older drugs. In addition, the SSRIs have some new and different side effects described below that were not publicized when they were first released.

Because of their favorable safety record and diminished side effects, the SSRIs have truly captured the antidepressant market. More money was spent on Prozac in 1995 ($2.5 billion) than was spent on all other antidepressants in 1991 ($2.0 billion). One reason for the upsurge in popularity is that primary-care physicians now feel comfortable prescribing antidepressants because the SSRIs are so safe. As a result, many depressed patients who would not think of going to a psychiatrist or psychologist receive SSRIs from their family physicians.

Because the SSRIs are used so widely and have received so much media attention, many people believe they are incredibly powerful and almost magically effective. But this is simply not the case. For some depressed people the SSRIs are very effective. For many others they are only somewhat effective. And often they do not seem to have any antidepressant effects at all. It is the same story with all currently available antidepressants—they are valuable tools to fight depression, but they

ANTIDEPRESSANT MEDICATIONS

are often not the entire answer and they are certainly not a panacea for what ails you.

The fact that the SSRIs are not more effective than the older drugs has caused scientists to reconsider the validity of the "serotonin" theory of depression. According to this theory, a deficiency of serotonin in the brain causes depression, and an increase in serotonin should reverse it. If this theory is valid, the SSRIs should cause depressed patients to become undepressed almost immediately—but Prozac can take as many as five to eight weeks to become effective. Regardless of what causes depression or why antidepressants work, the SSRIs have been helpful to many depressed individuals.

Doses of SSRIs

The doses of the five SSRIs are listed in Table 24.1 on page 487. Unlike the older antidepressants, which are often prescribed in doses that are too low, the SSRIs are often prescribed in doses that are unnecessarily high. Because they have so few side effects, doctors feel comfortable prescribing high doses and may prescribe more than is really needed. For example, although 23 mg to 80 mg per day was the dose range initially recommended for Prozac, a single dose of 10 mg per day is sufficient for many patients. Once they are feeling better, many patients need only 5 mg per day, or even less. These smaller doses are much less expensive and produce fewer side effects.

These low doses are effective because Prozac stays in the body for a much longer period of time than most other drugs—as long as several weeks. When you take Prozac, your blood level continues to increase each day because the Prozac leaves your body so slowly. After a while your blood level becomes quite high. This is why you may only need a tiny dose after you have been taking Prozac for several weeks or more.

To understand this better, let's imagine that you are trying to fill a bathtub with water, and the Prozac you are taking is like the water going in. However, there is a tiny hole in the bottom of the tub, so it takes quite a while to fill the tub up. Over time the water level increases, because more water goes into the tub than goes out. Once the tub is filled up, you don't need to put so much water in to keep the bathtub full.

The water level can be compared to the level of the Prozac in your blood. After 4 to 5 weeks the water level finally gets up to the correct therapeutic range. Now you can turn the faucet down quite a bit so that the level in the tub does not overflow. This is why you can reduce the dose of Prozac after you have been on it for several weeks. Paradoxically, you are now taking much smaller doses than when you first started taking the Prozac, but your blood level is far higher.

Technically, scientists say that "steady state" has been reached. This means that the blood level remains more or less constant, because the amount you take each day is similar to the amount that your body eliminates each day. The other four SSRIs do not have this property, because they leave the body much faster than Prozac. You generally cannot reduce the dose after several weeks.

The effectiveness of very low doses of Prozac is now well known among the psychiatric profession, but I first learned this from my patients soon after Prozac was released onto the market. Many patients told me that after they had been on Prozac for a month or two, they seemed to need only tiny doses, often as little as one tenth of a pill per day, and sometimes even less. At first I thought these patients had overly lively imaginations, but soon many patients were reporting the same thing. I advised them to take one Prozac pill, grind it up, and dissolve it in water or apple juice to store in the refrigerator. Then they adjusted their dose of Prozac by drinking a certain amount of the fluid each day. Say, for example, that you have dissolved one 20mg pill in some apple juice and you drink one tenth of the juice each day; this would correspond to a dose of 2 mg per day. But if you try this, make sure you label the juice clearly so that no one drinks your Prozac for breakfast! Also, make sure you talk it over with your doctor and that he or she approves of what you are doing.

After you stop taking Prozac, it will stay in your body for a long time, because it leaves your body so slowly. This would be like a bathtub that takes an extraordinarily long time to empty out after you pull the plug because the drain is plugged up. After you are no longer taking the Prozac, significant levels will remain in your blood for as many as five weeks or more before the drug is entirely cleared out of your system. Many medications can be dangerous to mix with Prozac (as well as the other SSRIs), so you must not take these medications until you have been off the Prozac entirely for at least five weeks. For example, tranylcypromine (Parnate) is an antidepressant known as an MAO inhibitor that will be discussed below. Tranylcypromine (as well as other MAO inhibitors) can cause dangerous and potentially fatal reactions if mixed with Prozac.

The other SSRIs, such as citalopram (Celexa), fluvoxamine (Luvox), sertraline (Zoloft) and paroxetine (Paxil) leave the body more rapidly than Prozac, but they are still metabolized rather slowly. If you stop taking one of these drugs, your body needs approximately one day to get rid of one half of the amount. It will take approximately four to seven days for most or all of the drug to leave your body. This is slow, but much faster than Prozac. Therefore, these other SSRI drugs do not build up to such high levels in your blood after you have been taking them for more than a few weeks. Because they go in and out of your blood more rapidly, they are usually taken several times per day, whereas Prozac can be taken once a day.

Age can also influence your dose requirements if you are taking an SSRI. For example, blood levels of citalopram (Celexa), fluoxetine (Prozac), and paroxetine (Paxil) are approximately twice as high in older individuals (over 65 years of age) than in younger individuals. If you are taking one of these drugs and you are over 65, you will need a lower dose. Blood levels of sertraline (Zoloft) are also higher in older individuals, although the differences are not as pronounced. In contrast, fluvoxamine (Luvox) blood levels do not seem to be affected by age.

Sometimes gender can play a role as well. For example, the blood levels of fluoxetine (Prozac) are 40 to 50 percent lower in men than in women. Similarly, young men develop blood levels of sertraline (Zoloft) that are 30 to 40 percent lower, on the average, than young women. Men may need relatively higher doses of these drugs, whereas women may need relatively lower doses.

Health problems can also influence your dose requirements. Individuals with liver, kidney, or heart disease may not get rid of SSRIs as rapidly, and so smaller doses may be needed. Make sure you ask your doctor about this if you are being treated for a liver, kidney, or heart ailment.

Side Effects of SSRIs

The most frequent side effects of the five SSRIs are listed in Table 24.5 on page 517. As noted above, the side effects of the SSRIs are milder than the older drugs, and this is the reason for their enormous popularity. They are less likely than the tricyclic antidepressants to cause dry mouth, constipation, or dizziness. They do not stimulate the appetite when you first start taking them; if anything, some patients taking SSRIs lose weight in the beginning. Unfortunately, when the SSRIs are taken for a prolonged period of time, their side effects sometimes increase. For example, some patients taking them report increases in appetite and weight gain after a while, even though they lost weight at first.

Some of the most common and troublesome side effects of the SSRIs include nausea, diarrhea, cramping, heartburn, and other signs of stomach upset. Approximately 20 to 30 percent of patients reported these symptoms in the earliest studies with the SSRIs.* Table 24.5 shows that fluvoxamine (Luvox) is the most likely to cause constipation, whereas sertraline (Zoloft) is more likely to cause diarrhea. Patients taking paroxetine (Paxil) and sertraline (Zoloft) are more likely to complain of a dry mouth because of the anticholinergic effects of these drugs. In some studies, as many as 20 percent of the patients taking paroxetine (Paxil) reported dry mouth. (However, the percentages in the table are much lower because the placebo effects have been subtracted out.)

Most of these effects on the stomach and intestinal tract tend to occur in the first week or two and then disappear as the body adjusts to the medicine. In addition, if you start an SSRI at a low dose and then increase the dose gradually, these side effects are less likely to occur. Taking the medication with meals can also help. (The tricyclic and tetracyclic drugs discussed in the previous section can also be taken with meals to minimize any adverse effects on the stomach and gastrointestinal tract.)

The SSRI drugs occasionally cause headaches when you first start to take them. The rates for headache seem to be the highest for fluoxetine (Prozac) and fluvoxamine (Luvox); in contrast, the rates for citalopram (Celexa), paroxetine (Paxil), and sertraline (Zoloft) appear to be no greater than the rates of headaches reported by patients who take placebos. Excessive sweating has also been reported, especially with paroxetine (Paxil), but this is not usually severe. Patients taking high doses of the SSRIs may also complain of tremors, and this side effect seems to be equally common among all of the SSRI drugs.

Although initially reported as a "rare" side effect, it is now clear that delayed time to orgasm is quite common for men and women taking SSRIs. Many patients also complain of a loss of interest in sex or an inability to achieve an erection. These side effects were reported in fewer than 5 percent of patients during the premarketing research trials. However, now that the drugs are widely used, we know that these side effects can occur in 30 to 40 percent of patients, and even more according to some experts. The sexual side effects may be a reasonable trade-off if the

---

*You will notice that the percentages of patients reporting stomach upset in Table 24.5 are a little lower than 20 to 30 percent on average. This is because the percentages in the table represent the differences between the rates for the actual drug minus the rates for patients taking placebo medications.

TABLE 24.5
SIDE EFFECTS OF SSRI ANTIDEPRESSANTS

Note: This table was adapted with permission from Preskorn (1996) and from the prescribing information for citalopram. Only the more common side effects of each drug are listed. The numbers in the table represent the percent of patients receiving the drug who reported each side effect minus the percent of patients on placebo who reported the same side effect.

	Fluoxetine (Prozac)	Fluvoxamine (Luvox)	Paroxetine (Paxil)	Sertraline (Zoloft)	Citalopram (Celexa)
number of patients on drug	1,730	222	421	861	1,063
number of patients on placebo	799	192	421	853	446
General Symptoms (%)					
headache	5	3	0	1	—*
dizziness	4	1	8	5	—
nervousness	10	8	5	4	1
tiredness	6	17	14	8	8
difficulty sleeping	7	4	7	8	1
weak or fatigued muscles	6	6	10	3	—
tremor	6	6	6	8	2
Mouth, Stomach and Intestinal Tract					
dry mouth	4	2	6	7	6
loss of appetite	7	9	5	1	2
nausea or upset stomach	11	26	16	14	7
diarrhea	5	0	4	8	3
constipation	1	11	5	2	—
Other					
excessive sweating	5	0	9	6	2
Sexual					
loss of interest in sex delayed or no orgasm	Specific comparative data on the sexual side effects of the SSRIs were not available. However, it appears that 30 to 40 percent of patients receiving SSRIs do experience some sexual side effects.†				

*A dash means that the incidence of this side effect was not greater than placebo.

†During the initial drug testing studies, patients were not asked about sexual side effects. Consequently, the estimates of sexual side effects in the *Physicians Desk Reference* are far too low.

Adapted from Preskorn, S. H.: (1996) *Clinical Pharmacology of Selective Serotonin Reuptake Inhibitors*. Cadde, OK: Professional Communications, Inc.; Schatzberg, A. F., Cole, J. O., & DeBattista, C. (1997). *Manual of Clinical Psychopharmacology*, Third Edition. Washington, DC: American Psychiatric Press.

drug helps you overcome your depression. Keep in mind that a loss of interest in sex can also be a symptom of depression itself. In addition, you will probably not need to stay on the drug indefinitely. Once you are feeling better and you stop taking the SSRI, your sexual functioning should return to normal.

You might wonder why these side effects were not noted in the pre-marketing research studies. At the 1998 Stanford Psychopharmacology Conference, one of the speakers jokingly mentioned that drug companies seem to have a "don't ask, don't tell" policy about certain kinds of adverse effects, including sexual side effects. I think this policy is unfortunate, because the FDA (and potential consumers) may be given an overly rosy picture about the effectiveness, side-effect profile, and safety of a new drug. After the drug has been in widespread use for several years, a different picture often emerges.

The adverse effects of the SSRIs on sex are so predictable that one of these drugs, paroxetine (Paxil), is now recognized as an effective treatment for men who experience premature ejaculation. Some people do not experience a delayed orgasm on SSRIs. Others experience it but are not bothered, and some actually view it as a benefit. If this is a problem for you, you should discuss it with your doctor before discontinuing the medication on your own. It might be possible to reduce the dose without a loss of the antidepressant effects. In any case, many available antidepressants do not have this side effect.

Several drugs can be combined with an SSRI in an attempt to combat sexual difficulties. Four which show promise include bupropion (Wellbutrin in doses of up to 225 mg to 300 mg per day), buspirone (BuSpar, 15 to 30 mg per day), yohimbine (5 mg three times daily), or amantadine (100 mg three times daily).

Citalopram (Celexa), one of the newest SSRIs on the American market, may have fewer sexual side effects than the other SSRIs, as seen in Table 24.5. In addition, there is the hope that it will be more effective for severe depressions than the SSRIs. It will be interesting to see if citalopram (Celexa) is more effective and does actually have fewer side effects after the drug has been in widespread use for a period of time. Sometimes marketing claims when drugs are first released turn out not to be supported by clinical experience or by subsequent research by independent investigators.

Among the SSRIs, fluoxetine (Prozac) appears to be the most activating (stimulating), although fluvoxamine (Luvox) seems almost as likely to cause this side effect. Because fluoxetine (Prozac) is stimulating, it is sometimes given in the morning and at noon rather than at bedtime. The stimulation can often be a benefit to depressed patients who feel tired, sluggish, and unmotivated. On the other hand, fluoxetine (Prozac) and fluvoxamine (Luvox) can cause anxiety or jitteriness in as many as 10 to 20 percent of patients. These side effects can sometimes create additional difficulties for depressed patients who already have these kinds of symptoms.

The stimulating effects of fluoxetine (Prozac) are not necessarily bad even for anxious patients. Anxiety and depression nearly always go hand in hand to a certain extent, and many patients need treatment for both kinds of problems. Patients with significant anxiety, such as chronic worrying, panic attacks, or agoraphobia, are often the ones who complain that fluoxetine (Prozac) makes them feel more nervous initially. I tell these patients that the nervousness they feel is a good thing, because it shows the drug is working in the brain. I encourage them to stick with it, because in a few weeks or less they may notice a significant improvement in their depression as well as their anxiety. Most anxious patients have been able to stick with the fluoxetine (Prozac), and the predicted improvement often does occur. This illustrates how a positive attitude can sometimes help patients overcome drug side effects.

Although any of the SSRIs can cause trouble with sleeping, not all of them are as stimulating as fluoxetine (Prozac). In fact, paroxetine (Paxil) and fluvoxamine (Luvox) can be quite sedating for some patients. In other words, these drugs will tend to relax or tire you instead of stimulating you the way fluoxetine (Prozac) does. They might be good choices if insomnia is a major aspect of your depression. Paroxetine (Paxil) is sometimes given two hours before bedtime so that the maximum sleepiness occurs at the time you ordinarily go to sleep. Note, however, that patients taking paroxetine (Paxil) are also somewhat more likely to complain of weak or fatigued muscles. Citalopram (Celexa) and sertraline (Zoloft) appear to be halfway in between—they do not typically cause excessive stimulation or sedation, but are more neutral in this respect.

In the section below on serotonin antagonists, I will describe an antidepressant called trazodone (trade name Desyrel) which has calming, sedative properties. Trazodone can be given in small doses (50 to 100 mg at bedtime) to patients who are taking SSRIs. This has three potential benefits: (1) the calming effect of trazodone reduces the nervousness caused by the SSRIs; (2) trazodone can be given at bedtime to improve sleep; (3) trazodone sometimes boosts the antidepressant effects of the SSRI and increases the likelihood of recovery.

In spite of these advantages, I usually try to treat patients with one drug at a time. This avoids any extra side effects and minimizes the possibility of adverse drug interactions. In my experience, treatment with one drug at a time is usually successful. If you reduce the dose of any SSRI, you can often minimize the side effects without having to add additional drugs. I will address the problem of using more than one drug toward the end of this chapter.

For example, if you are starting fluoxetine (Prozac) and you are bothered by nervousness, insomnia, or upset stomach, you can take a lower dose and increase the dose more gradually. In addition, if you have been on fluoxetine (Prozac) for several weeks or more, there is an excellent chance you can reduce the dose, often quite dramatically. This will often minimize the side effects without interfering with the antidepressant effects of this drug. As noted above, this is because levels of fluoxetine (Prozac) build up after a period of time, so the same dose may produce far more side effects because your blood level has become so much higher. There is really no need for large doses or excessively high blood levels of any of the SSRIs, because low doses have been shown to be just as effective.

SSRI Drug Interactions

A number of common drug interactions for the SSRIs are listed in Table 24.6 on page 521. The table shows that many other psychiatric drugs can interact with the SSRIs, including antidepressants, major and minor tranquilizers, and mood stabilizers. Important interactions with nonpsychiatric drugs are also listed. If you are taking an SSRI and one or more additional drugs at the same time, you should review this table. Make sure you also ask your physician and pharmacist about any drug interactions you should be aware of. This includes prescription as well as nonprescription drugs.

As you can see, SSRIs have a tendency to cause the blood levels of other antidepressants to increase. This is because the SSRIs slow down the metabolism of these other drugs in the liver. In some cases this could be dangerous. For example, the combination of an SSRI with a tricyclic antidepressant can potentially cause abnormal heart rhythms. Although this complication is rare, the effects on the heart can be serious. The combination of an SSRI with bupropion (Wellbutrin) can increase the risk of seizures—an uncommon but serious side effect of

TABLE 24.6
DRUG INTERACTION GUIDE FOR SSRI ANTIDEPRESSANTS

Note: This list is not exhaustive; new information about drug interactions comes out frequently. If you are taking an SSRI and any other medication, ask your doctor and pharmacist if there are any drug interactions.

Antidepressants

Drug	Comment
tricyclic and tetracyclic antidepressants	SSRIs can cause TCA levels to ↑; abnormal heart rhythms can result
SSRI antidepressants	not usually combined; ↑ in SSRI blood levels can result
monoamine oxidase inhibitors (MAOIs)	serotonin syndrome*
serotonin antagonists [trazodone (Desyrel) and nefazodone (Serzone)]	blood levels of nefazodone or trazodone and their metabolite (mCPP) may ↑ and cause anxiety
bupropion (Wellbutrin)	↑ risk of seizures; caution required
venlafaxine (Effexor)	may cause ↑ in levels of venlafaxine
mirtazapine (Remeron)	no information available as yet

Antihistamines

Drug	Comment
terfenadine (Seldane) and astemizole (Hismanal)	fluvoxamine (Luvox) may ↑ levels of terfenadine and astemizole; fatal heart rhythms can occur
cyproheptadine (Periactin)	may reverse the effects of SSRIs

Diabetes Medications

Drug	Comment
tolbutamide (Orinase)	fluvoxamine (Luvox) may ↑ levels of tolbutamide; low blood sugar may result
insulin	fluvoxamine (Luvox) may cause ↓ in blood sugar; insulin levels may need to be adjusted

Heart and Blood-Pressure Medications

Drug	Comment
digoxin (Lanoxin) and digitoxin (Crystodigin)	↑ in blood levels of digitoxin and potential toxic effects including mental confusion

Information in this table was obtained from several sources including the *Manual of Clinical Psychopharmacology* (Schatzberg et al. [1997]) and *Psychotropic Drugs Fast Facts* (Maxmen et al. [1995]). These excellent references are highly recommended.

*This is a dangerous and potentially fatal syndrome which includes rapid changes in vital signs (fever, oscillations in blood pressure), sweating, nausea, vomiting, rigid muscles, myoclonus, agitation, delirium, seizures, and coma.

Heart and Blood-Pressure Medications

Drug	Comment
medications for high blood pressure	levels of beta-blockers including metoprolol (Lopressor) and propranolol (Inderal) also used for angina may ↑, leading to excessive heart slowing and ECG abnormalities; calcium channel blockers including nifedipine (Procardia) and verapamil (Calan) may also ↑, leading to more potent effects on blood pressure
medications for abnormal heart rhythms	SSRI may ↑ risk of abnormal heart rhythms when combined with drugs to control heart rhythms, such as flecainide (Tambocor), encainide, mexiletine (Mexitil), and propafenone (Rythmol)

Other Psychiatric Drugs

Drug	Comment
benzodiazepines (minor tranquilizers), including alprazolam (Xanax), diazepam (Valium) and others	levels of benzodiazepines may ↑; excessive drowsiness or confusion; lower doses of benzodiazepines may be needed, fluvoxamine (Luvox) has strongest effect, but problems have also been reported with fluoxetine (Prozac); clonazepam (Klonopin) and temazepam (Restoril) may be safer than alprazolam (Xanax) and diazepam (Valium)
buspirone (BuSpar)	may enhance the effects of SSRIs; however, fluoxetine (Prozac) may reduce the effectiveness of BuSpar, some patients with obsessive compulsive disorder who received this combination experienced a worsening of symptoms
lithium	↑ or ↓ levels may result; may lead to lithium toxicity at normal lithium levels
l-tryptophan	can cause agitation, restlessness, and upset stomach as well as the serotonin syndrome

Other Psychiatric Drugs	
Drug	**Comment**
major tranquilizers (neuroleptics) such as haloperidol (Haldol), perphenazine (Trilafon) and thioridazine (Mellaril)	blood levels of major tranquilizer may ↑ leading to increased side effects; fluvoxamine (Luvox) may be the safest SSRI to combine with neuroleptics; risperidone (Risperdal) and clozapine (Clozaril) may block the antidepressant effects of the SSRIs
methadone (Dolophine)	fluvoxamine (Luvox) leads to ↑ in blood levels
mood stabilizers and anticonvulsants	SSRIs, especially fluvoxamine (Luvox) and fluoxetine (Prozac), can cause ↑ in levels of carbamazepine (Tegretol) and phenytoin (Dilantin). The combination of either SSRI with phenytoin can cause phenytoin toxicity.
Other Medications	
Drug	**Comment**
alcohol	increased drowsiness
caffeine (in coffee, tea, soda, chocolate)	fluvoxamine (Luvox) causes levels to ↑; excess nervousness may result
cisapride (Propulsid)	fluvoxamine (Luvox) may ↑ levels of cisapride; fatal heart rhythms can occur
cyclosporine (Sandimmune; Neoral) (an immunosuppressive drug used in organ transplants)	levels of cyclosporine may ↑
dextromethorphan (a cough suppressant in many over-the-counter medications)	hallucinations reported with fluoxetine (Prozac), possible with any SSRI
tacrine (Cognex)	fluvoxamine (Luvox) leads to ↑ in blood levels
theophylline (Bronkaid)	fluvoxamine (Luvox) leads to ↑ in blood levels and can produce toxic effects, including excess nervousness
tobacco (smoking)	levels of fluvoxamine (Luvox) may ↓
warfarin (Coumadin) (a blood thinner)	fluvoxamine (Luvox) may ↑ levels of warfarin (Coumadin); increased bleeding may result. The increased bleeding can also result without any changes in the prothrombin test (this bleeding test is used to monitor the dose of warfarin). This is because the SSRIs can also impair clotting through their effects on blood platelets, whereas warfarin affects the clotting proteins.

bupropion. However, as noted above, bupropion is often added to an SSRI in low doses to minimize the sexual side effects of the SSRIs. This can usually be done safely. Make sure you inform your physician if you have any history of head trauma or seizures, because this particular drug combination may not be advisable for you.

The interaction of an SSRI with an MAOI antidepressant (described below) is extremely dangerous regardless of the dose of either drug. This combination can result in the potentially lethal *serotonin syndrome* described on page 534. In addition, both SSRIs and MAOIs can require a considerable period of time to clear out of your body after you have stopped taking them. If you stop taking Prozac and then start an MAOI several weeks later, it can trigger the serotonin syndrome because Prozac would still be present in your bloodstream. Similarly, if you start Prozac within two weeks of stopping an MAOI, this may also trigger the serotonin syndrome. The effects of the MAOIs last only one to two weeks, so you will not have to wait as long when you switch from an MAOI to an SSRI.

A number of other important interactions which are listed in the table involve common drugs that many people take for a cold or flu, diabetes, high blood pressure, allergies, and so on. For example, dextromethorphan is a cough suppressant in many over-the-counter cold preparations. When combined with an SSRI, dextromethorphan can cause visual hallucinations. This has been reported with fluoxetine (Prozac) but could theoretically occur with any SSRI. Also, two common antihistamines, terfenadine (Seldane) and astemizole (Hismanal), can produce abnormal and potentially fatal heart rhythm abnormalities when combined with certain SSRIs, and a third antihistamine called cyproheptadine (Periactin) can block the antidepressant effects of an SSRI.

Make sure you review this table if you are taking an SSRI. If you have any questions, discuss them with your doctor and pharmacist. The SSRIs are safe for the overwhelming majority of individuals who take them. With a little good teamwork between you and your doctor, your experience with an SSRI can be positive.

MAO INHIBITORS

The Table of Antidepressants on page 485 lists four drugs known as monoamine oxidase inhibitors (MAOIs). They include isocarboxazid (Marplan),. phenelzine (Nardil), selegiline (Eldepryl), and tranylcypromine (Parnate). The MAOIs were the first antidepressants that were developed, but they fell into relative disuse when the newer and safer compounds emerged. They can be quite dangerous if mixed with a number of common foods (such as cheese) and medicines (including many common over-the-counter cold, cough, and hay-fever drugs). They require fairly sophisticated medical skills on the part of the prescribing doctor.

In recent years the MAOIs have experienced a much deserved resurgence of popularity because they are often remarkably effective for patients who do not respond to other kinds of antidepressants. Many of these patients have experienced so many years of chronic depression that their illness has become an unwelcome lifestyle. The beneficial effects of the MAOIs can sometimes be quite impressive.

The MAOIs can also be particularly effective in "atypical depressions" characterized by these types of symptoms:

- Overeating (as opposed to a loss of appetite in classic depression)
- Fatigue and sleeping too much (rather than trouble sleeping)
- Irritability or hostility (in addition to the depression)
- Extreme sensitivity to rejection

Patients with "atypical" depression sometimes also emphasize chronic feelings of fatigue as well as a "leaden paralysis." It is not clear whether this really represents a subtype of depression or simply a particular group of symptoms that any depressed individual might experience.

Studies conducted at Columbia University suggest that the MAOIs may be better than the tri- and tetracyclic antidepressants for patients with these kinds of symptoms. The MAOIs can also be remarkably effective when high levels of anxiety accompany the depression, including phobias (such as social phobia), panic attacks, or hypochondriacal complaints. Patients with recurrent obsessive thoughts and compulsive, ritualistic, nonsensical habits (such as recurrent hand washing or repetitive checking of door locks) may also experience relief when treated with MAOIs.

They can be helpful when chronic anger or impulsive self-destructive behavior accompanies the depression. Patients with these features are sometimes diagnosed as having borderline personality disorder. Although these individuals can sometimes be quite difficult to treat, I have seen many who were dramatically helped by the MAOIs. Of course, all patients who take MAOIs must agree to follow the dietary restrictions and medication guidelines religiously. If a patient is unreliable or does not agree to this, other types of medications should be used instead. Unfortunately, some patients with borderline personality disorder tend to be impulsive and somewhat unreliable, and so they cannot take this type of medication.

The way the MAOIs work is different from that of the other antidepressant drugs. Most antidepressants increase the levels of neurotransmitters such as serotonin and norepinephrine in the synaptic regions between two nerves. In contrast, the MAOIs seem to work by preventing the breakdown of chemical messengers like serotonin, norepinephrine, and dopamine within the nerves. As a result, levels of these messengers build up inside the nerve terminals, and they are released into the synapses in much higher concentrations when the nerves fire. This results in a greater stimulation of the nerve at the other side of the synaptic junction.

The MAOIs require careful medical management and close teamwork with your doctor. They are well worth the effort because they can sometimes lead to profound mood transformations, even when other drugs have been ineffective. Because the MAOIs may cause increases in blood pressure, they are not usually recommended for individuals over 60 years of age or individuals with heart problems. In addition, they are not usually prescribed for individuals with significant cerebrovascular disorders, such as strokes or aneurysms, or individuals with brain tumors. Paradoxically, though, they can sometimes be used with individuals with high blood pressure because they usually cause the blood pressure to fall.* Consultation with a cardiologist is necessary to make sure there are no dangerous interactions with your other blood-pressure medications.

Like other antidepressants, the MAOIs usually require at least two or three weeks to become effective. Your doctor will probably want to obtain a medical evaluation before starting you on this type of drug. This evaluation may include a physical examination, a chest X ray, an electrocardiogram, a blood count, blood-chemistry tests, and a urinalysis.

Doses of MAOIs

These doses are listed in Table 24.1 on page 487. The two most commonly prescribed drugs for depression and anxiety are tranylcypromine (Parnate) and phenelzine (Nardil). One of the MAOIs, isocarboxazid (Marplan), is no longer available in the United States but is available in

---

*You will learn below that the MAOIs can cause dangerous blood-pressure elevations, but this is only if you take one of the forbidden foods or medications. Usually, the MAOIs cause a mild drop in blood pressure.

some other countries, including Canada. In addition, selegiline (Eldepryl) is rarely used for depression but is often used in small doses (5 mg to 10 mg per day) in the treatment of Parkinson's disease. It is just starting to be used for depression and some other psychiatric disorders, although in higher doses than for Parkinson's disease, as indicated in Table 24.1. Although the Food and Drug Administration (FDA) has not yet approved selegiline for use in psychiatric disorders, recent studies indicate that it can also be effective for patients with atypical depression as well as those with chronic, severe depression.

A common error with the MAOIs is to prescribe too big a dose too soon. For example, the usual dose range for tranylcypromine (Parnate) is 10 mg to 50 mg per day. Some doctors prescribe larger doses, but I have seen many patients respond to just 10 or 20 mg per day. Because the MAOIs can have some toxic side effects, it is prudent to start them at low doses, to increase very slowly, and not to push the dose too high. I usually start the patient on just one pill per day of an MAOI for the first week, and then increase to two pills per day. If the patient does not respond to a reasonable dose, say 30mg or 40mg pills per day, I usually do not increase the dose further but instead try an alternative medication along with a different psychotherapeutic strategy.

How long should you stay on an MAOI if it does not seem to be working? If you have not had a fairly dramatic response after three or four weeks, as confirmed by your weekly scores on the mood tests in Chapter 2, then you have probably given the drug a fair trial. You might respond better to another type of drug or to the cognitive therapy techniques described in this book.

How long should you stay on an MAOI if you do respond favorably? As with any antidepressant, you have to discuss this with your physician, and many different approaches are currently in vogue. Some physicians believe that patients need antidepressants indefinitely to correct a "chemical imbalance," but I have not usually found this necessary. Patients nearly always do well when they discontinue their MAOIs after a reasonable period of feeling good. Sometimes this may be as short as three months, sometimes as long as six to twelve months.

As with most antidepressants, you should taper off an MAOI gradually so there will be no withdrawal effects. Tapering too rapidly has caused some patients to experience sudden manic reactions. Suddenly going off selegiline can cause nausea, dizziness, and hallucinations, so one has to be especially careful to taper slowly.

What if you go off the MAOI and then get depressed again in the future? If you have responded to an MAOI in the past, you may respond more rapidly if you take the same MAOI again in the future. I have had many patients who experienced a positive response to an MAOI (usually Parnate) and continued to feel undepressed for many years after they stopped taking the drug. Eventually, a few of them become depressed again and call for a "tune-up" appointment. I always give them the first available appointments. If they sound quite depressed, I tell them to start the medication again. I also tell them to start doing their psychotherapy homework again, especially the exercise of writing down and challenging their negative thoughts. When I see them a few days later, many of them are already feeling better. Some of them tell me that they begin to improve in as little as one day or less when they take the MAOI for the second time. I believe that the medication as well as the cognitive therapy contributes to the rapid improvement.

I have not seen this rapid response with other types of antidepressants and do not know why it sometimes happens with MAOIs. Several patients have explained that their bodies seem to "recognize" the effects of the MAOI right away, especially the pleasurable stimulation that tranylcypromine (Parnate) causes. This helped them "remember" what it was like not to feel depressed. In a few cases the improvement in mood came within an hour or two of the first pills they took. In the majority of cases, one or two cognitive-therapy sessions seemed to reverse the relapse of depression.

Side Effects of MAOIs

The most frequent side effects are listed in Table 24.7 on page 529. As noted above, tranylcypromine (Parnate) tends to be stimulating. Its stimulating effects can be especially helpful to depressed individuals who feel tired, lethargic, and unmotivated. Tranylcypromine (Parnate) may provide them with some much needed go power. Because it tends to be stimulating, it can also cause insomnia. In order to minimize this, the entire dose can be taken once a day in the morning or in divided doses in the morning and at noon. The latest recommended time to take it is 6:00 P.M. Phenelzine (Nardil) is less stimulating and may be an attractive option for patients who feel too stimulated by tranylcypromine (Parnate).

The other side effects of the MAOIs are similar to those of the tricyclic and tetracyclic drugs, but they are usually mild, especially when they are taken in low doses. As you can see in Table 24.7, the MAOIs do not have

TABLE 24.7
SIDE EFFECTS OF MONOAMINE OXIDASE INHIBITORS*

Note: This list is not comprehensive. In general, side effects that occur in 5 or 10 percent or more of patients are listed, as well as rare but dangerous side effects.

Side Effect	Sedation and Weight Gain	Light-Headedness and Dizziness	Blurred Vision, Constipation, Dry Mouth, Speeded Heart, Urinary Retention	Common or Significant Side Effects[†]
Brain Receptor	histamine (H₁) receptors	alpha-adrenergic (α₁) receptors	muscarinic (M₁) receptors	
isocarboxazid (Marplan)	+	+++	0 to +	headache; changes in heart rhythm and rate; overactivity or mania; tremor; jittery; confusion; memory problems; insomnia; edema; weakness; sweating; upset stomach; delayed orgasm
phenelzine (Nardil)	+	+++	0 to +	dizziness; headache; fatigue; trouble sleeping; weakness; tremor; twitching; dry mouth; upset stomach; constipation; weight gain; delayed orgasm; jittery; euphoria; trouble in starting urine; swelling; sweating; rash

*The + to +++ ratings in this table refer to the likelihood that a particular side effect will develop. The actual intensity of the side effect will vary among individuals and will also depend on how large the dose is. Reducing the dose can often reduce side effects without reducing effectiveness.
†Many of the side effects of the MAOIs can often be reduced or eliminated by reducing the dose. They usually have very few side effects, and can often be quite effective at small doses.

Side Effect / Brain Receptor	Sedation and Weight Gain / histamine (H_1) receptors	Light-Headedness and Dizziness / alpha-adrenergic (α_1) receptors	Blurred Vision, Constipation, Dry Mouth, Speeded Heart, Urinary Retention / muscarinic (M_1) receptors	Common or Significant Side Effects
selegiline (Eldepryl)	0	+	+	(limited information available);* nausea; weight loss; delayed orgasm; confusion; dry mouth; dizziness; possibly other side effects
tranylcypromine (Parnate)	0 to +	+++	0 to +	overstimulation; euphoric or manic feelings; restlessness; anxiety; trouble sleeping; tiredness or weakness; twitching; tremor; muscle spasms; upset stomach; loss of appetite; constipation; diarrhea; headache; delayed orgasm; numbness or tingling; swelling; racing heart; blurred vision

*This is because this drug is usually prescribed for patients with Parkinsonism who take many other drugs, and also have many symptoms due to their illness. Therefore, it is difficult to determine how frequently selegiline would cause side effects in depressed individuals. At higher doses, the side effects of selegiline are probably very similar to the other MAOIs.

strong effects on the muscarinic receptors. Consequently, they are not likely to cause dry mouth, blurred vision, constipation, or a delay in starting urine flow. Weight gain also does not seem to be so much of a problem with these drugs, although some patients experience an increased appetite. Weight gain appears to be less of a problem with tranylcypromine (Parnate) than phenelzine (Nardil). Because tranylcypromine is stimulating, it may actually reduce your appetite, as do some of the SSRIs, including fluoxetine (Prozac).

Some patients experience light-headedness when standing suddenly because these drugs have relatively strong effects on the alpha-adrenergic receptors. If dizziness does develop, the interventions described previously can help. These include: (1) ask your doctor if you can lower the dose—often you can still maintain the antidepressant effect; (2) get up more slowly and exercise your legs by walking in place immediately before you stand; (3) wear support stockings; (4) drink adequate fluids and make sure you eat enough foods with salt to maintain your body's electrolytes.

Like most antidepressants, the MAOIs can sometimes cause a rash, although I do not recall ever seeing this. A loosening of the stool or constipation might also occur. Some patients report an upset stomach. Taking the medication with meals can alleviate this. Other patients report muscle twitches, but this is usually not dangerous. If you experience muscle pains, cramps, or tingling fingers—side effects I have never observed—a daily dose of 50 to 100 mg of vitamin B6 (pyridoxine) may help. This is because MAOI drugs may interfere with pyridoxine metabolism, so taking extra pyridoxine may compensate for this effect. Some doctors recommend taking vitamin B6 routinely if you are on an MAOI.

The MAOIs sometimes interfere with sexual functioning, especially in higher doses. Some patients experience a decreased interest in sex and difficulties maintaining an erection or achieving orgasm. In this regard, the MAOIs are a lot like the SSRIs. The sexual side effects probably result from their effects on serotonin receptors in the brain and spinal cord, but this is not known for sure. Although the sexual side effects can be disconcerting, these difficulties may be a worthwhile trade-off if the medication is having a beneficial effect on your mood. You should be reassured that the sexual side effects are dose-related and usually disappear entirely when you are no longer taking the MAOI.

One young man I treated actually found the sexual side effects to be helpful. He reported that he had always had a problem with premature ejaculation. Once he started taking tranylcypromine (Parnate), the problem disappeared. In fact, he reported he could make love for prolonged periods of time. He said his girlfriend thought this was a great miracle, and he advised me to buy stock in the company that manufactured the drug!

One pleasurable side effect of an MAOI is an excessively positive re-action to the drug. In other words, quite a number of patients not only overcome their depressions but begin to feel euphoric or high. This is not necessarily bad, but in some cases may become so extreme that the patient experiences the symptoms of mild mania. In the rare patient with a history of bipolar manic-depressive illness (patients with previ-ous extreme highs and lows that were not caused by drugs or alcohol), an MAOI may trigger a full-blown manic episode. This is actually true of most antidepressants, and not just the MAOIs.

If you do start to feel unusually happy, keep in touch with your pre-scribing doctor to make sure these feelings do not get out of hand. In my experience, this is not usually a serious problem—the euphoric feel-ings provide a welcome relief from the depression and tend to dimin-ish in a week or so. The euphoric feelings also respond to a reduction in dose.

Dr. Alan F. Schatzberg and his colleagues* have pointed out that some patients seem drunk or intoxicated when taking MAOIs. Patients may also feel confused and have trouble with coordination. These ad-verse reactions are more likely when the doses are pushed to very high levels. Obviously, the dose should be reduced immediately if these toxic effects develop.

Two of the MAOI drugs, phenelzine (Nardil) and isocarboxazid (Marplan), can have negative effects on the liver. Therefore, your doc-tor may want to do a blood test to monitor levels of certain enzymes that reflect liver function before you start these drugs, and then again every few months while you are taking them. Patients with liver dis-ease or abnormal liver function tests are usually advised not to take any of the MAOIs, including tranylcypromine (Parnate).

Dr. Schatzberg and his colleagues have also pointed out that selegi-line (Eldepryl) may have fewer side effects than the other MAOI drugs, at least at low doses. At low doses selegiline seems less likely to cause dizziness when standing, sexual problems, or difficulties sleeping. However, it is much more expensive than the other MAOIs, and in

*Schatzberg, A. F., Cole, J. O., & DeBattista, C. (1997). *Manual of Clinical Psychopharmacology,* Third Edition. Washington, DC: American Psychiatric Press.

most cases the others will do the job just as effectively. In addition, the side effects of all MAOI antidepressants tend to be minimal at lower doses. In my experience, many patients have responded favorably to low doses of the MAOIs, so selegiline may not really have any significant advantages.

As you will learn in the next section, all the MAOIs can cause dangerous blood-pressure elevations when patients ingest certain forbidden foods or drugs. Selegiline is less likely to have this effect, but only if it is taken in small doses (10 mg per day or less). Larger doses of selegiline are often needed for psychiatric problems. At these higher doses it is necessary to observe the same dietary and drug precautions that you would observe with any of the MAOIs. This is unfortunate because it was initially hoped that depressed patients would be able to take selegiline and not have to restrict their diets so religiously.

Hypertensive and Hyperpyrexic Crises

In rare cases the MAOIs can produce two types of serious toxic reactions if they are not used properly. This is why so many doctors avoid using them. With good education and preventive medications, the MAOIs can be administered safely, but you will need to study this section carefully if you are taking an MAOI.

One of the dangerous reactions is called a *hypertensive crisis. Hyper-* means high and *tensive* refers to blood pressure, so a hypertensive crisis is a sudden increase in your blood pressure. Increases in blood pressure are not usually dangerous and can occur in many normal situations even if you are not taking medications. For example, when you are lifting weights, your blood pressure can easily rise into the range of 180/100 or higher at the moment you are straining and exerting maximum effort to raise the barbell. Our bodies are used to these temporary elevations in blood pressure. However, if you are on an MAOI and eat one of the forbidden foods, your blood pressure may increase to dangerous levels and remain elevated for an hour or more. If you continue to eat the forbidden foods that interact with the MAOIs, sooner or later a vessel in your brain can rupture because of the mechanical stress. This would cause a stroke, certainly an excessive price to pay for taking an antidepressant.

The initial symptoms of a ruptured or leaking vessel in your brain can include an excruciating headache, a stiff neck, nausea, vomiting, and sweating. As the bleeding continues, paralysis, coma, and death can occur. Because of the danger of hypertensive reactions, your doctor will check your blood pressure at each session. The risk of a stroke is higher in individuals over 60 because our arteries become less resilient with age and are more likely to tear or rupture when subjected to the stress of a sudden increase in blood pressure. Regardless of your age, you will need to monitor your blood pressure and watch your diet carefully when taking an MAOI.

These hypertensive crises are sometimes also called *noradrenergic crises* because they are thought to be due to an excessive release of norepinephrine. Norepinephrine is a transmitter substance used by nerves in your brain and in your body. Hypertensive crises usually occur if you eat certain forbidden foods that contain a substance called tyramine or if you take one of the forbidden drugs that I will describe in detail below. If you are careful, the risk of a serious hypertensive crisis is very small.

The other dangerous reaction to an MAOI is called a *hyperpyrexic crisis*. *Pyrexic* refers to fire, or fever. The patient with a hyperpyrexic crisis may develop a high fever along with a number of alarming symptoms that can include sensitivity to light, rapid changes in blood pressure, rapid breathing, sweating, nausea, vomiting, rigid muscles, jerking and twitching, confusion, agitation, delirium, seizures, shock, coma, and death. A hyperpyrexic crisis is sometimes also called a *serotonin syndrome* because it is due to an abnormal and dangerous increase in levels of serotonin in the brain. A hyperpyrexic crisis occurs when the patient takes certain forbidden medications that must not be combined with the MAOIs. These drugs cause an increase in levels of serotonin in the brain. Obviously, a hyperpyrexic crisis requires immediate discontinuation of the MAOI along with emergency medical treatment. The treatment may include intravenous fluids and treatment with the serotonin antagonist, cyproheptadine (Periactin), at a dose of 4 mg to 12 mg.

Several decades ago when MAOIs first became available, doctors were not as aware of the blood-pressure elevations that resulted from eating foods containing tyramine or from taking the kinds of drugs described below, and so these hypertensive reactions were more common and severe. Nowadays, extreme hypertensive and hyperpyrexic reactions are quite rare. I am personally aware of only one patient, treated by a colleague in Boston, who developed a stroke due to a hypertensive crisis (noradrenergic syndrome) while taking an MAOI. I have had about half a dozen patients over the years who called me because they suddenly developed elevated blood pressure. I told each of them to go to a local hospital emergency room for observation. In every case the blood pressure quickly subsided without any treatment besides observation. None of these patients experienced any adverse effects. I have never seen a patient who developed a hyperpyrexic crisis while on an MAOI.

Because we know a great deal about what causes these two kinds of reactions, they can be avoided. If you are taking an MAOI, educate yourself by studying the following sections carefully. You will have to avoid taking certain types of drugs and exercise a little self-discipline in your diet in order to be safe. You will find it is well worth the extra effort required to protect yourself.

How to Avoid a Hypertensive or Hyperpyrexic Crisis

There are two important keys to preventing a hypertensive or hyperpyrexic crisis if you are taking an MAOI. First, you must obtain a blood-pressure cuff and monitor your own blood pressure carefully. Second, you must carefully avoid certain foods or medications (including some illicit drugs) that will predictably trigger these reactions. I will describe these forbidden foods and medicines in detail below. You will see that the substances that can trigger a hypertensive crisis are somewhat different from the substances that can trigger a hyperpyrexic crisis.

You can obtain a blood-pressure cuff at your local pharmacy so you can monitor your own blood pressure whenever you want. Practice using the cuff. Although it may seem a little awkward or confusing at first, you will find that it gets pretty easy to take your blood pressure after you have practiced a few times. In my practice I have required every patient taking an MAOI to do this. In the rare situation that a patient did not want to go to the trouble of obtaining a cuff and learning how to use it, I have refused to prescribe an MAOI.

Initially you can monitor your blood pressure once a day or even twice a day if you are so inclined. After you have been taking the MAOI for several weeks, you do not need to monitor your blood pressure so frequently. Once a week is usually sufficient. You can check your blood pressure if you forget and eat one of the forbidden foods. You can also check it if you feel woozy or nauseous or if you get an excruciating or severe headache. We all get headaches from time to time, and they rarely ever indicate a stroke. However, if you have a blood-pressure cuff, you can check your blood pressure and make sure it is not dangerously elevated.

If your blood pressure goes up to a dangerous level, you should call your doctor or go to an emergency room. How much elevation is dangerous? Blood pressure consists of two numbers. The higher number is called the *systolic* blood pressure, and the lower number is called the *di-*

astolic blood pressure. A value of 120/80, for example, would be considered normal for most people. Most emergency room doctors would not be particularly concerned until these numbers reach in the range of 190 to 200 / 105 to 110. At that level they might observe you carefully and monitor your blood pressure every few minutes. Most of the time, an elevated blood pressure subsides without treatment. If your blood pressure continues to rise, the ER doctor could give you an antidote (such as phentolamine or prazosin) to lower your blood pressure back to a safe range.

The best time to take your blood pressure is about one to one and a half hours after you have taken the medication. About a quarter of my patients have noted modest blood-pressure elevations at this time even if they have not eaten any of the forbidden foods in Table 24.8 on page 537 or taken the medicines in Table 24.9 on page 540. These increases are not usually extreme or dangerous—a 20- or 30-point elevation in the systolic blood pressure is typical. Nevertheless, in those cases I have recommended stopping the medication because these patients seem overly sensitive to the blood-pressure effects of the MAOI. It just did not seem worth the worry and risk, especially since a different antidepressant might be just as effective.

Foods to Avoid

Hypertensive crises may occur if you eat foods (see Table 24.8 on page 537) that contain a substance known as tyramine. If you are taking an MAOI, too much tyramine can interfere with your brain's ability to regulate your blood pressure. Tyramine causes nerves to release more norepinephrine into the synaptic regions that separate them from the postsynaptic nerves. These postsynaptic nerves may become overly stimulated when too much norepinephrine is released. Because these nerves help to regulate blood pressure, all the extra norepinephrine that is released can cause a dangerous and sudden increase in blood pressure.

You will recall that an enzyme called monoamine oxidase (MAO) is located inside the presynaptic nerves. This enzyme usually destroys any excess norepinephrine that builds up inside these nerves and prevents them from releasing too much norepinephrine when they fire. But the MAOI drugs block this enzyme, and so the norepinephrine levels inside these nerves increase substantially. When you eat foods containing tyramine, all that extra norepinephrine suddenly spills into the synaptic region, causing a massive stimulation of the nerves that regulate your blood pressure.

TABLE 24.8
FOODS AND BEVERAGES TO AVOID IF YOU ARE TAKING A
MONOAMINE OXIDASE INHIBITOR (MAOI)*

Foods to Avoid Completely

Cheese, particularly strong or aged cheeses (cottage cheese and cream cheese are allowed)

Beer and ale: particularly tap beers, beers from microbreweries, and strong ales

Red wine: especially Chianti

Brewer's yeast tablets or yeast extracts (Breads and cooked forms of yeast are safe. The yeast extracts from health food stores are dangerous. Yeast extracts may be found in certain soups. Some powdered protein diet supplements contain yeast extracts.)

Pods of fava beans, also called Italian green beans (regular green beans are safe)

Meat or fish that is smoked, dried, fermented, unrefrigerated, or spoiled, including:

• Fermented or air-dried sausages, such as salami and mortadella (some experts state that bologna, pepperoni, summer sausage, corned beef, and liverwurst are safe)

• Pickled or salted herring

• Liver (beef or chicken), especially old chicken liver (fresh chicken liver is safe)

Overripe bananas or avocados (most fruits are completely safe)

Sauerkraut

Some soups, including those made from beef bouillon or Asian soup stocks (e.g., miso soup); tinned and packet soups are felt to be safe, unless made from bouillon or meat extracts

Foods or Beverages That May Cause Problems in Large Amounts

White wine or clear alcohol, such as vodka or gin

Sour cream

Yogurt: must be pasteurized and less than 5 days old to be safe

Soy sauce

NutraSweet (the artificial sweetener)

Chocolate

Caffeine in beverages (coffee, tea and soda) and chocolate

Foods or Beverages Once Thought to Cause Problems
Which Are Probably Safe in Small Amounts

Figs (avoid overripe figs)

Meat tenderizers

Caviar, snails, tinned fish, pate

Raisins

*Modified from B. McCabe and M. T. Tsuang, "Dietary Considerations in MAO Inhibitor Regimens," *Journal of Clinical Psychiatry, 43,* (1982): 178–81.

If you watch your diet carefully, the likelihood is high that you will experience no adverse blood-pressure elevation. The most common forbidden food is cheese, especially strong cheese. You will have to give up pizza and grilled-cheese sandwiches for a while if you are taking an MAOI.

Most of the forbidden foods contain the breakdown products of protein—including tyramine. So, for example, freshly cooked chicken is perfectly safe, but cooked leftover chicken that has been sitting for a few days can be dangerous because tyramine forms when the meat decomposes. One of my patients on tranylcypromine (Parnate) ate some leftover chicken that had been in the refrigerator for several days. Soon after eating it, he experienced a significant elevation in blood pressure. This was because the chicken had partially decomposed due to effects of bacteria while the chicken sat around. Fortunately, he was not harmed, but this experience served as a useful warning. The fermented or partially decomposed meats on the list in Table 24.8, such as strong sausage or smoked fish, as well as strong cheese, may contain large amounts of tyramine and can be especially dangerous. Some experts also advise against eating Chinese food while taking MAOIs. This may be due to the soy sauce, the monosodium glutamate, or other ingredients.

How much tyramine is necessary to cause a hypertensive reaction? This varies quite a bit from person to person. On average, foods containing at least 10 mg of tyramine will be sufficient to cause a hypertensive crisis if you are taking phenelzine (Nardil). As little as 5 mg of tyramine can trigger it if you are taking tranylcypromine (Parnate). Which foods contain this amount of tyramine? Well, most beers contain less than 1.5 mg, and many contain less than 1 mg, so you would have to drink several beers to run a significant risk. However, some ales contain 3 mg of tyramine per serving, and some tap beers can also be particularly risky. For example, one serving of Kronenbourg, Rotterdam's Lager, Rotterdam's Pilsner, or Upper Canadian Lager contains between 9 and 38 mg of tyramine. So even one glass of these beers could be dangerous.

Cheeses can also vary greatly. Processed American cheese contains only about 1 mg of tyramine per serving, but Liederkranz, New York state cheddar, English Stilton, blue cheese, Swiss cheese, aged white cheese, and Camembert all contain more than 10 mg per single serving.

Suppose you eat one of the forbidden foods by accident, and then you check your blood pressure and discover that it does not go up. What does this mean? There is a lot of individual variation in the sensitivity to the effects of the forbidden foods. You may be one of those individuals who is significantly less likely to react with an elevation in blood pressure. However, you should not become complacent, because these hypertensive reactions are unpredictable. If you cheat and eat the forbidden foods from time to time it is a lot like playing Russian roulette. You may get away with it for a while and then discover that you have experimented once too often. For example, you may eat a slice of pizza on nine separate occasions without any increase in blood pressure, and conclude that it is safe to eat pizza. But this can be very misleading, because the tenth time you may experience a sudden and severe increase in blood pressure. It is not known why this happens, but it does underscore the importance of consistent self-discipline if you are taking an MAOI.

Medications and Drugs to Avoid

A number of prescription drugs, nonprescription drugs, and street drugs that can cause a hypertensive or hyperpyrexic crisis when combined with MAOIs are listed in Table 24.9 on page 540. These reactions are dangerous, and so you must carefully avoid these drugs. Some of the medications that interact with MAOIs do not cause such severe reactions. For example, caffeine may cause you to become more jumpy and jittery than usual. Moderate amounts of caffeine are reasonably safe, however. (You may think of caffeine as more of a food than a drug, but it is a mild stimulant regardless.)

The list of drugs that interact with MAOIs includes:

- Most antidepressants—virtually any of them can be dangerous
- Many anti-asthma drugs
- Many common cold, cough, allergy, sinus, decongestant, and hay-fever medications that contain sympathomimetic agents (discussed in detail below) or dextromethorphan, the cough suppressant. You will have to check labels carefully, because many over-the-counter drugs contain these substances.
- Drugs used in the treatment of diabetes—they may become more potent than usual if you are taking an MAOI and cause your blood sugar to fall more than expected
- Some drugs used in the treatment of low or high blood pressure—both types of drugs can in some cases cause blood-pressure elevations when combined with MAOIs
- Mood stabilizers and anticonvulsants
- Some painkillers, including some local and general anesthetics
- Sedatives (including alcohol) and tranquilizers—they may have

TABLE 24.9
PRESCRIPTION DRUGS AND OVER-THE-COUNTER MEDICATIONS TO AVOID IF YOU ARE TAKING A MONOAMINE OXIDASE INHIBITOR (MAOI)*

Note: This list is not exhaustive; new information about drug interactions comes out frequently. If you are taking an MAOI and any other medication, ask your doctor and pharmacist if there are any drug interactions.

Antidepressants

Drug	Comment
tricyclic antidepressants,[†] especially desipramine (Norpramin, Pertofrane) and clomipramine (Anafranil)	some (e.g., clomipramine) may cause a hyperpyrexic crisis or seizures; others (e.g. desipramine) may cause a hypertensive crisis
tetracyclic antidepressants, especially Bupropion (Wellbutrin)	hypertensive crisis (noradrenergic syndrome)
SSRIs (all are extremely dangerous)	hyperpyrexic crisis (serotonin syndrome)
other MAOIs	hyperpyrexic crisis (serotonin syndrome); hypertensive crisis (noradrenergic syndrome)
serotonin antagonists, including trazodone (Desyrel) and nefazodone (Serzone)	hyperpyrexic crisis (serotonin syndrome)
mirtazapine (Remeron)	hypertensive crisis (noradrenergic syndrome)
venlafaxine (Effexor)	hypertensive crisis (noradrenergic syndrome)

Asthma Medicines

Drug	Comment
ephedrine, a bronchodilator contained in Marax, Quadrinal, and other asthma drugs	hypertensive crisis
inhalants which contain albuterol (Proventil, Ventolin), metaproterenol (Alupent, Metaprel), or other beta-adrenergic bronchodilators	blood pressure elevations and a rapid heart; beclomethasone and other nonsystemic steroid inhalers are generally safer
theophylline (Theo-Dur), a common ingredient in asthma drugs	rapid heart and anxiety

*Information in this table was obtained from several sources including the *Manual of Clinical Psychopharmacology* (Schatzberg et al. [1997]) and *Psychotropic Drugs Fast Facts* (Maxmen et al. [1995]). These excellent references are highly recommended.

†Many patients have been successfully treated with a combination of an MAOI and a tricyclic antidepressant under close observation, but such drug combinations are dangerous and require a high level of expert supervision.

Cold, Cough, Allergy, Sinus, Decongestant and Hay Fever Medications (including tablets, drops, or sprays)

Drug	Comment
antihistamines: terfenadine (Seldane-D)	can cause an increase in MAOI blood levels
dextromethorphan can be found in many cold and cough medications, especially any drug with DM or Tuss in its name. These include Bromarest-DM or -DX, Dimetane-DX cough syrup, Dristan Cold & Flu, Phenergan with Dextromethorphan, Robitussin-DM, several Tylenol cold, cough, and flu preparations, and many others	hyperpyrexic crisis (serotonin syndrome); may also cause brief episodes of psychosis or bizarre behavior
ephedrine can be found in Bronkaid, Primatene, Vicks Vatronol nose drops, and several other asthma and cold medications.	hypertensive crisis (noradrenergic syndrome)
oxymetazoline (Afrin) nose drops or sprays used to treat nasal decongestion	hypertensive crisis (noradrenergic syndrome)
phenylephrine can be found in Dimetane, Dristan decongestant, Neo-Synephrine nasal spray and nose drops, and many other similar preparations, including some eye-drop medications	hypertensive crisis (noradrenergic syndrome)
phenylpropanolamine is contained in Alka-Seltzer Plus Cold and Night-Time Cold medicine, Allerest, Contac decongestants, Coricidin D decongestants, Dexatrim appetite pills, Dimetane-DC Cough syrup, Ornade Spansules, Robitussin-CF Sinarest, St. Joseph Cold Tablets, Tylenol Cold medicine, and many others	hypertensive crisis (noradrenergic syndrome)

Cold, Cough, Allergy, Sinus, Decongestant and Hay Fever Medications (including tablets, drops, or sprays)	
Drug	**Comment**
pseudoephedrine can be found in Actifed, Allerest No Drowsiness formula, Benadryl combinations, CoAdvil, Dimetane DX cough syrup, Dristan Maximum Strength, Robitussin DAC syrup, Robitussin-PE, Seldane D tablets, Sinarest No Drowsiness, Sinutab, Sudafed, Triaminic Nite Light, and numerous Tylenol allergy, sinus, flu, and cold preparations, as well as several Vicks products including NyQuil, to mention just a few	hypertensive crisis (noradrenergic syndrome)
Diabetes Medications	
Drug	**Comment**
insulin	may cause a greater drop in blood sugar
oral hypoglycemic agents	as above
Medications to Treat Low Blood Pressure (for patients in shock)	
Drug	**Comment**
sympathomimetic amines including: • dopamine (Intropin) • epinephrine (Adrenalin) • isoproterenol (Isuprel) • metaraminol (Aramine) • methyldopa (Aldomet) • norepinephrine (Levophed)	hypertensive crisis (noradrenergic syndrome) because these drugs cause blood vessels to constrict
Medications for High Blood Pressure	
Drug	**Comment**
guanadrel (Hylorel) guanethidine (Ismelin) hydralazine (Apresoline) methyldopa (Aldomet) reserpine (Serpasil)	These blood-pressure medications may cause a paradoxical increase in blood pressure when combined with MAOIs

Medications for High Blood Pressure	
Drug	**Comment**
beta-blockers	may be more potent when combined with MAOIs, leading to a greater than expected drop in blood pressure and dizziness when standing
calcium channel blockers	appear to be reasonably safe when combined with MAOIs. Check with your doctor and monitor blood pressure closely. Watch for a greater than expected drop in blood pressure
diuretics	watch for a greater than expected drop in blood pressure. May increase blood level of the MAOI
Mood Stabilizers	
Drug	**Comment**
carbamazepine (Tegretol)	hyperpyrexic crisis (serotonin syndrome); MAOI may cause carbamazepine levels to fall, so epileptics may experience seizures
lithium (Eskalith)	can cause hyperpyrexic crisis (serotonin syndrome) in animal studies
Painkillers and Anesthetics	
Drug	**Comment**
anesthetics: general	tell your anesthesiologist you are on an MAOI; if possible, discontinue the MAOI two weeks before elective surgery
	muscle relaxants such as succinylcholine and tubocurarine may have a more pronounced or prolonged effect; general anesthetics such as halothane may lead to excitement, excessive depression of the brain, or hyperpyrexic reactions
anesthetics: local	some contain epinephrine or other sympathomimetics—make sure you tell your dentist you are taking an MAOI
cyclobenzaprine (Flexeril) (a muscle relaxant used to treat muscle spasm)	hyperpyrexic crisis (serotonin syndrome) or severe seizures

Painkillers and Anesthetics	
Drug	**Comment**
meperidine (Demerol)	a single injection can cause seizures, coma, and death (serotonin syndrome); most other narcotics, including morphine and codeine, have been used safely with MAOIs

Sedatives and Tranquilizers	
Drug	**Comment**
alcohol	may have enhanced sedative effects, especially when combined with phenelzine (Nardil); this could be hazardous when driving or operating dangerous machinery
barbiturates (such as phenobarbital)	enhanced sedative effects as described above
buspirone (BuSpar)	enhanced sedative effects as described above
major tranquilizers (neuroleptics)	enhanced sedative effects as described above; some neuroleptics may cause a drop in blood pressure when combined with MAOIs
minor tranquilizers (benzodiazepines) such as alprazolam (Xanax), diazepam (Valium), and others	enhanced sedative effects as described above
sleeping pills	enhanced sedative effects as described above
l-tryptophan	hyperpyrexic crisis (serotonin syndrome); blood-pressure elevations; disorientation, memory impairment, and other neurologic changes

Stimulants (Pep Pills) and Street Drugs	
Drug	**Comment**
amphetamines ("speed" or "crank") cocaine benzedrine benzphetamine (Didrex) dextroamphetamine (Dexedrine) methamphetamine (Desoxyn) methylphenidate (Ritalin)	hypertensive crisis (noradrenergic syndrome) is possible; methylphenidate considered somewhat less risky than the amphetamines

Weight Loss and Appetite-Suppression Medications	
Drug	**Comment**
cylert (Pemoline)	drug interactions have not been studied in humans; great caution should be used; some experts report that Pemoline has been combined with MAOIs in some cases
fenfluramine (Pondimin)	hyperpyrexic crisis (serotonin syndrome)
phendimetrazine (Plegiline)	hypertensive crisis (noradrenergic syndrome)
phentermine and some over-the-counter medications	hypertensive crisis (noradrenergic syndrome)
phenylpropanolamine (Acutrim)	hypertensive crisis (noradrenergic syndrome)
stimulants (listed above)	hypertensive crisis (noradrenergic syndrome)
Other MAOI Drug Interactions	
Drug	**Comment**
caffeine (in coffee, tea, soda, chocolate)	probably safe in moderate amounts; avoid large amounts; may cause blood-pressure elevations, a racing heart, and anxiety
disulfiram (Antabuse) (used to treat alcoholism)	severe reactions when mixed with an MAOI
L-dopa (Sinemet) (used to treat Parkinson's disease)	hypertensive crisis (noradrenergic syndrome)

more pronounced effects than usual when you are taking an MAOI. The increased sleepiness could be hazardous if you are driving.

- L-tryptophan—the natural amino acid
- Stimulants (pep pills) and street drugs
- Many weight-loss (appetite-suppressing) medications
- Caffeine, which is present in coffee, tea, many sodas, hot cocoa, and chocolate. Caffeine is also present in a number of prescription and nonprescription medications such as Cafergot suppositories and tablets, Darvon compound-65, No-Doz, Fiorinal, Excedrin, and many other cold or pain preparations.
- Disulfiram (Antabuse), used to treat alcoholism
- Levodopa, used in the treatment of Parkinson's disease

Drugs that are categorized as sympathomimetics are particularly dangerous because they are contained in many over-the- counter drugs for common ailments such as colds. They are called sympathomimetics because they tend to mimic the effects of the sympathetic nervous system, which is involved in the control of blood pressure.

Several sympathomimetic drugs are found in large numbers of prescription and over-the-counter cold preparations, cough medicines, decongestants, and hay-fever medications. These include ephedrine, phenylephrine, phenylpropanolamine and pseudoephedrine.

Ephedrine can be found in Bronkaid, Primatene, Vick's Vatronol nose drops and several other cold and asthma medications.

Phenylephrine can be found in Dimetane, Dristan decongestants, Neo-Synephrine nasal spray and nose drops, and many other similar preparations.

Phenylpropanolamine is contained in Alka-Seltzer Plus Cold medicines, Contac decongestants, Coricidin D decongestants, Dexatrim appetite-suppressant pills, Dimetane-DC cough syrup, Ornade Spansules, Robitussin-CF, Sinarest, St. Joseph Cold Tablets, and many other cold medicines.

Pseudoephedrine can be found in Actifed, Advil Cold & Sinus, Allerest No-Drowsiness formula, Benadryl combinations, Dimetane DX cough syrup, Dristan Cold Maximum Strength, Robitussin DAC syrup, Robitussin-PE, Seldane D tablets, Sinarest No Drowsiness, Sinutab, Sudafed, Triaminic Nite Light, and numerous Tylenol allergy, sinus, flu, and cold preparations, as well as several Vicks products including NyQuil, to mention just a few.

Some cold and cough preparations contain dextromethorphan. This is not a sympathomimetic drug, but a cough suppressant. Dextromethorphan is on the list of forbidden medications because it can cause a hyperpyrexic crisis. Dextromethorphan can be found in any drug with DM or Tuss in its name, as well as many preparations without these suffixes. A few examples are Bromarest DM or DX, Dimetane DX cough syrup, Dristan Cold & Flu, Phenergan with Dextromethorphan, Robitussin DM, several Tylenol cold, cough, and flu preparations, and many other medications as well.

Because so many common over-the-counter medications contain sympathomimetics or dextromethorphan, it is nearly impossible to keep up with all of them. You can best protect yourself by reading the warning labels that come with these medications and by checking with your doctor or pharmacist before you combine any of them with an MAOI.

Diabetics taking MAOIs need to know that the MAOIs may also cause blood levels of insulin as well as some oral hypoglycemic agents to increase. As a result, your blood sugar may fall more than expected. This can cause a hypoglycemic reaction, with dizziness, faintness, sweating, and so forth, because your brain does not get enough sugar from your blood. Your doctor may have to adjust the doses of your diabetic medications if you are on an MAOI.

Any of the MAOIs can lower your blood pressure, and so they can intensify the effects of other blood-pressure medications your doctor has prescribed, including diuretics and beta-blockers. The MAOIs can also cause the blood levels of a number of blood-pressure medications to increase. This also tends to intensify their effects. As noted above, some blood-pressure medications can have the paradoxical effect of causing an increase in blood pressure if you are taking an MAOI. Make sure you let your doctor know about the MAOI. Many major tranquilizers (neuroleptics) can also cause blood pressure to fall, and MAOIs can increase this effect as well.

Some painkillers must be avoided if you are taking an MAOI. For example, a single injection of the painkiller meperidine (Demerol) has been known to cause seizures, coma, and death in patients taking MAOIs. Other opiates, including morphine, are thought to be safer. Most mild nonprescription painkillers, such as aspirin or Tylenol, are also thought to be safe as long as they contain no caffeine. However, cyclobenzaprine (Flexeril), which is commonly used to treat local muscle spasms, can cause fever, seizures, and death. This drug should be avoided entirely.

Many local and general anesthetics can also interact with the MAOIs. Some local anesthetics contain epinephrine or other sympathomimetic drugs that can create hypertensive reactions. Inform your dentist that you are taking an MAOI so she or he can choose a local anesthetic that will be safe for you. If you require elective surgery while on an MAOI, it would be best to discontinue the MAOI for one or two weeks prior to the surgery. Some general anesthetics, such as halothane, can cause excitement or excessive sedation as well as hyperpyrexic reactions when combined with an MAOI. The muscle relaxants used by anesthesiologists, such as succinylcholine or tubocurarine, may also have more potent effects. Make sure you inform your anesthesiologist if you are taking an MAOI.

Sedative drugs, including alcohol, major tranquilizers (neuroleptics) and minor tranquilizers, barbiturates, and sleeping pills, can interact with MAOIs. This is especially true for phenelzine (Nardil). Because phenelzine also tends to be sedating, it can enhance the effects of any other sedative agent. You should try to avoid combining MAOIs with sedative drugs because the sleepiness you experience could be hazardous, especially if you are driving or operating dangerous machinery.

L-tryptophan is another sedative agent that should not be combined with MAOIs because it can cause a hyperpyrexic crisis (serotonin syndrome). L-tryptophan is an essential amino acid that is present in certain foods such as meats and dairy products. It used to be available in health-food stores and has been actively promoted as a natural sedative agent to help people with insomnia. It has also been used as a treatment for depression, but the evidence for its antidepressant effects is meager at best. Following ingestion, L-tryptophan rapidly accumulates in the brain, where it is converted into serotonin. If the dose of L-tryptophan is large enough, you will begin to feel sleepy. If you are taking an MAOI, the increase in brain serotonin may be massive. This is because your brain cannot metabolize the excess serotonin when you are on an MAOI, so the levels of serotonin can escalate to dangerous levels, triggering the serotonin syndrome.

However, some researchers have purposely treated depressed patients with an MAOI plus 2 to 6 grams per day of L-tryptophan in an attempt to make the MAOI treatment more effective. The purpose of these augmentation strategies is to convert a drug nonresponder into a drug responder. Some studies have indicated that this combination can be more potent than treatment with an MAOI alone. Such a treatment is somewhat dangerous, and should probably be administered by experts and reserved for patients with very difficult, resistant depressions.* Dr. Jonathan Cole and his colleagues (Schatzberg et al. [1997]). have given doses of 3 to 6 grams of L-tryptophan to patients who had been taking an MAOI for several weeks or more. They observed some early signs of the serotonin syndrome in these patients, suggesting the potential benefits of this drug combination may not be worth the risk.

In animal studies, the combination of lithium with an MAOI can also cause the serotonin syndrome. This is because lithium causes L-tryptophan to enter the brain more rapidly. L-tryptophan is present in the foods we eat, and a large meal can contain as much as 1 gram of L-tryptophan. If you combine lithium with an MAOI, you may get a large increase in serotonin in your brain following meals. However, some doctors have added lithium to an MAOI if the MAOI has not been effective, in just the same way they might add L-tryptophan to try to augment the antidepressant effect of the MAOI. If you receive lithium plus an MAOI, you must be monitored closely to make sure you do not develop any symptoms of the serotonin syndrome, such as fever, tremor, jerking of the muscles, or confusion.

MAOIs are often combined with lithium for another reason. Bipolar patients with abnormal episodic mood elevations as well as depression are often maintained indefinitely on lithium or another mood stabilizer, as described below. During the depressed phase of the cycle, many bipolar patients need an antidepressant as well as lithium to reverse the depression. The MAOIs, as well as many other kinds of antidepressants, have been used safely and successfully in this way. However, patients need to be monitored closely for signs of hyperpyrexic crises as well as episodes of mania, which can occur on rare occasions when bipolar patients receive antidepressants.

Stimulants, pep pills, and weight-loss pills are especially dangerous when combined with MAOIs. Some of these drugs are categorized as

*A patient with a "difficult" or "resistant" depression is simply one who does not readily respond to the usual treatments. If your doctor tries many antidepressant drugs and you do not improve, your doctor will naturally conclude that your depression is more difficult than usual to treat. However, you may respond nicely to another type of treatment. I have treated large numbers of patients who had years and years of unsuccessful treatment with a wide variety of drugs prior to seeing me. Many of these "difficult" patients recovered when I used cognitive therapy techniques like those described in this book.

No single treatment is a panacea for everyone. That's why it is important to have lots of approaches available, including many different kinds of medicines and many different kinds of psychotherapeutic methods as well. The term "different strokes for different folks" is right on target in the context of depression treatment!

sympathomimetics, and they can cause hypertensive crises. For example, methylphenidate (Ritalin), which is widely used for the treatment of attention deficit disorder in children and adults, is a sympathomimetic that could have this effect. Several commonly abused street or prescription drugs are also sympathomimetics. These include the amphetamines such as benzedrine, dexedrine, and methedrine (also known as speed or crank) and cocaine. Amphetamines used to be prescribed for weight loss, but their abuse potential is so high that most doctors no longer prescribe them for this purpose. However, a number of the newer popular weight-loss drugs can also be quite dangerous when mixed with MAOIs. For example, phentermine (Adipex, Fastin) · can cause hypertensive reactions and fenfluramine (Pondimin), the controversial weight-loss drug that was recently in vogue, can lead to hyperpyrexic crises.

Caffeine is also a mild stimulant. It can cause racing of the heart, an irregular heartbeat, or increased blood pressure if you are taking an MAOI. Although coffee, tea, soda, and chocolate all contain caffeine, they are not strictly forbidden, especially in moderate amounts, because their effects are usually mild. Nevertheless, you should avoid caffeine in large quantities because it could precipitate a hypertensive crisis. Some experts recommend a daily maximum of two cups of coffee or tea, or two sodas. In addition, if you monitor your blood pressure with a blood-pressure cuff, as described above, you can see whether that cup or two of coffee you love in the morning is actually causing a rise in blood pressure. If so, you should cut down or give up caffeine completely while you are on the MAOI.

You can see in Table 24.9 that L-dopa (levodopa), which is used in the treatment of Parkinson's disease, can also cause increases in blood pressure when combined with an MAOI. However, patients with Parkinson's disease are sometimes treated with the MAOI selegiline, as well as other medicines. If these patients also receive L-dopa, it should be started at a very small dose and increased slowly while checking the blood pressure.

As noted above, most of the forbidden drugs have warning labels to indicate they can be dangerous when combined with some antidepressant medications. If you are taking an MAOI, check the warning labels carefully before you take any new drug, and always check with your druggist or doctor as well. For a detailed list of drugs that cause hypertensive reactions for patients on MAOIs, see pages 157-160 of *Psychotropic Drugs Fast Facts* by Drs. Jerrold S. Maxmen and Nicholas G.

Ward (Maxmen et al. [1995]). The *Physician's Desk Reference* (PDR)* also lists dangerous drug interactions for any prescription medication you may be taking. It is available in any library, drugstore, or medical clinic.

The lists of forbidden foods and medications may seem somewhat confusing or overwhelming. If your doctor prescribes an MAOI, he or she can give you a card to carry in your wallet that lists the foods and drugs to avoid. When in doubt, you can check the card. Some experts advise patients on MAOIs to carry Med-Alert cards so that emergency room doctors will know in case an MAOI patient is in an accident or found unconscious and in need of emergency treatment. Then the doctors can take appropriate precautions when administering anesthesia or prescribing other drugs.

Remember that the chemical effects of an MAOI remain in your body for as much as one or two weeks after you stop taking it. This is why you must continue to observe the drug and dietary precautions for at least two weeks. I would suggest that you actually wait a bit longer. Then you can begin to eat the forbidden foods, such as cheese, in small amounts at first, followed by blood-pressure checks. If your blood pressure is not affected, you can gradually increase the amount you eat until your diet is back to normal. Similarly, if you are switching from an MAOI to another antidepressant, you will have to be completely drug free for two weeks after you take your last MAOI before starting the new antidepressant.

The same is true if you are starting an MAOI after you have taken another medication. You will have to wait for a period of time, depending on which medication you took. You will recall that you have to wait at least five weeks after going off Prozac because this drug remains in your blood for a prolonged time. Most of the other SSRIs are cleared out of your body more rapidly than Prozac, and so a two-week waiting period is usually sufficient. Some antidepressant drugs, such as nefazodone (Serzone) and trazodone (Desyrel), leave your body even faster, and you may have to wait only one week. Always check with your physician before making any changes in your medications.

By now you may be asking if it is worth taking an MAOI with all its complications and dangers. This question is especially relevant these days, when so many newer and safer drugs are available. Usually, I would try at least two other drugs first. The SSRI drugs in particular often help the same types of patients that used to benefit from the

*Arky, R. (Medical consultant). (1998). *Physician's Desk Reference*, 52 Edition. Montvale, NJ: Medical Economics Company, Inc.

MAOIs. I would like to emphasize, however, that in my experience MAOIs can usually be administered safely. I have prescribed them for many patients over the years. When doses are kept at a modest level, the side effects tend to be minimal. And when the MAOIs do work, their effects can be phenomenal.

In fact, some of my most impressive successes with medications have been with these MAOI drugs, especially tranylcypromine (Parnate). In addition, I have used these drugs with difficult patients who had experienced many unsuccessful treatments with drugs as well as psychotherapy. The degree of improvement was sometimes extreme, and these positive experiences with MAOIs have made a strong impression on me. I believe the enthusiasm of the physicians who use the MAOIs is quite justified. If your physician suggests a medication of this type, it might prove to be well worth the necessary extra effort (taking your blood pressure daily), sacrifice (no pizza!), and self-discipline (avoiding certain foods and medicines).

One last note is that a newer and safer MAOI drug, moclobemide, is available in other parts of the world, including Canada, Europe, and South America. Unlike the MAOIs described above, the effects of moclobemide do not persist in your body after you stop taking it. In addition, it does not seem to interact with tyramine in the diet to nearly the same degree. Dr. Alan Schatzberg and his colleagues have pointed out that moclobemide appears to have very few side effects and that the risk of serious drug interactions is relatively low. Psychiatrists hope that moclobemide or another new MAOI called brofaromine will eventually be marketed in the United States.

SEROTONIN ANTAGONISTS

Two antidepressant drugs on the table on page 555 are classified as *serotonin antagonists.* They are trazodone (Desyrel) and nefazodone (Serzone). They seem to act somewhat differently from most other antidepressants. Trazodone and nefazodone can boost serotonin by blocking its reuptake at nerve synapses, much like the SSRIs. However, these drugs have less potent effects on the serotonin pump than the SSRIs, or even the older tricyclic antidepressants, and this is probably not how these drugs achieve their effects.

Trazodone and nefazodone appear to block some of the serotonin receptor sites on post-synaptic nerve membranes. At least 15 different kinds of serotonin receptors have been discovered in the brain. The two receptors blocked by trazodone and nefazodone are called the 5-HT₂A and 5-HT₂C receptors. 5-HT is simply shorthand for serotonin; the number and letter after the 5-HT identify the specific type of receptor. Trazodone and nefazodone indirectly stimulate another type of serotonin receptor called the 5-HT₁A receptor. This receptor is thought to be important in depression, anxiety, and violence. According to one theory, the stimulation of these 5-HT₁A receptor sites might explain the antidepressant effects of trazodone and nefazodone. In addition, trazodone and nefazodone are effective anti-anxiety drugs. If you tend to be nervous and worried, like many depressed individuals, these medications may be especially helpful for you.

Doses of Trazodone and Nefazodone
The starting dose for trazodone is 50 to 100 mg per day. Most patients do well on 150 mg to 300 mg per day. The starting dose for nefazodone is 100 mg twice per day. The doses of both drugs can be increased very slowly over several weeks to a maximum of 600 mg per day.

Both nefazodone and trazodone have short half-lives. The half-life is the time it takes your body to get rid of half of a drug that is in your system. A drug with a short half-life leaves the blood fairly rapidly and must be taken two or three times per day. In contrast, a drug like Prozac, with an extremely long half-life, leaves your body slowly, and needs to be taken only once per day.

As with any antidepressant, you should monitor your mood with tests like the ones in Chapter 2 while taking trazodone and nefazodone. This will show whether the drugs are working, and to what extent. If you have not improved substantially after three or four weeks, it may be wise to switch to another drug. Although withdrawal symptoms are quite rare for these medications, taper off nefazodone and trazodone slowly. This is good advice with any antidepressant.

Side Effects of Trazodone and Nefazodone
The most common side effects of these two drugs are listed in Table 24.10 on page 555. One common side effect is stomach upset (such as nausea). This is also common with the SSRIs and other drugs that stimulate the serotonin systems in the brain. An upset stomach is more likely when nefazodone and trazodone are taken on an empty stomach, and so it can be helpful to take them with food, just like the SSRIs.

Trazodone and nefazodone also cause dry mouth in some patients.

Both drugs can also cause a temporary drop in blood pressure when you stand up, resulting in dizziness or light-headedness. Trazodone is much more likely to cause these problems than nefazodone. Elderly people are more prone to dizziness and fainting, and so nefazodone may be a better choice for them. As discussed above, several precautions can alleviate this problem: get up more slowly; walk in place when you get up so as to "pump" blood back to your heart from your legs; use support stockings; and take adequate amounts of fluid and salt to prevent any dehydration. Talk to your doctor if you have problems with dizziness or other side effects; she or he may be able to lower the dose.

Another major side effect of trazodone is that it makes you sleepy. This is why it is best taken at night. If you are taking another antidepressant, your doctor may also prescribe a small dose of trazodone at bedtime in order to promote sleep. This is because some antidepressants, such as Prozac and the MAOIs, tend to be stimulating and may interfere with sleep. Trazodone is not addictive, and it will not cause dependency or addiction the way some sleeping pills do. The calming, sedative effects of trazodone also help to reduce anxiety. If you tend to be worried and high-strung, this may be a good drug for you. Nefazodone is much less sedating than trazodone, and is not a useful medication for insomnia. In fact, it can occasionally have the opposite effect of causing restlessness.

Another adverse side effect of trazodone is called *priapism,* or an involuntary erection of the penis. Fortunately, this side effect is quite rare, occurring in approximately one male patient out of 6,000. It has only been reported in a few hundred cases so far. Personally, I have never seen a case of priapism, but men who take trazodone should be aware that it is remotely possible. If the priapism is not treated right away, it can lead to damage of the penis and permanent impotence (the inability to get an erection). Some patients require surgery to correct the priapism. Injecting a drug like epinephrine directly into the penis can sometimes counteract the priapism if you catch it quickly enough. If this unusual side effect does occur, or if you are beginning to notice an erection that will not go away, contact your doctor or go to an emergency room right away. Nefazodone, on the other hand, does not cause priapism.

Priapism sounds frightening, but I do not mean to discourage men from taking this medication. If you read the *Physician's Desk Reference* (52 ed., 1998) carefully, you will see that there is a remote chance of a dangerous side effect from nearly any drug you take, including aspirin. Pri-

TABLE 24.10
SIDE EFFECTS OF SEROTONIN ANTAGONISTS*

Note: This list is not comprehensive. In general, side effects that occur in 5 or 10 percent or more of patients are listed, as well as rare but dangerous side effects.

Side Effect Brain Receptor	Sedation and Weight Gain histamine (H_1) receptors	Light-Headedness and Dizziness alpha-adrenergic (α_1) receptors	Blurred Vision, Constipation, Dry Mouth, Speeded Heart, Urinary Retention muscarinic (M_1) receptors	Common or Significant Side Effects
nefazodone (Serzone)	+ to ++	++	+	dry mouth and throat; headache; tiredness; insomnia; nausea; constipation; weakness; dizziness; blurred vision; abnormal vision; confusion
trazodone (Desyrel)	+++	++ to +++	0	dizziness; dry mouth and throat; upset stomach; constipation; blurred vision; headache; fatigue; sleepiness; confusion; anxiety; priapism (rare; see text)

*The + to +++ ratings in this table refer to the likelihood that a particular side effect will develop. The actual intensity of the side effect will vary among individuals and will also depend on how large the dose is. Reducing the dose can often reduce side effects without reducing effectiveness.

apism is a very unlikely side effect of trazodone and can be treated at any emergency room if you act rapidly when the symptom first develops.

Some patients taking these drugs report visual "trails" or afterimages when they are looking at objects that are moving. Similar in some respects to the visual images reported by individuals who take LSD, this side effect is also quite unusual but not dangerous. These visual trails are more common with nefazodone than with trazodone and occur in slightly more than 10 percent of patients taking this drug. They often improve over time.

Drug Interactions for Trazodone and Nefazodone

As noted earlier, some drug combinations can be dangerous because one drug causes the level of the other drug in your blood to become excessively high. Nefazodone has the effect of raising the blood level of a number of drugs. These include commonly prescribed drugs for anxiety, including many of the minor tranquilizers such as alprazolam (Xanax), triazolam (Halcion), buspirone (BuSpar) and others. As a result, you should be very cautious when combining these drugs with nefazodone, because you could become excessively sleepy.

Trazodone will also enhance the sedative effects of other sedative drugs because trazodone itself will make you sleepy. Consequently, trazodone or nefazodone can enhance the sedative effects of any drug that makes you sleepy, such as alcohol, barbiturates, sleeping pills, painkillers, some major tranquilizers (neuroleptics), and some antidepressants. Be very cautious if you combine any sedative agents with nefazodone or trazodone, especially if you are driving or operating dangerous machinery.

There are several other things you should know about if your doctor decides to combine trazodone or nefazodone with another antidepressant. Nefazodone can increase the levels of several tricyclic antidepressants in your blood, especially amitriptyline (Elavil), clomipramine (Anafranil), and imipramine (Tofranil), so the doses of these drugs may need to be lower than usual.

If nefazodone is combined with one of the SSRIs, there is the possibility that a metabolite of nefazodone called mCPP (m-chlorophenylpiperazine) could build up in your blood. This substance may lead to agitation or feelings of panic or unhappiness. If you are switching from an SSRI to nefazodone, mCPP could also build up because the effects of the SSRIs can persist in your body for several weeks after you stop taking them. Neither trazodone nor nefazodone should be combined with an MAOI antidepressant because this combination could trigger the dreaded serotonin syndrome (hyperpyrexic crisis) described previously.

If you are taking nefazodone, make sure you inform your psychiatrist about any blood-pressure medication you are taking, and inform your general medical doctor as well. Your blood pressure may drop more than expected if you combine trazodone with a blood-pressure medication. If your blood pressure does drop too much, you may notice dizziness when you suddenly stand up. Many psychiatric medications can also lower the blood pressure, including many of the tricyclic antidepressants as well as a number of the major tranquilizers (neuroleptics). If these drugs are combined with trazodone or nefazodone, the drop in blood pressure may be pronounced.

Trazodone can also cause increased blood levels of the anticonvulsant phenytoin (Dilantin) as well as the heart medication digoxin (Lanoxin). These combinations can lead to toxic blood levels of phenytoin or digoxin. Make sure your doctor monitors your blood levels of phenytoin or digoxin carefully if you take trazodone.

The effects of trazodone on the blood thinner warfarin (Coumadin) are unpredictable. The levels of warfarin may increase or decrease. If the warfarin level increases, you may have a greater tendency to bleed, and if it decreases, your blood may have a greater tendency to clot. Your doctor can monitor any changes with blood tests and adjust the dose of warfarin if necessary.

Even more dangerous are the previously described interactions between nefazodone and two commonly prescribed antihistamines that are given for allergies (terfenadine, trade name Seldane) and astemizole (trade name Hismanal). Nefazodone causes the levels of these two antihistamines to increase, which can result in potentially fatal changes in heart rhythms. Nefazodone should not be combined with cisapride (trade name Propulsid, a stimulant for the gastrointestinal tract) for the same reason—sudden fatal heart failure can result.

BUPROPION (WELLBUTRIN)

Three other types of antidepressant drugs are listed in Table of Antidepressants on page 485. These include bupropion (Wellbutrin), venlafaxine (Effexor), and mirtazapine (Remeron). They are somewhat different from each other and from the antidepressants already discussed.

Bupropion was supposed to be introduced in the United States in 1986, but its release was delayed until 1989 because a number of patients with bulimia (binge eating followed by vomiting) who were treated with this drug had seizures. Further studies indicated that the danger of seizures was related to the dose of bupropion and that the risk was much lower for patients who did not have eating disorders, and so the drug was released again. Because of the seizure risk, the manufacturer recommends that bupropion not be prescribed to anyone with a history of epilepsy, a major head injury, a brain tumor, bulimia, or anorexia nervosa.

Bupropion does not affect the serotonin system in the brain. Instead, it seems to work by potentiating the norepinephrine system, much like the tricyclic antidepressant called desipramine (Norpramin). There is also some evidence that it may stimulate the dopamine system in the brain, but these effects are weaker, and it is not clear if they contribute to the antidepressant effects of bupropion. Nevertheless, bupropion is sometimes classified as a *combined noradrenergic-dopaminergic antidepressant,* because of its effects on the norepinephrine and dopamine systems.

Bupropion is used to treat depressed outpatients and inpatients over the entire range of depression severity. Preliminary studies suggest that it may also be useful for a number of other problems, including smoking cessation, social phobia, and attention deficit disorder. The widespread effects of bupropion do not mean this drug is special, however. Nearly all antidepressants have been reported to be at least partially effective for a wide array of problems including depression, all of the anxiety disorders, eating disorders, anger and violence, chronic pain, and many other problems as well. One possible interpretation for these findings is that antidepressant medications may not really be antidepressants per se. Instead, their effects on mood may simply represent a consequence of their more widespread effects throughout the brain.

A new use for bupropion is to enhance the effects of the SSRI antidepressants. Suppose that you are taking a drug like Prozac, but you have not responded to it adequately. Instead of switching to a new drug, your doctor may add a low dose of bupropion. In doses of up to 225 mg to 300 mg per day, Bupropion has been added to SSRI antidepressants in an attempt to combat the sexual side effects of SSRIs, such as loss of libido and difficulties in having orgasms.

In my clinical experience, the effects of these drug combinations have often been disappointing. I usually prefer to try another medication rather than combining drugs when a medication does not work. I am personally concerned that in some instances patients may be in danger of being overly medicated by physicians who are a bit too enthusiastic about adding more and more drugs in larger and larger doses. Also, because I rely so heavily on psychotherapeutic interventions, I do not feel as much pressure to find a solution from drugs alone.

Doses of Bupropion

You can see in Table 24.1 on page 489 that the usual dose range for bupropion is 200 to 450 mg per day. At doses below 450 mg, the risk of seizures appears to be about four patients per 1,000. However, the risk is ten times higher at doses above 450 mg per day—four patients per 100 experience seizures. Whenever possible, keep the dose in the lower range to minimize the chance of seizures. In addition, no single dose should ever be greater than 150 mg.

Side Effects of Bupropion

The most common side effects of bupropion are listed in Table 24.11 on page 560. Unlike the tricyclics, bupropion does not cause dry mouth, constipation, dizziness, or tiredness. It also does not stimulate the appetite. This is a big bonus for patients who have been bothered by weight gain. However, some patients have reported upset stomach (nausea).

Bupropion is also somewhat activating and can cause insomnia. Therefore, it may be relatively more effective for depressed patients who feel tired, lethargic, and unmotivated—the stimulating effects of bupropion may help get you moving.

Drug Interactions for Bupropion

Because bupropion can substantially increase the risk of seizures, it should not be combined with other drugs that can also make a person more vulnerable to seizures. This includes the tricyclic and tetracyclic antidepressants, the SSRIs, the two serotonin antagonists (trazodone and nefazodone), and many of the major tranquilizers (neuroleptics). In addition, there is a greatly increased risk of seizures when alcoholics suddenly stop drinking or when individuals abruptly stop taking minor tranquilizers (benzodiazepines such as Xanax or Valium), barbiturates, or sleeping pills. Bupropion is therefore especially risky for alcoholics and for individuals taking sedatives or tranquilizers regularly.

Many nonpsychiatric drugs (for instance, corticosteroids) can also increase the risk of seizures. Therefore, great caution must be exercised if bupropion is combined with any of these drugs, especially if the dose

TABLE 24.11
SIDE EFFECTS OF OTHER ANTIDEPRESSANTS*

Note: This list is not comprehensive. In general, side effects that occur in 5 or 10 percent or more of patients are listed, as well as rare but dangerous side effects.

Side Effect† Brain Receptor	Sedation and Weight Gain histamine (H₁) receptors	Light-Headedness and Dizziness alpha-adrenergic (α₁) receptors	Blurred Vision, Constipation, Dry Mouth, Speeded Heart, Urinary Retention muscarinic (M₁) receptors	Common or Significant Side Effects
bupropion (Wellbutrin)	0 to +	0 to +	0 to +	dry mouth; sore throat; upset stomach; loss of appetite; stomach pain; sweating; headache; insomnia; restlessness; tremor; anxiety; sweating; dizziness; rash; ringing in ears; seizures
venlafaxine (Effexor)	0	0	0	dizziness; dry mouth and throat; upset stomach; loss of appetite; constipation; sweating; headache; drowsiness; insomnia; anxiety; weakness; tremor; blurred vision; problems with orgasm; loss of interest in sex; abnormal dreams; increased blood pressure

*The + to +++ ratings in this table refer to the likelihood that a particular side effect will develop. The actual intensity of the side effect will vary among individuals and will also depend on how large the dose is. Reducing the dose can often reduce side effects without reducing effectiveness.

Side Effect Brain Receptor	Sedation and Weight Gain histamine (H₁) receptors	Light-Headedness and Dizziness alpha-adrenergic (α₁) receptors	Blurred Vision, Constipation, Dry Mouth, Speeded Heart, Urinary Retention muscarinic (M₁) receptors	Common or Significant Side Effects
mirtazapine (Remeron)	+++	++	+ to ++	dry mouth; increased appetite and weight gain; constipation; sleepiness; dizziness. **Warning:** Consult your doctor if you develop signs of an infection (such as fever). This could indicate a rare fall in the white cell count, a rare but dangerous side effect. Can also cause increased blood levels of cholesterol and triglycerides

of bupropion is high. Make sure you check with your pharmacist or druggist about drug interactions if you are taking any other medication along with bupropion.

There are several other kinds of drug interactions you need to consider if you are taking bupropion:

- Barbiturates can cause the level of bupropion in the blood to fall. This could make the bupropion ineffective.
- Phenytoin (Dilantin) can also cause bupropion levels to fall. However, phenytoin is most often prescribed for epilepsy, and so patients taking phenytoin are not likely to receive bupropion.
- Cimetidine (Tagamet) may increase bupropion levels in the blood. This can increase the likelihood of side effects or toxic effects, including seizures.
- Bupropion must not be combined with the MAOIs because of the risk of a hypertensive crisis.
- L-dopa increases the side effects of bupropion; caution is required when these drugs are combined. This is because both drugs increase norepinephrine and dopamine levels in the brain, although through different mechanisms.

VENLAFAXINE (EFFEXOR)

This is a relatively new antidepressant that is in a distinct class from other antidepressant medications. Released in 1994, it is called a *dual uptake inhibitor* or *mixed uptake inhibitor*. This has a very simple meaning. It leads to increases in two types of chemical messengers (also called neurotransmitters) in the brain—serotonin and norepinephrine—by blocking the pumps that transport them back into the presynaptic nerves after they are released into the synapses.

This capacity to increase levels of two different types of chemical messengers is actually not new. Many of the older and cheaper tricyclic antidepressants, such as Elavil (amitriptyline) also do this. The more important difference with venlafaxine is that it has fewer side effects because it does not stimulate the histaminic, alpha-adrenergic, and muscarinic brain receptors that cause tiredness, dizziness, dry mouth, and so forth. However, as you will see below, venlafaxine has quite a number of side effects of its own.

It has been claimed that the onset of action is faster with venlafaxine because of its dual effects on serotonin and norepinephrine receptors. This does not seem particularly likely because the older tricyclic antidepressants also have these dual effects, but do not have rapid antidepressant effects. Research is now in progress to try to determine if venlafax-ine really does work any more rapidly. Although a faster-acting antide-pressant would represent an important breakthrough, we should probably not be too optimistic. As noted above, claims about the supe-rior properties of new antidepressants have often not been substantiated by further research. In addition, venlafaxine must be started at low doses and increased slowly to minimize the side effects. For most patients this prevents the drug from having any rapid antidepressant effects.

Studies are in progress to examine the larger question of whether drugs with dual action have stronger antidepressant effects than SSRIs for certain types of patients, especially severely depressed patients who are hospitalized. This is important because a number of studies suggest that the SSRIs (such as Prozac) which are now so popular have not been particularly effective for more severely depressed patients. In one study, venlafaxine was more effective than Prozac in the treatment of inpa-tients with *melancholic* depression. Melancholic depression refers to a more severe depression with many organic features, such as waking up too early and a loss of appetite and sexual drive. Individuals with melancholic depressions may also have anhedonia along with feelings of guilt that can become extreme or even delusional. Anhedonia refers to a severe loss of the capacity to experience pleasure or satisfaction.

Like all antidepressants, venlafaxine has been used for a number of other disorders. These include chronic pain as well as adult attention deficit disorder (ADD). Remember that nearly all antidepressants have been used for a great variety of disorders, so it is not likely that the ef-fects of venlafaxine are superior for chronic pain or for ADD.

Doses of Venlafaxine

Some experts recommend starting venlafaxine at 18.75 mg twice per day, which is only half the starting dose recommended by the manufac-turer, in order to minimize the likelihood that nausea will develop. Then the daily dose can be slowly increased by 37.5 mg every third day until a total dose of 150 mg per day or above is reached. Most patients respond to a total dose of 75 mg to 225 mg per day. Higher doses tend to be more effective, but they are also associated with more side effects.

Venlafaxine has a short half-life, meaning that it leaves your body in a matter of hours. Therefore, you must take the medication two or three times per day to maintain an adequate level in your bloodstream.

The manufacturer has recently marketed an extended (slow) release version of venlafaxine (called Effexor XR) that you need to take only once per day, which is more convenient. In Table 24.1 the extended-release capsules appear to be more costly, but this is an illusion. For example, the average wholesale cost of 100 of the 75mg capsules of Effexor is $118.66, whereas the cost of 100 of the 75mg extended-release capsules is $217.14, or almost twice as much. When I first saw these figures, I concluded that the extended-release capsules were almost twice as expensive.

But let's see what happens in a real-life situation. Suppose your dose is 75 mg per day. You could take one of the 37.5mg pills in the morning, and a second 37.5mg pill in the evening, for a total cost of $2.17 per day. Alternatively, you could take one of the 75mg extended-release pills once per day. The cost of one of the 75mg extended-release pills is $2.17, so the cost of the medication turns out to be the same. Either way, Effexor is very expensive, since the daily dose may be as high as 375 mg per day. The high price is especially striking when you compare the cost of Effexor with the cost of many of the generic tricyclic antidepressants that are just as effective and available for less than ten cents per day.

As with any antidepressant, it is best to taper off venlafaxine slowly. At least two weeks are recommended, and some patients require as much as four weeks.

Side Effects of Venlafaxine

The side effects of venlafaxine are listed in Table 24.11 on page 560. As you can see, they are similar to the SSRI compounds described above. The most common side effects of venlafaxine are nausea, headache, sleepiness, insomnia, abnormal dreams, sweating, nervousness, and tremors. Venlafaxine can also cause the same types of sexual difficulties as the SSRIs, including a loss of interest in sex and difficulties in achieving orgasm. These sexual side effects tend to be quite common, just as with the SSRIs. In spite of the claim that venlafaxine has fewer side effects than the older tricyclic antidepressants, it can nevertheless cause dry mouth and dizziness in some patients. The dizziness is particularly likely if you go off the drug too quickly.

One distinct side effect seen with venlafaxine is an increase in blood pressure. However, these increases are typically seen only at higher doses (225 mg per day or above). At doses less than 200 mg per day, the likelihood of an increase in blood pressure is only about 5 percent. The probability increases to 10 or 15 percent at doses greater than 300 mg per day. Blood pressure increases of 20–30 mm of mercury have been observed, for example. If you have problems with blood pressure, this drug may not be a good choice for you. If you do take it, you and your doctor should monitor your blood pressure carefully.

Drug Interactions for Venlafaxine

Because venlafaxine is relatively new, information about its interactions with other drugs is still relatively limited. Venlafaxine appears to be less likely to interact in adverse ways with other medications you are taking. Several drugs may cause blood levels of venlafaxine to increase, and so lower doses of venlafaxine may be needed. These include:

- Some tricyclic antidepressants
- The SSRI antidepressants
- Timetidine (Tagamet)

Venlafaxine may cause the blood levels of several of the major tranquilizers to increase. These include trifluoperazine (Stelazine), haloperidol (Haldol), and risperidone (Risperdal), and so lower doses of these drugs may be needed. In theory, these drugs could also cause blood levels of venlafaxine to increase.

Venlafaxine must not be combined with MAOI antidepressants because of the danger of serotonin syndrome (hyperpyrexic crisis). Remember that it takes up to two weeks for the effects of an MAOI to clear out of your body, so a two-week drug-free period is required. In contrast, if you go off venlafaxine and then start taking an MAOI, a one-week drug-free period should be sufficient, because venlafaxine leaves the body fairly rapidly.

MIRTAZAPINE (REMERON)

Mirtazapine (Remeron), which was released in the United States in 1996, also enhances both norepinephrine and serotonin activity, but through a different mechanism than venlafaxine. Premarketing studies suggest that mirtazapine may be effective for mildly depressed outpatients and for more severely depressed inpatients as well. It may also be particularly helpful for depressed patients who are very anxious or nervous.

Doses of Mirtazapine

The dose range for mirtazapine is 15 to 45 mg per day. Most physicians prescribe a smaller amount at first (7.5 mg per day) and then slowly increase the dose. Because mirtazapine causes sleepiness in more than half of the people who take it, it can be given once a day at bedtime. Some physicians report that mirtazapine is less likely to cause sleepiness when the dose is increased. This is the opposite of what you might expect intuitively. It is because the drug may have some stimulating effects at the higher doses. We will have to wait until there is more clinical experience with this drug to see if this is really true.

Side Effects of Mirtazapine

The side effects of mirtazapine are listed in Table 24.11 on page 561. You can see that it blocks the histaminic, alpha-adrenergic, and muscarinic receptors in much the same way that the older tricyclic antidepressants do. Therefore, the side-effect profile of mirtazapine is very similar to the tricyclics, especially amitriptyline, clomipramine, doxepin, imipramine, and trimipramine (see Table 24.2). The more common side effects include tiredness (54 percent of patients) noted above, increased appetite (17 percent), weight gain (12 percent), dry mouth (25 percent), constipation (13 percent), and dizziness (7 percent). Keep in mind that these figures are somewhat inflated because they do not take into account the placebo effect. For example, 2 percent of patients on placebo also report weight gain, and so the true incidence of weight gain that can be attributed to the mirtazapine would really be 10 percent. Mirtazapine is not likely to cause stomach upset, insomnia, nervousness, and sexual problems commonly seen with the SSRIs.

Mirtazapine has some unique adverse effects. It can, in rare cases, cause your white blood cell count to fall. Because these cells are involved in fighting off infections, this could make you more vulnerable to a variety of infections. If you develop a fever while taking this drug, make sure you contact your physician immediately so that he or she can obtain a complete blood count. Mirtazapine can sometimes cause an increase in levels of blood fats such as cholesterol and triglycerides. This could be a problem if you are overweight or have a heart condition or if your cholesterol and triglycerides levels are already elevated.

Drug Interactions for Mirtazapine

Because mirtazapine is relatively new, very little information about drug interactions is available. It must not be combined with the MAOI antidepressants because of the risk of the serotonin syndrome (hyperpyrexic crisis). Because it can be quite sedating, it will enhance the effects of other sedative drugs. These include alcohol, major and minor tranquilizers, sleeping pills, some antihistamines, barbiturates, sleeping pills, many other antidepressants, and the anti-anxiety drug busiprone (BuSpar). The increased sleepiness you experience when these substances are combined with mirtazapine could lead to difficulties with coordination and concentration. This might be hazardous when driving or operating dangerous machinery.

Mood Stabilizers

LITHIUM

In 1949 an Australian psychiatrist named John Cade observed that lithium, a common salt, caused sedation in guinea pigs. He gave lithium to a patient with manic symptoms and observed dramatic calming effects. Tests of the effects of lithium in other manic patients yielded similar results. Since that time lithium has slowly gained in popularity throughout the world. It has been used successfully in the treatment of a number of conditions, including:

- Acute manic states. Although lithium is used to treat patients with severe mania, they are usually treated with more potent, faster-acting drugs at the same time until the severe symptoms of mania have subsided. These other drugs include the antipsychotics (also known as major tranquilizers or neuroleptics) such as chlorpromazine (Thorazine), as well as benzodiazepines (also called "minor tranquilizers") such as clonazepam (Klonopin) or lorazepam (Ativan). Once the severe manic symptoms subside, the other drugs are discontinued, and the patient continues taking the lithium to prevent future mood swings.
- Recurrent manic and depressive mood swings in individuals with bipolar disorder (manic-depressive illness). Lithium has significant preventative effects, and the likelihood of future manic episodes is reduced.
- Single episodes of depression. Lithium is sometimes added in smaller doses to an antidepressant drug that is not working in order to try to improve its effectiveness. I will describe this and other augmentation strategies later in the chapter.
- Recurrent episodes of depression in patients without manic mood swings. Lithium maintenance may help to prevent recurrences of depression following recovery. Some studies indicate that the preventative effects of long-term lithium treatment may be similar to the effects of long-term treatment with an antidepressant such as imipramine. However, the preventative effect does not work for all depressed patients. Lithium is probably more likely to prevent depressions in patients with a strong family history of bipolar (manic-depressive) illness.

- Individuals with episodic anger and irritability or outbursts of violent rage.
- Individuals with schizophrenia. Lithium can be combined with an antipsychotic medication, and the combination may be more effective than the antipsychotic medication alone. The improvement seems to occur in schizophrenic patients whether or not they also experience mania or depression.

You should keep in mind that in all of these conditions, lithium is sometimes helpful but rarely ever curative. Like most medications, it is a valuable tool but not a panacea.

As noted above, manic-depressive illness is sometimes also called bipolar illness. "Bipolar" simply means "two poles." Patients with bipolar illness experience uncontrollable euphoric mood swings that often alternate with severe depressions. The manic phase is characterized by an extremely ecstatic, euphoric mood, inappropriate degrees of self-confidence and grandiosity, constant talking, nonstop hyperactivity, increased sexual activity, a decreased need for sleep, heightened irritability and aggressiveness, and self-destructive impulsive behavior such as reckless spending binges. This extraordinary disease usually develops into a pattern of uncontrollable highs and lows that can come on unexpectedly throughout your life, so your physician may recommend that you continue to take lithium (or another mood-stabilizing drug) for the rest of your life.

If you have experienced abnormal mood elevations along with your depression, your physician will almost definitely prescribe lithium or another comparable mood-stabilizing drug. Some studies suggest that if you are depressed and have a definite family history of mania, you might benefit from lithium even if you have never been manic yourself. However, most physicians would first prescribe a standard antidepressant and observe you carefully. Although antidepressants do not usually cause euphoria or mania in people with depression, they can occasionally have this effect in individuals with bipolar illness (manic-depressive illness). The mania can begin as quickly as 24 to 48 hours after starting the antidepressant.

In my clinical practice, the development of a sudden and dangerous manic episode after starting an antidepressant has been quite rare, even in patients with bipolar illness. Nevertheless, if you have a personal or family history of mania, it is conceivable that you could experience this side effect. Be sure to tell your doctor about this so you can receive careful follow-up after starting an antidepressant. Your family, too, should be alerted to this possibility. Family members are often aware of the development of a manic episode before the patient realizes what is happening and can alert the doctor that a problem has developed. This is because the distinction between normal happiness and the beginning of the mania may be unclear to the patient. Furthermore, mania feels so good at first that you may not recognize it as a dangerous side effect of the medication you are taking.

Doses of Lithium

As shown in Table 24.1, lithium comes in 300mg dosages, and normally three to six pills per day in divided doses are required. Initially, your doctor may prescribe the lithium three or four times per day. Once you are stabilized on lithium, you may be able to take half your total daily dose in the morning and half before you go to bed. This twice a day schedule is more convenient.

Sustained-release capsules containing 450 mg are also available. Because these drugs are released more slowly in the stomach and gastrointestinal tract, they may cause fewer side effects, and they are more convenient because you don't have to take them so often. However, their increased cost, as compared with generic lithium, may not justify taking them. Furthermore, many patients have reported that the side effects of the inexpensive, generic brands of lithium are not any different from the more expensive slow-release brands.

Like the other drugs used for treating mood disorders, lithium usually requires between two and three weeks to become effective. When you take lithium for a prolonged period of time, its clinical effectiveness seems to increase. Thus, if you take it for a period of years, it may help you more and more.

Unfortunately, there appears to be a group of individuals who do well on lithium, stop taking it, become symptomatic again, and then find that the lithium is less effective when they start taking it again. This is one reason why you should not stop taking lithium, or any other medication, without first consulting with your doctor.

Lithium Blood Testing

Too much lithium in your blood can cause dangerous side effects. In contrast, if your blood level is too low, the drug will not help you. Because lithium has only a narrow "window" of effectiveness, blood-level testing is required to make sure that your dose is neither too high nor too low. Initially, your doctor will order more frequent blood tests so that she or he can determine what the proper dose should be. Later on, when your symptoms have stabilized, you will not need the blood tests nearly as frequently.

If you are not experiencing severe mania, your doctor may order lithium blood tests once or twice a week for the first few weeks, then once a month. Eventually, blood tests every three months may be sufficient.

If you are being treated for a more severe episode of mania, more frequent blood tests will be required. This is because higher blood levels of lithium are usually needed to control the severe symptoms. In addition, your body tends to get rid of lithium more rapidly during an episode of mania, so larger doses may be needed to maintain the proper blood level. As noted above, during a manic episode your doctor will almost definitely want to combine lithium with more potent drugs for the first few weeks until your symptoms have subsided.

Your blood must be drawn eight to twelve hours after your last lithium pill. The best time for a blood test is first thing in the morning. If you forget and take your lithium pill the morning of a blood test, *don't take the test!* Try again another day. Otherwise, the results will be misleading to your doctor.

Body size, kidney function, weather conditions, and other factors can influence your lithium dose requirement, so blood tests should be performed on a regular basis when you are on lithium maintenance. Your doctor will probably try to maintain your blood level at somewhere between 0.6 and 1.2 mg per cc, but this will vary with your symptom level. During an episode of acute mania, your doctor will want to keep your blood level closer to the top of the therapeutic range. Some doctors feel that levels as low as 0.4 to 0.6 mg per cc can be effective to help prevent an episode of depression or mania when you are feeling good. Certainly, there are many fewer side effects at the lower blood levels. Patients with chronic irritability and anger may also respond to lithium at lower blood levels, even if they don't suffer from clear symptoms of manic-depressive illness.

Other Medical Tests

Prior to treatment, the doctor will evaluate your medical condition and order a series of blood tests and a urinalysis. These blood tests will usually include a complete blood count, tests of thyroid and kidney function, electrolytes, and blood sugar. Your thyroid functioning should be tested at six-month or yearly intervals while you are taking lithium because some patients on lithium develop goiters (a swelling or lump on the thyroid gland) or underactive thyroid glands. Your kidney function must also be evaluated from time to time because of kidney abnormalities reported in some patients taking lithium. Your doctor may order an electrocardiogram (ECG) before you start taking the lithium, especially if you are over 40 or if you have a history of heart problems. Your doctor will also need to know about any other drugs you are taking, because some of them may cause elevations in your blood lithium level. These include certain diuretics as well as some anti-inflammatory drugs such as ibuprofen, naproxen, and indomethacin. You will learn below that some drugs can have the opposite effect of causing your lithium level to fall.

Side Effects of Lithium

The side effects of lithium are listed in Table 24.12 on page 572 and compared with the side effects of two other mood stabilizers I will discuss below. As you can see, lithium tends to have many side effects. Most of them are mildly uncomfortable but not serious.

Starting with the effects on the muscles and nervous system first, lithium can cause a fine tremor of the hands and fingers in 30 to 50 percent of patients. This tremor will be present when your hands are resting and often worsens when you do something purposeful with your hands. For example, the tremor can make it more difficult to hold a cup of coffee or to write clearly. The severity of the tremor is related to the dose and may be more severe when lithium is prescribed along with one of the tricyclic antidepressants, which can also cause tremor.

The tremor is one of the major reasons that some patients stop taking their lithium. An anti-tremor drug called propranolol (Inderal) can be given if the tremor is especially severe and troublesome, but it is my policy to avoid prescribing additional drugs whenever possible. A reduction in the lithium dose can also help.

If your doctor does prescribe propranolol, the usual dose to reduce a lithium tremor is 20 to 160 mg per day, given in divided doses. It is best to start with small doses and increase gradually. The smallest effective dose is best. This is because propranolol can have other effects, including a slowing of the heart, a drop in blood pressure, weakness and fatigue, mental confusion, and upset stomach. Propranolol can also cause breathing difficulties and must not be given to patients with asthma. It is also contraindicated for patients with Raynaud's disease. Metoprolol (25 to 50 mg) or nadolol (20 to 40 mg), drugs similar to propranolol, have also been used to treat lithium tremor.

TABLE 24.12
SIDE EFFECTS OF THE MOOD STABILIZERS*

Category	lithium	valproic acid	carbamazepine
Muscles and Nervous System	tremor problems with coordination tiredness mental slowing or dulling memory loss	tremor problems with coordination tiredness weakness	dizziness problems with coordination tiredness weakness
Stomach and Gastrointestinal Tract	upset stomach weight gain diarrhea	upset stomach weight gain abnormalities in liver function pancreatitis	upset stomach abnormalities in liver function dry mouth
Kidneys	nephrogenic diabetes insipidus (excessive urination and thirst) interstitial nephritis, leading to (usually mild) renal insufficiency		syndrome of inappropriate secretion of antidiuretic hormone (SIADH)
Skin	rash hair loss acne	rash hair loss	rash
Heart	ECG changes		abnormal heart rhythms
Blood	increased white blood cell count	decreased platets with bleeding problems	decreased platelets with bleeding problems bone marrow failure (rare)
Hormonal	hypothyroidism	menstrual changes	decreased levels of thyroid hormones (T3 and T4)

*Information in this table was obtained in part from the *Manual of Clinical Psychopharmacology* (Schatzberg et al. [1997]) and *Psychotropic Drugs Fast Facts* (Maxmen et al. [1995]). These excellent references are highly recommended.

Lithium may cause tiredness and fatigue initially, but these effects generally disappear with time. Some patients complain of mental slowing or forgetfulness, particularly younger individuals. The forgetfulness has been confirmed by memory testing. Antidepressants that have anticholinergic properties, such as Elavil, can also cause forgetfulness. Complaints about these mental changes are very common and cause many patients to stop taking their lithium. Memory difficulties seem to be more pronounced at higher lithium blood levels, as might be expected, and often improve when the dose is reduced.

Along the same lines, some patients complain of weakness and fatigue. These symptoms often indicate an excessive lithium level. A blood test and dose reduction may be indicated. Extreme sleepiness with mental confusion, a loss of coordination, or slurred speech suggests a dangerously elevated lithium level. Discontinue the drug and seek immediate medical attention if such symptoms appear.

Some patients express the fear that they may lose their creativity when they start taking lithium. This is especially of concern for artists and writers who have used their highs and lows as a source of painful inspiration for creative expression. Indeed, many well-known painters and poets through the centuries suffered from manic-depressive illness, and their dark or euphoric moods were clearly reflected in their work. However, three-quarters of patients on lithium report that it does not seem to reduce their creativity, and in some cases their creativity increases.

Turning next to the digestive system, lithium can cause an upset stomach or diarrhea that is most troublesome during the first few days of treatment. These side effects usually disappear with time. It may help to take the lithium with food or to take it in three or four divided doses throughout the day, so that your stomach isn't hit with a large dose all at once. It can also help to increase the dose of lithium more slowly. In rare cases lithium can cause vomiting and diarrhea at the same time, and your body may become dehydrated because of all the fluid loss. This can make your blood levels of lithium higher, and so the drug becomes more toxic. This in turn can cause more nausea and diarrhea, creating a vicious cycle. Medical attention may be needed to make sure you are adequately hydrated until the episode has passed.

Unfortunately, many patients on lithium experience weight gain; this is another common reason patients stop taking the drug. Dr. Alan Schatzberg (1997) has suggested that this problem will be greater if you are already overweight. The weight gain results from the stimulation of your appetite by lithium. This is often very difficult to control. Obviously, if you exercise more and eat less, the weight gain can be prevented or reversed, but this is often much easier said than done! If the weight gain is excessive or troublesome, switching to an alternative mood stabilizer such as carbamazepine may be helpful.

Increased thirst and frequent urination can also occur when taking lithium. In some cases patients develop intense thirst from urination that is so frequent and voluminous that the lithium must be stopped. This condition, known as *nephrogenic diabetes insipidus (NDI)*, results from the effects of lithium on the kidneys. It is usually reversible when the lithium is stopped. In some cases, adding certain types of diuretics can also help. This is not intuitive, since we usually give diuretics to *increase* urination, but in the case of NDI, some diuretics can have the opposite effect. Careful lithium monitoring must be performed, because these diuretics can cause increases in plasma lithium levels. Mild forms of increased urination probably occur in half to three-quarters of patients who take lithium.

Lithium can cause a form of kidney damage called *interstitial nephritis.* This term simply means inflammation or irritation of the kidney tissue. When first reported, psychiatrists were quite alarmed about this complication. Subsequent experience has indicated that although the problem may occur in 5 percent or more of patients who take lithium for many years, the degree of kidney impairment is usually mild. Your doctor will nevertheless want to monitor your kidney function periodically while you are on lithium. He or she will order two blood tests called the creatinine test and the blood urea nitrogen (BUN) test once or twice a year. These tests can be performed at the same time you are having your blood drawn for your lithium test. If the BUN and creatinine tests indicate a change in kidney function, your doctor may request a consultation with a urologist and order a 24-hour creatinine-clearance test. This is a more accurate test of kidney function. You will have to save all your urine for 24 hours in a special bottle that the laboratory will give you. The results will help your doctor evaluate if it will be safe for you to continue taking lithium. In most cases you will be permitted to continue, but keep in mind that at least three good alternative mood stabilizers are now available.

An occasional patient on lithium develops a rash, and patients with psoriasis often experience a flare-up of the condition. This may require consultation with a dermatologist, switching to another brand of lithium, going off lithium temporarily, or switching to one of the other mood-stabilizing medications. Acne may worsen during lithium treatment. This can be treated with antibiotics or retinoic acid, but in some cases the lithium has to be stopped. Some patients complain of hair loss, but the hair usually grows back whether or not the patient continues taking lithium. It is interesting to note that lithium-related hair loss occurs primarily in women, and hair can disappear from anywhere on the body. Hair loss is sometimes a sign of hypothyroidism (see below), and so your doctor may order a thyroid blood test if the problem persists.

Lithium can cause a variety of changes in an electrocardiogram (ECG), but these are usually not serious. Older patients, as well as those with heart disease, should have an ECG taken before they start on lithium, as noted above. The ECG can be repeated once you are stabilized on lithium to see if there are any changes in heart rhythm that might be a cause for concern.

You can see in Table 24.12 that lithium can also cause an increase in your levels of white blood cells. These are the cells that normally fight infection. A normal white blood cell count is in the range of 6,000 to 10,000 per cc. The white blood cell count in patients on lithium typically increases to the range of 12,000 to 15,000, elevations that are not considered dangerous. However, if you go to a physician because you are ill, make sure you remind him or her that you are taking lithium and that the lithium may cause a false elevation of your white blood cell count. Otherwise, your doctor may wrongly conclude that you have a serious infection when you actually do not.

Finally, lithium can affect thyroid functioning in as many as a fifth of patients. As noted above, one common effect is an increase in the size of the thyroid gland (called a goiter) without any changes in thyroid function. Other patients develop increases in the levels of thyroid stimulating hormone (TSH) in the blood. This indicates that the thyroid gland has gotten sluggish, and the body is trying harder to stimulate it to produce more thyroid hormone. As many as 5 percent of patients on lithium will develop hypothyroidism, and this may require treatment with thyroxine (0.05 mg to 0.2 mg per day), a thyroid hormone replacement. Hypothyroidism is more common in women than in men.

Lithium Drug Interactions

As shown in Table 24.13 on page 576, lithium interacts with many other drugs. Make sure you review this list with your physician if you are taking other medications at the same time you are taking lithium. Remember that over-the-counter drugs as well as prescription drugs can cause drug interactions.

TABLE 24.13
LITHIUM DRUG INTERACTIONS*

Note: This list is not exhaustive; new information about drug interactions comes out frequently. If you are taking lithium and any other medication, ask your doctor and pharmacist if there are any drug interactions.

Drugs Which Cause Blood Lithium Levels or Lithium Toxic Effects to Increase

ACE (angiotensin-converting enzyme) inhibitors:	antibiotics:	antifungal agents:	diuretics (thiazides):	mazindol (Sanorex)
benazepril (Lotensin)	ampicillin (Omnipen)	metronidazole (Flagyl)	chlorothiazide (Diuril)	methyldopa (Aldomet)
catopril (Capoten)	spectinomycin (Trobicin)	calcium channel blockers:	hydrochlorothiazide (Alsoril)	non-steroidal anti-inflammatory drugs:
enalapril (Vasotec)	tetracycline (Achromycin)	diltiazem (Cardizem)	diuretics (potassium-saving type):	diclofenac (Voltaren)
fosinopril (Monopril)	anticonvulsants:	nifedipine (Procardia)	amiloride (Midamor)	ibuprofen (Advil)
lisinopril (Prinivil, Vestril)	carbamazepine (Tegretol)	verapamil (Isoptin)	spironolactone (in Aldactazide)	indomethacin (Indocin)
quinapril (Accupril)	phenytoin (Dilantin)	diuretics (loop type):	ketamine	ketoprofen (Orudis)
ramipril (Altace)	valproic acid (Depakene)	ethacrynic acid (Edecrin)	low-salt diet	piroxicam (Feldene)
alcohol		furosemide (Lasix)		phenylbutazone (Butazolidin)

*Some information in this table was obtained from *Psychotropic Drugs Fast Facts* (Maxmen et al. [1995]), pp. 213–15. This book is an excellent source of information on psychiatric medications.

Drugs Which Cause Blood Lithium Levels or Lithium Toxic Effects to Decrease

acetazolamide (Diamox)	caffeine (in coffee, tea, soda, chocolate)	osmotic diuretics
bronchodilators:	corticosteroids:	sodium bicarbonate
albuterol (Proventil)	hydrocortisone (Cortef)	salty foods
aminophylline (Mudrane)	methylprednisolone (Medrol)	urea
theophylline (Bronkaid)		

Other Lithium Drug Interactions

Drug	Effect	Drug	Effect
antipsychotic agents: chlorpromazine (Thorazine) haloperidol (Haldol) thioridazine (Mellaril)	may cause increased lithium toxicity or increase the likelihood of neuroleptic malignant syndrome (NMS) (quite rare)	digitalis (Crystodigin; Lanoxin)	abnormal heart rhythms and heart slowing
		hydroxyzine (Atarax, Vistaril)	abnormal heart rhythms
		tricyclic antidepressants	increased likelihood of tremor

The drugs near the top of the table may cause lithium levels in the blood to increase. This can lead to more side effects, including lithium toxicity. The dose of lithium may need to be reduced to maintain blood levels in the proper range. The drugs that cause increased lithium levels include several drugs commonly used in the treatment of high blood pressure, such as the so-called ACE inhibitors, the calcium channel blocking agents, and methyldopa (Aldomet). The calcium channel blocking agents in particular may lead to greater lithium toxicity, with symptoms such as tremor, loss of coordination, nausea and vomiting, diarrhea, and ringing in the ears. Caution is required if you combine lithium with any of these drugs.

Many common non-steroidal anti-inflammatory drugs (NSAIDs) such as ibuprofen (Advil, Motrin, and other trade names) can also cause lithium levels to increase. Several antibiotics can raise lithium levels, as does the common antifungal agent metronidazole (Flagyl), which is often used to treat vaginal infections. Several anticonvulsants are also listed in the top portion of Table 24.13. If you are taking any of these medications, you might need lower doses of lithium.

If you have high blood pressure, you may also be treated with a diuretic (or water pill). Some diuretics cause lithium levels to increase. The loop diuretics and potassium-saving diuretics in Table 24.13 do not increase lithium levels as much as the thiazide diuretics that are listed there. Not all diuretics cause lithium levels to rise. For example, osmotic diuretics, which work a little differently from the others, can have the opposite effect of causing lithium levels to fall.

Your doctor may prescribe a low-salt diet if you have high blood pressure. However, a low-salt diet can cause lithium levels to rise. This is because your kidneys will excrete less salt in an attempt to preserve it. Since lithium is chemically very similar to table salt, your kidney will also excrete less lithium. By the same token, if you are sweating a great deal during the summer months, this can have the same effect of depleting your body of salt and causing your lithium levels to increase. Once again, your kidneys will try to preserve salt and lithium as well. Make sure you maintain an adequate intake of salt to compensate for the salt you will lose if you are sweating a great deal.

The opposite effect can also occur. If you eat too much salt, it can cause lithium levels to fall. This is because your kidneys sense that there is too much salt in your blood and try to get rid of it. Your kidneys excrete more lithium along with the extra salt.

In contrast, the drugs listed in the middle of Table 24.13 have the opposite effect of causing lithium levels in the blood to fall. As a result, lithium can lose its effectiveness. You can see that several drugs used in the treatment of asthma reduce serum lithium levels. Caffeine also has the same effect, so if you are a heavy coffee drinker, you may need to cut down on coffee or take higher doses of lithium. Corticosteroids, which are used for many conditions, including poison ivy, can also cause lithium levels to fall. The dose of lithium may need to be increased to maintain blood levels in the proper range.

A number of other lithium drug interactions are also listed in Table 24.13. Psychiatrists used to think that the combination of lithium with certain antipsychotic medications (especially haloperidol) greatly increased the risk of a toxic effect called NMS (neuroleptic malignant syndrome). NMS consists of severe muscle rigidity and confusion along with elevated temperature, profuse sweating, increases in blood pressure, rapid heartbeat and breathing, trouble swallowing, abnormal kidney and liver function, and other symptoms. Although any patient on an antipsychotic drug runs a small risk of developing NMS, recent clinical experience has indicated that the likelihood of NMS may be increased only slightly when antipsychotics are combined with lithium. Lithium is now often used in combination with antipsychotic drugs and may enhance their effects, as described above.

As with most psychiatric drugs, pregnant women should avoid lithium, if possible, because its use has been associated with birth defects involving the heart. This is not an all-or-nothing issue, and the potential benefits must be weighed against the potential hazards. The risk of a heart defect known as Ebstein's anomaly is 20 times greater than normal in mothers who take lithium, but the likelihood is still less than 1 percent. Other birth defects can also occur, especially when lithium is used during the first trimester of pregnancy. In addition, lithium (as well as some other psychiatric drugs) is secreted in human milk and should be avoided by nursing mothers. If lithium is needed, breast-feeding should be avoided.

If you or your doctor have any questions about lithium (as well as the other mood stabilizers described below), the lithium information center at the Madison Institute of Medicine, Madison, Wisconsin, can often help.*

---

*The Madison Institute of Medicine, 7617 Mineral Point Road, Suite 300, Madison, WI, 53717; 608-827-2470 phone; 608-827-2479 fax; email: infoctrs@healthtechsys.com. They can do literature searches and supply pamphlets, reprints and other information for a modest fee.

VALPROIC ACID

Valproic acid is usually used in the treatment of epilepsy but was recently granted FDA approval for the treatment of bipolar disorder, especially acute mania. As shown in Table 24.1 on page 490, this drug is prescribed in one of two forms: valproic acid (Depakene) or the slightly more expensive divalproex sodium form (Depakote). Studies comparing valproic acid with lithium indicate that the two drugs are comparably effective. Valproic acid, like lithium, also appears to be effective in preventing or reducing future manic episodes. The drug may be especially effective in the treatment of the rapid-cycling form of bipolar disorder. It can help patients who experience mania and depression at the same time (so-called *mixed states*), as well as patients who experience the more common forms of bipolar disorder. It is probably less effective in the prevention and treatment of depression than in the prevention and treatment of mania.

Doses for Valproic Acid

Start valproic acid gradually in order to minimize the side effects. The dose on the first day might be 250 mg administered with a meal. During the first week the dosage can be gradually raised to 250 mg given three times a day. As with any medication, the dose you receive may be slightly different, depending on your size, gender, and clinical symptoms. For example, a man who weighs 160 pounds might be started on 500 mg twice a day.

During the second and third weeks the dose may be slowly increased further. Most patients end up with a total daily dose in the range of 1,200 to 1,500 mg, given in divided doses (for example, 400 mg three times per day). Individual doses can vary widely. Some patients respond to as little as 750 mg per day, and others need as much as 3,000 mg. As with any drug, doses outside the normal range are occasionally needed.

Some improvement should be observed within two weeks of attaining a therapeutic blood level. If you respond to valproic acid, your doctor may suggest that you remain on it for an extended period of time, just like lithium.

Blood Testing

Your doctor will order blood tests to adjust your dose of valproic acid. Initially your doctor may order a blood test once a week until your dose and blood level are stabilized. After that you will need a blood test only every month or two.

The blood should be drawn approximately 12 hours after your last dose, just like the lithium blood test. Most patients take valproic acid in divided doses twice a day. If so, the blood can be drawn in the morning before you take your first daily dose. Most physicians think that a blood level of 50 to 100 mcg per ml is therapeutic, but others are comfortable with blood levels up to 125 mcg per ml, especially if the patient is acutely manic. Of course, more side effects are observed at higher blood levels.

Prior to treatment, your doctor will probably order a blood test to check your liver enzymes, a bleeding test, and a complete blood count (which includes a platelet count). These additional blood tests are performed because in rare cases valproic acid can cause hepatitis (an inflammation of the liver) as well as bleeding problems. From time to time after you have been on valproic acid, your doctor will repeat these tests to make sure that no changes have occurred. Many physicians feel that it is necessary to check the blood count and liver enzymes only every six to twelve months, especially if the patient has been educated to immediately report any signs or symptoms that indicate a liver inflammation, as described below. You should also tell your doctor if you notice any excessive bleeding or easy bruising.

Temporary increases in liver enzymes have been reported in as many as 15 to 20 percent of patients during the first three months of treatment. In most cases these elevations are not considered serious. Nevertheless, if your liver enzymes do change, your doctor will probably reduce the dose of valproic acid and continue to monitor your liver enzymes. Your doctor will also want you to be educated about the symptoms of hepatitis so you can contact him or her immediately if they develop. Jaundice is the classic symptom. Jaundice is a condition in which your urine becomes dark and your skin and eyes become yellow in color. When the liver becomes inflamed, the pigment that normally causes your bowel movements to become brown gets backed up in your blood, staining your eyes, skin, and urine. In addition, your bowel movements become pale, because the dark pigment is not secreted into your intestinal tract the way it normally is. Other symptoms of hepatitis include fatigue, nausea, a loss of appetite, tiredness, and weakness. Fortunately, hepatitis only rarely complicates treatment with valproic acid and can usually be treated successfully, especially if you notify your physician right away.

Although the liver inflammation is nearly always mild, it is important to watch carefully for these symptoms because they could, in theory, progress to fatal liver failure. This complication has been observed in infants; fortunately, it is rarely seen in adults. It usually occurs in individuals taking other anticonvulsants at the same time. In fact, some experts assert that it has not been seen in adults who take only one anticonvulsant.

Side Effects of Valproic Acid

The side effects of valproic acid are listed in Table 24.12 on page 572. On the average, valproic acid is usually better tolerated by patients than lithium because it has fewer side effects.

Sleepiness is a common side effect. Taking more of your daily dose in the evening before you go to bed can often prevent the sleepiness from being problematic. Valproic acid can also cause stomach upset, which can take the form of nausea, vomiting, cramping, or diarrhea. These effects on the gastrointestinal tract are less common and can often be helped by taking a drug like Pepcid twice a day. Drs. J. H. Maxmen and N. G. Ward indicate that the frequency of stomach upset is greater with valproic acid (15 to 20 percent) than with the enteric-coated divalproex sodium (10 percent) tablets, and so a switch to divalproex sodium may help if these symptoms are troublesome.

Valproic acid can also cause tremor. As with lithium, this effect can sometimes be helped by reducing the dose or by adding one of the beta-blocking drugs (see the discussion of lithium tremor above). Other uncommon side effects include a loss of coordination and weight gain.

Valproic acid can cause a rash in 5 percent of patients, much like the two other mood stabilizers listed in Table 24.12. Some patients have also reported hair loss, and if this develops you should discontinue the drug (after discussing this with your doctor, of course) because it can take several months for the hair to grow back. The hair loss is thought to be due to the fact that valproic acid can interfere with the metabolism of zinc and selenium. Vitamins containing these two metals can be taken to try to prevent this. Dr. Alan Schatzberg and his colleagues recommend the vitamin supplement Centrum Silver for this purpose.

As many as one fifth of women have reported menstrual irregularities while on valproic acid. This may be due to the fact that it can cause blood levels of the relevant hormones to fall, resulting in impaired ovulation. Paradoxically, valproic acid can also cause certain oral contraceptives to fail, so in theory you could become pregnant. Make sure you discuss this possibility with your doctor if you are taking oral contraceptives.

Valproic acid, like a number of other anticonvulsants, may lead to birth defects and should usually not be taken during pregnancy. The deformities include a cleft lip, clotting abnormalities, spina bifida, and others. During the latter phases of pregnancy (the third trimester) valproic acid can cause liver toxicity for the developing baby, especially when blood levels are greater than 60 mcg per ml. Make sure you inform your doctor if you think there is any chance you could become pregnant while taking this drug.

Special precautions are indicated for women under 20 who receive long-term treatment with valproic acid. Some studies have suggested that they may be more likely to develop polycystic ovaries and increased levels of male sex hormones, but the actual incidence of this complication is not known.

Drug Interactions for Valproic Acid

Valproic acid does not seem to have as many drug interactions as lithium or carbamazepine. Because valproic acid can cause sleepiness, it can enhance the effects of other sedative drugs such as alcohol, major and minor tranquilizers, barbiturates, or sleeping pills. These combinations could be hazardous, especially when driving or operating dangerous machinery. In addition, valproic acid can cause substantial increases in blood levels of barbiturates, causing extreme sedation or intoxication. Valproic acid may also cause levels of diazepam (Valium) to rise. The depression of the central nervous system can be serious, and so great caution must be exercised if these drugs are combined with valproic acid.

As noted above, valproic acid can interfere with bleeding and clotting, and so caution needs to be exercised if it is combined with other drugs that interfere with bleeding or clotting, such as warfarin (Coumadin) or aspirin. In addition, valproic acid can lead to increased blood levels of warfarin. This can also increase the tendency to bleed.

Some caution should be exercised when valproic acid is combined with a tricyclic antidepressant (especially nortriptyline and amitriptyline) because the blood levels of the antidepressant may increase. Your doctor may want to order a blood test to check the level of the antidepressant so the dose can be adjusted if necessary.

Several types of drugs can cause levels of valproic acid to increase. These include:

- Antacids
- Non-steroidal anti-inflammatory drugs such as aspirin, ibuprofen (Advil, Motrin), and others

- Cimetidine (Tagamet)
- Erythromycin (Erythrocin)
- Felbamate (Felbatol), an anticonvulsant
- Lithium; valproic acid also causes lithium levels to rise, and so the toxic effects of both drugs can increase.
- Some antipsychotic drugs, especially phenothiazines such as chlorpromazine (Thorazine)
- SSRI antidepressants such as fluoxetine (Prozac) and fluvoxamine (Luvox)

If you are taking any of these drugs with valproic acid, your doctor may need to reduce your dose of valproic acid.

Some anticonvulsants, such as carbamazepine (Tegretol), ethosuximide (Zarontin), phenytoin (Dilantin), and possibly phenobarbital (Donnatal) can cause blood levels of valproic acid to fall, and so doses of valproic acid may need to be increased. At the same time, valproic acid can cause the levels of carbamazepine, phenytoin, phenobarbital, and primidone (Mysoline) to increase, and so the doses of these drugs may need to be reduced when they are combined with valproic acid. Patients with difficult cases of bipolar illness may be treated with more than one mood stabilizer, and some careful attention to these complex drug interactions is needed.

Finally, the antibiotic rifampin (Rifadin) can cause blood levels of valproic acid to fall. This antibiotic is used in the treatment of tuberculosis, and is also used as a two- to four-day preventative treatment for individuals who have been exposed to patients with certain types of meningitis.

CARBAMAZEPINE

Carbamazepine (Tegretol) was introduced in the 1960s as a treatment for a certain type of epilepsy that originates in the temporal lobes of the brain. In the 1970s Japanese investigators discovered that carbamazepine was helpful in treating manic-depressive patients who did not respond to lithium. Although the FDA has not yet officially approved carbamazepine for the treatment of mania and depression, it appears to be helpful for half of the bipolar (manic-depressive) patients who have failed to respond to lithium. Carbamazepine can be combined with lithium or with one of the major tranquilizers (also known as neuroleptics) in order to enhance the effects of these drugs in the treatment of mania.

Carbamazepine can also be helpful for some rapidly cycling manic-depressives. These individuals have more than four manic episodes per year and can sometimes be challenging to treat. Some studies have also suggested that carbamazepine may be helpful for manic-depressive patients who experience anger and paranoia during their "high" phases. Finally, some psychiatrists report that carbamazepine may be helpful in the treatment of patients with borderline personality disorder when severe anxiety, depression, and anger coexist with impulsive, self-destructive behavior such as wrist slashing. However, in one of these studies, the psychiatrists thought the carbamazepine was helpful, but the patients did not agree. This makes it hard to draw firm conclusions about the drug's effectiveness.

Nearly all the studies of carbamazepine have been conducted on patients who were also taking other drugs at the same time, such as lithium or a neuroleptic. These drugs can also have effects on mania. Dr. Alan Schatzberg (1997) and his colleagues have pointed out that this makes it difficult to evaluate the true effects of the carbamazepine. This is also why the FDA has been reluctant to approve of the drug as a primary treatment for mania—because the safety and effectiveness of the drug in the treatment of mania have not yet been demonstrated through large, well-controlled studies.

Doses for Carbamazepine

The beginning dose of carbamazepine is 200 mg twice daily for two days. It may then be raised to 200 mg three times a day for five days. After this the dose is gradually increased by 200 mg per day every five days up to a total daily maximum of 1,200 mg to 1,600 mg.

Carbamazepine usually takes at least one to two weeks to be effective, as do many psychiatric medications. If it is helpful, your doctor will probably suggest you stay on the drug for a longer period of time to prevent a relapse of the mania.

Blood Testing

Carbamazepine blood testing is required, just as it is for the mood stabilizers lithium and valproic acid. You will need a blood test every week for the first two months. After that you will need a blood test every one or two months. The results will guide your doctor in the amount she or he prescribes. The usual effective blood level for carbamazepine is in the range of 6 mg to 12 mcg per ml, but some experts recommend blood levels in the range of 6 mg to 8 mcg per ml for most patients with depression or mania. Like any drug, there are fewer side effects at lower doses, but if the blood level gets too low, the drug loses its effectiveness.

Levels of other drugs in your blood may fall if you are taking carbamazepine. This is because carbamazepine stimulates certain liver enzymes, so your liver clears these drugs out of your system faster than usual. One of the drugs that is affected by carbamazepine is carbamazepine! In other words, after you have been on the drug for several weeks, you may find that you need a larger dose to maintain the same blood level. This is because your liver begins to metabolize the carbamazepine more rapidly, so it leaves your body faster.

Your doctor will probably want to check the blood levels of certain liver enzymes before you start the carbamazepine, and from time to time when you are on it. This is because carbamazepine may cause an elevation of the level of liver enzymes in your blood, indicating possible liver inflammation or damage. Earlier you learned that valproic acid can have similar effects on the liver. Some elevation of liver enzymes occurs in most patients taking carbamazepine, but this is not usually a cause of concern. However, you will still want to watch out for any signs of hepatitis, described in the previous section on valproic acid (see page 580).

Your doctor will also order frequent complete blood counts while you are taking carbamazepine. This is because carbamazepine may cause a drop in your red blood cells, white blood cells, or platelets. These cells are all produced by your bone marrow, and carbamazepine can sometimes make the bone marrow less active. Each type of blood cell serves a different function. The white cells help to fight infections. If you did not have enough white cells, you would be more vulnerable to infections. As noted above, a normal white blood cell count is in the range of 6,000 to 10,000. If your white cell count falls below 3,000, your physician will immediately consult with a hematologist (blood specialist). Roughly 10 percent of patients taking carbamazepine experience a drop in the white blood cell count, and levels below 3,500 are common. You should be reassured to know that a drop in the white blood cell count rarely develops into a serious problem. If carbamazepine is helping you, most doctors will continue prescribing it as long as your white cell counts are above 1,000. However, white cell counts below this level can be extremely dangerous, so your physician will monitor your blood count more frequently if your white cell count starts to drop.

Levels of red blood cells and blood platelets may also fall if you are taking carbamazepine. The red blood cells carry oxygen, and the platelets cause bleeding to stop. If your red blood cells fell to very low levels, you would experience anemia. You might appear pale and feel fatigued. If your platelets fell to low levels, you might experience an increased tendency to bleed. Dr. Alan Schatzberg and colleagues (1997) state that some changes in the blood count are expected and emphasize that routine blood counts along with good patient education are the best ways to monitor them. If you are taking carbamazepine, make sure you let your doctor know immediately if you develop any symptoms suggesting a change in your white cells, platelets, or red blood cells. These include fever, sore throat or sores in your mouth (indicating possible infection), bruising or bleeding (indicating a possible drop in the platelets in your blood), or fatigue along with pale lips and fingernails (suggesting anemia).

On extremely rare occasions, carbamazepine can cause a dangerous and potentially fatal failure of the bone marrow. In these cases all your blood cells may drop to dangerously low levels. Recent estimates of these severe bone marrow failures range from approximately one patient in 10,000 to 125,000, so you can see that this complication is very rare.

When carbamazepine was first introduced, this possibility frightened many physicians who were understandably reluctant to use the drug. Neurologists have been by far the largest group of doctors prescribing carbamazepine because it can be so valuable in the treatment of epilepsy as well as trigeminal neuralgia (facial nerve pain). Neurologists have now had vast experience with this drug and are quite comfortable with its use. More psychiatrists are also starting to recognize that this medication can be used safely.

Side Effects of Carbamazepine

A number of common or significant side effects of carbamazepine are listed in Table 24.12 on page 572. Tiredness is the most common side effect, especially at the start of treatment. A third of patients experience tiredness, and some (5 percent) also complain of weakness. Raising the dose more slowly can minimize these effects. Usually the drowsiness wears off over time. The drowsiness is usually not due to anemia, but just to the sedative properties of the drug.

Approximately 10 percent of patients report dizziness, especially when standing. This is due to a temporary drop in blood pressure because blood tends to pool in your legs when you rise. This can usually be minimized by standing more slowly and exercising your legs (such as walking in place) immediately when you stand up.

Carbamazepine can sometimes cause problems with coordination. This has been reported in as many as a quarter of the patients. They may appear a bit intoxicated and tend to stagger when walking. This sometimes indicates that the dose is too high. Other symptoms of an excess dose include double vision, slurred speech, mental confusion, muscle twitches, tremor, restlessness, and nausea, along with slowed or irregular breathing, a rapid heartbeat, and changes in blood pressure. Immediate medical attention is required if these symptoms occur, because in extreme cases overdoses can lead to stupor, coma, and death.

You may also experience nausea and vomiting at first. These effects are usually temporary and can be managed by raising the dose more slowly and by taking the medication with food. They are less common than with valproic acid or lithium. After several weeks most patients who have taken carbamazepine do not report these effects.

Like the tricyclic antidepressants, carbamazepine can sometimes cause dry mouth or blurred vision. This is because the carbamazepine blocks the cholinergic receptors in the brain. These anticholinergic effects are of special concern to patients with glaucoma who have increased pressure in their eyes because the carbamazepine may cause the glaucoma to worsen. If you have glaucoma, you should have your intraocular pressures monitored closely while taking carbamazepine (or any drug with anticholinergic properties).

A side effect that involves the kidneys is called the syndrome of inappropriate secretion of antidiuretic hormone (SIADH), or water intoxication. Patients develop a great increase in thirst along with mental confusion and a fall in the levels of sodium in the blood. This side effect has been reported in as many as 5 percent of patients taking carbamazepine. If you develop excessive thirst, your doctor may order an electrolyte test to see if your sodium has dropped. He or she may want to reduce the dose, change to a different medication, or treat you with a drug called demeclocycline (Declomycin). This drug can often correct the problem of low sodium levels in your blood. Your doctor will probably monitor your kidney function from time to time by checking your levels of blood urea nitrogen (BUN) and creatinine.

Carbamazepine can have some adverse effects on the heart. If you are over 50 years of age, you should have an ECG before starting the drug. The test should be repeated after you have been stabilized on the drug to make sure no changes of a serious nature have occurred. Carbamazepine often causes a slowing of the heart. These changes appear to be more common in older women. If you have a history of heart disease, you may do better to take another mood-stabilizing drug with fewer effects on the heart, such as valproic acid.

As many as 5 to 10 percent of patients taking carbamazepine develop a rash. All of the mood stabilizers (as well as most antidepressants) can cause a rash, but this is somewhat more common with carbamazepine. It sometimes helps to avoid direct sunlight (which may provoke the rash in some cases), to take an antihistamine, or to change to a different brand of carbamazepine. This is because you may be allergic to an ingredient in the pill other than the carbamazepine itself. On extremely rare occasions, two very severe and potentially fatal skin rashes (called Lyell's syndrome and the Stevens-Johnson syndrome) have been reported in patients taking carbamazepine. Make sure you report any severe skin changes to your doctor immediately.

Like many other psychiatric drugs, carbamazepine can cause birth defects, especially spina bifida. A number of other fetal abnormalities have also been reported recently, especially when the drug is taken during the first trimester of pregnancy. Therefore, the potential benefit must clearly outweigh this risk if the drug is taken during pregnancy. The risk appears to be significantly higher when carbamazepine is combined with other anticonvulsants. If a pregnant woman definitely needs the drug, some experts recommend folic acid supplements to reduce the likelihood of birth defects.

Carbamazepine is secreted in mother's milk. The concentration of carbamazepine in the milk is approximately 60 percent of the concentration in the mother's blood, and so the issue of nursing must be discussed with the pediatrician.

Drug Interactions for Carbamazepine

As seen in Table 24.14 on page 590, many drugs can influence the blood level of carbamazepine, and vice versa, so you and your physician will have to be very careful in this regard. At the top of the table are listed those drugs that cause carbamazepine levels and toxicity to increase. If you are taking any of these, your doctor may need to reduce the dose of carbamazepine. For example, many of the macrolide antibiotics (erythromycin is a common example) can double the blood levels and toxicity of carbamazepine.

Some drugs, such as diuretics (water pills) and other anticonvulsant medications, can cause levels of carbamazepine to fall. Your physician may have to give you a larger dose of carbamazepine to compensate for this.

TABLE 24.14
CARBAMAZEPINE DRUG INTERACTIONS*

Note: This list is not exhaustive; new information about drug interactions comes out frequently. If you are taking carbamazepine and any other medication, ask your doctor and pharmacist if there are any drug interactions.

Drugs Which Can Cause Carbamazepine Levels or Toxic Effects to Increase

acetazolamide (Diamox)	antibiotics (other):	calcium channel blockers:	lithium

acetazolamide (Diamox)

antibiotics (macrolides):
azithromycin (Zithromax)
clarithromycin (Biaxin)
erythromycin (Pediazole)
troleandomycin (Tao)
other macrolides

antibiotics (other):
doxycycline (Vibramycin)
tetracycline (Achromycin)
ketoconazole (Nizoral)
isoniazid (INH)

anticonvulsants:
valproic acid (Depakene, Depakote)

antidepressants (SSRIs):
fluoxetine (Prozac)
fluvoxamine (Luvox)
sertraline (Zoloft)
others

antidepressants (other):
nefazodone (Serzone)
cimetidine (Tagamet)

calcium channel blockers:
diltiazem (Cardizem)
verapamil (Calan)
danazol (Danocrine)
dextroprophoxyphene (Darvon)

lipid-lowering drugs:
gemfibrozil (Lobid)
isonicotinic acid
niacinamide
nicotinamide

lithium
mexiletene (Mexitil)
prednisolone (Delta-Cortef)
propoxyphene (Darvon)
terfenadine (Seldane)
viloxazine

Drugs Which Can Cause Carbamazepine Levels to Decrease

anticonvulsants:
ethosuximide (Zarontin)
phenytoin (Dilantin)
primidone (Mysoline)

barbiturates:
phenobarbital
others

diuretics
fentanyl (Duragesic)
major tranquilizers (neuroleptics):
haloperidol (Haldol)
methadone

*Some information in this table was obtained from *Psychotropic Drugs Fast Facts* (Maxmen et al. [1995]), pp. 213–15. This book is an excellent source of information on psychiatric medications.

Blood Levels of the Following Drugs May Fall When Combined with Carbamazepine

acetaminophen (Tylenol)
antibiotics:
doxycycline (Vibramycin)
cyclosporine
(Sandimmune; Neoral)
anticonvulsants:
phenobarbital
primidone (Mysoline)
phenytoin (Dilantin)
valproic acid (Depakene,
Depakote)

antidepressants:
bupropion (Wellbutrin)
imipramine (Tofranil)
others
antipsychotics (neuroleptics):
haloperidol (Haldol)
others

benzodiazepines (minor
tranquilizers):
alprazolam (Xanax)
clonazepam (Klonopin)
others
corticosteroids:
dexamethasone (Decadron)
methylprednisolone
(Medrol)
prednisolone (Delta-
Cortef)

emergency intubation drugs:
pancuronium (Pavulon)
vecuronium (Norcuron)
fentanyl (Duragesic)
mebendazole (Vermox)
methadone (Dolphine)
oral contraceptives
theophylline (Theo-Dur)
thyroid hormones
warfarin (Coumadin)

Other Carbamazepine Drug Interactions

Drug	Effect
clozapine (Clozaril)	increased possibility of bone-marrow suppression
digitalis, digoxin (Lanoxin)	levels rise, may cause toxicity including slowing of the heart
MAOI antidepressants	serotonin syndrome (fever, seizures, coma)

Just as certain drugs can cause blood levels of carbamazepine to rise or fall, carbamazepine can change the levels of other drugs you are taking. Blood levels of the drugs listed next on the table may fall when combined with carbamazepine. This is because it stimulates the liver enzymes that metabolize these drugs. As a result, the liver gets rid of these drugs more rapidly than usual. This would be equivalent to pulling out the plug while you are trying to fill the bath; the water may not rise to the proper level.

One important example is birth control pills. The consequence of the decreased blood level is that the pills may become ineffective and you may become pregnant. Other drugs listed in the table that may fall when combined with carbamazepine include some antidepressants, antipsychotic drugs, anticonvulsants, antibiotics, thyroid hormones, and others.

Sometimes the drug interactions work in both directions. A drug may cause the blood level of carbamazepine to fall, and carbamazepine may in turn cause the blood level of the other drug to fall. For example, if you are taking an antipsychotic medication like haloperidol (Haldol), which is often also given for mania, the haloperidol may cause the level of carbamazepine to fall in your blood. At the same time the carbamazepine may cause your blood level of haloperidol to drop substantially. As a result, it may seem that neither drug is working properly, and the mania may not be controlled adequately. Your physician may need to do blood tests to determine the levels of both drugs so that the doses can be adjusted properly. Carbamazepine probably has similar effects on some other antipsychotic drugs as well.

Finally, several other potentially dangerous drug interactions with carbamazepine are listed at the bottom of the table. In particular, carbamazepine must not be combined with any of the MAOIs because of the risk of the potentially fatal serotonin syndrome.

Although Table 24.14 is lengthy, it is not comprehensive because new drugs and new information about drug interactions are constantly emerging. Only a small percentage of the potential drug interactions have been studied for any drug, and our knowledge about these interactions is rapidly expanding. Other drugs may have important interactions with carbamazepine, so make sure your physician knows of all the medications you are taking. Ask specifically if any of them interact with carbamazepine.

OTHER MOOD-STABILIZING AGENTS

Until recently lithium, valproic acid, and carbamazepine were the main drugs used for the treatment of bipolar illness. Recently, a host of new drugs has been synthesized which may soon be available to treat patients with this disorder. Many of these new drugs are actually anticonvulsants that were designed for the treatment of epilepsy. At least two of them are already being used in the treatment of bipolar, manic-depressive illness, and many others will undoubtedly become available in the next several years. It seems likely that at least some of them will provide powerful new tools for treating bipolar illness and possibly other psychiatric disorders as well.

These new drugs (as well as the three mood stabilizers discussed previously) are quite different from antidepressants because they do not significantly increase levels of serotonin, dopamine, and norepinephrine in the brain. Instead, they seem to stimulate a transmitter substance called GABA (gamma-aminobutyric acid) or inhibit a transmitter substance known as glutamate. GABA and glutamate are used by a large percentage of the nerves in the brain. The anticonvulsants that stimulate GABA tend to cause sleepiness. Medications in this category include valproic acid as well as gabapentin (Neurontin), tiagabine (Gabitril), vigabatrin (Sabril), and several others. The anticonvulsants that inhibit glutamate tend to cause stimulation and anxiety. Medications in this category include felbamate (Felbatol), lamotrigine (Lamictal), topiramate (Topamax), and several others.

Although it is not known for certain why or how these drugs prevent epilepsy or stabilize manic-depressive illness, it is known that the GABA system and the glutamate system in the brain tend to compete with one another. This may be why drugs that stimulate GABA or inhibit glutamate are helpful for epilepsy and for bipolar illness.

Most anticonvulsant drugs also inhibit sodium transport across nerve membranes in the brain. Sodium, as you know, is present in table salt. It is known as an ion, because it carries a positive electrical charge when it is dissolved in a fluid. The electrical impulses of nerves result when tiny ion channels in the nerve membranes open up and positively charged ions like sodium and potassium suddenly rush across the membrane. These ion fluxes create the electrical impulses in the nerves. Because these drugs inhibit the sodium channels, they may stabilize nerve conduction in the brain by making nerves less excitable. Because nearly all anticonvulsants have this property, they are sometimes classified as *sodium blockers.* The sodium-blocking effects may also explain why these new drugs can prevent seizures and stabilize manic-depressive illness.

Of course, all new drugs have unforeseen benefits and hazards, and the new anticonvulsant drugs are no exception. Quite a bit of testing will be necessary before we can identify which ones have most promise for patients with epilepsy and bipolar illness. There is considerable excitement about one of the new drugs, called gabapentin (Neurontin), because it seems to have very few side effects, an excellent safety record, and few if any toxic interactions with other drugs. In addition, it does not require blood testing like the three mood stabilizers discussed above.

So far the FDA has approved only gabapentin for the treatment of epilepsy. Although it has not yet been officially approved for psychiatric disorders, many psychiatrists are beginning to prescribe gabapentin for patients with difficult bipolar illness who have not responded to other medications. Its eventual role will have to be determined by clinical experience as well as controlled-outcome studies.

At least eight studies of the use of gabapentin in mood disorders were published in 1997, and many more will undoubtedly be published in subsequent years. In these studies gabapentin was reported to be effective for many patients with bipolar illness. Gabapentin also appeared to have antidepressant and anti-anxiety properties, and it may be useful in the treatment of chronic pain (including migraine headaches), as well as PMS (premenstrual syndrome), panic disorder, and social phobia as well.

Doses of Gabapentin

The current dose of gabapentin for epilepsy is 300 mg to 600 mg three times daily, for a total dose range of approximately 900 mg to 2,000 mg per day. In studies of bipolar patients, the average dose was about 1,700 mg per day, with some investigators giving doses as high as 3,600 mg per day.

The absorption of gabapentin from the stomach and intestinal tract is not affected by food. However, the antacid Maalox can reduce the absorption of gabapentin from the stomach by about 20 percent. Therefore, you should wait at least two hours after taking Maalox before you take gabapentin.

About half of a dose of gabapentin disappears from the body within 5 to 7 hours, so it must be taken several times per day rather than all at once. If you take a high dose of gabapentin on a single occasion, a smaller proportion of the dose will be absorbed from your stomach and intestinal tract into your blood. For example, only 75 percent of a single 400mg dose is absorbed, as compared with 100 percent of a 100mg dose. From a practical point of view, this should not be a concern since you would be taking the medication several times per day in divided doses.

There is no evidence that men and women require different doses because of differences in metabolism, but individuals over 70 years of age may need only about half the doses used for younger people. This is because of changes in kidney function that occur with aging. Because the kidneys excrete gabapentin, individuals with impaired kidney function will require smaller doses.

Unlike lithium, carbamazepine, and valproic acid, blood testing does not appear necessary with gabapentin. This is another advantage of this medication.

Side Effects of Gabapentin

The main side effects are listed in Table 24.15 on page 596. They include sleepiness, noted above, along with dizziness, tremor, problems with coordination, and weight gain, along with some visual side effects. All of these are more pronounced at higher doses. Overall, the side-effect profile of gabapentin is very favorable, especially when compared with the other currently available mood stabilizers.

In the studies cited in Table 24.15, gabapentin was given to patients with epilepsy who were already receiving one or more other anticonvulsants. Therefore, the side effects that were actually due to the gabapentin were lower. The best way to get a more realistic estimate of any side effect is to subtract the percentage seen in the placebo group from the percentage seen in the gabapentin group. For example, 11 percent of the gabapentin group experienced fatigue, whereas 5 percent of the placebo group did. The difference in these two numbers is 6 percent, so this is a better estimate of the true incidence of fatigue that can be attributed to gabapentin.

Like nearly all psychiatric drugs, pregnant women should use gabapentin with great caution. Although there are no well-controlled studies of the effects of gabapentin on the developing fetus in pregnant women, fetal abnormalities have been observed when gabapentin was administered to pregnant mice and rabbits. Although animal studies do not always predict human responses, gabapentin should be used in pregnancy only if the need is great. Although it is not yet known if gabapentin is secreted into human milk, many drugs are secreted into

TABLE 24.15
SIDE EFFECTS OF GABAPENTIN (NEURONTIN)

Note: This table was adapted from the 1998 *Physician's Desk Reference* (PDR). In these studies, gabapentin (543 patients) or a placebo (378 patients) was given to individuals with epilepsy who were already taking at least one other drug for epilepsy. The side effects in individuals not taking other drugs are likely to be less. Only the more common side effects are listed.

	Gabapentin (n=543)	Placebo (n=378)
	Digestive System	
weight gain	2.9%	1.6%
dry mouth	1.7	0.5
upset stomach	2.2	0.5
	Energy	
fatigue	11.0	5.0
sleepiness	19.3	8.7
	Nervous System	
dizziness	17.1	6.9
trouble with coordination	12.5	5.6
tremor	6.8	3.2
slurred speech	2.4	0.5
memory problems	2.2	0.0
	Eyes	
nystagmus (tremor of the eyes)	8.3	4.0
double vision	5.9	1.9
blurred vision	4.2	1.1

human milk; consequently, gabapentin should probably not be used by mothers who are nursing. Certainly, you should discuss this risk with your physician.

Drug Interactions for Gabapentin

Gabapentin has one unusual and desirable property. It is not metabolized by the liver, but is excreted unchanged by the kidneys directly into the urine. For this reason it does not seem to interact in adverse ways with other drugs. You will recall from previous discussions that all the antidepressants and mood stabilizers have fairly complicated interactions with lots of other drugs. This is because these drugs compete with each other for certain metabolic enzymes in the liver. With gabapentin this is not a problem, so it is much safer to combine it with other medications. In fact, many experts believe that gabapentin has no metabolic interactions at all with other drugs. One benefit is that gabapentin can be combined with other mood stabilizers for patients with difficult cases of bipolar illness or epilepsy who have not responded to other medications.

The properties of gabapentin are certainly very appealing. Is there a down side? Sometimes, problems with a new medication surface after it has been in widespread use for a period of time and the initial excitement has worn off. Gabapentin may be no exception. One concern, already voiced by some neurologists and psychiatrists, is that it may not be particularly effective for either epilepsy or bipolar illness. This would be disappointing, since the drug has so few side effects or interactions with other drugs. A colleague with considerable experience with gabapentin told me she is using it primarily to help anxious patients with insomnia, because it has excellent sedative and relaxing properties and is not habit forming. Unfortunately, she feels it may not be powerful enough to be a primary mood stabilizer for bipolar patients; its value may be in combination with other medications.

As for other new anticonvulsants, lamotrigine (Lamictal) has also been approved by the FDA for the treatment of epilepsy. Like gabapentin, lamotrigine has been used in the treatment of treatment-resistant bipolar illness. Dr. Alan F. Schatzberg and colleagues (1997) point out that very few formal studies of lamotrigine have been conducted in psychiatric patients, and so the reports of its effectiveness are still mainly anecdotal. In addition, lamotrigine has some significant and troubling side effects. In particular, rashes and skin reactions occur in as many as 5 percent or more of the adults taking lamotrigine. While most of these rashes are not dangerous, lamotrigine can cause a severe and life-threatening skin reaction known as the Stevens-Johnson syndrome in 1 to 2 percent of cases. These skin reactions are more common in pediatric patients than in adults, and so lamotrigine should not be given to individuals under 16 years of age. Taking lamotrigine at higher doses or in combination with other drugs, such as valproic acid, may make these feared skin reactions more likely. In pre-marketing trials, five patients taking lamotrigine died from liver failure or multi-organ failure.

Lamotrigine causes many other side effects such as headache and neck pain, nausea and vomiting, dizziness, loss of coordination, sleepiness, trouble sleeping, tremor, depression, anxiety, irritability, seizures, speech problems, memory difficulties, runny nose, rashes, itching, double vision, blurred vision, vaginal infections, and others. Lamotrigine also has a number of interactions with other drugs because it is metabolized by the liver. Because it has many side effects, including some dangerous ones, lamotrigine must be used with great caution. Until we learn more, it should probably be reserved for patients who have failed to respond to the better-established mood stabilizers discussed above.

What If My Antidepressant Does Not Work?

As I have emphasized, I would recommend taking mood tests like the Burns Depression Checklist and the Burns Anxiety Inventory in Chapter 2 so you can monitor your response to any treatment, including medications or psychotherapy. You can take these tests once a week, or even more frequently, and keep track of your scores. Your scores will show if, and to what extent, the treatment is working. The goal of treatment is to get these scores reduced substantially. Ultimately, you will want your scores to be in the range considered normal, and ideally in the range considered happy.

If a drug doesn't help, or only helps somewhat, what should you do?

1. Make sure you have given the drug a fair trial. Ask yourself:
   • Is the dose adequate?
   • Have you taken the drug for an adequate period of time?
2. Make sure there are no drug interactions that are preventing the antidepressant from being effective. Remember that other drugs can cause your blood level of an antidepressant to fall, even if you are

taking the correct dose of the antidepressant. Inform your doctor about any other drugs you are taking.

3. Your doctor may consider one of the augmentation strategies discussed below.

4. If these procedures are not successful, your doctor may discontinue the medication and try another type of antidepressant.

5. Psychotherapy along the lines described in this book, either alone or in combination with an antidepressant, can often be far more effective than treatment with drugs alone.

Let's examine each of these principles. First, you need to be certain the dose is sufficient. If for any reason your blood level of an antidepressant is too low, then the probability of a positive drug response will be diminished. However, a dose that is too high might also be less effective. This is because the side effects at excessively high doses may counteract the antidepressant effects. Concerns about the doses of antidepressant drugs are important because different people metabolize these drugs quite differently. In other words, given a particular drug at a particular dose, different people can have dramatically different levels of the drug in their blood. In fact, the levels of a tricyclic antidepressant may differ by as much as 30 times in two different people. This can happen even if the two people are the same sex, height, and weight.

These differences in blood levels can result from differences in the ways people absorb a drug from their gastrointestinal tracts and from differences in how fast people get rid of a drug from their blood. Genetics can play a role. For example, approximately 5 to 10 percent of the Caucasian population in western Europe and the United States lack the liver enzyme called CYP2D6 (in the P450 family), and 20 percent of the Asian population lack the enzyme called CYP2C19.* These two enzymes help to metabolize a wide variety of drugs including many antidepressants. Individuals who lack either of these enzymes may develop dramatically higher blood levels of certain antidepressants because their liver enzymes cannot get rid of these drugs nearly as rapidly as the average individual.

Medical conditions such as liver, kidney, or heart disease can have an impact on the blood level of antidepressants. Age can also be important. On average, children and elderly individuals require lower doses

*Preskorn, S. H. (1997). Clinically relevant pharmacology of selective serotonin reuptake inhibitors. *Clinical Pharmacokinetics, Suppl. 1:* 1-21.

of most medications including antidepressants. You may recall, for example, that individuals over 65 may develop blood levels of several SSRIs, citalopram (Celexa), fluoxetine (Prozac), and paroxetine (Paxil), that are approximately 100 percent greater than the blood levels of younger individuals taking identical doses. Sometimes gender can play a role as well. As noted previously, men may develop blood levels of fluoxetine (Prozac) or sertraline (Zoloft) that are 30 to 50 percent lower than women taking similar doses.

Weather, your personal habits, or other medications you are taking can sometimes influence blood levels of antidepressants or mood stabilizers. For example, if you sweat a great deal during the summer, your blood level of lithium may rise, so your doctor may need to reduce the dose. If you are a smoker, your body will break down tricyclic antidepressants more rapidly because of the effects of nicotine. Consequently, you may need a higher dose of these antidepressants. Many other drugs that can also cause a rapid breakdown of tricyclic antidepressants are listed in Table 24.5. In contrast, some drugs in this table can slow the metabolism of tricyclic antidepressant drugs by the liver, leading to excessively high blood levels of the antidepressants. Remember that these drug interactions can work both ways: an antidepressant may affect the level of activity of other drugs you are taking, and vice versa.

Before you and your doctor decide that a particular drug is not working, make sure that you review the dose with him or her. Ask about the possibility of drug interactions if you are taking more than one drug. Your doctor may want to order a blood test to ensure that the level in your blood is adequate. Blood-level testing is more commonly done for the mood stabilizers and for the tricyclic and tetracyclic drugs than for other types of antidepressants listed in Table 24.1.

If the blood level is adequate and you have been taking the medication for a sufficient period of time but your antidepressant is still not working, your doctor may try switching you to a different type of antidepressant or try an augmentation strategy. This involves adding a small dose of a different drug to try to boost the effect of the antidepressant. A complete discussion of all the drugs that are used for augmentation is beyond the scope of this book. I will describe a couple of them to give you a feel for this approach. Interested readers may want to consult the excellent reference by Schatzberg and his colleagues (1997).

Two drugs commonly used for antidepressant augmentation are

lithium, a drug you've learned about in this chapter, and a thyroid hormone called liothyronine (also known as Cytomel, or T3). Your doctor may add 600 mg to 1,200 mg per day of lithium carbonate or 25 to 50 micrograms per day of liothyronine to your antidepressant for several weeks if it has not been working adequately. As noted above, lithium is usually used to treat bipolar illness (manic-depressive illness), and liothyronine is used to treat people with underactive thyroid glands. However, in this case the goal is different—the purpose of adding a small dose of lithium or liothyronine is to make the antidepressant more effective. It is not clear why lithium and liothyronine sometimes have this effect.

A liothyronine trial usually lasts for one to four weeks. If you respond positively, your physician may continue the liothyronine for two more months. Then she or he will then probably taper you off the augmentation medication over one to two weeks.

The dose of lithium used for augmentation is adjusted with a blood test so that your blood level remains in the range of around 0.5 to 0.8 mEq per L. These levels are a little lower than the levels used to treat patients who are experiencing mania. The lower levels have the advantage of having fewer side effects. The lithium augmentation trial will generally last for two weeks. Positive results have been reported when lithium was combined with tricyclics, SSRIs, and MAOIs. Research studies suggest that as many as 50 to 70 percent of all patients who do not respond to an antidepressant may respond more favorably when lithium is added. If there is no improvement in your depression, your doctor will probably discontinue the lithium as well as the antidepressant and try another medication.

Some doctors use antidepressant combination therapy for patients with difficult depressions. For example, one new approach is to add an SSRI when a tricyclic does not work, or to add a tricyclic when an SSRI does not work. This combination can cause large increases in the blood level of the tricyclic medication, and so your doctor may decrease the tricyclic first and then check your tricyclic level with a blood test after you start the SSRI. Your doctor may also order an ECG to make sure there are no adverse effects on your heart.

An MAOI might also be combined with a tricyclic antidepressant as a combination antidepressant strategy. This is an advanced form of treatment for a specialist to administer, and requires careful teamwork between you and your doctor. You will recall that dangerous reactions can result from combining MAOIs with other antidepressant drugs or with lithium. Although the *Physician's Desk Reference* (52 ed., 1998) advises against such drug combinations, Schatzberg and colleagues (1997) report that the combination can be safe and helpful to some patients who fail to respond to single medications. To maximize safety, these investigators recommend: (1) the MAOI and tricyclic should be started at the same time; (2) clomipramine should be avoided; (3) the safest tricyclics to use in combination with MAOIs appear to be amitriptyline (Elavil) and trimipramine (Surmontil); (4) among the two commonly prescribed MAOIs, phenelzine (Nardil) appears to be safer than tranylcypromine (Parnate) to use in combination with a tricyclic.

My experience with these antidepressant combination and augmentation strategies is limited, but I have not been impressed with the results. I have tried lithium or thyroid augmentation with a number of patients, but none of them seemed to improve. I was not encouraged to continue with this approach. However, if a depressed patient has failed to respond to an adequate trial of several antidepressants, one at a time, from different chemical classes, then a combination of antidepressants or an augmentation strategy might be worth a try.

If you have received an adequate dose of an antidepressant for an appropriate period of time and you are not responding, what antidepressant should you try next? Many physicians will switch you to an antidepressant of a completely different class to maximize the chance of a positive response. This idea makes good sense, since the different antidepressants have slightly different effects on the brain. If you have failed to respond to an SSRI such as fluoxetine (Prozac), your doctor may want to try a tricyclic such as imipramine (Tofranil), for example. Prozac selectively activates the serotonin systems in the brain, whereas imipramine has effects on many different systems.

If you switch to another drug, you will usually need to taper off your current drug slowly so as to prevent any withdrawal effects. Antidepressants are not addictive, and they do not cause craving when you stop taking them. However, they need to be discontinued slowly to prevent uncomfortable withdrawal reactions. For example, the tricyclics can cause insomnia and upset stomach if you go off them abruptly.

There may be a mandatory waiting period when you are switching from one drug to another. This is because the two drugs might be dangerous if mixed together, and the effects of the first drug may persist for a while after you have stopped taking it. The most classic example would be switching from an SSRI, such as fluoxetine (Prozac), to an MAOI, such as tranylcypromine (Parnate). As noted above, the combination of these two drugs can cause the serotonin syndrome, which is occasionally fatal. In addition, both types of drugs clear out of the body slowly, and so a drug-free period is necessary before switching from one to the other. When switching from Prozac to Parnate, this waiting period may be five weeks or more. When switching from Parnate to Prozac, the waiting period will be at least two weeks. With some combinations of drugs, however, a waiting period is not necessary. Check with your doctor about this.

Suppose that all these strategies fail to bring about an optimal antidepressant response. What then? In my experience this is not unusual. I have seen lots of patients who were treated for years with all kinds of medications and yet they were still severely depressed. Early in my career, I realized that drugs did not provide the answer for many people. That is why I devote so much of my career to the development of new psychotherapeutic techniques, such as those described in this book. I wanted to have more tools available than just drugs.

In my experience, the idea that a pill alone will solve your problems and bring you joy is not productive. In contrast, the willingness to use these cognitive therapy tools, often in combination with a compassionate, persistent, and creative therapist will often lead to substantial improvement.

Other Drugs Your Doctor May Prescribe

The antidepressants I have described are the ones that in my opinion clearly help treat depression. I will describe several types of drugs that you might want to avoid, although there are exceptions to this rule.

MINOR TRANQUILIZERS (BENZODIAZEPINES)

Some doctors use minor tranquilizers or sedatives to treat nervousness and anxiety. The benzodiazepines include many familiar drugs such as alprazolam (Xanax), chlordiazepoxide (Librium), clonazepam (Klonopin), clorazepate (Tranxene), diazepam (Valium), lorazepam (Ativan), oxazepam (Serax), and prazepam (Centrax). Minor tranquilizers may be added to the mix of drugs your doctor prescribes if you are depressed. Because most depressed patients also experience anxiety, this practice is unfortunately quite common.

I usually do not recommend minor tranquilizers because they can be addictive, and the sedation they produce might make your depression worse. In my experience, anxiety can nearly always be treated successfully without using these drugs. Two highly esteemed colleagues from Canada, Dr. Henny A. Westra from the Queen Elizabeth II Health Sciences Center and Dr. Sherry H. Stewart from Dalhousie University, recently reviewed the world literature on the treatment of anxiety disorders with cognitive behavioral therapy versus medications. Based on their careful analysis of many clinical outcome studies, the authors recommended treatment of anxiety disorders with cognitive behavior therapy instead of medications.* The authors concluded that cognitive behavioral therapy without drugs is a highly effective and long-lasting treatment for anxiety. They emphasize that benzodiazapines may give some limited relief, but only for a short period of time, tend to lose their effectiveness over time, and are very difficult to discontinue.

Although the benzodiazepines such as Ativan, Librium, Ritrovil (available in Canada) Valium, and Xanax and others can have wonderfully calming effects almost immediately after you take them, the main problem is that these relaxing effects do not last. As soon as the drug leaves your body a few hours later, there is a high likelihood you will feel nervous again. In addition, if you take these drugs daily for more than a few weeks, you may experience withdrawal effects when you try to go off them. The most common withdrawal symptoms are anxiety, nervousness, and trouble sleeping. Ironically, these are the exact reasons you started taking the drug in the first place. These withdrawal symptoms trick you into thinking you still need the drug, and so you start taking it again. This is how the pattern of drug dependency develops. Fortunately, antidepressants are also effective in treating anxiety, as are cognitive and behavioral therapy techniques, and these treatments are not addictive. This is why I avoid the benzodiazepines in the treatment of depressed or anxious individuals.

There are other reasons to avoid minor tranquilizers in the treatment of anxiety. One of the cardinal principles of treatment is that anxious individuals must face their fears and surrender to their fears in order to

---

*Westra, H. A., & Stewart, S. H. (1998). Cognitive behavioral therapy and pharmacotherapy: Complementary or contradictory approaches to the treatment of anxiety? *Clinical Psychology Review*, 18 (3), 307-40.

overcome them. For example, if you have a fear of heights, you may have to climb to the top of a ladder and stand there until the anxiety goes away. I could give you dozens of examples of patients who have experienced dramatic improvement or even complete recovery when they faced their fears in this way. Anxious individuals who face their fears often feel tremendous relief because they discover the fears were not realistic in the first place. This realization may not occur if you are simply taking tranquilizers and not facing your fears. Even if you do manage to face your fears with the help of minor tranquilizers, medication can reduce the effectiveness of your efforts. In fact, when doctors prescribe tranquilizers for anxious patients, there is the danger that this will reinforce the idea that the fears really are dangerous and that the uncomfortable symptoms must be suppressed. These messages are the very antithesis of the newer exposure therapies that have shown so much promise in the treatment of anxiety.

If your doctor has been prescribing a benzodiazepine, or suggests this type of medication, you should discuss the pros and cons. Remember that you are the consumer, and your doctor is working for you. You have every right to discuss your treatment in a frank and respectful way. This sense of teamwork and collaboration is important.

Many prescription sleeping pills can also be addictive and are easily abused. They can lose their effectiveness after only a few days of regular use. Then greater and greater doses may be required to put you to sleep. This can lead to a pattern of drug tolerance and dependency. If you take them daily, these pills can disrupt your normal sleep pattern. Severe insomnia is a withdrawal symptom, and so every time you try to stop taking the pills you will falsely conclude that you need them even more. Thus, they might greatly worsen your sleeping difficulties.

In contrast, there are several sedative medications that enhance sleep without requiring increased doses. In my opinion, these drugs represent a superior approach to treating insomnia in depressed individuals. Three that are often prescribed for this purpose are 25 to 100 mg of trazodone (Desyrel) or doxepin (Sinequan) or 25 to 50 mg of diphenhydramine (Benadryl). The first two are antidepressants that require a prescription. Benadryl is an antiallergy medication that is now sold without a prescription. Make sure that you consult with your doctor before taking any medication, even one that is sold over-the-counter, to make sure there are no dangerous drug interactions with other medications you are taking. Remember that many over-the-counter drugs, like Benadryl, were once available only by prescription, so they can be just as dangerous as prescription drugs. The new anticonvulsant, gabapentin, also has sedative and anti-anxiety effects without being habit-forming, and some doctors are prescribing it for this purpose.

If you are having trouble sleeping, you may have personal problems that make it hard to get to sleep. It could be anything—a problem at school or work, or a conflict with a family member or friend. Some people sweep these problems under the carpet so they won't have to deal with them. Then they develop a variety of symptoms instead. Some people become anxious, others have trouble sleeping, and some develop aches and pains that have no organic causes.

It is better to try to identify and solve the problem rather than masking it with tranquilizers or sleeping pills. In our culture, the idea of a quick cure is tremendously appealing to patients and physicians alike. It is easy to prescribe a drug that will make the problem go away. This contributes greatly to the enormous popularity of sleeping pills and minor tranquilizers.

STIMULANTS

How about the "pep pills" (stimulants) such as methylphenidate (Ritalin) and the amphetamines that used to be so commonly prescribed for weight loss? It is true that these drugs can produce a temporary stimulation or elation (much like cocaine), but they can also be dangerously habit-forming. When you come down from the temporary high state, you may tend to crash and experience an even more profound sense of despair. When given chronically, these drugs can sometimes produce an aggressive, violent, paranoid reaction resembling schizophrenia.

I have not prescribed stimulants for depressed patients (or for any other problem) because of my concerns about these drugs, but this is clearly an area of controversy. Some psychiatrists do prescribe stimulants for elderly depressed patients under certain circumstances, and they are quite popular for treating hyperactive children and adolescents. If your doctor recommends taking such pills, you should certainly discuss the pros and cons. You might also want to obtain a second opinion if you feel uncomfortable about the treatment.

There are exceptions to this rule, like any. Because of its energizing properties, some doctors add methylphenidate (Ritalin) to a tricyclic antidepressant. This combination may be helpful for some patients who are very sluggish and unmotivated. However, methylphenidate also inhibits the breakdown of most tricyclic antidepressants by the liver, and so the blood level of these other antidepressants will increase. This may lead to greater side effects and may require a reduction in the dose of the antidepressant.

ANTIPSYCHOTIC MEDICATIONS (NEUROLEPTICS)

What about the antipsychotic medications (also called neuroleptics or major tranquilizers)? Some of the older drugs in this category include chlorpromazine (Thorazine), chlorprothixene (Taractan), haloperidol (Haldol), fluphenazine (Prolixin), loxapine (Loxitane), mesoridazine (Serentil), molindone (Moban), perphenazine (Trilafon), pimozide (Orap), thiothixene (Navane), thoridazine (Mellaril), and trifluoperazine (Stelazine). Some of the newer drugs include clozapine (Clozaril), olanzapine (Zyprexa), quetiapine (Seroquel), risperidone (Risperdal), sertindole (Serlect), and ziprasidone (trade name not yet available). These agents are usually reserved for patients with schizophrenia, mania, or other psychotic disorders. They do not play a major role in the treatment of most depressed or anxious patients. Pills that combined an antidepressant with an antipsychotic medication have been marketed and promoted in the past, but most clinical studies have not documented any superior efficacy in the treatment of depression.

Only a minority of depressed individuals benefit from antipsychotic agents. These include depressed patients who are delusional—that is, patients who draw false and highly unrealistic conclusions about external reality. For example, a depressed patient might have the delusion that there are worms in his or her body or that there is a conspiracy against him or her. Elderly depressed patients seem more likely to develop paranoid delusions. Depressed patients who are extremely agitated and cannot stop pacing sometimes benefit from the antipsychotic agents as well. However, the major tranquilizers may also cause a worsening of the depression because of their tendency to cause sleepiness and fatigue.

In addition, unlike most antidepressants, many of the antipsychotic medications carry the risk of an irreversible side effect called tardive dyskinesia. This is an abnormality of the face, lips and tongue; it involves repetitious, involuntary movements, such as smacking the lips over and over, or grimacing. The abnormal movements can also sometimes include the arms, legs, and torso. The major tranquilizers can also cause a number of other alarming but reversible side effects. Therefore, these drugs should only be used when they are clearly needed so that their potential benefit outweighs the potential risk.

Polypharmacy

Polypharmacy refers to the practice of prescribing more than one psychiatric drug at a time to a particular patient. The idea is that if one drug is good, two, three, or more will be even better. Doctors may combine antidepressant drugs with other types of antidepressants as well as with ·other types of drugs, such as minor and major tranquilizers. The patient ends up taking a cocktail of many different types of drugs.

Polypharmacy used to be frowned upon. Now the practice has become more accepted, and many psychiatrists routinely prescribe two or more drugs for many of their patients. In contrast, if a family physician is treating your depression, then she or he is much less likely to prescribe more than one psychiatric medication at a time. This is because a family doctor is usually more concerned with your medical problems and much less aggressive in the treatment of emotional problems.

In some instances polypharmacy can be helpful in the treatment of mood disorders. For example, I have described several augmentation strategies that might boost the effectiveness of an antidepressant. Also, the occasional use of a second medication can combat a drug side effect. Rational polypharmacy might also be helpful when a patient has separate disorders that both require treatment. For example, a patient with schizophrenia may also be depressed and benefit from a combination of an antipsychotic medication along with an antidepressant. A bipolar manic-depressive patient may receive an antidepressant in addition to lithium during an episode of depression. During an episode of mania, the doctor may prescribe a neuroleptic or a benzodiazepine in addition to lithium to combat the acute symptoms.

Despite these specific instances, I am usually not in favor of polypharmacy in the treatment of depression or anxiety because of the increase in side effects, drug interactions, and costs. In addition, polypharmacy tends to convey the message that all the patient's problems can be dealt with by drugs. The patient may take one or two drugs for depression, one or two additional drugs to treat the side effects of the antidepressants, one more drug to treat anxiety, and so on. And if the patient is angry, she or he may get yet another drug, such as a mood stabilizer, to treat the anger.

The patient may end up in a rather passive role as a kind of human test tube. You may think I am exaggerating, but I have seen numerous patients who were in just this position. They were taking lots of drugs with lots of side effects but were receiving very little benefit from any of them. I have treated many of these patients successfully with cognitive therapy and no drugs or cognitive therapy and only one antidepressant.

I believe that some psychiatrists rely too much on drugs. Why is this? One problem is that most psychiatric training programs strongly emphasize biological theories about depression and stress the importance of drug treatments for depression and other disorders. In addition, a great many of the continuing-education programs for psychiatrists in practice are sponsored by drug companies, and the focus of these conferences is nearly always on medications. The psychiatric journals, too, are filled with expensive drug company advertisements promoting the benefits of the latest medications for depression or anxiety—but I have never seen an ad promoting the latest psychotherapy technique. This is because there is simply no money to pay for such an ad! Drug companies also fund a great deal of the research on medications that appears in psychiatric journals, and concerns have been voiced about the potential conflict of interest inherent in such arrangements.

I do not mean to sound like a rabble-rouser! This is not a black-or-white issue. Clearly, the excellent research conducted by the pharmaceutical industry has been an enormous boon to the psychiatric profession and to individuals suffering from psychiatric disorders. My concern is that the emphasis on drugs sometimes seems excessive. Unfortunately, some psychiatrists do not have good training in the newer forms of psychotherapy, including cognitive behavioral therapy, which can be so helpful for individuals suffering from depression and anxiety. When a patient does not respond to medications, the main response of the psychiatrist may be to increase the dose or add another medication because this is what the psychiatrist has been trained to do. And when a patient complains of an adverse side effect, the psychiatrist may decide to add some other drug as an antidote—because that is what she or he has been trained to do. The result in some cases is that patients end up taking more and more drugs in larger and larger doses—without any real benefits. This is when polypharmacy can get out of hand.

When I was a psychiatric resident, I used to have the idea that if only I could find the right "magic bullet" (in other words, the right pill), I could help every patient. In those days we treated our patients with pill after pill after pill but very little psychotherapy. My clinical experience has taught me over and over again that this model is not sufficient— many patients simply did not recover, no matter how many drugs I used, singly or in combinations.

To make matters worse, most psychiatrists do not require patients to take mood tests, like the ones in Chapter 2, between therapy sessions to track progress. As a result, the psychiatrist may conclude that the patient is being "helped" by a drug when the patient has not really improved substantially. To my way of thinking, treating patients without session-by-session assessments is anti-scientific and represents a barrier not only to good treatment but to progress in the field.

Some psychiatrists and many patients are almost exclusively committed to these biological theories and treatments for depression. They may discount the value of other approaches, sometimes with a religious fervor. A number of well-known psychiatrists are quite outspoken in this regard. The intensity of these debates about psychotherapy versus drug therapy is sometimes more reminiscent of a power struggle for turf than an intellectual search for the truth. Fortunately, there is a growing and healthy trend showing that all of our current psychiatric drugs are limited in their effectiveness. In addition, there is an increasing recognition that a combination of medication with the newer forms of psychotherapy (including cognitive behavioral therapy and others) usually provides a more satisfactory outcome than does treatment with drugs alone.

Antidepressant drugs can help some individuals, but many patients do not respond adequately. When they don't, I would prefer to switch into a different gear and use cognitive therapy or a combination of cognitive therapy and one antidepressant medication at a time. Most depressed people have real problems in their lives, and at times nearly all of us need a compassionate, healing relationship with another human being to talk things out. The idea that drugs alone should work to cure depression and anxiety may be appealing, but this approach is often ineffective.

To be fair, an exclusive focus on psychotherapy alone can be just as biased. I have had patients who did not respond to many psychotherapeutic interventions—week after week their depression scores and anxiety scores on the tests in Chapter 2 did not change. Sometimes I prescribed an antidepressant while we continued working with a variety of psychotherapeutic strategies. Within several weeks the depression and anxiety often began to improve, and the psychotherapy suddenly began to work better. In these cases I was glad to have the medications available.

A final problem of polypharmacy is that many patients are unassertive. Even though they feel uncomfortable about all the drugs they are taking, they may sometimes assume that "the doctor knows best." This is understandable. The doctor does have a great deal of training, and the patient's knowledge is usually limited. In addition, the patient often admires the doctor and respects his or her advice. But in psychiatry and psychology, treatment approaches are far more subjective and varied than in internal medicine, where the treatments are more precise and uniform. Your feelings about the treatment are important, and you have every right to share these feelings with your doctor.

This review of drug-prescribing practices obviously represents my own approach. Your physician's ideas may differ. Psychiatry is still a blend of art and science. Perhaps someday the "art" will no longer be such a prominent ingredient. If you feel uncertain about your treatment, ask your physician questions. State your concerns and urge your doctor to explain the treatment in simple terms you understand. After all, it's your brain and body that are at risk, not the doctor's. The sense of teamwork and collaboration are important to successful treatment. As long as the two of you agree to a rational, understandable, and mutually acceptable strategy for your therapy, you will have an excellent chance of benefiting from your doctor's efforts to help you.

25

◆

The Complete Consumer's Guide to Anti-Anxiety Medications

In this chapter I describe a variety of medications that have been used in the treatment of anxiety disorders. These include the barbiturates, powerful sedative drugs that were the first developed 75 years ago, and meprobamate (Miltown), the first real "tranquilizer" that became enormously popular after its release in the mid-1950s. During the next decade, the benzodiazepines were marketed for the first time. This class includes medications such as diazepam (Valium), alprazolam (Xanax), and many others. The benzodiazepines quickly captured the lion's share of the anti-anxiety medication market because they were safer than barbiturates or meprobamate, and they are still in widespread use today. I also discuss several other types of drugs that are used for anxiety, including antihistamines such as Benadryl, buspirone (BuSpar), and two types of drugs used by cardiologists in the treatment of hypertension or other cardiac problems. These include the beta-blockers such as propranolol (Inderal) and the anti-hypertensive drug clonidine (Catapres).

However, the bottom line of the chapter is this: I do not usually use these medications in the treatment of anxiety disorders for a variety of reasons. First, most anxious patients can be treated successfully with the newer forms of cognitive behavioral therapy (CBT) described in this book. CBT can be administered without medications, or it can be combined with one of the antidepressants described in the last chapter. The antidepressants tend to be reasonably safe and effective, and they do not have some of the hazards associated with the drugs described in this chapter. For example, the barbiturates, meprobamate, and the benzodiazepines are wonderfully relaxing and they take effect almost immediately, but they can be quite addictive, especially if taken over a period of time. They tend to reduce the symptoms temporarily, but the underlying problem does not go away. Then when you try to go off these drugs, you may experience a withdrawal syndrome. The withdrawal symptoms include nervousness, worry, jitteriness, and insomnia, as well as other symptoms. These symptoms can be quite intense, and they are virtually identical to the symptoms of anxiety the patient was trying to treat in the first place. Many patients conclude that they still need to continue taking these drugs, and so the addiction intensifies. The other drugs in this chapter are not addictive, but they have other problems I will describe. These include a lack of effectiveness as well as other hazards.

Barbiturates

These drugs were introduced in the early 1920s and were first used in the treatment of insomnia and epilepsy. Thirty to forty years ago barbiturates were the only drugs available to sedate anxious and agitated patients. They include Amytal (amobarbital), Butisol (Butabarbital), Mebaral (mephobarbital), Nembutal (pentobarbital), phenobarbital, Seconal (secobarbital), and Tuinal (secobarbital and amobarbital). These drugs have calming properties, but they can be quite dangerous. High doses can produce intense sleepiness, anesthesia, coma, and even death. Barbiturates can be very intoxicating and are commonly sold in the streets by junkies, who call them "downers." They are very addictive. Except in rare or unusual situations, they are no longer used in the treatment of mood problems such as anxiety, panic, or depression.

Meprobamate (Miltown)

This drug was first marketed in the mid-1950s, when it received substantial media attention as the first true tranquilizer. It is about as effective as the newer tranquilizers like Valium, but it will produce sleepiness and a loss of coordination in high doses. Meprobamate can also cause addiction and physical dependence. Strong withdrawal effects, such as convulsions and delirium, can occur if you suddenly withdraw from doses of only 3,200 mg/day, or twice the recommended upper dose range.

Meprobamate is not in widespread use today, but it is occasionally prescribed for the rare anxious patient who becomes restless and agitated when taking the minor tranquilizers. Some practitioners prescribe meprobamate at bedtime in doses of 400 to 800 mg for patients with insomnia.

Minor Tranquilizers (Benzodiazepines)

When these drugs were introduced in the 1960s, they dramatically changed the treatment of anxiety. At one point the minor tranquilizers accounted for nearly 90 percent of the prescriptions written for anxiety. Psychiatrists wrote only 20 percent of these prescriptions. Internists, family practitioners, and obstetricians wrote the vast majority.

These remarkable statistics reflect the fact that most patients who suffer from anxiety and panic attacks do not know that their symptoms are the result of stress and conflicts in their lives. Indeed, many are overwhelmingly convinced that a medical problem is causing their symptoms. Although most physicians are aware that most of these patients have marital or personal problems that are causing the symptoms, the doctors may be pressed for time and lack the professional training to do any counseling. This may create an unfortunate tendency to rely excessively on prescription medications. In addition, both the doctor and the patient may see the need for psychotherapy as a somewhat stigmatizing and threatening sign that the patient is deeply disturbed. Even in this day and age, a referral to a psychiatrist or a psychologist may be seen as a last resort. As a result, the patient's personal problems frequently get overlooked entirely.

The real danger is that you might rely on tranquilizers as an escape from your problems or as a way of camouflaging your feelings. The tendency to avoid upsetting situations is almost universal, and tranquilizers can sometimes feed into this pattern. Instead of facing up to your fears and grappling with conflicts at work or with your spouse, you may simply increase the dose in the hope that you will feel better.

TABLE 25.1
NAMES AND DOSES OF ANTI-ANXIETY MEDICATIONS

Note: The dose ranges in this table are only estimates. Your physician may recommend higher or lower doses. The benzodiazepines can be addictive, especially when taken daily for several weeks or more. Higher doses create more intense physical dependence. The potency column compares the drugs to clonazepam, the most potent benzodiazepine. For example, 40 mg of chlordiazepoxide is equivalent to 1 mg of clonazepam. This means that chlordiazepoxide is one fortieth as potent as clonazepam. The more potent drugs may be more addictive.

Generic Name	Trade Name	Total daily dose range (mg/day)	Available sizes (mg)	Potency (clonazepam dose equivalents)
Benzodiazepines (Minor Tranquilizers)				
alprazolam	Xanax	1–6	0.25/0.5/1.0	½
chlordiazepoxide	Librium	15–75*	5/10/25	1/40
clonazepam	Klonopin	0.5–5.0	0.5/1.0/2.0	1
clorazepate	Tranxene	15–60	3.75/7.5/15	1/30
	Tranxene-SD	15–60	11.25/22.5	
diazepam	Valium	2–40	2/5/10	1/20
halazepam	Paxipam	40–160	20/40	1/80
lorazepam	Ativan	1–6	0.5/1/2	¼
oxazepam	Serax	30–120	10/15/30	1/60
prazepam	Centrax (discontinued)	20–60	5/10/20	1/60
Other Anti-Anxiety Drugs				
buspirone	BuSpar	10–60	5/10	NA†
meprobamate	Equanil	400–1,600	200/400	1/3,200
	Miltown	400–1,600	200/400/600	1/3,200
Antihistamines				
diphenhydramine	Benadryl	50–100	25/50	not known
hydroxyzine pamoate	Vistaril	200–400	25/50/100	1/400‡
hydroxyzine benzoate	Atarax	200–400	10/25/50/100	1/400
Beta-Blocking Agents				
atenolol	Tenormin	50–150	50/100	NA§
nadolol	Corgard	40–240	40/80/120/160	NA
propranolol	Inderal	30–240	10/20/40/60/80/90	NA
Alpha-Agonists				
clonidine	Catapres	0.2–0.6	0.1/0./0.3	NA

*Some experts recommend a maximum daily dose of 60 mg for anxiety. Doses for acute alcohol withdrawal are much higher: 50–200 mg per day, but these high doses are usually administered under close medical supervision in an emergency room.
†It is difficult to compare the potency of buspirone with the benzodiazepines. Buspirone does not have the rapid anti-anxiety effects of benzodiazepines but takes two to four weeks to work. Further, there is no clear-cut dose-response effect with buspirone. In other words, larger doses do not necessarily have greater effects.
‡The antihistamines are not true anti-anxiety agents, but a 400mg dose of hydroxyzine is about as sedative as a 1mg dose of clonazepam.
§Because the beta-blocking drugs and alpha agonists are not true anti-anxiety agents, their potencies cannot be compared with clonazepam. They actually block some of the physical symptoms of anxiety, such as tremor or a speeding heart.

The most widely prescribed minor tranquilizers are the benzodi-azepines. Their chemical and brand names and dose ranges are listed on page 615. They are used mainly for stress and anxiety, but they are also used for muscle tension (headache and back pain), insomnia, epilepsy, preoperative anesthesia, and alcohol withdrawal. One of the benzodi-azepines, alprazolam (Xanax), has been reported to have some antide-pressant properties and is often prescribed for patients who suffer from anxiety plus depression. Other benzodiazepines are also often pre-scribed for patients suffering from depression and anxiety.

Unfortunately, alprazolam is extremely addictive, and uncontrolled withdrawal can cause seizures and even death. The other benzodiazepines can also be quite addictive. Nevertheless, these drugs are not as danger-ous as the barbiturates. They are also less likely to be abused because they don't cause as much sleepiness and intoxication as the barbiturates.

Doses of the Benzodiazepines

The doses of the benzodiazepines are listed in Table 25.1 on page 615. Doses higher or lower than those listed in the table may be used. In general, I recommend the lowest possible dose for the shortest possible period of time to minimize the chance that physical dependence on these drugs will develop.

The benzodiazepines are most useful if you need temporary relief for se-vere anxiety or insomnia while you are making constructive changes in your life. Because of the addictive potential of all these drugs, some experts do not recommend using them beyond 1 to 2 weeks if the anxiety has come on rather recently because of a stressful situation, and I would certainly con-cur with this recommendation. When the anxiety symptoms have existed for six months or more, treatment may be extended for as long as 1 to 2 months. Keep in mind, however, that withdrawal effects may occur when treatment is extended beyond a few weeks. The *Physician's Desk Reference* emphasizes that minor tranquilizers have no proven effectiveness beyond four months' use, but many physicians believe this estimate is too liberal.

The minor tranquilizers can be used in one of two ways. First, you can take them occasionally as needed for anxiety or insomnia. For ex-ample, I have had a number of patients who took the smallest dose of a benzodiazepine, or even half a pill, when they felt stressed or had dif-ficulties getting to sleep. They took only one to three pills per week and did not abuse them. Second, you can take a minor tranquilizer reg-ularly, on a fixed schedule throughout the day for a maximum of one or two months. Then you can slowly taper off the drug entirely.

You should be aware that some psychiatrists prescribe large doses of tranquilizers for much longer periods of time for patients suffering from anxiety or panic attacks. For example, some psychiatrists have prescribed daily doses as high as 10 mg or more of Xanax for panic disorder, and these high dose levels are often maintained for a year or more. This is an enormous dose of alprazolam! I strongly prefer to keep the dose low and the duration brief, so that the chances of a serious addiction problem with dangerous withdrawal symptoms are minimized. I do not claim that the use of high doses is always wrong, but I do question this trend, especially when patients are not exposed to the new kinds of psychotherapy for anxiety disorders which can speed recovery and make the use of medications unnecessary.

Side Effects of the Benzodiazepines

Most of the minor tranquilizers have very few or no side effects aside from slight sleepiness, and this can usually be reduced or eliminated by lowering the dose. Excessively high doses can impair mental concentration and coordination and slow down your heart, especially when combined with other sedative agents such as alcohol. That's why high doses of tranquilizers can be quite dangerous when mixed with large amounts of alcohol. Side effects such as dizziness, weakness, decreased coordination, nausea, and forgetfulness have been reported, but small or moderate doses rarely cause significant side effects. Elderly patients who take these drugs have a greater risk of hip fractures due to falling.

A number of very fast-acting benzodiazepines that are not listed in the table are used as sleeping pills. These drugs are not essentially different from the drugs on the table except that they have a rapid onset of action, and so they can help you fall asleep at night. One of these fast-acting benzodiazepines, triazolam (Halcion), was the subject of a great deal of media attention for causing aggression and a loss of control. Although this topic is controversial, I have also seen uncharacteristic aggressive behavior in several patients taking alprazolam (Xanax). Although aggressive behavior is not a common side effect of the benzodiazepines, I believe it can occur, especially with those like alprazolam or triazolam that act more rapidly. In large doses some of the benzodiazepines may also cause amnesia for the events that occur after you take these drugs. Amnesia is not usually a problem, however, especially when the doses are modest.

Addiction

As noted above, the benzodiazepines can be extremely habit-forming. If you take high doses of any of them over a long period of time, your body may become dependent on the drug. Then when you try to get off the drug, you may experience withdrawal symptoms such as insomnia, anxiety, extreme restlessness, shakiness, clamminess, sweating, and racing of the heart, upset stomach, or diarrhea. You may also feel confused and overly sensitive to light and sound. These withdrawal symptoms may make you think that you still need the drug, and so you start taking it again. This is how you can so easily get hooked on these drugs. The sudden withdrawal from high doses of minor tranquilizers can lead to epileptic seizures and death.

The withdrawal symptoms usually begin somewhere between 1 to 7 days after you take the last dose of the medication. However, fast-acting drugs like alprazolam are an exception. Because alprazolam goes in and out of the blood very quickly, some patients experience a rush of relief when they take it, followed by an increase in anxiety several hours later when it starts to wear off. These anxious symptoms are actually a form of withdrawal.

Tapering very slowly from these drugs can minimize some of the withdrawal symptoms. Some experts recommend no more than 10 percent dose reduction per day, and many physicians would reduce these medications even more slowly than that. No matter how slowly you reduce the dose, you may have to put up with some symptoms of nervousness, jitteriness, and difficulties in sleeping during the withdrawal phase. Fortunately, these symptoms usually improve or disappear completely after you have been entirely drug-free for three weeks or more.

Some studies have indicated that group cognitive behavioral therapy during drug discontinuation greatly increases the likelihood of becoming drug-free. In addition, if you need to taper off alprazolam, your physician may switch you to a longer-acting drug like clonazepam first. Your total daily dose of clonazepam will be one half your total daily dose of alprazolam because clonazepam is twice as potent on a mg per day basis, as you can see in Table 25.1. It takes about one week to make the transition from alprazolam to clonazepam, and then the drug tapering can begin. Because clonazepam leaves the body far more slowly, the withdrawal symptoms tend to be a little smoother and gentler. However, many patients also find withdrawing from clonazepam very difficult.

Two of the drugs, alprazolam (Xanax) and lorazepam (Ativan), are more potent than most of the others and require lower doses. These two drugs appear to have particularly intense withdrawal symptoms and are especially likely to cause addiction if you take them in large doses for a prolonged period of time. There are reports that oxazepam (Serax), which is less potent and requires a higher dose, may produce fewer withdrawal symptoms, but this has not yet been clearly proven in controlled studies.

Individuals with a history of alcoholism or addiction to drugs are at increased risk of abusing benzodiazepines. Impulsive patients with personality disorders may also be at greater risk of becoming dependent on these drugs. The benzodiazepines should generally not be prescribed for these patients unless there is a strong reason to do so.

Drug Interactions*

A number of drugs can cause blood levels or effectiveness of the benzodiazepines to decrease. These include:

- Antacids—the rate of absorption from your stomach and intestinal tract may be decreased. Try to take the antacid and the benzodiazepine at least one hour apart.
- Barbiturates—they can cause the liver to metabolize the benzodiazepines more rapidly, and so the blood levels can fall. At the same time, the barbiturates and benzodiazepines increase each other's sedative effects.
- Asthma medications, such as aminophylline and theophylline, may antagonize the effects of benzodiazepines.
- Birth-control pills may cause blood levels of some benzodiazepines to increase and other benzodiazepines to fall. Check with your physician or pharmacist.
- Caffeine antagonizes the effects of the benzodiazepines because it makes you feel jittery.
- Carbamazepine (Tegretol) stimulates the metabolism of benzodiazepines by the liver, so blood levels of the benzodiazepines may fall by as much as 50 percent.
- Physostigmine (Antilirium) reverses the effects of benzodiazepines and is sometimes used to treat overdoses.
- Rifampin (Rifadin)—this antibiotic may reduce the effects of diazepam.
- Nicotine can cause the blood levels of benzodiazepines to fall.

A number of drugs can cause blood levels or effectiveness of some of the benzodiazepines to increase. These include several drugs that affect the heart or blood pressure, such as digitalis, amiodarone (Cordarone, a heart-rhythm drug) and several beta-blockers, including metoprolol

*The information about benzodiazepine drug interactions was drawn from several sources including Dr. J. S. Maxmen and N. G. Ward's excellent *Psychotropic Drugs: Fast Facts* (New York: W. W. Norton, 1995) as well as *The Pill Book* (New York: Bantam Books, 1998) and the *1998 Physician's Desk Reference* (PDR).

(Lopressor, a medication for high blood pressure) and propranolol (Inderal). Several anti-fungal medications such as fluconazole (Difulcan), ketoconazole (Nizoral), miconazole (Monistat), and several macrolide antibiotics, including clarithromycin (Biaxin), erythromycin (many brand names), troleandomycin (Tao), as well as isoniazid (INH, an anti-tuberculosis medication) can also cause the effectiveness or blood levels of benzodiazepines to increase.

Of course, any sedative drug can increase the sedative effects of benzodiazepines. The combination can lead to excessive sedation and even difficulties breathing in extreme cases. Sedative drugs include other benzodiazepines as well as alcohol or sleeping pills, barbiturates, major tranquilizers, painkillers, and antihistamine.

Many antidepressants also have sedative properties, and some antidepressants (e.g., SSRIs such as fluoxetine as well as some tricyclics) may cause an actual increase in the blood levels of benzodiazepines. The mood stabilizer valproic acid (Depakene, Depakote) can cause diazepam levels to increase.

Several other drugs may also intensify the blood levels or intoxicating effects of the benzodiazepines. These include cimetidine (Tagamet, for stomach acid), oral contraceptives (as noted above, they may cause increases or decreases in benzodiazepines), probenecid (Benemid, an anti-gout drug) and proxyphene (Darvon, a pain medication).

Finally, the benzodiazepines may have effects on a number of other drugs. These include:

- Alcohol or other sedative drugs—as described above, the sedative effects will be more potent and the combinations can be quite dangerous.
- Digoxin (Lanoxin, a heart medication)—blood levels and toxicity of digoxin may increase, particularly after alprazolam, clonazepam, and diazepam, so careful blood-level testing of the digoxin will be needed.
- Levodopa (L-dopa or Laradopa, used for Parkinson's disease)—the effects of levodopa may be decreased by some benzodiazepines.
- Phenytoin (Dilantin, an anticonvulsant)—the blood levels and toxicity of phenytoin may increase.
- Primidone (Mysoline, an anticonvulsant)—clorazepate may cause the levels of primidone to increase, and the combination may cause depression and aggressive behavior.
- Scopolamine (Transderm Scop)—intramuscular lorazepam may cause increased sleepiness, hallucinations, and irrational behavior.

- Tricyclic antidepressants—alprazolam may cause the levels to increase by 20 to 30 percent.

In summary, the benzodiazepines can have wonderful, fast-acting, calming effects with very few side effects. If it weren't for their considerable addiction potential, they would be ideal drugs. The following guidelines are helpful if you are taking a minor tranquilizer:

1. You should not stay on a minor tranquilizer for more than a week or two unless it proves to be tremendously helpful. Since there is a danger of addiction, the corresponding benefit must be great. If the drug isn't helping you a great deal, there's simply no reason to keep taking it, especially since other highly effective and less risky treatments exist.
2. Any adjustment in the dose—whether it's an increase or a decrease—must be gradual.
3. No matter how effective the drug is, you cannot stay on it indefinitely. The longer you stay on it, and the higher the dose, the more likely that you will become addicted. This can make the withdrawal extremely difficult. Therefore, limit the length of treatment to one to three months at most. Use this time to work hard on the problems in your life.
4. You must avoid alcohol and other sedative drugs. The effects of the combined sedatives may be excessively potent. This can lead to intoxication and depression of the central nervous system.
5. As noted above, I have occasionally observed an increase in aggressiveness in mild, unassertive patients who are taking minor tranquilizers such as alprazolam (Xanax). They suddenly become quite courageous and begin telling people off, including me! A little bit of increased assertiveness can be therapeutic, but too much can be a bad thing. Watch out for sudden hostile outbursts if you are taking any minor tranquilizer.
6. Do not drive or operate dangerous machinery until you find out how the drug affects you. The precaution applies to any medication that affects your mind.
7. Inform your physician if you are pregnant or planning to become pregnant. The use of tranquilizers during early pregnancy should always be avoided because of the risk of congenital malformations. Since these drugs can be present in human milk, you may have to stop nursing if a tranquilizer is prescribed.
8. Do not take more than your physician has prescribed. If you feel the

urge to take more and more pills to cope with personal problems, or to get high, inform your physician immediately. Some counseling could prevent the development of addiction.

9. There are many drug interactions, so make sure you tell your doctor or pharmacist if you are taking any other drugs.

This approach is conservative and sensible. Remember that most antidepressants can be extremely effective for patients with anxiety disorders and have none of the addiction problems associated with the minor tranquilizers.

CLONAZEPAM (KLONOPIN)

Clonazepam is a benzodiazepine worthy of special mention. It is listed in the *Physician's Desk Reference* as an anticonvulsant and has been used by neurologists in the treatment of epilepsy. Psychiatrists have used clonazepam in the treatment of anxiety disorders, including panic attacks. It also appears to have antimanic properties, and can be used along with lithium in the treatment of manic-depressive illness.

Clonazepam (Klonopin) is excreted very slowly; it takes thirty to fifty hours for half a dose to be eliminated from the body. For this reason the drug provides a very smooth effect throughout the day—in contrast to a drug like Xanax, which leaves the body quite rapidly. Since clonazepam can be given just once or twice a day, it is more convenient. Preliminary reports treating panic disorder with this drug were promising, and for a period of time there was a great deal of enthusiasm about clonazepam. Initially, psychiatrists believed it was less addictive than a short-acting drug like alprazolam (Xanax). Since the onset of action of clonazepam is more gradual than alprazolam, clonazepam is less likely to produce a high when you take a pill. Further, because it does not go out of the blood so rapidly, it is less likely to produce feelings of anxiety and craving several times a day when the blood level drops. For the same reason, psychiatrists believed that it would be easier to withdraw from clonazepam than from the short-acting drugs. Since it goes out of the body so slowly once you stop taking it, the withdrawal effects (such as anxiety and insomnia) were thought to be more tolerable.

Although these hopes for clonazepam were high, many clinicians are now less enthusiastic about this drug. The criticisms that minor tranquilizers only mask the symptoms in part seems valid, since the symptoms of anxiety usually return, often with great intensity, when patients stop taking the minor tranquilizers. In addition, clinicians with a great deal of experience with clonazepam have reported it can also be very difficult for patients to withdraw from. For these reasons most clinicians have now largely switched to antidepressants in the treatment of panic and other anxiety disorders. The SSRIs and the MAOIs have been used extensively and with good success. Although these antidepressants may take longer to work, they are non-addictive. My own clinical experience with them has been quite favorable.

Busiprone (BuSpar)

Buspirone (BuSpar) is an anti-anxiety drug that is chemically distinct from the benzodiazepines. Although it is not known how BuSpar works, it is known to stimulate a serotonin receptor in the brain known as the 5HT-1A receptor. The effects on this receptor may contribute to its anti-anxiety properties. Deficiencies in brain serotonin are also theorized to play a role in depression. You might therefore expect that BuSpar would have antidepressant effects, since it stimulates the serotonin system. In fact, it does have some modest antidepressant effects that are thought to be greater than a placebo.

BuSpar has some potential advantages over the minor tranquilizers:

- In moderate doses BuSpar does not cause significant sleepiness or impaired alertness or coordination.
- It does not cause addiction, because it does not make you euphoric.
- You can go off BuSpar, unlike the minor tranquilizers, without experiencing any withdrawal effects. (However, as a general rule, you must taper off all psychiatric drugs slowly, and this includes BuSpar.)
- It does not appear to be especially dangerous when mixed with alcohol or other sedative agents. In fact, it has been used with some success in the treatment of patients with anxiety and alcoholism.

Clinical experience with BuSpar indicates that it is a safe drug. Unfortunately, its effectiveness in clinical tests has been questioned. It is thought to be only somewhat effective for generalized anxiety and social phobia (shyness) and even less effective for other forms of anxiety such as panic attacks or obsessive compulsive disorder. Even those who advocate the use of BuSpar acknowledge it may take the edge off the anxiety but is not likely to eliminate the anxiety entirely. My own clinical experiences with this drug have been disappointing.

Many patients with anxiety have been treated with the minor tran-quilizers (benzodiazepines) described above. You will recall that when pa-tients take these drugs for more than a few weeks and then try to withdraw, there is an increase in anxiety for a period of time. BuSpar is not effective in treating the anxiety that results from benzodiazepine withdrawal. This may have contributed, perhaps unfairly, to the impres-sion that BuSpar is not a particularly effective drug. In addition, patients who are dependent on minor tranquilizers may feel the need for the high or the rush of relief they get when taking a drug like alprazolam (Xanax). They do not get this rush from BuSpar. Consequently, some anxious pa-tients complain they do not like BuSpar.

It is occasionally combined with an SSRI antidepressant such as flu-oxetine (Prozac). This is because fluoxetine can cause increases in anxi-ety during the first few weeks, and BuSpar can sometimes help reduce this anxiety. BuSpar has also been combined with SSRI antidepressants in an attempt to boost the effectiveness of the SSRI, and it may also help to combat the sexual side effects of the SSRIs.

Doses of BuSpar

The usual starting dose of BuSpar is 5 mg twice daily. This can be grad-ually increased by 5 mg per day every two to three days, as needed, up to a maximum dose of 60 mg per day. The optimal dose for most pa-tients appears to be between 20 and 30 mg per day in divided doses. Some experts recommend pushing the dose to the range of 30 mg to 60 mg per day. The drug should begin to work in one to two weeks and will become maximally effective in three to four weeks.

Side Effects of BuSpar

The most common side effects include dizziness, light-headedness, nausea, headache, nervousness, restlessness, and excitement. It has also been re-ported to cause dry mouth, vomiting, diarrhea, blurred vision, ringing in the ears, weakness, tiredness, trouble sleeping, weird dreams, and some other side effects as well. These are usually mild and are not a problem for the patient.

Drug Interactions for BuSpar

It is not known if BuSpar affects the metabolism of other drugs. You should inform your physician of any other prescription or nonprescrip-tion drugs you are taking, especially drugs that affect the brain. BuSpar can cause the levels of the antipsychotic agent haloperidol (Haldol) to increase. It may also increase the bleeding time in patients treated with warfarin (Coumadin). In one case the combination of BuSpar with trazodone (Desyrel) caused liver inflammation. BuSpar must not be combined with MAOI antidepressants because the combination may lead to dangerous blood-pressure elevations.

Other Precautions

Food delays the absorption of BuSpar in the stomach and intestinal tract, but increases the total amount of the pill that is absorbed into your bloodstream. Therefore you should be consistent in how you take this drug—either always with food or always on an empty stomach. Although you can drink alcohol when you are on BuSpar, you should do so only in moderation. Do not drive or operate dangerous machinery until you find out how the drug affects you.

Inform your physician if you are pregnant or planing to become pregnant or if you are breast-feeding an infant. Fetal abnormalities were not observed in pregnant rats or rabbits that received doses of BuSpar 30 times greater than human doses (when adjusted for weight). This is encouraging, but the results of animal studies do not always apply to humans, and there is very little data on the risk in pregnant women. Consequently, the drug should be used during pregnancy only if absolutely needed.

In conclusion, BuSpar is a very attractive medication for anxiety because it is safe and non-addictive and has rather mild side effects. Unfortunately, it may not be particularly effective for some patients. If BuSpar helps you, and the side effects are minimal, the fact that it will not cause addiction makes it an attractive alternative to the minor tranquilizers.

Beta-Blockers

Some people with anxiety, panic attacks, or phobias experience uncomfortable physical symptoms such as rapid heartbeat, tingling fingers, tremors, sweating, or rapid breathing. These symptoms are caused by stimulation of the autonomic nervous system, which controls the internal organs such as the heart, sweat and salivary glands, and digestive system. Drugs such as propranolol (Inderal), nadolol (Corgard), and atenolol (Tenormin) are called *beta-blockers* because they inhibit part of the automatic nervous system. These drugs are used primarily by cardiologists to slow the heart, to reduce high blood pressure, and to prevent angina (a type of chest pain associated with poor blood flow to the heart). Beta-blockers are also sometimes used in the treatment of migraine headaches.

These drugs can block some of the physical symptoms of anxiety, such as palpitations, sweating, and tremors. In fact, beta-blockers were banned in Olympic competition because of their effectiveness in reducing the hand tremors of target shooters. You will recall from our discussion of lithium that propranolol and other beta-blockers are sometimes used to treat the tremors that often develop in patients taking lithium. Although the Food and Drug Administration has not yet officially approved the beta-blocking agents for the treatment of anxiety in this country, propranolol has been used to treat anxiety in England since the mid-1960s.

Some American physicians also prescribe propranolol for anxious patients. Recent reports indicate that beta-blockers are most effective for anxiety disorders like stage fright or social phobia. For example, some physicians might prescribe a small dose of propranolol for someone to take before they have to give a speech in public. In this case it can be prescribed in a low dose prior to the anxiety-provoking situation. For this type of anxiety, the drug does not need to be taken continually. At least one expert has stated that evidence for effectiveness in these situations is quite weak and has suggested that these may simply be placebo effects.* Others have reported that beta blockers can be helpful for performers (e.g., musicians).

It seems likely the propranolol is more effective at blocking the physical symptoms of severe anxiety, such as the racing of the heart, the trembling of the fingers, the sweating, and so forth. It may not have any true anti-anxiety effects on the emotional or "psychic" symptoms of anxiety, such as feeling afraid, nervous, worried, or panicky. Therefore, if you are more of a worrier, and are not overwhelmed by physical symptoms, then this drug is not likely to be helpful to you.

In Chapter 2 the Burns Anxiety Inventory lists the physical symptoms of anxiety in questions 18 to 33. When you take the test, review your scores on these questions. These are the kinds of symptoms that may be helped, at least in part, by a beta-blocker.

Doses of Propranolol

The usual starting dose of propranolol is 10 mg twice daily. This can be gradually increased to 80 to 160 mg per day. Patients receiving propranolol for the treatment of high blood pressure may receive doses as high as 240 mg per day, but Schatzberg and colleagues emphasize that anxious patients rarely need this high a dose. Propranolol is usually

---

*Schatzberg, A. F., Cole, J. O., & DeBattista, C. (1997). *Manual of Clinical Psychopharmacology, Third Edition.* Washington, DC: American Psychiatric Press.

taken in divided doses throughout the day, and it is important to be consistent in taking the drug at the scheduled times.

Food increases the amount of propranolol that is absorbed from the stomach, so it is usually taken on an empty stomach. However, it is not wise to skip your dose, and so it is better to take it with food in case you forget and eat first. If you forget your dose entirely, do not double up and take twice the normal amount at the time for your next dose. Simply take the normal amount instead.

Blood tests are not necessary to monitor the beta-blockers, but your physician must take your blood pressure to determine your heart rate, and listen to your heart and lungs with a stethoscope before you start these drugs. Your doctor should check your heart and blood pressure periodically when you are taking the drug.

As with the minor tranquilizers, limiting the length of treatment to a relatively short period is probably best. If you are taking propranolol for anxiety or for lithium tremor, your doctor may keep you on the drug for a much longer time, and so far there have been no reports on major side effects or toxic reactions.

Although it is not addictive, you should taper off the drug very slowly over a period of approximately two weeks. Sudden withdrawal after you have been taking it regularly can lead to heart and breathing problems, with a rapid or irregular heart beat, increased blood pressure, chest pain, sweating, and breathing difficulties.

Side Effects of Propranolol

One of the most common side effects is impotence (difficulties with erections) in males. This side effect is fortunately reversible. The beta-blockers can also cause a drop in blood pressure along with dizziness, weakness, fatigue, mental confusion, and stomach upset in some patients. In addition, they can cause spasm of the airways and must not be given to patients with asthma or with Raynaud's disease, a disorder in which the toes and fingers get cold, pale, and painful. Finally, you might become depressed while taking beta-blockers. These depressive reactions may possibly be triggered by the feelings of fatigue.

Drug Interactions for Propranolol*

There are many drug interactions for propranolol and the other beta-blockers. Some drugs cause propranolol blood levels to increase, while

*The information about propranolol drug interactions was drawn from several sources including Dr. J. S. Maxmen and N. G. Ward's excellent *Psychotropic Drugs: Fast Facts* (New York: W. W. Norton, 1995) as well as *The Pill Book* (New York: Bantam Books, 1998) and the *1998 Physician's Desk Reference* (PDR).

others cause them to fall. Conversely, propranolol can cause the side effects or blood levels of other drugs to increase or decrease. Make sure you tell your physician and pharmacist about any other drugs you are taking. Ask if there are drug interactions that you should be aware of.

- Many drugs cause propranolol levels or effects to increase. These include acebutolol (Sectral, another beta-blocker), alcohol, amiodarone (Cordarone, a heart-rhythm drug), antipsychotic drugs (including chlorpromazine, cimetidine [Tagamet], thioridazine, thiothixene, and others), calcium channel-blocking agents, digitalis, disopyramide (Norpace, a heart-rhythm drug), flecainide (Tambocor, a heart-rhythm drug), hydroxyzine (Atarax, Vistaril, an antihistamine), isoproterenol (Isuprel, used to treat shock and asthma), furosemide (Lasix, a diuretic), oral contraceptives, phenytoin (Dilantin, an anticonvulsant), proxyphene (Darvon, a pain medication), and quinidine (a heart-rhythm drug).
- Many drugs can cause propranolol levels or effects to decrease. These include albuterol (Proventil, used for asthma), alcohol, antacids (aluminum and magnesium hydroxides), anticholinergic drugs (because they speed up the heart, they can prevent the heart-slowing effects of beta-blockers), antidiabetic agents, aspirin, and other anti-inflammatory drugs such as indomethacin (Indocin) and other NSAIDs, barbiturates, carbamazepine (Tegretol), MAOI antidepressants, rifampin (Rifadin, an antibiotic), smoking, and tricyclic antidepressants.

Propranolol and other beta-blockers affect many drugs. The blood levels, therapeutic effects, and side effects of the following drugs may increase or decrease:

- Acebutolol (Sectral, another beta-blocker)—both acebutolol and propranolol will have more powerful effects on the blood pressure (which will fall).
- Anesthetics—there are complex interactions with general and local anesthetics. Check with your physician. Beta-blockers may increase the effects and side effects of anesthetics. Heart problems during surgery may be more likely. Local anesthetics containing epinephrine should be avoided in patients taking propranolol.
- Asthma medications, including albuterol (Proventil), aminophylline (Mudrane), ephedrine (Valtornol), isoproterenol (Isuprel), theophylline (Bronkaid)—the effectiveness of these drugs may be impaired by beta-blockers such as propranolol. Propranolol may block the effects of these drugs, so that they will not do a good job relieving the spasm of the bronchioles in the lungs.

- Diabetes medications—propranolol may mask the signs of low blood sugar (such as dizziness, sweating, and rapid heart). In addition, it may interfere with the action of oral hypoglycemic medications.
- Antihistamines—the effects may be reduced by beta-blockers.
- Anti-hypertensive medications—the effects may be increased by beta-blockers.
- Anti-inflammatory medications—the effects may be reduced by beta-blockers.
- Anti-psychotic medications (including chlorpromazine, thioridazine, and thiothixene)—the blood levels and effects may be increased.
- Benzodiazepines (minor tranquilizers)—their effects may be more potent.
- Calcium channel blockers such as diltiazem (Cardizam), verapamil (Isoptin), and others that are used for hypertension)—the effects of these drugs may be increased, and they may also increase the effects of some beta-blockers. This may lead to complex interactions, including a slowing of the heart, increased blood pressure and impaired heart function. Check with your cardiologist.
- Clonidine (Catapres, used for hypertension)—when you go off clonidine, there may be a severe increase in blood pressure if you are taking propranolol.
- Cocaine—propranolol may cause an irregular heartbeat.
- Digitalis—the heart rate may be slowed substantially when combined with propranolol.
- Epinephrine (Primatene)—an increase in blood pressure along with a slowing of the heart.
- Glucagon—the effects on blood sugar may be reduced.
- Lidocaine (Xylocaine, a local anesthetic and heart-rhythm drug)—the blood levels and effects may be increased.
- MAOI antidepressants—should not be combined with propranolol.
- Marijuana—propranolol may block some of the effects.
- Methyldopa (Aldomet, an anti-hypertensive)—an increase in blood pressure may result when combined with propranolol.
- Phenylephrine (Neo-Synephrine)—hypertension may result. Even the phenylephrine in eye drops can be dangerous to patients on propranolol. One case of a fatal stroke has been reported in a patient using this combination.
- Prazosin (Minipress, an antihypertensive)—use cautiously because the initial effects on blood pressure may be more potent if you are taking propranolol.
- Quinidine—beta-blockers may cause an increase in blood levels,

leading to a drop in blood pressure, a slowing of the heart, and light-headedness.

- Reserpine (Serpasil, a blood-pressure medication)—increased effects, with sedation and a drop in blood pressure.
- Terbutaline (Brethine, an anti-asthma drug)—levels may increase or decrease; propranolol blocks the beneficial effects on the bronchioles in the lungs.
- Thyroid hormone replacements—may be blocked by propranolol.
- Tocainide (Tonocard, a heart-rhythm drug)—may lead to heart failure when combined with propranolol.
- Tricyclic antidepressants—the levels may fall and depression may increase.
- Tubocurarine (a muscle blocking agent used in surgery)—the effects may be prolonged by propranolol.
- Warfarin (Coumadin, a blood-thinning agent)—the blood levels and effects on bleeding may be increased by propranolol.

Other Precautions

Although beta-blockers do not cause intoxication or addiction, they can be hazardous if you have a cardiac problem because they cause a slowing down of the heart. For these reasons they should be used only under careful medical supervision. Propranolol and other beta-blocking agents should be avoided or used with caution if you have asthma because they may block the beneficial effects of asthma medications on the lungs, as noted above. They should be avoided or used with caution in patients with heart failure or abnormal heart rhythms. Finally, propranolol should be used in caution with patients with kidney or liver disease because the blood levels on a given dose may be much higher. This last precaution applies to all drugs.

An overdose of propranolol can be quite dangerous. Victims should always be taken to the emergency room along with the bottle containing the drugs.*

In summary, propranolol is a powerful drug usually used in the treatment of cardiac problems, and it should not be taken lightly. You can see that it has many effects on the body and a number of side effects, and lots of complex interactions with other drugs. In addition, its effects on anxiety are not powerful. Propranolol is not usually a drug of first choice for most anxious patients, especially when so many other effective approaches are available. As noted above, this includes the

*Silverman, H. M. (Editor-in-Chief). (1996). *The Pill Book*. New York: Bantam Books.

newer cognitive and behavioral psychotherapies as well as other medications such as the antidepressants.

Clonidine (Catapres)

Clonidine (Catapres) has been approved by the FDA for the treatment of high blood pressure, but some psychiatrists have used it to treat withdrawal from opiate and other forms of addiction and also for anxiety and panic disorder. Understanding how clonidine works helps put this drug in better perspective. Clonidine stimulates alpha-2 receptors on nerves throughout the body that use norepinephrine as their chemical transmitter. These nerves are called noradrenergic nerves. The result of the stimulation of the alpha-2 receptors by clonidine is that the rate of firing of the nonadrenergic nerves slows down and so less norepinephrine is released from them. Essentially, clonidine turns these nerves down by pressing the brakes, so to speak, so the nerves become less excitable.

During intense anxiety or drug withdrawal, the activation of these noradrenergic nerves accounts for many of the physiologic effects of anxiety, such as a racing heart, sweating, dilated pupils, or tremor. Because clonidine turns these nerves off, it tends to block these effects. Clonidine is probably better at blocking these physiologic effects of anxiety than the subjective, emotional feelings of fear, worry, nervousness, panic, and so forth. The same can probably be said of the beta-blockers discussed previously.

Clonidine was originally tested as a treatment for mania, since one theory holds that mania results from excess activity in the noradrenergic systems in the brain. Although some early reports using the drug in open trials were promising, it has not turned out to be a particularly useful drug for treating mania in double-blind controlled studies. In research studies it has also been tried for a variety of anxiety disorders associated with strong physiologic arousal. These include panic disorder, post-traumatic stress disorder, and phobias. Clonidine has also been tested in Tourette's disorder (tics which often consist of rapid, purposeless movements) in at least two studies.

The doses of clonidine are listed in Table 25.1 on page 615. Schatzberg and colleagues recommend starting at 0.1 mg twice daily and increasing by 0.1 mg every day or two to a total dose of 0.4 to 0.6 mg. These experts do not recommend indefinite treatment with clonidine because many patients develop drug tolerance—in other words, the same dose of clonidine no longer has the same beneficial effects.

The most common side effects are sleepiness and fatigue, which occur in up to one third or more of patients. Some experts recommend giving the medication in two divided doses in the morning and at bedtime, with two-thirds of the daily dose at bedtime so that the sleepiness and other side effects will not be a problem during the daytime. When you stop taking clonidine, you must do so slowly to prevent a sudden increase in blood pressure. Sudden withdrawal can also cause a racing heart, anxiety, headaches, and sweating, and can be life threatening.

Other common side effects of clonidine include dry mouth, stuffy nose, upset stomach and loss of appetite, constipation, weight gain, a loss of interest in sex, blurred vision, burning eyes, dry eyes, weakness, headaches, and others. Of course, because it is used to treat high blood pressure, it often causes a drop in blood pressure, so you may experience dizziness when you stand up. Clonidine can also cause abnormal heart rhythms, so your doctor may order an ECG before and after you start the drug to make sure there are no adverse effects.

If you take clonidine, you should be aware of a number of drug interactions. Any other medication you take for high blood pressure may have an additive effect with clonidine, so your blood pressure may drop too low. During the rebound phase, when you taper off the clonidine, the rebound increase in high blood pressure may be particularly severe, particularly if clonidine is combined with a beta-blocker. Combining clonidine with other drugs that affect the heart or blood pressure, such as verapamil (Isoptin), may cause abnormalities in the heart rhythm, including heart block.

Because clonidine is a sedative drug, it should not be combined with other sedative drugs because the combined depressive (sedative) effects may be too great. This includes alcohol, sleeping pills, major and minor tranquilizers, and so forth.

Tricyclic antidepressants should not be combined with clonidine because they may block its effects. This can have the same effect as abrupt withdrawal from clonidine, and may trigger a sudden and dangerous increase in blood pressure. A number of drugs may also block the effects of clonidine, so that your blood pressure may rise. These include stimulants like caffeine and cocaine, as well as the narcotic antagonist naloxone (Narcan). Beta-blockers can also sometimes have this effect.

In contrast, diuretics can cause an increase in the effects of clonidine, so your blood pressure may drop. Marijuana may have the same effect.

In studies of pregnant animals, even very small doses of clonidine damaged the developing fetuses. In addition, clonidine is secreted into mother's milk. Women who are nursing, pregnant, or thinking of becoming pregnant should avoid this drug unless there is some overwhelming reason to take it.

In summary, although clonidine has been tested in research studies for a variety of psychiatric disorders, it has not emerged as a drug of first choice for the treatment of anxiety. While it does reduce some of the physical symptoms of anxiety, its effects on the emotional symptoms of anxiety do not appear to be particularly strong. Keep in mind that clonidine is a potent sedative. It is quite possible that it has few if any true anti-anxiety effects besides its sedative properties and its effects on the physical symptoms. This may explain why tolerance to the anti-anxiety effects often develops after patients have been taking clonidine for a period of time.

Clonidine also has a number of uncomfortable side effects, interacts with several other drugs, and poses some considerable risks, particularly during withdrawal. For most patients, other types of safer and more effective medications, as well as the newer drug-free cognitive and behavioral psychotherapies for anxiety, probably represent more attractive treatment choices.

Antihistamines

Antihistamines, such as Vistaril and Benadryl, are ordinarily prescribed for the itching associated with skin allergies. They have mild sedative and anti-anxiety properties, but they are not widely used for anxiety because they are not especially potent. They cause dry mouth and may make other sedative drugs, such as alcohol, more potent. One significant advantage of antihistamines is that they are not habit-forming and there are no significant withdrawal symptoms. Thus they may be useful for people with mild anxiety. Some of my patients with insomnia have found that Benadryl is a mild and safe sleeping medication.

Major Tranquilizers (Also Called Neuroleptics or Anti-psychotic Agents)

The major use of anti-psychotic medications is the treatment of schizophrenia (which is characterized by delusions, hearing voices, or the belief that others are plotting against you) as well as mania (an uncontrollable "high" not caused by drugs and often requiring hospitalization). The drugs are also used in the treatment of psychosis associated with other mental disorders or medical conditions. These drugs are not particularly effective in the treatment of depression or anxiety disorders. They should usually not be used for these disorders because they have a number of uncomfortable and dangerous side effects that far outweigh any potential benefits.

Some of the older drugs in this class include acetophenazine (Tindal), chlorpromazine (Thorazine), chlorprothixene (Taractan), fluphenazine (Prolixin), haloperidol (Haldol), loxapine (Loxitane), mesoridazine (Serentil), molindone (Moban), perphenazine (Trilafon), pimozide (Orap), promazine (Sparine), thiothixene (Navane), thoridazine (Mellaril), and trifluoperazine (Stelazine). Some of the newer drugs include clozapine (Clozaril), olanzapine (Zyprexa), quetiapine (Seroquel), risperidone (Risperdal), sertindole (Serlect), and ziprasidone (trade name not yet available).

For Therapists (and Curious Patients) Only: How to Deal with Difficult Patients

26

•

The Ingredients of Therapeutic Success—and Failure!

Several years ago, I became curious about the reasons why some patients felt so much better at the end of therapy sessions. What was the key to the more successful sessions, in which there was an improvement in mood and self-esteem and a decrease in depression, anxiety, or anger? Dr. Jacqueline Persons—who was then a student and is now a colleague practicing in Oakland, California—and I designed an experiment to learn more about this. We hypothesized that patients would feel better at the end of a session if they felt cared about and understood by their therapist, and if there was an actual change in their negative thinking patterns during the session. These two dimensions reflect the degree of empathy and rapport (the "nonspecific" aspect of therapy) as well as the effectiveness of the cognitive interventions (the "specific" aspect). We also hypothesized that patients with certain diagnoses, such as "borderline personality disorder" (see page 472), would experience relatively less improvement in any particular session because of their chronic feelings of resentment and difficulties with trust.

We studied the degree of empathy, the percent of reduction in belief in Automatic Thoughts, and the degree of emotional improvement in a randomly selected group of patients at the beginning and end of their therapy sessions. As we had predicted, patients who felt cared about and understood by the therapist, and those who reported the greatest decreases in the amount they believed their negative, self-critical thoughts, reported the greatest improvement in feelings of depression, anxiety, guilt, and anger at the end of their sessions. Patients with personality disorders in addition to depression and anxiety reported significantly less improvement.

The magnitude of these effects was large. Together, these three factors—empathy, the percent of change in the degree of belief in negative thoughts, and the presence or absence of a personality disorder—accounted for 89 percent of the variance (or variability) in the degree of emotional change during sessions. This meant that we had almost entirely accounted for the reasons why patients felt better, worse, or unchanged during therapy sessions.*

This result was surprising. We sometimes think of human emotions and the therapeutic relationship as mysterious, sacred, unmeasurable, unknowable. It doesn't seem that what goes on during psychotherapy sessions could be precisely measured or that the results could be predicted in the way we can make accurate predictions in the "hard" sciences like biology or astronomy.

From a clinical perspective, the results were *not* so surprising. I had had a strong hunch that there were usually only two reasons why patients did not feel they were being helped: Either they didn't feel cared about and understood—indicating a lack of empathy and trust—or they weren't making any real headway in modifying the negative, self-critical thoughts that were making them feel so depressed. The research indicated that these two causes of therapeutic failure—a lack of empathy or a lack of successful technique—operated independently of each other. This means that some patients may feel you have lots of brilliant techniques to help them, but they may feel a lack of warmth and caring, which makes them annoyed and mistrustful. They may feel that you are talking *at* them rather than truly comprehending how awful they feel. Other patients may feel you're the most wonderfully sympathetic person in the world—there's really good chemistry between you—but they aren't helped much in their sessions because you aren't giving them the tools they need to modify their pessimistic thinking patterns.

*Therapists interested in learning more about this study can consult: J.B. Persons and D.D. Burns, "Mechanisms of Action of Cognitive Therapy: Relative Contributions of Technical and Interpersonal Interventions," *Cognitive Therapy and Research* 9, no. 5 (1985): 539–551.

Empathy. A failure of empathy can occur for one of two reasons. Patients may think you haven't really listened and heard how bad they feel, or they may feel angry because of something you did or said that rubbed them the wrong way. They may feel annoyed because:

- You were late for a session or answered the phone during a session.
- You charged for a missed visit.
- You made a comment that sounded sarcastic or hurtful.
- Your therapeutic strategy struck them as dishonest, phony, or superficial.
- You seemed rushed and uncaring.

Patients are often extremely inassertive and may not express these negative feelings. This will sabotage the therapy. These patients may need to make the therapy fail, as a way of thwarting you and letting you know indirectly how let down and hurt they feel.

Some patients may feel belittled because you are trying to problem-solve prematurely, at a time when they still need emotional support and caring. Since the newer therapies—such as cognitive and behavioral therapy—are rich in technology, the human dimension can get lost in the shuffle. Therapists may be too eager to swoop in and help patients turn things around. Patients may not be ready for this. They may need you to listen and to show concern. This is a potential problem at the beginning and throughout therapy.

There are two ways to tune in to the lack of empathy. At the beginning and end of every session, I try to ask each patient for positive and negative feedback. At the beginning I might say, "I'd like to hear your positive and negative feelings about the therapy so far. Let's start with the negatives first. Was there anything about our last session that turned you off? When you listened to the tape of the session, was there anything I said that was confusing or that rubbed you the wrong way?" After I hear what the patient has to say, I go on to ask, "I'd also like to hear if there was anything that was helpful to you." I ask similar questions at the end of each session.

If the patient appears tense but denies any negative feelings, I might say: "I have the feeling you might be a little uncomfortable, even though you say there were no problems during the session. Let me ask you this: If you *were* a little annoyed with me or dissatisfied with the therapy, would it be easy or difficult for you to tell me?" If the patient says "Difficult," then you can say, "I wonder, then, if you're having some difficulty right now. I know it can be hard to tell someone when you feel ticked off, but I believe that this can make our work much more rewarding and effective."

In addition, I ask the patients to fill out the Empathy Scale after each session and to give it to me at the beginning of the next session. I would urge you to copy this form, which appears on page 507, and to give copies to your patients. The first ten questions are similar to the Empathy Scale which Dr. Persons and I used in our research. Answers of 3 on questions 1, 3, 5, 7, and 9 as well as answers of 0 on questions 2, 4, 6, 8, and 10 indicate that the patient feels liked and understood by you. Other answers usually indicate negative feelings which need to be explored and expressed so the therapy doesn't get stuck. If you don't get all 0's and 3's on the report, I would explore the patient's feelings about you. If you get a 2 on questions 1, 3, 5, 7, or 9, you may think, "That's not so bad." However, you may be lulled into complacency if you think this way. Even slightly less than optimal responses can reveal strong negative feelings. This may be condemnation through faint praise!

I've noticed a strong reluctance among therapists to use this form with patients. It's as if we don't want to hear the bad news. If you don't believe me, ask yourself this question right now: "Do I plan to copy the Empathy Scale and hand it out to my patients starting this week?" I guarantee that the form will provide surprising, unexpected information that is vital to successful treatment, and that you cannot get this information in any other way. Furthermore, the form is quick and easy to fill out and interpret.

If you don't plan to use it, or if you feel ambivalent and uncommitted, ask yourself why. It may be that you are afraid of conflict and criticism. This is a very human reaction, and many therapists do feel this way. I know that there are times when I find it difficult to be criticized by an angry patient. It's particularly upsetting when I know that I haven't done as good a job as I'd like. Maybe I was annoyed and sounded cold or judgmental and made a sarcastic remark. It hurts to have this pointed out! You can get used to criticism by eliciting it over and over. The fear tends to diminish, in much the same way that an elevator phobia will diminish when you finally get on the elevator and stay on it for a while. Once you become comfortable with patients' negative reactions, the therapy will become more effective and more rewarding.

Some therapists think they are too sophisticated and sensitive to

EMPATHY SCALE*

Using the scale from 0 to 3 below, rate the EXTENT TO WHICH YOU FEEL EACH OF THESE STATEMENTS IS TRUE TODAY.

0—I do not feel this statement is valid
1—I feel this statement is somewhat valid
2—I feel this statement is moderately valid
3—I feel this statement is extremely valid

_____ 1. I feel that I can trust my therapist.

_____ 2. Sometimes my therapist does not seem to be completely genuine.

_____ 3. My therapist thinks I'm worthwhile.

_____ 4. My therapist pretends to like me more than he or she really does.

_____ 5. My therapist is friendly and warm toward me.

_____ 6. My therapist does not seem to care what happens to me.

_____ 7. My therapist usually understands what I say to him or her.

_____ 8. My therapist does not understand the way I feel inside.

_____ 9. My therapist is sympathetic and concerned about me.

_____ 10. My therapist sometimes acts condescending and talks down to me.

PATIENT'S REPORT OF THERAPY SESSION

Was there anything that was said during the session which irritated you, rubbed you the wrong way, or which you disagreed with? Describe any negative feelings you had during the session:

_____

_____

_____

_____

_____

_____

_____

Was there anything in today's session that was particularly helpful or useful? Was there anything you learned or would like to develop further? Outline any key points that were covered:

_____

_____

_____

_____

_____

_____

_____

need a tool like the Empathy Scale. They believe, wrongly, that they can sense intuitively when patients feel angry or uncared about. Nothing could be further from the truth. Studies have indicated that therapists' estimations of how empathetic and caring they are during therapy sessions are poorly correlated or completely uncorrelated with patients' ratings how empathetic and caring their therapists are.* This means that although you feel that you were being extremely supportive and that you listened with sensitivity and compassion during a particular session, there may be no greater than a random chance that the patient will feel cared about or will report that you listened and understood how he or she was feeling.

These surprising findings have intriguing theoretical and practical implications. First, they indicate that our patients' thoughts—rather than our actual behavior—dominate the way they feel about us. A depressed college student named Ted once asked if I cared about him. I told Ted that I did like him and respected him greatly. He began sobbing and appeared enraged. When I asked Ted what he was thinking, he said: "Even my shrink can't see what a fraud I am!" Even though I thought I had expressed genuine caring, Ted did not feel cared about. His self-esteem was so low, and his feelings of mistrust and resentment were so strong, that he did not accept what I said.

The practical implication is obvious—you have to *ask* patients repeatedly about their positive and negative feelings about you, and you have to look at ratings on the Empathy Scale. You will discover many negative reactions that you were not aware of, and you will have a chance to deal with them. But if you are a therapeutic ostrich and you keep your head buried in the sand, you won't know how the patient really feels about you. The therapy will get stuck and you will get frustrated because no matter how hard you try, the patient just won't seem to respond.

Good therapists dance back and forth constantly between technique and empathy, depending on the signals they receive from the patient on a moment-by-moment basis throughout the session. There are times when patients just want to ventilate. You may see a sudden change in the facial muscles as tears well up: the patient is looking for a signal—"Is it okay for me to cry?" If you are sensitive to this,

*For a review article, see: P. E. Orlinsky and U.I. Howard, "Process and Outcome in Psychotherapy," Chap. 8 in *Handbook of Psychotherapy and Behavior Change*, 3rd ed., S. L. Ossfield and A. E. Bergin, eds. (New York: Wiley, 1986).

you will encourage the patient to let the tears flow. You will listen and provide support.

Some patients are angry at the world. It makes no difference if their complaints appear to be irrational—they need to get these feelings out. They feel inadequate, panicky, desperate, hopeless, and bitter. They want you to see the world through their eyes without judging them or insisting that their feelings are illogical or distorted. This process creates bonding and feelings of trust that are crucial to the success of the therapeutic process. Once you can grasp the world through your patients' eyes and fully comprehend the traps that they feel caught in, your subsequent interventions will be more sensitive and successful. You can help them from *within*, rather than attacking their faulty cognitions from *without*.

Patients will often feel angry with you. Some of their reasons may be valid. You may have inadvertently made a mistake or said something that upset them. You may have made a comment that had a sharp edge because you felt frustrated. Some of the reasons for their anger may be distorted. Many patients have difficulty trusting and getting close to others, and these feelings may get projected onto you. A man may have the belief that he is unlovable and will inevitably be rejected. He may filter all your actions through this lens and constantly look for little signs of rejection and dislike. He may act hostile and provoke fights because he is so sure you will ultimately reject him.

To make matters worse, many patients fear conflict. They are unassertive and extremely reluctant to express these feelings openly and directly. Instead, they become evasive or argumentative. They may cancel sessions at the last minute, fall behind in paying their therapy bills, or "forget" to do their self-help assignments between sessions. They may complain that you aren't helping and insist that they are hopeless. All these can be signs that the patient is angry with you. If these feelings are aired and worked through, they won't sabotage the therapeutic process. Indeed, they can enhance the therapy greatly.

The matter is even more complicated because therapists, being human, are also imperfect. We bring our own vulnerabilities and shortcomings to the therapeutic process. There's a popular myth that people who pursue careers in psychology or psychiatry are neurotic and insecure and are looking for help. I think this is often true. Most of us have fears and wounds from the past which may make us vulnerable to criticism and personal conflict. I have seen these reactions in most of the therapists I have trained, and I have seen them in myself. We're all human, and therapy can be extraordinarily stressful at times. It's easy to get frustrated and anxious and to feel inadequate and threatened. We share many of the same inhibitions and irrational beliefs that plague our patients. We fear criticism. We fear anger. We feel ashamed of our shortcomings. Right? These emotional barriers can interact with a patient's fears and create a negative emotional climate that will interfere with the therapeutic relationship. Learning to deal with these difficulties can make the therapy far more effective.

Technique. Even when the feelings of rapport are adequate, therapy can fail when the technical aspect of treatment is insufficient. A patient could come to sessions for months and months, complaining about depression and anxiety. He or she could tell you how dissatisfying life is. You could listen and understand and express great caring and emotional support. The patient might like and respect you greatly. But if there are no specific, effective interventions to help the patient change these negative patterns of thinking and behaving, there will be no tangible improvement in his or her mood and outlook.

There are three reasons for a technical failure. First, you may not have negotiated meaningful goals for the therapy or developed a specific, workable agenda at the beginning of each therapy session. This is the commonest reason why therapy fails, and therapists are frequently unaware that this is the source of the difficulty. The patient may vaguely want to feel less depressed, without having defined any concrete problems—such as a troubled marriage or career—that he or she wants help with.

A second reason for a technical failure is that even when there is a specific problem, you and the patient may not yet have come up with the best strategy for resolving it. The patient may procrastinate at work or at school. You may try a few interventions and discover that none of them work. Then you may give up and conclude that the patient doesn't really want to change, so you succumb to a more passive role as a friend and listener.

Suppose your patient has a self-defeating belief such as "I deserve to suffer because of the abortion I had many years ago," or "I will never again feel truly happy or fulfilled because I was rejected by someone I loved," or "I must be perfect in everything I do," or "It is terribly dangerous to express my inner feelings to others," or "I'm basically inferior because other people are so much more intelligent and attractive and successful than I am." You may try one, two, three, four, or more cognitive techniques and discover that the patient is still trapped in the same belief system. Helping the patient modify dysfunctional attitudes and negative thinking patterns requires creative, persistent therapeutic effort. In Chapter 6 I described numerous cognitive techniques that can help patients modify negative thoughts and self-defeating attitudes. You may need to be relentless in trying a myriad of approaches until you finally discover the combination to the lock. If you give up prematurely, the door to the safe may never open.

Motivation. A third reason why therapy can fail is that patients may have mixed motives about getting better. Often what we see as a "problem"—such as the patient's obesity, depression, and excessive dependency on her parents—may actually be a "solution" to her fears of intimacy, sexuality, and growing up. Helping her to resolve these "problems" through dieting and other self-help exercises may be met with resistance if you have not conceptualized her deeper concerns and fears of change. You need to ask what her life would be like if she *did* get better. Is she prepared to deal with men's sexual advances? Does she really want to leave home and face the world alone? Her despair and overeating may be painful and humiliating, but these habits may also be old friends that are familiar and reliable. We do not readily say good-by to dear friends. The predictable pain of obesity, loneliness, and low self-esteem may in some ways be preferable to the terrifying fear of taking risks and moving forward with one's life.

In the following chapters I will describe techniques that my associates and I have developed for dealing with difficult patients. We are excited by the clinical and theoretical challenges these patients present. When therapy is stuck, the solution often involves substantial growth for the therapist and for the patient. I hope that you will share the excitement we feel and that your eyes will be opened to new ways of understanding and dealing with these challenges!

27

•

Empathy:
How to Establish Rapport with the
Critical, Angry Patient

Therapists at all levels of experience seem to have one overwhelming concern: How can I deal with difficult patients? The cognitive, behavioral, and interpersonal techniques illustrated in *The Feeling Good Handbook* work well for about two thirds of the patients that my colleagues and I see in our clinic. These patients describe their problems and share their feelings openly. The therapist listens and shows concern and proposes a variety of approaches that might help. The patient and therapist respect each other and work productively toward a solution.

For the other third of the patients, it's not nearly so easy. Therapy gets bogged down. These patients may complain that their therapists aren't helping or don't care or don't understand. They may feel hopeless, and they are often unclear about what they want from therapy. They frequently feel unmotivated and may appear to resist their therapist's efforts.

I suspect that you can think of many difficult patients you have treated through the years. You may have felt frustrated with these patients, disappointed in the results and insecure about your own level of skill.

These therapeutic impasses frequently result from a lack of therapeutic empathy. Although most therapists feel that they have good interpersonal skills and believe they communicate well, this is often not the case. Whenever I do workshops or teach groups of psychiatrists and psychologists, I ask therapists to demonstrate in a role-play how they would respond to an angry, evasive, critical patient. The therapists almost invariably get defensive. They appear stiff and formal. This is not something I have occasionally observed, but something I nearly *always* observe. It makes no difference if the therapist is a novice or a full professor with an international reputation as an expert in communication! When you see how therapists actually relate to difficult patients, the deficiencies sometimes become uncomfortably obvious.

I once did a full-day cognitive therapy workshop for a small group of highly experienced psychiatrists and psychologists in New York, along with one of my colleagues, Tony Bates. The participants all had illustrious careers in teaching, research, and clinical practice. At the beginning of the workshop, I decided to quickly review basic interpersonal skills before we moved on to specific cognitive and behavioral techniques. I asked if the participants felt comfortable dealing with critical, demanding, angry patients. They all indicated that this was familiar territory. Several of them had written and taught extensively on the subject. I told them I thought that one important principle was not to get defensive but to empathize and draw patients out so they would feel it was safe to express their angry feelings. The workshop participants unanimously agreed that this was crucial. I suggested that I could pretend to be a hostile patient and I would criticize each of them, one at a time. I told them that all they had to do was to use the three listening techniques described in Chapter 19:

1. **The disarming technique:** You find some truth in what the patient says, even if the criticism seems somewhat irrational. For example, if an angry patient says that you "don't understand," you could sincerely agree that you don't understand him or her as well as you would like and ask for more information in a friendly way.

2. **Thought and feeling empathy:** You show that you understand how the patient is thinking by paraphrasing what the patient tells you. You try to grasp how the patient is feeling, and you reflect this back. To continue with the previous example, you might say,

"Feeling understood by someone who cares is one of the most important things in the world. It sounds like I haven't really understood you very well yet. You might be feeling mistrustful and frustrated with me. Are you?"

3. **Inquiry:** You use gentle, probing questions to draw the patient out and validate your interpretation ("Are you?"). You can encourage the patient to share more of his or her angry feelings and you can indicate your willingness to listen and to try to comprehend. You want to convey an attitude of curiosity rather than defensiveness.

In addition, the three self-expression skills described in Chapters 19 and 21 can be useful:

1. **"I feel" statements:** Let the patient know how you feel about what he or she is saying. This will make you appear more genuine and real. For example, if the patient says he's ticked off because the therapy is a waste of time and money, you can let him know that you feel concerned. You might say that you also feel frustrated because the therapy seems to be at an impasse just now.

2. **Changing the focus:** Instead of focusing on the content of the patient's criticisms, you draw attention to the dysfunctional interpersonal process and share your feelings about this. For example, if a patient is excessively aggressive and hostile, you might say, "I'm feeling attacked right now. I sense that we're arguing instead of working together. Your criticisms and feelings are important, and I want to hear what you have to say, but I feel there's a lack of trust and teamwork between us. I wonder if you also feel this way. Do you?"

3. **Stroking:** You can remind the patient that you do respect him or her and that you feel optimistic that you can work together successfully, even though you may both be feeling some tension or annoyance with each other. This will let the patient know that it's okay to be angry with you and will relieve any fears of rejection, which could make the conflict escalate.

The participants all agreed that these techniques made good sense. They emphasized that this was precisely how they ordinarily responded to angry, critical patients. I asked them to demonstrate these listening and self-expression skills. I walked around from person to person, saying things like "Dr. Smith, I feel as if you don't care about me. All you seem to care about is getting paid."

I was amazed—as were the participants—that *not one* of the therapists was able to respond effectively. Every one of them got defensive! Dr. Smith got tense and said, "But I *do* care about you." This, of course, is argumentative; he contradicted me instead of drawing me out. At first I thought this was a fluke, so Tony Bates and I demonstrated the listening and self-expression skills. The participants continued to have rather serious difficulties. What would you have said if you were the therapist? Put your response here:

_____

_____

_____

_____

Here's one approach. You might say: "It sounds as if you feel that I don't care about you, and that I seem more interested in getting paid than in helping [thought empathy]. That must be really upsetting [feeling empathy]. I wonder if you might be annoyed with me [inquiry]. I know I'd be upset if I felt someone was exploiting me to make money [disarming]. Can you tell me more about this [inquiry]?"

The therapists agreed this was a more effective response, and they all wanted to try again. I continued playing the role of an angry patient and came up with more criticism and accusations. I said, "Dr. Jones, I don't feel as if I'm getting any help with my problems. All you do is nod your head and say 'Hmm' or 'Tell me more.' " The results were similar. Dr. Jones sounded stiff and defensive. He nodded and said, "Mmm . . . tell me more"! What would you say if you were the therapist? Put your ideas here:

_____

_____

_____

_____

You might say, "You don't feel you're getting any real help with your problems [thought empathy]. I think you're right—things do seem bogged down [disarming]. I'm frustrated, too ['I feel' statement]. It seems like we're arguing instead of working together [changing the focus]. Can you tell me a little more about the problems we're not solving [inquiry]? I'd also like to hear more about things I've said that have turned you off [inquiry]."

We ended up working for half the day on the basic listening and self-expression skills that we had planned to review in ten minutes! And even then, it seemed as if we were still just scratching the surface.

This group was not unique. Psychologists, psychiatrists, and therapists from a variety of persuasions have all had similar difficulties. Unless you are extraordinarily gifted, your communication skills could probably be improved as well.

You can enhance your skills with a method I have developed, called script writing. In the late 1970s it dawned on me that there were many moments in therapy sessions that I was not handling in a satisfactory manner. A patient would complain, and by the end of the session it was clear that the problem was still unresolved. Although I often felt I was handling the difficulties in a reasonable way, the patient still felt annoyed and we both left the session feeling dissatisfied.

On the train coming home from work, I would reconstruct from memory a brief excerpt of what had gone on. I wrote down what the patient said, what I said in response, what the patient said next, and what I said. This amount of dialogue—two consecutive statements by the patient and two of my responses—was sufficient to illustrate the conflict. The patient was generally frustrated and annoyed with the therapy. Although my statements initially seemed quite helpful and logical, I could readily see that I was not using good listening and self-expression skills. I often discovered that my statements were subtly sarcastic or defensive, or that I was "helping" when I should have been listening. I would revise the dialogue and try to write down more effective responses.

The next day, I would study the revised dialogues again. I often discovered that my revised responses were equally ineffective, so I revised them again. I would often consult with a colleague and ask, "How would you have handled this? What would you have said?" Eventually I would come up with an approach that I was more comfortable with. The next time I saw the patient, things usually went much better. I did this over a period of months, and the exercise proved to be extremely helpful. The listening skills and self-expression skills became more and more naturally my way of responding to these difficult moments in therapy.

If you use the script-writing method, I strongly encourage you to show your responses to a colleague. It's an inherent part of human nature to be blind to our own foibles. You may come up with a response to a patient's criticism that you think is just wonderful, and you may not tune in to the fact that it sounds phony or subtly controlling. You may be invalidating the patient's feelings. I cannot emphasize this enough.

Let's practice this technique now. Suppose a patient says, "I didn't like it when you answered the phone during the last session." What would you say?

_____

_____

_____

_____

_____

Some therapists might get defensive ("I don't usually take the phone, but my secretary buzzed me because it was an emergency"). Others would try to solve the problem by saying, "In the future, I can ask my secretary to hold the calls during your sessions." These responses have two serious flaws. First, the therapist may be feeling somewhat tense and is trying to disguise this by sounding "professional." This will irritate the patient. Second, the therapist hasn't drawn the patient out and given him or her the chance to express the negative feelings. The therapist indicates that the discussion has ended and there's nothing more that needs to be talked about. The therapist has suddenly cut off the communication and appears to be protecting him- or herself from the patient's anger. The patient may conclude that negative feelings are too upsetting to talk about.

You may think, "Oh, I wouldn't do that! Only a novice would do that!" But I know of very few therapists who don't unwittingly fall into this trap.

A more effective reply might be, "You may feel that I'm ignoring you and not putting a high priority on your problems [thought empathy]. I know if someone interrupted my sessions to answer the phone, I would feel a little ticked off [feeling empathy]. Do you [inquiry]?" This would encourage the patient to share his or her feelings and would acknowledge that you have feelings too. In the discussion that follows, you could ask the patient what he or she likes and dislikes about you. This may help the patient get over the hurdle of expressing anger to another human being. These feelings often provide a window to the patient's deeper fears and feelings of inadequacy.

Now I want you to try. First, think of a difficult, hostile patient who's dissatisfied with the therapy. Have you thought of someone? Good. Now write down an upsetting comment the patient made that you felt you didn't handle as well as you would like:

_____

_____

_____

_____

Now write down what you said next:_____

_____

_____

_____

Analyze your statement. Can you see why it was ineffective? Ask yourself if you were argumentative and contradicted what the patient said. Did you sound defensive? Sarcastic? Phony? Critical? Rejecting? Show your response to a colleague who will be honest and who's not afraid to criticize you. Ask him or her to point out why your statement was ineffective and to suggest an alternative one.

Finally, substitute a revised response. What could you have said instead? Try to utilize the listening and self-expression skills described earlier. Try to draw the patient out and to create a safe emotional environment so that he or she can express angry, desperate feelings without shame and without the fear of being judged or rejected by you. Try to see the world through the patient's eyes. You may need to express your feelings tactfully, genuinely, and openly. If you feel put down or inadequate or frustrated, say so, but do it in a friendly way. Your goal is not to elicit sympathy or to make the patient feel guilty, but to give vital information that will be helpful to him or her. You use your own reactions as a mirror, so the patient can see how he or she is affecting you.

Put your revised response here:_____

_____

_____

_____

_____

The other day I had a long session with a critical, intelligent woman named Ronda, who has felt depressed and bitter for many years. She was on the attack during most of the session. No matter what I said, it didn't seem to work. As the session wore on, I felt more and more drained and inadequate. I felt embarrassed and humiliated. I felt inept and lame. Just before she left, she indicated that the session had been a waste of time and money.

As the therapist, what would you have said?

_____

_____

_____

_____

I told Ronda that I felt inadequate. I said I felt as if every sentence that came out of my mouth was wooden and useless to her. I said that although I usually felt I had something to offer, it didn't seem that way today. I told her I felt excluded and shut out, and that I felt angry with her. I said I wanted to give her something positive and I believed that the therapy could be successful, but I felt thwarted in my efforts. I said that she also seemed angry and mistrustful and I wondered if she ever had a similar problem with other people, or if it just happened with me.

My motive was not to get back at her but simply to share my feelings. She left in a huff and didn't make another appointment. I was too embarrassed to ask if she wanted to schedule one. I wondered if I would ever see Ronda again.

The next day she called the office to set up a session. She asked the secretary to tell me that she'd made the decision to keep trying. The next time I saw her, she reported that her depression score had fallen by more than half (indicating a substantial improvement in her mood) when she was waiting to catch the train after the session. She gave me a note describing her reaction to what I thought was a terribly inept session. In the note, she said the session had been helpful because she was able to deal with her anger in an up-front way. Although we were fighting, she felt she was being direct and holding her own. She said that simply being angry and open with me was a relief, and that she had had a flash of insight when I said that I felt excluded and shut out. She said that she felt vulnerable and wounded and needed greater emotional support from me. She said that if I would explore the pain she felt in a gentle way, it would be easier for her to open up.

We often feel ashamed of these moments when therapy seems to fail, because we feel that we are supposed to be successful. But there's really no such thing as a "failure." Those moments of desperation and frustration are an inherent and necessary part of the creative therapeutic process. When you and your patient feel the angriest and the most defeated, you may be the closest you have ever been to each other and to the source of the difficulty. Often when you immerse yourself in the patient's desperation and allow yourself to experience the hopelessness the patient perceives, you are just a stone's throw from the solution. Sometimes you have to see and touch the wall of impossibility before you discover how to slip around it or climb over it or tunnel underneath it.

A second way to enhance your interpersonal skills is to role-play with a group of three or more therapists who want to learn together. You can make a list of barbed comments that you have heard from patients, such as:

"Of *course* I'm not angry with you!"

"Aren't you a little young, doctor?"

"I feel as if you don't care about me."

"The therapy seems a little superficial."

"I read in the paper that some people have chemical depressions. Maybe that's why I'm not getting better."

"You don't seem to understand what's really bothering me."

"You always seem to be in a rush."

"You seem to be siding with my spouse."

"You're one of the best 'mechanics' in the business."

I'm sure you can come up with lots more of these! One of you can play the role of the patient and one can play the role of the therapist. The others can watch. After a minute or so of role-playing, the "patient" can provide feedback about what he or she liked and disliked about the therapist's communication techniques and interpersonal style. Did the therapist express a concern for the patient? Did he or she encourage the patient to express the angry feelings? Did the therapist seem genuine? Was the therapist accurately tuned in to what the patient actually said and felt? Did the patient feel cared about? The therapists who observe the role-play can also provide constructive suggestions.

You will be shocked to find that you will usually get poor ratings from the "patient" and from your peers who are watching! If your ego can't take it, then this approach is definitely not for you! But if you dare to expose your shortcomings to the scrutiny of other therapists, then you will have the chance to enhance your therapeutic skills and to grow.

When I do this exercise with a group, I make it abundantly clear that we're working together in a spirit of mutual trust to reveal our insecurities and shortcomings to each other. The goal is to feel closer and more comfortable with our humanity and with our limitations. We are there to talk about our failures, not to show off. If you confront your fears of being judged, the process can be exhilarating, and your therapeutic skills will develop enormously!

•

28

Agenda Setting:
How to Make Therapy Productive
When You and Your Patient
Feel Stuck

At a workshop I conducted recently at the annual meeting of the American Psychiatric Association, one of the participants asked this question: "Dr. Burns, I have this patient named Susan. I've been working with Susan for eighteen months, but we don't seem to be getting anywhere. She's depressed and she has a terrible self-image. She has a real problem with her weight. Sometimes she binges and then she starves herself. Susan is very resistant and won't follow any of my suggestions. What can I do to help her?"

How would you answer this question? It's the most common question I hear from the therapists I train and from those who attend professional workshops. I won't ask you to write out your answer to this one, but I want you to stop and think about it for a moment before you read on.

Have you thought about how you'd answer the question? I asked the doctor what specific problem Susan asked for help with in their most recent therapy session. He replied, "I don't know. I don't think I've ever asked Susan that question."

This may explain why the therapy is bogged down. He may want to help Susan lose weight or develop better personal relationships, but she may not have the same agenda. She may feel bad because she's unpopular and can't get the boys at school to pay attention to her. She may be interested in learning how to flirt and getting the boys to chase her. She may feel angry and bossed around by her parents and want help in dealing with them. She may feel she's fine and is in therapy only because her parents are pressuring her to be there. If you and your patient are on different wavelengths and are not working on a common problem, the therapy has little chance of success.

This is an incredibly common therapeutic pitfall. The patient complains that you aren't helping, but it may not be clear to you, or to the patient, what problem you're supposed to solve. How can you possibly help someone if the two of you haven't agreed on whether the patient really wants help and, if so, what he or she wants help with? As basic as this might seem, these issues are frequently overlooked.

At the beginning of each therapy session, I encourage patients to set an agenda for the session. I ask what problems they want to work on that day. Usually this is straightforward. Patients may want to review the Daily Mood Logs they have been working on between sessions, or they may want suggestions about how to deal with specific problems in their lives. Sometimes it is not so easy. Patients may be evasive or vague about what they want help with. If you let this go unnoticed and unchallenged, the therapy is almost certainly doomed to failure.

This difficulty can be overcome with a technique called "agenda setting." Agenda setting has two components. First, you and the patient need to agree on the specific problem he or she wants help with in each session. Second, you need to agree on the methods you will use to solve the problem.

The problem must be specific and concrete, or it cannot be dealt with. For example, a woman may want help with her depression. She says her goal in therapy is to feel better about herself. This sounds specific, but it really isn't. I would ask her to tell me about the problems in her life that she feels bad about. Is she worrying about her marriage? School? Her career? Let's suppose she has a career problem. I would want to know more about it. What is the problem? Is her boss too critical? Does she procrastinate? Does she get panic attacks at work? I would want to know:

- What day did the problem occur? What time of day was it?
- Where did the problem occur? Whom was she with? What was going on?
- What her life would be like if the problem was solved—what would be different?

Once you have defined the problem, you need to agree on the methods you will use to attack it. What are you expected to do? To listen? To teach communication skills? To help her identify and to talk back to her negative thoughts? Does she want you to prescribe a medication? All these issues need to be spelled out and negotiated. After all, therapists aren't magicians, and we don't just say "presto" to make problems disappear. We have certain skills to offer. Patients have the right to know what these skills are and to decide if they want to make use of them.

As a part of this negotiation, it's important to agree on what the patient is expected to do during the sessions and between sessions. You might expect her to keep a daily journal of her negative thoughts between sessions, to fill out the depression and anxiety tests weekly and to show the results to you, and to bring a cassette tape so that each session can be recorded and she can listen to the tapes between sessions. Your list of requirements may differ, depending on your therapeutic orientation and the type of problem the patient wants help with.

Some patients are vague and not used to defining problems in a precise way. I recently saw a 22-year-old woman from New York. Sue is single, very attractive, slim, and intelligent. She's lonely and says her life is dull. Sue was referred by her mother, who'd read *Feeling Good*. She felt that Sue was unhappy and would benefit from cognitive therapy. That, of course, was one strike against me: Sue didn't come because she had made the decision herself and felt strongly motivated to change. Therefore her basic mind-set seemed to be: "I'm not really sure I want to be here. You've got to prove that you can help me."

During the sessions Sue was quiet and asked appropriate questions, but she rarely talked about herself. I found that I was easily seduced into talking a great deal and answering all her questions. She appeared interested but played the devil's advocate. She asked questions like "What makes you think cognitive therapy can help me?" If you were the therapist, how would you answer this question?

_____

_____

_____

_____

I might say, "I'm not sure the therapy can help you. I'm hopeful we can work together, but I need to find out specifically what you want help with first. Then we can discuss a variety of approaches that might appeal to you." The purpose of this response is to avoid getting into a salesman's role. If you try to persuade her that you can help her, you will almost surely fail. For one thing, you don't know yet if you can help her because you don't have the vaguest notion of what, if anything, she wants help with!

I encouraged Sue to describe a specific problem. Eventually she came up with several:

1. Fears about the future.

2. Obsessing too much about things.

3. Not having any fun in life.

As the therapist, what would you say next? Put your ideas here:

_____

_____

_____

_____

I asked Sue to choose one problem to work on first. I was unwilling to make that choice myself, because that would be my agenda rather than hers. She reluctantly chose "Not having any fun in life." She didn't seem especially happy with her decision. What

would you do next? Check the strategy that makes the most sense
to you:

_____   Explore her reluctance.

_____   Suggest ways she might have more fun in life.

_____   Explore conflicts that might make it hard for her to have fun.

_____   Ask her to tell you more about the problem—for example,
           what kinds of fun is she missing out on?

_____   Ask how she thinks you might help her.

_____   Other:

_____

_____

_____

_____

I believe that each approach has merit, but I explored her reluctance first. Why is she reluctant? If we don't talk about her negative
feelings, she may dig in her heels and resist me. That's precisely what
I'm trying to avoid.

Sue said she was reluctant because she didn't want to work on
trivial, day-to-day problems but wanted to get to the "deeper issues
at the heart of the matter." She said she wanted to know why she was
"like this." However, she had no idea what these "deeper issues"
might be and she left that up to me. What would you say next?

_____

_____

_____

_____

There could be many effective responses. You could ask what she
meant by the "heart of the matter" or "being like this." I decided not

to do this, since I'd covered that territory a number of times already and her answers had tended to be vague. She would usually say that she was basically fine but wasn't always quite as happy as she wanted to be, and she would add that she obsessed about the future too much.

Instead, I said: "The deeper issues are important, but I've found it works better to work on a specific, practical, concrete problem first. As we solve one problem, we may begin to understand what some of these deeper issues are. If we try to work immediately on the deeper issues, we may ramble on and on in a vague way that won't be helpful to you." Once she agrees to work on a specific problem, I might show her how to fill out a Daily Mood Log, and I would illustrate the "Vertical Arrow Technique" (see page 122). This might help us unearth the "silent assumptions" at the root of her difficulties.

I asked Sue if what I said made sense, and if she wanted to continue working on the specific problem of "not having enough fun in life." She agreed to pursue this theme. As the therapist, how would you proceed? How would you help her work on "not having enough fun in life"?

_____

_____

_____

_____

I would want her to be more specific. The problem is still far too general. I might ask:

- What type of fun is she missing?
- Whom would she like to have more fun with?
- What happens when she tries to have fun?
- When would she like to have more fun?

I suspect you can think of a number of equally good questions that would help to clarify the problem.

I asked *when* she wanted to have more fun. She looked puzzled and then said, "Today." I asked, "What time today?" She seemed taken aback, and said "Right now." I replied, "Right now? You mean that the problem is that the therapy sessions aren't any fun? Should we play cards, or what?" This admittedly sarcastic response was intended to jar her into being more specific. If she laughed, I would know it's okay to use a little humor. If she appeared hurt, I would apologize.

Sue said she wanted to have more fun when she took the train back to New York that evening after her session. What would you say next?

_____

_____

_____

I would still want more specific information. What is her idea of having fun on the train? Are there times when taking the train isn't any fun? We generated a list of activities that people might consider to be fun on a train:

- Talking to some interesting people
- Reading a good book
- Getting work done
- Drinking cocktails in the club car

She decided that it would be fun to find some interesting people to talk to. What would you say next?

_____

_____

_____

I would still want her to make the problem more specific. Does she want to talk to *anyone*? Or does she really mean that she wants to meet a cute and eligible young man? How would she go about talking to someone who interested her? What problems would she encounter? How could I help her with these problems? Would she be willing to follow through with some of my suggestions, even if they might make her a little anxious?

Sue is not difficult in the sense that she's hostile or argumentative or defensive. However, she is difficult in the sense that she's not used to dealing with real problems in a practical, direct way. She tends to be vague and unfocused. If you allow her to talk on and on, she might be in therapy for months or years without making any real changes. Can you see how easy it would be to fall into this trap with her? In contrast, if you gently but forcefully encourage her to define a real, tangible problem that she wants help with, the chances for rapid and significant improvement are great.

Sue said that sometimes when she tried to talk to people, the conversation got dull and she couldn't think of anything to say. She was worried that this would happen to her on the train. I suggested that she could tell the other person they seemed interesting and admit that she couldn't think of anything to say. She could also tell them that she wanted to learn more about them. Sue agreed that this statement would be rather bold and would probably open things up quickly, but she said it would take courage to be so direct. We role-played various ways of flirting and talking to cute guys. Sue did a good job and grasped all the ideas I proposed. We talked about the importance of being less serious and a little more outrageous in the way she related to men. She seemed to enjoy the session.

As you can see, most of these interventions focused on communication training. The next time I see Sue we may need to use cognitive techniques to deal with any fears and inhibitions that make it difficult for her to open up to others. She may be perfectionistic and have rigid expectations for herself that make it hard to lighten up and have fun. These are probably some of the "deeper issues" that she wants to deal with. However, we will be moving from the specific problem—such as feeling anxious when she talks to a cute guy on the train—to the more general problem, such as the fear of making a fool of herself or the belief that she should always be poised and in complete control of her feelings.

The point of this example is to illustrate that therapy can become productive and meaningful when you push for a specific agenda. This session was admittedly an easy one because Sue was motivated and cooperative. As long as I provided the appropriate guidance, she was willing to follow my lead.

Let's assume that you're my patient and you want help with procrastination. Our session might proceed like this:

DAVID: So you'd like help with your procrastination? Can you tell me what you're procrastinating about?

YOU: Oh, everything, Doctor!

DAVID: Well that's a tall order for me—to help you with "everything." I'm afraid I may not be quite up to it. Now if there's one thing you're procrastinating on, maybe I could help you with that. Then you could use the same tools to get more motivated and productive in other areas of your life.

YOU: Well, one thing would just be a drop in the bucket. What good would that do?

DAVID: Possibly no good at all. I think you're saying that helping you with one thing is not really very appealing to you. Is there anything else I could do to be helpful to you?

YOU: Are you saying you can't help me with my procrastination?

DAVID: No, I'd love to work with you on this problem. But I've never figured out how to work on more than one thing at a time. I really wouldn't know how to help you with "everything." After all, we only have forty-five minutes to work together today. But we might make a start if you were willing to work on just one problem.

Notice that I'm beginning to negotiate with you about how we will work together. I'm not going to jump in and try to help you until it becomes clear that what we're doing makes sense. I won't buy into your agenda of solving *all* your procrastination problems today. We only need one problem to work on. We might continue like this:

YOU: Okay. Well, how about my problem of not going to classes? I've skipped so many that I'm on probation. I've just got to get out of bed and get to classes.

DAVID: That's a problem we could work on together. Are you sure you want help with it?

YOU: Oh, yes. Oh, absolutely!

DAVID: What time would you like to be helped?

YOU: Oh, all the time! I almost never go to classes.

DAVID: Once again, "all the time" is a pretty tall order, and it's probably too much for an old man like me. You might need a younger and more energetic therapist. But if you'd like help going to *one* class, I'd be interested in helping you.

YOU: Okay, I need to go to history class. Can you get me to go to history?

DAVID: I doubt I could make you do anything you didn't want to do, and I can assure you I wouldn't dream of trying. But if you really want me to help you get to your history class, I'll be glad to see how I might help. But tell me, history class is probably really boring to you, and I'll bet you have some very good reasons for not going. Can you tell me why we should be working on this problem?

Can you see the reason for this intervention? I'm not sure yet that you really want to solve this problem. Maybe your real agenda is to take a year off from school. Maybe you feel stubborn and coerced by your parents. You may express your anger indirectly, by rebelling and refusing to make a commitment to school. If I don't clarify your motivations, I may become like a parent who pressures you while you resist. This won't be helpful for you or rewarding for me! We'll just end up feeling frustrated with each other.

Let's assume that we have dispelled these concerns and you have convinced me that you really do want help going to history class. Then I would continue like this:

DAVID: Okay, I can see that you genuinely want help with this. When would you like me to help you go to history class? When is the next class scheduled?

YOU: At 8:00 tomorrow morning.

DAVID: Eight a.m.! That's awfully early in the morning. You'd have to get up by 7:00 or 7:30. Are you sure you want to do that?

YOU: Oh, yes. I've just got to go.

DAVID: Okay, what kind of help would you like?

YOU: I don't follow.

DAVID: I don't know what kind of help you need. Do you need help waking up? Getting out of bed? Do you need help walking to class?

YOU: Well, I just can't seem to get motivated. I get up but I get distracted by other things. I just read novels.

DAVID: It makes good sense to read a novel, because going to class will be upsetting when you're so far behind. I can see why you don't feel motivated. I'm still not sure what kind of help you'd

like. Would you like to hide your novels so you won't feel so
tempted? Should we make a list of the advantages and disadvantages of going to class in spite of the fact that you don't feel like
it? Or should we look at some of your negative thoughts so we
can find out why going to class is so upsetting to you? Do any of
these ideas make sense to you?

Notice that I've presented you with a menu of methods we might
use in dealing with the problem. These are the two essential components of agenda setting—selecting a specific problem the patient
wants to solve, and agreeing how we will tackle the problem. When
these two criteria are not fulfilled, therapeutic failure is probable.
When they are fulfilled, the chances for success are high.

Some patients will resist establishing a meaningful therapeutic
agenda because they are mistrustful and have mixed feelings about
being in therapy. They may project the message "Help me, I'm
desperate! By the way, I will resist you and fight you every step of
the way."

These individuals are often reluctant to ask for help and unclear
about the problems they want help with. Agenda setting may be
traumatic for them, but it's absolutely essential. The following
dialogue illustrates this process. The patient is a moderately
difficult adolescent girl who is demanding and uncooperative. She
feels angry and depressed but isn't clear on the problem she wants
help with.

DAVID: Can you tell me what you'd like to work on in today's
session? Are there some problems you'd like help with?

NATALIE: I've just been feeling really depressed and I don't know
what to do.

DAVID: So you've been feeling depressed and you don't really know
what to do. Can you tell me what you've been feeling depressed
about?

NATALIE: Well, I seem to have a lot of problems with . . . like . . .
everything. My whole life seems pretty awful.

DAVID: That sounds pretty upsetting. You feel depressed, and everything seems just awful. I'd like you to tell me more about the
way you feel.

I am empathizing with Natalie. She may need some time to
ventilate and to share her feelings. I would encourage her to tell me

how awful her life seems. I would be sympathetic and I would not challenge her. This might go on for five or ten minutes, or for a full session or two.

After Natalie has had sufficient time to get her feelings out and she sees that I am trying to understand her and am not judging her, we would come back to the issue of agenda setting. I would want to know what particular problems Natalie wants help with. I might introduce this by saying, "Well, Natalie, we have been talking for a period of time about some of the problems in your life. I think I can understand how bad you feel. One way we can work together would be for you to pick out one of the problems you'd like some help with. Then I can teach you some techniques that might help you solve this problem. In time, we'll work on all of your problems. Does this appeal to you? Is there a particular problem you might like to work on in today's session?"

NATALIE: I guess that sounds fine. One problem, I think, would be the one with my boyfriend 'cause it's the most confusing one.

DAVID: Okay, that's a good one to start on. Tell me about the problem with your boyfriend. Can you be a little bit more specific? What's going on? What is it that bothers you?

NATALIE: Well, we are always fighting. Nothing seems to work. We never get along. There's always something to fight about.

DAVID: Oh, I see. I guess you fight an awful lot and you have trouble getting along. Can you tell me about a recent fight that you've had that you'd like some help with?

NATALIE: Well, on Friday my parents told me I had to baby-sit and I couldn't go out. He got really upset because we planned to go out that night. Then I felt really helpless.

DAVID: Oh, I see. You were caught in kind of a no-win situation. On the one hand, your parents were putting pressure on you to baby-sit, and on the other hand your boyfriend was putting pressure on you to go out with him. Am I reading you right?

NATALIE: Yeah, I guess that's it.

DAVID: Is this something you might want to work on?

NATALIE: I don't know.

DAVID: Perhaps we could work on how you negotiate your duties with your parents or how you talk to your boyfriend when you both feel upset.

NATALIE: No. I just want it to be better.

DAVID: Let's see. You want it to be better but you don't want to work on how to talk to your parents or your boyfriend when you feel upset?

NATALIE (angrily): *You're* the therapist! *You* tell me what to do!

Natalie is getting a little hostile and evasive. I would empathize for a period of time and try to find out why she's annoyed with me. Once I have explored her angry feelings, I would encourage her to zero in on the problem she wants help with.

DAVID: You say that I'm the therapist and I should know what to do. In fact, I do have lots of ideas about how to solve different kinds of problems, and I'd really love to tell you about them. I'm a little confused because I'm not sure what problem you'd like help with. I'm puzzled because I don't know if you want some help on how to communicate with your boyfriend or with your parents, or if you'd like some help dealing with your negative feelings, or if you just want to talk so I can be a good listener.

NATALIE: Tell me how to talk to him so that we don't fight. I can't do it myself and I need help.

Now Natalie is being cooperative. She is saying that she does want help with communication. I might teach her the self-expression and listening skills that are described in chapters 16 through 18.

Let's assume that Natalie isn't so cooperative. She may keep complaining and thwarting my suggestions. She may be vague about what she wants help with.

NATALIE: Well, I don't really know. Why don't you just help me? You should know what will work best.

DAVID: Okay. Well, one thing that might help would be some communication training. Another thing might be for me to help you turn some of your negative thoughts and feelings around. Do any of these ideas appeal to you?

NATALIE: I don't even know what those things are. Why don't you just help me with my problems?

DAVID: Okay. Can you tell me about the problem that you'd like to have some help with? What is the problem as you see it?

NATALIE: I already told you! You must not be listening to me very well. Are you?

As the therapist, what would you say to Natalie at this point? Put your ideas here:

_____

_____

_____

_____

At this point I would empathize. She has told me that I am not listening to her feelings. I might say something like this: "You're telling me that I am not really listening to you [thought empathy]. You seem frustrated with me [feeling empathy]. Are you [inquiry]? Maybe that happens when you talk to your parents and your boyfriend, too. I understand that you are upset because your boyfriend and your parents were mad at you and they were making demands on you. Is there something that I might not have understood [inquiry]?"

NATALIE: Well, I *told* you I am having problems with my boyfriend and my parents. I don't know what to do and I just need some help.

DAVID: Yes, you want some help with your boyfriend and with your parents. I think you might feel like you weren't treated very fairly. That part is very clear to me. It's a good problem and I think we can work on it together. I need you to help me break it down into smaller pieces so I can know the best way to help you. We could talk about how you feel, or we could talk about some solutions to these problems with your boyfriend and your parents. Do any of these suggestions appeal to you?

NATALIE: I think you really are a stupid therapist. You're really annoying me a lot. How come you can't just give me some help with my boyfriend or my parents? How am I supposed to know what we should do?

What would you say to Natalie at this time? Put your ideas here:

_____

_____

_____

_____

I might say, "You say that I'm a stupid therapist. Once you get to know me better, you may see that I'm even stupider than you think! I would like to help you, and I think I have some tools that can help you, but I am feeling a little unsure of what you want. I admit that I am perplexed. You seem annoyed with me, and I'm not sure how you would like to proceed. For example, if you told me you wanted help cooking, I might ask if you wanted help with cakes or with roasts. Once I knew what the trouble was, I could suggest a solution. By analogy, I need to know if you want to work on the problem with your boyfriend or your parents first. Can you tell me a little bit more about this? I need your help."

NATALIE: Well, I don't want to hear about cooking, I want to hear about my boyfriend and me. We're just not getting along and I don't know what to do. We're always fighting and it's stupid.

DAVID: You know, that's a common problem. A lot of people fight with people they care about because they don't know how to deal with angry feelings and conflicts. I think this is something we could work on together. Maybe we could talk about what goes on when you and your boyfriend are fighting. Would that appeal to you?

NATALIE: Fine. If you think *that* will work! Is that what *you* want to do?

What would you say to Natalie at this point? Notice that she still seems to be on the attack. Her voice has a sharp edge. What is going on? What would you say to her now? Put your ideas here:

_____

_____

_____

_____

I would comment on her tone of voice instead of dragging her along reluctantly. I might say, "You still sound pretty annoyed with me, and you seem to have some doubts about my suggestions. It may not be the way you really want to proceed. I don't want to push you into something you don't feel good about. Maybe you're not sure that you want to learn how to communicate with your boyfriend any differently."

NATALIE: Well, how will that help me? What will that do? What is this technique?

DAVID: I believe that good communication involves learning to express your feelings and learning to listen to what the other person is trying to say. That's good communication. Bad communication is when people argue and get defensive and go around and around in circles and never get anywhere. This is what most people do. In fact, that's kind of what we've been doing. We're both feeling frustrated because we're not working together as a team. We're bickering. Communication training shows you how to change this. It would take a number of sessions to teach you how to express your feelings in a more effective way and to listen better when your boyfriend expresses his feelings. This might help you deal with your angry feelings more effectively. I am not saying that you *should* do this, I'm just saying that this is one thing that might be helpful. You'd have to work hard, but I believe you could learn it. Does that appeal to you?

NATALIE: But why should I have to, when the problem isn't my fault? I'm not doing anything wrong. I get blamed for everything, but it's not my fault! It was unfair for him to get mad. My parents shouldn't make me baby-sit at the last minute. My parents are hopeless.

At this point, the reason for Natalie's angry resistance becomes more obvious. Write down your hypothesis about why Natalie is reluctant to engage more productively in the therapy:

_____

_____

_____

_____

I believe that Natalie feels scapegoated and blamed unfairly. As a result, she's got her heels dug in. I reflected this to her.

DAVID: So, you think that the problems aren't your fault. There's clearly some truth in that. You may feel that if we did some communication training it would mean that some of the problems *are* your fault. You don't like that idea very well. That probably annoys you. Your parents sent you in for treatment, so it looks like you're the sick one who's to blame for everything. Am I reading you right? I know I'd be real ticked off if that happened to me.

NATALIE: How can it be my fault? My boyfriend is such a stupid asshole. He doesn't let me do anything I want to do. He's always telling me to do this and do that, just like my parents.

DAVID: It sounds like you are really frustrated with all of them. They're all bossing you around. Is this true?

NATALIE: Of course! I already told you that!

As a therapist, what would you say now?

_____

_____

_____

_____

I would ask about the annoyance in her voice. She was just beginning to open up, and now she suddenly sounds angry and mistrustful again.

DAVID: I feel like you're a little frustrated with me again. Are you?

NATALIE: It doesn't have anything to do with you!

DAVID: I see. You say that your problems don't have anything to do with me. That's certainly true.

NATALIE: When you say something, you always agree with me. I don't know what you're doing to help me!

DAVID: I feel frustrated because it seems like I'm not connecting with you in the way I'd like to. I'm trying to get you to zero in on a problem so that we can work together. I feel pushed away. I would like to help you, but I feel like you won't let me. Are you aware of that? You seem annoyed with me. Maybe we need to talk about that a bit more and see if we can clear the air before we work on your problems at home. Could you tell me more about this? Are you uncomfortable with me?

It may be a mistake to rush prematurely to a specific agenda. It may be better to back off and listen to Natalie's complaints about me, her boyfriend, and her parents. Her core conflict seems to be "Nobody treats me right." Her response is to get mad and to pout, and she's mistrustful and reluctant to change.

The therapist must dance back and forth constantly between active, empathetic listening and gentle, persistent agenda setting. She will predictably get angry every time I ask what the problem is and how she wants to work on it. The very question is a challenge to her defense. Her posture toward the world may be "You don't love me. It's all your fault. I will punish you until you love me more. I will complain angrily and withdraw until you admit your wrongdoing and give me the love and respect I deserve."

It's possible that Natalie will not come around. She may get so frustrated that after two or three sessions she'll drop out of treatment. On the other hand, if the therapist combines warmth and gentleness with a firm, persistent request for her to define a problem to work on, the chances for success will be enhanced.

She may drop out of therapy prematurely. You may be disappointed, but the termination may be therapeutic. You have laid your cards on the table and said, "Here are some ways we may be able to work together. There are many other ways as well. Do any of these ideas make sense to you? Is there a chance that we can work together? If you would like to be in therapy with me, then I'm convinced we can find a way to work together successfully. Would you like to?" I think this message should be presented in a kindly, flexible, and encouraging way.

Premature dropout could be due to several reasons, and you can review them with patients who seem uncommitted. They may dislike you and find it difficult to tell you. The ideas and strategies you are suggesting may not appeal to them. There may be something embarrassing that they are afraid to talk about. They may be frightened and mistrustful. They may find the therapy sessions upsetting, or they may have financial difficulties and feel the therapy is too costly.

As you review these possibilities, you can ask if any of them sound correct. If so, you can offer to help the patient find a solution. Several additional ideas might help:

1. You might consult with a colleague and role-play how you interact with the patient. You might discover that you were missing

the boat or coming across in a sarcastic or defensive way. It might be that you're missing a powerful positive or negative transference reaction that needs to be explored. The consultation might give you an idea of how to approach the situation differently.

2. You might ask the patient's permission to allow another therapist to sit in as a co-therapist on one or more sessions. This could be a more experienced colleague or a student therapist. The co-therapist might also have individual sessions with the patient. Two heads can be better than one, especially when working with difficult patients. However, it's important that the two therapists respect each other and work together as a team so that the patient's efforts at splitting and playing people off against each other are not successful. In addition, you need to make it clear that you would like to remain the primary therapist. Emphasize that you're not trying to get rid of the patient by shuffling him or her off to a colleague.

AGENDA-SETTING EXERCISE

In Chapter 27, I described how a group of two or more therapists can learn cognitive and behavioral techniques. One therapist can volunteer to play the role of the patient, and a second therapist can volunteer to be the therapist. The others in the group can observe and provide feedback.

The "therapist" begins by asking what specific problem the "patient" would like to work on in today's session. The "patient" is instructed to be purposefully vague. The therapist's job is to try to get the patient to describe a specific, real problem, and to determine what kind of help the patient wants. This could involve modifying a dysfunctional attitude like perfectionism or a communication problem like getting defensive when criticized. You can stop the action every minute, so that the "patient" and the observers can give specific positive and negative feedback.

You will be surprised to discover that most people in the therapist role will do quite poorly. They will be unable to define an adequate therapeutic agenda with a patient who is only moderately difficult. You will see right away that some therapists will get tense or defensive. Others will fail to listen and will respond to something the patient didn't really say. Some therapists will get nervous and talk too much. Once the error has been pointed out, try again or do a role reversal.

In setting the tone for the group, it's important to remind the participants that most of us have clay feet and that we all fantasize that other therapists are far more talented and effective. The purpose of the group training is to grow and to reveal our inadequacies without having to feel ashamed. If we can trust each other and share our vulnerabilities, the group experience can be exhilarating.

I enjoy the process of group training because it makes me feel more human and much closer to my students and colleagues. And, of course, the potential for rapid learning is enormous. There's also another reward: When you play the role of the patient, you can pretend to be one of your most difficult patients, one you feel annoyed with. You can act just as whiny and uncooperative and hostile as you want! This can be cathartic. You can get your frustration and aggression out of your system. In addition, by putting yourself in the patient's shoes, you will see the impact of the therapist's efforts to respond to you. This will make you more aware of effective and ineffective therapeutic interventions.

Let's review some of the principles illustrated in this chapter. First, what did you like or dislike about the techniques and concepts that I illustrated? List what you disliked or disagreed with:

_____

_____

_____

_____

Were there some ideas you found helpful? List them here:

_____

_____

_____

_____

What communication techniques can you use when a patient gets angry and critical of you?

1._____

2._____

3._____

4._____

5._____

These are empathy, the disarming technique, inquiry, "I feel" statements, and stroking.

After you have empathized and allowed the patient to ventilate, you will need to agree on an agenda. What are the two most important aspects of agenda setting?

1._____

2._____

You need a clear and specific description of the problem the patient wants help with, and a consensus about which therapeutic methods you will use to solve the problem.

29

♦

Self-Help Assignments:
How to Motivate Patients Who
Sabotage the Therapeutic Process

One of the most common problems that cognitive and behavioral therapists encounter is the patient's lack of compliance with self-help assignments between sessions. These assignments can take many forms, including:

- Taking a mood test, such as the Burns Anxiety Inventory or the Burns Depression Checklist, each week to monitor one's progress
- Bringing a cassette tape to the session and listening to the tape of the session at home
- Keeping a journal of negative thoughts with the Daily Mood Log
- Bibliotherapy—reading articles or book chapters that may be relevant to one's problems
- Practicing self-expression skills or listening skills with friends and family members
- Scheduling more productive and satisfying activities
- Confronting a feared situation or a phobia through gradual exposure or flooding
- Doing an experiment or conducting a survey to test the validity of a dysfunctional attitude

- Taking an antidepressant medication and obtaining necessary blood tests to monitor the dose

Some patients seem to "forget" these assignments, while others wage a more open rebellion and angrily refuse to participate in them. Solving this problem is of vital importance. In a recent study published in the journal *Cognitive Therapy and Research,* Dr. Jacqueline Persons and I reported a strong positive correlation between compliance with these self-help assignments and therapeutic improvement. By the time of completion of therapy, patients who regularly did at least some self-help assignments had an average 80 percent reduction in Beck Depression inventory scores. In contrast, those who did not do these assignments averaged zero percent improvement. This striking finding suggests that compliance with self-help assignments may be the most important predictor of therapeutic success.

The problem of compliance is also of great interest because it brings cognitive and behavioral therapists back to the old, unresolved issue of resistance. Why do some patients come for help and then sabotage the therapeutic process? How can we motivate these patients to collaborate more actively with us?

The first thing to ask yourself when a patient isn't doing the self-help assignment is whether the purpose, nature, and importance of these assignments have been spelled out adequately. Many people think of psychotherapy as something that occurs in the therapist's office. You sit or lie on the couch and share your feelings with a therapist who listens and asks questions. You presumably improve because of the insights you gain and the emotions you express during these sessions. The idea that you would be asked to do self-help assignments between sessions may seem strange to some people.

At my unit, all new patients receive a copy of the "Concept of Self-Help" memo at the completion of their intake evaluation (see page 694). They are asked to read and fill out this memo and give it to their therapist at their first session. The memo emphasizes the importance of self-help assignments and describes the types of assignments that may be utilized in the course of therapy. The memo asks whether or not patients are willing to participate in this aspect of the therapy ("yes," "no," or "needs discussion" are the response options). They are also asked how many minutes per day they are willing to spend on the self-help assignments, how many days per week they are willing to do them, and the number of weeks they are willing to keep it up. The answers to these questions can alert the therapist right away that compliance may be a problem. For example, some patients are evasive and do not fill out this section of the memo. I gently confront them with this so we can negotiate the issue of self-help assignments prior to the beginning of the actual therapy.

The memo concludes with a list of reasons why they may not want to do these self-help assignments. They are asked whether each reason describes them "not at all," "somewhat," "moderately," or "a lot." A review of the responses can make the therapist and patient more aware of why the self-help assignments might be a problem. Since I made it a policy that every patient at my clinic must complete the memo and review it with his or her therapist at the beginning of therapy, the degree of adherence of self-help assignments seems to have increased substantially.

A lack of homework compliance may occur because you did not make it clear precisely what you wanted the patient to do or why you asked him or her to do it. Toward the end of a session, I will frequently make a written list of what I've asked the patient to do. I review this list with the patient to make sure there's no miscommunication. At the beginning of the next session I review the list and go over the patient's homework, so they'll know I am serious about it and am interested in what they've done. I try to accentuate the positive, and I compliment them on what they've done so they won't feel ashamed or fearful of my criticism.

If the self-help homework was clearly assigned and the patient failed to comply, you can ask why. Maybe you haven't properly identified the problem the patient wants help with. Maybe the patient was uncomfortable with the methods you advocated. During one of her first therapy sessions a woman told me that she wanted to work on the problem of whether to continue to build her own interior decorating business or to work full-time for a local company that had repeatedly asked her to join their firm. I asked her to list the advantages and disadvantages of each possibility so we could review it during the next session.

She seemed sheepish at the next session and had not completed the assignment. She said she was annoyed with me and ambivalent about being in treatment. She said that the career problem was not at all crucial, and she felt that she needed to talk about her dissatisfaction with her husband. She owned up to the fact that she'd been having an affair with her neighbor. She said that rationally she knew he wasn't good for her, but she didn't feel ready to give up this relationship. She was afraid I'd judge her and tell her she had to be faithful to her husband.

Part of the problem, as you can see, is the need to negotiate what she most wants to work on. In addition, a transference issue may be emerging. She seems concerned that I may look down on her and tell her what to do, and she may not trust me. I will need to explore why she is dissatisfied with her husband. What are the problems in her marriage? What therapeutic methods will we use to deal with these problems? I will also need to do some active listening. Can she tell me about her negative feelings about the therapy? Are there things I said or did that turned her off? Are there other people who have tried to boss her around and tell her how to run her life?

Some patients may be clear about the problem they want help with, but they may have mixed feelings about the therapeutic methods you advocate. In Chapter 8 I described a severely depressed nurse who felt angry and frustrated with the way she was treated by the hospital staff, the physicians, and the patients. When I listened to her description of several problems at the hospital, it seemed to me that her complaints were valid. I felt her anger was frequently a healthy and appropriate response to a genuinely irritating situation.

I suggested that we might work on communication skills so she could learn to express her feelings more effectively. I explained that if she opened up a little more, she wouldn't have to go around being resentful because of all the feelings she kept bottled up. She reacted very negatively. She said that she didn't want to be angry with people. She said she wanted me to use cognitive techniques so she could achieve greater emotional control and not react so angrily.

I was uncomfortable with her request. I was concerned that she was already overcontrolled and inassertive. Although cognitive techniques could help her change the way she thought and felt during conflicts with others, this didn't seem to be the whole answer, because it might just feed her belief that she should never be upset with anyone. She had an intense fear of conflict and was convinced that any expression of her feelings would be inappropriate and would get her into trouble.

It took us several sessions to reach a compromise on this point. She agreed to tell people a little bit about how she felt, as an experiment. Fortunately she got positive responses from her co-workers, which boosted her mood and made her more animated and committed to the therapy. She saw that being more open with people, though frightening, could be important and helpful to her.

Sometimes failure to do self-help assignments may be a form of passive aggressiveness. The patient is saying, "I don't like you. I don't feel cared about. Therefore I'll go on strike. I won't play ball with you." The quickest way to find out is to ask them to fill out the Patient's Report of the Therapy Session (see pages 507–508). Low ratings for warmth and trust will tip you off that they feel annoyed with you. You can encourage the patient to talk about these negative feelings with the communication techniques described in Chapter 25. Once these feelings are aired, the patient will often be willing to cooperate and work with you again.

Sometimes patients won't do the self-help assignments because they feel hopeless and convinced that they cannot get better. This attitude operates as a self-fulfilling prophecy, because once they give up, the therapy gets stuck. It's important to identify feelings of hopelessness because they can also lead to suicidal impulses.

If your patients fill out the Burns Depression Checklist weekly (or an equivalent self-assessment instrument, such as the Beck Depression Inventory), you can simply glance at item 2, which assesses hopelessness, as well as item 15, which assesses suicidal thoughts. If the responses indicate that the patient feels hopeless or suicidal, then you can explore these feelings during the session. (Ways of assessing the seriousness of suicidal impulses are described on page 40.)

Let's assume that a patient says there's no point in doing the self-help exercises because nothing could possibly help. You have asked the appropriate questions and determined that the patient isn't actively suicidal. What would you say next? Put your ideas here:

_____

_____

_____

_____

_____

You could say, "It sounds as if you feel that your problems are so severe that nothing could help you [thought empathy]. Is this true [inquiry]? It's also possible that you're not comfortable with me or with the therapy [inquiry]. Maybe I did or said something that made you feel turned off. Does any of this ring true [inquiry]?"

Note that I am emphasizing the listening skills. Patients are frequently very unassertive. They may be afraid to tell you how they feel, and they may communicate indirectly—by missing a session, by coming late, by failing to do the self-help exercises, or by insisting that they're hopeless. You need to lift the rock so you can see what's lurking underneath. Often you will find resentment hidden in the shadows.

Now suppose the patient feels hopeless and discouraged, but he or she is not angry with you. What would you say or do next? Remember that the patient is not doing any self-help assignments. Put your ideas here:

_____

_____

_____

_____

Answer: I can think of three strategies, and there are undoubtedly many more. One suggestion would be to tell the patient to *maintain* the belief that he or she is hopeless, but to test this belief over an appropriate period of time, such as ten weeks. During that time the patient can agree to do the self-help exercises and to fill out the Burns Depression Checklist every week as a way of assessing progress. Ask the patient how much the score on the test would have to improve to prove that he or she *is* getting better. The advantage of this strategy is that you and the patient can work together productively instead of getting involved in a debate about whether or not the therapy can be helpful.

A second strategy involves agenda setting. Ask the patient what he or she *specifically* wants help with, and how he or she would like to proceed. Is there a marital problem? What kind? Is there a problem with procrastination? With the career? You must spell out precisely what the patient wants help with before you can decide whether you can be of help.

It's important that you both agree that the therapeutic methods are appropriate. Maybe the patient is asking for something you're not comfortable with. If a man asked me to explore his childhood to find out why he had an elevator phobia, I would say that I wasn't an expert in psychoanalysis and I couldn't do an adequate job. I would let him know that I did want to work with him. I would be eager to find a way that we could work together that would be mutually satisfactory, but I would not agree to any approach that didn't make sense, given my theoretical orientation and skills. I might tell him that if we got on the elevator together, and stayed on it for about thirty minutes, he might get anxious at first and then he would probably start to feel better. The anxiety might even disappear completely. I would say that this made a lot more sense to me than probing for causes. I would add that nobody even knows the cause of elevator phobias, but that the problem can usually be corrected. If the method I suggested made sense we could proceed.

A third response to a hopeless patient would be to ask why he or she is coming to therapy. What does he or she want from you? There's something basically illogical about coming to a therapist, paying a good fee for the time, and then announcing that the therapist cannot help. What's going on? I would caution you to pursue this line of inquiry *cautiously*, and to express concern for the patient, because this line of inquiry could sound flippant or disrespectful. I would say that I was committed to the patient and felt confident that we could work together successfully, but that I felt puzzled and needed to know why the patient was there and what he or she wanted. Maybe the patient doesn't want to be in therapy but feels coerced to come. You could explore this dynamic and help the patient decide if he or she wants to continue working with you.

You may discover that the patient has no real desire to be in therapy with you. A psychiatry resident at the University of Pennsylvania was asked to treat a hostile young man with a diagnosis of schizoid personality disorder who had been referred by a dermatologist. Apparently, the patient had been to numerous dermatologists for a skin problem and the referring doctor sensed that there were significant emotional problems. I would suspect that the patient was angry and was compulsively going to dermatologists because of a fixation with his skin instead of dealing with the problems in his life.

He was resentful and uncooperative and told the psychiatric resident that she couldn't help him. She felt annoyed and frustrated with him and didn't know how to proceed. If you were the therapist, what would you say next to the patient?

_____

_____

_____

_____

Answer: I would say, "Can you tell me what it is you want help with?" The patient's response was, "I've got an itch." If you were the therapist, what would you say next?

_____

_____

_____

_____

Answer: I would say, "I can imagine that an itch would be quite uncomfortable [feeling empathy]. Can you tell me what type of help you're looking for? [inquiry]" This is the crux of the issue. What in the world *is* he looking for? Did he want her to scratch it? I apologize for my sarcasm, but I want to emphasize how crucial it is to negotiate a specific agenda. The issue is, how will you and the patient work together?

You could ask the patient if there were tensions at home or problems in his life that he wanted to talk about. More than likely, he will reject this and terminate therapy. If so, at least you have tried to clarify what kind of help he wants and attempted to find some common ground.

Another attitude that can get in the way of doing self-help assignments is the fear of change. Some patients are ambivalent about getting better. They vaguely want to feel better, but they are terrified of what this might mean. A new patient suddenly quit doing homework assignments after the first couple of sessions. She told me: "Dr. Burns, when you said the patients who do the assignments have an average of 80 percent improvement as compared with zero in those who don't, I suddenly got cold feet. I couldn't motivate myself to do the assignments anymore. I got scared that the therapy would work and that things would start to change." If you were the therapist, what would you say next? Put your ideas here:

I would ask, "What is it that frightens you about getting better [inquiry]? What do you think might happen [inquiry]?" It turned out that she was afraid of getting too close to people, including her husband. She said she was "a closed person" and didn't feel comfortable opening up. Her intake diagnoses confirmed this, since in addition to chronic depression she had a diagnosis of "avoidant personality disorder." She said, "My family never thought I'd actually marry Hal. They thought I'd cancel out at the last minute. I like freedom, and Hal and I do our own thing. If we get too close, it might cause problems. If I maintain a distance, I can stay in my own little world. People tell me I should communicate more openly, but I don't really want to let the walls down."

If you were the therapist, what would you say next?

I would explore her fear. What does she think would happen if she got too close to her husband? I might ask if there are some problems we could work on together that would be a little less threatening to her.

Some patients may resist doing self-help assignments because of strong dependency needs and feelings of entitlement. This is especially true of those with a diagnosis of borderline personality disorder. They may have strong needs to be loved and cared about, and they may feel angry and entitled to better treatment from the world. They may resist doing self-help assignments because they do not believe that they can learn to be happy and to function in a more self-reliant manner. They may feel that they should not have to assume any responsibility for their negative feelings and unsatisfactory relationships. Their personal lives may reveal a pattern of loneliness and rejection, and they are often excessively dependent on others for emotional and financial support.

These patients may be extremely ambivalent toward you. They may idealize you at first and then become angry when you do not meet all their needs for love and affection. Because they have difficulties expressing these feelings openly and directly, they may act them out instead. They may miss sessions, stop doing self-help assignments, make suicidal threats, slash or burn their wrists, legs, or stomachs, or engage in other impulsive, self-destructive activities.

The angry, coercive motivation behind these actions is usually pretty transparent. A young man named Sam described how threatening and self-destructive he got whenever he was frustrated. He told me that once, while holding a gun to his own head, he had called a prior therapist and made admittedly unreasonable demands. He told the therapist that he would pull the trigger if the demands were not met.

Sam called me once, just as I was about to jump in a taxi to appear on a local television show. I was tense because I was on the verge of being late. Sam knew of this appearance because it had been announced in the *TV Guide*. Sam said, "Dr. Burns, I want to thank you for all the help you've given me. You've been great and I've really appreciated all your efforts. I'm just calling to say good-by. I finally realized I was hopeless, and so I've decided to commit suicide while you're on the show. I know you need a twenty-four-hour notification to cancel appointments, so I wanted to let you know not to expect me at tomorrow's session. By the way, I'm out of town, in a phone booth, with a hose from my car's exhaust pipe into the front window, so there's nothing you can do to stop me. It will be useless to call the police, so you don't need to worry about me. Good-by and have a terrific show."

I was furious and told Sam I expected him to keep his appointment and that I wanted him to come in for an emergency session right away. However, he wouldn't stay on the line and hung up on me. On the way to the show I felt intense guilt and panic. I thought, "I must be a terrific phony. How can I talk about *Feeling Good* when my patients are dropping dead like flies?" This reaction illustrates how uncanny these patients can be when they are angry. They sense our greatest vulnerabilities and stick the dagger in the bull's-eye! But my anxiety turned into anger as I thought about the situation. I told myself, "I'm not going to let Sam do this to me. I'm going to have a great show in spite of him." During the show, I told the audience that we are all subjected to great stress at the times we least expect it and described what had just happened to me. This revelation made it easier for the people in the audience to open up about the problems in their own lives. The show went unusually well.

When I returned to my office, the phone was ringing. It was Sam. He congratulated me and said he had watched the entire show. He said it was my best TV show so far. He let me know he would be there shortly for his emergency appointment.

Patients like Sam often make therapists feel guilty and insecure. You may make the mistake of trying too hard to please them. They tell you that the therapy cannot help, that you do not care about them, and that there's no point in doing the self-help assignments. They insist you just don't understand. So you try harder. You propose a new strategy. They complain that they have already tried it and insist that it "just won't work." On and on the battle goes, and you get more and more frustrated. No matter how hard you try, they just won't cooperate or respond to your efforts.

It's important not to buy into this common power struggle. Suppose a woman who has failed to do the homework says, "These silly assignments won't do me any good anyway. I don't think you can help me. You don't really care about me." How would you respond?

_____

_____

_____

You could say, "It sounds like you feel I don't care about you and you think the self-help exercises won't be helpful to you [thought empathy]. You may be upset with me and disappointed in the treatment [feeling empathy]. Are you [inquiry]?" Notice that you're drawing her out instead of defending yourself or trying to be helpful.

Suppose she says, "I know you can't help me. Nobody can. I'm a horrible human being." What would you say next?

_____

_____

_____

_____

"You seem to be really pessimistic that we can work together, [thought empathy], and extremely unhappy with yourself [feeling empathy]. I'm concerned about how desperate you seem to feel ['I feel' statement]. I'm committed to you [stroking], and I hope we can work together ['I feel' statement]. I wonder if you do want to work with me [inquiry]. Do you [inquiry]? The self-help exercises are an important component of therapy ['I feel' statement]. Do you think this is something you will be willing to do [inquiry]? Is this the type of therapy you want [inquiry]?"

Notice that instead of trying to sell yourself to her, you're asking if she wants to work with you. The implication is that therapy is a negotiated relationship which must be satisfactory to both parties. If she says she doesn't want to do her part, and if she will not make a minimal commitment to the therapy, then it may be appropriate to question whether ongoing therapy with you is indicated. It's never wise to pursue people who are playing hard to get and putting you at a distance. This leads to endless grief and frustration, If, however, you *agree* that the therapy may not make sense, then you reverse the dynamics. You toss the ball back into her court. Let her try to persuade you that you should work together.

Now suppose she tells you that she just "can't" do the self-help assignments. She says that writing down her negative thoughts is too upsetting. She tells you she just can't do any self-help assignment at home. If you were the therapist, what would you say to her? Put your ideas here:

_____

_____

_____

_____

You might say, "You couldn't write down your negative thoughts because you got too upset when you tried [thought empathy]? When did this occur [inquiry]? Can you show me the written exercise you started when you got so upset [inquiry]?"

The purpose of this statement is to pin her down. I suspect that she really didn't try to do the self-help assignments. She just assumed the exercise would be upsetting, so she avoided it. In the unlikely event that she did begin a Daily Mood Log, you could help her complete it in the office. If she didn't even try, she might protest that she just "can't" fill out a Daily Mood Log on her own. She might explain that it's too difficult or protest that she can't think of any negative thoughts. What would you say next if you were the therapist? Put your ideas here:

_____

_____

_____

_____

I would ask her if she "can't" do the exercises or if she doesn't want to. I would explain that I could help her with any difficulties she's having, to make sure she understands each step of the self-help exercise. I would add that I was concerned that this may not be the real issue, and that we might be missing the point. She may not be strongly committed to doing the self-help exercises, and she may simply have difficulties telling me this for fear that I'll be angry with her.

Let's assume she acknowledges that she doesn't want to do self-help exercises at home. She says she doesn't think they'll help, or she thinks she "can't remember" to do them, or she makes some other excuse. What would you say next?

_____

_____

_____

_____

I would ask if she is committed to working with me, but I would be careful not to sound too rejecting. I might make a statement like this: "Jane, I'm hopeful that we can find an answer to this problem, because I would like to work with you. I believe we can work together successfully, if that's what you want. Most therapists would only ask you to come to sessions and talk, and they wouldn't ask you to do self-help assignments between sessions. That may be the type of therapy that you want and need. However, that's not my forte. The success of the therapy that I do strongly depends on whether you're willing to do things to help yourself between sessions. You certainly have every right not to do the self-help assignments, but I doubt that we will make any tangible progress. Tell me, do you think I'm the person you want to work with? Does this type of therapy make sense to you, given how hard it is for you to help yourself?"

Now she has to persuade you that she does want to work with you. She may *not* want to work with you. If so, you can refer her to a colleague with a different style and orientation. But if she does decide to stay, you've made it clear that the two of you will have to negotiate this issue in a way that makes sense to both of you.

Some patients refuse to do the self-help assignments because they don't like to be told what to do. You may have to resort to a little reverse psychology to turn this problem around. A 32-year-old man named Jerold was referred to me after ten years of unsuccessful psychotherapy for chronic depression. He felt resentful toward the world. During the first session Jerold told me he had difficulties attracting women. He complained bitterly about how lonely and unhappy he was. He insisted he was a "hard-boiled egg" and a hopeless loser no woman would want. His previous psychiatrist had suggested he read my first book, *Feeling Good.* Jerold said the "gimmicks" in the book couldn't possibly help him. He said he didn't want to do any "homework" exercises between sessions. He said I was probably just another "rip-off artist" like the two other "shrinks" who took his money and did nothing for him.

I felt a little uneasy after the session! I dreaded seeing him again, because it seemed the treatment was going to be a real uphill battle. I imagined trying to drag him forward while he sat back, refusing to cooperate and complaining that my efforts were no good. The scenario I foresaw was this: Jerold holds up the hoop and I jump through. Jerold says, "That's no good!" and holds it up a little higher. I jump through again! Then he says, "That wasn't any good, either!" Eventually I get exhausted, and ask myself, "Why in the world am I jumping through this hoop?"

I felt that Jerold's resentful, stubborn style might be protecting him from something he was afraid of. As long as he refused to cooperate, he wouldn't have to take a chance of getting his hopes up and risk getting hurt. If I rejected him or if the therapy was unsuccessful, he wouldn't feel let down because he could say, "I knew this all along."

After thinking about this problem, I called him at home very early on the morning of his second session. I told him I had thought about what he had said and concluded he was right. I said it sounded as if he didn't really want to work with me, and if he wanted, he could cancel that day's session and he wouldn't be charged for it. I told him I was willing to work with him, but he should know that I was an extremely demanding therapist and I insisted that all my patients had to work their fingers to the bone doing homework assignments between sessions. I told him it sounded as if this didn't appeal to him and that it might not make sense for him to have such an aggressive and demanding therapist. I explained that I would ask him to do all kinds of things he might not really want to do, like asking women for dates and keeping a journal of his negative thoughts. I told him I could refer him to a number of fine therapists who would be happy to listen to him without making any demands on him whatsoever. I told him I was also a "hard-boiled egg" and I felt that he deserved a better and more patient therapist.

Jerold begged me to continue my work with him! He told me he would be one of my hardest-working patients if only I'd give him a chance!

This was the start of what turned out to be a challenging and rewarding therapeutic experience. Jerold worked feverishly and faithfully at anything I asked him to do between sessions. His depression was greatly reduced after three sessions, and he began work on the tougher problem—his difficulties forming intimate relationships. He continued faithfully in his therapy and made great strides in his career and in his personal relationships.

When my second book, *Intimate Connections*, was released, I had to go out of town for two weeks for a promotional tour. When therapists go out of town, some patients feel hurt, rejected, and angry, and they may act out these feelings. Leaving for a book tour can seem particularly selfish and insulting, because it can appear as if I'm trying to promote myself and ignoring the needs and feelings of my patients. When I said good-by to Jerold, he simply shook my hand and said, "I'll miss you." There were tears in his eyes and he wished me success. I was touched by his vulnerability. Not bad for a couple of hard-boiled eggs!

THE CONCEPT OF SELF-HELP*

The purpose of treatment is to *feel* better, to *understand* why you got depressed or anxious, and to learn to *master your moods* so you can cope with your problems more effectively in the future.

There are several reasons why you may feel better as a result of your therapy:

1. You may experience a mood lift because you learn something that helps you solve a personal problem.

2. You may appreciate the support of a therapist who understands you and approves of you.

3. You may benefit from an antidepressant medication.

4. You may do things to help yourself between therapy sessions, such as scheduling more productive or pleasurable activities, becoming more assertive with people, writing down your negative thoughts and substituting more positive ones, or reading a self-help book.

Some of the newer forms of therapy are unique in emphasizing a structured self-help program to help you feel better, to become more productive, and to improve your relationships with people. Research and clinical experience have confirmed that the speed of your improvement can depend on your willingness to do self-help assignments. People who are unwilling to help themselves are often very slow to improve. In contrast, people who make an effort to participate in a systematic self-help program generally make the most rapid gains.

For this reason, it's crucial for you to decide whether you are willing to make an effort to help yourself as part of your treatment. Please answer the following questions and return this memo to your therapist so you can review it together.

1. I understand that my therapist emphasizes a self-help program as a key to personal growth.
   _____ yes _____no _____needs discussion

2. I am willing to do things to help myself between therapy sessions.
   _____ yes _____no _____needs discussion

3. The amount of time between sessions I agree to spend is _____ minutes per day (fill in).

4. I am willing to do this _____ days per week, and to continue working in my own behalf for at least _____ weeks (fill in).

*Copyright © 1984 by David D. Burns, M.D., from *The Feeling Good Handbook*, copyright © 1989

Self-Help Forms and Methods

The following is a brief review of some of the types of self-help forms and methods that are commonly used by patients involved in therapy. It is not comprehensive but is just intended to give you an idea of what is available.

1. **Activity Schedules:** A variety of forms are available to help you organize and utilize your time more productively.

2. **Daily Mood Log:** This form will help you change negative thoughts that lead to sadness, anxiety, anger, guilt, and frustration.

3. **Checklist of Cognitive Distortions:** This is a list of the ten types of twisted thinking that most frequently give rise to painful feelings. You can use it in conjunction with the Daily Mood Log to help you pinpoint the distortions in your negative thoughts.

4. **The Pleasure-Predicting Sheet:** This is a form for predicting and assessing the amount of satisfaction you get from various activities that have a potential for pleasure, achievement, learning, or personal growth. This can help you test and modify certain self-defeating attitudes that can make you vulnerable to depression and anxiety, such as:

   - I cannot feel happy and fulfilled if I'm alone.
   - I cannot feel satisfied unless I do things perfectly.
   - I cannot be truly happy unless there's someone in my life who loves me.

5. **The Anti-Procrastination Sheet:** This form can help you overcome procrastination. You break a task down into its smallest component parts and predict how difficult and satisfying each part will be, between 0 (the least difficult or satisfying) and 100 (the most). Then you do each part and record how difficult and satisfying it actually turned out to be. Things you've been putting off frequently turn out to be considerably easier and more enjoyable than you predicted.

6. **Bibliotherapy:** Many useful self-help books and pamphlets are available which can speed up your recovery. Some of these have to do with self-esteem, sex, assertiveness training, or other topics relevant to personal growth. Your therapist might be able to suggest some titles that would be especially valuable to you.

7. **The Burns Depression Checklist (BDC):** This is a 15-question multiple-choice inventory that acts as an "emotional thermometer" to measure the amount of depression you are experiencing. It can be filled out and scored in two or three minutes. While you are in therapy for depression, you can take the BDC test once a week to monitor your progress.

8. **The Burns Anxiety Inventory (BAI):** This is a 33-question multiple-choice inventory that measures the symptoms of anxiety and panic. Like the Burns Depression Checklist, it can be filled out and scored in several minutes. Taken weekly, it can help you monitor your progress in therapy.

9. **Communication Training:** During therapy sessions, your therapist can teach you specific verbal skills by role-playing difficult situations with you and demonstrating appropriate responses. Common areas of difficulty include dealing with people who are angry and excessively critical, as well as with complainers and people who make excessive demands on you. You might need to work on how to say no graciously, how to ask for a date, how to interview for a job, how to listen better, how to flirt, how to handle rejection, or how to communicate with people who refuse to talk to you. Once you have mastered a specific verbal skill in the office, your therapist can help you devise actual practice experiences outside the office.

10. **Decision-Making Form:** This form allows you to weigh the advantages and disadvantages of various options in a systematic manner when you are faced with a difficult decision.

11. **Empathy Scale:** This form allows you to give your therapist positive and negative feedback about each therapy session. You can fill it out after a session and give it to your therapist at the beginning of the next session. This will bring any negative reactions to the attention of your therapist so they won't build up and undermine your treatment. The resolution of these conflicts can improve your relationship with your therapist and give him or her valuable information about the best way to be helpful to you.

12. **Taping of Sessions:** Many patients find it very beneficial to tape their sessions so they can listen to the tapes at home between sessions. During a productive session you may discover many exciting insights about yourself or learn to solve problems that

have been troubling you. During the session these new ideas may all seem perfectly clear, but an hour or two later you may have trouble recalling what seemed so important and useful at the time. As you listen to the tape, you will have the opportunity to review these ideas again. Many patients listen to the tapes of especially good sessions numerous times. They report that the tapes can be more helpful than the actual sessions themselves.

When you listen to a tape, you may discover that you had a tendency to ignore or discount what the therapist said, even though you felt convinced during the session that you were listening carefully. At times it can be uncomfortable to hear yourself, because you will notice certain negative habits that you weren't aware of. Listening to yourself takes courage, but it can be an important growth experience. You may also become aware of mistakes your therapist is making. Be sure to share this feedback at the next session.

Twenty-Five Reasons for Not Doing Self-Help Assignments

The following are some of the reasons why you may have difficulty doing self-help work between sessions. There is some overlap between a number of the categories, and you will probably discover that several of them apply to you. These same attitudes may make you less productive and successful in other areas of your life. Once you pinpoint the problem that is holding you back, you can work with your therapist to develop a strategy for overcoming it.

After each of the following descriptions, put a check (✓) in the box that indicates how accurately it describes the way you feel.

1. **The love addiction:** You may feel convinced that love and closeness are the keys to happiness, so you can't conceive of finding satisfaction as a result of learning to cope with your problems on your own. Self-help techniques may seem cold and mechanical. You may resent having to help yourself because you feel convinced that the best way to overcome your depression involves sharing your feelings with a therapist or friend who cares about you and supports you.

   This problem or attitude describes me:

   _____ not at all   _____ somewhat   _____ moderately   _____ a lot

2. **Perfectionistic thinking:** You may feel that if you don't do things perfectly, there's no point in doing them at all. This attitude can defeat you in several ways. You may feel you have to do your self-help exercises so thoroughly and perfectly that you feel too overwhelmed to try. In fact, even five to ten minutes a day of self-help work can contribute enormously to your improvement. You may be afraid that if you make a mistake or don't complete an exercise properly, you will appear incompetent or stupid. In fact, you're permitted to make as many mistakes as you like, because your therapist is teaching you something new. You can learn from your mistakes. You may also feel that a particular exercise must lead to a dramatic change in the way you feel, or else it wasn't successful. Actually, you can learn a lot from self-help exercises that don't make you feel better, if you will review your efforts with your therapist.

Perfectionism describes me:

____ **not at all** ____ **somewhat** ____ **moderately** ____ **a lot**

3. **The fear of disapproval:** You may be afraid that your therapist will think less of you when s/he reviews your self-help efforts. You may think your negative thoughts and feelings are shameful or foolish. Paradoxically, this attitude may bring about the disapproval you're trying so hard to prevent. Since your therapist's primary job is to help you design and carry out a self-help program that will help you get in better control of your life, s/he might feel frustrated about your unwillingness to try to help yourself. This could make you feel disapproved of, and even less like doing the assignments.

The fear of disapproval describes me:

____ **not at all** ____ **somewhat** ____ **moderately** ____ **a lot**

4. **Putting the cart before the horse:** You may have the belief that motivation comes before effective action, so you wait around until you feel like doing something. Since the motivation doesn't come, you end up doing nothing.

Actually, action must frequently precede motivation. Since depressed people often feel lethargic and unmotivated, you may have to make a decision to do something constructive whether or not you feel like it. Once you get started, you will often feel more motivated.

Putting the cart before the horse describes me:

____ **not at all** ____ **somewhat** ____ **moderately** ____ **a lot**

5. **Unexpressed anger:** You may resent something your therapist said or react negatively to his or her personality. Instead of expressing these feelings in a direct and open fashion, you may avoid the problem and express your feelings indirectly—by cancelling sessions at the last minute, by being argumentative, or by not completing the self-help assignments you agreed to do. This can make the feelings of tension worse, and you may eventually drop out of treatment entirely.

Avoiding conflicts when I feel angry describes me:

_____ not at all _____ somewhat _____ moderately _____ a lot

6. **Hopelessness:** One of the most painful aspects of depression and anxiety is the illogical sense of hopelessness that many patients experience. You may feel as if your problems and suffering will go on forever, no matter what. In spite of the fact that your therapist is convinced that your prognosis for recovery is excellent, you may believe that all your efforts are pointless and doomed to failure. Then you give up and do nothing. Consequently, nothing changes. This reinforces the belief that you're hopeless.

Hopelessness describes me:

_____ not at all _____ somewhat _____ moderately _____ a lot

7. **Coercion sensitivity:** You may at times feel that people are trying to force you to do various things. You may think that friends or family members are being pushy and bossy or are trying to control you. Consequently you may dig in your heels and resist them, because you don't want to give in. Then they get frustrated and put more pressure on you. You, in turn, feel stubborn and even more determined not to let them control you.

I sometimes feel as if people are bossing me around.

_____ not at all _____ somewhat _____ moderately _____ a lot

8. **Fatalism:** You may be convinced that your moods are governed by forces that are beyond your control, such as hormones, drugs, biorhythms, fate, God, or the way other people treat you. Consequently there seems little point in trying to learn to master your moods. If you become passive and don't try, you will continue to feel that you can't control your feelings or solve your problems.

Fatalism describes me:

_____ not at all _____ somewhat _____ moderately _____ a lot

9. **Fear of blame:** Some people believe that if they accept the idea that they are responsible for their emotions, it follows that they will be blamed for them. Since they don't want to feel blamed, they resist assuming any responsibility for their feelings or their problems, and they refuse to do anything to help themselves.

I am afraid of accepting responsibility for my negative feelings:

____ not at all ____ somewhat ____ moderately ____ a lot

10. **Internal vs. external expectations:** You may feel the need to meet the expectations of your parents, your spouse, your boss, etc. You might base your self-esteem on the amount of praise or criticism you get. When you're criticized, you might feel inadequate, resentful, guilty, or anxious. This is so uncomfortable that it seems preferable to adopt a low profile and do nothing at all. The less you do, the less you can be criticized for. You try to keep everybody's expectations at an absolute minimum, so that no one will get their hopes up and then be disappointed.

The fear of letting other people down describes me:

____ not at all ____ somewhat ____ moderately ____ a lot

11. **Resistance to a structured fast-acting approach:** Some people feel that personal growth and insight must involve a long process of disclosing your feelings and childhood memories to a therapist over a period of years. The idea of trying to achieve your emotional goals in a limited period of time, using a structured training program, may strike you as gimmicky and superficial. You may tend to write off cognitive and behavioral techniques that focus on the here-and-now as "fads" or as psychological "Band-Aids" rather than as new developments that could speed up the process of psychotherapy, just as penicillin improved the treatment of pneumonia.

I believe that any rapid treatment for a mood problem will be superficial:

____ not at all ____ somewhat ____ moderately ____ a lot

12. **Self-labeling:** Some people justify putting things off because they think of themselves as "lazy" or they call themselves "procrastinators." These labels set up the expectation that you will continue to be unproductive because of a deeply ingrained and irreversible aspect of your personality. You may even find that your family and friends buy into the passive, helpless role you

play. During a martital therapy session, a severely depressed woman announced: "I think I need a cigarette." Her obedient husband immediately picked up her pack of cigarettes from the table, took one of them out, placed it in her mouth, and lit it for her. His behavior rewarded her for acting as if she couldn't do anything for herself and had to be waited on.

I think of myself as "lazy" or as a procrastinator:

_____ not at all _____ somewhat _____ moderately _____ a lot

13. **Different priorities:** Some people are genuinely overcommitted and either forget to do their self-help assignments or feel that they can't budget any time for them. You may feel overwhelmed and believe that the exercises your therapist suggests will only add to your burdens instead of helping you solve your problems.

I feel overwhelmed by everything I have to do:

_____ not at all _____ somewhat _____ moderately _____ a lot

14. **Entitlement:** Some people feel they're entitled to happiness and fair treatment from others. They deeply resent the implication that they are responsible for the way they feel, and they think they shouldn't have to work hard to improve a difficult situation. They often think that other people don't treat them right. They resist therapy because it seems "unfair" that they should have to put out any effort to feel better. As one woman put it, "Why should I have to change? My husband is the one making me miserable!"

I believe that I am entitled to feel happy and that I shouldn't have to work on my problems:

_____ not at all _____ somewhat _____ moderately _____ a lot

15. **Fear of change:** Some people, in spite of their misery, fantasize that any change in the status quo might be even worse. The anxiety associated with change appears so great that the current painful state of affairs seems preferable. You may think that your personal identity depends on feeling depressed, angry, or inadequate, and so you may feel reluctant to give up your symptoms. As one woman put it, "I think I *like* being depressed and feeling sorry for myself."

I sometimes feel afraid to change my life:

_____ not at all _____ somewhat _____ moderately _____ a lot

16. **Shame:** You may have a number of painful feelings and problems that you find it difficult to share with your therapist, such as alcoholism, a sexual indiscretion, or an angry reaction to something the therapist said. The therapy may not seem relevant if you don't share this information with your therapist.

There are problems that I might feel ashamed to share with my therapist:

____ not at all ____ somewhat ____ moderately ____ a lot

17. **Emotional reasoning:** This is one of the commonest distortions that can undermine your self-help efforts. You might reason: "I feel worse. Therefore, I must not be getting anywhere in my therapy." You might also tell yourself, "I *feel* hopeless. Therefore, I must *be* hopeless." The tendency to reason from the way you feel can be quite unrealistic and self-defeating, because your emotions will often result from distorted thoughts that have no more validity than the grotesque images in the curved mirrors at an amusement park. Virtually all patients have setbacks and feel hopeless or unmotivated at times, but this doesn't mean they can't improve.

When I feel bad, I often give up on things:

____ not at all ____ somewhat ____ moderately ____ a lot

18. **Low frustration tolerance:** Many individuals find it difficult to stick with a task if they don't get immediate results. If they reach a plateau, or if they experience a setback, they give up. Since a number of ups and downs are an inevitable part of treatment, or practically any activity, it would be to your advantage to learn to increase your frustration tolerance so that you can have the persistence required for optimal results.

I often give up on things when I feel frustrated with my progress:

____ not at all ____ somewhat ____ moderately ____ a lot

19. **Superman/Superwoman:** You may think that if you ask for help, it means that you're "weak" or "inferior." If your therapist tries to help you, you may feel the urge to resist and come up with something entirely different that you alone thought of. This is just as illogical as going to a tennis coach and then refusing to follow through on his or her suggestions. If you insist on hitting

the ball in your own way, your style may be quite original, but you may not win as many matches!

This attitude describes me:

____ not at all ____ somewhat ____ moderately ____ a lot

20. **Lack of direction:** During periods of depression, some individuals experience slowed thinking and have difficulty concentrating. At these times you may have trouble figuring out what's bothering you and find it difficult to think of anything positive to do to help yourself.

This problem describes me:

____ not at all ____ somewhat ____ moderately ____ a lot

21. **The "realism" of depression:** Some people who are depressed are reluctant to work at getting better because they are convinced their problems are real and that their misery is inevitable. They may feel there's no point in writing down their negative thoughts or trying to learn to think more positively because they think this means ignoring reality or getting involved in the "Power of Positive Thinking."

I believe that psychotherapy cannot help me because my problems are real:

____ not at all ____ somewhat ____ moderately ____ a lot

22. **Reluctance to give up negative feelings:** Some people are reluctant to give up feelings of anger, guilt, depression, or anxiety because they believe that these emotions are healthy or beneficial to them. A psychologist who was petrified about failing her licensing examination didn't want to give up worrying because she was convinced it was helping her in some way, even though she was so nervous that she couldn't study. A woman who was considering separating from her husband didn't want to give up her anger and depression and suicidal urges because she felt that if she did, she'd get complacent and stuck in a bad marriage.

Sometimes I feel that I don't really want to let go of my negative feelings:

____ not at all ____ somewhat ____ moderately ____ a lot

23. **The medical model:** If you go to a doctor because of a cough or a fever, you generally expect him to diagnose the problem and

prescribe a medicine that will correct it. All you have to do is get plenty of bed rest and wait for the cure to take care of itself. Similarly, many people feel that a chemical imbalance has caused their mood problems and that only a drug could make them better. Therefore, the idea of dealing with their problems or doing self-help assignments does not appeal to them.

I am convinced that only a medication can make me feel better:

_____ not at all _____ somewhat _____ moderately _____ a lot

24. **Passivity:** Some people feel that just talking to a therapist every week should be enough to make them feel better. This expectation may lead to disappointment. Your therapist can help you pinpoint the causes of the problem and develop a step-by-step plan for solving it, but ultimately you will have to work actively on your own to carry out that plan.

I sometimes feel that just going to therapy and talking about my problems should be enough to make things better:

_____ not at all _____ somewhat _____ moderately _____ a lot

25. **Summary:** After reading this memo, you may have a better understanding of the advantages and disadvantages of doing self-help assignments in therapy. Please indicate how you now feel about this.

I feel convinced that doing self-help assignments will be an important part of my recovery:

_____ not at all _____ somewhat _____ moderately _____ a lot

Index

You are invited to visit Dr. Burns' website at http://www.FeelingGood.com. This website contains information about:

- Dates and locations for upcoming lectures and workshops by Dr. Burns.
- Audiotapes for the general public.
- Training tapes for mental health professionals (including CE credits).
- Links for referrals to cognitive therapists around the country.
- A description of Dr. Burns' new *Therapist Toolkit 2000*.
- Links to other interesting sites.
- New information of potential interest to patients, therapists, and researchers.
- "Ask the Guru." You can submit questions to Dr. Burns about mental health topics. Answers to selected questions are posted in a column format.

Workshops and Lectures by Dr. Burns

Dr. Burns offers workshops and lectures for mental health professionals and for general public audiences as well. For a list of dates and locations, you are invited to visit Dr. Burns' website at http://www. FeelingGood.com

Audio Tapes for Mental Health Professionals

STRATEGIES FOR THERAPEUTIC SUCCESS: MY TWENTY MOST EFFECTIVE TECHNIQUES (8 CASSETTES–12 CE CREDITS AWARDED)

In this two-day intensive workshop, Dr. Burns illustrates the most valuable therapy techniques he has developed during 25 years of clinical practice, training and research.

FEELING GOOD: FAST & EFFECTIVE TREATMENTS FOR DEPRESSION, ANXIETY AND THERAPEUTIC RESISTANCE (4 CASSETTES–5.25 CE CREDITS AWARDED)

Dr. Burns describes the basic principles of CBT and illustrates state-of-the-art treatment methods for depression and anxiety disorders. He also illustrates how to deal with difficult, mistrustful, unmotivated, or angry patients who seem to sabotage treatment

FEELING GOOD TOGETHER: COGNITIVE INTERPERSONAL THERAPY (4 CASSETTES–5.75 CE CREDITS AWARDED)

In this workshop, Dr. Burns shows how to modify the attitudes that sabotage intimacy and lead to anger and mistrust. He illustrates, step-by-step, how to work with individuals who can't get along with their spouses, family members, friends, or colleagues at work. He also explains how to deal with patients who blame others for their personal relationship problems.

RAPID, COST-EFFECTIVE TREATMENTS FOR ANXIETY DISORDERS (4 CASSETTES–5.5 CE CREDITS AWARDED)

In this workshop, Dr. Burns shows you how to integrate three powerful models in the treatment of the entire spectrum of anxiety disorders, including Generalized Anxiety, Panic Disorder (with or without Agoraphobia, Phobias, Social Anxiety, Obsessive-Compulsive Disorder, and Post-Traumatic Stress Disorder (including victims of childhood sexual abuse).

You may order the audio tapes for professionals or for the general public by calling 800-810-9011 or by visiting this web page: http://www.lima-associates.com

Treatment and Assessment Tools for Mental Health Professionals

THERAPIST'S TOOLKIT

Includes hundreds of pages of state-of-the-art assessment and treatment tools for the mental health professional. Purchase includes licensure for unlimited reproduction in your clinical practice. Site licenses are available.

You may learn more about the toolkit and ordering procedures at Dr. Burns' website—http://www.FeelingGood.com